Unionist Politics and the Politics of Unionism
since the Anglo-Irish Agreement

Unionist Politics and
the Politics of Unionism
since the Anglo-Irish Agreement

Feargal Cochrane

revised edition

CORK **cup** UNIVERSITY PRESS

First published in 1997 by
Cork University Press
Crawford Business Park
Crosses Green
Cork
Ireland

© Feargal Cochrane 1997
revised edition 2001

British Library Cataloguing in Publication Data
A CIP catalogue record for this book is available from
the British Library

ISBN 1 85918 259 3 paperback

First edition typset by Seton Music Graphics Ltd, Co. Cork
Revisions for second edition typset by Tower Books, Ballincollig, Co. Cork
Printed by ColourBooks Ltd., Baldoyle, Co. Dublin

Contents

Preface
(first edition)

The Anglo-Irish Agreement (AIA) was the most important British government initiative in Ireland since the introduction of the Government of Ireland Act in 1920. From the unionist perspective, it represented the greatest threat to their position since the Home Rule legislation at the beginning of the century. As such, the unionist campaign against the AIA provides a fascinating insight into the dynamics of unionist ideology, as the crisis, and particularly the unionist inability to cope effectively with it, stretched the fabric of unionist politics to breaking point. This book analyses the political evolution of Ulster unionism from the signing of the Anglo-Irish Agreement on 15 November 1985 to the present day. It aims to examine what lies at the core of the unionist identity. What are the central dynamics of the ideology? What does the Union mean to unionists? How has unionist strategy evolved since the AIA? What is the likely medium-term future for the unionist ideology?

The unity forged out of the identification of external aggression began to break down as the anti-Agreement campaign progressed. The main reason why the unionist monolith began to disintegrate was because it was never more than an illusion to begin with. As this book demonstrates, unionism is an umbrella term for a hugely diverse community. While unionists can often appear to be a homogenous group, unionist electoral cohesion masks a wide variety of cultural and political goals.

This book was inspired by my belief that the political muscle of unionism declined steadily from the prorogation of Stormont in 1972 to the point that, on 15 November 1985, the British government signed the Anglo-Irish Agreement and gave the government of the Republic of Ireland a consultative role in the administration of Northern Ireland. The objective of this study is to examine the unionist response to this dramatic shift in British policy-making towards Northern Ireland and investigate how, and with what success, the unionist community attempted to deal with what they perceived to be the biggest threat to their way of life since the Home Rule crisis at the beginning of the century. By examining the unionist response to the Anglo-Irish Agreement, it is possible to analyse the extent to which their struggle against the 'diktat' influenced their subsequent political behaviour. Chronologically, the bulk of the book concentrates on the period between 1985 and 1996, though frequent historical parallels are drawn. My intention is not to adjudicate on the morality or legitimacy of unionist political behaviour during the period so much as to examine the dynamics which underpinned that behaviour.

The central argument of the book is that the diversity of the ideology's social composition is both its strength and its weakness. While unionism's electoral cohesion has invested it with a considerable degree of political power, especially when combined with apprehension about the constitutional position of Northern Ireland, this has been more than offset by its negative by-products. The desire to encompass as wide a support base as possible has resulted in a church so broad that, far from singing from the same hymn sheet, many do not actually believe in the same God. A consequence of the desire to get everyone under the unionist umbrella is that there is little which unites unionists other than their allegiance to the Union. As a result of their social diversity, the ideology contains not only people who advocate alternative political tactics and strategies, but people who disagree fundamentally about who they are and where they want to go. This has produced a negative dynamic within the ideology which tends to become more apparent during periods of political uncertainty. While political cohesion can be maintained when reacting against proposals which unionists commonly regard as repugnant, such as the AIA, it tends to disintegrate when they have to chart a more positive course, as many disagree about the desired destination. Like two people fighting over the steering-wheel of a motor car, the result is normally unpleasant for both parties.

This study also illustrates the extent to which the unionist community has been hampered by the uneasy coalition of interest groups who took shelter under the collective umbrella. The diversity of the ideology's composition combined with the unique cocktail of their historical experience has left an indelible mark upon the collective psyche. At its root, modern unionism is profoundly insecure, and with good reason. From their initial organised entry into Ulster at the beginning of the seventeenth century, unionists have felt threatened by external aggression, either from their immediate neighbours or from the malicious policies of the British government. This threat, whether real or imagined, has continued at varying degrees of intensity ever since. However, this book is not a wholly negative audit of contemporary unionism. One of its main themes is to chart the learning curve embarked upon by many unionists during the period. While unionists may not have altered any of their fundamental beliefs or principles, many of them have become much more skilful operators in the political process and are now capable of conducting a more intelligent strategy to attain their political objectives.

To date, no significant study of the unionist reaction to the AIA has been published, and consequently the detailed narrative of the anti-Agreement campaign contained in this book serves as an important historical record. In addition to explaining *what* happened, this study attempts to provide a theoretical explanation of *why* unionists reacted in the manner they did and the lessons that experience provided both to the unionist community and to policy-makers. The unionist campaign against the AIA illustrated that the gradual breakdown of unionist unity, which resulted in the periodic eruption of both intraparty and interparty factionalism, was not simply the product of personality clashes or a structural division between political parties (though these were important) but was a reflection of fundamental socio-economic and cultural differences within the ideology. The frustrations which built up over the course of the anti-Agreement campaign were directly related to the diverse composition of the ideology. Whilst all were disillusioned by the general lack of success, some wanted the campaign to progress in a more militant direction, whereas others, fearing that this would have negative long-term effects, lobbied for a de-escalation of street politics. As all concerned realised the importance of unity, they were caught in a loveless marriage, each partner pulling in conflicting directions but conscious of the fact that they were unable to achieve any of their objectives without at least the tacit support of the rest of the unionist community.

The AIA was drafted with considerable skill. The lack of any identifiable target which could be used to motivate the unionist community, other than the Maryfield secretariat, increased the frustration and apathy at grassroots level. The fact that they seemed to be fighting an invisible enemy, together with the failure of the AIA to deliver upon the grandiose promises laid out in the joint communiqué which accompanied the Agreement, led many within the unionist community to the,conclusion that it did not present such a threat to their social and cultural position as had originally been feared. The apathy and disappointment with the anti-Agreement campaign made it increasingly difficult for the political leadership to mobilise grass-roots opposition and maintain party discipline. Eventually, the continuance of street politics became impractical as it proved difficult to rally sufficient numbers to prevent attendances from looking embarrassingly sparse. This forced the leadership of the unionist coalition to adopt a more orthodox strategy and develop alternative political proposals which might replace the AIA.

The text falls into three broad sections. The first deals with the origins of the AIA and attempts to unpack the dynamics of unionist political and cultural identity. The second provides a detailed narrative of the unionist campaign against the Anglo-Irish Agreement, illustrating the theoretical arguments made in previous chapters. The third section examines unionist political behaviour since the Brooke-Mayhew talks of 1992, the lessons which the ideology has learned since the AIA and the likely medium-term future for the ideology and the Union they cherish.

My research benefited greatly from the kind assistance of senior figures in both of the main unionist parties, many of whom gave up their time to reflect on political events since the signing of the Agreement. I am extremely grateful to those individuals whose help provided me with a fresh insight into the period and provided a rich and interesting seam of primary source material. The study also benefited from gaining an external perspective on the unionist ideology. This was provided by interviews with representatives of both the SDLP and senior Southern Irish political figures. My discussions with former Taoiseach Garret FitzGerald proved enormously valuable, not only in providing background information on the negotiations which led to the signing of the Agreement itself, but also by illustrating how the unionist political community was perceived by one of the co-signatories of the AIA in 1985.

This book evolved out of my PhD thesis which was researched while at the Department of Politics, Queen's University, Belfast. A special word of thanks is due to Professor Vincent Geoghegan, who supervised my PhD and has continued, beyond the call of duty, to provide valuable advice during the course of this long and often frustrating project. I am extremely grateful to Professor Geoghegan for the help he has given me during the past few years.

I would also like to thank Professor Paul Arthur for his assistance and for providing many useful comments on some of the early material contained in the book.

Thanks are also due to The Linen Hall Library and particularly the Political Collection within that institution which has built up an unparalleled archive that is an essential habitat for any researcher concerned with Irish history or politics. A special word must go to the staff of the Political Collection, and in particular Yvonne Murphy and Ciaran Crossey, who were always helpful in guiding me through the almost overwhelming wealth of material contained in the Collection. I would also like to thank Robert Bell, the former Curator of the Collection, for his help with initial aspects of the project.

The book also benefited greatly from the many politicians, journalists and academics who gave up their time to speak to me. I am extremely grateful to them for their assistance.

Most of the manuscript was written while teaching in the Department of Politics, Queen's University, Belfast. I would like to thank all of my former colleagues and those students who enthusiastically discussed their ideas on the development of the unionist ideology.

The usual health warning applies in that all of the views expressed in the book are those of the author and any shortcomings are my responsibility alone.

Sara Wilbourne of Cork University Press dealt expeditiously with the preoccupations of the neurotic author and maintained a judicious eye on the development of the manuscript.

Finally, and most importantly, I would like to thank my family. My mother, Roisin Cochrane, provided unstinting (and unpaid) secretarial assistance, maintaining and cataloguing a cuttings file. Her joy at seeing her son every week was doubtless given a bitter-sweet quality by the quantity of newspapers under his arm, yet this task was carried out with characteristic thoroughness, efficiency and good humour. I would also like to thank my father for putting up with our numerous late-night political debates, which helped me crystalise my thoughts while possibly depriving him of sleep! This book is dedicated to mum, dad and my brother Niall for their support and encouragement.

Feargal Cochrane
June 1996

Preface
(second edition)

Much water has flowed under the bridge since the first edition of this book was written in 1996. Since the book was published in 1997, Northern Ireland has witnessed the political roller-coaster of the multi-party negotiations at Stormont; the Good Friday Agreement (GFA) of April 1998; the stop-start nature of the Agreement's implementation; the rise and fall of the GFA's institutions; internal feuding within the Ulster Unionist Party (UUP) for much of the period and ultimately, a challenge to David Trimble's leadership of the UUP led by senior members of his party.

The central argument within the book, that the diversity of the unionist ideology's composition is both its greatest strength and its greatest weakness, remains true today, in fact is probably more apparent in 2000 than it was in 1997. While time has moved on in the intervening period, the dynamics of unionist politics have changed little. These are ultimately characterised by fear and insecurity, political pessimism, conflicting ideas about where unionism should be going, confusion over political strategy and consequently, internecine internal conflicts over policy direction.

Despite these unfortunate dynamics, there is also a more positive story to tell about unionist politics than was the case hitherto. Perhaps the biggest development in unionist politics over the period since 1997 was provided by a more proactive and positive style, notably absent from the earlier years. This was epitomised by the participation of the UUP in political negotiations with Sinn Féin. It was also demonstrated by the willingness of David Trimble, most of his party, and the majority of the unionist community at the subsequent referendum, to take 'a risk for peace' and support the Good Friday Agreement. While unionists may not have altered any of their fundamental beliefs or principles, many of them have become much more skilful operators in the political process and have demonstrated their capacity to conduct a more intelligent strategy to attain their political objectives. This second edition of the book will illustrate that the journey for those unionists who wished to become insiders rather than outsiders in the political process was a long and painful one.

Unsurprisingly, it was a journey undertaken with varying degrees of enthusiasm. Many unionists proved to be reluctant debutants and found it difficult coming to terms with the challenges and opportunities the peace process has brought with it. While many recognised the need for political reform and welcomed the opportunity to take devolved responsibilities away from Westminster control and back to a Stormont administration, they have never quite been able to free themselves from political insecurity and fear of the future. As a consequence, instead of seizing the opportunities they had helped to create, unionism became increasingly paralysed and was sucked inexorably back into previous patterns of behaviour. This book illustrates the slow and difficult journey unionism faced after 1985 in moving from being outsiders to becoming insiders in the political process. This journey neared its destination towards the end of 1999 with the establishment of a new Northern Ireland Executive at Stormont led by the UUP's David Trimble as First Minister. One of the saddest aspects of this story for the unionist community (and for the nationalist community also) is that having reached their goal of securing devolved power within the United Kingdom, internal tensions within the UUP resulted in the suspension of the institutions that had been set up and the return of devolved powers to Westminster. Unionists might argue that Sinn Féin were responsible for the suspension of the GFA, though this argument is difficult to justify within the terms of the Agreement. While the institutions of the GFA were subsequently restored, their position, at the time of writing, is less than secure.

This second edition of the book includes a fully revised and updated conclusion to bring the story forward. This looks at unionist politics before and after the Good Friday Agreement of April 1998 and examines the internal fracturing within the UUP that accompanied the stuttering implementation of the Agreement. While much of the narrative content in the concluding chapter is new, it tells a similar story to the rest of the book about the dynamics within unionist politics. While some have recognised the need for change, others fear it. Rather than being demanded of unionist leaders, progressive political behaviour is often engaged in cautiously for fear of incurring damage to the leader's authority. This has been the case since the 1960s and, as the second edition of the book will illustrate, has changed little at the beginning of the twenty-first century.

The revised concluding chapter of this second edition was written while teaching politics at the Richardson Institute, within the Department of Politics and International Relations at Lancaster University. I would like to thank my colleagues in the Department for their encouragement and advice, particularly my Head of Department Gordon Hands, Hugh Miall, Roger Mac Ginty, David Denver, Gareth Davies, Alan Warburton and Gerd Nonneman.

I am also indebted to former colleagues within the Centre for the Study of Conflict at the University of Ulster in Coleraine, for their ideas and encouragement. Special mention is required for Professor Seamus Dunn, Professor Valerie Morgan, Helen Dawson, Alison Montgomery, Ruth McIlwaine and Gregory Irwin, colleagues who have become close friends.

Thanks are also due to my mother, Roisin Cochrane (see preface to first edition). She is still organising my cuttings file and is still unpaid!

Feargal Cochrane
October 2000

Abbreviations

AIA	Anglo-Irish Agreement
CDP	Campaign for a Devolved Parliament
CEC	Campaign for Equal Citizenship
CLMC	Combined Loyalist Military Command
CRP	Campaign for a Regional Parliament
DUP	Democratic Unionist Party
GFA	Good Friday Agreement
IGC	Intergovernmental Conference of the AIA
IRA	Irish Republican Army
NIO	Northern Ireland Office
PUP	Progressive Unionist Party
RUC	Royal Ulster Constabulary
SDLP	Social Democratic and Labour Party
UDA	Ulster Defence Association
UDP	Ulster Democratic Party
UDR	Ulster Defence Regiment
UFF	Ulster Freedom Fighters
UPRG	Ulster Political Research Group
UUC	Ulster Unionist Council
UUP	Ulster Unionist Party
UULF	United Ulster Loyalist Front
UVF	Ulster Volunteer Force
UWC	Ulster Workers' Council

PART I

CHAPTER 1

The Anglo-Irish Agreement: Origins and Interpretations

Staging posts of the Anglo-Irish Agreement

> We will listen for a while. We hope we will get an agreement. But then the government will have to make some decisions and say, having listened to everyone, we are going to try this or that, whichever we get most support for.[1]

These words were spoken by Margaret Thatcher shortly after becoming Prime Minister and can be seen in retrospect as the first indications of a more radical approach to the Northern Ireland 'problem'. The Anglo-Irish Agreement, which was signed on 15 November 1985, was not a sudden departure from the containment goals of direct rule, but was actually the product of five years of diplomacy between Britain and Ireland. The summit meetings held in May and December 1980 between Margaret Thatcher and Taoiseach, Charles Haughey, marked the inauguration of a new period of co-operation between the two governments. After the May meeting, Haughey reaffirmed that it was the policy of his government to achieve Irish unity through consent, but added significantly that constitutional change in the status of Northern Ireland would only come about with the consent of the majority of the people in Northern Ireland. The ambiguous phrase in the joint communiqué issued after the talks on 8 December, that the two governments were to give consideration to 'the totality of relationships within these islands', was exploited by Haughey to imply a strengthening of the Irish dimension.[2] Having witnessed the recent collapse of the Atkins Talks, (these discussions, aimed merely at achieving some level of consensus rather than an overall solution to the conflict, were convened by the Secretary of State in January 1980 but abandoned in November due to their lack of progress) unionists interpreted this communiqué as containing an implicit and deliberate threat from the British Prime Minister that continued intransigence would not be in their interests.

After the December summit, several joint studies were commissioned by the two governments to examine the possibility of new institutional structures which would improve security and economic co-operation. The results of these Anglo-Irish studies were reported the following year when Garret FitzGerald (who had replaced Charles Haughey as Taoiseach in June 1981) met Margaret Thatcher at Downing Street on 6 November. It was decided at this meeting that an Anglo-Irish Intergovernmental Council would be established to provide institutional evidence of the growing links between the two countries. In practical terms, this would involve regular meetings between the two governments at ministerial and official levels to discuss matters of common concern.[3]

However, despite these formal signs of official *rapprochement*, conflict remained within the Anglo-Irish relationship and the 'road to Hillsborough' proved to be a rocky one. As Paul Arthur has commented, the relationship was fluid and unpredictable, with both London and Dublin operating with one eye on their internal constituencies and the other on external and thus uncontrollable events.[4] Certainly, the relationship between the two governments was influenced by their realisation that an alliance of some description was necessary to secure internal political support, yet this often proved an uncomfortable partnership.

The need to maximise internal political support and pander to the domestic and perhaps ephemeral concerns of public opinion has always been a key element in the development of Anglo-Irish relations. Whatever the constitutional niceties or stated policy positions may be, in practical terms Northern Ireland has always been a foreign policy matter for both the British and Irish governments and within the mind-sets of their respective populations. Public opinion in both states has usually been driven more by economics than by history. Economic recession, unemployment and the prevailing social issues of the day have normally exercised the public mind to a greater extent than the situation in Northern Ireland, and this naturally has been reflected in the policy priorities of the two governments. The financial crisis facing the Republic during the early 1980s and the accompanying political instability (three general elections in eighteen months during 1981–82) forced Northern Ireland off, or at least further down, the political agenda, with Dublin's attention being focused on unemployment, inflation and emigration. Recession was also biting hard in Britain, and consequently Anglo-Irish relations were neglected by a government mesmerised by its own monetarist policies and battle with the trade unions.

The republican hunger-strike in the summer of 1981 increased the strain between London and Dublin, not so much over the principle of 'political status' as due to the insensitivity of the British reaction. Again domestic needs were sovereign, as the Irish administration had little choice but to criticise the British government who were widely perceived by the Irish electorate as behaving in a gratuitously vindictive and cruel manner.

In his book examining the external background to the AIA, Adrian Guelke concentrates on the extent to which international pressures, especially those which emanated from Washington, exerted influence over British policy-making towards Northern Ireland.[5] He argues that quite apart from alienating Dublin, the hunger-strike dealt a severe blow to the policy which the British government had been pursuing since ending 'special category status', namely attempting to depict the IRA as mercenary terrorists. As the water in the lake of moral legitimacy clouded up, so international pressure increased on the British government to resolve the conflict.

> The hunger strike was a severe challenge to Britain's international standing over the issue of Northern Ireland. In particular, the mass mobilisation of opinion in Catholic areas behind the prisoners' demands destroyed the credibility in the outside world of the Government's representation of those engaged in political violence in Northern Ireland as terrorists . . . In its aftermath, there was considerable relief that the strike had not done even greater damage to Britain's position and particularly that President Reagan had resisted pressure for American intervention.[6]

If Anglo-Irish relations were cool in the wake of the hunger-strike, then the temperature fell to subzero levels during the Falklands War in the summer of 1982. Irish criticism of the sinking of the Argentinian warship, the *General Belgrano*, led to a sharp deterioration in relations between Britain and the Republic, further complicating policy towards Northern Ireland. British hostility towards the Republic over its neutral stance on the Falklands was not helped by the activities of the IRA, particularly by bomb attacks in London which killed eleven soldiers in the Household Cavalry and in the band of the Royal Green Jackets. Sinn Féin's success in the Northern Ireland Assembly elections in October 1982 further shocked British public opinion and placed more strain on relations between the two governments. This litany of disputes between Britain and Ireland which characterised the early 1980s cheered unionist hearts, their reasoning being that, the louder the megaphone diplomacy between the two countries became, the more likely it was that Thatcher would protect and defend unionist interests, namely the constitutional link between Great Britain and Northern Ireland.

In retrospect this logic can be seen to have been seriously flawed, as despite the periodic frostiness of Anglo-Irish relations a broad consensus did emerge. Both sides came to the view that the most propitious way of managing Northern Ireland was through co-operation with one another and the establishment of new political structures which would resolve conflict between the two governments. Both administrations were beset by financial crises and political problems which were the result of economic recession. Both were eager to distance themselves from the Northern Ireland conflict, not only because it seemed to be unsolvable, but also because there were other issues on the political agenda which commanded a higher priority. Northern Ireland had long since become a drain on the resources of the British Treasury; Britain was under pressure from the White House to legislate its way out of the impasse, yet saw all its efforts to establish internal political structures founder on the rocks of sectarian politics. What better way to deflect international pressure than to make friends with Dublin? If it was impossible to solve the problem internally, through either a military defeat of the IRA or the achievement of political institutions capable of securing cross-community support, then the best alternative appeared to be an agreement with the government of the Republic which would minimise the political importance of Northern Ireland in the domestic affairs of both countries.

The New Ireland Forum

If the British government was frustrated by the failure of successive political initiatives, the latest being Secretary of State James Prior's scheme for 'rolling devolution' within the Northern Ireland Assembly, then nationalists were equally disappointed. The Social Democratic and Labour Party (SDLP), who must share part of the blame for this failure, were particularly anxious to find a political platform given their absence from the Assembly. There can be little doubt that the SDLP's refusal to take their seats at Stormont was not based solely on the structure of the initiative. It is true that from a nationalist perspective the Assembly was inadequate, as it was designed to be an internal settlement with no designated Irish dimension. To understand the other factors behind the SDLP's lack of enthusiasm for Prior's scheme, we must look back to the summer of 1981 and particularly the republican hunger-strike. The deaths of ten republican prisoners in the H-Blocks was one of the most emotive (and thus important) political/religio-cultural events of the previous fifty years, a blood-sacrifice which created martyrs whose influence remained long after their temporal deaths. Sinn Féin seized the opportunity to make both internal and international capital from the hunger-strike, and their electoral success enabled them to set the political agenda until the mid-1980s. It was this growth in Sinn Féin's political muscle, and not the merits or otherwise of the plan for rolling devolution, which decided the SDLP's strategy in 1982. A 'holier than thou' row broke out within the nationalist camp, reminiscent of that which was endemic within the unionist community, concerning who were the legitimate political guardians of the Catholic population and who possessed the map which would navigate Ireland's journey out of the current conflict. Lacking the political space to participate meaningfully in the Assembly for fear of losing votes on their 'green' wing to Sinn Féin, the SDLP faced something of a dilemma. How were they to remain outside this latest political initiative without appearing the laggard, a negative party exercising a veto over political dialogue and possible progress? In short, how were the SDLP to escape the criticism that they were guilty of the very sins previously committed by the unionist parties?

The New Ireland Forum was established in 1983 in an effort to offset such criticism, divert the attention of supporters who may have felt upset that the abstentionist tactic had excluded them from the levers of power and, most importantly, emphasise that the SDLP and not Sinn Féin was the legitimate voice of Northern nationalism. Devised by John Hume, the initiative proposed that leaders of 'constitutional' nationalist opinion would meet and seek to agree a common position within the nationalist community, which could then be debated with the unionists. The agreed remit was to establish a means whereby 'lasting peace and stability could be achieved in a New Ireland through the democratic process'. The main unionist parties were invited to attend but declined. Sinn Féin were not invited.

The eleven months of debate which followed provided the disparate Catholic/nationalist factions both North and South with a platform from which to impress their respective electorates. The SDLP were able to demonstrate that they had the ear of the Irish government and the blessing of all those within the Irish political process. Southern politicians were able to use the Forum debates to illustrate their concern for 'the fourth green field' and to comment upon the administration of justice in Northern Ireland. The Catholic Church (though initially reluctant to be subjected to public accountability) welcomed the opportunity to bolster constitutional nationalism, undermine the political progress of Sinn Féin and fight their own corner with regard to social issues such as education.

It would be overly cynical to simply deride the New Ireland Forum as nothing but a mutual appreciation society since real differences did exist. The political divisions which emerged during the course of the Forum's deliberations would suggest that the participants were not in the business of reassessing their opinions, which presumably was the point of the exercise. Instead, all concerned sought to ensure that the *New Ireland Forum Report* coincided as closely as possible with their own party position on Northern Ireland. Charles Haughey was the least subtle in this respect, issuing an ultimatum that, as a price of his continued participation in the process, the final report would have to go a long way towards meeting the traditional Fianna Fáil demand for a united Ireland. The result was a mishmash, which illustrated that the lengthy debates had done little to resolve the differences that had existed before the process began. As Anthony Kenny put it, 'the document which appeared in May 1984 was uneven, ambiguous and not entirely consistent'.[7]

Setting aside the inadequacies of its conclusions, the *New Ireland Forum Report* should be seen as an important marker in the evolution of the non-physical-force nationalist tradition. Hidden away behind the headline-grabbing constitutional proposals was a recognition of the existence of a rival tradition in the community and a commitment to a political settlement capable of securing the agreement of the unionist population. Paragraph 5.2 of the report states that 'the political arrangements for a new and sovereign Ireland would have to be freely negotiated and agreed to by the people of the North and by the people of the South'.[8] This language of inclusiveness can also be interpreted in a less charitable light. Arthur Aughey regards paragraph 5.8 of the report as an example of the sinister intentions which lay beneath the soothing rhetoric of 'constitutional' nationalism in 1984. Paragraph 5.8 states:

> Constitutional nationalists fully accept that they alone could not determine the structures of Irish unity and that it is essential to have unionist agreement and participation in devising such structures and in formulating the guarantees they required. In line with this view, the Forum believes that the best people to identify the interests of the unionist tradition are the unionist people themselves. It would be thus essential that they should negotiate their role in any arrangements which would embody Irish unity. It would be for the British and Irish governments to create the framework and atmosphere within which such negotiations could take place.[9]

Aughey interprets this, not as an appeal to unionists to participate in a fair debate, but as an appeal to the British government to go over the heads of the unionist community and embark upon a prescriptive strategy within which unionist politicians would be forced to negotiate. In this analysis, the AIA was the logical offspring of the Forum. 'The argument of the deed of 15 November 1985 is already intimated in the argument of Article 5.8.'[10]

The unionist reaction to the *New Ireland Forum Report's* three preferred options (a unitary state, a federal or confederal arrangement, and joint authority) was understandably frosty. Both the Ulster Unionist Party (UUP) and Democratic Unionist Party (DUP) asked the rhetorical question, 'what's in it for us?' Any analysis of the report must elicit the response that there was not a lot in it to attract the unionist community. Despite John Hume's assertion that the *New Ireland Forum Report* was not meant primarily as an overture to unionism, but rather as a clarification of the nationalist position, the fact remains that it was riddled with vague phrases which did little to reassure those already suspicious of the duplicitous intentions of the authors. The report was visionary rather than practical, with frequent references to a 'New Ireland' but few specifics about what this actually meant or how it would be brought about. The UUP's response to the Forum came with the publication in November 1984 of *Opportunity Lost*. Written by Peter Smith (one of the leading liberal thinkers within the party at the time), it rejected all of the Forum's proposals as repugnant to the unionist community and was particularly scathing of the joint authority scenario, commenting that this was indicative of a hidden agenda.

> It is in the provocative nature of the introduction of joint authority that the real danger lies. Unionists would see it as a first step to a united Ireland. . . .
> It is a measure of the Forum's lack of understanding of Northern Unionism and, therefore, a clear demonstration of the way in which it tackled its task, that it could put forward such a nonsensical 'solution' to the problem. It is simply unbelievable that any serious student of Northern Ireland could imagine that such an idiotic scheme could work.[11]

The DUP's answer to the *New Ireland Forum Report* was equally hostile. *The Unionist Case: The Forum Report Answered* declared that joint authority was a half-way house to a united Ireland and that the proposal exposed the real intentions of the SDLP to be akin to those of Sinn Féin in all but method.

The UUP had pre-empted the *New Ireland Forum Report* with proposals of their own in a document entitled *The Way Forward*, which was published in April 1984. While to some extent this was designed as an alternative to nationalist ideas, it provided a rare example of forward thinking within the unionist community. For once, policy ideas were initiated by unionists and debated in a thoughtful manner, rather than as a hurried and recalcitrant reaction to a British initiative. *The Way Forward* sought to find a role for the Northern Ireland Assembly, as it was obvious by this time that legislative powers were unlikely to be devolved to it from Westminster. It proposed that the Assembly should be given a greater administrative function, assuming the duties of the unelected area boards for health and education. Control of these regional services would be divided amongst committees composed on a proportionate basis, thus encouraging minority participation. 'The absence of any party with an overall majority in the foreseeable future would necessitate those compromises and bargains between participating parties which are the essence of real politics.'[12]

This is a rather optimistic argument, however, given that nationalists do not see the DUP and UUP as distinct entities, but rather different brands of the same product. It is likely therefore that they would consider such committees to have a built-in unionist majority and thus to constitute a pre-1972 Stormont administration in microcosm. Safeguards for the Catholic population were not specified but were to be enshrined in a bill of rights, which it was hoped would prevent an abuse of power and discriminatory practices by devolved institutions. It was reiterated that executive interference by the Republic of Ireland would be intolerable in any new political arrangements. *The Way Forward* did take a step towards recognising the nationalist identity by advocating the promotion and state funding of Irish cultural events, with the ambiguous proviso that such funding should reflect the level of public participation.

Not to be outdone, the DUP followed its castigation of the Forum with the more constructive *Ulster: The Future Assured*. This document was less apologetic than that of the UUP about its desire to see the restoration of majority rule and it advocated a more comprehensive form of devolution. It proposed a system of Cabinet government which would be formed by the leader of the largest party and would be answerable to an assembly. A number of departmental committees, whose members were to be appointed proportionally, would act as a check on the executive by scrutinising government legislation. In order to safeguard the rights of the minority, the DUP proposed that, in the event of a bill being rejected by a departmental committee, it would then require a weighted majority of 60 per cent in the assembly before it could become law.[13] It was also suggested that legislation which was considered discriminatory could be referred by the Secretary of State to the Judicial Committee of the Privy Council, provided that such action received a minimum of 30 per cent support within the assembly. Enthusiasm within the nationalist community for the unionist proposals was mild; this is not surprising given the wide gulf that existed between these and the conclusions of the *New Ireland Forum Report*, which was presumably an accurate reflection of nationalist political aspirations at the time.

The Kilbrandon Committee

The British reaction to the Forum underwent an interesting metamorphosis from cautious optimism to outright condemnation. The Secretary of State, James Prior, gave both *The Way Forward* and the *New Ireland Forum Report* a cautious welcome in a House of Commons debate on 2 July 1984. His speech emphasised that the constitutional position of Northern Ireland would not change until the majority of its citizens wished it to do so, but also pointed out to the unionists that a closer relationship was required between the UK and the Republic. Prior declared rather prophetically in light of later events that the establishment of an intergovernmental body might be a useful means of improving this relationship. However, there were others within the Tory party who saw the *New Ireland Forum Report* in much less favourable terms. One of the more vociferous, Ivor Stanbrook, denounced it as 'a humbug, a deceit, a snare, and a delusion'.[14]

An unofficial inquiry, headed by Lord Kilbrandon, was set up by the British Irish Association to determine what political arrangements would satisfy the main aspirations of both *The Way Forward* and the *New Ireland Forum Report*. The committee, which began its deliberations in May 1984, was composed of several academics, a journalist and politicians from the main parties. Their report, *Northern Ireland: Report of an Independent*

Inquiry, was published on 1 November 1984 and proposed a number of reforms which it was hoped would establish some middle ground between the two communities. A bill of rights was proposed in order to safeguard the rights of the minority, while it was suggested that potentially inflammatory legislation such as the Flags and Emblems Act could be replaced by laws with a less sectarian interpretation. Other proposals included a reform of the justice system with the abolition of Diplock courts and the introduction of trial by two judges, one from the United Kingdom and another from the Republic.[15] The central principle which lay behind the Kilbrandon Report was that a trade-off was necessary, whereby in return for increased security co-operation, the government of the Republic would be granted some say in the administration of justice in Northern Ireland. This equation – that an increased effort to thwart the IRA equals a greater say for the Irish Republic in matters affecting the welfare of the minority community in Northern Ireland – was also the basic rationale behind the Anglo-Irish Agreement. The Kilbrandon Committee, however, could not agree on the extent to which Dublin should be involved in the affairs of Northern Ireland and as a result produced majority and minority proposals. The minority were anxious to ensure that Irish involvement did not extend to the point that it compromised British sovereignty in Northern Ireland and favoured joint authority only in specific areas such as tourism, industry, energy and transport. They rejected power-sharing, declaring that the Assembly should only be given local government powers to be exercised through a committee system, rather than through a devolved executive.

The majority of the Kilbrandon Committee, on the other hand, were less squeamish about Dublin involvement and were happy to promote the idea that the Republic should have an executive as well as a consultative role in the government of Northern Ireland. Their proposals included the suggestion that Irish representation on the Northern Ireland Police Authority would increase the legitimacy of that institution in the eyes of the Catholic population and would satisfy Dublin's penchant for 'hands-on' involvement. Recognising that direct rule was not an acceptable form of government, the majority concluded that the only long-term solution lay in some form of legislative devolution. They were faced, of course, with the structural problem which had beset all other attempts at establishing a devolved administration. Given the Protestant majority which had existed within Northern Ireland since partition, together with the bipolar political division, how could power be devolved 'democratically'? How could sufficient safeguards be introduced to protect nationalists from unionist domination without this resulting in a nationalist veto over executive authority? 'If the executive takes decisions by majority votes, the majority ascendancy can be replicated within the Cabinet; if unanimity is required, the minority can hamstring the government.'[16] In an attempt to overcome this dilemma, the Kilbrandon majority proposed a scheme which it termed 'co-operative devolution', whereby power would be devolved – on a 'rolling' basis – to a democratically elected assembly, with subsidiary roles for both London and Dublin. At the head of this new political structure was to be a five-person executive, composed of the Secretary of State for Northern Ireland or their deputy, the Irish Minister for Foreign Affairs or their deputy, and three representatives from Northern Ireland elected by the voters of the region. These were to be nominated in such a way that two would represent the majority community and one would articulate the concerns of the minority. In practical terms, therefore, Britain would hold the balance of power between the two sides and could act as umpire in the event of political disagreement. It was hoped that these structures would be designed in such a way as to diminish the veto power of both sides and create a more positive attitude towards the political process.

Although the Kilbrandon Report was publicly ignored by the British government, its importance in determining future policy towards Northern Ireland should not be underestimated. The correlation between its concluding remarks and the structure of the Anglo-Irish Agreement is not sheer coincidence. In making the point that any new political arrangements must avoid ambiguity and set out precisely the form of the new structures so as to avoid the charge that such reforms contained a 'hidden agenda', the report concluded:

> We believe, as does the Forum sub-committee, that the most appropriate form [of providing institutional reassurance] would be a treaty between the two Governments, terminable, with due notice, by either side, but deposited with the United Nations. Throughout the duration of the Treaty, sovereignty will remain with the United Kingdom, and should it be revoked, all powers conferred on representatives of the Irish Government will revert to the UK Government.[17]

The Joint Communiqué

If the British government paid little public attention to the Kilbrandon Report, the same could not be said of the unionists who denounced it as a 'Trojan Horse' designed to get rid of the Ulster Defence Regiment (UDR). DUP deputy leader Peter Robinson offered the most pithy response, managing to condemn both the Kilbrandon and Forum reports in a single sentence: 'If you have to comment on a document that is absolute nonsense – as the New Ireland Forum was – then naturally your document will be nonsense.'[18] Meanwhile, relations between the two governments continued to improve. On 19 November 1984 the second summit of the Anglo-Irish Intergovernmental Council took place between Garret

FitzGerald and Margaret Thatcher. This summit was memorable for two conflicting reasons. Firstly, the joint communiqué published after the summit was a diplomatic building-block towards the Anglo-Irish Agreement. The communiqué set out the joint objectives being sought by both governments which were to find institutional form in Hillsborough a year later. In addition to rejecting the validity of any attempt to achieve political change through violent means, the Taoiseach and the Prime Minister agreed upon the following principles:

> The identities of both the majority and minority communities in Northern Ireland should be recognised and respected, and reflected in the structures and processes of Northern Ireland in ways acceptable to both communities.

> The process of government in Northern Ireland should be such as to provide the people of both communities with the confidence that their rights will be safeguarded.

> Co-operation between their two Governments in matters of security should be maintained and where possible improved.[19]

The second reason for the importance of this summit was not contained within the official communiqué, but occurred during the press conference which followed. It was here that Margaret Thatcher gave the definitive response of the British government to the *New Ireland Forum Report* and, unwittingly, undermined the declared goals of the communiqué.

> I have made it quite clear – and so did Mr Prior when he was Secretary of State for Northern Ireland – that a unified Ireland was one solution that is out. A second solution was confederation of two states. That is out. A third solution was joint authority. That is out. That is a derogation from sovereignty. We made that quite clear when the Report was published.[20]

Whatever prompted this outburst (possibly a knee-jerk reaction to the IRA bombing of the Grand Hotel at the Tory party conference in Brighton a month earlier), it sent shock waves through the Irish community. Thatcher, not so much by what she said but rather in the way that she said it, had ironically added fuel to the republican argument, namely that the British were not reasonable people and would not get out of Ireland until they were forced out. FitzGerald's recollection of the Chequers meeting was that it was a stormy though in the end amicable series of discussions.

> She remarked that this was the best discussion that we had ever had. Without enthusiasm, I agreed. . . . We drove back to London with very mixed feelings. The negative character of much of the discussion was disturbing. It seemed clear to us that the British Ministers had decided to scale down the scope of any agreement to something that would provide no basis for any attempted amendment of articles 2 and 3, to which I had become strongly committed. Moreover, what they had in mind would have

a totally inadequate impact upon the alienation of the nationalist minority in Northern Ireland.[21]

Having at least further crystalised the matters upon which they disagreed, if achieving little substantive progress, the two sides agreed to meet again early in the new year. Thatcher's initial suggestion that they should meet the following spring illustrated that in the true tradition of British prime ministers her main priorities lay elsewhere. Shocked by this laid-back attitude, FitzGerald warned Thatcher that such a gap would be 'disastrously dampening'[22] and he secured a commitment to meet in London in January. The two sides then worked out an agreed communiqué the broad thrust of which – as outlined above – was that, while significant differences still existed between the two governments, positive steps were being taken to achieve further agreement. It would appear from FitzGerald's account that Thatcher's denunciation of the three Forum options resulted from her characteristic inability to give an ambiguous answer to a direct question rather than any pre-planned strategy to torpedo the negotiations. FitzGerald had sent an observer to the British press conference which took place an hour before his own and, although his emissary had to return to brief him before Thatcher had finished speaking, the general tenor of her remarks were agreeable.

> Margaret Thatcher had described our meeting as 'the fullest, frankest and most realistic bilateral meeting I have ever had with the Taoiseach'. In reply to questions she had agreed that the two identities in Northern Ireland merited equal respect, if not equal recognition, and she later added that the minority did not think their identity was fully reflected in the structures and processes of Northern Ireland. And she had volunteered off her own bat that the security issues we had discussed included prisons and judicial issues as well as policing.[23]

FitzGerald's man would have been well advised to have waited for the final verse. Anxious to hear the 'spin' which the media were putting on Thatcher's briefing before going into his own press conference, FitzGerald attempted to listen in to the BBC six o'clock news but it appears that everyone was conspiring against him.

> Because of interference from a pirate radio station I was not able to catch much of what was said about our meeting in the opening minutes of the news, but I had the impression that near the end of the press conference she had rejected a confederation of two states and also joint authority. I went in to my press conference a few minutes late somewhat less happy than I had been before listening to the BBC but quite unprepared for the hurricane that was about to hit me. It very quickly became apparent that the helpful and positive comments the Prime Minister had made up to a late point in her press conference, as well as the positive elements in the

communiqué itself, had been rendered totally irrelevant by the manner in which she seemed to have dealt with the three Forum models.[24]

Irish and British diplomats immediately set about massaging the egos which had been bruised by Thatcher's rather patronising tone and began to work together to find some means of securing an institutional manifestation of the common objectives outlined in the 1984 communiqué.

Towards a New Treaty

One of the most important contributions to the debate which followed this diplomatic débâcle was provided by the academic lawyers Kevin Boyle and Tom Hadden, with their publication *Ireland: A Positive Proposal*.[25] They argued that a new treaty was necessary, not only as a means to remove communal suspicion and improve human relationships within Northern Ireland, but just as importantly as a mechanism to redefine the British–Irish axis and specifically their relationship over a disputed territory. Boyle and Hadden suggested that the constitutional status of Northern Ireland should be enshrined within the treaty so as to avoid ambiguity and consequent suspicion on either side that this was merely a first step towards either 'Dublin rule' or nationalist capitulation and acceptance of partition. Their wording contained the provision that the constitutional status of Northern Ireland was a matter for the majority within Northern Ireland, whether that be Orange or Green.

> The Governments of the United Kingdom and of the Republic of Ireland, recognising that Northern Ireland is a territory in which there are two communities with divided loyalties and in which special arrangements are required to ensure that those loyalties can be fully expressed . . . have therefore resolved:
>
> (1) to take further measures to secure the common concerns of their peoples and to ensure co-operation and harmony in future relations without prejudice to the independence or the sovereign rights of both states;
>
> (2) that there shall be no change in the constitutional status of Northern Ireland as part of the United Kingdom until a majority of the people in Northern Ireland desire a change;
>
> (3) that appropriate measures shall be taken by both sides to guarantee the rights and interests of both communities in Northern Ireland and that if at any time in the future a majority of the people of Northern Ireland should vote to join a united Ireland, corresponding measures shall be taken by both states to guarantee the rights and interests of both communities within a unitary Irish state.[26]

As a means of improving security co-operation, Boyle and Hadden suggested reforms to the judicial system which would maximise its flexibility and enable it to deal more effectively with the IRA. Their plan envisaged a facility allowing the police forces of both jurisdictions to cross the border, while judges from one administration could sit in the courtroom of another in any case with a cross-border element. An Anglo-Irish inter-parliamentary tier was proposed which would monitor the progress of such reforms and help to resolve any disputes which might arise as a result of the new arrangements. Central to Boyle and Hadden's proposals, therefore, was the idea that any new constitutional arrangements for Northern Ireland must be more proactive, relying less on the vagaries of the internal partici-pants for success. The key here was primarily London–Dublin agreement, the rationale being that unionist–nationalist and Protestant–Catholic agreement would emerge, once the benefits of the former became obvious.

In July 1985, a report commissioned by the SDP–Liberal Alliance appeared under the title *What Future for Northern Ireland?* The Alliance Commission, like its Forum and Kilbrandon predecessors, concluded that the Northern Ireland conflict could not be solved without an Irish dimension. They too illustrated their wish to externalise the issue by taking the Northern Ireland actors out of the equation. They identified the major sticking point to be not in the accommodation of intercommunal differences within new political structures but rather how such structures would relate to those outside Northern Ireland. The stress fractures in the power-sharing executive of 1974 were not created by the sharing of power within Northern Ireland but by the Council of Ireland and the perception of the unionist community that they were not playing on a level pitch. Consequently, the Alliance Commission suggested that, while an Irish dimension was essential, it should have a London–Dublin axis rather than a Belfast–Dublin axis and would best be facilitated within a British–Irish parliamentary council. What the commission failed to realise was that the relationship between the unionist community and London was not the same as that between the nationalist community and Dublin. While Northern nationalists have traditionally viewed the Southern government – however erroneously – as a protector of their collective interests, unionists have no such illusions about the British government. Their insecurity about the intentions of the state to which they claim loyalty has left unionists feeling isolated and vulnerable. Given the conditional loyalty which is a result of such insecurity, it was highly unlikely that they would regard the Alliance Commission's proposals as a levelling of the playing field.

The unionist response to the avalanche of proposals for political reform which had surrounded them for the preceding six months, and which contained very little for them to enthuse over, came with the third report of the Northern Ireland Assembly Devolution Report Committee. This report, compiled by Sir Frederick Catherwood and published in October 1985, recommended an extension of legislative devolution to the existing

Assembly, with a bill of rights to protect minority interests. Legislative proposals considered discriminatory were to be referred to the Secretary of State, providing such a course of action received a minimum of 30 per cent support in the Assembly. The Catherwood plan, weighing in at a modest three pages, was given scant attention by anyone outside the unionist community and was ignored by the policy-makers. In truth, the Catherwood Report was simply a rehash of *The Way Forward* and contained little evidence of new ideas within unionism.

By the summer of 1985 it was clear to most observers that some new political initiative was being considered and, given the Anglo-Irish dialogue of the preceding five years, all the signs were that any new settlement would contain a greater role for the Southern government. The two unionist parties had by this time formed a pact to co-ordinate opposition to newly elected Sinn Féin councillors on local councils. This coalition was later to become a crucial element in the unionist campaign of opposition to the AIA. Desperate to pre-empt a deal, the DUP and UUP formed a joint working party in August, whose brief was to repel any agreement that proposed to give Dublin a say in the affairs of Northern Ireland. Later the same month, Ian Paisley and James Molyneaux wrote to Margaret Thatcher expressing their profound anxiety about the impending initiative. The letter contained the veiled threat of violence, arguing that the unionist leaders were the last hope for constitutional politics and the only remaining barrier to civil war. If the rumours about Dublin involvement were true, then unionist politicians would lose credibility and the paramilitaries would take control. The political climate therefore made Paisley and Molyneaux 'fearful for the future of constitutional politics'. In September, they sent a second letter to the Prime Minister, complaining that the Vatican had been briefed by the Irish government about recent developments in Anglo-Irish relations while British 'citizens' in Northern Ireland were kept in the dark by their own government. Thatcher was chastised for her dismissive attitude towards the unionist community. 'The Pope is to know more about your deliberations than Unionist members of the British Parliament.'[27] The letter also contained the prophetic announcement that any new Anglo-Irish initiative would result in a secretariat in Belfast, staffed by Irish and British civil servants. The unionist leaders made it clear in the letter that they would be willing to consider any 'reasonable' proposal for the protection of minority interests – short of seats in Cabinet – in any new devolved administration, together with the possibility of Belfast–Dublin discussions to consider matters of mutual interest.[28]

Alas, the time for negotiation had passed. Thatcher's mind was made up and she was about to deliver on her promise of 1979.[29] She had tried various schemes (the Atkins Talks and rolling devolution in the Northern Ireland Assembly) in the hope of reaching an agreement. Failing to secure any such agreement, the Prime Minister was now going to impose her own 'solution'.

The motives and principles of the Anglo-Irish Agreement

> The three men primarily responsible, Sir Robert Armstrong, Sir Geoffrey Howe and Douglas Hurd, work easily together. They have similar world views and similar personalities. None of them has any enthusiasm for the Union. They see Northern Ireland as an encumbrance – a drain on the economy and an obstacle in foreign relations.[30]

The Anglo-Irish Agreement, signed by Margaret Thatcher and Garret FitzGerald at Hillsborough Castle on 15 November 1985, was unquestionably the most important political initiative in Northern Ireland since the power-sharing executive of 1974. (The text of the Agreement is reproduced in Appendix I.) The two leaders signed a formal treaty to be lodged with the United Nations, whose aim, as declared in the joint communiqué, was to be:

> Promoting peace and stability in Northern Ireland; helping to reconcile the two major traditions in Ireland; creating a new climate of friendship and co-operation between the people of the two countries; and improving co-operation in combating terrorism.[31]

Why was the Agreement signed? Was it, as stated, an attempt to bring peace and stability to Northern Ireland, or did more Machiavellian principles underpin its birth? How could it be that Margaret Thatcher, who had previously been considered by unionists to be a friend of the Union and only a year earlier had said 'Out Out Out',[32] had turned around and 'sold them out'? If she condemned the three models of government proposed by the *New Ireland Forum Report* on the grounds that they compromised British sovereignty, how could she now grant Dublin a formal role in the governing of Northern Ireland?

John Bruton, a member of the Irish government at the time and later Taoiseach, provides the Irish government perspective at its most basic. Speaking in February 1996, over ten years after the signing of the Agreement, he emphasised the necessity for Dublin to formalise its role in Northern Ireland and to represent nationalist grievances to the British government.

> It was designed to give an institutional recognition to the fact that the nationalist community in Northern Ireland had a loyalty to an all-Ireland idea, a concern about their minority status and the way that they were being treated, and a need for the Irish government to act as a guarantor of their rights and of their position.[33]

Garret FitzGerald's recollection was that, almost immediately on Thatcher's re-election in 1983, he authorised his diplomatic adviser Michael Lillis to conduct private soundings with British officials to determine how receptive the government were likely to be to overtures from Dublin and simultaneously to make them aware of the Irish government's commitment to progress. FitzGerald describes a subsequent meeting with Thatcher at Chequers on 7 November as constructive, though he seemed more concerned with getting a process started which would place Northern Ireland on the British government's agenda before it became submerged under more immediate domestic priorities, rather than looking for any substantive progress on issues of political reform within the six counties. From his own account this approach would appear to have succeeded.

> Many months were to elapse . . . before we learnt that in discussions with her Ministers and senior civil servants at Chequers after our departure, Margaret Thatcher had instructed that consideration be given to preparing for a major new initiative on Northern Ireland.[34]

Thatcher had expressed her agreement that to do nothing might well be worse than attempting an initiative; the shape of that initiative, however, was originally seen by Thatcher as being aimed primarily at security co-operation, and only later developed into a more ambitious policy aimed at political reform.

Academic opinion of the governments' motives in signing the AIA is divided. Anthony Coughlan, in his incisive though ominously titled book *Fooled Again?*, rejects the suggestion that the Agreement was signed to promote peace and stability.

> The Agreement ushers in a new phase in Anglo-Irish relations. It adds the ire and humiliation of northern unionists to the discontent of northern nationalists. That it will bring peace and stability to the Six Counties – the main claim for it at its launching – seems a self-evident absurdity. If the IRA are bombing and shooting because the British will not leave Ireland, why should they stop because Garret FitzGerald and John Hume tell the British they can stay?[35]

Coughlan's central argument is that the AIA was designed to suit the interests of the two sovereign governments in London and Dublin rather than the people of Northern Ireland. From this perspective, the political problem for both governments was not that of finding constitutional structures which would accommodate the two communities, but rather how a 'foreign policy' could be devised for Northern Ireland which would facilitate a more efficient management of the conflict and thereby relieve domestic pressure on the two governments. Coughlan suggests that the Irish government saw the AIA as a means of revitalising the Fine Gael–Labour coalition and alleviating the tension in domestic politics which was the result of a flagging economy. This, he claims, and not an objective concern for the political problems in the North of Ireland, was the motive which lay behind the Irish signing of the Hillsborough Agreement.

> The Irish government needed a publicity coup. A year before the Taoiseach had been humiliated by Mrs Thatcher's 'Out, Out, Out' to the Forum options. . . . A second dismissal would publicly destroy him. His government lagged 19 points behind Fianna Fáil in the polls. The economy and public finances were worsening weekly. . . . Young people were again emigrating in large numbers. An atmosphere of hopelessness was abroad in the land. The Taoiseach's liberal credentials had been destroyed by his precipitating a painfully divisive national referendum on abortion. A north–south breakthrough would distract attention from all this. It might yet save the day for the coalition.[36]

Similarly, according to Coughlan, the British viewed the AIA as a means of wrapping the 'Irish problem' in cotton wool. The improved relationship with Dublin would reduce the actual problem, namely the military threat of the IRA, while the political kudos which was certain to flow from the initiative would improve Britain's relations with the rest of the world. The situation in Northern Ireland which had tarnished Britain's image for the previous twenty years would no longer be a point of embarrassment between Britain and its allies and would, most importantly, relieve the constant pressure from the United States to do something constructive.[37]

However, Garret FitzGerald's recollection of the period does not support this analysis. His account of discussions with Secretary of State Tom King in September 1985 confirms the notion that the two governments were attempting to move in different directions, rather than simply implementing an agreed master-plan for their mutual benefit:

> . . . an NIO representative said that he had been directed by the Secretary of State to say that he was very concerned in regard to the presentational impact of the Secretariat. The first couple of meetings of the joint body and the location of the Secretariat should not at the outset be in Northern Ireland but rather in London, leaving open the question of where they should be located after that. The NIO intervention came as a bombshell, not merely to us but, it was clear, to other members of the British team. The whole agreement as it had emerged over such a long period clearly hinged on the role of the Secretariat and on its location at the centre of the administration of Northern Ireland in Belfast, and this attempt to re-open this fundamental issue was, to say the least, maladroit.[38]

FitzGerald's account of his relations with Tom King during the run-up to the signing of the AIA would suggest that the British were becoming worried at the thought of unionist political opposition and Protestant paramilitary violence, and the British desire for a 'soft launch'[39] of the Agreement was at cross-purposes with the Irish government's view. FitzGerald's meeting with King on 6 November 1985 suggested an incredibly fluid situation considering the importance of the political initiative.

> Tom King, infuriatingly, went back once again to the question of what the Secretariat would actually be doing. With whom would it be in contact? And how it would do business? These matters had of course all been settled during the previous discussions, as was pointed out. . . . After this long and inconclusive discussion, and with the proposed signing date of the agreement barely a week away, I wrote to Margaret Thatcher to summarise our position as it had evolved and to stress the urgency of speedily finding a solution to the intergovernmental differences on the issue. . . . And I concluded by saying that on both sides we were now approaching fundamental decisions about whether to proceed or not with what was now before us.[40]

When it was suggested to FitzGerald that far from being a Machiavellian power-play[41] there appeared on the contrary to be a degree of chaos surrounding the negotiations, he replied that this was a final attempt to prevent the British from reneging on earlier commitments.

> The NIO by that stage began to worry about the effects of it and wanted to have the Conference not meeting here [Belfast] and to postpone the Secretariat's establishment. They wanted to go back upon what had been agreed, and we had obviously to resist that because these were essential elements of the Agreement, and that caused problems. So we had to take a very tough line in the end to make sure things worked out, and that paid off when eventually they conceded ground. But it was really a bit difficult at the end when suddenly they went back on what had already been settled, as we thought. That was our perception.[42]

FitzGerald's recollection of the negotiations leading up to the signing of the Agreement would suggest a haphazard affair, not an elaborately choreographed event designed to achieve a sequence of pre-planned responses. It may be worth reflecting that if the political elites were clever enough to engage in the sort of lateral thinking many have credited them with over the AIA they would surely have solved the conflict long ago. While Irish politics lends itself to paranoid vistas, it is clear that those taking the political decisions had relatively modest objectives. Margaret Thatcher has stated that her motives were uncomplicated:

> I started from the need for greater security, which was imperative. If this meant making limited political concessions to the South, much as I disliked this kind of bargaining I had to contemplate it. But the results in terms of security must come through.[43]

Another point which puts a dent in the Machiavellian thesis concerns the actual prosecution of the AIA by the two governments. The interminable disputes which followed its introduction over security co-operation and the administration of justice suggest not so much a well-thought-out policy initiative between two governments working in tandem towards the same hidden agenda, as two competing pressure groups who wanted different things out of the relationship.

In her assessment of the success of the AIA, for example, Thatcher employs the sole criterion of security co-operation to make a judgement. She does not seem concerned about the administration of justice or nationalist attitudes to the state, or a metamorphosis in Northern Ireland's political landscape, but instead appears to view the AIA as a lubricant to ease extradition and protect British policy from international criticism.

> The fact remained that the contribution which the Anglo-Irish Agreement was making to all this [security] was very limited. The Unionists continued to oppose it – though with less bitterness as it became clear that their worst fears had proved unfounded. It never seemed worth pulling out of the agreement altogether because this would have created problems not only with the Republic but compromised our position with broader international opinion as well. Still, I was disappointed by the results. The Patrick Ryan case [In December 1988 the Irish Attorney General refused to extradite Fr Ryan to Britain on the grounds that public statements by senior government ministers including Margaret Thatcher, had precluded his chances of receiving a fair trial] demonstrated just how little we could seriously hope for from the Irish.[44]

Some commentators have suggested that security concerns do not explain the motives behind the signing of the AIA, as violence was much worse in the mid-1970s than in the mid-1980s. It is true that the most intense phase of political violence was in the early seventies, during the early days of direct rule and after the fall of the power-sharing executive. The policy of 'Ulsterisation' (a British government policy preference introduced in the mid-1970s for using regional, i.e. RUC/UDR personnel, rather than 'security forces' from Britain) resulted in a considerable reduction in the number of British soldiers being killed, while the IRA changed both its structure and strategy, becoming more selective in its choice of targets. These changes amounted to the achievement of 'an acceptable level of violence', while the AIA, in raising the political temperature, actually increased the level of political violence and necessitated greater involvement of the British army in the conflict.[45] However, there were other elements in the security picture which were less positive. It was not the *actual* level of violence which motivated the two governments so much as the fear that those who were perpetrating it were gaining in strength and capability. While republican violence may have decreased, the IRA was much stronger in other ways. Their reorganisation into a cell structure of active service units had rendered them almost impervious to British infiltration and lessened the damage which could be done by informers. They had become much more sophisticated in their ability to accrue revenue and transform this – through international links with Libya – into military hardware. Finally, they had made significant strides in their technological capability, and were thus able to mount more politically significant attacks such as that on the Conservative party conference in Brighton in 1984. This worry about what the IRA were *capable* of doing in the future rather than what they were doing at the time functioned as a sword of Damocles in the minds of British policy-makers. The Brighton bombing shocked the British government and the statement by the IRA Army Council that, although they had been unlucky on that occasion, Margaret Thatcher would have to be lucky all of the time, made the security situation a pressing and immediate problem for those who previously considered themselves to be untouchable. The Anglo-Irish dialogue which had been taking place in earnest since 1983 was always likely to lead to some sort of agreement between the two governments, but, despite her public chutzpah, Thatcher and her government were rattled by the Brighton bomb and consequently became more amenable to the Irish government's analysis that political reforms and security improvements were both necessary elements of any new initiative.

In addition, there was a fear that the 'armalite and ballot-box' strategy announced by Sinn Féin's Danny Morrison in the early eighties was bearing fruit. The Irish government in particular seemed to be worried, not only about the IRA's military potential, but that Sinn Féin's brand of militant republicanism was going to eclipse the constitutional nationalism of the SDLP and therefore pose a political threat to the *status quo* both north and south of the border. This point is linked to the fact that the dynamics of the AIA and the motives of the political actors lay not in the mid but in the early 1980s. FitzGerald's recollection of his reasons for wanting a new political initiative would tend to substantiate this point.

> Sinn Féin had gained relative to the SDLP, to the point where shortly after my return to office [November 1982] I was advised that at the forthcoming British general election they could conceivably win three or four seats, as against one or two for the SDLP. I was told also that the two communities in the North were more polarised than ever, and that the security situation had deteriorated. . . . I had come to the conclusion that I must now give priority to heading off the growth of support for the IRA in Northern Ireland by seeking a new understanding with the British government.[46]

It is clear from FitzGerald's account of events that the dynamics of the AIA from the perspectives of both governments lay in the potential threat of militant republicanism dictating the political agenda in Northern Ireland.

> The Northern Ireland Committee of the Government reviewed our strategy at a meeting on 15 January [1985], and John Hume came to see us on the

sixteenth en route to his meeting in London with Margaret Thatcher. We knew that he had recently become more confident that the SDLP could hold its own against Sinn Féin in the May local elections, but we urged him not to present himself as overconfident about this and thus seeming to write off the Sinn Féin threat, for it was the perceived menace of the SDLP losing ground to Sinn Féin that had provided in the first instance the underlying logic of the agreement we were seeking with the British government.[47]

As FitzGerald later explained, while fears about Sinn Féin eclipsing the SDLP (which were the original dynamic in 1982–83) appeared unfounded in 1985, this rationale was gradually being overtaken by a new agenda. Referring to a meeting between Peter Barry, Douglas Hurd and Geoffrey Howe on Monday, 4 February 1985, FitzGerald pointed out the metamorphosis that had taken place since 1983:

> By this point it was clear that the fear that Sinn Féin might defeat the SDLP at the local elections in May no longer concerned us or the British as much as it had done; the Provisionals [sic] were not now expected to threaten the SDLP's position as had been feared in 1983 and 1984. But the negotiations had now gained a momentum of their own, and the joint fear of Sinn Féin electoral success had gradually been replaced on both sides by a positive hope of seriously undermining its existing minority support within the nationalist community.[48]

To sum up the motives which lay behind the signing of the AIA, it would be accurate to conclude that a proactive mood evolved due to a combination of favourable circumstances together with political actors eager to grasp the opportunities which developed. Both administrations were beset by economic crises and needed to reinvigorate their flagging popularity. Both were concerned about the security situation and the potential escalation of political instability. The British and Irish governments had established sufficient rapport to know they could do business with one another and were attracted by a scheme which did not require the active participation or support of those in Northern Ireland for its survival.[49] Previous policy initiatives, from the Sunningdale Agreement to the Northern Ireland Assembly, required the support or at least acquiescence of the internal actors for their success. The Hillsborough Agreement was more prescriptive, the key to its survival being the maintenance of diplomatic harmony between the two governments. This was the central genius of the AIA and, as we shall see later, the ability of the two sovereign governments to manipulate externally a framework for an internal solution insulated their policy from attack by those most likely to be unhappy with it.

Interpreting the Anglo-Irish Agreement

Before looking in detail at the unionist response to the AIA, it may be useful to provide an outline of exactly what was signed at Hillsborough Castle on 15 November 1985. In general terms, a compromise was reached between the British and Irish governments whereby in return for a formal recognition by Dublin of the legitimacy of Northern Ireland (notwithstanding Articles 2 and 3 of the Irish constitution) London agreed to confer with the Southern government on all matters that affected the rights of the nationalist minority within Northern Ireland. This did not mean – in strict terms at least – that the British had to take any notice of anything Dublin had to say. The Agreement was an international treaty lodged with the United Nations and not a piece of legislation, though a motion of support was passed by the House of Commons by 473 votes to 47 on 27 November, while a similar motion was passed in Dáil Éireann by the narrower margin of 88 votes to 75. One of the most impressive dissections of the Agreement has been provided by Tom Hadden and Kevin Boyle.[50] They correctly declare that the 'Agreement represents the most significant and carefully prepared development in the relationship between Britain and Ireland since the partition settlement of the 1920s.'[51]

Article 1 of the Agreement declared that the constitutional status of Northern Ireland was based upon the consent of the people in Northern Ireland and that this would remain unchanged until a majority of the people consented to such change; this clause moved Charles Haughey to denounce the Agreement with the following declaration:

> It represents an abandonment of Irish unity and a copper-fastening of the partition of our country. It will not bring peace or stability but only serve to prolong violence and strife . . . The Agreement is in total conflict with the Constitution, and in particular Articles 2 and 3 . . . For the first time ever the legitimacy of the unionist position, which is contrary to unification, has been recognised by an Irish government in an international agreement . . . The British guarantee to the unionists has been reinforced by the Irish government, and the government has also endorsed the British military and political presence in Ireland. . . . what is proposed is that the Irish government by becoming involved in the existing British administration in Northern Ireland, however tenuously, will afford that administration an acceptance, an endorsement and an approval, which constitutionally they cannot and should not do. The Inter-Governmental Conference only formalises an existing right of the Irish government to make its views known, but in return we have given everything away . . . The impression is given to our friends around the world that we are now fully satisfied about the situation in Northern Ireland, that they need no longer be concerned about us and that we have finally accepted the British presence in Ireland as valid and legitimate . . . It is a triumph for British diplomacy which undermines the very basis of constitutional nationalism.[52]

The legality of the AIA, questioned by Haughey, was later to be tested in the Irish Supreme Court by UUP members Chris and Michael McGimpsey, the object being to prove its incompatibility with Articles 2 and 3 of the constitution. The eventual outcome of this case – *McGimpsey* v. *An Taoiseach* (1990) – ruled that there was nothing in the AIA which weakened the status of the six counties as part of the national territory, and thus the unionist case was disallowed. While the unionists lost their legal challenge, the Supreme Court judgment reinforced the political significance of Articles 2 and 3 within the unionist community by pointing out that their achievement was a 'constitutional imperative'. The view that the terms of the AIA were consistent with the *achievement* rather than merely the *existence* of the Republic's constitutional aims reinforced unionist fears about the Agreement. Notwithstanding Haughey's opinion, the AIA can be interpreted in such a manner, as Article 1(c) sets out a mechanism (unity by consent) for the establishment of a 'united' Ireland.

When Garret FitzGerald was asked whether he was ever worried about the constitutionality of the Agreement (even though he was out of government when the McGimpseys brought their case against it), he replied 'No'. He said that his administration was extremely careful during the drafting stage to ensure that they did not move away from the existing position, because of that very difficulty. '. . . we stuck to the Sunningdale wording and that is why we stuck to it, because it had been through our courts and had been upheld already.'[53]

In his book *Ulster: Conflict and Consent*, Tom Wilson commented that the Irish government's refusal to compromise on Articles 2 and 3, by accepting the legitimacy (as opposed to merely the reality) of the Northern Ireland 'state' and writing this into the text of the AIA, did not decrease unionist fears that Dublin was intent upon regaining the six counties. He suggested that Irish intransigence over this reform produced an inevitably negative reaction from Protestants in Northern Ireland and was largely responsible for their almost unanimous rejection of the Agreement.

> If this *de facto* recognition had been accompanied by *de jure* recognition – that is to say, by the removal of Article 2 from the Irish Constitution – the situation in 1985 would have been transformed. The British Government might well have pressed for such a change during the negotiations. Even if, in the end, it had been thought right to accept an Irish refusal to change in order to save the Agreement, the British Government could have made it clear, in its public announcement, that it accepted this refusal only with reluctance.[54]

However, Wilson's analysis is factually incorrect. His assumption that the Irish government were reluctant to compromise on Articles 2 and 3, despite the best efforts of the British administration to convert them to a more flexible approach, does not correlate with the recollection of

FitzGerald, who points out that it was actually the British who tried to dissuade *him* from attempting to amend Articles 2 and 3 by means of a constitutional referendum. Pointing out the difficulties which a written constitution presents to the executive, FitzGerald revealed that although he wanted a referendum on the articles as part of the political package, the British government vetoed this on the grounds that he might lose the referendum and thus wreck the whole initiative.

> We were not worried about the constitutionality, but we recognised that the formula we had used was from the Unionist point of view less than fully satisfactory because we had to be very careful about our courts. If we were not going to change Articles 2 and 3, we had to be careful, and we couldn't get British support for that because they were afraid we would lose the referendum. At that meeting in November '84, [Chequers summit, 19 November 1984] I asked to see Margaret Thatcher privately, and beseeched her to understand the importance of [Articles] 2 and 3 and that we had to have an Agreement which would enable us to put them to a referendum as we would never satisfy the Unionists unless we removed them. The whole next day they backed off that, and that was that.[55]

One of the most important innovations of the Agreement was enshrined within Article 2, which announced the establishment of an Intergovernmental Conference (IGC) to deal on a regular basis with political matters, security and related matters, legal matters including the administration of justice and the promotion of cross-border co-operation. The IGC was intended to include the Secretary of State for Northern Ireland and a representative from the Republic, expected to be the Minister for Foreign Affairs, and the conference would be serviced by a permanent secretariat to be stationed at Maryfield on the outskirts of Belfast.[56] Article 2 added weight to the arguments of those who interpreted the AIA in terms of the Machiavellian model described earlier, with its statement that the Irish government could put forward its views and proposals on matters within the conference, insofar as such matters were not the responsibility of a devolved administration in Northern Ireland. This argument – that the AIA was designed to coerce the unionists, prevent them saying no, and force them to come to some sort of compromise with the nationalist community – was denied by Tom King in a BBC interview shortly before the end of his period as Secretary of State for Northern Ireland.[57] As we shall see later, such denials cut no ice with the unionist community, many of whom adhered to the belief that the AIA was designed in such a way that power-sharing would result from their desire to remove the odious influence of Dublin in the affairs of Northern Ireland. Beyond recognising that the Agreement represented a compromise between the British and Irish governments, it is difficult to determine precisely what the new role of Dublin was to be. While applauding the general motives of the AIA,

Fortnight magazine commented that, although it was easy to give a simple summary of the new policy,

> . . . it is much more difficult to give a detailed analysis of the agreement. It is drafted not in the precise language of constitutional lawyers but in the flexible language of politicians. Almost everything has been left open. The British and Irish Governments have agreed to confer on certain specified matters in the new Anglo-Irish Ministerial Conference. They have not committed themselves to anything.[58]

The question of what precisely had been signed at Hillsborough was complicated by the two governments saying different things about its significance. Did the IGC provide the Irish government with a purely consultative role, or did it represent an involvement in executive action and decision-making? Garret FitzGerald recommended the AIA as being practically the realisation of one of the Forum options: '. . . as near to Joint Authority as one can get'.[59] The Republic's Minister for Justice Michael Noonan was equally triumphant about the deal, declaring that: 'In effect we have been given a major and substantial role in the day-to-day running of Northern Ireland.'[60] Needless to say Margaret Thatcher was making very different noises, maintaining that the Irish role was purely consultative and that the constitutional position of Northern Ireland had not been altered by the Agreement. 'Far from representing any threat to the union of Northern Ireland with the United Kingdom, the Agreement reinforces the Union.'[61] The Tory backbench MP Julian Amery criticised the AIA in the House of Commons for its ambiguity, its inconsistency and its attempt to 'be all things to all men'. 'The nationalists are being told that the agreement is a step towards the re-unification of Ireland, while the unionists are being told that it is a guarantee of their remaining in the UK.'[62] Aughey, in an acute analysis, maintains that the differences between the two governments in both the tone and the substance of their respective positions were not an accident but rather a deliberate fudge designed to placate the conflicting desires of their domestic audiences. 'The interests of the British government have been served by playing down the constitutional significance of the Agreement while the reverse has been true for the Irish government. Neither side is being entirely truthful or accurate in the presentation of their case.'[63]

O'Leary suggests that the significance of the AIA is best understood negatively, in that it was not three of the things it was claimed to be. It did not constitute joint authority, that is, an exact sharing of sovereignty over Northern Ireland between the two signatories. Secondly, it did not put the unionists on notice that a reunification of Ireland would be enacted on an as yet undetermined date. Thirdly, the AIA did not, as Charles Haughey had claimed, represent a *de jure* abandonment of the Republic's constitutional claim to Northern Ireland.

If the Anglo-Irish Agreement is not formal joint authority, neither a formal notice to Unionists of eventual reunification, nor the formal abandonment of territorial irredentism by the Irish Republic, then what is its constitutional significance? First, it is the formalisation of inter-state co-operation; second, a formal notice that while the Unionist guarantee remains, Unionists have no veto on policy formulation within Northern Ireland; and, third, the formalisation of a strategy which binds the Irish Republic to a constitutional mode of reunification which is known to be practically infeasible, and therefore facilitates the end of the Nationalist monolith in the Republic's politics.[64]

This is clear-sighted analysis, though the significance of the Agreement is only really appreciable in retrospect, as the AIA was in essence a frame-work or process for resolving differences rather than 'a substantive edifice of agreement'.[65] The extent to which the Republic's role impinged upon British sovereignty in Northern Ireland, if at all, could only be judged after the IGC had been in place for some time due to the flexible language used in the Agreement. The commitment to resolve differences by seeking consensus, for example, could mean anything from just a little more consultation than before to a mode of informal joint authority by London and Dublin over the internal affairs of Northern Ireland. Back in 1985, however, few unionists were in any doubt about the role which had been conceded to the Irish Republic. Almost universally they rejected it as a product of 'Perfidious Albion', an undemocratic 'diktat' designed to undermine their constitutional position (and by implication their social, religious and economic position) within the United Kingdom.

The initial unionist response

We pray this night that thou wouldst deal with the Prime Minister of our country. We remember that the Apostle Paul handed over the enemies of truth to the Devil that they might learn not to blaspheme. O God, in wrath take vengeance upon this wicked, treacherous lying woman; take vengeance upon her, Oh Lord, and grant that we shall see a demonstration of thy power.[66]

The editorial in the *Belfast News Letter* on the morning after the signing of the Agreement illustrates through a combination of fear and anger the shock felt by the unionist community. 'At Hillsborough yesterday the ghosts of Cromwell and Lundy walked hand in hand to produce a recipe for bloodshed and conflict which has few parallels in modern history.'[67] Unionists felt betrayed not only because they saw the Republic being given a formal role in the internal affairs of Northern Ireland (even a consultative input was obnoxious to them, though many unionists believed that the Agreement went beyond that, regardless of British reassurances to the contrary) but also because of what they saw as the underhand way in which their 'birthright' had been given away, without even a nominal consultation with their elected representatives. At a special sitting of the Northern Ireland Assembly the day after the Agreement was signed, James Molyneaux used a seasonal metaphor which caught the general mood and expressed a widespread concern: 'We are going to be delivered, bound and trussed like a turkey ready for the oven, from one nation to another nation.'[68]

The Alliance Party's John Alderdice agreed that the AIA represented a fundamental shock to the unionist system which it took them a while to recover from. Speaking over ten years after its introduction, he recalled:

> It was like a bereavement, because first of all there was a kind of numbness, then a sense of anger and blame, then a kind of wandering around in uncertainty as to where to go next and what to do next. Then quite interestingly, a shift towards integration, and that's not surprising from a psychological point of view. We call it 'identification with the lost object'. What happens is, when someone who is important to you dies, what you tend to do is identify with it and hold on to a lot of things about the person who's gone. So, whenever this bereavement occurred, where any sense of trust of the British government and establishment was broken, the response, paradoxically, was to overattach itself. And so you got the rise of the CEC [Campaign for Equal Citizenship], the rise of the Conservative Party, an increasingly integrationist stance by the Ulster Unionist Party and so on, which may appear paradoxical but is quite understandable in psychological terms.[69]

Many unionists felt humiliated as much by the manner of their treatment by the British government as by the content of the policy itself. Twelve days after the signing of the Agreement, UUP MP Harold McCusker made an electrifying speech to the House of Commons which provides a definitive expression of the emotional bond felt by many Ulster unionists towards Britain.

> The Agreement deals with my most cherished ideals and aspirations. . . . I stood outside Hillsborough, not waving a Union flag – I doubt whether I will ever wave one again – not singing hymns, saying prayers or pro-testing, but like a dog and asked the Government to put in my hand the document that sold my birthright. They told me that they would give it to me as soon as possible. Having never consulted me, never sought my opinion or asked my advice, they told the rest of the world what was in store for me. I stood in the cold outside the gates of Hillsborough castle and waited for them to come out and give me the Agreement second hand. . . . I felt desolate because as I stood in the cold outside Hillsborough castle everything that I held dear turned to ashes in my mouth. Even in my most pessimistic moments, reading the precise detail in the Irish press on Wednesday before, I never believed that the Agreement would deliver me, in the context that it has, into the hands of those who for 15 years have

murdered personal friends, political associates, and hundreds of my constituents.[70]

It has since been made clear that the lack of consultation with the unionist leaders was requested by the British government, against the better judgement of Dublin who wanted to bring them in on the process. Commenting six years after the signing of the Agreement, Garret FitzGerald made it clear that the impetus for keeping unionists outside the process came from London rather than Dublin and that this lack of consultation fuelled unionist misunderstanding (such as that displayed by McCusker) as to the intent of the new policy.

> I suppose the difficulty was that we had no means of explaining to them the rationale of the Agreement. We did have contacts with them, but we were inhibited from telling them what was in the Agreement by virtue of the fact that the British would not forgive us if we did. They took the view that the unionists should not be told. When we pressed them in September [1985] that perhaps more briefings should be given, they said 'no'. So that inhibited us.[71]

When asked in February 1996 if he thought that the governments should have consulted the unionist political community to a greater extent, Taoiseach John Bruton's reply echoed that of his predecessor. He commented that as he had not been directly involved in the drafting of the AIA he could not provide an authoritative response to the question, but added:

> In the first instance, the task of consulting unionists on the Anglo-Irish Agreement would appear to have rested with the British rather than the Irish government. The question as to why adequate consultation didn't take place would first and foremost have to be answered by the British government. Having said that, of course, the more people are consulted about something the more is the likelihood that they might agree to it.[72]

After the Agreement was ratified, the unionist coalition decided to make the Northern Ireland Assembly the spearhead of their immediate response; this was a questionable move as the government were looking for an excuse to get rid of the Assembly due to the non-participation of the SDLP. Thatcher had tired of the Prior initiative as well as the man himself, and by the beginning of 1986 was more interested in the London–Dublin axis and the political benefits this might bring to her administration than in flogging a horse which had obviously expired in 1982. Possibly realising that the Assembly was doomed anyway, the two main unionist parties were determined to use the remaining days of its existence to 'debate' the iniquities of the Agreement.

On 5 December, Ian Paisley proposed a motion to set up a 'Committee on the Government of Northern Ireland' with a remit 'to examine the implication of the Anglo-Irish Agreement for the government and future of

Northern Ireland and the operation of the Northern Ireland Constitution Act 1973, and the Northern Ireland Act 1982'.[73] To accommodate this committee, the normal meetings of the Assembly and its scrutiny committees were to be suspended, except for the Finance and Personnel Committee which was to investigate the effect that the Agreement would have on the provincial civil service.[74] This blatant breach of the Assembly's remit as laid out in the 1982 Act precipitated the formal withdrawal of the Alliance Party and removed the last vestiges of credibility from an institution whose legitimacy was already wafer-thin. The *First Report from the Committee on the Government of Northern Ireland*, published on 29 January 1986, considered in detail the implications of the IGC, and whether or not its role went beyond granting consultative rights to the Irish government. The committee contrasted the conflicting statements of the two prime ministers, Thatcher on the one hand declaring that the IGC 'will have no executive authority either now or in the future'[75] while FitzGerald commented in the Dáil that it was 'going beyond a consultative role, but necessarily, because of the sovereignty issue, falling short of an Executive role'.[76] The Assembly committee concluded that the IGC

> . . . is acting as an executive for most of the time on the matters referred to it. This institution is unique, it is not formally a condominium or joint sovereignty arrangement, it does not have as yet, the external trappings of a joint authority. But the Committee is of the opinion that it is a joint authority in embryo. If it develops and establishes its own procedures and precedents, then within its 'field of activity' and in accordance with its precedents it will become the effective government of Northern Ireland.[77]

With characteristic mistrust of British government motives the committee chose to accept Garret FitzGerald's rather than Margaret Thatcher's explanation of the scope of the Agreement. They went on to declare that, even if the British Prime Minister were correct in her analysis that the AIA provided only consultative rights to the government of the Irish Republic, this in itself was a change in the constitutional status of Northern Ireland. 'At its very lowest the agreement concedes a right of consultation: it is therefore, even at that level, an encroachment upon British sovereignty.'[78]

The *First Report* characterised the AIA as an attempt to coerce unionists by means of 'carrot and sticks' into accepting power-sharing with the SDLP. They argued that the 'carrot' was contained within Article 2(b), which stipulated that those matters which were devolved would not be within the remit of the Irish government. The committee regarded the 'sticks' as being enshrined in Articles 5(c) and 10(b), which provided that in the absence of devolution the Irish government could put forward views and proposals within the IGC on all transferred matters. There can be little doubt that the AIA was designed to act as a catalyst for devolved power-sharing between the unionist and nationalist communities within

Northern Ireland. However, the unionists saw it as a sign of British treachery and of an ultimate intention to completely disengage. Claims by Thatcher that the AIA enshrined the status of Northern Ireland for the first time in an international treaty did nothing to mollify the insecurity felt by the unionist community. The *First Report* condemned Article 1(a) as a vague statement which could be interpreted in a number of ways, and which did not (unlike the Sunningdale declaration) explicitly state what Northern Ireland's position was within the United Kingdom. 'The Committee is of the opinion that Article 1 is the weakest statement yet of the position of Her Majesty's Government.'[79]

Regardless of its semantics and the question of whether or not it gave a consultative or executive role to the Southern Irish government, the Agreement shocked many unionists because they finally realised that they were an unwanted child. Despite the frequency with which they acted as fodder for the British war machine, the realisation dawned on many unionists in November 1985 that they remained part of the United Kingdom on sufferance, a residue of Britain's imperial past and a diplomatic loose-end yet to be tied up. The unionist perception after the AIA was that, despite assurances to the contrary, they were not as British as the people of Finchley but were rather as British as the people of Hong Kong. This feeling of betrayal is embodied in the following statement by William McClure, a member of an Independent Loyal Orange Lodge deputation who gave evidence to the Grand Committee. His comments, while typical of unionist sentiment at the time, also demonstrate the level of unionist insecurity and his empathy with what he considered to be another besieged minority betrayed by the British government.

> I believe that this Agreement is a victory for the IRA. . . . Margaret Thatcher was bombed to the negotiating table. She went there because of the IRA campaign, she went there because she was attacked in Brighton. . . . In the same way that Margaret Thatcher sold out the white people in Rhodesia, she is prepared to sell out the Unionist and Loyalist people of Northern Ireland. She said at Hillsborough that she was a Unionist and a Loyalist. I say that Margaret Thatcher is neither a Unionist nor a Loyalist; by her act that day she destroyed the Union as we know it.[80]

The Grand Committee's reaction to the AIA was typically bullish, due in large part to the misconception of the unionist leadership that their co-operation would be necessary for the survival of the policy. However, as has already been pointed out, the AIA was unlike other British initiatives in that it did not rely on the acquiescence of internal actors. Confident that the government would not be able to ignore the voice of a million Protestants, the Grand Committee decided unanimously that not only would they refuse to countenance any new power-sharing deal with the SDLP, but that proposals which they themselves had previously put forward for devolved government would be withdrawn for the duration of the Agreement.

> The Committee is unimpressed at this crude form of blackmail. It considers that it is pointless to submit to it and so fasten the chains of this framework more firmly around the people of Northern Ireland. Devolution within the terms of the Agreement is a trap and the parties in the Committee are determined to avoid any form of devolution within the framework of this Agreement. Consequently the various schemes for devolution considered by the Devolution Report Committee, including the *Catherwood Plan*, are withdrawn and no longer operative while this Agreement subsists.[81]

It is clear that the AIA was the most significant policy initiative in Northern Ireland since partition and that unionists of all shades were implacably opposed to it and determined to undermine its workings. The identification of external aggressors (especially ones so familiar to them as the Irish and British governments) produced a terrific cohesion within the unionist community which was already institutionalised in the joint unionist pact. Regardless of their many differences, here was something that everyone could unite against. The old slogans of 'No Surrender' and 'Ulster Says No' came readily to the tongue and became consistent themes in the unionist 'guttural muse'. However, this unity was a chimera which obscured the rich social and intellectual diversity within the unionist community and it was the interaction of that diversity with the anti-Agreement campaign which illuminated the nature of the unionist identity.

Notes

1   P. Bew and H. Patterson, *The British State and the Ulster Crisis: From Wilson to Thatcher* (London, 1985), p. 112.
2   A. Kenny, *The Road to Hillsborough: The Shaping of the Anglo-Irish Agreement* (Oxford, 1986), p. 37.
3   ibid., p. 38.
4   P. Arthur, 'Anglo-Irish Relations Since 1968: A Fever Chart Interpretation', *Government and Opposition*, Vol. 16, (1983), pp. 157–74.
5   A. Guelke, *Northern Ireland: The International Perspective*, (Dublin, 1988).
6   ibid., p. 94.
7   Kenny, *The Road to Hillsborough*, p. 41.
8   T. Hadden and K. Boyle, *The Anglo-Irish Agreement: Commentary, Text and Official Review* (London and Dublin, 1989), p. 7.
9   A. Aughey, *Under Siege: Ulster Unionism and the Anglo-Irish Agreement* (Belfast, 1989), pp. 50–1.
10   ibid., p. 51.
11   Kenny, *The Road to Hillsborough*, p. 58.
12   ibid., p. 61.
13   ibid., p. 62.
14   ibid., p. 66.
15   ibid., p. 71.

16 ibid., pp. 74–5.
17 ibid., p. 77.
18 ibid., p. 81.
19 ibid., p. 82.
20 ibid.
21 G. FitzGerald, *All in a Life* (Dublin, 1992), pp. 521–2.
22 ibid., p. 521.
23 ibid., p. 522.
24 ibid., p. 523.
25 K. Boyle and T. Hadden, *Ireland: A Positive Proposal* (London, 1985).
26 ibid.
27 E. Moloney and A. Pollak, *Paisley* (Dublin, 1986), p. 391.
28 C. O'Leary, S. Elliott and R. Wilford, *The Northern Ireland Assembly 1982–1986: A Constitutional Experiment* (London, 1988), p. 188.
29 See note 1.
30 *Times*, 5 December 1985.
31 Northern Ireland Assembly Papers, No. 237, Vol. I, Appendix A, p. 97.
32 Thatcher did not actually say this though it has become an effective shorthand of her comments.
33 John Bruton, interview with author, 21 February 1996.
34 FitzGerald, *All in a Life*, p. 478.
35 A. Coughlan, *Fooled Again? The Anglo-Irish Agreement and After* (Cork and Dublin, 1986), p. 7.
36 ibid., p. 19.
37 ibid., pp. 19–20.
38 FitzGerald, *All in a Life*, pp. 557–8.
39 ibid., p. 557.
40 ibid., pp. 558–9.
41 As suggested by Anthony Coughlan in *Fooled Again?* and more recently by Brendan O'Leary and John McGarry in *The Politics of Antagonism: Understanding Northern Ireland* (London, 1993).
42 G. FitzGerald, interview with author, 8 April 1992.
43 M. Thatcher, *The Downing Street Years* (London, 1993), p. 385.
44 ibid., p. 413.
45 O'Leary, 'The Anglo-Irish Agreement: Statecraft or Folly?', *West European Politics*, 10(1)(1987), p. 14.
46 FitzGerald, *All in a Life*, p. 462.
47 ibid., p. 529.
48 ibid., p. 532.
49 Brendan O'Leary puts this succinctly: 'One reason why both British and Irish officials like the Anglo-Irish Agreement is that its survival seems much less dependent upon the actors within Northern Ireland than previous attempted solutions.' O'Leary, 'Anglo-Irish Agreement: Statecraft or Folly?', p. 25.
50 Hadden and Boyle, *Anglo-Irish Agreement*.
51 ibid., p. 1.
52 Dáil Debate, 19 November 1985, in *Irish Times*, 20 November 1985.
53 G. FitzGerald, interview with author, 8 April 1992.
54 T. Wilson, *Ulster: Conflict and Consent* (Oxford, 1989), p. 196.
55 G. FitzGerald, interview with author, 8 April 1992.
56 O'Leary et al., *Northern Ireland Assembly*, p. 189.
57 *The View from the Castle* (BBC [NI], 1988).

58   *Fortnight*, No. 230 (December 1985), p. 3.
59   Coughlan, *Fooled Again?*, p. 11.
60   ibid.
61   House of Commons Debate, 26 November 1985, in Coughlan, *Fooled Again?*, p. 18.
62   Coughlan, *Fooled Again?*, p. 16.
63   Aughey, *Under Siege*, p. 53.
64   O'Leary, 'Anglo-Irish Agreement: Statecraft or Folly?', pp. 6–7.
65   Kenny, *The Road to Hillsborough*, p. 101.
66   Rev. Ian Paisley addressing his congregation at the Martyrs Memorial Church in Belfast on the Sunday following the signing of the Anglo-Irish Agreement, in P. Bew and G. Gillespie, *Northern Ireland: A Chronology of the Troubles 1968–1993* (Dublin, 1993), pp. 188–9.
67   O'Leary et al., *Northern Ireland Assembly*, p. 190.
68   P. Arthur and K. Jeffery, *Northern Ireland Since 1968* (Oxford, 1988), p. 18.
69   Dr John Alderdice, interview with author, 7 February 1996.
70   Kenny, *The Road to Hillsborough*, pp. 102–3.
71   Garret FitzGerald, interview with author, 8 April 1992.
72   John Bruton, interview with author, 21 February 1996.
73   O'Leary et al., *Northern Ireland Assembly*, p. 191.
74   ibid., p. 191.
75   Speech made by Margaret Thatcher in the House of Commons on 26 November 1985, in Kenny, *The Road to Hillsborough*, p. 113.
76   Speech made by Garret FitzGerald in Dáil Éireann on 19 November 1985, in Kenny, *The Road to Hillsborough*, p. 105.
77   *First Report from the Committee on the Government of Northern Ireland*, Northern Ireland Assembly Papers, No. 237, Vol. I, p. 46.
78   ibid., p. 52.
79   ibid., p. 40.
80   ibid., Vol. II, p. 47.
81   ibid., p. 66.

CHAPTER 2

The Unionists of Ulster:
An Ideological Analysis

Who are the loyalists of Ulster? . . . They are loyal to Britain yet ready to disobey her; they reject clerical tyranny yet oppose secularism; they proclaim an ideology of freedom and equality, except for Catholics; they revere law and authority, then break the law.[1]

Unionist ideology contains diverse interest groups with little in common other than a commitment to the link with Britain. While this position remains relatively cohesive during periods of constitutional crisis when they can articulate what they do not want (namely a weakening of the link with Britain), the coherence of the ideology begins to disintegrate when unionists are forced to establish a consensus for political progress. The tensions created by conflicting perceptions of their political environment and how they should tackle these external forces were exacerbated by the realisation that many unionists were committed to the Union for different reasons. While some regarded it in isolationist terms, as a guarantor of Protestant religio-cultural hegemony, others saw Northern Ireland as simply another region of Britain which should be governed in precisely the same manner as the rest of the country. These conflicting perceptions of identity inevitably spilled over into alternative political objectives, with the former group demanding the restoration of legislative devolution based on majority rule, while the latter advocated full political integration with the rest of the United Kingdom. Between these two poles lay a number of other objectives such as power-sharing, administrative devolution and various schemes for regionalism which combined both legislative and administrative features. The nett result of this multiplicity of objectives was political stagnation. The emphasis placed on unionist unity precluded any one objective – over and above that elusive goal of securing the Union – being given priority. Although the DUP were unified behind a coherent policy – majority rule – the UUP were not prepared to accept it. There were two main reasons for this: firstly, many in the party found majority rule an unpalatable philosophy and secondly, those who were not against it on principle realised – quite correctly – that it was no longer a practical option in terms of reaching a negotiated settlement with the SDLP and the British government.

This chapter presents a critical review of recent academic literature on Ulster unionism. The various hypotheses presented are tested against the first-hand responses of leading members of the unionist political community. The narrative seeks to explain the dynamics of the unionist ideology and the complex motivations which underpin unionist political behaviour.

The roots of modern unionism

The seeds of modern Ulster unionism were sown after the 1798 rebellion, when the liberal Presbyterian merchants of Ulster began a process of *rapprochement* with the Protestant ascendancy and became estranged from the Catholic population. Before the Act of Union in 1800, the wealthy merchant class in the north-east of Ulster resented their exclusion from political power and were envious of the landed gentry who could instigate legislation detrimental to their interests. The Act of Union, however, together with rapid industrialisation and economic change in Ulster, especially the growth of Belfast's cotton industry, contributed to a shift in Presbyterian politics as their fortunes were now inextricably bound up with the British economy. The decline in liberal sentiment after 1798, due to the failure of the rebellion, the anti-liberal excesses of the French revolution and the realities of Catholic political mobilisation, led to a shift in Presbyterian political thought. Economic self-interest was an underlying force (though not the only force) behind these changing political attitudes, facilitating and in some cases causing a revision of traditional allegiances. It is not an unusual law of political motion, nor is it an illegitimate one, for individuals or ethnic groups to follow what they perceive to be their own self-interest. Thus the Presbyterians, who had sympathised with their Catholic neighbours while they shared some of their legal and political difficulties, gradually drew closer to the conservative Anglicans once these had begun to dissipate.

A good starting point for examining unionism's historical legacy and the extent to which environmental circumstances fashioned its ideological identity is provided by Jennifer Todd. She has commented that the unionist ideology is essentially an umbrella organisation under which two distinct groupings exist. The first, Ulster loyalism, sees itself primarily as a self-contained cultural community with a secondary political allegiance to the British state. The other strand is an Ulster British tradition which defines itself as being an integral part of Greater Britain with a secondary regional patriotism for Northern Ireland.[2] This group consider themselves to be as British as natives of London or Sunderland, with a fondness for their 'Irishness' which is akin to that felt by those on the 'mainland' for their own regional differences, such as the Cockneys in London or the Geordies on Tyneside.

This perspective was illustrated by the response of UUP councillor, Michael McGimpsey, when he was asked to explain why he was a unionist. It was put to him that his political philosophy appeared to be a secular one based largely on a pragmatic assessment of the political environment, a perception of advantage which concluded that the Union was the best political vehicle to secure the economic prosperity of Northern Ireland. His response provides a perfect illustration of the Ulster British tradition, rejecting the subliminal belief of his more radical unionist colleagues that Northern Ireland is a self-contained nation.

> As I see it, I'm an Irish Unionist. I'm Irish, that's my race if you like. My identity is British, because that is the way I have been brought up, and I identify with Britain and there are historical bonds, psychological bonds, emotional bonds, all the rest of it you know. I'm not so much anti-united Ireland as I am pro-Union with Britain, and I would be quite prepared to take a united Ireland tomorrow, if somehow the whole of Ireland could have some form of Union grafted [on] . . . But to talk of independence in Northern Ireland, Northern Ireland is not a country, Northern Ireland is a province of Ireland and it is a province in the UK and I think that the notion of a national identity or group identity or racial identity or cultural identity here is a nonsense. We have a particular ethos OK, but it draws so heavily from the Irish and from the British that I think independence is a nonsense.[3]

Todd builds upon her previous work in an article published in 1988[4] by identifying three specific aspects of Ulster Britishness, the first being a cultural commonality and distinctive regional identity with the rest of the people in Northern Ireland. The second characteristic could be termed civic unionism, a celebration of and commitment to state structures such as Westminster, the monarchy, the health and education systems, even the physical infrastructure. The Irish-Canadian academic John Wilson Foster epitomises this strand within unionist thought in his contribution to *The Idea of the Union*, a publication which bills itself as 'a manifesto in favour of the constitutional link between Northern Ireland and Great Britain'.

> The constitutional union of the four portions of the kingdom best expresses the historic and contemporary realities of my cultural and ethnic kinship, as well as safeguarding the citizenship and civil rights I wish to have the continued privilege of enjoying. My pro-Union position does not of course erase the strong sense of neighbourhood I feel with the southern Irish and with northern nationalists, nor the many contexts in which I properly regard Ireland as an unpartitioned island.[5]

The third element of Todd's findings has been defined as a 'supremacist aspect of some unionists' British identity',[6] a glorification of the history of Empire and British military adventures (however exaggerated or sanitised), and, as identified by David Ervine of the Progressive Unionist Party (PUP), a tendency at times to 'want to be more British than the British them-selves'.[7] John McGarry and Brendan O'Leary have stylishly summarised this aspect with the comment:

> It includes such attributes as proclaiming the merits of being part of a great imperial power as opposed to a small independent neutral nation; assuming British culture to be the acme of civilisation and Irish culture to be the converse; asserting Protestantism to be incontestably superior to Catholicism; regarding Britain as the epicentre of liberty, democracy and justice by contrast with benighted Ireland; and taking opposition to British institutions as a sign of ineffable backwardness, amorality, immorality, or cultural immaturity.[8]

The Ulster loyalist tradition, meanwhile, is firmly rooted in their Presbyterian ancestry, and the ideals and values which permeate radical loyalist behaviour are heavily influenced by this historical legacy. The environmental circumstances of the Presbyterian settler community left an indelible stamp on their collective psyche which has influenced their subsequent activity. Upon their arrival in Ireland, the Scottish Dissenters felt isolated and vulnerable, squeezed as they were between the orthodox Episcopalians in the Church of Ireland and the sheer numerical dominance of the Catholic Church, both of whom regarded Presbyterianism as heresy. In addition to this the settlers were in a minority even in the nine counties of Ulster, which created the feeling of physical and economic insecurity. These environmental factors were naturally exacerbated by political events such as the constitutional uncertainty which surrounded the accession to the British throne of James II, an occurrence which appeared to signal their downfall until William of Orange's victory at the Boyne. This insecurity produced a desire for independence and a siege mentality identified by Lyons when he commented that 'The settlers who struck their roots in the region, did so under conditions of maximum insecurity and this insecurity became a permanent part of their psychology.'[9] In later years, such insecurity proved to be a successful breeding ground for the Orange Order, evangelical religion and cultural isolationism within the Ulster loyalist community.

Recent academic literature tends to reinforce this observation, with McGarry and O'Leary declaring that

> . . . there has been a persistent Ulster 'loyalist' tradition, which despite its self-description, is much less loyal to Britain than the British unionists, and more equivocal about the national identity of Ulster Protestants. They display 'settler insecurity', and their primary imagined community is themselves. Their loyalty is to the Crown, rather than Parliament, provided the Crown defends Protestant liberties in Ulster.[10]

While the authors are broadly correct in their analysis, this chapter will demonstrate that their sweeping generalisations about concepts such as loyalty to the Crown and the dynamics of Protestantism overlook important nuances within this section of the unionist community.

Many contemporary observers, such as Garret FitzGerald, perceive political Protestantism to be a dichotomy between moderates and extremists. When asked to elaborate upon his Irish Identities Dimbleby Lecture of 1982 in which he argued that unionism was not a monolithic creed, he defined the difference in terms of two rival groupings.

> There is unionism and there is loyalism basically, the unionists are mostly in North Down I think! There, there is an upper-middle class who go into the army, go over to universities in Britain, which is unionism; but when you go beyond that into so-called loyalism, it is loyalty to Ulster not to the Union with Britain and it is mis-described as unionism which causes a lot of confusion for everybody. We can deal with unionism; loyalism is more difficult to deal with, because it is divisive within their own community.[11]

FitzGerald's comments demonstrate an inability to appreciate the complexities of unionist ideology. As shall become apparent in the rest of this chapter, such a simplistic division hides a multilayered phenomenon which almost defies categorisation. Todd has emphasised that the competing political agendas of the Ulster loyalist and Ulster British traditions have been central to unionism's development as a reactive ideology, capable of describing what it is against – for example Home Rule, the Anglo-Irish Agreement or the Frameworks Document – but incapable of articulating a positive political programme without destroying the fragile coalition of separate interest groups contained within it. In Todd's analysis, therefore, the central anomaly of unionism is the group solidarity and political strength of unionists when faced by an external enemy and their corresponding weakness during periods of relative stability, witnessed by their inability to develop a consensus over core principles and political objectives. The Rev. Martin Smyth was asked whether the unionist protest against the Anglo-Irish Agreement was hampered by the multiplicity of objectives enshrined in the differing cultural perspectives of unionists such as Ian Paisley and John Taylor. Smyth conceded the point when asked if political progress was made difficult by the fact that every time unionism tried to move forward, everybody wanted to go in different directions.

> I do, I think that is one of the difficulties as I've said in two gatherings over the last weekend. I had asked the folk, 'if you were Jim Callaghan or if you were John Major, what would you do?' Going back to the time during the Convention [1975], when I was carrying on discussions with [John]Hume and [Paddy]Devlin after the Convention, and we were having a reasonable rapport, I'm not saying complete agreement but a reasonable rapport, and then for their own purposes, some DUP folk went mad, and that meant that Callaghan had to deal with the problem. 'Oh, do I go down this road'

where, using the worst possible scenario, a third of the people . . . didn't want to be British. Then out of the two-thirds, there was a division. 'What would you do?' So you just, 'when in doubt, do nowt'. So yes, I have no difficulty in accepting that has been one of the difficulties in getting progress.[12]

Radicals and pragmatists

The role of fundamentalist evangelical religion is a key feature of radical unionism and is central to its reactive nature, the political subtext of such Bible-Protestantism being that the enemies of today have remained unaltered from the enemies identified during the eighteenth century. Liberalism such as that represented by the ecumenist movement is regarded by this tradition within unionism as a movement designed to make Ulster Protestants compromise, not just in their political habits but in their spirituality as well. This fear of liberalism and compromise can again be seen in terms of unionism's historical legacy, in that the battle between the 'Old Light' and the 'New Light' dramatised in Belfast by Henry Cooke and Henry Montgomery in the nineteenth century is still being waged today. This was brought into sharp focus in December 1982 when a Presbyterian minister in Limavady, the Rev. David Armstrong, was attacked for allowing a Catholic priest to deliver Christmas greetings to his congregation. Wesley McDowell, Limavady's Free Presbyterian minister, castigated Armstrong upon his arrival for being 'a charismatic, a compromiser, and a Romaniser'.[13] This perspective has created a political and philosophical rigidity within radical unionism (a less problematic definition than 'loyalism') where politics is seen as a struggle to maintain socio-cultural hegemony and religious liberty. As external political motivations have remained constant in this analysis, the way to achieve political success is seen in terms of what worked in the past.

The following extract from a discussion between Clifford Smyth, a former DUP activist, and Dr Gordon Gray, a leading Presbyterian theologian, which took place outside a World Council of Churches conference in Geneva, illustrates the tendency for 'religion' to militate against unity within the Protestant community. It also presents an example of how radical Protestant thought is locked into its political position by an inflexibility derived from religious certainty. Pragmatism in the political sphere is rendered impossible, as this would only serve to dilute their distinctive cultural identity and, perhaps more importantly, would endanger the free exercise of their religion and thus imperil their chances of being granted eternal salvation.

 . . . . : Away from the conference chamber, which I had declined to enter because of my opposition to shared worship between Roman Catholics and Protestants, I spoke to Dr Gordon Gray. I'm in a sense disappointed to find you as a Presbyterian here at this ecumenical conference.

G: Well that's your problem not mine, for I think it's a wonderful thing to be here. We are affirming the same Biblical faith as Calvin affirmed. Involvement in conferences of this kind in no way means a compromise of our Reformed tradition . . .

S: You see I wouldn't accept that, I would contend that Calvin's concern was to establish clarity in matters of religious thought, and when we come to a conference like this, there's considerable confusion and ambiguity about the basis of membership, and what really constitutes a Christian.

G: Have you been in the conference itself?

S: Well I haven't been in the conference . . .

G: Have you been at any other conferences for instance?

S: No I haven't been at any comparable conferences, but what I have done is studied the issue in very considerable detail . . .

G: Studied what issue?

S: The issue of ecumenism, in the modern world. I have maintained opposition to the ecumenical movement from [sic] a very considerable length of time, going back years, and in the early days I was taught that the ecumenical movement was really a Romeward trend, and I don't believe, if you look at the situation, that can seriously be disputed, that really ecumenism is moving back under the shadow of Rome.

G: Well now, you're using two terms there, a Romeward trend, and under the shadow of Rome. I would ask you to justify those terms.

S: Right, well what I mean by that is that we are moving into an age when there will be a confederation of churches, with the Pope as the head, like a kind of Queen of the Commonwealth; now that's not my statement, that's the statement of one of the bishops who is very ecumenical in his thinking . . . This is what they're aiming at.[14]

It would be easy to sneer at this warped logic as evidence of a classic unionist Neanderthal man, a bigot in bigot's clothing to whom the word 'compromise' would appear to be anathema. To do so would be to misunderstand the integrity and serious implications represented by this strain of unionist thought. For many radical Protestants, such religious conviction lies at the centre of their political activity, with the battle for electoral support being merely an extension of the battle for souls. It should not be surprising to learn that such concrete religious beliefs produce a concrete political ideology which is unwieldy, inflexible and unadaptable to changing circumstances. Journalists Ed Moloney and Andy Pollak quote a former member of the Free Presbyterian Church as an example of how politics and religion are inextricably linked within the DUP, with the church being the engine room of the party's electoral machine.

> They bring an evangelical fervour to electioneering because electioneering is part of the crusade, because it's spiritual warfare, part of their spiritual work. Some more pious church members do object saying it's all unspiritual and worldly, but at election time, their objections count for nothing and the whole church becomes centred round it. It's the same battle for God and Ulster, that's the key.[15]

Religion also acts as a hindrance to unionist unity, as despite the increasing secularisation of the DUP during the 1980s it still plays an important role in policy formulation. This is not so much because of the doctrinal semantics of fundamentalist Protestantism, but because of the political aspects of dogmatic theology. Radical unionism, such as that exhibited above by Clifford Smyth, has a much greater number of political absolutes which are non-negotiable than have the more secularly orientated Ulster Unionist Party. The DUP have to fit developments in their political environment into their existing matrix, or world view. This leads to an extrapolation of events to the degree where their political vision descends into paranoid delusion. The Machiavellian intent of antagonistic world forces headed by the Vatican, the American government and the European Union are all continually conspiring against Ulster Protestantism. Consequently, any political movement by the British government is often seen as a product of these antagonistic forces and must therefore be resisted. This penchant within the DUP for conspiracy-theory politics was illustrated by Ian Paisley during an interview conducted several years after the signing of the AIA. When asked to explain why Margaret Thatcher changed her mind so dramatically from her response to the three options of the New Ireland Forum to endorsing the Agreement barely a year later, the DUP leader recited what has become a familiar litany.

> I believe that Enoch Powell is right in saying that Washington had a big say in bringing it about. But I think that we are getting away from the real lobby. The real lobby came from the Vatican. The real lobby came from the Church of Rome. The Church of Rome throughout the world was preaching against the unionist position for years, and using their pulpits, and their newspapers, and the vast machinery of the Roman Catholic political machine that emanates from the Vatican, as a lever against everything that Ulster Protestants stand for. I can see that influence in Europe, because the European Parliament is largely a Roman Catholic Parliament. . . . I go to the source, and I believe the source is the Roman Catholic Church.[16]

The Ulster Unionist Party is generally less hysterical in its political analysis and is usually capable of determining where its best interests lie, even if being unable to achieve them. Michael McGimpsey's analysis of why the AIA was signed does not allude to the web of international intrigue outlined by Paisley, but regards it purely as a matter of British domestic policy-making: 'I think clearly Thatcher decided that something radical had to be done, and that is where the Agreement came from; it might have been partly the child of the Forum, but it was primarily the result of the Brighton bombing.'[17]

In contrast to the radical unionist perspective, the Ulster British ideology (to use Todd's terminology) has a primary cultural identification with Great Britain and a secondary regional loyalty to Northern Ireland. This tradition is much less insular, viewing the British connection in terms of technological progress and the effects of the British welfare state on society's health and education. The cultural perspective of this strand of the ideology does not emphasise the mythical figures of the seventeenth century; rather its adherents see themselves bound up in and integrated into the 'British Family' through institutionalised linkages such as industrial connections, trade union organisations and British social welfare policies, which encourage them to view life from a British perspective. The historical legacy also plays an important part in the formation of the Northern Ireland British identity, as family and military connections have created a bond between Ulster and Britain, although this is increasingly becoming a one-way relationship. In addition, the emphasis on Britain's imperial history as taught in the state (*de facto* Protestant) school system and the importance placed on the part played by Ulstermen in Britain's imperial wars, especially at the Somme, have contributed to a cultural identification with those in the rest of the United Kingdom. This identity is reinforced by their view of the Republic of Ireland, as while they conceive of themselves as being progressive, liberal and democratic, they view the Southern Irish as being regressive, conservative and authoritarian. This strand of unionist philosophy was outlined by John Taylor when the Ulster Unionist MP for Strangford was asked whether his unionism revolved primarily around a political allegiance to Britain derived from a perception of potential economic advantage, or rather emanated from a cultural affinity with the people and institutions of the UK.

> Oh it would be more cultural, and loyalty to the Crown, and . . . obviously the kind of society, a sectarian Catholic state which would apply here if we had a united Ireland, we see this in the Republic. Even Garret FitzGerald, the man who signed the Anglo-Irish Agreement, was open enough to say that the South of Ireland was a sectarian state. We couldn't live in that kind of climate here in Northern Ireland as part of the Republic. There are a large number of reasons why one is a unionist, there is the loyalty to the Crown, there is your whole historic background, the fact that one's families for hundreds of years have been connected with the British army, and, of

course, there is also the economic advantages. . . . There are economic advantages for everyone, Catholic and Protestant, but as I say, that is not the only factor that is the guiding philosophy for being a unionist. I think I would still be a unionist even if the economy hadn't progressed in the way it did.[18]

Edward Moxon-Browne proposes an economic hypothesis to account for the divisions within unionism between radicals and pragmatists. He argues that those who see themselves as British are likely to be upper-class Protestants, with the lower social orders being more attached to a regional 'Ulster' identity. This argument is based on the premise that middle- and upper-class Protestants have benefited from the Union in terms of economic and political power, whereas the lower socio-economic groups who have not prospered to the same degree would not feel the same cultural or institutional affinity. In this analysis, the unionist identity is seen as being primarily based in economic materialism. 'For the Protestant, national identity is a pragmatic issue, it is based on perceptions of advantage.'[19] Moxon-Browne uses data from the 1978 Social Attitudes Survey to illustrate the division within the unionist ideology, as the results showed that two-thirds of the Protestant community viewed themselves as British while approximately 20 per cent favoured an Ulster identity. This does not explain, however, why large sections of the working class profess to having a British identity, or why the Democratic Unionist Party has become increasingly professionalised. These young, urban, upwardly mobile middle-class Protestants are not changing their political philosophies in line with the growth of their material prosperity. Evidence of this fact was provided by the DUP chief whip, Nigel Dodds, when asked to define the central principles of unionism from his point of view. Dodds, a lawyer and graduate of Cambridge University, emphasised not so much a cultural affinity with subjects in the rest of the UK as a desire to retain the link with Britain as a means of preserving the existing cultural ethos within Northern Ireland. The subtext of this rhetoric is that unionists have a strategic political allegiance to Britain for so long as it guarantees the existing Protestant hegemony and prevents the dilution of the region's specific cultural identity through an increase in Dublin's political influence in Northern Ireland.

Well the general principle of unionism, I suppose, is the maintenance of the union with Britain. My view is that at the end of the day, we have got to preserve a British way of life in Northern Ireland. That means seeking at all times to preserve the Union, but if we are forced out of the Union or the Union becomes untenable, then we must preserve that by looking at some form of independence, but certainly not being absorbed by the Irish Republic.[20]

In the past, socio-economic criteria such as those forwarded by Moxon-Browne functioned as a useful shorthand for an understanding of unionist motivations. However, time has moved on and the picture has become increasingly complex. Few of the activists and supporters of the Progressive Unionist Party, for example, are tax exiles from Northern Ireland, yet they display none of the 'little-Ulsterism' which materialist explanations might expect. When asked to define the central principles of unionism from his point of view, the Shankill Road community worker and PUP activist Billy Hutchinson provided a response which could just as easily have come from a prosperous businessman from Northern Ireland's 'gold coast' in North Down.

> For me unionism is quite simple. It's about maintaining the link with the rest of the United Kingdom and I don't think that it's any more or any less. As somebody who was brought up in a Protestant tradition and a very pro-British tradition, my links are East–West politically. I would have links with working-class communities in Liverpool, Glasgow, Manchester and London. I have also been brought up in that whole British democracy thing, the Westminster model. . . . So for me, it's not about being a Protestant or anything else and it's not about being an Orangeman . . . pure and simple I think unionism is about the link with Britain and it's as simple as that.[21]

Moloney and Pollak support Moxon-Browne's class-based view up to a point, suggesting that the confessional element within the DUP (by 1981, 89 per cent of DUP councillors were also Free Presbyterians) illustrates a major difference between radical unionists and those of an Ulster British disposition. Their perception of the class difference within the unionist ideology may be more appropriately described as a conflict between materialism and anti-materialism. While many mainstream Ulster British unionists, such as those who inhabit the Ulster Unionist Party, support the Union for social and economic reasons and have a cultural affinity with the rest of the UK,

> The DUP view of the Union is much more fundamental. They regard it principally as a mechanism through which they can best avoid absorption into a Roman Catholic Irish Republic with the resulting destruction of the Bible Protestantism that they hold so dear.[22]

Moloney and Pollak emphasise the importance of the conditional loyalty exhibited by many Northern Ireland Protestants and argue that the professed willingness to rebel against Westminster is due to a deep-rooted independent sentiment fashioned by the conditions of their entry into Ulster in the seventeenth century. Their examination of the DUP tends to negate the viability of the economic hypothesis proposed by Moxon-Browne, with the influx of young urban graduates being particularly significant. These articulate and ambitious 'Duppies' came to prominence after the 1982 Assembly elections, and '. . . their emergence has produced two distinct strands in the DUP'.[23]

The old guard was largely rural and had a basic education, fundamental Protestantism and a belief in Ian Paisley, whilst the new guard, personified by Peter Robinson and Sammy Wilson, was mainly urban, well educated and less directly connected to the Free Presbyterian Church. The early 1980s witnessed the secularisation of the DUP under the careful steward-ship of Peter Robinson, who, like Desmond Boal before him, had convinced Paisley that the party could not expand unless it transcended its Free Presbyterian base. Robinson made himself indispensable to Paisley through his organisational expertise, a fact recognised by the rank and file membership: 'Whatever else he is, Ian is not a great man for the details of organisation. It was Peter who was really responsible for making the DUP into what it is now.'[24] Robinson's political base is East Belfast, an urban constituency with a much smaller proportion of Free Presbyterian members than rural areas such as North Antrim. Built upon the employment centres of Harland and Wolff, and Shorts, East Belfast is predominantly composed of working-class Protestants who find the dogmatism of Free Presbyterianism less attractive than the lower middle classes and rural Protestants who populate its pews. Although their loyalism is equally virulent, it contains little of the restrictive puritanical fervour so apparent within Free Presbyterianism. The suggestion that the DUP can be separated into two groups, religious bigots and secular bigots, is itself something of a simplification. Ian Paisley Jnr contends that the significance of religion within the DUP is rather more complex.

> I think that the DUP markets itself and has always marketed itself to certain sections of the unionist community. First of all, traditional Protestant unionism, I think, is one of the mainstays of the DUP. That doesn't necessarily mean a religious thing but it certainly means that those things which people see traditionally as being very much part of their identity, their whole ethnic mix of being a Protestant evangelical, even though they might go and play the National Lottery and go to the pub at the weekend, at the end of the day their granny or their mother was a good evangelical woman and that's something which they go back to as a touchstone of normality.[25]

Clearly, the changing social profile of the DUP has influenced the political significance of religion within the party. An example of this cultural gap was provided by Castlereagh Borough Council's decision to hold a refer-endum on the issue of whether the Dundonald Ice-Bowl should be allowed to open on a Sunday. The East Belfast DUP incurred the wrath of the Protestant fundamentalist group, The Lord's Day Observance Society, as under Peter Robinson's influence the council's main preoccupation was to keep the rates down through maximising the use of the amenity and reflect public wishes, rather than take a dogmatic and unpopular stand on religious grounds. This controversy was a testament to the success with which Robinson has separated the DUP from the Free Presbyterian Church in East Belfast.

> When he looked at East Belfast and the votes he needed to win and sized up the hard core DUP in it – which basically boiled down to the Free Presbyterian Church – he hadn't a hope of winning it. So he had to broaden the base to bring in people whose loyalty was to the party not the Church and to give him credit he worked incredibly hard to do it.[26]

Robinson's professionalisation of the DUP was accompanied by an influx of young articulate graduates into the party. Emerging during the Assembly elections of 1982, these Young Turks owed their primary allegiance to Robinson rather than Paisley and represented a new faction within the party. The traditional DUP members, those left over from its predecessor the Protestant Unionist Party, were often poorly educated, had a simple unquestioning faith in fundamentalist Protestantism and regarded Ian Paisley as a deity. By the early eighties the character of the membership was changing, with new supporters attracted by a more strident approach to politics, the increased prospects of advancement through the ranks of the party and the outlet for radical socio-economic opinions. This group contained a nursery of young talent including Nigel Dodds, Jim Wells, Jim Allister, Alan Kane and Sammy Wilson, and they appealed to people on secular grounds, with the religious metaphors and evangelical sentiment of the 'old guard' being less evident within their political vocabulary.

Gender imbalance in unionist politics

One consistent feature of this influx of new blood into the DUP was its gender profile. The only women of any significance who came into the foreground of the party were those connected by either blood or marriage to more famous relatives. While the DUP has a number of female elected representatives in local government, few women have gained a substantial profile within this section of radical unionist politics. Iris Robinson is the partner of the DUP deputy leader and was elected to Castlereagh Borough Council as a DUP representative, eventually, due to her own ability, becoming leader of the council. Elizabeth Seawright was elected to Belfast City Council as an independent after the assassination of her husband George Seawright, a former DUP councillor who was expelled from the party for extreme remarks he made about 'incinerating' Catholics. Perhaps the most obvious and interesting example is provided by Rhonda Paisley, daughter of the party leader. As a Belfast City councillor during the late 1980s and early 1990s, she undoubtedly had the highest media profile of any woman within the DUP. This was only in part a consequence of her family ties and probably owed more to another genetic inheritance, namely her gift for staging publicity stunts, such as letting off a rape alarm in the council chamber when a Sinn Féin councillor was trying to speak. Rhonda Paisley personified the culture clash within the DUP between old and new, and this struggle, together with the adversarial nature of the debate in local government, saw her leave active political life in 1992. Paisley was a young, well-educated ambitious woman, with impeccable contacts for political advancement. Though being for many years a practising Free Presbyterian,[27] her social attitudes may have seemed too modern, her lipstick too red and her skirts too short for some of those of a more traditional bent within the party. While nationalists may have perceived her as simply another anti-Catholic bigot and a chip off the old block, a radically different perspective between her and many of her colleagues became apparent when it came to women's issues. One example of this was a row in April 1989 over the siting of two statues in Amelia Street in Belfast city centre and Paisley's support of a motion in Belfast City Council to provide grant assistance of £15,000. The statues depicted two prostitutes in a commemoration of Belfast's local history, as in the past the street had been a thoroughfare for that particular trade in the city. While most of the DUP on Belfast City Council saw this proposal as an outrageous tribute to immoral practices, Paisley, as a feminist and practising artist herself, regarded it as an artistic expression of a contemporary social issue. Rev. Ivan Foster (who was not a member of the council) condemned the decision, claiming that God viewed prostitution as 'wickedness', while Paisley commented that her support for the work was 'a personal one'. Inevitably, the paradoxes inherent in simultaneously advocating dogmatic politics and personal liberalism could not be sustained. In February 1992, Rhonda Paisley announced that she did not intend to defend her seat on Belfast City Council at the district council elections the following year.

> Politics is not my future and there's no point pretending it is. . . . I dread council meetings and I always leave exhausted. People can push and shove me all they like but I'm not going to stay in politics any longer than I have to. I want to paint and I intend to give it my best shot now.[28]

Aside from socio-cultural differences between the 'new women' in the party such as Rhonda Paisley and the 'Stepford wives' (the more traditional social profile of rural matronly housewives with good cooking skills but a basic education and limited independent careerism), the very nature of politics in Northern Ireland has produced a male-dominated environment. While politics is a profession where women are underrepresented generally, due to both anti-social working conditions and deliberate exclusion by the 'clubby' elite who often control candidate selection, this is a much more pronounced phenomenon in Northern Ireland than in either the Republic or Great Britain. The reasons for this are both historical and social. The main political organisations in contemporary Northern Ireland politics either evolved out of violence or were formed in reaction to that violence. As those engaged in the violence – either directly though republicanism and loyalism or peripherally in the peaceful protest of the civil rights demonstrations or the less peaceful counterdemonstrations – were largely male, it was they who dominated the political structures. In addition, political activism in Northern Ireland during the armed conflict between 1969 and 1994 carried a much greater personal risk for those involved than is normally the case in more stable societies and this did little to encourage women to enter the political arena. Because the political debate has taken place in an atmosphere of violence and has rarely deviated from the central issue of the region's constitutional future, such 'debate' has exuded machismo and testosterone, as anyone who has attended Belfast City Council during the period could attest to. While it would be unreasonable to assume that women are any less concerned about the constitutional issue, it would be fair to suggest that the democratic deficit which has existed since the introduction of direct rule in 1972 (with power over socio-economic issues resting not with local politicians but with unelected officials and various quangos) has acted as a disincentive to female involvement in the political life of the region.

> At the beginning of this century James Connolly described the Northern Ireland woman as 'the slave of a slave'. . . . This graphic phrase is no less fitting today. . . . Women in Northern Ireland tend to marry young, start their families soon afterwards and remain by strong family networks. They are not helped to examine in any critical way their domestic role in the home, or indeed their relationship to their husbands and their families: rather they are socialised into a strong maternal role directed to 'keeping the family together', 'making ends meet' and servicing political campaigns largely determined by men.[29]

In social terms Northern Ireland is a very patriarchal and conservative society where 'family values' is one concept which unites both Catholic and Protestant and the woman's role in society is seen in more traditional terms than in Great Britain. One of the few issues which unites 'the two communities' concerns legislation on moral issues such as abortion (which remains illegal in Northern Ireland despite being legal in the rest of the UK), divorce and sex education. There was, for instance, common opposition from the SDLP, UUP and DUP to the opening of the Brook Clinic in Belfast in September 1992.[30] Despite such 'official' opposition, the clinic had a considerable amount of cross-community support among women in the North and has developed a successful service in the region. 'On the opening day, the Reverend Ian Paisley arrived to preach his message of damnation, but he beat a hasty retreat after a number of women outside the entrance started dancing to the hymn "Rock of Ages" when it came blaring over his sound system.'[31]

Given this propensity for social conservatism, there is nonetheless a noticeable underrepresentation of women in unionist politics as compared with their nationalist counterparts.[32] One historical reason for this was that in the struggle to resist Home Rule in Ulster at the beginning of the century, unionism was formed as a political movement dedicated to resisting this legislation through extraparliamentary means. The formation of the Ulster Volunteer Force (UVF) and signing of Ulster's 'Solemn League and Covenant' were not considered activities suitable for women. Many of those who signed the covenant did so in their own blood and pledged to fight to the death over the issue. As few people thought that women should give such a pledge, a separate register was opened, in which the female population could record their support for the cause. Other organisations within unionism which provide a link between the past and the present exhibit a similar patriarchal if not patronising culture. The Orange Order is an obvious example with its pseudo-military regalia and structure, where the vast majority of the membership is male. The widespread presence of Freemasonry (a less visible and less vulgar organisation than Orangeism but perhaps a more powerful one) within the Protestant middle and upper classes is another bastion of male exclusivity within the unionist community.

Evangelical religion has also done little to encourage women to come forward into the political arena. While there are few overt examples where women candidates have been discriminated against because of their gender, the fact that one of the major unionist parties is led by the moderator of the Free Presbyterian Church has been reflected in the political culture. Ian Paisley commented during one of his early battles with a particularly troublesome female parishioner that; 'when you meet a devil wearing trousers it's bad, but a devil wearing a skirt is ten times worse'.[33] While Rhonda Paisley was able to enter the fast-track to advancement within the party, she was the exception rather than the rule. Within this culture, women are rarely seen as equals who deserve access to the same levers in society as their male counterparts, but as inherently different 'creatures' whose function in society should reflect that fact. They should be home-makers rather than house-builders, nurses rather than mechanics, whose God-given function is to look after their husbands and rear their children rather than build independent careers. Those women who subscribe to this agenda (and obviously many do not) are unlikely to build profiles within unionist politics.

Clearly something is fundamentally wrong with a society where over 50 per cent of the population is composed of women, yet which has no female MPs or MEPs and in which only 11 per cent of local government councillors are female.[34] However, while women are underrepresented generally (and particularly so within unionist politics) at the top level, their influence permeates grass-roots politics and community work to a much greater degree.

> Disadvantaged by having no elected female politicians in either the parliaments of Westminster or Brussels, women turned instead to a wide range of activism within the more informal settings of the community and voluntary sectors. Within the 'democratic deficit' of Northern Ireland, this is where the real political activism has taken place and where some of the most talented political women can be found. Rather than pursue the more official road of electoral politics, a road from which many of them have been alienated because of its uncompromising and stagnant style of politics, they have chosen instead to become the effective agents of change in their work with women at the more grass-roots level.[35]

In view of the present level of political debate within Northern Ireland, it is clearly time for both unionist and nationalist parties to develop inclusive mechanisms which provide an outlet for women to participate in the mainstream political process. The debate has already begun. At a conference in September 1995, May Blood of the Shankill Women's Forum indicated that the old attitudes would have to change. 'This isn't good enough. We invited seven councillors from the area to explain their views on women's rights and the lack of women in politics and only one has bothered to turn up.'[36] The UUP's Chris McGimpsey, the lone councillor who did turn up, recognised the difficulties which women faced in gaining a voice in the political system in general and within unionist politics in particular. *Irish Times* journalist Suzanne Breen reported McGimpsey's account of the problems encountered by women in the UUP.

> Mr McGimpsey said that his party had recently established a 'women and consumer affairs committee'. Even setting up a body with so unsatisfactory a title had been a battle. 'Initially it was just to be a consumer affairs committee with special reference to women – presumably because they buy the groceries on a Friday.' When the UUP debated women's rights at its annual conference earlier this year, it degenerated into 'men standing up and taking the piss out of women'.[37]

Evidence of the dissatisfaction at the traditional parties' response to the lack of women in mainstream politics was apparent with the formation of the Northern Ireland Women's Coalition to contest the Forum elections held on 30 May 1996. This cross-party body was more a single-issue interest group than political party, taking advantage of the unique electoral arrangements of 30 May[38] to highlight the gender imbalance in Northern Ireland politics and do something to remedy the situation, while bringing a more pragmatic perspective to the hackneyed debate of the more traditional parties. In comparison to the sterile dialogue going on between unionism and nationalism, separate political structures such as the Women's Coalition may be an effective way, not just of augmenting female representation in the political process, but of redressing the male-dominated cultures prevalent within the existing political organisations in Northern Ireland.

Social diversity within the DUP

Evidence of the tensions within the DUP – between the young, urban, politically secular element, and the older, predominantly rural, overtly evangelical/Free Presbyterian contingent which had originally formed the backbone of the DUP (especially in its former manifestation as the Protestant Unionist Party) – is provided by a comparison of the alternative cultural identities expressed by Sammy Wilson and former DUP member Rev. Ivan Foster. It was suggested to Wilson that there were those within the DUP who would claim to be a Protestant first, and a unionist only for as long as this advanced Protestantism in Northern Ireland. When asked if he would accept the hypothetical situation where the monarch was removed as constitutional head of state in Britain and replaced by an elected president who was not a Protestant, Wilson replied that this would not be sufficient cause for him to withdraw his loyalty from the state.

> Yes, I mean, I don't think my unionism depends upon whether the King or Queen is a 'Prod' or what. Probably the Protestantism that the Queen espouses might be a bit different from the Protestantism I would espouse anyway, so I'm not so sure that it makes all that much difference. No, I mean, my unionism is based much more on the historical connection that there is between this part of the island and the rest of the United Kingdom. It is based on the fact that my identity is more with the rest of the United Kingdom, whether that's culturally or religiously or whatever. . . . I think that one has also got to say that there is a negative reason for it as well, and the negative reason is I don't believe that any unionist would get a fair deal in the Irish Republic. I have no evidence, despite all the promises that have been made, that they are going to change their society.[39]

Wilson's rhetoric contrasts sharply with that of the Rev. Ivan Foster, whose language abounds with religious metaphors and whose primary motivation is evidently the preservation of a fundamentalist-orientated Protestant culture within Northern Ireland. This was brought sharply into focus when he denounced proposed education reforms (what later became the Education Reform [NI] Order 1990) and specifically the emphasis upon cultural heritage studies and education for mutual understanding on the grounds that these represented an attempt by the British government to indoctrinate Protestant children. In describing Dr Brian Mawhinney (the then Education Minister for Northern Ireland) as 'a latter-day Pharaoh' who sought, with the 'stealth of the assassin' and under the 'guise of the educator', to compromise the teaching of true Protestant Christianity, Foster highlighted the strong isolationist element within the DUP.

It would appear that the strategy that Pharaoh adopted, because he feared the growing strength of the Israelites, and felt that it would not suit his purpose just to mount a massacre against the adults, he decided to control them through their children by killing off the all-male children that were born, and thus he could control the nation. . . . I have no doubt that there is an attempt being made to control the thinking, the political thinking particularly, of the Protestant people in Northern Ireland, and where better to make an attempt to do that than in the classroom.[40]

When it was suggested to Foster that these reforms sought to encourage understanding and tolerance of opposing cultures and were aimed at dispelling myths and folklore which fed the sectarian strife in Northern Ireland, his response exhibited the inherent insecurity and fear within some sections of the unionist community. Here we have a classic exposition of a defensive, reactionary ideology, battling against what it perceived to be an aggressive external community. In this analysis, the ultimate aggressor was considered to be the Catholic Church, with the Vatican controlling the European political actors, including of course the policies of the British government. The Machiavellian world which people such as Foster inhabited determined that Northern Ireland was at the top of the Vatican's agenda, and thus the subtext of political reforms introduced by the British government was to eradicate Bible-Christianity in Northern Ireland and thereby reduce the religious and political liberty of the Protestant community. The extent to which Foster's political opinion was informed by his theological critique was demonstrated by his reply to the suggestion that debunking traditional attitudes to opposing religious faiths would lead to greater social harmony. His political opposition to this education reform was the direct result of his religious belief that Catholicism was heresy and was therefore unlikely to be truthful in its interpretation of itself:

> When you see that plan [for educational reform] translated into action, then you begin to suspect what is actually being planned. How can I ask the Roman Catholic Church to paint for me an accurate picture of itself, when, if it did that, it would cause the mass of its people immediately to reject it as no church of Jesus Christ, but a church of the Anti-Christ?[41]

Foster's attitude to political progress again demonstrates the tendency for rigidity to flow from theological certainty, making this strand of the ideology inflexible, unwieldy and incapable of changing its strategy to cope with altered political circumstances. Foster disagreed with the contention that peace could only be achieved when all sections of the community agreed to respect the beliefs and aspirations of their political opponents. His reply to the suggestion that the classroom was a suitable place to begin this process of *rapprochement* between the two sectarian blocs illustrates once again the negative dynamic produced by dogmatic theology. The application of these strict criteria to the political arena tends to vitiate the possibility for moderation because compromise is seen not as a diplomatic solution to an intractable problem, but rather as a way of ensuring that everyone ends up in the wrong.

> Sir, if divisions are to be healed in this province, they are to be healed by each and every one of us coming to the truth. Each and every one of us finding out where we should be standing. Not us all taking a step in each other's direction and arriving on middle-ground, because middle-ground might be still the wrong ground. I believe what is needed in this country is a spiritual reformation, a spiritual revival, a return to Bible-Christianity, and it is all the more surprising that a man like Dr Brian Mawhinney, who I understand was brought up amongst the Plymouth Brethren, and who should therefore have some understanding of what Bible-Christianity is all about, should now be promoting an ecumenical venture of this nature which is designed to change the whole face of Ulster Protestantism, change it, never to be unchanged and brought back again to the allegiance that it once had to the Word of God. It's an attempt to destroy Ulster Protestantism forever.[42]

Any comparative analysis of Foster's rhetoric and that of his former colleague Sammy Wilson would suggest that even within the DUP respective legitimations of the Union differed greatly. It should be noted here that Foster's subsequent resignation from the DUP in protest against the slow pace of the anti-Agreement campaign provides further evidence to support the contention that the DUP's increasing urbanisation and secularisation was being reflected in its policy-making. A testimony to this change was provided by the pact with the UUP, a strategic compromise which created internal tensions between the rural Free Presbyterian grass-roots element and the urban working/middle-class contingent who regarded this arrangement as a necessary evil for political progress.

Another complicating factor within the DUP was provided by class divisions between the party's urban working-class heartlands and the increasingly middle-class composition of the leadership and, more importantly, the conflicting political agendas of the rural middle-class Free Presbyterian voters and their urban working-class secular brethren. Clifford Smyth argues that the extent to which the DUP became a working-class party is a matter for conjecture, commenting that it is impossible to prove Paul Arthur's hypothesis that 'Political Paisleyism was proletarian, but religious Paisleyism attracted lower middle-class congregations which crammed the ample car park with their Cortinas.'[43] While recognising that a distinction does exist between Paisley's church supporters and his political supporters, Smyth contends that '. . . it is a topic which defies statistical quantification and remains therefore a matter of observation'.[44] While the influx of young blood was initially encouraged by Paisley as he needed to broaden the base of the party, the long-term benefits for his own position were questionable. The professionalisation of the DUP augmented the power base of Robinson and diminished Paisley's authority within the party, hitherto insulated through his leadership of the Free Presbyterian Church. The dangers of creating the overmighty subject were to become apparent after the signing of the Anglo-Irish Agreement, as Paisley found it increasingly difficult to control the party and recognised with mounting frustration that it was often Peter Robinson who was setting the political agenda of the DUP.

The conflict within the DUP between secular and fundamentalist factions hampered the party's development as disagreements began to erupt over tactics such as civil disobedience. This was to become particularly obvious after the Hillsborough Agreement, when the inconsistency of party policy suggested that it emanated from more than one source. Although there is a deep-rooted independent sentiment in radical unionism which has grown out of the conditions of their entry into Ulster in the seventeenth century, it does not follow that Moloney and Pollak's summary of this strand of the ideology accurately reflects the reality of unionist political motivation.

> The readiness of Protestants to rebel against Westminster, as well as the occasional manifestations of an independent Ulster sentiment, has its roots here. It is a deep strain in Northern Ireland Protestantism and Paisley has successfully tapped it. His followers' first allegiance is to Protestantism, not to the Union. Their official slogan is: 'For God and Ulster'. As Paisley has often told his supporters: 'The Alliance party is the political wing of ecumenism but the DUP is the political wing of evangelical Protestantism.'[45]

While this could certainly be said to be representative of the DUP in their former manifestation as the Protestant Unionist Party, the changes in personnel and the increasing urbanisation of the party base have complicated the picture. As Sammy Wilson's testimony concerning the basis of the Union would suggest, a degree of secularisation has taken place which has been reflected in DUP policy-making. Ironically perhaps, Ian Paisley Jnr displays attitudes more similar to the secular modernisers than to those traditionally associated with his father. Paisley Jnr, a well-educated, Belfast-born young professional, was asked about the importance of religion in the equation of allegiance. While stressing the importance of the Protestant religion in his personal life and moral code, he differentiates between private ethics and public political manifesto.

> Obviously I'm a very passionate Protestant and I've a very strong Protestant religious view and it's not just a Protestant class view, a Protestant sociological view, it's a Protestant religious view. That's a very personal thing

for me. But, I think that religion comes into Britishness and comes into unionism, for me anyway, only to the point that I believe that religious freedoms are cherished more underneath Britishness, and have more ability to flourish, adapt and to actually exist than they would have . . . under a single Irish nation.[46]

When asked if the hypothetical scenario whereby the British monarchy were abolished and replaced with an elected president who was not a Protestant would present grounds for leaving the Union, Paisley Jnr gave the same response as his party colleague Sammy Wilson.

Not at all. Not at all. Let's face it, we had a Lord Protector you know? We had our revolution, we had our quasi-Presidency . . . and that failed and the British state adopted . . . the constitutional monarchy which we have obviously in adapted form today. So I don't think it would be grounds for me to get out.[47]

When Peter Robinson was asked to outline the central principles of his cultural identity, his response suggested that there is more to the DUP than simply being the 'political wing of evangelical Protestantism'. Asked the same question as Paisley Jnr about the importance of Protestantism and the monarchy to his allegiance to the Union, Robinson commented that such a scenario 'may not in itself, automatically cause one to recoil from being within the United Kingdom, but it removes one of the pegs that holds down our unionism'.[48]

Those politicians who style themselves as representing the views of former loyalist paramilitaries and those who have traditionally been seen as a more insular, intolerant and religiously bigoted element within the unionist community appear to be more flexible on questions such as the monarchy and religion than Peter Robinson. When Gary McMichael, the leader of the Ulster Democratic Party, was asked to define the central principles of unionism from a personal perspective, he replied that 'My unionism is not based upon a protection of my Protestant identity, it's based upon the practical needs of the people of Northern Ireland – all the people.'[49] When asked specifically about his attitude to the replacement of the British monarch with an elected president who was not a Protestant, he exhibited a pragmatic, secular attitude: 'I don't believe that we maintain the Union for as long as the Union retains its Protestant character. That doesn't come into my thinking because I want to see religion taken out of politics.'[50] David Ervine took a similarly prosaic approach: 'I'd be interested in his politics rather than his religion. I'm not interested.'[51]

Attitudes to the monarchy as an essential ingredient of their political allegiance are by no means fixed within the unionist population. Apart from the above testimony, there are elements of the Protestant working class which take an ambivalent view. It should be said that in general terms a devotion to the monarchy (as opposed to the extended royal family) is still strong within urban Protestant communities. However, although the Progressive Unionist Party has a picture of the Queen hanging on the wall of their party headquarters on the Shankill Road in Belfast (it is not a recent likeness), Billy Hutchinson was able to say that '[personally], I would have to say that I'm not even sure that I'm a monarchist. I'm not loyal to any monarchy. What I'm loyal to is my class and also my political beliefs.'[52] David Ervine espouses a similar view, emphasising that his unionism was based more in present-day membership of a liberal democracy (albeit an imperfect one) than in any romantic attachment to a historical figurehead. 'My definition of unionism is very simple . . . and it is merely that I am a citizen of the United Kingdom – no more no less.'[53] He went on:

> It would be ridiculous of me to take a magic wand and just rub the Queen and the royal family out, they are aspects of our society that many many people have a fondness for. . . . Essentially I'm not an elitist and therefore don't like anybody else who is, or don't like any other system that espouses that elitism.[54]

It is clear that to simply define unionism as being a dichotomy between moderates and extremists, as Garret FitzGerald has done, is little more than a caricature of the ideology which does not address the nuances within it. Many of those whose extremism has in the past resulted in their engaging in political violence are in some instances more open-minded than those within the DUP who have pursued more moderate forms of political behaviour. Consider the following responses of David Ervine of the PUP and Peter Robinson of the DUP when questioned about their cultural identity. Though anxious to differentiate between his geographical situation and cultural iconography, Ervine stated that, as far as he was concerned,

> I haven't really got a problem in terms of someone calling me Irish. But if I felt that that were being done to my detriment, then I would define exactly what it was for them and say 'look this is not the case. I firmly believe myself to be British'. We are a peculiarity in that we're both.[55]

The deputy leader of the DUP takes a much more defensive and absolutist position than Ervine, indicating that his cultural identity is a product of what he considers to be an antagonistic counterculture and malign irredentist nationalist project on the other part of the island.

> I resent people suggesting I'm Irish. My wife would throw a tantrum if anybody called her Irish. And that's simply because of not wanting to be associated with this country whose government has been their foe for the last twenty-five odd years.[56]

The complexity of this issue was illustrated when Ian Paisley was asked a similar question. The DUP leader, whom we might expect would be the embodiment of old-style Ulster loyalist sentiment, exhibited a different perspective than that expressed by his deputy leader. 'I was born in the island of Ireland. I have Irish traits in me – we don't all have the traits of what came from Scotland, there is the Celtic factor . . . and I am an Irishman because you cannot be an Ulsterman without being an Irishman.'[57] One of the most eloquent explanations of the apparent conundrum for working-class Protestants in defining their identity within the context of being British while living within an Irish cultural inheritance was provided by Patricia Anderson of Ballybeen Community Theatre. Commenting on her participation in a seminar on the Protestant cultural identity in Northern Ireland organised by the Ulster People's College in Belfast, Ms Anderson illustrates the extent to which some people in the unionist community have come to terms with their dual identity.

> At first it was a bit scary because I didn't want to admit I was Irish. I didn't want anything to do with being Irish, I was British. But then I learned that I am Irish and I can reclaim all my Irishness, the Irish dancing, the Irish language, everything. That's as much part of me as it is to anybody in the nationalist community. I'm very proud to be a Protestant and very proud to be British, but I'm also very proud to be able to sit here and say, 'I'm Irish too' and have as much right to be as anyone.[58]

The pundit's view: a critical assessment of the academic literature

Unionism as Ethno-nationalism

This should be taken to mean a definition of unionist political behaviour which is primarily motivated from a sense of belonging to an ethnic and/or national community within Northern Ireland, with a consequent right to exercise self-determination autonomously. Such unionists are liable to emphasise local/regional characteristics such as religion, culture and historical experience over merely a political allegiance specifically to the Union with Great Britain or, more broadly, the liberal-democratic ideals and principles which that regime is held to represent.

Casting a sociologist's eye on the subject, Steve Bruce attempts to explain the differences between nationalist and unionist political behaviour by contending that Catholic nationalists in Northern Ireland form part of a nation, while Protestant unionists are essentially an ethnic group. This assumption provides the basis for an identity crisis thesis, with Bruce arguing that, devoid of the cultural richness and diversity available to Catholic nationalists, Protestant unionists are forced to articulate their identity in terms of religious exclusivity. In this analysis, nationalist security about their cultural identity has allowed them to secularise their ideology and decouple their Catholicism from their nationalism (for example, marxist republicanism), whereas unionists, by virtue of being a smaller and more vulnerable ethnic group, have not been able to do likewise. According to Bruce, no secure cultural identity is available to unionists outside the confines of evangelical Protestantism. As unionism in this analysis is seen as being primarily concerned with avoiding absorption into the Irish Republic and thereby becoming an even more vulnerable minority, there is a gravitational pull within the unionist community during periods of constitutional uncertainty towards the most vivid expressions of Protestantism. For Bruce, therefore, it is this inability to perceive a common identity outside the boundaries of their religious observance which explains the importance of Protestantism in unionist politics.

> A people need a shared ideology if they are to remain a people. Although the minority in the North does draw on religious symbolism, Catholics do not need religion. Three-quarters of a united Ireland already exists within travelling distance. Nationalism is so well-established as to provide a strong source of identity. Ulster loyalists, however, need their evangelical religion because it is the only viable source of a shared identity. After all, they want to be British, but the British do not want them. They are loyal, but loyal to what? The only coherent set of ideas which explains the past, which gives them a sense of who they are, which makes them feel justifiably superior to Catholics, and which gives them the hope that they will survive, is evangelical Protestantism.[59]

There are a number of reasons why Bruce's arguments are ultimately unsatisfactory, not least of which is that he appears to suggest that the terms evangelical Protestant and unionist are synonymous. His assertion that this strand of Protestantism is the most natural constituency from which the unionist ideology is composed is highly contentious. One could ask why it is then, if this is the case, that the Ulster Unionist Party enjoys a significantly greater amount of electoral support from the Protestant community (even during times of crisis such as the post-AIA period) than does the DUP. Secondly, Bruce's equation of evangelical Protestantism with Ian Paisley and the DUP does not take account of that party's increasing secularisation. Nor does it explain why Ian Paisley, the personification of the politician motivated by religious conviction, has steadily lost control of his party, to the point that in the mid-1990s he is merely the dominant presence within it, rather than having the omnipotent influence he enjoyed in the late 1970s. If Bruce's thesis was correct, we should have seen a rapid and dramatic increase in support for the DUP after the signing of the AIA, as frightened unionists rushed to hide behind the skirts of this shared religious identity. The fact that this did not occur brings us to the most important problem with Bruce's argument, namely his analysis of Protestantism and unionism. For his thesis to work, Bruce is forced to adopt reductionist criteria in his definition of these terms. Although he astutely points out that the democratic nature of Protestantism fosters political disputes, due to the absence of an ultimate moral authority other than the Bible, individually interpreted,[60] he does not explain how the heterogeneous nature of Protestantism has produced conflicting cultural identities.

Bruce has suggested that the conflict within unionism was due to a two-pronged suspicion of the Protestant middle class. On the one hand, the working-class element was wary of the elite nature of the Ulster Unionist Party leadership, and argued on populist grounds for higher wages, better housing and more welfare provisions. The second group were suspicious of the UUP's lack of evangelical piety, and they wanted to bring a greater theological aspect to unionism. However, Bruce's depiction of Protestants as an ethnic group, sharing common historical experiences, traditions, values, beliefs and symbols, creates a one-dimensional view of unionism which does not correspond with reality. It is clear that unionists *do not* all share a common cultural language, but are split in religious terms along denominational lines, are divided over their support for Protestant institutions such as the Orange Order and the Ulster Defence Association (UDA), and, more fundamentally, are divided over whether Northern Ireland is a nation with the right to self-determination or merely another region of the United Kingdom.

Clearly there are problems with this. Bruce proposes that the central organising principle of unionism is provided by the unifying force of evangelical Protestantism; certainly this is a factor but only one of many and hardly the dominant one. Bruce pursues his own argument to self-destruction and reduces what is a complicated and multifaceted community to a caricature of itself. Fellow sociologist Colin Coulter does not overstate the case against Bruce:

> [he] fails to grasp the genuinely diverse and complex character of unionism.
> . . . In reality unionism does not possess a single essence, but rather exists as
> a single formation that accommodates a number of divergent and
> contradictory ideological impulses and political interests sharing little in
> common save for a commitment to the Union itself.[61]

John McGarry and Brendan O'Leary are less charitable. Giving him the rather unflattering 'handle' of 'sociologist of religion', these carnivores of the political science jungle charge Bruce with an 'unprofessional use of data' over his argument that Protestant resistance to a united Ireland was motivated primarily by religious reasons.[62] His psephological endeavours are equally patronised. Bruce is implicitly accused of academic bias over his use of untypical election results (a concentration on personality-driven European rather than Westminster elections) to explain DUP popularity. 'To sustain his thesis Professor Bruce seems intent on exaggerating the DUP's support. . . . The lesson is simple: sociologists of religion, over-ambitious to apply their insights, should be more cautious with electoral data.'[63] To be fair to Bruce, his more recent work has tip-toed away from his bald assertion in 1986 that 'the Northern Ireland conflict is a religious conflict' and that it was people's adherence to 'competing religious traditions which has given the conflict its enduring and intractable quality'.[64] In his 1994 book on Protestant paramilitary attitudes, Bruce returns to the above statement to add the caveat that the connection between politics and religion in Northern Ireland is 'complex'.[65] However, impaled on a 'cleft-stick' of his own whittling, he continues to overemphasise the importance of what is in reality a minor branch in the unionist political tree.

> The key point is the centrality of evangelicalism for the Ulster loyalist's sense of ethnic identity. It defines the group to which he belongs, it figures large in the history of that group, it legitimates the group's advantages (such as they are), and it radically distinguishes the group from its traditional enemy.[66]

My evidence would suggest that the obverse is the case. It is clear from the testimony of former loyalist paramilitaries and members of the DUP that, although religion plays an important part in their personal lives and cultural iconography, it forms a more complex component of their political calculations.

Other concepts in Bruce's recent work are even more problematic. His assertion that 'for many Protestants in Northern Ireland, Ulster loyalism has displaced the Ulster Britishness which was common prior to the present conflict'[67] does not stand up to empirical examination. In fact the reverse is true. The Social Attitudes Survey (1990) compared responses to the question of whether people in Northern Ireland felt themselves to be British, Irish, Ulster or Northern Irish over a time-span of twenty-one years. In 1968, 39 per cent of Protestants regarded themselves as British while 32 per cent opted for an Ulster identity. In 1978 the figures were 67 per cent and 20 per cent respectively. In 1986, the numbers describing themselves as British stood at 65 per cent (amazingly, in spite of the introduction of the AIA the previous year) while only a mere 14 per cent described themselves as having an Ulster identity and 11 per cent opted for the more neutral 'Northern Ireland'. In 1989, those Protestants describing themselves as British had risen to 68 per cent with only 10 per cent defining themselves as 'Ulster' and 16 per cent as 'Northern Irish', a total of 26 per cent for a regional identity.[68]

An accompanying note for Bruce's conclusion that an Ulster identity is gaining ground at the expense of the British variant within Protestant politics displays an alarming methodology:

> . . . given that the percentages can vary a great deal according to just how the question was asked, *we are forced to rely rather on our intuition*, and mine

is that, while the number of Protestants who actually want an independent state remains small, the number who think it might be the only alternative to a united Ireland, and who are therefore reconciling themselves to it, has increased over my period of interest in Northern Ireland. [emphasis added][69]

Apart from the obvious point that conclusions are arrived at by virtue of personal whim rather than empirical evidence, Bruce seems to confuse the *cultural* concept of an Ulster versus British identity with the *political* will to consider independence in a doomsday situation. As this chapter has illustrated, these concepts overlap, with members of the DUP and UUP who espouse a commitment to essentially British identities also being willing to consider independence as a last resort. The bar-room bravado in which such sentiments are often uttered may dissipate when the practical realities become obvious, but if it came to it, this alternative would be undertaken by most unionists with a heavy heart. Few would look positively upon it as the achievement of a cultural objective.

Unionism as Secular Rationalism

This should be understood as defining those unionists whose politics are motivated by easily quantifiable criteria, for example an identification with the institutions and declared philosophy of British parliamentary democracy, an assessment of the most beneficial economic model for Northern Ireland, or a cultural empathy with British sport, arts and media. Such unionists rarely carry around the same amount of weighty historical, religious or cultural baggage as their ethno-nationalist colleagues and generally place their regional identity within a Greater British context.

An alternative explanation to Bruce's religious reductionism has been provided by Sarah Nelson with the suggestion that the dynamic within unionism in the 1970s was class based: 'Class tensions and resentment within the Protestant community began to be openly expressed, and the Civil Rights slogan "Fifty years of unionist misrule" was increasingly heard from the lips of working class loyalists.'[70]

Clifford Smyth has pointed out that opposition to the Ulster Unionist Party could not be explained in class terms alone, as illustrated by Ernest Baird and Reg Empey, former members of the pseudo-paramilitary Vanguard Party,[71] both of whom were vigorous in their criticisms of mainstream unionism but were also prosperous businessmen.[72] In more recent times David Trimble, now the leader of the UUP and formerly a founder member of the Ulster Clubs[73] and the Vanguard Party, embodies the capacity of radical unionism to cross class barriers. When questioned, for example, about what he regarded as being the central principles of unionism, his response intimated that the Union was a strategic political allegiance (by definition conditional) of Ulster Protestants to a community with which they shared a psychological and cultural affinity.

> I suppose one does put the Union pretty high up, but one doesn't say that the Union is an absolute end in itself. I regard unionism as being an all-class political alliance, of the Ulster British people, formed for the purpose of defending their position within the Union. But the Union is seen as the best political vehicle for the development in social, economic and political terms, of the Ulster British people.[74]

When pressed as to whether he saw the Union in terms of a political rather than a cultural allegiance, Trimble replied that, while there was a strong cultural cohesion which sustained the Union, this could not be relied upon indefinitely and thus other political structures may have to be contemplated outside the present constitutional arrangements to preserve the politico-cultural hegemony of the unionist community.

> It's both [political and cultural]. It is cultural, I mean it's obviously cultural because the British community here do feel themselves to be cultural in all respects, in virtually all respects in that sense British, so there is a very strong cultural affinity, and there are the political and economic things as well. The only reason why I put a question-mark against the Union is because one knows that a union requires two parties, and that if the English – and I am using the word English deliberately – if the English should decide to say, 'well that is all very well, you feeling yourselves to be British, all your history and background and all the rest, that is all very well, but frankly we don't want the Union anymore and we want to end it' . . . in that case we would say that we cannot unilaterally sustain the Union, and so one has to say that there is, in the last analysis, another goal, which is to find some other political structure as a means of advancing the well-being and continuing existence of the Ulster British people.[75]

Again we can observe in Trimble's definition of unionism a defensive mentality which emanates from the realisation that the state to which he gives his allegiance, the UK, is at best ambivalent about its desire to maintain the relationship. The fear that the state to which they express a loyalty (with varying degrees of conditionality) does not accept them as wholly legitimate members of that state has encouraged a separatist culture within the unionist community.

Perhaps the ultimate example of secular rationalism is to be found within the cross-community Alliance Party, where the concerns of an ethno-Ulster nationalist culture are clearly of little relevance. Alliance is at the outer limits of the ideology and the opposite pole to those who inhabit the most extreme recesses of unionist ethno-nationalism. Recognising this fact I asked the party leader, Dr John Alderdice, if he would define Alliance as being a unionist party in the traditional sense.

No, I wouldn't. It certainly is a party which currently takes a pro-Union position, that is to say that we believe that the best social and economic interests of the people of Northern Ireland are served by remaining within the United Kingdom. . . . But remaining within the United Kingdom is not some article of faith for us. In other words, if it became clear that the best social and economic interests of the people of Northern Ireland would be served by another arrangement, and that was something that we felt and that the people of Northern Ireland felt, then we would [look at] the political dispensation, whether that was to a united Ireland or a region within a Europe of the Regions or whatever. That's not an issue or a problem from our point of view. But we feel that at this point it is quite clear that the best interests are served by remaining within the UK.[76]

When Alderdice was asked if he would distinguish Alliance from the other unionist parties on the basis that, while they would have, to varying degrees, a cultural identification with the Union, his party made a purely pragmatic assessment which was devoid of sentiment, he ironically used a historical analogy to clarify his position.

Well, pragmatism, yes, is a very important part of it but there are certain political principles involved too. I mean if you go back to Northern Ireland coming into being, you had essentially three groups of people. You had Conservatives and Unionists, who wanted the Union to be maintained and that meant no devolution, it meant a centralised form of government and so on. Then you had nationalists, who at the end of the day wanted Ireland as a whole to leave the United Kingdom and be a separate independent republic. Then you had liberals, and the liberal view was for Home Rule, the term devolution is the one that we use now. So, if there had been an Alliance Party then it would have been saying: 'we want Home Rule on a power-sharing basis within the United Kingdom'.[77]

Notwithstanding the assertions of Alderdice that his party was temperamentally neutral on the Union, many within the nationalist community in Northern Ireland would view them as 'unionists with breeding', those people whom the wife of the former Cabinet minister Alan Clark referred to, in a separate context entirely, as coming 'from above stairs'. While this may be an unfair assessment and an inaccurate caricature of the party, it would not be the first time that communal stereotyping fashioned political attitudes within Northern Ireland. In a final attempt to get to the bottom of the precise position of Alliance within the secular-rationalist strand of unionism, Alderdice was asked if his party had a particular cultural outlook on the Union as opposed to the political definition he had provided. Aside from adhering for the moment to the political institutions of the British state, did Alliance have any cultural position on the Union which would exhibit a bond not reflected in their attitudes towards the Southern Irish state?

That's not a particular issue for us. We are in this state at present and therefore there's a commitment to the institutions of the state within which we are. If we were part of a united Ireland our commitment would be to the institutions of that state. We are loyal to whatever state we are a part of at that time.[78]

This response is important. Here we have the distinction between those on the periphery of the ideology and those at the centre. While members of the Alliance Party may define their loyalty as the exercise of *real politik*, a formal addendum to the political reality they happen to find themselves in, unionists who are wholly a part of the ideology see this as central. Which state they belong to is the starting point from which all else is to be understood and synthesised rather than a footnote. Unlike Alderdice, their loyalty is non-transferable, and the feeling that they are going to be delivered from one state to another state has, in extreme cases, led to violent confrontations with the state to which they claim to be loyal.

Contractarianism and Statehood

Contractarianism defines unionism as an ethnic group whose relationship with the rest of the United Kingdom is a quirk of historical development and has become a cold legalistic agreement where loyalty to the state is conditional upon adequate behaviour by the executive. Statehood is a definition of unionism which rejects the idea that its adherents are motivated by narrow criteria of nationhood such as identity, religion, colour, race and cultural symbolism; rather they are organised around a commitment to the preservation and enhancement of liberal democratic structures and values, which only states can provide and nations destroy.

David Miller's account of the dynamics of unionism is rooted in a historical perspective and remains one of the most provocative (if rather outdated) works on the ideology to date.[79] The propensity within radical Protestant politics to illustrate the conditional nature of their loyalty is central to Miller's thesis and requires detailed examination as this provides further evidence of the regressive nature of the unionist ideology. Miller prefaces *Queen's Rebels* by quoting Robert Bradford as presumably the personification of conditional loyalty: 'The time might come when Ulstermen would have to become Queen's rebels in order to remain citizens of any kind.'[80]

While being a convenient means of defying state authority yet remaining at least nominally loyal to that state, the phenomenon of conditional loyalty has concrete historical foundations. These stretch back to the sixteenth-century tradition of public banding, i.e. entering into 'bands' for mutual protection, which was originally a response by the gentry to a prolonged spell of weak central government. The Scottish Kirk entered into such an arrangement in an attempt to combat the anti-Presbyterian tendencies of the monarchy. Bands such as the National Covenant of 1638, organised in opposition to the new prayer book, came to be regarded as tripartite contracts between God, his people, and the King.[81] It has some relationship to the democratising nature of the Reformation, the emphasis on individualism which this engendered, and the liberalism of the time which stressed man's inherent rationality (as this would be required to determine when a covenant had been breached). Miller suggests that loyalty is reduced to a matter of private ethics, with political obligation being no more than a business arrangement. In the event, therefore, of the ruler breaking his side of the bargain, the ruled are absolved of their duty to comply with his wishes.[82] One of the earliest examples of conditional loyalty was provided in 1689, when the fortified town of Derry issued a resolution declaring that the Catholic troops of James II would not be allowed into the city. As the following statement indicates, despite blatantly defying the king's authority, they still viewed him as their legitimate sovereign.

> That as we have resolved to stand upon our guard and defend our walls, and not to admit of any Papist whatsoever to quarter among us, so we have firmly and sincerely determined to persevere in our duty and loyalty to our sovereign Lord the King, without the least umbrage of mutiny or seditious opposition to his royal commands . . . God Save The King.[83]

This emphasis on religious distinction is of central importance to the conditional nature of radical Protestant politics, and provides evidence to support the argument that 'loyalty' to Britain is given for so long as it sanctions the existence of the 'Protestant nation'. The cultural heritage of many radical unionists is not therefore seen in terms of their position as a colony of the British Empire, or as a member of the Commonwealth. Theirs is a separatist culture, reminiscent (in their eyes) of the value system of nineteenth-century Britain, but one which in reality bears little relation to the secular Britain of today. In Miller's analysis, one of the key elements of this culture is the Protestant religion, as it serves to identify those who subscribe to the group and provides a useful regenerative function. For those who understand their culture in terms of their religion, any hint of a threat to the dominance of the latter amounts to an attack upon their cultural identity. An interesting corollary may be observed between this view and the emphasis placed by Patrick Pearse upon the Gaelic revival. Pearse argued that the cultural struggle was pre-eminent in the fight for national independence, as without the Irish language and Irish customs it would be impossible to identify a separate nation and this would reduce the need for separate political structures. In the same way, many unionists have argued that a dilution of Protestantism will reduce Northern Ireland's claim to be culturally distinct from the rest of Ireland. This is why many unionists emphasise their religion when discussing their cultural identity, and point out that loyalty is dependent upon the preservation of Protestantism in Britain, as only then can it be guaranteed in Northern Ireland. This sentiment was expressed in 1976 by George Graham, a former DUP Assemblyman, when he declared that:

> My loyalty is to the British Throne being Protestant. I have no loyalty to any Westminster government. I have no loyalty to a government which prorogued a democratically elected government, destroyed our security forces, and left us prey to the IRA. Nor have I a loyalty to a British government going over the heads of our people, conniving and double-dealing behind our backs with a foreign government.[84]

From Miller's perspective, therefore, the conditional aspect of Ulster loyalism is the greatest paradox within the ideology. He argues that their interpretation of Britishness was not a patriotic nationalistic sentiment, nor a sense of community with the people of Great Britain. In essence it was a loyalty to the monarch and constitution for as long as they guarded the rights of the loyal Ulster people. Paul Arthur and Keith Jeffery largely concur with Miller's analysis, commenting that the powerful loyalist tradition of 'public banding' is based in a lack of confidence in Britain's determination to sustain the Union.[85] It was precisely this belief, for instance, which led William Craig, a former unionist Cabinet minister, to comment after the demise of Stormont in 1972 that the Ulster loyalists were an 'old and historic community' for whom the Union with Britain had never been an end in itself but '. . . was always a means of preserving Ulster's British tradition and the identity of her Loyalist people'.[86] Loyalty therefore to this tradition in unionism meant a primary identification with the people and territory of Northern Ireland, rather than with those within the United Kingdom as a whole. As a consequence of this isolationist perspective, some radical unionists tend to embrace the cultural identity of the Ulster Protestant in its rawest and most mythical form, namely through the Orange Order and fundamentalist religion. The folk heros within this band of radical unionism are the defenders of the faith and the preservers of the culture such as William of Orange, Rev. George Walker, and Rev. Henry Cooke. The isolationism within this strand of unionism has produced a curious mixture of insecurity and complacency, which has generally resulted in political stagnation. The eternal fear of being abandoned by Britain and delivered into the joint clutches of Dublin and Rome has been accompanied within radical unionism by the belief that the nature of the forces ranged against them have remained constant. The certainties provided by doctrinaire theology were translated into the political sphere, the result being that traditional assumptions were not questioned, changing political circumstances were not recognised, and the unionist ideology did not learn to adapt or innovate to meet the volatile political environment of twentieth-century Britain.

John Taylor, deputy leader of the Ulster Unionist Party, commented upon this weakness within unionism, arguing that the assumption of his more radical colleagues within the DUP that the Union was a one-way relationship had been detrimental to unionist political fortunes as their behaviour had alienated the other partner in the relationship. When Taylor was asked if he shared Miller's view that a social contract existed between Britain and Northern Ireland, he disagreed, preferring the more organic analogy of both communities being contained within the same family than the cold legalistic one of an arrangement between separate parties.

> Oh, it is not a social contract, it is like a marriage certificate. Any marriage requires two partners, and if one partner opts out, the thing collapses. The United Kingdom is made up of a partnership between Great Britain and Northern Ireland – after all, that is what it even says on our passports, the United Kingdom of Great Britain and Northern Ireland. Northern Ireland is not part of Great Britain but it is part of the United Kingdom – and for that partnership to survive, it isn't simply dependent on people in Northern Ireland voting unionist or being pro-British, it also depends on those who live in Great Britain wanting to retain the partnership. So it's a two-way operation and not just one-way. I think that is a great weakness in the unionist family here in Northern Ireland, that they seem to think that so long as they are strongly pro-British here, everything is well, but in fact that is a very blind approach to the real basis of the relationship. The basis of the relationship does depend on the unionists of Northern Ireland having public support in Great Britain as well.[87]

From this perspective, the tendency within radical sections of the unionist community has been not only to misread the basis of the relationship between Britain and 'Ulster', but also to fail to understand the antipathy felt towards them in the rest of the UK and to look to the past when dealing with crises of the present. The political tactics of Ian Paisley, for example, have often mirrored those of Sir Edward Carson (though with less success) in the latter's opposition to Home Rule, with the repetition of the 'Carson Trail Rallies', the establishment of the 'Third Force' mimicking the formation of the 'Ulster Volunteer Force' and, after the AIA, a repeat of Carson's 'Solemn League and Covenant' of 1912.

In essence, therefore, the unionist identity crisis is derived from their unilateral declaration of 'love' for the 'mother country' which has never been fully reciprocated. Commenting retrospectively on the period, Garret FitzGerald argued that this 'sense of being besieged', the fear of their external environment, led to a culture of political irrationality within the unionist community, which was emphasised in the aftermath of the Anglo-Irish Agreement.

> The fact is that there is a reason for the unionist attitude, and it is that they have felt under threat from the beginning. They have never felt that the

threat has gone away. They have misperceived it at some times possibly, but once people feel under threat, reason goes out the window, and they have found it impossible to identify their interests and to pursue them, by virtue of all the time reacting simply negatively against a perceived threat, sometimes in existence, sometimes not. That can happen to any group; I mean the Israelis are also a bit irrational at times and don't necessarily pursue their own interests, or even identify them in the long run. Fear is a great destabiliser for rationality.[88]

It was realisation of the fact that they were 'unwanted children' which diminished the trust of the unionist community in the country to which they gave their allegiance. David Trimble personifies this belief that the Britishness of Northern Ireland is not an objective reality but is subject to the whim of fickle politicians in Westminster.

> I regard myself as a unionist who is aware of the fact that I cannot unilaterally insist that the Union be continued, that there might be – there are not yet, I don't actually ever think there ever will be, but one has to acknowledge the possibility that there will be – circumstances where the other party to the Union would wish unilaterally to end it.[89]

This statement ties in with Miller's perception that the unionism of Protestant Ulster was never a feeling of cultural 'oneness' with the Greater British community, but a tactical political alliance. This was not however an allegiance to the British state, to its parliament, or even to its monarch, but to those constitutional arrangements which were vital to the maintenance of the Ulster Protestant way of life. The basis of the Union, therefore, was a contract between two separate parties, and not an internal agreement between members of the one family. In essence, this definition of the Union was supported by David Trimble, who emphasised not that unionists were simply a section of the United Kingdom separated by geography, but rather that they were a specific cultural community where loyalty to Britain was granted on a *de facto* basis, rather than Northern Ireland belonging in a *de jure* manner to the UK.

> Yes, there is a sort of contract relationship. I'm sure you have read David Miller's book . . . I don't agree with all of Miller's book but I think it is quite interesting. But the idea of a covenant – I use that word instead of contract – is of course very very central to Presbyterian theological thinking, and a lot of people's political thought – it is true here, it has been true elsewhere as well – is closely related to their theology.[90]

As Miller has pointed out, the problem with perceiving loyalty to the state in contractarian terms lay in its subjective interpretations. The forces of modernisation had resulted in political change to the extent that sovereignty was no longer vested in a single person, the monarch, but was now replaced by a parliament responsible to the people. Ironically therefore the liberal-democratic institutions which Ulster Protestants placed so much emphasis upon augmented their feelings of insecurity and contributed to their isolationist political culture.

> The people are fickle, and it is a fundamental feature of the British Constitution that parliament is incapable of giving binding promises: any law enacted by one parliament can be repealed by the next. . . . The Parliament Act forced upon the consciousness of Ulster Protestants the fact that they could find reassurance of their fundamental rights neither in a felt sense of co-nationality with any people – British or Irish – nor in the capacity of British institutions to give promises which came up to their own exacting standards of honesty.[91]

The endemic (and not unjustified) paranoia of the unionist community which emanates from constitutional uncertainty has highlighted the conditional nature of their loyalty, as their obedience is based upon a two-way relationship, a social contract or covenant with the government. The following statement by Ian Paisley in the *Protestant Telegraph* could be cited in support of the contractarian thesis: 'Government is not a one-way street. It is a civil contract in which each party has a duty.'[92] The belief that the Union is founded upon a contract (at least from the unionist perspective) rather than mutual trust and cultural commonality has fed the virus of political insecurity within unionism. It has produced frequent declarations that the actions of the 'mother country' have jeopardised the position of the Ulster Protestant community and so broken the contract between the rulers and the ruled, thus legitimating unconstitutional behaviour.

However, though intellectually more diverting than Bruce's one-dimensional characterisation of Ulster unionism, this theoretical edifice is built upon foundations which are just as shaky. The main problem with Miller's contractarian theory is its negation of unionism's cultural identification with Britain, even if this is largely a one-way unreciprocated relationship to a mythical British community which owes more to Kipling's Britishness than to the multicultural Britain of the late twentieth century. It is rather too mechanistic to simply interpret the dynamics of unionism as the autonomous exercise of political self-interest grounded in pseudo-legality. Ian Paisley Jnr's response when asked about the central principles of unionism provides a classic example and demonstrates the complex pattern within the unionist fabric of allegiance.

> Number one, I believe in the principles of the Union, those principles being that the Union is best for everyone; that it offers and facilitates everybody's cultural, political and economic outlook better than any other option that appears to be available. Therefore I'm a unionist for practical reasons. But I'm also a unionist for very emotional reasons as well. My whole cultural/political philosophy I think is based in a very, not only nostalgic idea of what the past means, but also a very profound identity with the principles

of Protestantism, with the principles of freedom, with the principles of civil and religious liberty and all those things which I think make up the cross-mix which is both a Protestant identity and indeed then a unionist political identity.[93]

It is undoubtedly the case that many unionists, especially (to use Todd's classification) in the Ulster British tradition, do regard themselves as having a close social and cultural affinity with the rest of Britain. Many unionists would regard themselves as being British in the manner of the Scottish or Welsh, with a subordinate regional loyalty to Northern Ireland, and they feel hurt that this is not accepted by the ruling elite at Westminster. Sammy Wilson, for instance, sees no reason why constitutional arrangements cannot be established in Northern Ireland similar to those in other regions of the UK, taking account of the regional differences between Northern Ireland and the 'mainland' while allowing for the devolution of specific responsibilities.

> The first principle of my unionism is that I want to remain part of the United Kingdom. That is the bedrock of my belief. But, I believe that there is wide diversity within the United Kingdom, and I am not just talking about the diversity between Northern Ireland and the rest of the United Kingdom. It is now quite apparent that the Scots feel the same, the Welsh feel the same, even people in the North of England feel the same, and therefore the kind of unionism that I would want to see would allow for an expression of that diversity, and allow for some kind of institutional expression of the diversity as well. It would therefore be bolstered by a devolved – I'll call it an institution, I don't want to call it a parliament, some people would think that is too grandiose – but some devolved institution here in Northern Ireland, that would have real decision-making powers which would reflect, first of all, the wishes of people in Northern Ireland, and the particular flavour of politics here in Northern Ireland.[94]

However, it is clear that the status of Northern Ireland within the United Kingdom is not the same as that of Scotland or Wales. This has nothing to do with the legal niceties of the situation or any ceding of sovereignty occasioned by Britain's signing of the Anglo-Irish Agreement, but is rooted in cultural and historical factors. Miller has pointed out that Northern Ireland's position within the UK is not comparable with that of Scotland or Wales, due to its isolationist political culture. The Ulster Protestant community 'has evoked a kind of group loyalty incompatible with acceptance of the full implications of British nationality'.[95] Miller determined that it was the forces of modernisation and economic progress which were the root cause of the differences between Northern Ireland's relationship with England, and that of Scotland and Wales.

Despite its many advantages as a political theory of unionism, Miller's thesis presents hypotheses which do not always correlate with the reality of unionist motivations. In his examination of the Home Rule period, for example, he states that unionists did not feel a cultural affinity with the rest of the UK.

> The dilemma of the Ulster Protestant community derived from both their conception of political obligation and their rights of citizenship in contractual terms. Lacking a genuine feeling of co-nationality with the British people, they could not entrust their fate to 'safeguards' which depended on the willingness of that people to intervene in Irish affairs to rectify abuses.[96]

In his contention that unionists lacked 'a genuine feeling of co-nationality with the British people', Miller seems to be confusing objective fact with the perceived reality of the situation from the unionist point of view. He may be correct in his assertion that a common culture did not exist between the unionists and the English; however this was not reflected in contemporary unionist feelings (however irrationally such feelings were arrived at). The fact was that unionists *did* feel as much a part of the empire (and thus by extension part of a mythical British nation) as did the English during the Home Rule period and they still do to a large degree. It is unlikely for instance that they would have volunteered for slaughter at the Somme had they not felt themselves to be an intrinsic part of the empire, or not felt a strong cultural affinity with the 'mother country'. The unionist perception of the First World War was that it was a fight to preserve civilisation and the British Empire, their empire. This does not presuppose, of course, that their perception was an accurate one, or that they were accepted as being an integral part of the empire by its other constituent parts or within the 'mother country' itself. Tom Hennessey, writing about Ulster unionist identity at the end of the nineteenth century, substantiates this point.

> As in Great Britain, Ulster unionists, and Irish unionists in general, consistently defined themselves as being part of a British national community sharing a specifically British historical heritage. . . . The British imperial experience, that 'consciousness of great shared events' which created a communal myth of national identity, was apparent throughout unionist rhetoric at this time.[97]

Coulter casts a healthily sceptical eye over Miller's thesis and finds it wanting in several respects. He challenges Miller's claim that the contractarian element within unionist political thought is anachronistic in the modern liberal-democratic polity. Western society has not, in Coulter's analysis,

> . . . resolved to the satisfaction of its citizenry those vital constitutional issues that pertain to the nature and limits of government and of political obligation. . . . The modern liberal democratic state has, in reality, proved incapable of satisfactorily resolving the problematic matter of the relationship between government and governed. Indeed, far from having

been rendered obsolete, such issues of citizenship have in fact returned to the centre stage of political debate in recent times.[98]

Miller is seen as putting the theoretical cart before the horse. The oddity about the unionist–British relationship is not that Ulster unionists have erected conditions to their loyalty which find expression in periodic demonstrations of defiance against state authority. The anomaly is instead presented to be the conditional loyalty of successive British governments to the concept of the Union and to the unionist community in Northern Ireland. The kernel of Coulter's argument is that it was Britain's historic inability to provide an unequivocal definition of Northern Ireland's constitutional status which fashioned the supposed deviance of unionist political behaviour.

> In view of the uncertainty that shrouds the constitutional future of Northern Ireland within the Union, it would seem both rational and inevitable that the unionist community should have remained so profoundly concerned with constitutional matters. . . . Suspecting that the intentions of Westminster regarding the Union are far from pure, the unionist community has inevitably withheld from the government its unqualified consent, as to do otherwise would place it in a singularly vulnerable position.[99]

For Coulter, therefore, the contractarian element in modern unionism is a rational and salient political tactic, a behavioural trait fashioned out of an antagonistic political environment, whereas for Miller it is a structural residue of unionism's historical evolution and 'Ulster's' unique economic development, which has served ever since to poison their relationship with the 'mother country'.

A full-scale assault on Miller's assumptions was launched by Arthur Aughey, who declared that his interpretation

> . . . chooses the wrong foundation upon which to build, and is therefore substantially misconceived. It constructs an argument on grounds congenial to nationalism, and so it is not surprising that unionism appears woefully inadequate as a political doctrine.[100]

Aughey's critique of Miller asserts that the crisis within unionism does not revolve around the anomaly of conflicting identities, but is rather a consequence of the British government's insistence on denying them the democratic rights of statehood and the basic right to participate in the political process. What Miller sees as an identity crisis fashioned out of cultural confusion, Aughey represents as a product of stunted political development born out of the Government of Ireland Act and the establishment of a regional administration in Northern Ireland. Aughey takes issue with Miller's articulation of conditional loyalty, arguing that it is the definition of a political absolute which does not exist.

If conditional loyalty is at the centre of political behaviour, Miller has left one major question unanswered in his exposition: namely, what is unconditional loyalty? Of course, he cannot really answer this question for it falls into that category of absolutes which is outside the scope of politics.[101]

Of course the point Aughey is making here, namely that nobody's loyalty to the state is unconditional, is a valid one,[102] and he cites the example of militant republicanism as evidence of this fact. The IRA in this analysis are manifestly not loyal to the existing Irish nation, but to an idealised version of it which does not yet exist. However, Aughey's use of this example to support his argument illustrates a misunderstanding of Irish republicanism, as unlike the unionists, they do not accept the Government of Ireland Act, republicans do not accept the partition of Ireland and they do not accept what is legally termed the Republic of Ireland to be the 'Irish nation'. This belief that the state is not a complete manifestation of the Irish nation is recognised by the constitution and thus, in theory at least, by the state itself. It is not a case therefore, as Aughey suggests, of militant republicans giving conditional loyalty to the government of the twenty-six counties; they do not give any loyalty to it at all, although they do accept it as a *de facto* if not *de jure* reality. It could perhaps be said in Aughey's defence that regardless of a nation-state's cultural homogeneity, there comes a point when citizens will decide either individually or collectively to withdraw their loyalty to the government or sovereign.

> The Obligation of Subjects to the Sovereign, is understood to last as long, and no longer, than the power lasteth, by which he is able to protect them. For the right men have by Nature to protect themselves, when none else can protect them, can by no Covenant be relinquished. . . . The end of Obedience is Protection.[103]

Thomas Hobbes did not design this covenant with the unionists in mind, but commented that everyone had the right to withdraw their loyalty to the state in the last resort (in this case during a period of life-threatening political instability). Aughey is therefore correct in his assertion that the observation of social contracts and covenants between the rulers and the ruled was not the unique preoccupation of the unionist community. The riots which occurred in Britain's inner cities in the early 1980s would testify to the fact that unionists were not alone in their propensity to exhibit conditional loyalty to the state should sufficient alienation occur between the government and the governed. However, despite Aughey's objections to Miller's thesis and his declaration that unionism 'is no more conditional in its loyalty than any other rational political doctrine',[104] it could justifiably be claimed that the ambiguity of unionist loyalty to the state is pronounced to an unusual degree. Aughey's view that the loyalty of everyone is conditional is not shared by Enoch Powell for example, who points out the anomaly of seeking to belong to a particular state while refusing to obey the laws of that state. When asked to comment upon the legitimacy of the unionist campaign of civil disobedience against the AIA, Powell declared that a prerequisite of citizenship of a particular state was the acceptance of and obedience to the legitimately made laws of that state, regardless of how unpalatable these laws were considered to be. Powell argued that whilst a case could be made for unlawful protest action against legislation which had been influenced by the Dublin government through the AIA,

> . . . you then get yourself into the great difficulty, that, claiming to be part of a country, you reject its law, and also you get into the difficulty of picking and choosing between one law and another, and saying, 'now is this law a consequence of, or in any way influenced by the Anglo-Irish Agreement, or isn't it?' Now I can see that the law on public order [Public Order Act 1987] was professedly influenced by the Anglo-Irish Agreement, but still there is the difficulty of claiming to belong to a state and not obeying its laws. . . . My view was that the law was still binding, and that if one claimed to belong to the United Kingdom, one was admitting that one was still bound by the law of the United Kingdom.[105]

Powell's contention that the individual owed a loyalty to the legislative institutions of the state to which they gave allegiance stands at variance, however, with more radical sentiments within the Ulster Unionist Party. David Trimble, for instance, rejects the dictum of parliamentary sovereignty, arguing that such fundamental concepts could not be institutionalised in such a manner.

> I've never actually personally subscribed to the view that parliament is absolutely sovereign. . . . I have always regarded sovereignty at the end of the day, as resting in the people, and parliament just happens to be the present central institution within our constitution.[106]

When it was put to him that the loyalty of some unionists to Britain was dependent upon the monarch remaining Protestant, Trimble went on to assert that conditional loyalty was not an anachronism, but evidence of a liberal-democratic polity.

> I'm not sure that the people who say that they are loyal to the monarch so long as it's a Protestant have actually thought the matter through, although what they are saying is strictly speaking accurate. That is the Act of Settlement, and people here who celebrate the Glorious Revolution are very deeply conscious of the fact that loyalty is conditional. That is the bedrock of the British constitution, there is no unconditional loyalty, but loyalty is conditional. . . . I mean otherwise we simply wouldn't be a democratic state at all.[107]

Aughey's dismissal of Miller's conditional loyalty thesis as the product of a false premise, a concern with the nation rather than the state, was accompanied by an attempt to provide unionism with a new coherence. The starting point for his more positive critique came with the suggestion that the central dynamics of the ideology have been misinterpreted by academics who mistakenly understand unionism in terms of nationalist criteria. Aughey rejects Terence Brown's assertion that unionism suffers from an impoverished identity, lacking the 'complex, rich, emotional identity' of nationalism.[108] His point is that to measure unionism against nationalism will inevitably result in misunderstanding as the two ideologies are fundamentally different in nature: '. . . the point is that unionism does not claim to be an entire philosophy of life but a rational political idea. To criticise it in such terms is to do so according to the assumptions of nationalism.'[109]

What Aughey does not mention is that unionist demands for the preservation of the Union have been substantially based (in recent years at least) on the argument that they are a culturally distinct community from the rest of Ireland. As Garret FitzGerald remarked, '. . . they try to have it both ways, both in and out of the UK'.[110] Unionists do not simply declare that they have a political allegiance to Britain, but maintain that this is based on the desire to preserve the distinctive cultural and religious heritage of unionism. 'The average Loyalist today would state without hesitation that his first loyalty was to Ulster rather than to the United Kingdom parliament.'[111] In a similar vein, Sarah Nelson quotes a former unionist councillor as saying that unionism for him was about preserving the distinctness of Northern Ireland, rather than integrating it into the UK.

> I joined the party from a love of Ulster, its customs, character and heritage. Unionism to me always meant 'Ulster first'. This I felt was the true unionism in the tradition of Carson and Craig. Our leaders were weak allowing Britain to interfere when it was clear they had lost any loyalty to Ulster.[112]

It could of course be pointed out that this speaker totally misunderstands both the political philosophy of Edward Carson and the balance of power between London and Belfast. Carson in fact disliked many of Ulster's local characteristics and particularly the culture of Orangeism, their speeches reminding him of 'the unrolling of a mummy. All old bones and rotten rags.' The point is, however, this is a perception of identity widely held within the unionist community. As there is no law of political motion which declares that the depth of a person's beliefs is directly related to the rationality by which they are reached, the important factor to consider when discussing perceptions of identity is not intellectual coherence so much as the degree of consensus. Aughey rejects the contemporary orthodoxy that the unionist ideology is handicapped by a crisis of identity, this too being the product of nationalist misrepresentation. He quotes the following response of a loyalist bandsman, questioned by *New Society* about his identity, but reinterprets the message to deny the identity crisis thesis.

> Well, I'd like to call myself British, a British person like. But you look deep into it like, I'm Irish . . . because Northern Ireland like. You don't hear the English going round and saying, 'I'm British'. They'd turn round and say 'I'm English' . . . like the Scottish . . . I'd like to classify myself as a British person – if anybody asks me my nationality I'd turn round an' say, 'British' . . . I hate calling myself Irish, myself like . . . but it's a thing you have to face up to. It's the truth, you look at yourself, you're living on one island.[113]

Rather than accept the apparently obvious explanation that this individual is profoundly confused about his identity, Aughey chooses to depict the bandsman as a latter-day Platonic philosopher-king, who exhibits

> . . . a profound modern political wisdom – a wisdom which the identity-advocates ignore or are simply unable to recognise. For the confusion, such as it is, appears not to lie in the stumbling formulations of unionism but in the narrow perversity of the whole idea of the politics of identity.[114]

Aughey concludes that unionists are more interested in *statehood* than in *nationhood*. Their preoccupation is not to psychoanalyse themselves as nationalists do, in terms of cultural 'oneness' or diversity using the cultural totems of language, religion, etc.; the concern of unionists is primarily to integrate themselves into the modern British state. 'The identity of unionism has little to do with the idea of the nation and everything to do with the idea of the state.'[115] Having established that the unionist community is more interested in belonging to a state than a nation (despite evidence to the contrary as expressed through the Orange Order et al.), Aughey goes on to argue that states are not based on concepts of nationhood and do not, in fact, 'depend upon any form of substantive identity at all'. The modern state, he says, 'has transcended its dependence on extrinsic legitimations such as race, nation or religion, and is grounded in the political universals of right and the rule of law'.[116] Historian James Loughlin correctly points to the practical deficiencies in Aughey's theoretical conception of the state as an underpinning dynamic within unionist politics.

> [The] notion that the state can be conceptualised in terms of the political universals of 'right and the rule of law', abstracted from the emotions of nationalism, is not very convincing. Indeed, while Aughey notes that Robert McCartney employed the Union Jack in his campaign literature at the general election of June 1987, 'against his better judgement', its use in this context is instructive. It is impossible to dissociate the national flag from notions of national identity and it is impossible to imagine the state without also imagining the national flag.[117]

In his desire to rationalise the equal citizenship argument, Aughey rather misses the point that states and nations are intrinsically linked to one another and in a time of crisis the nation will prove to be a much stronger social coagulant than the state. The break-up of the Soviet Union could be cited as supporting evidence here, as the various factions which previously made up that political unit are not organising around the 'Holy Grail' of liberal democracy. Instead, old nationalities which had been submerged within the state for seventy years have re-emerged in their original form, dusted themselves down, and are prepared to protect the interests of what they define as their nation. The war in the former Yugoslavia is another obvious example. Here, ethno-nationalist antagonism, which had remained relatively dormant during the Cold War and under Tito, has re-emerged from hibernation, and the Serbs, Croats and Muslims continue to define themselves and their enemies in terms of their ethnicity and how this interacts with their shared history. While Aughey is correct to point out that states are political rather than cultural arrangements, he fails to mention that more often than not it is the forces of nationality, language, colour, religion, history and social cohesion due to threat from external enemies which bind the state together. In other words, are states not simply the political manifestations of nations, groups of nations, or parts of nations? As Emerson noted, the nation '. . . has in fact become the body which legitimises the state'.[118] States certainly do not exist (as Aughey suggests) as a result of liberal democracy – indeed, a significant number of these geographical units known as states studiously ignore concepts such as the 'political universals of right and the rule of law'.

In reality, many unionists exhibit a concern with identity/culture rather than merely an abstract desire for citizenship and liberal-democratic principles. Regardless of how benign the Irish Republic becomes or the extent to which it liberalises its social policies, unionists are unlikely to seek citizenship of it. As this chapter has demonstrated, unionism is not based solely upon rationalism, or on political, social and economic self-interest. At its most fundamental, it is based on a sense of *belonging*. In addition to seeing the Union as a protector of civil liberties, religious expression and economic well-being, there is a complex web of historical, emotional and psychological bonds (though these are largely unreciprocated) which underpin the dynamics of unionist political behaviour.

Two examples will suffice to demonstrate that many unionists are motivated by exactly the same symbolic forces which drive Irish nationalism. Consider the reaction to the decision by Queen's University of Belfast in 1994 to abandon the playing of the British national anthem at its graduation ceremonies, thus bringing the institution into line with the practice in the rest of the United Kingdom. The letters column of the *Belfast Telegraph* was dominated by this issue for months afterwards, while a unionist rally was organised and attended by several leading politicians in an attempt to pressurise the university to reverse its decision. Obviously this example of integration with the 'mainland' was not one which they found to their taste. Consider also the events in Portadown during the Protestant marching season in July 1995 and specifically the 'Siege of Drumcree'. The picture of unionists chasing the RUC across fields was more reminiscent of old-style triumphalism than democratic citizenship and is difficult to square with the claim that unionism is essentially motivated by a desire to adhere to the liberal values enshrined within the British state.

Aughey's concern to differentiate between statehood and nationhood, illustrated in the following two statements, is motivated out of a desire to demonstrate that unionists are entitled to equal citizenship with the rest of the freedom-loving residents of the United Kingdom.

> If the autonomous principle of the modern state is taken to be right (in the Hegelian sense), then the relevant political concept is neither religion nor nation but citizenship. The United Kingdom is a state which, being multi-national and multi-ethnic, can be understood in terms of citizenship and not substantive identity (which helps to account for the bandsman's muddle). . . . The imperial notion of '*civus Britannicus sum*' has transformed itself into the democratic ideal of different nations, different religions and different colours, all equal citizens under the one government. It is to this notion that intelligent unionism, which embraces both protestants and catholics, owes allegiance. . . . The character of unionism must be understood in terms of this idea of citizenship; and the longer that protestant unionists and catholic nationalists are denied local state power, the more important it becomes as a universal organising political value.[119]

> . . . nationality assumptions and notions of loyalty based upon them rather confuse the motivation of unionist politics. . . . unionism is concerned primarily with the quality of citizenship within the Union; it is nationalists who are agitated by ideas of nationhood and its extent. The political cohesion of the United Kingdom – its 'identity' if you like – cannot lie in loyalty to the nation. There is no British nation; there are only British citizens. Loyalty, if it means anything, must mean loyalty to the idea of the Union: the willing community of peoples united not by creed, colour or ethnicity but by recognition of the authority of that Union.[120]

Whether or not Aughey's various hypotheses carry any validity (his explanation of the unionist identity crisis, denial of the peculiarities of unionist conditional loyalty, and differentiation of nation and state, are not totally convincing), the fact is that his thesis concerning the dynamics of unionist politics is not reflected in the political reality of Northern Ireland. Coulter arrives at a reasonable conclusion.

> The essential shortcoming of Aughey's account derives from his provision of an abstract and idealised characterisation of unionism that fails to take on board the realities of unionist motivation and political practice. While the political aspirations of many unionists may very well stem from their adherence to abstract ideals of citizenship, they are also motivated by substantive identities such as nationality and ethnicity. Anyone who has ever witnessed an Orange parade or engaged flesh and blood unionists in conversation regarding their political beliefs could hardly draw a different conclusion. . . . The abstract and idealised interpretation of unionism provided by Arthur Aughey is indicative of an inconsistency in his approach that bespeaks an ideological prejudice.[121]

As Coulter rightly points out, whilst Aughey's unionism may be more about equal citizenship within the UK than the preservation of some cultural heritage, this could not be said of many others within the unionist community. For them, intangible concepts such as 'citizenship' are of secondary importance to the preservation of their cultural heritage and religion. The Republic of Ireland, for example, believes in the pantheon of western liberalism, in citizenship and natural justice, as much as does Britain (for example, its single transferable vote electoral system is more democratic in terms of the correlation between votes cast and seats won than its British counterpart). Yet some unionists are violently opposed to joining it and this is not simply as a result of the 1937 constitution and failed efforts to reform it. The political allegiance of unionism to Britain is not, therefore, solely based upon a desire to live in a western democracy (when given the opportunity from 1921 to 1972 unionists built a political system which was anathema to modern liberal-democratic theory) but is founded variously upon a wide range of assumptions, from being the best means of preserving their cultural distinctiveness from the rest of Ireland to being the optimal strategy for maintaining the region's economic prosperity.

Aughey defines his own unionism as if it is representative of the ideology as a whole. It is not. It may be a vision of unionism, it may be a more effective or legitimate expression of unionism, but it is not the reality of present experience. The majority of unionists *are* concerned about their identity, their culture, their religion, and their history, as of course are nationalists. They are not concerned with fitting into the multicultural multiracial Britain of the late twentieth century. It is not sufficient to condemn the majority of such unionists as ideological interlopers who merely hijacked unionism for their own ends. It is too trite to suggest that the devolution experiment which lasted from the beginning of the state until 1972 was '. . . not a victory for unionism; it was a victory for unionists'.[122] In other words it was led by a small group of sectional interests unable to take the longer view, aided and abetted by successive British governments.

More recently Aughey has shown signs of a more considered, less dogmatic, approach, although he comes to similar conclusions.

> It may be countered that the interpretation so far is a one-sided view and does not do full justice to the character of unionism; that it ignores a deep current of political thought which places more emphasis upon an 'Ulster identity' than upon British citizenship; and that this current of thought is indeed separatist, is concerned to attain an explicit form of self-determination even to the extent of going for independence. Of course that current does exist and finds expression in a number of popular ways from bar bravado to the waving of Ulster flags. And there is no doubt that it is a legacy of 50 years of unionist government at Stormont.[123]

As this chapter has sought to indicate, there is a significant degree of 'doubt' that separatist sentiment within the unionist community was simply the product of the Government of Ireland Act and the Stormont administration. This strain in unionism, which Aughey rightly identifies, can be traced much further back than 1920. The Orange Order, for instance, was established long before Northern Ireland came into existence and it was not set up to lobby for liberal-democratic constitutional reform, or as a sister organisation to anything on the British 'mainland'. The nearest corollary in fact to the Orange Order in Britain would be the Freemasons, hardly an example of the British liberal-democratic polity much alluded to by the equal citizenship lobby. Similarly, the political by-product of evangelical Protestantism in the nineteenth century was separatist. The Great Revival of the 1850s fostered the notion that Ulster Presbyterians were a distinct community from both Catholic Ireland and Anglican Britain, a notion which, as we have already seen in this chapter, still prevails today.

John Whyte summed up the weakness of Aughey's critique and the equal citizenship case as a whole with his comment that the communal tensions in Northern Ireland transcend political institutions such as the party structure, and lie rather in the unique cocktail of its history.

> The argument that the main difference between Northern Ireland and the rest of the United Kingdom lies in their party systems is not convincing. Nowhere else in the United Kingdom are communal tensions remotely so severe as they are in Northern Ireland. Nowhere else does one find the lethal mixture of a large minority with a well-founded and deeply felt sense of grievance, and a narrow majority with justifiable anxieties about what the future may hold. There are nationalists in Scotland and Wales, but they do not display the bitter sense of injustice felt by nationalists in Northern Ireland and, apart from a tiny fringe, they do not resort to violence. There are racial tensions in some English cities, but these do not call into question the nature of the State. The truth is that Northern Ireland is different, and the

notion that special institutions are required to meet the contending needs and aspirations of its two communities is reasonable.[124]

A similar line to Aughey has been taken by Patrick Roche and Brian Barton, who suggest that unionism has been maligned by the devious agenda of nationalist ideologues. They condemn Joe Lee's study (*Ireland 1912–1985*) as a one-dimensional analysis which fails to understand the wider complexities of the ideology.

> Lee's perception of Ulster unionism is rooted in the most offensive of nationalist stereotypes: unionism is the political expression of nothing more commendable than a 'racial imperative'. Lee's book is an example of a failure to liberate the understanding of unionism and the politics of Northern Ireland from nationalist mythology and stereotype.[125]

Roche and Barton seek to redress what they regard as an imbalance in Irish historiography in favour of the nationalist critique. 'Nationalist ideologues have propagated, with virtual complete success since the late 1960s, an image of Northern Ireland as a "failed political entity".'[126] The problem with this analysis is that it suffers from the very disease it ascribes to nationalist commentaries. The Roche and Barton critique is littered with phrases such as 'the nationalist argument' and the 'nationalist story', as if there was simply one monolithic perspective articulated by Irish nationalists. Indeed after one such sweep of their broad ideological brush, concerning the rationale of discrimination during the 1920–72 period, they commented that 'according to the nationalist story' discrimination was a conspiracy to subjugate Catholics, and promptly juxtaposed this with the views of Michael Farrell on the subject. While Farrell's contribution to an understanding of the Stormont period should not be underestimated, it would be fair to say that he occupies one particular strand of Irish nationalist opinion. Roche and Barton attempt to refute Farrell's analysis by suggesting that allegations of discrimination have been grossly exaggerated by nationalist historians. They cite the comment of the pro-Union economist Tom Wilson that because no one complained about discrimination the level cannot have been as high as 'the nationalist story' has subsequently alleged.

> In 1970 the Stormont Government appointed a Commissioner of Complaints and it might have been expected that a large number of complaints about discrimination in housing would have been brought before him. . . . There was only one case in which discrimination was alleged. If discrimination had been as widespread as persistent republican propaganda has led so many people in Britain and the Irish Republic to believe, it is inconceivable that only a single case would have been brought before him.[127]

This is clearly an absurd argument to propagate. Could the same criteria be used to argue that, as nationalists made little use of the Police

Complaints Board, little opposition existed within the Catholic community towards the security forces? The existence of institutional structures such as a housing ombudsman is not of itself going to provide reliable empirical evidence with which we can accurately determine the extent of discrimination during the Stormont regime. It could be argued, for example, that the low level of complaints from the Catholic community over housing allocation cited by Wilson demonstrates that alienation amongst the minority community had reached such a level that they had lost all faith in the system and were not even availing of the opportunities which did exist to air their grievances.

Notwithstanding the claims of Wilson, Roche and Barton, and Arthur Aughey that unionism has been falsely ascribed an identity crisis by nationalist historians, this is a conspiracy theory which holds little credibility. It is clear that politico-cultural identity within unionism is diverse to the point that it defies categorisation. There is a crisis of identity within the ideology, derived from the historical inheritance of unionism and the overriding sense of insecurity which this experience has engendered. The existence of an antagonistic state on the other part of the island (at times imagined, at times real) has been gradually accompanied by hostility to the unionist cause within the country to which unionists express an allegiance and from the rest of the world.

As this chapter has sought to demonstrate, the desire for unity fashioned from such insecurity constantly precluded progressive political behaviour, as the complex assortment of diverse interest groups and individuals which existed under the ideological canopy of unionism were unable to develop a coherent political programme. The fact is that the Union means different things to different people. Whilst one unionist may regard it, in accordance with Miller's characterisation, as a contract with Britain to protect the religio-cultural heritage of Ulster Protestantism, another might see it as simply another region of the United Kingdom, separated merely by geography and the unwillingness of successive British governments to incorporate what Wilfred Spender termed 'North West Britain' into the rest of the kingdom. These different perceptions of cultural identity had obvious political consequences, resulting in conflicting notions about where unionism should be going, and how its political strategy should develop. The lack of cultural homogeneity, when combined with the self-imposed structural partition within unionism and the conflict which accompanies the idiosyncrasies of human nature, led to intellectual incoherence and political stagnation. The next chapter will demonstrate the way in which the diversity of cultural identities in the unionist community has been reflected in diverging political analyses and conflicting political strategies within the ideology.

Notes

1   S. Nelson, *Ulster's Uncertain Defenders: Protestant Paramilitary and Community Groups and the Northern Ireland Conflict* (Belfast, 1984), p. 9.

2   J. Todd, 'Two Traditions in Unionist Political Culture', *Irish Political Studies*, 2 (1987), pp. 1–26.

3   Michael McGimpsey, interview with author, 16 October 1991.

4   J. Todd, 'The Limits of Britishness', *The Irish Review*, 5 (1988).

5   J. W. Foster (ed.), *The Idea of the Union* (Vancouver, 1995), p. 59.

6   J. McGarry and B. O'Leary, *Explaining Northern Ireland: Broken Images* (Oxford, 1995), p. 121.

7   David Ervine, interview with author, 20 November 1995.

8   McGarry and O'Leary, *Explaining Northern Ireland*, p. 121.

9   F. S. L. Lyons, *Culture and Anarchy in Ireland 1890–1939* (Oxford, 1982), p. 134.

10   McGarry and O'Leary, *Explaining Northern Ireland*, pp. 111–12.

11   Garret FitzGerald, interview with author, 8 April 1992.

12   Rev. Martin Smyth, interview with author, 22 November 1991.

13   D. Armstrong and Hilary Saunders, *A Road Too Wide* (Basingstoke, 1985), p. 83.

14   Clifford Smyth, *A Protestant Pilgrimage* (Ulster Television, 1989)

15   E. Moloney and A. Pollak, *Paisley* (Dublin, 1986), p. 272.

16   Rev. Ian Paisley, *The History-Makers* (BBC Radio Ulster, 22 January 1989).

17   Michael McGimpsey, interview with author, 16 October 1991.

18   John Taylor, interview with author, 30 September 1991.

19   E. Moxon-Browne, *Nation Class and Creed in Northern Ireland* (Aldershot, 1983), p. 8.

20   Nigel Dodds, interview with author, 2 December 1991.

21   Billy Hutchinson, interview with author, 20 November 1995.

22   Moloney and Pollak, *Paisley*, p. 271.

23   ibid., p. 295.

24   ibid., p. 290.

25   Ian Paisley Jnr, interview with author, 9 November 1995.

26   Moloney and Pollak, *Paisley*, p. 293.

27   She reportedly resigned from the Free Presbyterian Church at the beginning of the 1990s to the dismay of her father. *Daily Express*, 3 February 1992.

28   ibid.

29   L. Edgerton, 'Public Protest, Domestic Acquiescence: Women in Northern Ireland', in R. Ridd and H. Callaway (eds.), *Caught up in the Conflict: Women's Responses to Political Strife* (London, 1986), p. 61.

30   The Brook Clinic provides a range of family planning services and sex education for young people in Northern Ireland.

31   Talk by Inez McCormack to Boston Public Library Symposium on Irish Women, 9 March 1993, quoted in 'Women in Northern Ireland' by C. B. Shannon in *Chattel, Servant or Citizen: Women's Status in Church, State and Society*, ed. by M. O'Dowd and S. Wichert (Belfast, 1995), p. 250.

32   'In the 1993 local government elections [in Northern Ireland] women constituted 14% of Official Unionist and 10% of Democratic Unionist candidates. These percentages are comparable to the ratio of women candidates for the SDLP which had 16% and Sinn Féin 11.5%. The latter figure was down 4% from 1989, undoubtedly a result of the frequency of assassination attempts on Sinn Féin councillors in recent years.' ibid., p. 249.

33   Moloney and Pollak, *Paisley*, p. 36.

34   Shannon, 'Women in Northern Ireland' p. 250.

35 M. McWilliams, 'Strategy for Peace and Justice: Reflections on Women's Activism in Northern Ireland', *Journal of Women's History*, Vol. 6, No. 4/Vol. 7, No. 1 (Winter/Spring 1995), p. 30.

36 *Irish Times*, 22 September 1995.

37 ibid.

38 The 30 May elections were to a forum which would then send delegates to all-party talks (including Sinn Féin in the event of a renewed IRA ceasefire). The electoral system was a hybrid between the normal single transferable vote form of proportional representation and a variant of the list system. One key advantage of the 30 May election from the point of view of smaller parties such as the Women's Coalition was that no deposits had to be paid in order to stand in the election and thus the exercise was not a severe financial burden on those likely to lose deposits in several constituencies.

39 Sammy Wilson, interview with author, 20 November 1991.

40 Rev. Ivan Foster, *Talkback* (BBC Radio Ulster, 10 February 1989).

41 ibid.

42 ibid.

43 Clifford Smyth 'The Ulster Democratic Unionist Party: A Case Study in Religious Convergence' (PhD thesis, Queen's University, Belfast, 1983), p. 214.

44 ibid., p. 214.

45 Moloney and Pollak, *Paisley*, p. 271.

46 Ian Paisley Jnr, interview with author, 9 November 1995.

47 ibid.

48 Peter Robinson, interview with author, 8 November 1995.

49 Gary McMichael, interview with author, 22 November 1995.

50 ibid.

51 David Ervine, interview with author, 20 November 1995.

52 Billy Hutchinson, interview with author, 20 November 1995.

53 David Ervine, interview with author, 20 November 1995.

54 ibid.

55 ibid.

56 Peter Robinson, interview with author, 8 November 1995.

57 Rev. Ian Paisley, in J. Loughlin, *Ulster Unionism and British National Identity Since 1885* (London and New York, 1995), p. 217.

58 *For God and Ulster? Protestant Voices from the North* (RTE Television, May 1996).

59 S. Bruce, *Fortnight*, No. 242 (July–September 1986), p. 6.

60 S. Bruce, *God Save Ulster! The Religion and Politics of Paisleyism* (Oxford, 1986), p. 57.

61 C. Coulter, 'The Character of Unionism', *Irish Political Studies*, 9 (1994), p. 7.

62 McGarry and O'Leary, *Explaining Northern Ireland*, p. 197.

63 ibid., pp. 200–1.

64 Bruce, *God Save Ulster!*, p. 249.

65 S. Bruce, *The Edge of the Union: The Ulster Loyalist Political Vision* (Oxford, 1994), p. 22.

66 ibid., p. 25.

67 ibid., p. 30.

68 P. Stringer and G. Robinson (eds.), *Social Attitudes in Northern Ireland 1990–1991* (Belfast, 1991), p. 25. See also McGarry and O'Leary, *Explaining Northern Ireland*, p. 110, Table 3.3.

69 Bruce, *Edge of the Union*, p. 159.

70 Nelson, *Ulster's Uncertain Defenders*, p. 25.

71 Ulster Vanguard was originally set up on 9 February 1972 by the former Stormont Minister for Home Affairs William Craig as a right-wing militant pressure group within the Unionist Party. On 18 March 1972 Craig led a rally in Belfast's Ormeau Park

attended by 60,000 supporters where he talked of 'liquidating' the enemies of Ulster and threatened a unilateral declaration of independence from Great Britain. Essentially this was a quasi-fascist movement with Craig assuming the role Oswald Mosely occupied within the British Union of Fascists in the 1930s.

72 Smyth, 'Democratic Unionist Party', p. 71.

73 The Ulster Clubs were set up by radical unionists in the rural areas of Northern Ireland after the signing of the Anglo-Irish Agreement in November 1985. This was an attempt to provide both organisation and muscle to the unionist campaign against the initiative. In their conscious mimicry of the Ulster Clubs established by Sir Edward Carson in the fight against Home Rule at the beginning of the twentieth century, they represented a classic example of unionism's tendency to look back to victories of the past in order to deal with crises of the present. They openly admitted their intention to engage in violence as a means of achieving their political objectives and their slogan was 'hoping for the best but preparing for the worst'. Northern Ireland's independent political review *Fortnight* magazine carried a profile of the Ulster Clubs' Chairman and leading activist Alan Wright under the headline 'Is this man bluffing?' It turned out that he was – he later left active politics and went to Bible college.

74 David Trimble, interview with author, 3 October 1991.

75 ibid.

76 Dr John Alderdice, interview with author, 7 February 1996.

77 ibid.

78 ibid.

79 D. Miller, *Queen's Rebels: Ulster Loyalism in Historical Perspective* (Dublin and New York, 1978).

80 ibid., p. 1.

81 ibid., p. 12.

82 ibid., p. 5.

83 ibid., p. 23.

84 Bruce, *God Save Ulster!*, p. 251.

85 P. Arthur and K. Jeffery, *Northern Ireland Since 1968* (Oxford, 1988).

86 ibid., p. 46.

87 John Taylor, interview with author, 30 September 1991.

88 Garret FitzGerald, interview with author, 8 April 1992.

89 David Trimble, interview with author, 3 October 1991.

90 ibid.

91 Miller, *Queen's Rebels*, p. 102.

92 Rev. Ian Paisley in *Protestant Telegraph*, 19 March–1 April 1977, in ibid., p. 6.

93 Ian Paisley Jnr, interview with author, 9 November 1995.

94 Sammy Wilson, interview with author, 20 November 1991.

95 Miller, *Queen's Rebels*, p. 46.

96 ibid., p. 103.

97 T. Hennessey, 'Ulster unionist territorial and national identities 1886–1893: Province, island, Kingdom and empire', *Irish Political Studies*, 8 (1993), pp. 29–30.

98 Coulter, 'Character of Unionism', p. 3.

99 ibid.

100 A. Aughey, *Under Siege: Ulster Unionism and the Anglo-Irish Agreement* (Belfast, 1989), p. 20.

101 ibid., p. 23.

102 See also Coulter, 'Character of Unionism', p. 5.

103 Thomas Hobbes, *Leviathan*, Ch. 21, p. 14.

104 Aughey, *Under Siege*, p. 23.

105 Enoch Powell, *The History-Makers* (BBC Radio Ulster, 5 February 1989).
106 David Trimble, interview with author, 3 October 1991.
107 ibid.
108 T. Brown, *The Whole Protestant Community: The Making of a Historical Myth* (Derry, Field Day Pamphlet No. 7, 1985), p. 8.
109 Aughey, *Under Siege*, p. 14.
110 Garret FitzGerald, interview with author, 8 April 1992.
111 John Taylor in David Miller, *Queen's Rebels*, p. 3.
112 Nelson, *Ulster's Uncertain Defenders*, p. 96.
113 Aughey, *Under Siege*, p. 15.
114 ibid., p. 16.
115 ibid., p. 18.
116 ibid.
117 Loughlin, *Ulster Unionism and British National Identity*, p. 221.
118 R. Emmerson, *From Empire to Nation: The Rise to Self-Assertion of Asian and African Peoples* (Cambridge, Mass., 1960), p. 96, in Miller, *Queen's Rebels*, p. 44.
119 Aughey, *Under Siege*, p. 19.
120 ibid. p. 24. Yes, but for many it only retained such authority for so long as the monarch remained Protestant and the state preserved the cultural ethos of Ulster unionism. Witness the comment in *Anglo-Irish Betrayal: What Hope Now For Loyal Ulster*: 'It must be stated quite clearly and unambiguously that Ulster's Loyalty is primarily to her Protestant Faith and to her Queen (and in that order!).'
121 Coulter, 'Character of Unionism', p. 16.
122 Aughey, *Under Siege*, p. 19.
123 A. Aughey, 'Unionism and Self-Determination', in P. Roche and B. Barton (eds.), *The Northern Ireland Question: Myth and Reality* (Aldershot, 1991), pp. 11–12; reprinted in Foster (ed.), *The Idea of the Union*, p. 16.
124 J. Whyte, *Interpreting Northern Ireland* (Oxford, 1991), p. 219.
125 Roche and Barton (eds.), *The Northern Ireland Question*, p. vii, referring to J. Lee, *Ireland 1912–1985* (Cambridge, 1989).
126 ibid., p. 8.
127 T. Wilson, *Ulster: Conflict and Consent* (Oxford, 1989), p. 130, in ibid., p. x.

CHAPTER 3

Divisive Visions

Strategic disagreements

The necessity of developing a coherent political alternative to the AIA exacerbated existing tensions within the unionist ideology. The coalition of interest groups existing under the ideological canopy of unionism, which could achieve unity in the face of a commonly perceived aggressor – in this case represented by the AIA – was unable to maintain this unity when political progress was contemplated. The divisions which emerged over political strategy were not merely driven by party rivalries or the associated personality clashes, but were rooted in quite fundamental ideological differences. Not unnaturally, unionist disagreement over their critique of the external political environment was reflected in their espousal of alternative political strategies. This problem was recognised by the DUP press officer Sammy Wilson, who emphasised the interparty discord when talking retrospectively about the anti-Agreement campaign. Wilson disagreed with the analysis that by 1991 the AIA was a 'dead letter' to the extent that, although it still existed on paper, it had not achieved its objectives as set out in the joint communiqué.

> Well, I think it would be too complacent to say it is a 'dead letter'. It is still there and it's hanging over us, and there are still things happening as a result of the Agreement which I believe are detrimental to unionists, and therefore I wouldn't like to say that it's a 'dead letter'. I think that it is never going to have the support of the unionist community and to that extent it is dead, because you can't have a form of government that is not recognised or not supported, even in a lukewarm fashion, by two-thirds of the community. But it is still a big threat, and that is why I believe that unionists cannot be complacent about getting rid of it.[1]

This belief in the Agreement's continuing political virility contrasts sharply with the perception amongst Ulster Unionists, who see it as increasingly impotent, an irrelevance in terms of its practical influence, but an obstacle to political progress. When Belfast Ulster Unionist Councillor and former honorary secretary of the party Michael McGimpsey was asked the same question as Sammy Wilson, to the effect that the AIA was no longer a political threat to the unionist community, he provided the opposite response.

> Oh the Anglo-Irish Agreement is going nowhere. It has produced nothing, it has done nothing for either side, so I think both governments recognise that it has got to be replaced. The question is how do you replace it, and that's what the 'Brooke Talks' were about. I think [Secretary of State Peter] Brooke's analysis is right, that the answer will come from some sort of agreement you know.[2]

This sentiment cross-cuts the liberal-conservative cleavage within the Ulster Unionist Party and is not simply a product of sanguine misinterpretation of the political environment. The Rev. Martin Smyth, for example, concurred with McGimpsey's analysis when asked if his position on the AIA was that it was dead in all but name. 'It would be my position, so much so that I wanted a slogan earlier, "the Agreement is dead, end the wake". But some folk thought that it wasn't a very nice slogan.'[3]

These conflicting perceptions of the AIA's importance inevitably coloured the political strategies which were considered to be most appropriate to the situation. The benign scenario facilitated James Molyneaux's 'long view' and encouraged the belief that, if they waited for long enough, the AIA would tear itself apart through its own internal tensions. The more malign analysis of the Agreement favoured by the vast majority of those in the DUP, however, required a much more active campaign against it. They believed that unionists could not simply wait for the accord to wither away, but had to strive to have it removed because it was gaining in strength and influence as time progressed. Sammy Wilson recognised the clash between the UUP's view of the Agreement and that of his own party, and he sought to substantiate the latter through a practical example.

> I would take a difference for example with the Official Unionists, who feel that there is no urgency to get into talks, there is no urgency to push things, because really if you lie about for long enough, the thing will wither . . . Well now I don't think that unionists can afford to be that complacent. The Agreement can still do a lot of damage if it is allowed, if unionists are prepared to sit back and take that kind of view. I think that we have got to continually say, 'look, this Agreement is bad, here are some of the bad things that have come out of it, here are some of the detrimental things that have come out of it', and that we have got to work for its removal. That shows itself and the difference between the two parties. Let me just give you one example. The Official Unionists would take the view that the merger of the UDR and the Royal Irish Rangers just happened to come about because of the defence cuts. We would believe that the defence cuts were a convenient cover, that it came about because of the pressure through the Agreement, by the Dublin government, to get rid of the UDR. Now if that is

the case, if we are right and they are wrong, you can't sit back and wait for the Agreement to wither, you have actually got to be out there doing something to get rid of it, because it is having detrimental effects on the unionist community anyway, even at present.[4]

While it could be argued that Wilson may not be representative of the DUP as a whole, he was the party's press officer and thus charged with giving the general as well as his individual perspective. Nevertheless, the existence of the joint unionist pact could be cited as evidence to support the point that, despite Wilson's remarks, the DUP were prepared to go along with the Ulster Unionist policy of 'masterly inactivity', a strategy which would surely not have been acceptable had the party been in agreement with Wilson's analysis. Indeed Ian Paisley has stated that the AIA was not as strong as it once was. 'The Anglo-Irish Agreement is not a healthy child and I think it will eventually have its demise.'[5] Despite such statements by the DUP leader, Wilson's analysis was substantiated by Nigel Dodds, the party's chief whip. When asked whether he agreed with the Ulster Unionist view that the AIA was no longer relevant in practical terms, because the British government had lost interest in trying to achieve its original aims and were now looking for a way out of it and a replacement for it, Dodds demurred, arguing that this was a much too optimistic reading of the political situation.

There is a different analysis being put forward by both parties. The Official Unionists tend to put forward the analysis that really, as time has gone on, the Anglo-Irish Agreement is getting weaker and our position is getting stronger, and there is now a change of heart and a change of mind [by the British government]. My view, and the view of our party, would be different. My view is, okay we may have stopped some things happening as quickly, but there is no doubt that the Anglo-Irish Agreement is firmly in place, and if we don't get a replacement for it, it will get stronger, and if you talk to civil servants and if you talk to the NIO, they are in no doubt that every day that passes the Anglo-Irish process gets stronger and more entrenched. You only have to look at the issues, I mean look at the UDR decision, the fair employment, the way decisions are now being made as a matter of course in Northern Ireland. . . . This idea that somehow it is now a 'dead letter' is a lot of nonsense, I mean it is there and it will get stronger and more entrenched, and whoever is the [Irish] foreign minister will continue to come in and say his bit. You know I think there is no future for unionists in closing their eyes to reality and pretending the trouble isn't there, they have got to face up to the reality and say, 'how are we going to deal with it?' Are we going to negotiate the Agreement away or find a replacement for it, or else if we can't do that, are we going to have a look, very realistically, at all the options? Now there are some unionists who, rather than take on the fight, or rather than face up to the problem, would say, 'well, if we get a select committee at

Westminster' and so on and so forth, 'we have won', and they are really selling everyone short.[6]

This statement, which ties in very much with the rhetoric of Sammy Wilson on the issue, would suggest that, despite statements to the contrary by Ian Paisley, the view of the party was that the AIA was still alive and kicking and chipping away at the foundations of the Union. When these criticisms of the UUP were put to Rev. Martin Smyth, he denied that his party was complacent or that it had underestimated the durability of the Agreement. He rejected the suggestion that the decision to merge the UDR with the Royal Irish Rangers had anything to do with the AIA on the grounds that there was no empirical evidence whatever to substantiate such an argument. In a counterattack against the DUP, Smyth went on to allege that they were involved in a cynical attempt to activate the Protestant defensive mentality in order to maximise their vote at the forthcoming 1992 general election.

> The DUP misread the situation completely and use it [for their own ends]. There is an election coming up remember, so they have got to go for the populist feeling. There is not a scrap of evidence that anyone has produced yet to support the view that the amalgamation of the two [UDR and RIR] were part of the Anglo-Irish Agreement, or even had been discussed at the conference. There are other philosophies on that level, and I believe we are seeing a massive reorganisation of the British armed forces, and the Agreement had nothing to do with the shutting down of the Scottish regiments, and the phasing out of the Royal Hampshires. . . . the Agreement cannot deliver what it set out to deliver, and sooner or later, and I would like to think sooner than later, something will be in its place.[7]

Irrespective of whose analysis was correct, this relatively minor issue can be seen in a wider context as indicative of the difference between the two main unionist parties. As will become clear in the following chapters, the unity of purpose to remove the AIA was not matched by a common perception of the existing political environment. The disagreement over what reasons lay behind the merger of two regiments in the British army, when replicated over other policy issues – for example the significance of the Public Order Act, the legitimacy and/or necessity of violence to achieve political goals – resulted in widespread disagreement within the unionist community. The consequence of this internal dissent was that the ideology could neither progress in a liberal/progressive manner and implement those reforms advocated by Ulster Unionists such as Peter Smith and Frank Millar, nor 'progress' in a conservative/regressive fashion, along the lines suggested by Jim Allister or Ivan Foster. The necessity of unity and unilateral action had its price, and that price was political ossification.

Strategic problems

The underlying reasons for the divisions which arose within the unionist ideology as the campaign against the AIA progressed were rooted in the observation by James Chichester-Clark, former Prime Minister of Northern Ireland and leader of the UUP, that the Unionist Party could hardly be called a political party as all that united those within it was a desire to remain part of the UK, thus 'you could really be any political complexion within that umbrella'.[8] More recently, Michael McGimpsey agreed that this socio-political diversity presented a problem for unionism which he preferred to characterise as an identity rather than an ideology. For him, there were many different versions of unionism with little in common other than a basic identification with Britain.

> Unionism is a very broad church and there are ideological differences right throughout it, not just on devolution versus independence versus integration, but also you have socialists and liberals and high Tories, extreme fascists even. So it is getting them all to work together [that] is the problem.[9]

This desire to attract as broad a coalition as possible to unionism was emphasised by James Molyneaux when he was asked to explain the main elements of his political strategy. He stressed that since he became leader of the UUP he had attempted to promote a cross-class secular party which would strengthen the Union with Britain. He pointed out that this was an act of extreme political bravery on his part which had been vindicated by increased support for the party. Molyneaux referred to a speech he made to the Friends of the Union conference in October 1991, when he stated that since 1979 his objective had been to establish a catch-all party which revolved around the common denominator of support for the constitutional link with Britain.

> I was going for the philosophy of the broad church party . . . and I spelled out quite clearly to the Friends of the Union conference that means that I see the Ulster Unionist Party having a mission and a responsibility to provide an umbrella for all the pro-Union people of Ulster, whether they be Protestant, Roman Catholic, or of no religion at all. If we say the Union is paramount, then everything else must take second place to that. . . . Again it is the 'long view', that we have got to the position now where, I think it is recognised, except by people who have a vested interest in doing us down, that we have been growing in strength, and we have been attracting support from all social sections of the community, and all the various so-called sectarian sides of the community.[10]

There is certainly a degree of truth in Molyneaux's assertion that the UUP is a broad-church party, though the extent to which this umbrella has been widened by Molyneaux himself is difficult to quantify. However, his declaration that the Ulster Unionist Party had widened its cross-community appeal under his leadership is a more difficult argument to sustain, as most studies indicate that there has been no significant increase in Catholic support for the UUP since the beginning of the present conflict.

The desire for unity which was so apparent throughout the anti-Agreement campaign brings us on to examine the self-perception of the unionist political community. Why is it, if unity is so important in strengthening the unionist position, that two separate party structures exist despite the avowed attempts by James Molyneaux to create as broad a coalition as possible? Does the existence of the UUP and DUP reflect the specific historical circumstances of the early 1970s which witnessed political disintegration over post-Stormont arrangements, and has this simply been perpetuated by personality conflicts between those involved, or is there instead an organic ideological difference between the two parties?

As Chapter 2 demonstrated, there are fundamental cultural and political differences within unionism which broadly, though not exclusively, correlate to party divisions. In social terms Democratic Unionists tend to be younger, more populist and to possess a closer link to fundamentalist Protestantism than their colleagues within the Ulster Unionist Party. In addition, as group participation in the political process is based upon competition for electoral support, the existence of separate political structures has produced its own rationality. As Paul Arthur and Keith Jeffery explained, the battle for electoral supremacy waged between the two main unionist parties throughout the 1980s

> . . . led to such acrimony and exaggerated pledges that a rational debate became impossible within the camp. As a result unionists tried to outbid each other in their claims to be the true loyalists. In turn this induced unrealistic expectations of what they might secure from the government in terms of their political future and it made them incapable of negotiating a meaningful compromise with their political opponents.[11]

The issue of the amalgamation of the two main unionist parties, for example, illustrates the multiplicity of cultural identities within the UUP. John Taylor regards the DUP as political vandals who go around stirring up trouble over outdated religious dogma and consequently diminishing support for the unionist cause in Britain and the rest of Europe. He sees their involvement in Northern Ireland politics as an obstacle to the chances of achieving a political settlement, and advocates that the UUP should have as little to do with them as possible.

> I of course would be one Member of Parliament in the Ulster Unionist team who would be rather hesitant about co-operating with the DUP. In fact, in more recent months [mid-1991], we have had these silly Brooke Talks, in which we have been involved with the DUP, and I have been trying to

distance myself as far as is reasonable, without letting the side down, on that issue, because I think one of our problems there again is that we are too closely linked with the DUP. I think we could make much more progress if we were on our own.[12]

When asked explicitly if he would recommend that the Ulster Unionists should end their alliance with the DUP, Taylor (speaking in 1991) made his feelings plain. 'Oh yes, oh, yes, oh I think that is one of the necessary ingredients to the overall settlement.'[13]

UUP leader David Trimble, on the other hand, represents a different strand which defies categorisation. A middle-class academic/politician who exudes a largely secular British orientation, yet he dallies with radical unionist movements committed to political independence and cultural isolationism, such as the Vanguard Unionist Party in the 1970s and the Ulster Clubs in the 1980s. Whilst recognising the importance of Free Presbyterianism in the DUP, Trimble contends that this is of more significance amongst party activists than for those who vote for it.

> There is the obvious difference, in that the Democratic Unionist Party is a party where the leading figures are members of the Free Presbyterian Church. The party organisation in the country is very much based on membership, not exclusively of course, but very much based on membership of the Free Presbyterian Church, so the DUP is a more confessional party than the OUP, which sees itself as a broad church. Although that is in terms of party activists. I have seen surveys of party support, which would seem to indicate that there is no strong difference in the social profile of the voters for the parties, although received wisdom has been that there was a certain difference in the social profiles.[14]

Notwithstanding the confessional element which he identifies, Trimble sees no distinction between the parties in terms of ideology. His view is that any differences which exist are the product of self-generating animosities between competing political structures in the battle for electoral support and not a reflection of cultural differences. Consequently, Trimble is keen to see an amalgamation of the two main unionist parties, partly perhaps because he thinks he has a chance of leading it, but primarily because he sees no inherent reason for the maintenance of two competing structures. When asked if he could see the Ulster Unionists and the DUP merging at some point in the future, he replied that he could easily envisage such a scenario in a post-Paisley environment, as without his leadership the DUP would not continue as an independent political party for a significant length of time. When it was suggested to Trimble that such a prospect would appal a great many people within the Ulster Unionist Party, he maintained that after Ian Paisley's political demise the internal fractures within the ideology would become less obvious.

I think that if Ian Paisley stepped in front of the proverbial bus, and I put that as a first requirement [as] nobody can see Ian Paisley agreeing to do anything else other than be top-dog, and nobody – hardly anybody – in the Ulster Unionist Party thinks he is fit to lead it, for a variety of reasons I hasten to add. Now if Ian stepped in front of the proverbial bus, I don't see the DUP lasting as a separate party. I see a substantial number of the present DUP moving into the Ulster Unionist Party. I see a handful of people in the DUP remaining outside, probably remaining outside political activity, and I think in that scenario, some of those Ulster Unionists who say, 'oh, I couldn't possibly work with x', might actually find that they never have to, that the people they would have to work with, are people they could work with.[15]

In a separate interview on Radio Ulster's *Talkback* in March 1989, Trimble asked a number of rhetorical questions as to why structural divisions existed within the ideology and concluded that the explanation lay in the historical legacy of the past rather than with the contemporary situation. His portrayal of the anti-Agreement campaign as a period of inter-party harmony was a typically idiosyncratic if scarcely accurate reading of the situation.

What it really brought to mind was the simple question, 'why are there two unionist parties today? Are these two parties serving any separate functions?' . . . In the past there were policy differences, [but] there have been no fundamental policy differences for three years. There have been difficulties created because we've got two structures and have to work within them, and the two structures give opportunities for mischief-making, but they don't do us any positive good. I don't think 'the-man-in-the-street' wants them, and I think there is an increasing impatience amongst 'the-man-in-the-street' with the continued existence of these two structures.[16]

However, when this argument was put to his colleague the Rev. Martin Smyth, it became clear that enthusiasm for the amalgamation of the two parties was not uniform throughout the UUP. Smyth took exception to the idea that if Paisley retired from active politics there would be an influx of Democratic Unionists into the UUP and suggested that the proposer of such a plan was out of touch with political reality.

Any unionist who said that is an absolute loony who doesn't actually know the realities of life. I mean this is mythology, it's the mythology – if we may use the church scene – [of] those who have been telling me now for forty years that the Free Presbyterian Church is dying. An institution has its own momentum. It will be a different party, I don't doubt that, but it will not dissolve. It may divide, but you will have DUP folk around for a long time, and whether it would have full electoral support is another issue, but the party will be there, and anybody who comes off with that sort of claptrap doesn't deserve to be called a politician. That is all I have to say to you.[17]

James Molyneaux took a rather more reserved tone, arguing that, whilst he would have no objection in principle to such a scenario, it would not be advantageous in electoral terms for an amalgamation of the two main parties to occur. He also pointed out that it would probably lead to further factionalism within the ideology with splinter groups occurring, and thus defeat the purpose of securing a unified party.

> Well Ian and I have talked about it, even in our lifetime. There is no power to bind our successors, but the conclusion we came to any time we did talk about it, given that you have people in my party who would say, 'we are not going to have anything to do with the DUP, we just won't wear it. If you are going to amalgamate with them, right, we are getting out.' You would have people in the DUP who would say, 'we are not going to have anything to do . . . [with the UUP] because they are the people who in Stormont sold us out in the bad old days . . . and they have still got the same gang there'. . . . You would end up then, with one party, maybe slightly bigger than the sum total of the two . . . bigger than our party, but you would have two other parties, one on either side of it. You would have one on the right wing in the social sense, you would have the left going off on a tangent, and saying that they were not having anything to do with anything other than very hard-line unionism. So instead of having two parties, you would have three.[18]

Not surprisingly, some members of the DUP were more animated in their opposition to the idea of a merger with the Ulster Unionists, objecting to it not just on practical grounds, but on the basis that they had a separate identity to the UUP. When Sammy Wilson was asked whether he thought that the DUP would disintegrate without Ian Paisley's charismatic leadership, he replied that the essential divisions between the two parties had not diminished despite the pact between them.

> No I don't. I think that there is a very very distinct identity in the DUP. I think that most people here in the DUP at the moment joined the DUP because they didn't see a future with the Official Unionist Party. They had fundamental disagreements and those fundamental disagreements are still there. Anyway, I believe that most people in the DUP, there wouldn't be any future for them within the Official Unionist Party. I could never see myself fitting neatly into the Official Unionist Party, the kind of compromises that are required, to keep that broad church you were talking about, I simply couldn't live with, and in an increasingly polarised society, there are more people within unionism who see compromise as a difficult thing to live with; therefore I think that they are always going to need to have some kind of distinct unionist identity, which the DUP is capable of providing. I am sure that there is this desire within the Official Unionist Party to try and get everybody under the one big umbrella again. I don't even believe that is good for unionism, because I think that that leads to the kind of lethargy that you had in the 1960s, which led us into the present situation.[19]

When Ian Paisley Jnr was asked whether the institutional divisions were purely an accident of history or a product of a more fundamental organic difference within the ideology, he suggested that the individualism inherent within the Protestant psyche lent itself more to factionalism than to unity. Protestants liked the right to argue, to put forward an alternative point of view, and to choose both in spiritual and in temporal affairs. Thus, why should there be one single political ideology when there was no single denomination called the Protestant Church? While recognising the importance of his father's personality in shaping the character and electoral base of the DUP, Paisley Jnr believes that the party has a particular ideological profile which distinguishes it from the UUP.

> I think there is [an ideological] difference. I think that the DUP tries to represent their view of what traditional unionist principles are. They very much see themselves in the light of Carson unionism, very much see themselves as the traditional unionist party, the party which is firmly in the Union. It's not prepared to have double standards in its dealings with Dublin, [it's] a very straight up and down 'like us or loathe us' party. And I think that is very different from the kind of broad church image . . . which the OUP try to market.[20]

When David Trimble's analysis – that the DUP was merely an extension of Ian Paisley's personality, and would find it very difficult to sustain itself as an independent political party in the event that he 'fell under the proverbial bus' – was put to Paisley Jnr, he agreed with the view of Sammy Wilson and Rev. Martin Smyth that the DUP had transcended this and had established its own identity.

> I think that if they were saying that in 1978, they may have had a chance of being realistic. The Democratic Unionist Party, it has been in existence now, it'll be its silver jubilee next year. We have a lot of young people in the DUP. Their fathers and mothers joined the DUP and left the OUP. The children are now in the DUP . . . because it's their party. You can't then just wipe that out and say 'no we're going back' because they wouldn't understand. . . . I also believe that because we have marketed ourselves on issues and because we tend to work as a party on those issues on the ground with regards to community advice centres . . . we tend then to get support because of the job we do and the service we provide, and whether it's a last resort social service we provide, the fact is it's there and people identify with that.[21]

When Trimble's analysis was put to Peter Robinson, he too denied that Ian Paisley was bigger than the party. In a response which approached humour, the East Belfast MP pointed out sardonically that Paisley was not the only popular figure within the organisation.

> Without being immodest, I think if you look at the support of the Democratic Unionist Party in Northern Ireland you will see it is not highest

in North Antrim but in East Belfast and Castlereagh. I can't see that that would change because Ian Paisley wasn't on the political scene.[22]

Another manifestation of this lack of unanimity within the unionist community can be found in the various political alternatives sought by those at the policy-making end of the ideology. As will become apparent in the chapters on the anti-Agreement campaign, the unionist coalition was disabled by the fact that once they began to look for positive strategies which would cripple the Agreement, or achieve its suspension through political negotiation, no alternative could be found which could secure interparty support. When Garret FitzGerald was asked to comment as an external observer upon unionism's apparent inability to establish a coherent political strategy on the AIA, he pointed to differences within the respective leaderships of the Ulster Unionist Party and the DUP. When interviewed in April 1992 for his recollections of the post-Agreement period, he was asked for his opinion on the differences within the ideology as represented by the existence of two party structures.

> Well, there are quite a lot of cultural differences, but you want to distinguish the leadership of each from the parties. Molyneaux is an integrationist who is a veteran parliamentarian . . . he belongs almost to the Redmondite tradition [of Irish nationalism], where the centre of gravity is London and Westminster, which is what killed the Irish Party, and it has damaged the OUP as well I think. He doesn't want devolution. Paisley is a devolutionist, but he doesn't want ever to be in government. He wants to be in opposition and has always wanted to be in opposition to an OUP–SDLP government that he could attack. But he has never been able to get that. Both of them, therefore, in the present situation want nothing to happen, because their personal power-bases depend upon nothing happening, and by doing nothing they can prevent anything happening. . . . But within each party obviously there are others with their own view. Peter Robinson is totally different. He wants power. Robinson's desire for power is, I think, quite a positive factor in the present context of Northern Ireland.[23]

Chichester-Clark's observation, that all which united unionists was a desire to retain the link with Britain (albeit for differing reasons), remained salient throughout the anti-Agreement campaign. Once positive alternatives were considered, and once progressive thought was engaged in, the various interest groups within the ideology began to move in differing if not mutually exclusive directions. The ultimate effect was to hamper the intellectual coherence of the ideology and diminish its political muscle against both the British government and internal actors, namely the SDLP and quasi-political groups on the radical fringes of the unionist community such as the UDA and the Ulster Clubs. These groups were never going to affect the main unionist parties in electoral terms, but their public opposition and ridicule of the anti-Agreement campaign diminished the political space available to constitutional unionism. This was recognised by Christopher McGimpsey when he commented that 'The spectre of Lundyism haunts all who are prepared to consider compromise, co-operation or conciliation.'[24] The inability of unionist politicians to 'run ahead of the mob' and provide leadership which would benefit the ideology in the longer term became a marked feature of unionist politics over the next three years.

Conflicting scenarios

This brings us on to an examination of how conflicting identities within unionism fashioned mutually exclusive political programmes. The search for alternatives to the AIA exposed the latent factionalism within the ideology as the various interest groups competed for control of party policy. Pressure groups emerged such as the Campaign for Equal Citizenship (CEC) and the Charter Group, arguing for integration and devolution, whilst the devolution camp was itself split between those who wanted the reinstatement of majority rule, others who wanted power-sharing, and those in the middle who favoured administrative devolution. The nett result was an incoherent political policy which failed to exercise the minds of either the SDLP or the British government. The absence of a credible strategy for political progress after three years of looking for one within the anti-Agreement campaign was recognised by David McNarry, a founding member of the pro-devolution Charter Group. A radio interview which preceded the 1989 European election revolved around the announcement by the Charter Group that they were considering putting up an opposition candidate to Jim Nicholson (the Ulster Unionist nominee) to give voters a chance to express their support for devolution. McNarry was asked how he could say that he favoured devolution when there were so many models of it supported by different factions within different parties. He conceded that this had had a debilitating effect on the fortunes of the ideology since the signing of the AIA and would continue to damage it if the leadership did not provide a coherent policy which the unionist community could rally around. The following conversation between the interviewer and McNarry would suggest that, whatever may have been proposed by lobbyists such as the Charter Group, they were not representative of the wider unionist political community at that time.

> I: Is there actually an appetite within the Ulster Unionist Party for devolution, or indeed one has to ask, having attended, as an observer, the party's last conference, is there even the desire and the appetite for political thought or discussion or consideration, because all one heard at that conference in Portrush before Christmas [1988 AGM] was 'no no no no no' to everything?

M: I think the fact is that some people prefer the soft option of, 'do nothing and you can't be blamed for any mistakes'. The fact is that the longer unionists sit on the fence, the longer John Hume is going to taunt them, and the longer that unionists fail to test the SDLP with any proposals, then the longer John Hume is going to flirt with aspirations and notions that do nothing to encourage unionists to trust the nationalist community. . . . I agree that so long as there are differences, splits and counter proposals inside unionism, we are letting the SDLP off the hook every time we talk in different voices. . . . It would be a tremendous step for me to say, 'this Unionist Party [UUP] that I believe in . . . is going nowhere because of one man and his leadership'.

I: But can you hang it on one man? After all, there is the Ulster Unionist Council, there are party conferences, Jim Molyneaux was cheered to the echo at that last party conference. You can't just hang it on one man?

M: We have one man in control of the Unionist Party. That is our problem. One man who controls every aspect of the Unionist Party. Now there are 800 people in the Ulster Unionist Council, and the question that I continually ask myself is, 'why is it that only 300 people turn up to cheer Jim Molyneaux? What is happening with the other 500? Are they like me, really couldn't be bothered?' . . . I believe that the officers of the Ulster Unionist Council have in fact damaged the Ulster Unionist Council, by allowing the leadership of Jim Molyneaux to continue as it has. . . . I have been quite prepared over these last couple of years to wait for Jim Molyneaux to tell me that he is right – well he keeps on telling me he's right – but to prove that he is right, that in fact Northern Ireland is gaining something from his leadership, and I am sorry to say that it is not. We are clutching at straws as a community. What I feel is that there is a great need to know where we are going in Northern Ireland. As a democrat, I am quite prepared to have devolution rejected, but I want it up front, I want the debate to be settled. I don't think the debate was settled at the Ulster Unionist conference [1988 AGM] when Ken Maginnis and Raymond Ferguson took a walloping, because I don't think that that was what that debate was about. That debate was, 'let's keep our positions, let's do nothing. Molyneaux's not taking any risks so what is there to lose?'

I: And he was delighted to say that he was not for moving. That was what gained him most applause, that he was standing still, wherever he is, and wasn't going to move, and that seemed to be extremely popular as far as I could see, with the delegates at that conference.

M: What I am going to say [is] that without a single coherent policy, unionism is bankrupt as a party in its thinking and in its way forward.[25]

The Ulster Unionist Party was being pulled in the opposite direction, meanwhile, by the Campaign for Equal Citizenship, who advocated a conflicting political strategy. Their philosophy was summed up by Robert McCartney at the organisation's first general conference on 1 November 1986. Here he put forward the thesis – later developed by Arthur Aughey in *Under Siege* – that 'provincial politics', the exclusion of Northern Ireland from the class-based system operating in the rest of the UK, had created sectarianism in the province.

> Our political masters on Stormont Hill have catalogued us as Protestants and Catholics. They are determined that we shall remain Protestants and Catholics. It is not enough for them that we are Protestants and Catholics in our religion: They have also determined that we must be Protestants and Catholics in our politics. . . . The sectarian conflict and siege politics of Northern Ireland only exist, because all the people of Northern Ireland have been deliberately excluded, for deliberate reasons of political expediency, from that enriching secular, pluralist culture. . . . We, the people of Northern Ireland, are not the political dinosaurs. The dinosaurs are those decayed imperialists in the British political establishment who have locked the people of Northern Ireland outside the politics of modern Britain. It is they who have decreed that we must be Protestants and Catholics in politics in a modern pluralist world. It is they, and the politically myopic mandarins who serve them, that have so arranged things, that the people of Northern Ireland cannot be Tories; they cannot be Socialists; they cannot be Liberals and Social Democrats – or even Communists, should they so choose.[26]

The tension between these competing philosophies of integration and devolution with Molyneaux in the middle trying to hold the party together resulted in stagnation, as movement in any direction would have resulted in a schism. A 'Task Force' was set up in 1987 by the two main parties in an attempt to ascertain what consensus if any existed within the unionist community for political progress. The main conclusion to emerge from the subsequent report, *An End to Drift*, was that something should be done to revitalise the anti-Agreement campaign. However, no consensus could be reached as to how this should be done or what changes should be made to policy direction by the unionist coalition. When Michael McGimpsey was asked for his opinion of the Task Force report, his reply indicated that the search for some sort of political consensus within unionism was still going on at the end of 1991. 'They had to set up the Task Force to try and rethink and you had the preferred options, trying to get some sort of gel on what unionists actually wanted. But it has been a very slow and tortuous process, though it is going on at the minute.'[27] The central cause of this disagreement over political constructs was a conflict in unionist self-perceptions as to their primary cultural identity, and intellectual squabbling over what political strategy was most likely to achieve this objective. This explains why two unionists such as Robert McCartney and Michael McGimpsey, both of whom could be categorised as being of the Ulster British tradition,[28] could advocate conflicting political programmes. McCartney emphasised that he did not subscribe to an isolationist Ulster culture, but regarded himself as living in a normal region of the UK, to which abnormal political arrangements had been applied.

> I am not an Ulster nationalist. I believe, and I hope, that I am a liberal democrat. It is not because of the Queen, or because of the Union Jack, that I feel my essential unity with the United Kingdom. It is because Britain is one of the great liberal democracies of the world. Indeed it has been the major source of liberal democracy for the world. I am British because I believe in the principles of liberal Parliamentary democracy and pluralism. I am not British upon the narrow sectarian ground of nationalism – Ulster or of any other kind.[29]

It seems incredible that McCartney, who built a political platform on the critique of anti-democratic constitutional arrangements perpetuated by successive British governments since 1920 and exacerbated after the signing of the AIA, should declare that his unionism was grounded in a love of the democratic traditions of that state. Despite the inadequacies of his argument, it is clear that McCartney exhibited an affinity with the cultural values and institutions of 'mainland' Britain which exceeded David Miller's characterisation of a mere contractarian relationship.[30] A similar cultural identity is displayed by Michael McGimpsey, yet the political strategy which he advocates is the direct opposite of integration.

> Everybody has a different perception of the best way forward. My idea, as I said to you, is . . . to go back to roughly 1968, because I think Stormont offered at least the framework. The inherent instability of Stormont was that a substantial minority within the community was excluded from the levers of power and naturally withheld their consent and that is what made the whole system unstable. . . . I think we need leaders in Belfast who are accountable. Our leaders aren't accountable, and that is the prime reason I see for devolution. Everybody gets a say, and the disadvantaged in Andytown and the disadvantaged in the Newtownards Road can at least get an input and have some sort of say, and make some sort of a difference. . . . Integration, as far as I'm concerned, just runs away from the problem. The problem lies within Northern Ireland and within Northern Ireland the problem will be solved, eventually.[31]

In essence what McGimpsey is saying is that devolution contains the only hope for lasting peace and stability within Northern Ireland. In his analysis, Stormont-style devolution failed because of those who were involved in it, not because of any inherent weaknesses of the system itself. This is a perception which contrasts sharply with McCartney's belief that,

What has passed for politics in Northern Ireland is a sorry business, of which many people in both communities are rightly ashamed. It is the game of Protestants versus Catholics. It is a mixture of sectarian huckstering and control by political patronage. It is a mean and uninspiring sectarian conflict, out of which nothing can develop, even if it were allowed to continue for a second hundred years.[32]

What is clear from the contradictory statements of McCartney and McGimpsey (aside from the obvious point that they represented conflicting tensions within the UUP) is that even unionists who shared a common cultural identity and rationale for the Union could not agree on the most appropriate strategy for political progress. Thus whilst self-perceptions of identity are a very important determinant in explaining the logic behind unionist thought processes and consequent behaviour, they are not the only factor.

The debate within unionism over political alternatives was not of course a simple dichotomy but rather a multipolarity, even within the so-called Ulster British community. John Taylor, who epitomises this strand of unionist philosophy (if a rather elitist version of it), rejects both McGimpsey's plan for legislative devolution based on power-sharing, and McCartney's advocacy of integration into the body politic of the United Kingdom. When Taylor was asked if he thought that James Molyneaux (then leader of the UUP) could actually deliver any political settlement based on devolution considering the overt factionalism within his party, he conceded that this conflict had damaged and was continuing to damage the political fortunes of the ideology.

Yes, this internal debate within the Ulster Unionist Party, which is unresolved, does not help us get a settlement. I take the line that it is not a simple comparison between devolution and integration. I really think the way forward is something in between. Now that is not to fudge the issue, but it is to be realistic. If you are talking about a devolved executive and government here, as Brooke is, . . . what the unionists have to understand, looking at this from the English point of view, is there is going to be no devolution in Northern Ireland, unless it is on a power-sharing basis, with a law-making body at Stormont, with a unionist, be it Mr Paisley or someone else, as Prime Minister, and with the nationalists, for example, with a minister in charge of the RUC, for example Seamus Mallon. Now that is the kind of theoretical approach the English have to solving Northern Ireland's problems. Paisley and Mallon in the same Cabinet, one as Prime Minister, one in charge of the RUC. . . . I don't think that Ian Paisley and Seamus Mallon could survive. I rather suspect that after one week they couldn't decide which flag to fly on the next new factory they were going to open. So a fully fledged devolved government at Stormont on a power-sharing basis is not a realistic way forward for Northern Ireland, and you will just be hurting the Ulster people more, because you will be raising their hopes, to create something which yet again collapses after a matter of weeks.[33]

It should be noted here that Taylor, who portrays the image of a benign and impartial bystander interested in achieving the most practical political settlement, ignores the fact that power-sharing devolution did not fail in the past of its own volition, but because of the dogmatic opposition to it of people such as himself. Nationalists might suggest that Taylor's record would demonstrate that his distaste for power-sharing bore no relation whatever to the relative merits of the initiative, but owed more to his fear of such a regime succeeding rather than failing. In February 1969, he was one of twelve unionist MPs who signed a statement calling for the resignation of Terence O'Neill as party leader and Prime Minister. It would appear that maintaining the unity of the Unionist Party (which was the ostensible reason behind this statement) was a higher priority for Taylor than supporting one of the few figures in the party who had some support within the nationalist community and was making some effort to introduce a more liberal and palatable regime for the Catholic community. From a nationalist perspective, as an Assembly member for Fermanagh and South Tyrone between 1973 and 1974, Taylor opposed the Sunningdale Agreement and the power-sharing executive, not on the grounds that it would not be practical, but because it was damaging to the power base of the unionist community and weakening the stranglehold of his party on political power. At a meeting of the UUC in February 1974, Taylor moved the motion attacking Brian Faulkner and the Agreement; the motion was carried and Faulkner resigned as party leader.[34] Taylor was against Sunningdale on the same narrow sectarian grounds as Ian Paisley, though he dresses this up as an exercise in *realpolitik*. The following extract from a political profile of Taylor does not overstate his credentials as a reactionary unionist of the 'not an inch' variety.

> On several occasions between 1972–74, he mentioned the possibility of negotiated independence for NI, stressing that this was very different from UDI. In April 1974, he said that, apart from integration, this might be the only option open to loyalists. A prominent Orangeman, he told the 12 July demonstration in Belfast in 1974 that a new Home Guard should be set up 'with or without London Government legislation'.[35]

It could perhaps be said in Taylor's defence that politicians are as likely as anyone else to change their views and develop a more mature critique of their political environment. There is the possibility, therefore, that the reasons for his opposition to power-sharing with an Irish dimension in 1974 are not the same as those which currently underpin his distaste for it. Nevertheless, his advocacy of devolution seems to be grounded in the realisation that legislative devolution will not only entail sharing power with nationalists, but also involve a substantial role for the government of the Republic of Ireland. A form of devolution which did not include law-making responsibilities, on the other hand, would lessen the need for Dublin's involvement in the structure of the initiative. Taylor's objection to political constructs along integrationist lines once again illustrates the subdivisions within Todd's definition of Ulster Britishness.[36] Both Taylor and McGimpsey, while not harbouring the belief that Northern Ireland is a nation, disagree with McCartney's integrationist view, with their belief that there are specific regional differences in Northern Ireland which have to be reflected in local political institutions. When Taylor was asked what type of devolved government he wanted to see established, he replied that he wanted a compromise between the two poles of total integration and legislative devolution.

> I think it is tremendously important to recognise that the political situation in Northern Ireland is not the same as in Kent, and to that extent the Northern Ireland Tories and that ilk are equally crazy, they want total integration. I think the idea of total integration is equally out, just as the power-sharing executive is out, so that's why I say it's not devolution or integration. I think both are an impossibility, because what you have got to recognise is that we have a special political situation here in Northern Ireland. . . . The answer therefore to me is that the Westminster parliament should be responsible for the law-making of Northern Ireland, the same way as it is for Scotland, Wales and England . . . so I would therefore go for integration insofar as law-making was concerned, but when it comes to the administration of the laws, then I think you have got to take on board the special problems within Northern Ireland. . . . What we need is an elected devolved assembly at Stormont, and there is where your devolution comes in, but it's going to be administrative devolution not legislative devolution. Being administrative devolution, it can have a committee for each department of government, because government is two things, government make laws with the consent of parliament . . . then the second role of government is to administer those laws, and it is that second role of government I want to see tackled in Northern Ireland on the basis of a devolved institution. . . . That is the kind of solution I would like to see. Northern Ireland remaining within the United Kingdom, the laws being made by Westminster, [and] the laws then being administered by a committee structure through an assembly at Stormont.[37]

When discussing exactly what sort of Irish dimension he envisaged in any future constitutional arrangements for Northern Ireland, and what role he thought the Republic of Ireland should play, Taylor exhibited none of the insular parochialism evident in his more radical colleagues. He demonstrated an understanding of the external political environment, although his conclusion was that Dublin had no right to even a consultative role in the internal affairs of Northern Ireland. The subtext of his rhetoric was that there should be co-operation between the two parts of Ireland, on the basis of common economic interests, but not in political matters concerning the administration of Northern Ireland.

> We have got to get some new relationship with the Republic of Ireland, because there is an Irish dimension now, like it or not, brought more upon us by the reality that we are in Europe, that 1992 means that there must be more things in common between Northern Ireland and the Republic than ever before. . . . We have a Common Fisheries Policy already. The little boats going out of Portavogie down the road here chase the same little fish that the little boats in the Republic chase in the Irish Sea, and they do it under the same grant schemes and under the same CFP. . . . There are so many things to be tackled, and the only proper way to do it is to create an institution . . . through which the new assembly at Stormont and Dáil Éireann in the Republic would be represented. . . . That is the Irish dimension I want to see, co-operation and not interference, and regrettably the Anglo-Irish Agreement creates a role of interfering for Dublin which I resent.[38]

This demonstrates a political absolute within the unionist community, namely that Northern Ireland is a legitimate legal entity owned by the United Kingdom and not, as the Republic claim (theoretically at least), part of their national territory over which they have a legitimate interest. The consequence of this is that unionists are only prepared to co-operate with the Republic on the basis of good-neighbourliness between two foreign states, rather than as overlapping political regimes. Despite Taylor's analysis of the prevailing political climate, and regardless of the disparities between his cultural identity and that of his more radical colleagues, the conclusion which he reaches over the role of Dublin in the affairs of Northern Ireland does not differ substantially from that of the DUP. Nigel Dodds for example, whilst disagreeing with Taylor's model of government for Northern Ireland, articulates a very similar sentiment on the legitimate parameters of Dublin's role in Northern Ireland politics. 'We were prepared to look at structures which would involve both Northern politicians and Southern politicians, but purely, and only, after Articles 2 and 3 had gone, and then only on the basis of matters of mutual interest.'[39] Similar sentiments were exhibited by Sammy Wilson, when he was asked to describe the main principles of unionism from his perspective.

> Since I want to live in peace in this island, and I don't really want to be at war with the people who live in the other country on the island, I believe that unionists should be able to find some accommodation with the Irish Republic. That requires an awful lot from the Irish Republic mind you; they have got to act as good neighbours and they have been far from good neighbours, over the last twenty years . . . I think that unionism should be

big enough to be able to embrace that and face up to the Irish Republic and say, 'yes, we believe that we have got a separate identity, we want to maintain that separate identity, but where there are areas of common concern we can work with you'.[40]

So, despite their conflicting cultural identities and advocacy of alternative political constructs, both John Taylor and Sammy Wilson agreed that the Republic was a foreign country and should be treated as such. This issue is at the opposite end of the spectrum to that of the Union with Britain. While most unionists would agree that both are inviolable, they have found it difficult to establish a political consensus between these two points.

The inability of the unionist ideology to develop common political constructs had a debilitating effect on the anti-Agreement campaign. Grass-roots activists became increasingly frustrated at what they saw as a directionless and muddle-headed leadership, unable to develop a coherent political strategy. This is not entirely fair on the unionist leadership, as they could not manufacture a consensus which did not exist. Whilst Aughey has commented that the ideology has failed to get its case across in a cogent manner to those outside the unionist community (notably the British government), he mistakenly attributes this to bad public relations and a failure to communicate their views to non-unionists.

> Unionism has been noted for its inarticulateness. This has little to do with the rhetorical skills of unionist politicians. It has to do with the ability of unionists to convey to others in an intelligible, defensible and coherent manner what they believe.[41]

However, the evidence of this chapter would suggest that Aughey is only partly correct in his assertion. It is true that unionism has in the past failed to get its case across in a lucid manner, but to suggest that a coherent set of beliefs existed in the 1980s and merely required articulation misses the point that it was precisely the absence of a unilaterally agreed agenda for unionism which prevented the clear exposition of their case. Even within the Ulster Unionist Party, as we have seen, there were those who advocated integration and others who favoured various forms of devolution, ranging from a power-sharing legislative assembly to one which was simply concerned with administrative matters.

The political constructs favoured by David Trimble provide yet another variation on the devolution theme, illustrating once again that the middle-class secular unionism represented by figures such as McCartney, McGimpsey, Taylor and Trimble, which has been described elsewhere as Ulster Britishness, has not prevented the development of conflicting political programmes. When asked what he considered to be the best form of government for Northern Ireland, Trimble replied that he favoured something in between legislative and administrative devolution.

> I do see it as having a form of regional administration. I think an appropriate form of government would be to perhaps have a form of district council set-up. . . . As to the full range of functions for that regional administration, particularly with regard to legislation, I would like to see a rethink of that. . . . I'm thinking of more than administrative devolution. I'm thinking of something that has some legislative functions, but not perhaps the full range.[42]

While it could be argued that such diversity and internal debate were signs of a vibrant political movement, this ceases to be of positive influence when the debate does not progress, but simply goes round in circles. This was the situation within the Ulster Unionist Party during the anti-Agreement campaign, as the need for unity precluded the development of a positive political strategy. Running alongside the 'masterly inactivity' of the UUP was the old-style traditional demand of the DUP for a return to legislative devolution based on majority rule. Nigel Dodds, when commenting retrospectively on the proposals put to Secretary of State Tom King by the two parties in January 1988, pointed out that majoritarianism remained the central principle in the Democratic Unionist conception of democracy. 'What we were basically saying was that we were prepared to consider within Northern Ireland a form of administration which enabled everyone that had representation in an assembly to have a real say in the running of the affairs of the country, in proportion to their strength in the assembly.'[43]

Ian Paisley expressed a similar perception of democracy in a radio interview conducted several years after the signing of the AIA. When questioned about his opposition to sitting alongside nationalists on a power-sharing basis in the Constitutional Convention of 1975, he declared a contentment with the 'winner take all' principle inherent in the British electoral system.

> I believe in the British democratic system. That is that those that can have a majority in the House are entitled to form the government. Those who haven't a majority in the House are entitled to be the opposition. Now I said, and I continue to say, that if certain unionists, if the Alliance Party, if the SDLP, can get a majority in an Assembly, freely elected in Northern Ireland, they are entitled to form the government. Not by the choice of a Secretary of State, but by the choice of the people at the ballot-box. . . . We were very liberal [in the Constitutional Convention Report compiled by unionists], we said that we would set up the committees to be fifty-fifty, we would give the SDLP important chairmanships. But those chairmanships of those committees . . . were scrutiny committees, they weren't the executive. The Cabinet would have been a majority-elected Cabinet.[44]

What Paisley omits to mention, of course, is that rarely in any other liberal democracy is there no rotation of government. It is unlikely that Paisley would support majoritarian democracy if that meant the permanent exclusion of the unionist community from political power. It is clear from statements such as those of Ian Paisley and Nigel Dodds that a great degree of cohesion exists within the DUP in favour of legislative devolution based on majority rule. The problem faced by the Democratic Unionists is not establishing a consensus for any particular model of government, but getting the Ulster Unionist Party to endorse their proposals. This support has not been forthcoming because of conflicting cultural and intellectual perspectives, together with the UUP's realisation that such ideas are totally unrealistic in practical terms. The DUP are unable to actively pursue their one-dimensional policy of legislative devolution because they do not have the political power to ignore the UUP and take unilateral action. Conversely the Ulster Unionists, who could disregard the DUP if they could gain sufficient support from their traditional electorate and hammer out a workable compromise with the SDLP, have not so far been able to demonstrate the necessary internal political cohesion to agree upon the most appropriate form of institutional reform for Northern Ireland.

There are those within the Ulster Unionist Party who maintain that the factionalism caused by commitment to contradictory political programmes, which damaged the political muscle of the ideology during the anti-Agreement campaign, has been resolved and that a more coherent policy has been established. Michael McGimpsey is in no doubt that the debate over integration versus devolution has been resolved within the party.

> Oh it has [been resolved]. Party policy is clearly for devolution. At a conference in Enniskillen a couple of years ago, David Trimble got up and proposed a motion on Orders in Council, and I got up and proposed an amendment on the devolution of proper powers, and it was carried overwhelmingly. So our party policy is devolution and Jim Molyneaux could clearly deliver devolution if he can get the right sort of deal.[45]

David Trimble was equally positive, claiming that intraparty agreement had been established within the UUP as a result of the Brooke Talks of 1991. He contended that, while the Ulster Unionists had been split during the initial years of the anti-Agreement campaign, these differences had been resolved by the early 1990s.

> There used to be a tension, it has to be said, there used to be a tension between devolutionists and integrationists within the Unionist Party . . . I think it has largely been resolved, and one of the very useful things, believe it or not, about the interparty talks [Brooke Talks 1991], is the ease with which we found we were able to get down to the detail of preparing policy statements and agendas for a future administration in Northern Ireland. There was no real problem, we found, when we got down to that, although we weren't being absolutely precise, but it was roughly along the lines that I

have being saying to you. . . . If there was the sort of devolved structure that Jim [Molyneaux] and the rest of us are thinking of, I am quite sure that it would be acceptable to the party. Some of those who think in black and white might say that it was really more like integration than devolution, and the others who think in black and white would say that it is more like devolution than integration. But I think the sort of regional administration we are thinking of would be acceptable to the party.[46]

Senior figures in the DUP such as Sammy Wilson remain unconvinced by assurances from people such as Trimble that the Ulster Unionists have sorted themselves out and have developed a coherent devolutionist policy. Wilson was asked whether the DUP found it difficult to deal with the Ulster Unionists after the signing of the AIA, due to the internal policy-wrangles between the devolutionist and integrationist factions which were raging within the UUP at the time. Commenting six years after the signing of the Agreement, Wilson responded to this question in a characteristically forthright and unambiguous manner. When asked whether there was a feeling in the DUP during the anti-Agreement campaign, as to whether Molyneaux could ever deliver a strategy based on devolution to his own party and present that to the DUP, Wilson's answer was blunt.

There has always been a feeling in the DUP, can the Official Unionists deliver anything, and I suppose of all the DUP hierarchy, I have been one of the most critical of the Official Unionists for this. . . . The internal divisions within the Official Unionist Party, especially between devolutionists and integrationists, were damaging, especially when it comes to the positive aspects of the campaign, as to what you could put forward as an alternative. I know that one of the questions that the [British] government was always asking was, 'well look, yes, you are dead keen for talks and we believe you are genuine in being dead keen for talks, but are the other ones [UUP] really keen? And if they get into talks, are they going to come up with some kind of mishmash of an integrationist solution that we know is a non-starter with the SDLP, and therefore is going to take us nowhere?' I can't answer that one, I think only the Official Unionists can answer it, and I fear that, as they have done on other occasions, they will put their internal party conflicts, and the resolution of those, first, and the good of the community as a whole, second.[47]

When Trimble's analysis – that the internal power-struggle was over, that the devolutionists had won and the integrationists had been vanquished – was put to Wilson, it is clear that he remained unconvinced.

I don't know that it has been resolved. I mean, I listened to Jim Molyneaux at his last party conference, waxing eloquent about the fact that soon we are going to have, what is it, select committees or something, in the House of Commons, and we might even get done away with Orders in Councils for certain things, and this is seen as a step forward, and not a word about devolution, and I ask myself, is the leader of the Official Unionist Party now saying that he would settle for the Agreement, with some minor tinkering in the House of Commons. I mean I don't know, really it is like trying to beat a sponge to try and get anything out of the Official Unionists on this. They tell you they are for devolution, but I get different vibes when I talk to individual members.[48]

This perception that the Ulster Unionists were still ambivalent in their commitment to devolution was corroborated by Wilson's DUP colleague Nigel Dodds. The DUP chief whip remained adamant that the articulation of pro-devolutionary rhetoric was a cosmetic exercise to hide the fundamentally integrationist tendencies of the leadership. When asked whether he thought the matter had been resolved, he replied:

I don't think it has. I mean I think Jim Molyneaux would like to see integration perhaps, but I think that it is clear from anybody who has any close dealings with them that there is this division between those who want devolution and those who want integration. They may be able to paper over the cracks but the cracks are there, and that is sometimes why they don't want to get into talks and so on, because that simply brings those differences to the surface, whereas we are very firmly a devolutionist party and have remained so very consistently.[49]

Whilst it must be borne in mind that the DUP are keen to promote an independent identity and may therefore have a vested interest in depicting the Ulster Unionists as integrationists and thus different to themselves, it is clear that animosity exists over policy direction and that the two parties have had difficulty establishing common ground on the issue of constitutional political reform.

To conclude, the unionist ideology has been beset by a number of fundamental problems, some of which were beyond its control, whilst others were a consequence of the actions and attitudes taken by the various political actors involved in decision-making during the anti-Agreement campaign. A conflict of identity does exist within unionism and the conflicting perceptions of identity have produced contradictory political programmes. Undoubtedly, the structural division between the two main parties has not helped coherent policy-making, firstly because the existence of two organisations becomes a self-perpetuating phenomenon with a logic of its own in the competitive environment of electoral politics. Secondly, the existence of two distinct organisational hierarchies makes decision-making a more cumbersome and unwieldy procedure and often entails compromise between two blocs, rather than simply translating coherent orders from the top of one organisation down to the bottom. David Trimble, one of the few Ulster Unionists who favours an amalgamation of the two parties and thinks that this will make unionism a more cohesive political movement and a more coherent ideology, agreed with the suggestion that the existence of two separate party organisations had damaged the anti-Agreement campaign.

> It did of course, because it meant that decision-making was complex and cumbersome. You could not have a simple decision-making process, and all sorts of committees had to be created and people had to be consulted, and that did slow things down. Some people were only prepared to go this far and others wanted to go that far . . .[50]

However, this structural division in the ideology is a symptom rather than the cause of disharmony. As is clear from Chapter 2, there is a wide diversity of opinion within unionism over what the Union is actually for. Some see it in isolationist terms as a means of preserving a religio-political Ulster culture, while others totally reject this and advocate the Union on the basis that Northern Ireland is simply another region of the UK. This second group, who have been loosely termed Ulster British in accordance with Jennifer Todd's classification,[51] can be further subdivided between those who seek complete integration into the political and administrative apparatus of the United Kingdom and those who, while sharing a very similar cultural identity to integrationists, advocate a recognition of the regional differences of Northern Ireland through local political structures. Here again there is a division between preferred political institutions ranging from legislative devolution based on majority rule (support for which is not restricted to the DUP) through to power-sharing with the nationalist community. Others want devolution restricted to administrative functions, whilst there are also those who would like to see something in between legislative and administrative devolution.

Clearly it can be seen that the unionist ideology is diverse to the point that it defies categorisation. There is a crisis of identity derived from environmental circumstances, namely the historical inheritance of unionism. The existence of an antagonistic state on the other part of the island has been gradually accompanied by hostility to their cause within the country to which they express an allegiance. The implicit message from Britain since the Home Rule period has been that the unionist community in Northern Ireland are somehow different to the other subjects within the United Kingdom.

> . . . it is the British government which has been primarily responsible for the deep trauma within the Protestant psyche, for its actions have engendered an increasing sense of betrayal, which twenty-five years on has led to the almost total estrangement of Protestant Ulster from 'mother' England. Most working-class loyalists now believe that their 'loyalty' counts for little on the mainland – Britain no longer wants them.[52]

To discuss the concept of identity at all is, of course, potentially a philosophical minefield. Who can say with any certainty where the emotional or intellectual boundaries between Britishness and Irishness ultimately lie? Perhaps one of the main problems for unionists is nailing down exactly where they fit in between Britain and Ireland. Their difficulty in determining the British–unionist relationship has been exacerbated by those who have taken a political allegiance to the Union and transformed it into a cultural one. The United Kingdom, as Arthur Aughey rightly points out, is a state rather than a nation,[53] that is it is a set of political arrangements rather than a culture, while its constituent parts, England, Scotland, Wales and (more problematically) Northern Ireland, are nations with distinct cultural differences. Consequently, from the 'mainland' perspective, when unionists describe themselves as being British in anything other than the legal sense, they are aspiring to a cultural common denominator which does not exist.

It could of course be countered that, notwithstanding the rivalry occasioned by sporting events, Scotland, Wales and England share common cultural bonds, viewing each other as British and by extension an associate member of their own nation, so why can the same attitude not extend to Northern Ireland? This is certainly an anomaly though the following reasons may be posited to account for it. Firstly, it may be linked to the fact that Ulster was primarily settled by Scots Presbyterians rather than English Anglicans. Had the latter become the dominant ethnic group in the region, it may have come more to resemble the culture of the 'motherland' and thus been accepted as an integral part of the 'extended nation'. Secondly, the explanation may lie in the modern definition of what constitutes a nation-state. It is possible that the geographical separation of Northern Ireland from Great Britain has fuelled the perception that its residents are something less than native British. Allied to this, of course, is the fact that the rights to ownership are much more controversial in Northern Ireland than in the case of Scotland or Wales and are still being contested, thus creating some doubt among the British about the validity of their presence. Finally, the cultural icons exhibited by unionists do not find an empathy with many of those on the British 'mainland'. To put it bluntly, few of those in Great Britain, with the exception of followers of Glasgow Rangers Football Club and an exotic collection of right-wing Conservative MPs, can distinguish between the two rival ideological projects in Northern Ireland. Many view the Irish, unionist and nationalist alike, as sharing a common culture of violent enmity, an incessant desire to march up and down the street, and a fetish for the seventeenth century. Paradoxically, those unionists such as Ian Paisley (one of the few Irish politicians recognisable to the majority of the British public) who spent their time shouting 'Ulster is British' were seen as inherently Irish. How 'Irish' it was to have unionists demonstrating their love for the Union by threatening rebellion. For the majority of those in Great Britain who can raise an interest, therefore, Northern Ireland is a different world, not an integral part of some mythical nationhood.

The cultural alienation which has taken place between Great Britain and Northern Ireland since the beginning of the century (of which the AIA and the Frameworks Document can be seen as examples) has created a constituency for political separatism in Britain and amongst the more radical elements within the unionist community. However, despite the repeated unwillingness of successive British governments to clasp Northern Ireland to the bosom of its body politic, some unionists have failed to get the message. The common theme of British policy towards the region from the Home Rule period to the AIA and beyond has been that Northern Ireland is not British on a *de jure* basis. What other partner to the Union has been told, for example, that it would be quite acceptable (if desired by a simple majority of 50% + 1) for it to secede and join another state? The present British Prime Minister John Major has unwittingly emphasised the situation by attacking the Labour Party's proposals for *devolution* in Scotland as damaging to the fabric of the Union. These proposals are in reality a mild concession to Scottish local democracy and self-government; they come nowhere near tinkering with the region's political sovereignty or facilitating the input of another state into Scotland's internal affairs. Yet, while Major expresses horror at the prospect of Scotland being given devolution, he finds himself able to sign an agreement with the Republic of Ireland stating that his government has no selfish strategic or economic interest in Northern Ireland remaining part of the Union.

Ian Paisley Jnr summarises the position perfectly and demonstrates a degree of political acumen which distinguishes him from some of his colleagues in the Ulster Unionist Party who adhere to the facile belief that Northern Ireland exists as a region of the UK on a similar basis to that enjoyed by Scotland.

> Look what they've done with Scotland. In 1992 they [the British govern-
> ment] produced a White Paper called *Scotland in the Union: A Partnership for
> Good.* It spoke about every government department having cognisance of
> and taking care to understand Scotland and Scottish interests. I would like
> that for Northern Ireland. I'd like to see a White Paper, instead of the
> Framework Document; I'd like to see a Framework Document called *Ulster
> in the Union: A Partnership for Good.* There's no uncertainty about that, it's a
> very clear ideological position. . . . and I think that the disinterest has done
> the most harm because it's alienated those people who are most willing to
> work for a better Union and it has also then encouraged those people who
> want to destroy the Union, whether legitimately or illegitimately, it has
> encouraged those people that their option is attainable.[54]

Some unionists have tried to rationalise this tale of unrequited love by suggesting that the parochial culture of Whitehall is not representative of attitudes in Britain as a whole. James Molyneaux argued that all the regions within the United Kingdom were treated with equal contempt by the policy-makers in London.

> We are in company with Scotland, with Wales, the north-west of England, the north-east of England, the midlands . . . The English around here [Westminster] in London and the south-east of England, south of the Wash to the Severn, that is England in their eyes. All those boys across in Whitehall work on that basis. 'Oh those bloody people from Liverpool, the way they are carrying on, couldn't we get rid of them?' Why for God's sake couldn't we hive them off to somebody else?[55]

The conflicting views within unionism about the health of their relationship with Britain was reflected in political uncertainty during the campaign against the Anglo-Irish Agreement. A comparison of the respective views of the UUP's John Taylor and David Trimble, for instance, illustrates that the analysis of the former led him to advocate measures which would not alienate the British public any further, while the latter's opinion that unionists were still held in high regard in Britain facilitated a more aggressive approach. Taylor maintained that sympathy for the unionist case had diminished markedly in Britain since the beginning of the century and was being exacerbated by the inability of some unionists to recognise that the social composition and political character of Great Britain had changed dramatically. He pointed out that unless these new circumstances were recognised, and unless the unionist community adapted their strategy and spoke to Britain in a political language it could relate to, then the unionist position within the Union would weaken still further.

> The English people themselves have changed. After all, more than 50 per cent of the babies born in London last year were born to immigrants [sic], a third of the second city in Britain, Birmingham, is now Muslim, and two of the big cities, Bradford and Leicester, are now majority Muslim. . . . That is why I say I do wish unionists in Northern Ireland would look more to the longer term trends. . . . Within England itself, there is now a new attitude towards Northern Ireland which is not as helpful as it was in the earlier part of this century. These are things which unionists have to take on board and decide their policies accordingly. . . . We are now seen as a place apart and the task of unionism is not to abandon our churches or what we believe in . . . but at the same time we have got to recognise that the English are a race apart and we have got to work with them if we want to remain in the United Kingdom.[56]

Trimble was rather more upbeat in his assessment of the public mood in Britain towards the unionist community. He disagreed with the suggestion that antipathy towards the unionists and Northern Ireland in general had reached a crisis point. While not denying that a change had occurred in the relationship between the North and the rest of the UK, Trimble sought to explain this change by arguing that the anti-unionist attitudes of the policy-makers were unrepresentative and did not reflect the views of wider public opinion.

> There has been a shift. I think we should identify just what the shift is. A lot of sympathy for Irish unionism – not specifically for Ulster unionism – a lot of sympathy for Irish unionism in England at the turn of the century was because the landed gentry, the aristocracy, was common between the two. There wasn't a significant difference between the Irish aristocracy and the English aristocracy. They were all part of the same families, they were closely related, went to the same schools, one person maybe owning estates in north England and someone else estates in Ireland, very often families would have estates in both places. So there was that close degree of sympathy which has gone, because the Irish aristocracy has either vanished, or like Lord Longford, become eccentric. There never was, I think, any close degree of sympathy between metropolitan aristocratic London and prole-tarian Belfast. . . . The lack of sympathy is there [metropolitan London]. If you go to northern England, you go to Scotland, you go to different sorts of mileu within England, there is still a very close sympathy. . . . If you are talking to the informed circles in London, you find a difference between that and Britain as a whole.[57]

While there is no doubting the sincerity with which Trimble expresses his view, it is difficult to find quantitative data to substantiate his argument. All the empirical evidence would suggest that the broad constituency of support in Britain for the maintenance of the Union which he alludes to does not exist. All the opinion poll evidence of recent years would suggest that Westminster's attitude is representative of Britain as a whole. The Gallup Political and Economic Index shows a consistent low level of support in Britain for Northern Ireland remaining part of the Union over a period of twelve years, ranging from 24 per cent in 1981 to 27 per cent in 1993.[58]

This conflicting analysis of Taylor and Trimble over the health of the Union had obvious implications for the conduct of the campaign against the AIA, which was bedevilled by contradictory political philosophies and mutually exclusive political objectives. Where one saw the AIA as inherently flawed and ultimately doomed, another viewed it as strong and vibrant with indeterminable longevity. While the former may therefore advocate an incrementalist policy, the latter considers a more active and militant approach to be essential. Whereas many Ulster Unionists favoured caution, in line with their cultural identification with the political and social institutions of the 'motherland', the majority within the DUP felt no such constraints. The former liked to wear the clothes of respectability and observe the etiquette of the Westminster regime, while the latter were locked into a zero-sum game of truth versus evil and right versus wrong. The following statement from Sammy Wilson of the DUP epitomises the difficulty in harmonising the conflicting perceptions of the two main unionist parties.

One has got to remember that the fight is a dirty fight, and we weren't the ones who made it dirty. I mean the British government made it dirty, and if that means at times you actually have to maybe get down in the muck, and do a bit of scraping and gouging, well then maybe you have got to do that, and if politicians aren't prepared to maybe get to that level, at stages, then they are maybe better just to say nothing, rather than do damage to the campaign which they have committed themselves to.[59]

While Wilson and many of his colleagues within the DUP denigrated the Ulster Unionists for not engaging in enough 'scraping and gouging', which they saw as the only means of getting rid of the Agreement, the analysis of the UUP was that such behaviour would ultimately prove to be counterproductive.

This disagreement within unionism over quite where they stand in the affections of the state they seek to remain members of still persists today and is a fundamental reason why several political strategies for progress can co-exist at any one time. The DUP attitude continues to exude defensiveness and a fear that Britain (or at least the establishment who make the policy decisions) want to break the Union but have not yet found a convenient mechanism for doing so which would prevent the outbreak of more political violence in the region. This was summed up by David Ervine's comment that unionists have always lived 'with a sense of siege'. This siege mentality, exemplified by the following statement of the deputy leader of the DUP Peter Robinson, makes it extremely difficult for the DUP to enter political negotiations as they do not trust the bone fides of their interlocutors whether they be Irish nationalists or the British government. The marriage analogy is an overused metaphor when discussing the unionist ideology. However, any spouse who distrusts their partner is in for a very uncomfortable relationship and eventually it becomes very difficult to determine whether suspicions are real or imagined. This problem was embodied by Robinson's response when asked about British attitudes towards Northern Ireland.

I think that it is the agenda of the establishment . . . in the UK that Northern Ireland for a very long period of time has been a problem, it's a problem that they can't solve and therefore it will be a problem that they will get rid of. They can't simply write Northern Ireland out of the Union, therefore they have to involve themselves in a process, and if they have accepted the premise that ultimately there will be a united Ireland . . . if the British government has accepted that view, then considering the close proximity of Northern Ireland to Great Britain, it becomes a political imperative for them that there should be a smooth transition. They don't want a civil war, they don't want civil unrest, therefore they set in train a process that gradually moves Northern Ireland from its position within the United Kingdom to being part of the Irish Republic. And they move that process as fast as they can but certainly not so fast as is going to cause unrest on its own. That's been the pattern of recent events, that's what the government is doing, they give you your medicine spoonful by spoonful and when they reckon that your stomach's ready to take another spoonful they'll give you it.[60]

Whether or not Robinson is correct, this image of the British government as a demonic nanny leaves such unionists ill-prepared to lead their community in a manner which either strengthens the long-term future of the Union, or strikes a deal with the nationalists who co-exist in the region. Contrast this political nihilism (which is not to say that it is not well founded) with the practical perspective of unionists such as David Ervine, of the Progressive Unionist Party. While recognising that the elite have become less than enamoured with the Union in recent years, his attitude is not that this represents a Machiavellian plot designed to shuffle the North into a united Ireland, but is rather a set of circumstances which can be reversed as long as unionists enter the debate.

> I would say that one of the most significant views that has to be considered of Northern Ireland is the Treasury view, which is the economics of Northern Ireland. That's bad enough without being bled to death by body-bags and bombings in London. And it must be a grinding-down process for many people who have an economy to look after and things like that. So I think rather than get angry about it let's understand it. I think that there is within the elite a sense that the loyalty of Northern Ireland and all the rest is great, but we're moving into a pragmatic world and pragmatic times and it's hard to afford.[61]

Ervine went on to say that the general public in Britain were largely ignorant of Northern Ireland and had no strong conviction about the Union either way. When asked whether this apathy and antagonism could be reversed given the peaceful environment presented by the republican and loyalist ceasefires, Ervine concurred.

> Yes I think there is a case where you can say that if there isn't the bleeding sore continuously, then those who switch off consistently may be inclined to look at it in a more sensible and rational way. I think we do ourselves and have done ourselves no favours, with a liberalising society in Britain and an entrenched and retreating society in Northern Ireland. . . . I think that a proper articulation based on the moral grounds of democracy and consent will certainly find seed within the British people. Of that I have no doubt.[62]

The disagreement between the two main unionist parties over the dynamics of their political environment strained the coalition to breaking-point. While the DUP were frustrated at what they considered to be a half-hearted commitment by the Ulster Unionists to civil disobedience and unconstitutional action, the UUP belief was that such actions would ultimately destroy the fabric of the Union. The antithesis of the DUP perspective was embodied by the following recollection of the UUP councillor Michael McGimpsey, when commenting on his reservations about the initial phases of the anti-Agreement strategy. 'The trick was to oppose the Agreement without breaking the Union, and all those devices were ultimately damaging the Union and ultimately getting nobody anywhere.'[63]

Clearly the intraparty and interparty conflict over long-term political objectives and short-term political strategy had a debilitating effect upon the unionist political community after the Anglo-Irish Agreement was signed in November 1985. The ideological disagreements which grew from differing perceptions of identity, the struggle between parochial isolationism and cultural integrationism, the conflicting intellectual analyses of those of similar cultural perspectives, and in some cases simple personality clashes – all combined in the mid-1980s to produce a cocktail of political incoherence. As Garret FitzGerald remarked when commenting on unionist strategy in the post-Agreement period, the ideology has been hampered by its inability to correctly perceive its long-term interests and pursue them, due to its preoccupation with short-term considerations.

> It is this extraordinary human capacity to walk yourself into fruitless acts you can't get out of, because you are not motivated by reason and pursuit of interests, but by fear. Nobody backs into a cul-de-sac who is being rational. You only do it because you are afraid, and then you find you can't get out of it. If you are rational you will find some other way out. The last place you will go is a cul-de-sac.[64]

These strains within unionism became evident during the campaign against the AIA as their potential muscle weakened due to the ideology's internal tensions and central incompatibilities.

Notes

1   Sammy Wilson, interview with author, 20 November 1991.
2   Michael McGimpsey, interview with author, 16 October 1991.
3   Rev. Martin Smyth, interview with author, 22 November 1991.
4   Sammy Wilson, interview with author, 20 November 1991.
5   Rev. Ian Paisley, *The History-Makers* (BBC Radio Ulster, 22 January 1989).
6   Nigel Dodds, interview with author, 2 December 1991.
7   Rev. Martin Smyth, interview with author, 22 November 1991.
8   P. Arthur, *Government and Politics of Northern Ireland*, 2nd edn (London, 1984), p. 61.
9   Michael McGimpsey, interview with author, 16 October 1991.
10 James Molyneaux, interview with author, 19 November 1991.
11 P. Arthur and K. Jeffery, *Northern Ireland Since 1968* (Oxford, 1988), p. 53.
12 John Taylor, interview with author, 30 September 1991.
13 ibid.
14 David Trimble, interview with author, 3 October 1991.

15 ibid.
16 *Talkback* (BBC Radio Ulster, 10 March 1989).
17 Rev. Martin Smyth, interview with author, 22 November 1991.
18 James Molyneaux, interview with author, 19 November 1991.
19 Sammy Wilson, interview with author, 20 November 1991.
20 Ian Paisley Jnr, interview with author, 9 November 1995.
21 ibid.
22 Peter Robinson, interview with author, 8 November 1995.
23 Garret FitzGerald, interview with author, 8 April 1992.
24 C. McGimpsey, 'Now for the Hard Part', *Fortnight*, No. 295 (May 1991), pp. 12–13.
25 *Talkback* (BBC Radio Ulster, 4 January 1989).
26 R. McCartney, *What Must Be Done* (Belfast, 1986), p. 2.
27 Michael McGimpsey, interview with author, 16 October 1991.
28 See J. Todd, 'Two Traditions in Unionist Political Culture', *Irish Political Studies* 2 (1987), pp. 1–26.
29 McCartney, *What Must Be Done*, p. 3.
30 D. Miller, *Queen's Rebels: Ulster Loyalism in Historical Perspective* (Dublin and New York, 1978). See Chapter 2 for a treatment of this issue.
31 Michael McGimpsey, interview with author, 16 October 1991.
32 McCartney, *What Must Be Done*, p. 1.
33 John Taylor, interview with author, 30 September 1991.
34 W. D. Flackes and S. Elliott, *Northern Ireland: A Political Directory 1968–1988* (Belfast, 1989), pp. 264–5.
35 ibid., p. 264.
36 Todd, 'Two Traditions', pp. 1–26.
37 John Taylor, interview with author, 30 September 1991.
38 ibid.
39 Nigel Dodds, interview with author, 2 December 1991.
40 Sammy Wilson, interview with author, 20 November 1991.
41 A. Aughey in P. Roche and B. Barton (eds.), *The Northern Ireland Question: Myth and Reality* (Aldershot, 1991), p. 1.
42 David Trimble, interview with author, 3 October 1991.
43 Nigel Dodds, interview with author, 2 December 1991.
44 *The History-Makers* (BBC Radio Ulster, 22 January 1989).
45 Michael McGimpsey, interview with author, 16 October 1991.
46 David Trimble, interview with author, 3 October 1991.
47 Sammy Wilson, interview with author, 20 November 1991.
48 ibid.
49 Nigel Dodds, interview with author, 2 December 1991.
50 David Trimble, interview with author, 3 October 1991.
51 Todd, 'Two Traditions', pp. 1–26.
52 Springfield Inter-Community Development Project, *Ulster's Protestant Working Class* (Belfast, 1994), p. 7.
53 A. Aughey, *Under Siege: Ulster Unionism and the Anglo-Irish Agreement* (Belfast, 1989), p. 18.
54 Ian Paisley Jnr, interview with author, 9 November 1995.
55 James Molyneaux, interview with author, 19 November 1991.
56 John Taylor, interview with author, 30 September 1991.
57 David Trimble, interview with author, 3 October 1991.
58 For a detailed analysis, see F. Cochrane, 'Any Takers? The Isolation of Northern Ireland', *Political Studies*, 42 (3) (1994), pp. 378–95.

59 Sammy Wilson, interview with author, 20 November 1991.
60 Peter Robinson, interview with author, 8 November 1995.
61 David Ervine, interview with author, 20 November 1995.
62 ibid.
63 Michael McGimpsey, interview with author, 16 October 1991.
64 Garret FitzGerald, interview with author, 8 April 1992.

PART II

CHAPTER 4

The Politics of Protest

If the British Government, through the Anglo-Irish Agreement tries to take our liberty away from us, then there is no other course of action open for the Northern Ireland people but to do what Lord Carson did and that is to resist by whatever force they can muster. . . . I appeal for the mobilization of the Ulster people. At the moment structures are being set up for that mobilization. . . . I will also be advocating the enlistment of the Northern Ireland people in a show of strength – dedicated to die if needs be rather than surrender to a united Ireland.[1]

In charting the course of the unionist campaign against the Anglo-Irish Agreement, this chapter will concentrate specifically on the campaign of civil disobedience and street politics which took place between 1986 and 1988. In addition to looking at what steps the unionist coalition took to 'smash' the Agreement, the chapter will pay particular attention to the divisions and fractures which resulted from such activity and indeed inactivity. The faction-fighting which emerged during this period was a direct result of the mutual realisation that the only chance of removing the AIA was through unilateral action. After 15 November 1985 these divisions were mitigated by the identification of an external enemy, which allowed all shades of opinion within the unionist family to forget their differences in order to fight against a greater evil. Once the initial shock had been absorbed by the unionist community and decisions had to be made concerning choices between alternative political strategies, the coalition began to fracture. The interparty and intraparty disputes which subsequently arose were not simply the result of personality conflicts, nor merely the protection of vested interests, but reflected the different socio-economic and cultural forces within the unionist community.

The myopic vision: unionist recollections

. . . the simple message had to be that we said 'no' to the Agreement. Under no circumstances was it acceptable, and you know the slogan 'Ulster

Says No' I think summed it all up, and even if people weren't too sure why they were saying 'no', it had to be pushed into their psyche that this was not acceptable to the unionist community, [and] could never be acceptable to the unionist community.[2]

It is beyond contention that the AIA came as an unpleasant 'bolt from the blue' for all unionists, not least the leaders of the two main political parties. They had been worried since the early 1980s that the thaw in Anglo-Irish relations would be translated into a political initiative, aimed at coercing unionists into accepting Dublin's involvement in the affairs of Northern Ireland. By the summer of 1985 they were certain that an Anglo-Irish deal was imminent, although its scope was greatly underestimated. The leader of the Alliance Party, John Alderdice, commented that

> . . . it was an extraordinary shock for them. For some reason they didn't believe it was coming. My predecessor and colleagues told unionists [over] a long period of time that if they did not reach an accommodation with nationalists that something like this was going to happen and [they] had created the circumstances for its inevitability. And yet, nevertheless, they seemed completely shocked.[3]

When asked what he knew and when he knew it, the UUP deputy leader John Taylor pointed out that he was aware before the rest of his party that the British and Irish governments were preparing a new agreement.

> Well there's a difference between the Unionist Party and myself. I was very conscious of it for about six months beforehand, maybe longer, and in fact I did try to excite public interest in the subject by several statements and speeches through 1985, – the first part of 1985 – but I regret to say that I think it was only in August or September of 1985 that the Ulster Unionist Party finally took on board what was happening.[4]

Taylor contends that a leading figure in the Ulster Unionist Party at the time convinced the leadership that Thatcher was a friend of the Union, and would not embark on any initiative which involved a derogation of British sovereignty over Northern Ireland:

> . . . people like Enoch Powell pooh-poohed the chances of such a thing occurring and said it was not possible, and to a certain extent Unionists were prepared to accept what Enoch Powell was saying, and trust that he was correct. In fact he was totally wrong, and they found out too late what was happening behind their backs and they then wrote to Mrs Thatcher as you know offering to enter into talks with the British Prime Minister and the Dublin government, and that offer was rejected.[5]

However, this allegation that Enoch Powell lulled the Ulster Unionists into a false sense of security has been denied by Rev. Martin Smyth, who claimed that the former South Down MP did not anaesthetise the critical faculties of the UUP in the months leading up to the signing of the Agreement. When asked whether he thought the UUP had become complacent due to Powell's analysis and would perhaps have been more on their guard had the Labour Party been in office, Smyth replied;

> No I don't think so. I don't think it's even a question of Enoch Powell at that particular level. There is this mythology of Enoch Powell, for example there is the mythology within Europe that he was against Europe and therefore Jim Molyneaux did what he wanted, the same sort of hypocrisy that is manifested when they say that Molyneaux has been led like a poodle behind Paisley. . . . There was not that faith that Margaret Thatcher would never let us down insofar as we are aware that diplomats have their own agenda. . . . What took us somewhat by surprise was the willingness to be conned again by Dublin, because we were told that we were going to get Articles 2 and 3 removed. . . . That is the surprise, that British diplomats and politicians were so gullible, thinking that they were cornering Dublin in the duplicity of the language of the Agreement.[6]

Despite Smyth's protestations, the DUP interpretation of events leading up to the signing of the Agreement was that the UUP fooled themselves into believing that they were well liked at Westminster and that the Conservative government would not sign any agreement with Dublin which would prove detrimental to the unionist position in Northern Ireland. Nigel Dodds, for example, was keen to differentiate between the analysis of his own party and that of the Ulster Unionists in the months leading up to November 1985. When asked whether he thought the unionists were lulled into a false sense of security due to Thatcher's unionist rhetoric, her reaction to the *New Ireland Forum Report* and events such as the Falklands War where the British army was sent thousands of miles to protect British subjects from foreign aggression, Dodds made clear that while some unionists may have started to trust the British government, those in the DUP were under no such illusions.

> There may have been Official Unionists who were persuaded by that, as undoubtedly there were, I mean Enoch Powell was very much an advocate of that, you know, 'put your trust in Westminster', and Jim Molyneaux himself was on record as saying he had the ear of the Prime Minister and he had assurances and so on. The DUP never believed that, and we were vindicated in that view with what happened.[7]

What emerges from talking to those unionists closely involved with the political situation in 1985 is that they were aware that something was going on between the two governments but were deeply shocked at the nature of the final Agreement. Michael McGimpsey's response, when asked at what point was he first aware that a radical new agreement had been reached, was:

On November 15th when it was announced. We got some whispers of it privately, about four to six weeks beforehand, but were assured by people who should have known that the two governments were really just talking and nothing radical was going to come out.[8]

Again there is implicit criticism here of the UUP leadership and disappointment that their reading of the political situation in 1985 was seriously flawed. When it was put to him that Enoch Powell's influence, together with Thatcher's response to the *New Ireland Forum Report*, the Falklands War and the Brighton bomb, had combined to create an air of complacency within his party, McGimpsey agreed that the unionists were slow to recognise the seriousness of the situation and had underestimated the degree of consensus between the two governments.

> I think certainly the accepted wisdom in the party was that time was on our side, and all we had to do was sit back and wait and that Margaret Thatcher would never do anything to harm unionists. I was a bit more sceptical about that but didn't actually anticipate what was coming. We had the Forum Report as you were saying and the famous 'Out, Out, Out' against the three options, but then between that and November we had the Brighton bombing, and I think clearly Thatcher decided then that something radical had to be done and that's where the Agreement came from.[9]

Garret FitzGerald's recollection that hints about the general shape of the forthcoming Agreement were being thrown out to unionists as early as February 1985 was rejected by McGimpsey. FitzGerald declared that both he and the British government had been 'flying kites' in the faces of unionist politicians from the beginning of the year and he had been surprised they had not picked up the signals. When McGimpsey was asked whether any rumours were circulating during this period, he replied that rumours were always circulating within the unionist political community, producing a neurosis which made it difficult for them to distinguish fact from fiction.

> There were no kites flown in my direction, and Chris [McGimpsey] and I were at the Forum, we had been up and down to Dublin before that and ever since. We are both members of the Irish Association; the Irish Association has a number of political seminars with people who . . . I'm quite sure knew what was going on in the background. Nobody ever threw a kite at us or told us. It wasn't until we had an Irish Association conference in the Culloden Hotel [Holywood Co. Down] at the beginning of September . . . and by that time there were rumours floating and some of the people told us that joint-authority was coming. Chris and I then got on to some of the politicians and said 'look, this is the rumour, how much truth is there in it?' And they came back and said 'none at all'. FitzGerald said that there was contact with unionists; I don't know, I've no knowledge of any contacts and

any of the politicians I've talked to were taken by surprise. Obviously they had suspicions, we all had suspicions, but then that is part and parcel of unionists' paranoia and it's very hard to know whether your suspicions are just merely in your mind, whether you have some basis for it or whether you are simply being paranoiac. . . . It's the unionist nightmare you know, that they are going to be sold out.[10]

David Trimble's recollection was similar to that of his more liberal colleague, his version of events being that during the period leading up to the signing of the Agreement, the unionists were relying on press speculation and whispers from the back-benches of the Conservative Party and did not have any direct information or briefing from government sources.

Certainly if you were looking at the press speculation, you would have expected that something big was coming, because there was plenty of such speculation and that was all that we were relying on. There was no direct information, no official briefing I should say. There were obviously some senior members in the Conservative Party and government who spoke to our members in the House [of Commons], but we had no direct knowledge.[11]

A very different story was provided by the leader of the Ulster Unionist Party at the time of the Agreement, James Molyneaux. He rejected criticisms that the UUP was unaware of the AIA until it was too late and did not do enough to get the unionist case over to British politicians before 1985, which may have prevented the Agreement being signed in the first place. When asked at what point he first realised that a radical new policy initiative was imminent, Molyneaux replied that he had known for the best part of a year that a new agreement was being planned, but was powerless to stop it.

Just after Christmas on the . . . I think it was the tenth or the fourteenth of January. . . . There was a curious idea put around, I don't know who started it, that Paisley and I were taken by surprise, but even the public utterances that we made right through that period would disprove that because, I mean, even the fact that we went to see Thatcher at the end of August to warn her that what was being proposed was unworkable and would do hideous damage and so forth. . . . The other thing too that we set up was a joint working party between the two parties to prepare for the worst on the basis of what was going on and what we were hearing privately and through the news industry.[12]

Despite Molyneaux's claim that he knew from the beginning of the year that moves were under way for a new agreement between the two governments, it seems strange that the leaders of the two main unionist parties waited until August to approach the British government about the matter. The two letters sent to Margaret Thatcher by the unionists in August and

September, and their visit to Downing Street which Molyneaux refers to, would suggest that while the unionists were aware that talks were taking place between the two governments, they had been assured by figures such as Enoch Powell that nothing would come of them because any substantial agreement would involve a commitment by the Irish government to repeal Articles 2 and 3 of the constitution, a price which, despite Garret FitzGerald's 'Constitutional Crusade', the unionists thought no Irish government would be prepared to pay, or could deliver even had they wanted to. It was only when they realised this precondition had been dropped by the British government that they belatedly attempted to lobby Downing Street by showering the Prime Minister with written correspondence. Molyneaux's statement that he realised a radical new policy was imminent at the beginning of 1985 also stands at variance with his speech to the Ulster Unionist Council on 30 March, when his attitude was upbeat to the point of optimism.

> So members of the Ulster Unionist Council, when you return to your constituencies later this day and you are asked by those who sent you here, 'what is the state of the Union?', tell them that the Union is secure because the Union is in safe hands.[13]

A few months after these encouraging remarks the AIA was signed and Molyneaux's tone changed dramatically. As he readily admits, by the time the unionists met Thatcher at Downing Street in August it was too late. The minds of the policy-makers had been made up and there was little the unionists could do to stop the Anglo-Irish train from leaving the station. Molyneaux rejected the suggestion that unionists had become complacent, pointing out that it wasn't a question of failing to get their message across to the British government, it was simply that their case had been ignored.

> It was clear to us that night that it was all up with it and that was as far back as August, because she [Thatcher] was sitting there stony-faced listening to what we were saying, but not conceding one word, not giving any inkling, but not denying anything that we were putting to her. I mean [we were] saying 'well look, are you going to do such and such a thing?' And she said 'well nothing has been agreed'.[14]

Molyneaux found an unlikely ally on this matter in Nigel Dodds, a former DUP lord mayor of Belfast. Dodds claimed that the unionists had been trying to get their case over to the British government since the early 1980s but had been studiously ignored by London.

> It wasn't a question of unionists being too late, it was a question of the British government deciding to exclude unionists completely from the process of politics in Northern Ireland. You remember that just three years prior to that, the Northern Ireland Assembly had been set up, tasked with

the job of trying to find a means of governing Northern Ireland, and it was carrying on that work, and in fact reported under Fred Catherwood, and yet the government didn't consider that at all, didn't take any notice of that, didn't take that on board or listen to the Assembly, it simply turned its back on it and ignored it. So I don't know if it was a question of not getting there early enough, the government made up its mind not to listen to what unionists were saying completely.[15]

Both Molyneaux and Dodds were right in believing that Thatcher's mind was made up by the summer of 1985. However, that is not to say that had the unionists made greater efforts to get their case across at an earlier stage, before the policy was set in concrete, they would not have met with a more sympathetic response. In view of the Anglo-Irish dialogue from 1980 onwards, the unionists would have been well advised to have put their case consistently and in a way that would not have alienated British policy-makers. In the event, their belligerent attitude as perceived from London (the Catherwood Report cited by Dodds was simply a reiteration of the existing unionist position and not, as he suggests, a sign of progressive thought) resulted in Whitehall politicians coming to the conclusion that if they could not do a deal with the unionists and get them to share power with the nationalists, they would do a deal with the Irish government and thus by proxy with the nationalist SDLP. This fact was admitted by Garret FitzGerald when he said that by March 1984 the British Cabinet had accepted the Irish analysis of the political situation in the North and had come to the conclusion that it might be more dangerous to do nothing than to attempt an initiative aimed at giving hope to the constitutional process.[16] The analysis which the Irish government sold to the British was that unionists were not interested in power-sharing with the nationalists and would have to be forced to do so, while the SDLP were rapidly being eclipsed electorally by Sinn Féin. It could be argued that had the unionists lobbied the British government at an earlier stage, they could have ensured that their analysis was the accepted wisdom within British governing circles in the mid-eighties. John Taylor has commented that the unionists did not do enough to get their case over in Britain, though like his party leader he was pessimistic about the chances of gaining concessions from Westminster.

> I personally feel that they should have made a greater effort to try and influence what was happening in London. I think that they placed far too much trust in Mrs Thatcher. On the other hand, as events proved, even when you caught on what was happening and tried to make an effort to influence what was occurring, there was a totally closed door. The London government was not prepared to talk to the Ulster Unionist Party, the talks with the Dublin government were strictly private and exclusive, there was no input allowed from the majority community in Northern Ireland.[17]

It is not difficult to have a degree of sympathy for Taylor's view as there was little they could do by 1985 to change the most substantial features of the new initiative. However, having been aware at the end of 1984 that a new policy was being considered, unionists should have at the very least developed a worst-case scenario. They should not have disregarded the Anglo-Irish dialogue because of a belief that the Irish would never tackle Articles 2 and 3, but should instead have worked out a strategy in the event that this precondition was dispensed with, as of course it was. Better still, the unionists could have directed their energies into ensuring that the British found it difficult to renege on the guarantees given to them. David Trimble has conceded that the unionists did not work hard enough and did not have their finger on the pulse of the British government to an adequate extent. When asked whether he thought the Ulster Unionist Party should have had its ear closer to the ground within British policy-making circles in 1985, he concurred:

> Obviously yes. I wonder though – and I did wonder this at the time – whether there was some deliberate misinformation being put out by the government. Now that's something that one can't exclude, and when one knows that senior officials and Cabinet ministers were reassuring unionist MPs, saying, 'oh nothing will happen unless the Irish agree to such and such which they won't agree to', I wonder if that was done just from a misreading of the situation, or whether there was an attempt to mislead, and lull into a false sense of security.[18]

Wilson has pointed to the shabby treatment unionists received from the British government in the run-up to the accord. 'During the eighteen months of negotiation, with two summits, that preceded the conclusion of the Agreement, no attempt was made to inform any of the Ulster leaders about the proposals under discussion or to seek their views.'[19] However, this analysis owes more to folklore than reality as not only did the Irish government give informal briefings to contacts within the unionist community,[20] but in addition the British government made an official approach to the Ulster Unionist Party offering them an opportunity – albeit a tainted one – to hear what was proposed and to put their views to the policy-makers at Westminster. Belated though this offer was, it could be argued that one way in which the unionists could have counteracted the meagre degree of consultation offered to them would have been to make full use of the opportunities which did come their way. It has since emerged, for example, that James Molyneaux was offered a Privy Council briefing on the Anglo-Irish Agreement by the British government, but refused to accept it on the grounds that he would not be allowed to discuss what he had been told with his colleagues, due to parliamentary convention. Thus, whilst Trimble and Wilson may have been correct in declaring that the unionists had no official information on the impending agreement from government sources, this was partly their own fault.

> The position was that the possibility of being briefed on a Privy Council basis would have come so late, did come so late, that the thing was set in concrete, I'm talking about the month of August. There was no point then in having a Privy Council type briefing, being shown the actual document, because all that would have happened was that you would have been muzzled, and you couldn't have gone back to your colleagues and said 'well I know, but I'm not allowed to tell you, but you'd better cool it', because you couldn't give any hint even as to what was in the document. So my position simply was, 'no, I see no point in that because you've already decided it'. That again answers this curious allegation that we didn't know until it actually happened, because knowing, as I did in August, before the Thatcher meeting – early August – what was going to happen, I flatly refused to look at the document or be told what was in the document, simply because there was nothing I could do about it. It was in its final form apart from one or two dots and commas and therefore there was no point in being muzzled and prevented from criticising it.[21]

To a certain extent Molyneaux was correct in viewing the offer of a Privy Council briefing to be a 'poisoned chalice' as the conventions of parliament would have prevented him from making use of the information he was given and this would obviously have placed him in a very embarrassing position with his colleagues. However, the DUP have criticised Molyneaux's decision not to take the briefing, a difference of opinion which illustrates the cultural differences within unionism examined in some detail in previous chapters. The DUP attacked Molyneaux's behaviour for two reasons. Firstly, they argued that, as there was a pact between the two main unionist parties, a decision of such importance should not have been taken unilaterally by Molyneaux without consultation with the DUP. Secondly, they claimed that the observance of such parliamentary etiquette was a luxury they could not afford. Nigel Dodds of the DUP took the view that Molyneaux should not have felt constrained by the conventions of Westminster, as the British parliament had betrayed the unionist community.

> I think if I were in his position, I would have used every opportunity, every weapon at my disposal, to try to expose first of all, and then secondly to bring down, something which would ultimately destroy the Union, and I would not have said, I mean this only emerged recently and there are conflicting reports, but I would have thought that his first priority would have been loyalty to Ulster rather than to anything else.[22]

The DUP view, therefore, was that the AIA had created an abnormal situation which absolved unionists from their responsibility to abide by the rules, whether in parliament, in local government or elsewhere. The

Ulster Unionists came from a completely different perspective, as illustrated by the following comment from Rev. Martin Smyth on the issue. When asked whether, given the way the AIA had been signed – without their consultation or consent – and considering that it was (according to the unionist analysis) a derogation of British sovereignty over Northern Ireland, he thought Molyneaux should have accepted the briefing and broken the convention not to disclose what he had been told, Smyth replied: 'Well, honourable people will not, and that is one of the problems. We have been seeking to be honourable and of course in the end that will be vindicated, it might take a long time but honour ultimately does come through.'[23] Whether or not Molyneaux's decision was the correct one, the unpalatable fact which unionists had to face in 1985 was that they had misread the intentions of the British government and would therefore have to reassess their position and provide the British policy-makers with an alternative more attractive than the deal they were negotiating with Dublin. Adherence to the belief that they could not be coerced into any new political arrangements saw unionist leaders reply to the Anglo-Irish process of the early to mid-1980s with a constantly vituperative invective. They were content to say that they would not countenance any political initiative which gave Dublin a say in the internal affairs of Northern Ireland, confident that this would be sufficient to steer policy-makers in a more acceptable direction. Little attempt was made to analyse the prevailing political climate, or establish a constructive dialogue with the British government until it was too late.

Some of those on the liberal wing of the Ulster Unionist Party later accepted that their party was complacent. One leading figure responded to an enquiry as to whether the UUP should have worked harder to get their case across in Britain by commenting:

> I don't think they worked at all. You are quite right, they were complacent and the argument was always that time was on our side, that eventually the IRA campaign would run out of steam, the IRA would be beaten and then some sort of normal politics would come back into the fray, and then some sort of cross-community agreement could be worked out. The argument was always so long as the Provos are bombing we will never get any sort of agreement, so they were complacent, just sitting back in what's often been described as masterly inactivity.[24]

Thatcher's meeting with Ian Paisley and Jim Molyneaux at Downing Street on 31 August 1985 cemented fears that an Anglo-Irish deal was imminent, yet the unionist response was one of defiance rather than conciliation.[25] As uncertainty grew in the months preceding the signing of the AIA, the familiar thread of conditional loyalty which runs through the ideology was the most consistent theme to be heard within the unionist community. The *News Letter* reported a television appearance by the UUP deputy leader Harold McCusker on 10 September 1985, when he illustrated the combustible nature of Unionist emotions in the period preceeding the signing of the AIA. McCusker displayed the limits of his loyalty when questioned about the impending Anglo-Irish deal, commenting that he would never again give unqualified support to the Crown forces.

> Mr McCusker said Ulster Unionists would resist by both constitutional and physical means any Dublin involvement in Northern Ireland affairs. Asked if this meant by force of arms, the Official Unionist deputy leader replied 'if necessary'. Pressed further and asked if this meant shooting British soldiers, Mr McCusker said it depended on what the government was doing and what those British soldiers were doing.[26]

Implicit in McCusker's statement was the idea that a social contract existed between the government and the people, and failure to abide by this contract de-legitimised the actions of the executive and the duty of the people to abide by the rule of law. McCusker declared that the terms of the Union could not be dictated by Britain alone, and that if the government acted in a manner which forced Northern Ireland out of the Union, then he, together with the rest of the unionist community, would be absolved of any responsibility for the laws laid down by that government.

> If those British soldiers were in this country to force me into a political settlement which under no circumstances would I agree with, then those soldiers would have to take the consequences, and their political leaders would have to take the consequences.[27]

Anxious not to be outdone in the field of gloomy predictions, the DUP deputy leader Peter Robinson issued another warning that the unionist politicians would become redundant if a London–Dublin deal was agreed. While such declarations may have been intended to scare British politicians, they also contained the implicit threat that unionism would seek to pursue its aims by paramilitary rather than political means. 'If politicians cannot produce the goods then there's always an alternative. IRA violence continued only because Republicans have learned the lesson that it works.'[28] The dire warnings from unionists about what would happen if the British government dared to ignore the wishes of the majority community and came to an agreement on the future of Northern Ireland without their consent illustrates the peculiar attitude of some Ulster unionists to British sovereignty. Peter Robinson's statement that any Dublin interference in the affairs of Northern Ireland would be taken as an act of war indicates not just the conditionality of his loyalty to Britain, but also invokes the idea that Northern Ireland was a nation in its own right and could therefore conduct its own foreign policy independently from the United Kingdom. If, for example, he viewed Northern Ireland as simply another region of the United Kingdom, then he would presumably wait for his national government to decide whether or not war should be declared. However, when 'cut to the quick', Robinson appears to see Northern Ireland as a separate nation with a politico-cultural allegiance to the United Kingdom rather than as an intrinsic part of it. He stated at a party dinner on 20 September 1985 that any concession to Dublin of a political role would be viewed by unionists as

> . . . just as much a declaration and act of war as a push to take over land by force. . . . The Government of the Irish Republic had better be warned that it shall be held accountable and will not be absolved from the consequences of such action.[29]

It was rhetoric such as this which alienated the British government from the unionists to such an extent that the policy-makers in London determined that negotiating with them would be a pointless exercise. As a consequence it was decided by Downing Street and the Northern Ireland Office (NIO) that the unionists should be kept in the dark about British intentions until a *fait accompli* could be presented to them. Evidence of this decision was illustrated by the former UUP Belfast City councillor Dorothy Dunlop's recollection of events which led up to the signing of the Agreement. Dunlop accused Tom King of attempting to mislead the unionists and cover up what they had already agreed with the Dublin government.

> Well I suppose we were first aware [of the AIA] in the autumn. . . . At that time I was in the Northern Ireland Assembly, and Tom King was recently appointed Secretary of State at that time, and we were having lunch with him at Stormont just at the beginning of that week, and we asked him, 'what about this Agreement?', and he said 'Oh, there is no Agreement. You don't need to worry, there is no Agreement.' Now that was within days of the Agreement being signed, and he said it because everything was agreed except some small point, and he could cross his heart and say there is no Agreement, when in fact 90 per cent of it was already agreed. . . .[30]

Emergence of the Ulster Clubs

Two things were clear from the embryonic campaign to halt the AIA, the first being the enormous cohesion present within the unionist community. Few voices were heard above the cacophony of indignation dissenting from the argument that the AIA must be stopped in its tracks. The second common theme which became apparent was the threat of violence, be it implicit or explicit, if the wishes of the unionist community were ignored. Although nearly every unionist politician was anxious to point out that they deplored violence and did not see paramilitary action as a legitimate means of achieving their political goal, most of them were nevertheless prepared to present the worst-case scenario in order perhaps to gain political leverage on the British government. There was widespread unity within unionism to the extent that an overwhelming majority wanted the Anglo-Irish express train derailed. However, when it came to the question of how this was to be achieved, the unionist coalition began to look less secure.

By the end of September 1985 it was clear that the usual tactics of declaring outrage, betrayal and imminent Armageddon were having little effect. The rhetoric of even the most bellicose amongst unionist politicians was failing to make any impact upon the policy process. It was consequently decided by a militant faction within unionism that conventional political behaviour would not be sufficient and needed to be supplemented by more exotic forms of extraparliamentary activity. On 24 September, it was announced that a network of 'defence groups' were to be set up to combat the Anglo-Irish talks. These 'Ulster Clubs', as they became known, were to be co-ordinated by the Portadown-based United Ulster Loyalist Front (UULF). The Ulster Clubs present a classic example of the propensity of radical unionism to resort to strategies of the past when faced with crises of the present. In 1912 unionists threatened to fight Britain in order to remain British and in 1974 they threatened the same. By invoking Edward Carson's Ulster Clubs the radicals were attempting to link the constitutional crisis of 1985 with that of 1912 and thus bestow legitimacy upon subsequent action. The chairman of the Ulster Clubs, Alan Wright, illustrated the Pavlovian response of many unionists and their inability to see that the prevailing political environment rendered such comparisons invalid.

> It's a case of history repeating itself. In 1893 when the first Home Rule Bill for Ireland was presented to Parliament, the Unionists got together and formed a Unionist Club. So we decided that we needed a structure that everyone could come together under.[31]

It would be wrong, however, to see the Ulster Clubs as merely an extension of the UDA or simply a rural branch of the predominantly urban paramilitary organisation. The familiar aspects of conditional loyalty were of course present, namely the idea that the social contract between the rulers and the ruled had been contravened to such an extent that the people were absolved from their responsibility to observe the civil law. The aim of the Ulster Clubs was not primarily to take up arms against the British government (though they maintained that this was one of a number of options), but to demonstrate that no political initiative could be imposed on Northern Ireland without the support of the unionist majority. Wright was at pains to point to historical precedent as an indication that the Protestant solidarity which brought down the power-sharing executive of 1974 would triumph once again.

> Obviously comparisons are being made with '74. We have to recall that in February 1974 the politicians went back with a massive mandate to smash

Sunningdale. But the politicians didn't smash Sunningdale. They started the momentum but the workers and the ordinary people reminded the government that it was still, very much loyalist fingers on all the buttons in this society. I believe that yes, it ultimately could mean that we will have to remind London, Dublin and the whole of the western world, who seem to be pro-nationalist at this time, that Ulster loyalists are still in control and will not be worked over.[32]

Wright argued that the Ulster Clubs were not simply a recruiting base for paramilitary organisations, but sought to gather together as wide a coalition as possible. The following statement illustrates the paradox of Wright's analysis, as he appears to recognise that the AIA was a result of unionist failure to present their case effectively outside the North of Ireland and present an attractive or even achievable alternative to the British policy-makers, yet his remedy is to retreat to an even more isolationist position.

We are a united movement and that of course involves Orangemen, Apprentice Boys, DUP, OUP, UDA members. It involves everybody but they're not representing organisations, they're coming together as individuals. It was the division among ourselves that brought about the Agreement. There is no doubt about that. Loyalists and Unionists have been divided. We see here today the culmination of 50 years work by nationalists, not 2 years work in Dublin. Fifty years of lobbying right across the world. A 50 year PR job. We haven't been doing that and we have to learn that lesson.[33]

While such rhetoric is not too far removed from that of the UDA, Wright placed more emphasis on his own moral rectitude than one normally expects from paramilitaries or their spokespersons. In an emotionally charged polemic he stressed his respect for law and order and for the government to which he deferred before 15 November, in the mistaken belief that it would reward his obedience by protecting the interests of his community.

. . . when Thatcher signed on the dotted line on the 15th November the respect disappeared. The love that we had for the British Government disappeared. And I can assure you that we are not bluffing. Alan Wright is a 31 year old man from Portadown. He's not in any political party. He's not in any paramilitary force. He's never been in bother with the law. He has never thrown a stone. He has never lifted a gun because he clung to the establishment. He trusted his government and that, incidentally, was after the murder of my father, the maiming of my sister, after the wrecking of my mother's home. Yet I sat back in the hope that my government would win. I trusted my government and it's sold me out.[34]

While few would doubt his sincerity, or the validity of the historical perspective that unconstitutional action had thwarted similar British initiatives in 1912 and 1974, Wright's analysis is less convincing in claiming that such tactics could combat the AIA. In reality Wright, together with those other unionists who participated in the Ulster Clubs, failed to appreciate the extent to which Irish politics had been marginalised since 1912. Northern Ireland was of little importance in British domestic politics and the friends of the Union were a very exclusive club, consisting mainly of radical elements on the right wing of the Conservative Party.

> If in the past the unionists were seen as rather quaint, even faintly ridiculous, now they are widely believed to be positively certifiable. This is not 1912, indeed the idiocy of the comparison only reflects in the British political mind both the Unionists' obsession with heroic exploits of the past and their psychotic delusions of self-importance. It's not just that gone are the days when the Union was the hub of party conflict in Britain – Lloyd George put an end to that – Gone too are the days when the Unionists carried political clout through their organic relationship with Conservatism. . .[35]

In retrospect, it is clear that the Ulster Clubs overestimated their political clout and were attempting to fight today's war with last month's battle-plan. The birth of the Ulster Clubs illustrated the degree of conflict within unionism over how they should attempt to thwart the impending agreement. A spokesperson for the UULF was reported as saying on 23 September that 'We are coming under extreme pressure to form these groups now. . . . But our committee decided to allow the main unionist leaders time to ensure that the democratic process would' work. That time is now running out'.[36] Ken Maginnis, however, was uncompromising in his attack upon the tactics of the UULF and he counselled people against attending their Belfast rally scheduled for the 23 November when the first Ulster Clubs were to be set up.

> I fear the self-appointed self-seekers who will take our young people and exploit their frustrations just as they did in the mid-70s and just as the IRA continues to do within its own community. I fear the protection rackets, the intimidation, the drinking clubs with the spin off for personal profit, and ultimately the relapse into sectarian murder which every God-fearing Protestant and Unionist rejects without equivocation.[37]

As illustrated in Chapter 3, conflicting cultural perspectives within unionism often produce contradictory political strategies. It follows that Maginnis's cultural *alter ego*, George Seawright, advocated an alternative way forward. The former DUP Assemblyman presented a typically doomsday scenario, commenting that he could not see how opponents of an Anglo-Irish deal could resist it in a non-violent fashion and he was consequently pessimistic about the future for constitutional politics. 'I know where I stand. It would be impossible in my view for loyalists to maintain their opposition to a deal in a non-violent context.'[38] Seawright said that a split in loyalist ranks in the wake of any summit was inevitable, as Paisley and Molyneaux would never sanction activity outside the political process. 'The split is already happening, and it is a bad thing for us to be divided when our attention should be directed at the Irish Republic, which has an unstable economy, and an unstable government.'[39]

The initial response of the UDA to the impending agreement was to encourage people to support the constitutional process. Deputy leader John McMichael was particularly anxious to deny that there would be a UDA-inspired paramilitary backlash and he urged people to support the two main unionist parties. 'The tactics used would be totally different from the strategy deployed to bring down the power-sharing executive and council of Ireland in 1974.'[40] By early December, however, divisions began to emerge within the UDA between the 'hawks' led by McMichael, who wanted to raise the political temperature of the Protestant population, thus boosting the ranks of UDA as a prelude to violent conflict with the British government, and the 'doves' who wanted to exhaust the political process before pursuing unconstitutional action.

> The authorities now believe that McMichael and [UDA leader Andy] Tyrie are contemplating ambitious and large-scale paramilitary actions against the Anglo-Irish agreement in the foreseeable future. The former has become less guarded in some of his briefings to the press, telling foreign journalists to expect civil war within a matter of months . . . the same [RUC] sources say that important sections of the UDA in Belfast are against this strategy, believing it to be unrealistic and over-ambitious.[41]

Differences were also apparent among unionists who occupied the constitutional arena, with the immediate political reaction to the Agreement being characterised by vivid religious imagery from the DUP which was generally not to be found in the language of UUP politicians, a fact which is again indicative of the cultural differences which exist between the two main unionist parties. The immediate response to the Agreement from the DUP combined accusations of British betrayal with references to the crucifixion of Christ. On the eve of the signing, when the scale of the proposal had become clear, Ian Paisley commented that Margaret Thatcher had finally turned her back on Northern Ireland and warned that such a policy would be met by firm opposition and hostility from the whole unionist community.

> Having failed to defeat the IRA you now have capitulated and are preparing to set in motion machinery which will achieve the IRA goal – a united Ireland. We now know that you have prepared the Ulster unionists for sacrifice on the altar of political expediency. They are to be the sacrificial lambs to appease the Dublin wolves. You can build your altar: You can use bent and corrupted law to ignite its fire; you can prepare to stifle truth with a propaganda of lies paid for out of the taxpayers' pocket; you can bring into Northern Ireland those who illegally and unconstitutionally claim

jurisdiction over this part of the Queen's dominions; . . . you can offer bribes to the Iscariots who in their day of betrayal always surface with hands outstretched for the blood money – but you can never break the spirit of Ulster unionism. Like the three Hebrew children we will not budge, we will not bend and we will not burn. This simple sum you will have to learn the hard way – six into 26 will never go. Before it is too late, desist from refusing Ulster the right to vote on these proposals. If you deny democracy you and you alone will be responsible for an aftermath too horrible to contemplate.[42]

This contrasts sharply with the following extract from a joint unionist statement which sets out the campaign against the AIA. This contains none of the lurid language characteristic of the DUP, restricting itself to the practicalities of the unionist response.

Yesterday, our Parliamentary parties agreed, as a first step, to withdraw all support and cooperation from the present government, and neither offer advice to, nor enter into communication with the Northern Ireland Office ministers who are now in harness with Dublin to rule over us. We recommend to our Assembly parties and our members in local government that they discharge their elected mandate subject to the same principle . . . we further call upon all members of our respective parties to withdraw immediately from every post or position on boards and agencies set up to assist or advise Northern Ireland ministers.[43]

Compare this joint approach with the advertisement published on 18 November in the *News Letter* by Ian Paisley entitled, 'FOR GOD AND ULSTER'. This was obviously aimed at a different constituency within the unionist community. The joint statement was meant to appeal to all those who sheltered under the unionist umbrella and was consequently restrained in tone in order to draw together as great a coalition as possible. The advertisement from Ian Paisley was clearly targeted much more specifically at a particular section of the unionist community. The vivid imagery and revivalist style indicates that it was designed to mobilise what could be described as the non-secular elements of unionist opinion. It was essentially an attempt to establish a link in the Protestant psyche between their religious inheritance and their political future.

'FOR GOD AND ULSTER'
Dr IAN PAISLEY M.P., AS AN ELECTED REPRESENTATIVE, CALLS ON ALL BIBLE BELIEVING PROTESTANTS TO SET ASIDE NEXT LORD'S DAY 24th NOVEMBER 1985, AS A SPECIAL DAY OF PRAYER FOR OUR BELOVED PROVINCE. A BASE BETRAYAL HAS TAKEN PLACE. THE RIGHT OF THE MAJORITY TO HAVE ANY SAY IN THE DUBLIN/ LONDON JOINT RULE OF OUR PROVINCE

HAS BEEN DENIED AND THE USE OF THE BALLOT BOX STOPPED. WE MUST TURN NOW TO THE GOD OF OUR FATHERS. THE WORD OF GOD PROMISES THAT WHEN WE ARE AT OUR WIT'S END AND CRY UNTO THE LORD IN OUR TROUBLE, HE WILL BRING US OUT OF OUR DISTRESSES. (SEE PSALM 107:27:28.) LET US, NEXT LORD'S DAY, AT OUR BEDSIDES, WITH OUR FAMILIES, IN OUR CHURCHES AND IN OUR HALLS, FERVENTLY, SIMPLY AND SINCERELY, CALL ON GOD. 'FOR WITHOUT FAITH IT IS IMPOSSIBLE TO PLEASE HIM: FOR HE THAT COMETH TO GOD MUST BELIEVE THAT HE IS, AND THAT HE IS A REWARDER OF THEM THAT DILIGENTLY SEEK HIM. (HEBREWS 11:6)[44]

Although there was widespread support within the unionist community for the idea of a pact between the two main political parties and an endorsement of the tactics (insofar as these were known) to defeat the Agreement, strains were apparent from the beginning of the campaign between those whose socio-economic and cultural backgrounds differed. These differences, which were initially submerged for the benefit of the group, gradually became more apparent due to the specific demands placed upon individuals by the anti-Agreement campaign and the lack of success of such protest action.

Uncertain revolutionaries

One of the first problems which the anti-Agreement campaign encountered was to mobilise street protest while at the same time harnessing such action to prevent it from escalating out of control. The overzealous elements which were the engine-room of demonstrations had to be restrained from riotous behaviour which might rebound upon the unionist campaign. Commenting several years after the period, Garret FitzGerald summed up the dilemma which unionists found themselves in after the Agreement was signed in November 1985.

> They couldn't challenge the Agreement. They had no means of challenging the Agreement, except by revolution, and they rightly were not prepared to go towards a revolution, so the whole thing was a waste of time. It couldn't succeed and therefore it was an enormous waste of energy and got them into another cul-de-sac.[45]

Five days after the signing of the AIA, unionist demonstrators physically attacked Tom King on a visit to Belfast City Hall, with an unedifying brawl ensuing between the protestors and the RUC. Reaction within the wider unionist community to the attack on the Secretary of State on 20

November illustrates the desire to curb the excesses of those anxious to display their defiance through a resort to violence. The *News Letter* editorial the following day criticised the undisciplined scuffle and advised that the first mass unionist rally scheduled for 23 November would have to be peaceful if it was going to be of any merit.

> A massive, dignified, peaceful protest will be an excellent way of demonstrating the anxieties and good faith of people who value the link with Britain. Physical attacks like those on Secretary of State Tom King at Belfast City Hall yesterday must be condemned without reservation; violence of any sort ultimately leads to anarchy and disaster.[46]

While there was widespread unionist support for the general objective of bringing down the AIA, there was disagreement from the beginning about the tactics which should be employed to achieve this common end. One of the first components in the anti-Agreement campaign, the mass rally of Saturday 23 November, illustrated the difficulty inherent within a strategy which, on the one hand, required an active street campaign to put pressure on the British government, while, on the other, necessitated restraint in order to preserve the fragile unionist pact. The *News Letter* was unequivocal in its condemnation of those who used the protest campaign as an excuse to damage property. The paper argued that such indiscipline would jeopardise the unionist campaign and reduce support for their cause both in their own community and among the few friends they could still call on in Britain and around the world. Under the headline 'High-rise vandals ignore plea', the paper reported incidents of vandalism by some members of the crowd during the mass rally at Belfast City Hall.

> Dozens of youths clambered up the scaffolding around the building [Robinson Cleaver's] ignoring repeated appeals from the platform to come down for their own safety. Some then burst through the thick plastic sheeting covering some windows, using knives the youths then went into the building where smashing glass and other loud sounds were clearly audible to the crowd. Later police went into the building, and 38 arrests were made.[47]

Strangford MP John Taylor condemned the violence associated with the mass demonstration, but argued that it was a much more effective propaganda tool than the boycott strategy, as it provided a public and undeniable exhibition of the mandate which unionists had to oppose the AIA. The rally at Belfast City Hall on 23 November was seen by many unionists as an overtly democratic and morally superior response to what they regarded as their shabby and cowardly treatment by the British government. Many of the key figures involved in devising the unionist strategy at the time have since remarked that their campaign was as legitimate an expression of 'people power' as that which took place in

Eastern Europe in 1990 and the former Soviet Union after the failed coup attempt against Mikhail Gorbachev in 1991. James Molyneaux recalled that while his enthusiasm for mass protests was overtaken by a concern that this would endanger the lives and property of people in Northern Ireland, it was nevertheless successful in demonstrating publicly the lack of consent for the Agreement in Northern Ireland. Molyneaux has also pointed out that the rally of 23 November had a significant impact upon the architects of the Agreement and left a lasting imprint in their minds about the strength of feeling within the unionist community and about the ability of the unionist leaders to mobilise their supporters.

> We had to enable them [the unionist community] to make manifest their rejection of the Agreement. I myself was against the second rally, the second year of it [15 November 1986] because I think it's always a mistake to try to repeat a success of that kind and because a senior Northern Ireland Office official had said to me when we were planning the second one, that it wasn't necessary . . . 'it's because you have imprinted that in our minds that it will never leave us or the Foreign Office, the fact that you could turn out a quarter of a million people out of a relatively small population'. A much bigger proportion than what Yeltsin was able to turn out in Moscow [in response to the failed coup attempt against Gorbachev] out of seventeen million. Anyway, it was necessary to do that, it was necessary to go through, not the motions, but to use every means we had of demonstrating that we had no intention of consenting.[48]

Molyneaux's colleague, South Belfast MP Rev. Martin Smyth, supports the 'people power' thesis, commenting that in retrospect the demonstration on 23 November was perhaps the most successful event of the whole anti-Agreement campaign.

> The success was first and foremost that Margaret Thatcher never realised there would be so much opposition, and at the level of peaceful protest, even the media had to admit, when one considers for example that she denounced it because it brought people onto the streets in Belfast, and yet she was the one who called for the Muscovites to come out in Moscow [to support Yeltsin and Gorbachev during the failed coup in 1991], and when you compare the response which she said was wonderful in Moscow, compared with the response in Belfast, pro rata, ours was twenty times more successful.[49]

Undoubtedly, 23 November acted as an important safety valve through which unionists of all descriptions were able to display their anger and resentment against the AIA. However, the failure of the rally to effect any practical changes in the operation of the new policy, let alone see it being replaced altogether, increased unionist anger against the British government.

Nineteen-eighty-six began with a Young Unionist march from Derry to Belfast, ironically mimicking the civil rights march of 1 January 1969 (albeit in reverse). The demonstration, which reached Belfast on Saturday 4 January, degenerated into violence at the gates of the Maryfield secretariat, much to the embarrassment of the UUP political leadership. The RUC, who were protecting the Maryfield complex, came under repeated attack from loyalists in spite of appeals from their leaders to stop. RUC cars were overturned and set alight by youths wearing balaclavas (indicating that this was a planned rather than spontaneous event), while gangs forced open the iron gates to the site, dismantled the barbed wire and steel fencing, and flung it at the police lines. In its editorial of 6 January, the *News Letter* condemned the violence surrounding the end of the march.

> All right thinking people will condemn the vicious attacks on RUC officers which left 23 injured. There can be no justification for such outrageous behaviour. The organisers of the fiveday march from Londonderry to Belfast and the subsequent protest rally at the secretariat offices were left with feelings of anger and shame by a few minutes of mindless thuggery.[50]

Emphasising again the different cultural perspectives within the unionist community over the legitimacy of civil disobedience as a tool of political protest, the paper went on to say that violence, especially that directed at the RUC, would be counterproductive to the unionist goal of smashing the AIA and would play into the hands of their enemies.

> Attacks on the RUC cannot be condoned. These must cease to prevent the strong case which the unionists have against the wretched agreement being wrecked by violence. . . . Unionist leaders must review their tactics and their relationship with other groupings to ensure there is no repetition of the disgraceful scenes at Maryfield.[51]

While the Ulster Unionists unequivocally condemned loyalist violence, their DUP colleagues were less inclined to so do. James Molyneaux attacked the riotous behaviour at Maryfield on 4 January and made it quite plain that he would not tolerate violent street protest as part of the anti-Agreement campaign. 'There can be no justification for the violence. There can be no excuse for it. I and my party condemn it unreservedly.'[52] Contrast this with the statement made shortly after the riot by DUP Mid-Ulster MP Rev. William McCrea, who made no secret of his view that there could be a legitimate reason for violence. McCrea told a party meeting in south Derry that the unionist community, 'may even yet have to fight the British to remain truly British'.[53]

The fear and anger which resulted from the AIA, together with frustration at the seemingly ineffective campaign against it, forced even those on the liberal wing of the UUP to retreat into the ideological bunkers dug by their more conservative colleagues. This may explain Ken Maginnis's outburst that, in the wake of the Maguiresbridge killings and the NIO policy of allowing the IRA a 'free hand', it was time for all loyalists to completely withdraw their support from the NIO regime and to assume responsibility for their own areas. 'We have got to challenge – and challenge in a militant way – the administration which allows this sort of thing to happen.'[54]

It is clear that emotional temperatures were at fever pitch. However, the immediate challenge was a constitutional one and came with the resignation of the fifteen unionist MPs from their Westminster seats to force a mock referendum on the Agreement. The by-elections, held on 23 January, were conducted on the basis of agreed candidates, thus ensuring that the fifteen MPs seeking re-election were the only unionist nominees for each seat. The SDLP, whilst supporting the AIA and anxious not to confer legitimacy on the unionist resignation tactic, were nevertheless keen on using the situation to their advantage and making political capital out of their increased popularity in the immediate post-Hillsborough nationalist euphoria. Consequently, they participated in the by-elections though they limited their involvement to the four constituencies where they had a reasonable chance of winning, namely Mid-Ulster, Newry and Armagh, Fermanagh and South Tyrone, and South Down. In order to avoid being returned unopposed in their ultra-safe seats, the unionists were forced to run a bogus candidate in four constituencies under the name of Peter Barry, the Irish Minister for Foreign Affairs. The by-elections saw unionists increase their percentage of the vote from 62.3 per cent in the 1983 Westminster election to 71.5 per cent. Although the unionists recorded 418,230 votes against the AIA (a mandate in anyone's language, encompassing 44 per cent of the total electorate), the Ulster Unionist Jim Nicholson lost his Newry and Armagh seat to SDLP deputy leader Seamus Mallon. The by-election tactic therefore produced a 'hollow victory' for the unionists, as the media concentrated on the personalities rather than the arithmetic in the poll. It may be a truism that elections – especially under the British system – are about winners and losers rather than ideas. Nevertheless, no matter how much the unionists declared otherwise, the by-elections did not significantly advance the anti-Agreement campaign. Rightly or wrongly the popular perception of victory and defeat in British elections is seats-orientated rather than votes-orientated. David Trimble later conceded that the by-elections did not work as well as expected, though he suggested that this was because of the media's interpretation of events rather than any dispassionate appraisal of the figures. It is interesting that when asked whether he thought the resignations were a success, Trimble began by saying that they were undertaken because similar tactics had worked in the past. This demonstrates, yet again, the regressive tendencies within the unionist ideology in that political action which proved successful in previous constitutional crises was attempted again, with little thought being given to the fact that other political variables had changed.

> The reason for that [the by-elections] was the belief that the February 1974 elections had been a tremendous boost for the campaign against Sunningdale, and it was an attempt to reproduce that. Inside Northern Ireland I think they were a success, because people inside Northern Ireland thought of them as a referendum and looked at the votes. The effect in London I think was muted because people in London are not accustomed to thinking in terms of votes and percentages; they think in terms of seats and they say 'ah you lost a seat'.[55]

It was put to Trimble that the by-elections were intended to influence external rather than internal opinion and, as such, the loss of Newry and Armagh tarnished any gains that were made in terms of votes cast against the Agreement. Trimble agreed that this was true to a certain extent, but commented that the unionists had deliberately put one of their Westminster seats at risk in order to have the by-elections seem as close to a referendum as possible.

> It took a bit of an edge off it. You know it's funny, from the London perspective, they wouldn't have noticed if we hadn't fought Newry and Armagh, if we'd fought the others. They wouldn't have noticed that, because they didn't notice the fact that Foyle wasn't being fought, and we put Newry and Armagh on the line knowing that it was probably going to be lost, in order to get it as close to a referendum as possible, although thinking in London still regards referenda as being, you know, not quite the proper thing. So they looked at seats, we looked at votes – I think that tells you something about the English.[56]

The Rev. Martin Smyth's assessment of the by-election tactic was similar to Trimble's analysis, his argument being that the Newry and Armagh seat was sacrificed to maximise the vote and that the results were subsequently hijacked by the media and made to look like a failure. 'People say we were very foolish because we lost Nicholson. We would have lost Nicholson anyway, Nicholson was only lent to us. . . . It looked like an own goal because the media did it that way.'[57] The attitude on the liberal wing of the Ulster Unionist Party was less sanguine, however, as illustrated by Michael McGimpsey's recollection that neither the by-elections, the mass demonstrations, nor anything else which they tried was making the British government waver in their determination to implement the AIA. McGimpsey declared that the success of the resignation tactic was limited to the theoretical level, in that, while highlighting the anti-democratic nature of British policy-making in Northern Ireland, it had little practical impact as the government were able to proceed with the AIA largely unhindered, under the aegis of parliamentary sovereignty.

It was successful insofar that the public perception throughout the Republic and throughout the mainland saw that the majority of people weren't going to have it. But under the constitutional arrangements we have in the UK, there is absolutely nothing that people here can do about an Act or a motion passed by the House of Commons. So they had the giant protest at the City Hall, everybody resigned in form the of a mock referendum, they had boycotts at parliament and had boycotts in the council chamber, but none of it made a button of difference, because those were the only outlets for them and those outlets were never really going to produce the goods as far as unionists were concerned so long as the government held firm.[58]

The DUP view as expressed by the party's deputy leader Peter Robinson was less fatalistic. For him the by-elections could have succeeded if the unionists had taken a much stronger line of opposition. Once again we see the conflicting cultural perspectives within the ideology, for whereas McGimpsey takes the view that the people of Northern Ireland are limited in their scope for opposition by Westminster legislation, Robinson feels that the unionist community could have changed the policy through solidarity and expressions of defiance against the government.

> If you allow almost a normal political situation to exist, first of all you are telling your own supporters that nothing is so urgent that we're going to disturb ourselves greatly. A view I expressed at the time was 'look, politics is over, resign our positions, let people know we're serious. If you don't accept this basis of government then don't give it the credence of your presence within it. Let's get out and let's make sure nobody takes our positions. Let's make it such an ugly event that nobody will want to stand in by-elections to take over from us.' I think we could have done that. You don't get crowds the size that we had in those days at the [Belfast] City Hall unless there was a very deep feeling in the Protestant psyche. . . . Unless you bring into play people power, you're not going to bring down a form of government. You have to make it clear that we are not prepared to be governed in this way and that effectively 'you can't govern without our consent.'[59]

If the by-elections of 23 January were something of a public relations disaster and did little to really put pressure on the British government to revise their commitment to the Agreement, it was hoped that the next big set-piece in the anti-Agreement campaign announced at the beginning of March would provide a demonstration of Protestant 'people power' that could not be ignored. An advertisement was placed with the *News Letter* which announced 'a day of action and protest' for Monday 3 March 1986. The text of this advertisement was secular in tone, declaring that the AIA had instituted Dublin rule and the government had ignored the 'popular will' of the people as expressed democratically through the ballot-box. Consequently it was up to all pro-Union supporters to join in the one-day constitutional stoppage to send 'an unmistakable signal to Westminster that Ulster means business'.[60] Under the photographs of the two Unionist leaders were calls for non-violence. James Molyneaux commented: 'There must be no violence in the course of this operation on Monday. The protest must be rigidly controlled and any irresponsible people weeded out.'[61] Ian Paisley declared: 'This should be a passive and voluntary demonstration. Violence and intimidation can play no part in our plan. We do not want the support of those who do not accept these conditions.'[62] There are a number of points to be made about 'A Call to Action', not the least being the low-key nature of the language used. Gone are the religious metaphors and lurid language characteristic of earlier DUP advertisements, suggesting that once again the primary aim was to embrace as wide a coalition as possible. The disclaimer notices which followed the advertisement are also interesting (and in light of subsequent events timely), for although one would have expected such qualification from Molyneaux, Paisley's disavowal of violent street protest was not entirely consistent with earlier statements. What is clear from this advertisement is that compromise had occurred on both sides with the realisation that each party needed the other. The UUP agreed to a one-day strike in the knowledge that this could have undesirable effects for the business community which formed a significant section of its support, while the DUP agreed to tone down their language and repudiate any violence which might result from the stoppage. A joint press conference held at the UUP's Glengall Street headquarters on 1 March, co-hosted by Ian Paisley and James Molyneaux, illustrated the different perspectives of the two party leaderships. The message coming from the press conference was that there should be no violence and that intimidation was not part of the strike-plan. However, there appeared to be a slight difference of emphasis between the two leaders. While Molyneaux said that there should be no roadblocks on 3 March, as these would be illegal, Paisley added that this did not rule out picketing, leaflet distribution and requests to people not to go to work. On a more ominous note, the DUP leader also told reporters that a 'blacklist' was being drawn up of companies and organisations attempting to browbeat employees into going into work. A note would also be taken, he claimed, of shops and businesses which stayed open, though he rejected suggestions that this was a form of intimidation.[63]

The attitude of the *News Letter* (an opinion-former in the unionist community which should not be underestimated) was broadly supportive, though it sided very much with the Ulster Unionist interpretation of what constituted a peaceful protest. 'The protest will be effective if it is carried out in a dignified and peaceful manner. There can be no room for intimidation, violence or sectarianism.'[64]

Despite appeals from the *News Letter* and the unionist political leadership, the 'Day of Action' of 3 March 1986 was neither a peaceful nor a constitutional stoppage. The RUC were fired on by loyalist paramilitaries on the Newtownards Road in east Belfast and on the Shankill Road in the west of the city, although no one was injured. Under the headline 'Youths on rampage in Belfast', the *News Letter* captured the mood in the wake of the mob violence which accompanied the protest.

> Hundreds of youths went on the rampage in Belfast city centre yesterday afternoon. In spite of appeals from Unionist leaders the mob broke away from the Death of Democracy rally and stoned shops and a car showroom. . . . Black smoke soon hung over the city's office blocks and the Unionist platform party, whose rally had just finished, appeared powerless to stop the rampaging mob.[65]

Reactions to the violence were varied, ranging from outright condemnation to justification and self-congratulation at the expression of the 'Protestant popular will'. Sammy Wilson condemned the looting, though he sought to contextualise it, alluding to the fact that it was an almost inevitable symptom of a deeper problem, namely the AIA. 'I suppose I can give a thousand explanations why something like this has happened but, in the end, the bottom line is that it just cannot be condoned . . .'[66] However, in the main the DUP were unrepentant, as illustrated by a statement issued by party headquarters the same evening. 'We've proved our point. Without the consent of Ulster Unionists joint authority cannot be successfully implemented.'[67] Justification of the rioting was not limited to the DUP, as the following statement by John Taylor would indicate. 'It is now time for the Government to take stock. The message today was that People Power had broken through.'[68] Nonetheless, the majority within the Ulster Unionist Party, including its deputy leader Harold McCusker, sought to distance themselves from the violent events which took place on 3 March and the damage which this had inflicted upon the unionist case. 'The day of protest is over. I don't think post-mortems will achieve anything. There are clear lessons for both Mrs Thatcher and for Northern Ireland politicians.'[69] Contrast this with the statement of DUP Assemblyman Jack McKee, at the Larne rally on the Day of Action itself, that violence might be necessary as a future tactic.

> Today's protest is just the first blow. There will be other days to come where we will have to take a stand, to continue the protest by other methods. Even if it means taking up arms for the defence of Ulster you are going to have to do that. There are many incarcerated in Ulster's jails for taking a stand in the past.[70]

Jim Allister's comment at the same Larne rally was equally unrepentant and implied that, whatever the leadership were trying to suggest, there were many (within the DUP at least) who were convinced that violent protest was both a legitimate and to some extent a necessary tactic in the unionist campaign. 'The Agreement will either destroy us or we will destroy it. We have shown today that we, loyalists, control this Province. Today the Prime Minister knows that we are not going to be trampled on.'[71]

Defiant statements such as those uttered by Allister and McKee were patently out of sympathy with the Ulster Unionist leadership, whose association with the events of 3 March angered the more moderate elements within their own constituency. The feeling which had been simmering for some time within the grass-roots of the UUP, that James Molyneaux was allowing the party to be dominated by Ian Paisley, finally came to the boil after the strike. There were those who believed that the Ulster Unionists were rapidly becoming the junior partner in the pact and that their party leader was merely rubber-stamping decisions taken by the leader of the DUP, decisions moreover which they profoundly disagreed with. Under the headline 'The night they put us back fourteen years', the *News Letter* reported on grass-roots opposition to the Day of Action and the antipathy shown towards the unionist leadership.

> The main emotion among loyalists yesterday was anger with strong criticism of Unionist leaders Jim Molyneaux and Ian Paisley. One woman said, 'Mr Paisley and Mr Molyneaux should have known this would happen. It was as bad as the riots back in '69. We are back to square one. The leaders didn't need a fortune-teller to know what would happen if they took the protest onto the streets.'[72]

Despite such resentment within some quarters of the unionist community, the DUP chief whip Jim Allister made a call for similar one-day strikes to be held each time the AIA Intergovernmental Conference took place in Belfast: '. . . we should now announce as policy that every day the Conference meets in Northern Ireland, it will be a day of protest action with mass stoppage of work and Province-wide demonstrations'.[73] This, of course, stood at variance with Molyneaux's position that he would not support strike action in the future due to the violence associated with the 3 March stoppage. Molyneaux recollects that he had been against the Day of Action from the beginning and could not sanction similar tactics in the future, on the grounds that such strikes were potentially destructive to lives and property and usually counterproductive to the political fortunes of unionism. When Molyneaux was asked if this was Ian Paisley's view and whether his anti-strike declaration had been met by any animosity from the DUP, he replied that the DUP leader was 'not all that enthusiastic about the strike' but was forced into it by the more militant members within his party:

> . . . some of the younger Turks did say you shouldn't have thrown that card away and I said, 'but how can you guarantee that you would prevent

the thing being hijacked by paramilitaries?', that is the central problem. The strike itself, if it had been possible to control it, would have been alright but then I knew in my heart of hearts that you couldn't do that and what I did was to, once it was inevitable, I had to take a strong line and then in the Assembly, which was meeting at that time, lay down the law that every Assembly member and every councillor of both parties would have to be out on the streets controlling the situation, which was to some extent successful, but there were far too many very regrettable incidents and that's the sort of thing that you couldn't risk again.[74]

Despite Molyneaux's attempt to downplay unionist reaction to his declaration that further strikes would not be sanctioned by his party, the reality was that the DUP were bitterly angry for two reasons. Firstly, they pointed out that, as there was supposed to be a pact between the two parties, Molyneaux should not have been making unilateral policy statements without consultation with the DUP. Secondly, they admonished Molyneaux on the grounds of practicality, arguing that such declarations were akin to trying to win a game of poker by showing your cards to the opponent. Sammy Wilson was particularly scathing in his criticism of Molyneaux's reaction to the strike, accusing him of political cowardice, although he was anxious to point out that the violence which accompanied the strike had been exaggerated. When asked whether Molyneaux had consulted his party before making his statement, Wilson replied:

No he didn't, he didn't. I mean I think that that is essentially the difference between the two parties. The first thing is that you've got to put the violence of 3 March into context. It was no more than what happened fairly frequently on a bad weekend in west Belfast. I was involved to very very late that night on what was happening on the Newtownards Road where the main focus of the riots was supposed to have been. There were a few skirmishes, there were a couple of lorries overturned, a few lamp-posts pulled over, but that is a common occurrence in parts of this city. There was a certain amount of media hype and Jim Molyneaux I think lost his nerve. . . . I think that when Jim Molyneaux, when he made that statement, he really gave the green light to the government, to sit back and not to take loyalists seriously.[75]

Wilson then went on to declare that Molyneaux's behaviour during this period was indicative of the cultural differences between the two main unionist parties. He implied that whatever the rhetoric of the Ulster Unionist Party during conditions of relative political stability, once a political crisis was imminent the UUP would prevaricate and sup- port the forces of the establishment rather than the people of Northern Ireland. The DUP by contrast were, according to Wilson, the party of the people and a true reflection of the community which they served and sought support from.

I think there is the difference between a party which has its roots firmly in the establishment, and a party like ourselves, which is not in any way connected with the establishment because we are a relatively new party and we've got people who basically come from a working-class background.[76]

Wilson's colleague Nigel Dodds denounced Molyneaux's action in a similar fashion, pointing out that it was totally counterproductive and had mitigated fears in London that political instability on such a scale could prove detrimental to the Agreement and possibly prevent its implementation. Dodds declared that the strike had scared the British government, and would ultimately have produced political leverage for the unionists had Molyneaux kept quiet. Instead, he argued, the British government were informed by Molyneaux that they were not really serious about their opposition to the Agreement and would not take any action which might lead to political instability. As a consequence, London were able to sit back and watch the posturing of the unionists in the knowledge that the UUP, at least, would 'pull back from the brink' before events got out of control.

My view is that it should have been kept as a weapon in our armoury, it should not have been thrown away in the way in which Mr Molyneaux did. I mean he came out, more or less straight away, and said 'never again', and let the government off the hook. I think it's clear that the one thing that government feared was that sort of popular reaction that would bring the public to a standstill, and I think that that was a fundamental error in the tactics that we used at that time.[77]

When asked whether he thought Molyneaux should have consulted the DUP before making his decision to oppose strike action in the future, Dodds replied in the affirmative and suggested that had he done so, the Ulster Unionist leader would have received very sound advice.

Well yes I think if he had consulted us he'd have got our opinion very clearly, because even if you do not want to use the strike weapon again, you don't openly declare that you're not going to do it. I mean, even if you felt, 'well okay, this is not something we're going to pursue', to come out publicly and say that destroys immediately the effect of having had the strike in the first place.[78]

Peter Robinson, the deputy leader of the DUP, takes a similarly critical line to his party colleagues, arguing that, to be effective, unconstitutional action needed to be bold and unapologetic, an option which Molyneaux effectively foreclosed with his declaration that similar protests would no longer form part of the anti-Agreement campaign.

I really believe that the campaign against the Anglo-Irish Agreement died on the evening of the Day of Action . . . [Molyneaux's statement] that he wouldn't support any event which could result in that kind of violence.

That kind of violence was events of a scale which would have hardly been reported on a day-to-day basis in Northern Ireland. Nobody was killed, nobody was injured, a few shops had their windows broken and a few cars were burnt, nothing of a major scale. But what it [Molyneaux's statement] did was give to the British government a clear message that this represents the limit of this man's opposition and that: 'we have nothing to worry about. He is not going to do anything, he's not going to lead people to do anything, therefore we needn't worry. All we have to do is really batten down the hatches and wait till the storm has passed.' And unless unionism had been going forward on a united basis it wasn't really going to be effective and Ian [Paisley] was left with the difficulty of either leading a full-blooded campaign which was what was needed and breaking with Molyneaux to do it, in which case unionist division would have occurred and that would have been counterproductive as well, so he was in a no-win situation. So yeh, I blame Molyneaux for wrecking the whole protest campaign.[79]

Molyneaux's decision not to sanction any further strike action was defended however by Rev. Martin Smyth, who argued that, whilst such tactics worked well in 1974, that did not necessarily mean they could be used to equal effect in 1986. When Smyth was asked whether he considered Molyneaux's decision to be a correct one, his reply emphasised once again the armour-plated nature of the AIA which insulated it from attack.

I can understand Jim's position, because he doesn't want to see his country destroyed. He realises that the strike is a weapon that you can use in particular circumstances. It was quite effective in '74, when you had local people who could be affected. All the Northern Ireland Office had to do [in 1985] was to withdraw behind their barricades . . . and at that particular time, we were fighting for the survival of the shipyard [Harland and Wolff], we were fighting for the survival of the aircraft factory, [Short's] two large engineering concerns, at a time when English shipbuilding was going to the wall and when even the aircraft industry was in the doldrums.[80]

This analysis is totally at variance with that of Peter Robinson who saw the May 1974 Ulster's Workers' Council (UWC) strike as a useful template for action against the AIA. While Smyth supported a policy which would not result in physical destruction or economic breakdown, Robinson's 'devil take the hindmost' mentality saw this as almost being a prerequisite for success.

I lived and worked through the period in politics from 1968 to the present day. I therefore have some experience of campaigns of opposition in the past. In the opposition to Sunningdale, the Ulster Workers' Council strike took probably about two weeks to bite before it had any effect on the factories in Northern Ireland, before its impact was such that lights were going off and so forth, it was a very slow build-up in terms of the strike. In one day of the Day of Action, we had reached about that period of time that had taken two weeks to come about in the early '70s. If we had got through with a united leadership, after that Day of Action, the government knew very well that what we were in effect in a position to do was to say: 'We are stopping our labour, everything in this Province is coming to a standstill, and until you sort out our constitutional position in a way that satisfies us, nothing will start again.' And you simply hold the province until it was satisfactorily resolved. I think that might have concentrated the mind of the British government in a way that years of opposition would never have done in any other form.[81]

Perhaps as a consequence of frustration within the unionist community at the lack of political progress, reports began to emerge of leadership crises within both of the major parties. Ken Maginnis denied that Molyneaux's position within the UUP was under threat, while rumours grew that Ian Paisley was increasingly being overshadowed by Peter Robinson. 'Over the past month there has been increased speculation that his [Paisley's] deputy Peter Robinson is now the "man in the driver's seat".'[82]

The UDA, meanwhile, were growing impatient at what they saw as an ineffective political campaign and sought to increase their prestige within the Protestant community by attracting those frustrated by the series of setbacks suffered by the unionist leadership since the signing of the Agreement. John McMichael, who was keen to carve out a higher political profile for his organisation, criticised Molyneaux and Paisley for, 'fiddling while Ulster burns'.[83] He suggested that the joint unionist pact was getting nowhere. 'The DUP has been holding back to keep the pact intact but the Glengall Street leadership is the slowest ship in the convoy.'[84] Commenting on the course of street politics to date, McMichael declared that the 'constitutional stoppage' of 3 March had been a success and that the violence which accompanied it was both minor and a direct result of the apathy of some unionist politicians.

> In areas where politicians shied away from their responsibility there was a lack of co-ordination which left people to do their own thing and that is what led to misunderstandings, frustration and in some cases violence. These back-peddlers did not go unnoticed.[85]

McMichael's criticism of the unionist political leadership was reflected in the UDA magazine *Ulster*, which warned that the constitutional path being followed by the unionist leadership and inspired by Enoch Powell was a shield to hide the fact that they had no idea what to do next. The politicians were prevaricating because they had no commitment to the sort of direct action which was necessary to defeat the Agreement.

> It would seem that the thinking of Molyneaux, Taylor and even Paisley is being directed along the lines of working within Westminster. In effect they

are merely stalling in order to try to think of some more 'nice' tactics to employ in order to avoid using nasty unconstitutional methods which will confront our enemies on our ground in the way that they fear and we understand. . . . The real danger to Ulster lies in the fact that if a coherent campaign of resistance is not embarked upon soon, the Anglo-Irish Agreement will become more cemented into our political infrastructure and thus more difficult to remove. With many of our unionist leaders lacking the guts necessary for the struggle, they will seek to achieve some sort of compromise rather than confront the government.[86]

The conflicting cultural perspectives within unionism over the meaning of the Union and the consequent disagreement over political tactics were highlighted by the Day of Action. Interparty friction grew when a row erupted between the Ulster Unionist councillor Alfie Redpath and the DUP, with Redpath attacking his DUP colleagues over their ambiguous denunciations of violence. The DUP press officer Sammy Wilson described Redpath's attack as 'scandalous and unfounded'. He challenged Redpath to produce evidence that they had instigated or condoned trouble, and accused him of playing into the hands of the NIO, which wanted to divide unionist opposition to the AIA. By playing the 'unionist unity' card, Wilson was challenging Redpath over the central strategy of the whole unionist pact against the Agreement. He had correctly calculated that unity would not be jeopardised by either party because some DUP politicians were ambiguous in their condemnation of Protestant paramilitary violence. Wilson recollects that from the very beginning of the unionist pact, the primary aim of the two parties was to present a united front and prevent division as this would destroy their common goal of getting rid of the Agreement:

> . . . the one thing we decided we'd have to do was to make sure that within the unionist community as a whole there was not a split, that there was increased opposition to the Agreement, and that the government wouldn't be able to sell the Agreement by getting some section of the unionist community to say, 'well, we think we could live with it and we could accept it and we could work with it'.[87]

The rioting in April in the wake of Keith White's death, a young Protestant man killed by a plastic bullet during rioting with the RUC in Portadown, marked an interesting point in the unionist coalition, as the DUP leader chose to respond in a manner which would please James Molyneaux and consequently risked alienating the radicals within his own party. Paisley denounced the rioting in unequivocal language, a marked contrast with his previously ambiguous position over the tactics which should be employed by unionists to defeat the AIA. 'Those who pretend to be Protestants and carry out such disgraceful acts as those we have witnessed on Thursday night are an utter and total disgrace, and [we] unreservedly condemn them.'[88]

The anti-Agreement campaign, combined with protests over the police rerouting of unionist demonstrations, inevitably produced friction with the RUC. While the UUP satisfied mainstream unionist opinion by condemning attacks on the police, the DUP leadership found themselves in a more difficult position. Paisley had successfully mobilised radical Protestant opinion, yet could not support their actions for fear of fracturing relations with the UUP. The DUP walked a precarious tightrope therefore, as on the one hand they tried to keep the pact intact and at the same time maintain their radical individualism, while on the other hand they attempted to avert the 'Grand Old Duke of York' syndrome. The paramilitaries, who had been suspicious of Paisley since the 1974 strike, were conscious that as in the past he might march Protestants to the brink, only to leave them there and retreat himself at the last moment. In this sense the joint pact endangered the DUP vote, as there was a very real risk that the need to keep the two parties together would alienate the DUP's young, radical, urban vote, and perhaps deliver them into the hands of less constitutional brands of unionism. The same risks applied of course to the Ulster Unionists, though the bulk of their support was by its very nature less demanding, requiring only an acceptable level of unconstitutionality which would not damage their real estate. The need to satisfy a number of very different audiences, the UUP on the one hand and the DUP grass-roots on the other, not to mention the British government and the more fastidious elements of his Free Presbyterian congregation, may help explain the rather schizophrenic nature of Ian Paisley's rhetoric during this period. For example, while condemning violence in April, he appeared to be condoning it by June. Speaking at an Ulster Clubs rally in Larne on 24 June he declared that he would not stand in the way of violent loyalist reaction to the Agreement.

> I give notice that if a Protestant backlash is the only thing that can destroy the Anglo-Irish Agreement, then I will not stand in its way to do the dirty work of a government which I neither recognise nor have one pinhead of respect for.[89]

Paisley declared that civil war was imminent, and not only was he prepared to give wholehearted support to those who would fight to retain their heritage but he would lead them into battle.

> If the British Government force us down the road to a united Ireland we will fight to the death . . . This could come to hand-to-hand fighting in every street in Northern Ireland. We are on the verge of civil war; when you take away the forums of democracy you have nothing left. We are asking people to be ready for the worst and I will lead them. . . . The people must prepare themselves as in the days of Carson, for a long struggle. . . . The Union is over.[90]

However, with that inconsistency which bespeaks a successful politician, he had changed his mind seven days later, announcing that the danger of civil war had receded. At his party's weekly press conference on 1 July, he attributed this to divine intervention in the shape of the Irish referendum on divorce. 'The mercy of God has brought us back from the brink. The civil war which was almost upon us has receded.'[91] Paisley's denunciation of attacks on the RUC in April was seen by some of his more radical critics as yet another occasion when his actions had failed to match the ferocity of his rhetoric. It is clear from the DUP annual conference of April 1986 that a division existed within the party on what their attitude should be to police enforcement of law and order. The irony of the debate over the role of the police, the use of plastic bullets and what attitude the party should take towards the RUC, was that many of the speeches made by delegates were not that far removed from those made by nationalist politicians ten years earlier.

> The RUC were hissed, the death of plastic bullet victim Keith White was condemned and there was a motion saying that the party's support for the police was not unconditional. But an attempt by Councillor Ethel Smyth to say she regretted the death of John Downes, [sic], the last Nationalist victim of a plastic bullet was shouted down by the Reverend William McCrea. 'No. No. I'll not condemn the death of John Downes. No Fenian. Never. No.'[92]

The disagreement expressed over this issue did not go unnoticed by the unionist press, the *News Letter* commenting that such dissent was unprecedented within the DUP. 'It was the first time at a DUP conference that there was such an open display of division within the Party's rank and file.'[93] Although his leadership address mended some fences within the party, Paisley was not able to mollify all opinion, with some delegates, such as Ballymoney member James Patterson, continuing to express their dissatisfaction. 'I believe for too many times we have been at the brink and turned back. This time my hope is that this party will pursue the fight to its ultimate conclusion.'[94]

Aside from personality conflicts, grass-roots dissent, interparty and intraparty faction-fighting, fractures also began to appear within the Ulster Unionist Parliamentary Party over the Westminster boycott policy, which angered the DUP and embarrassed the UUP leadership. The former Ulster Unionist MP for Newry and Armagh Jim Nicholson launched an attack on those Ulster Unionists who had returned to the House of Commons in defiance of the boycott. Nicholson joined UUP deputy leader Harold McCusker and DUP deputy leader Peter Robinson in criticising MPs John Taylor, Rev. Martin Smyth, Cecil Walker and Enoch Powell for breaking party ranks. Nicholson suggested there should be 'No creeping back' to Westminster until the Anglo-Irish Agreement was totally defeated,[95] while

Robinson launched a more blistering attack: 'John Taylor sneaked back to Westminster to speak in the House of Commons. He broke faith with his colleagues when we had our backs to the wall.'[96]

If there were tensions within and between the two main unionist parties over tactics in the summer of 1986, this was nothing compared to their relationship with the Protestant paramilitaries. Dismay at the slow pace of the anti-Agreement campaign, and the lack of success which it had so far achieved, led *Combat* magazine (the mouthpiece of the UVF) to compare the existing political leadership to that of Brian Faulkner and Terence O'Neill a generation earlier. Betraying its urban and working-class roots with a noticeably anti-clerical stance, the magazine attempted to tap a populist nerve in the loyalist community by blaming the political failures of unionism over the past twenty years on the leadership, rather than on the electorate who voted for them. It attacked the various elites who controlled the political institutions in Northern Ireland, accusing them of being both self-serving and incompetent in equal measure, and oblivious to the real needs of the Protestant community.

> For forty years Ulster was ruled by the biggest bunch of cretins outside Botha's Africa. They abused their mandate and the electorate allowed them to do so. All in the good name of Ulster of course. At first it was a Quasi-Military Junta. Captain O'Neill, Captain Long, Captain Ardill, Captain Lord Brookeborough, Major Lloyd Hall Thompson, Major Chichester Clarke, [sic], Captain Mitchell (ad infinitum). Now we are faced with a different form of leadership . . . a vicars' junta if you like. The Reverend Ian Paisley, Reverend Beattie, Rev. Coulter, Rev. Martin Smyth, Rev. Wm. McCrea, Rev. Ivan Foster (ad infinitum) plus an ambuscade of lay preachers and salvationists. Now anyone with an ounce of sense and a titter of wit in the field of political acumen must know that there has to be a radical change from all of that.[97]

While the paramilitaries were anxious to dissociate themselves from the unsuccessful tactics being pursued by the main unionist parties, they were also trying to apply pressure on their constitutional colleagues to adopt their analysis and step up the street politics aspect of the protest. Given the social profile and cultural outlook of the UUP, this was never a realistic hope.

Disillusionment with street politics

By the end of October 1986 the unionist political leadership was coming under fire from many grass-roots supporters on both sides who had grown disillusioned with the unionist pact. Criticism also came from the UDA after the two main parties announced that another mass protest rally would be held outside Belfast City Hall on 15 November to commemorate the first anniversary of the Agreement. The UDA leader Andy Tyrie commented that the unionist campaign had lost its initial vigour and needed an injection of fresh ideas. 'We need some new tricks, not the same old ones we always use. We've become too predictable.'[98] The inference Tyrie was making was that protest rallies were now insufficient, were incapable of dealing with the present crisis and that more militant action was necessary. Sources close to the Ulster Clubs had stated that Molyneaux and Paisley should step down in three months and make way for more dynamic leaders to emerge. UDA deputy leader John McMichael commented the following day that there was a great deal of resentment and frustration among unionist councillors and grass-roots loyalists at the way the protest was being organised. McMichael was particularly critical of the Westminster politicians and the leaders of the two main unionist parties for spending so much time outside Northern Ireland.[99] Speaking on BBC Radio Ulster's *Talkback* programme on 28 October, McMichael commented: 'There is no new thinking in it [the mass rally at Belfast City Hall]. . . . There seems to be a lack of a coherent, comprehensive campaign against the Agreement.'[100] McMichael said that the UDA was not boycotting the rally or calling on anyone not to attend it, but that their view was simply that a rally on its own was insufficient to achieve their objectives. 'It has to be the beginning of a campaign of resistance against the Agreement; that campaign has been totally absent since last November.'[101] Frank Millar, the UUP general-secretary, rejected the UDA's criticism, claiming that the proposed City Hall demonstration on 15 November would not be a waste of time. He said that the UDA were not representative of the majority of the unionist population and attacked what he called a dangerous build-up of tension, deliberately engineered by the extreme fringes of the unionist community.[102] While few would disagree that the UDA had a vested interest in raising the political temperature, Millar did not need to look outside the ranks of his own party for evidence of similar behaviour. David Trimble, then a law lecturer at Queen's University Belfast and a leading member of the Ulster Clubs, commented in early November that loyalists were coming very close to stepping outside the bounds of lawful protest. Trimble made it clear that he hoped DUP leader Ian Paisley was not going to 'do a Grand Old Duke of York act' over his reported plans for raising a citizens' army. The former Vanguard Party representative said the unionists were in a dilemma, because if they did nothing they would be walked upon and if they did something radical it would be a sign of disloyalty and would necessarily break the law.

> If you have a situation where there is a serious attack on your constitutional
> position and liberties – and I regard the Anglo-Irish Agreement as being just
> that – and where the Government tells you constitutional action is ineffec-
> tive, you are left in a very awkward situation . . . do you sit back and do

nothing, or move outside constitutional forms of protest? I don't think you can deal with the situation without the risk of an extra-parliamentary campaign. . . . I would personally draw the line at terrorism and serious violence. But if we are talking about a campaign that involves demonstrations and so on, then a certain element of violence may be inescapable.[103]

Although it would have been understandable had he avoided commenting on the UDA's criticism of the unionist political leadership for only recommending a mass demonstration in Belfast to commemorate the signing of the Agreement, Trimble went out of his way to make it clear that he sympathised with this view and with the position of the Ulster Clubs. 'The general reaction, not only of the Clubs' membership but of the party politicians was one of disappointment . . . there will be very great disappointment if something more substantial is not announced at the big Belfast City Hall rally on November 15.'[104] In its editorial column, meanwhile, *Combat* delivered its verdict on one year's protest against the AIA and declared that the joint unionist campaign had accomplished little and would achieve nothing of significance during the second year of the Agreement's existence.

Another Rally for the history books, another trek by loyal Ulstermen and women to the now familiar meeting place with its all too familiar sights . . . . and sounds. The bloodcurdling guldering of politicians threatening hell-fire, blood and damnation at 2.00 pm and the castigation of the mob at 2.30. We have all been here before, who would wish to go again? Surely it will be November 1987 before the same can be attempted yet again. And what of it? Where is it leading to? There's a short answer to that . . . nowhere. It's one great cul-de-sac to which the organisers will privately admit even if the crowd have not yet tippled to it! This Journal has gone along with the process for one year. Now there has to be a different approach. . . . The days of marching to God-knows-where are over.[105]

Advocates of a more radical campaign against the AIA were no doubt encouraged by a meeting in the Ulster Hall on 10 November, which announced the formation of a new 'loyalist army' under the leadership of Ulster Resistance. The meeting which was by invitation only was chaired by Belfast lord mayor Sammy Wilson and also had Ian Paisley, Peter Robinson and Ulster Clubs chairman Alan Wright on the platform. The invitations to the meeting bore the request: 'Dress should be suitable for a religious service.'[106] Perhaps it should have added that the emphasis would be on the Old rather than the New Testament. Most of the political figures on show were from the DUP although North Belfast MP Cecil Walker and Frazer Agnew of the UUP turned up against the advice of party leader James Molyneaux. Begging a 'fool's pardon', Walker claimed he was not aware that an 'army' was being set up and maintained that he was attending a normal meeting of committed unionists. Agnew, on the other hand, said that he would not be opposed to the formation of a 'citizen army' even if this went outside the law in certain circumstances.[107] A 'statement of intent', issued after the meeting, contains a classic exposition of unionist conditional loyalty as discussed in Chapter 2 and reflects the peculiar cultural cocktail discussed in earlier chapters of this study.

> We are not revolutionists or anarchists or murderers. We seek no fight with the forces of the Crown. Our cause is Ulster, the land of our birth. . . . We make it clear to the British and Eire governments, that Ulster Protestants will not sit idly by while our future heritage and freedom are taken from us. . . . No earthly power has the right to take from us our God-given heritage. Neither have we the right to surrender it. . . . We call on the men of Ulster to rally to the cause and to swell our ranks. . . . Our cause is just. Let us with God's help match its justice with our courage and resolution.[108]

This statement contains the familiar ingredients of radical unionist protest, namely protestations of loyalty to the Crown, the law-abiding nature of the Protestant community and the spiritual legality under the eyes of God of actions which might be illegal under temporal law. One of the main protagonists in the Ulster Resistance movement, the chairman of the Ulster Clubs, Alan Wright, claimed that his organisation had a membership of 12,000, spread across Northern Ireland in seventy-four clubs. Wright warned the unionist political leadership about going back on earlier promises to withdraw completely their consent from British political structures.

> That was their pledge to us last November. After the signing they said they would withdraw the consent of the Northern Ireland people plus every elected representative on every government body – this clearly has not happened. . . . The unionist leadership must complete this withdrawal and implement a massive campaign of civil disobedience . . . traditional unionism was shown in the 1912–16 period when it was unconstitutional and illegal to form an army. But faced with treachery as we are today I cannot see anything other than the Ulster people on the streets prepared to use legitimate force – only this will bring down the agreement.[109]

Wright went on to say that the tactics of the unionist leadership were worse than useless, and were playing into the hands of the British government.

> It's going to be disastrous for Northern Ireland if we are planning a third rally at City Hall. . . . The country is crying out for something other than a rally. The Government is delighted this is all that is being done. We need a complete change of heart and to upgrade the tempo.[110]

For their part, the DUP hoped that by supporting Ulster Resistance they could manipulate and harness what was essentially an inexperienced political leadership and thus align it more closely with the priorities of the DUP. Additionally, Paisley hoped that his donning of the red beret would re-establish his Carsonite credentials with the radical elements within his own party, who were becoming restless with the pace of the anti-Agreement campaign and disillusioned with the unionist pact. This was, it should be said, a symbiotic relationship, providing Ulster Resistance with a degree of legitimacy and respectability essential for the support of the God-fearing residents of rural Northern Ireland.

Predictably, the formation of Ulster Resistance was the final straw for some members of the UUP who felt that they could no longer defend a pact with the DUP. One of the few people who came out publicly at this point to recommend a formal break with the Democratic Unionists was Alan Chalmers, chairman of the Greater Belfast Young Unionist Association. He commented that the unionist pact was 'effectively at an end'.

> It is becoming increasingly recognised in our own community that the aims of the Ulster Unionist Party and the DUP are simply incompatible. . . . The DUP's actions in recent months have been nothing other than a catalogue of irresponsibility and the one thing which has disgusted me is that so few of our public representatives have been prepared to dissociate themselves from such behaviour.[111]

Chalmers commented that the DUP seemed intent on setting up an independent state; he accused its members of 'seeming to be increasingly intent on breaking all links with the mainland so they can set up a fourth rate nation independent Paisleyland'.[112] He also backed calls for the return of MPs to Westminster and for a rethink of the unionists' local government boycott.[113] Chalmers's condemnation of the DUP sparked off a predictable row within the ranks of the Greater Belfast Young Unionist Association, which saw the subsequent resignation of its vice-chairman Raymond Glass. Glass maintained that Chalmers was out of step with party policy and with the YUA, and should therefore consider his position. 'If Mr Chalmers finds the views of the Young Unionists as intolerable I would suggest he take the honourable course and join the Alliance Party where his anti-unionist bleatings will be more appreciated.'[114]

Barely a month later it was announced that all of the officers of the Greater Belfast Young Unionist Association, including its controversial chairman Alan Chalmers, had resigned from the movement. The resignations took place on 17 December, when Chalmers declared that he and his colleagues had stepped down before the Young Unionist Council changed its constitution to allow it to expel them. 'The Young Unionist movement is unrecognisable as the one I joined four years ago. It is steeped in its own hatred and anti-British bigotry and detests freedom of speech. I could not with honour remain in such a movement.'[115]

The latest event in the anti-Agreement campaign, meanwhile, added to the friction which had become endemic within the unionist community, as most of the publicity that surrounded the mass protest rally of 15 November at Belfast City Hall was concerned with the violence which took place. The demonstration was accompanied by widespread looting in Belfast city centre, during which violent confrontations broke out between loyalists and the police. RUC figures claimed that one man had died and 76 people were injured (28 civilians and 48 police), while 110 people were arrested, with charges ranging from riotous behaviour to arson and criminal damage. In the centre of Belfast 73 shops were attacked and a further 76 premises in the Greater Belfast area were damaged. A total of 14 were looted.[116] While the UUP were embarrassed by the violence which accompanied the first anniversary rally, the DUP viewed it as a legitimate means of exerting political pressure on the British government. As Sammy Wilson's recollection of events indicates, the DUP analysis was that the violence was a direct result of British policy-making and a steadfast refusal by London to accede to unionist demands as expressed democratically through the ballot-box. Wilson's argument was that Britain was creating the conditions for violence to prosper by ignoring the wishes of constitutional unionists and if violence erupted, responsibility for that violence lay with the British government.

> I think that if you feel that the law is disadvantageous to your community, if you feel that the law is an unjust law, if you feel that you've done everything within your ability as a parliamentarian to change the law, and still that has been ignored, then I believe that you've got to be prepared to consider other options. Anyway, street demonstrations are not outside the law, mass protests are not outside the law, and if they overspill into something else, because people have seen that those other tactics work, I don't think that the politicians who first of all organised the demonstrations should take responsibility for that.[117]

While the consequences of street politics were tearing the unionist pact apart, intra-unionist division was also hampering the anti-Agreement campaign. In the knowledge that a Westminster election was probable within the next eighteen months, many hopeful candidates began jockeying for position within the DUP. It was widely reported at the beginning of December 1986 that Belfast DUP councillor Nigel Dodds would run in North Belfast against Cecil Walker, while Jim Allister would fight Roy Beggs for East Antrim.[118] Possibly in an attempt to build his own electoral platform, Allister had become entangled in a public row with his party leader. This tells us as much about the extent to which Ian Paisley's internal authority had diminished as it does about the high-risk strategy being pursued by the former Assemblyman. Allister had criticised the conduct and tactics of Ulster Unionist MPs at Westminster, an attack which provoked his leader to condemn his colleague as 'foolish'. The row erupted after Allister had criticised Ken Maginnis for allegedly breaching joint policy by speaking on the Emergency Provisions Bill in the Commons on the evening of 16 December. Allister said that Maginnis's behaviour was deplorable and that if such action went unchecked by the leadership it would 'make a mockery' of the anti-Agreement protest. Paisley took the unusual step of chastising Allister in public after making it clear that Maginnis's intervention in the debate had been approved by both himself and James Molyneaux. Rejecting the suggestion that events at Westminster made the unionist parties look foolish, Paisley replied: 'It does not make anybody look foolish but Mr Allister. . . . He should have got in touch with the leadership of the party and then he would have known the exact position.'[119] Allister's political career did not recover, while Paisley had demonstrated that his primary goal was the preservation of the peace with Molyneaux and the UUP. This episode leaves one wondering how sincere was his involvement with Ulster Resistance and whether he would ever have followed through on his promise to lead 'the Ulster people' into battle in the fight to protect their common heritage. The articulation of his willingness to do so was the means by which he preserved the radical Protestant constituency, leaving Molyneaux free to satisfy the more moderate elements within the unionist community. Such sophistry was compounded by the actual tactics employed to defeat the AIA, as expressing one's loyalty to the state through disloyal behaviour and disregard for the laws of that state was a difficult if not illogical position to sustain. Yet, as Padraig O'Malley has argued, in an asylum insanity becomes the norm and irrationality may be the only sensible course of action.

> . . . in the past the threat of irrational action, i.e. fighting Britain to remain part of Britain was successful. In short, the threat of irrational action is a perfectly rational tactic when it achieves its desired purpose. The desired purpose in the present circumstance is to bring down the Hillsborough Agreement. It is, therefore, of little consequence to unionists at the moment if their actions to achieve this end actually weaken their position within the Union. They have a simple objective – not a grand strategic design. The latter, they believe will somehow emerge once the former is achieved.[120]

The tunnel vision which O'Malley identifies was not of course true of all those involved in the anti-Agreement campaign, as many sought (without much success) to begin a wider debate about the relevance of the unionist ideology in the 1980s. Peter Smith was one such progressive voice within the unionist community. As far back as December 1985, Smith had declared that unionists would have to learn to take a longer view if they were going to successfully defeat the Agreement and secure a lasting settlement which would preserve their interests. They may not have had much room for manoeuvre but they did have a fundamental choice to make.

> We can either retreat into ourselves and wait for Armageddon. Or we can take a long look at all the options and face up to the reality that funda-mental change requires a fundamentally new response. The objective must be not just to defeat the agreement but ensure that nothing like it ever happens again.[121]

From the unionist point of view it is a pity that Peter Smith's advice was not taken, as the subsequent history of the anti-Agreement campaign was riddled with progressive division in the joint pact and an abject failure to either damage the AIA or bring the British and Irish governments or Northern nationalists to the negotiating table on unionist terms.

A new year of protest against the AIA began with a series of bonfires throughout Northern Ireland to mark the launch of a petition to the Queen. However, reports of the event would suggest that enthusiasm for the tactic was lukewarm.

> About 20 fires lit up the night sky across the Province although most of them were poorly attended. Unionist councillors and MPs said the fires were symbolic and that a low turnout was no sign that opposition or anger at the accord had burnt out.[122]

While the leadership of the campaign were being admonished for running a lacklustre and unimaginative protest against the Agreement, there were those who condemned in equal measure, not just what the leadership had failed to do, but also what they had succeeded in doing. Jim Allister, for example, was quick to forecast that the petition to the Queen for a refer-endum on the Agreement would be rejected and that in the wake of such rejection, he hoped prominent unionists would face up to the 'inescapable requirement' for militant action.[123] Though there was a certain amount of ambiguity in this statement, as militant action could cover anything from industrial unrest to politically inspired murder, the general tone of Allister's comment was that the anti-Agreement campaign should get tougher, dis-pense with democratic conventions such as petitions, and use whatever extraparliamentary means as were necessary.

The fundamental problem facing the anti-Agreement campaign was that the unionist community had become accustomed to the AIA. Despite the rhetoric of the politicians, the new arrangements did not appear to threaten their everyday existence, or the practice of their religious or civil liberties. It consequently became increasingly difficult to sustain the momentum which the street demonstrations had given to the campaign. Looking back on the period, Peter Robinson accepts that the politicians did not sufficiently focus the protest on the people.

I think that if we had gone for it at an early stage the people would have responded. And one of the great difficulties with that campaign was that the nature, the way it was worked, left most of the protest to the politicians instead of giving the people something to do, and people therefore, just being observers, lost interest when the events became less interesting themselves.[124]

There was a fundamental difference between this perspective and that of certain sections of the unionist community upset by the sectarian by-products of the anti-Agreement campaign. A notable example of the difficulty in satisfying all parties within the unionist coalition was provided by a row which erupted between the Presbyterian Church and the DUP over the conduct of the petition to the Queen. The DUP reacted angrily to the passing of a resolution by the East Belfast Presbytery which expressed 'concern over the referendum canvass' and urged the political parties to give a clear undertaking that no records would be kept of those who refused to sign the petition. This statement by the Presbytery sparked off the obvious response from unionist politicians, Sammy Wilson commenting that it was a sad day when the East Belfast Presbytery:

> . . . started doing the SDLP and Alliance Party's dirty work and parroting the propaganda of republicans. . . . If the Presbytery have evidence of intimidation they should give it to the police and the political parties and we could identify the areas in which it is supposed to be happening . . . but if they have no evidence, they should keep their mouths shut. This is a political bid to scuttle the referendum canvass.[125]

Undaunted, Presbyterian Church criticism of the unionist campaign intensified towards the end of February 1987 when the moderator, the Right Rev. John Thompson, described unionist tactics against the Agreement as ill-conceived. 'Refusal to pay taxes, to attend parliament regularly, or to meet British ministers, while accepting all the benefits that accrue from the United Kingdom Government, is both counter-productive and morally questionable.'[126] Ian Paisley attacked these remarks in typical fashion, calling Thompson a compromiser who was advocating surrender 'dressed up in a robe of hypocrisy'.[127]

Public disorder

At the beginning of March 1987, Peter Robinson called for an escalation of the civil disobedience campaign, with a boycott of all rates demands together with television and motor licence payments. The renewed campaign was to coincide with the new public order legislation, which unionists saw as being a deliberate attempt to block all avenues of legitimate unconstitutional action open to them. Anxious not to be outdone by his deputy, Ian Paisley condemned the new public order legislation with an article in the *News*

Letter which declared that the new law was a product of the AIA, designed to destroy Protestant civil liberties. Speaking to the Young Democrats in Omagh, he declared:

> But now we see that the agreement is responsible for legislation which is destructive of our Protestant heritage and which removed a whole series of basic civil and religious liberties. . . . . A Protestant minister will no longer have the freedom to hold a religious open-air service and those who attempt to attend could also find themselves foul of these pro- posed laws. On the other hand, a republican flying the Eire tri-colour will have the same protection under the law as someone flying the national flag. These laws will have to be resisted with all the might of public protest. It must be said that Northern Ireland will not have enough soldiers, policemen, courts and jails to enforce laws based on tyranny and arbitrary power.[128]

Paisley's denunciation of what was to become the Public Order (NI) Order 1987 centred around its requirement that loyalist parades would have to give seven days' notice to the RUC rather than the five days demanded by existing regulations. This two-day extension may seem a rather trivial matter to the casual observer, but was regarded by many unionists as clear evidence of the hand of Dublin in the internal affairs of Northern Ireland and a particular attempt to inhibit Protestant civil liberties. Typically, Paisley responded to the impending legislation with defiance, advising that loyalist parades should not give any notice to the police in excess of that which they would normally provide. Once again this illustrates the cultural diversity within the ideology, as while Paisley and the traditional wing of unionism were incensed by the new Public Order Order, those of a more liberal disposition within the Ulster Unionist Party did not see it as an attack upon their way of life, but as a means of securing the rule of law in Northern Ireland. Michael McGimpsey recollects that the requirement to give the RUC a longer period of notification for parades was not a major worry so far as he was concerned.

> I don't see any problem, if you've got to give the police seven days as opposed to three days [notice for parades], then there's a one-day notice, but so what you know, you don't organise marches spontaneously. Alright, everybody should be allowed to march the streets, that's the first principle, but you're not allowed to march the streets if you are going to create civil unrest and disturbance.[129]

Peter Robinson, meanwhile, suggested that a series of freedom marches should be held across Northern Ireland when the new public order legislation was introduced. Robinson, speaking on 19 March, ruled out any further strike action against the Public Order Order, advocating instead that a series of 'acts of defiance' be held on the day that the legislation became law and that these should be maintained throughout the forthcoming year.[130]

In an attempt to regain the political initiative from the UDA and the Ulster Clubs and offset criticism from the ambitious and frustrated within their respective parties, Paisley and Molyneaux declared Saturday 11 April to be a 'Day of Defiance' against the new public order laws. This provides an interesting example of a situation where the UUP supported the DUP (albeit ambiguously) and agreed to the escalation of unconstitutional action, a fact openly admitted in a joint statement by the two leaders. 'There may be legal consequences for participating in such acts of defiance, but Ulster has a history of making sacrifices in defence of liberty.'[131]

The gauntlet was thrown down on 10 and 11 April, when individual politicians staged protest acts of defiance with MPs challenging the RUC to arrest them for defying the new Public Order Order. The MPs were scheduled to meet at the back of Belfast City Hall on 10 April in a united stand to set the scene for the Day of Defiance. However, a lack of co-ordination provoked criticism from hardline unionists, with the UDA saying that they were not consulted about the protests and would not be taking part in them. Harold McCusker urged people to break the law in the protests, but called on people to avoid violence or attacks on the police.[132] The UDA's lukewarm response to the Day of Defiance provoked a war of words between themselves and Ian Paisley on the eve of the region-wide protest. Comments made on the evening of 10 April by the DUP leader were seen as labelling loyalists not taking part in the action, including the UDA and Ulster Clubs, as faint-hearted. Paisley commented that the lack of enthusiasm of certain individuals for the latest protest was not due to apathy, or the fact that it had all been tried before with little success, but to their lack of personal courage and fear of the consequences of unconstitutional action. 'If people are afraid to take the penalty for defying this dictatorial law, that is just too bad. I'm not afraid. When it comes to action the men are separated from the boys. I have never asked anyone to do anything I would not do myself.'[133] The UDA responded to Paisley's taunt by saying:

> Mr Paisley has always managed to be abroad during critical periods such as the 1974 strike and during the struggle which raged for several weeks following last Easter. . . . Mr Paisley is correct when he says that, when it comes to action, the men are separated from the boys. Unfortunately, Mr Paisley has always been with the boys when action was imminent. Ulster has in recent years seen many would-be field-marshals who have, at the critical point, shown themselves to be field mice. Mr Paisley will learn quickly that Ulster people will no longer be used like Pavlov's dogs by people who have not the courage to fight, nor the intelligence and integrity to find a settlement.[134]

Paisley and many of his unionist colleagues soon found themselves facing the possibility of criminal charges over the illegal 'freedom march' through Belfast city centre on 10 April. This march was a dry run for the demonstrations planned in every constituency across Northern Ireland on 11 April. The MPs marching included Harold McCusker, Peter Robinson, Ken Maginnis, William McCrea, Roy Beggs, Clifford Forsythe, Cecil Walker, William Ross and the Rev. Martin Smyth, together with party leaders Ian Paisley and James Molyneaux. As an event, it was not that interesting, its most intriguing aspect being that three unionist MPs, James Kilfedder, John Taylor and Enoch Powell, were absent. Taylor said that he intended to lead a demonstration against the Public Order Order but he would not be breaking the law. As it turned out, the sum total of his activity was to hand in a letter of protest at Newtownards RUC station on the morning of 11 April whilst notifying people that there would be no marching either before or afterwards. 'We will simply gather outside the police station. I am totally opposed to breaking the law, even a law I disagree with.'[135] Taylor maintained that he had been given dispensation from his party leader to receive a delegation from the Northern Ireland meat industry in Strasbourg and thereby absent himself from the protest activities being engaged in by the rest of his colleagues. 'I am not opposed to what the MPs did in Belfast. It was simply that I had other urgent business and could not get back for it if I had wanted.'[136] In retrospect, however, Taylor appears less enthusiastic, commenting that token gestures such as the Day of Defiance were not an effective tactic.

> As far as the Day of Defiance is concerned, well quite honestly, I don't believe in one-day efforts. If you're going to have a period of defiance it should be a period of not just twenty-four hours. If it's only twenty-four hours, the authorities know they can sit back and do nothing and it's over at the end of midnight.[137]

The UDA were unimpressed with the latest attempt by the political parties to put pressure on the British government. John McMichael claimed that the apathy apparent on 11 April was a testament to the fact that the unionist leadership had lost the support of their community and thus their mandate to make policy for the unionist people. 'The lack of response to the call for a Day of Resistance particularly in the constituencies of the two party leaders can only be interpreted as an emphatic vote of no-confidence in their leadership against the Anglo-Irish diktat.'[138]

Fears began to emerge within the unionist leadership during March 1987 that the new Public Order legislation might split the main loyalist organisations over the coming marching season, due to the necessity to notify the RUC seven days in advance of all processions and demonstrations. Unionists were divided over their attitude to the new seven-day ruling, with Harold McCusker calling on his colleagues to ignore the new regulations in spite of calls from others in his party to abide by the change. 'I would appeal to all Orangemen to abide by the formalities that were in existence before the Public Order Order was passed. Then, traditional parades did not require formal notice and other marches a minimum of five days.' [139]

Paisley also called on Orangemen and other unionists to ignore the new directives on traditional parades and to ignore the seven-day ruling. However, his unionist colleagues John Taylor and Cecil Walker refused to take part or involve others in a law-breaking exercise. Taylor's reluctance to participate in the Day of Defiance illustrated a fundamental difference in his attitude to Westminster and the rule of law to that demonstrated by many of his parliamentary colleagues. He was asked, in light of his obvious disinclination to partake in the token law-breaking against the Public Order Order, whether he would obey the law even if it was a bad law. Taylor's reply provides further evidence of the cultural divisions within the unionist community and the way in which these often impacted upon political behaviour. It is clear that Taylor defined Northern Ireland, not as a separate cultural community where special rules of loyalty applied (a characteristic evident in certain strands of DUP political thinking), but as simply another administrative region of the United Kingdom.

> Well you see that was a law passed by parliament, it is the law of the land, and I accept the laws of the land as passed by the United Kingdom parliament. I didn't break that law, I didn't go to prison for example, I was the only MP who didn't go to prison. I don't believe in those kind of tactics, I don't think that suffering for two nights in a cold cell in the Crumlin Road [jail] is going to shake 10 Downing Street, and this is our trouble in the unionist family, they do these idiotic things.[140]

Reaction to the public order legislation illustrates the range of different opinions within unionism at the time, between those who saw it as a matter of little importance but a useful opportunity to motivate the unionist community and raise the profile of the protest campaign, and others who regarded it as anathema. The latter group viewed the Public Order Order as repugnant in theoretical terms, as a product of the AIA and thus Dublin interference, and in practical terms, as an attack upon the traditional civil liberties of the unionist community. Michael McGimpsey's recollection of the Day of Defiance would indicate that he subscribed to the first of these perspectives.

> I had no great conviction about defying it at all, I didn't see it as a point of principle. As I saw it, some unionists used it as an opportunity to defy the government, that they had tried all these other measures and it was only an anti-Anglo-Irish Agreement thing. . . . Maybe the Irish had a major input, I'm sure they had, but at the end of the day you have got to support law and

order and it's got to be a very crucial matter of principle for you to defy the law and I didn't see that as a crucial matter of principle.[141]

This contrasts sharply with David Trimble's perception of the public order legislation, which he denounced as a fundamental attack upon the Orange Order and the traditions of the Protestant community. It was not for him simply a semantic dispute over the number of days' notice to be given to the RUC in advance of street demonstrations, but was instead an attempt by the government to exert control over traditional Orange parades which had previously been free from such regulations.

The seven, five day, [notification] wasn't a problem. What was a problem was that certain traditional parades which had hitherto been exempt from a notice requirement were now being made subject to notice, because up until that Order a traditional parade was entirely free of any form of legal control. It was bringing traditional parades under legal control and that was consequently being interpreted – as that was the major change – we were saying, 'well they must be intending a major legal attack on traditional parades', and of course the majority, not all, but the majority of traditional parades are Orange parades. So people were saying, 'ah ha, they have decided to strike right at the heart of our dearest traditions.' That is what people felt, and that was their reaction to it.[142]

Trimble's attitude to the Day of Defiance illustrates a radically different view of unionism to that of colleagues such as McGimpsey or Taylor in that, although he did not contest the validity of legislation which came from the British parliament, he expressed a belief that he did not always feel morally obliged to obey the law. 'One has to say that what is law is what is enacted by parliament, and that's the case, that doesn't mean that there is an absolute duty to obey it at all times. I broke the Public Order Act myself a few times.'[143] James Molyneaux's recollection of the Day of Defiance was that the deliberate law-breaking by himself and his colleagues was a technical exercise consistent with their duties as parliamentarians. As they were not inciting their followers to do likewise, Molyneaux claimed that such action, since it was not indefinite, was a perfectly legitimate tactic in extraparliamentary lobbying of a dictatorial government who were bent upon trampling over the democratically expressed wishes of the Northern Ireland electorate. When asked whether he would defy a law if he considered it to be illegitimate, Molyneaux replied:

Well, no, laws made by parliament, you can make your protest against them, as we did for instance on the Public Order Act, we did a token operation there, confined to the Members of Parliament only, and we told everyone else we didn't want any of them to come out and break the law with us. . . . But the citizen, in my view, is under no obligation whatever to make a bad law work. He has to be bound by the law, he can make an initial protest, but he must not go around inciting other people to disobey the law.[144]

Paisley meanwhile, as he could not get at the architects of the new policy, attempted to 'shoot the messenger' by threatening to name police officers in parliament if he received evidence that they had been intimidating Protestants in the aftermath of the Day of Defiance. With typical if tasteless hyperbole, Paisley told a rally in Ballymoney that there was more freedom in Russia or in Nazi Germany than under the public order laws in Northern Ireland. He attacked UUP MPs Enoch Powell and John Taylor and Popular Unionist Jim Kilfedder for not attending the demonstration at the City Hall on 10 April, commenting: 'we will leave these people to one side and Ulster will go marching on'.[145]

In an effort to up the ante, DUP chief whip Jim Allister called for a series of rates strikes across Northern Ireland in the forthcoming year and urged the unionist leaders to make a clear commitment to step up the protest campaign.[146] The Rev. Ivan Foster meanwhile, speaking in Omagh, called for the termination of what he called the 'straightjacket' of the unionist pact. Foster also attacked DUP mayor of Ballymena Sandy Spence who failed to turn up for the rally on 11 April.

> The pact has failed to produce the necessary opposition to the agreement and it has failed to produce any real unity except of the worst kind as demonstrated by the DUP Mayor of Ballymena who appears to have imbibed some of the timidity of his OUP colleagues. . . . It appears that there is more concern about maintaining the pact than there is about opposing the Anglo-Irish agreement. At present the terms of unionist opposition are being dictated by the weakest members of the UUP since they must be placated in order to maintain unity.[147]

Foster was bitterly opposed to the idea of extending the unionist pact to cover the forthcoming general election as he feared this would smother any effective protest action by DUP members. Foster's attitude was shared by many of his colleagues in the party as Ian Paisley's authority was pushed to the limit over the issue. This row can be seen as evidence of the modernisation of the DUP, as a significant number within the party were no longer content to accept his leadership without question. Such a situation would have been inconceivable ten years earlier, when the party was little more than a political manifestation of the Free Presbyterian Church. In the 1970s Paisley's authority was unquestioned, either as moderator or as party leader, a situation he had achieved by creating the illusion that he was a synthesis of Moses and Nostradamus whose prophecies would always be fulfilled. In the latter half of the 1980s however, two factors were combining to diminish his control over both the policy and the personnel within the party. The first of these was the professionalisation of the DUP under the guidance of Peter Robinson, with an influx of well-educated young graduates into the party. The second factor which diminished Paisley's omnipotent position was his inability to do what he had promised and smash the 'diktat' on the anvil of Protestant political muscle. Entering a pact with the Ulster Unionists was a political necessity for Paisley, but bound him in the straightjacket of collective responsibility and prevented him from giving his followers what they wanted, namely a clear and simple plan to bring down the Agreement. The difficult balancing act Paisley had to perform between pragmatism and principle was read by many as vacillation and weakness. The new breed of ambitious career politicians such as Jim Allister, who did not feel that dissent was tantamount to heresy, combined with the old-style Free Presbyterians such as Ivan Foster over the electoral pact issue, to determine exactly how 'democratic' the DUP was. As it turned out, Paisley was not prepared to submit to any dissent on the matter. As the *News Letter* reported, he responded to this challenge by presenting his party with the ultimatum that they either defer to his political viewpoint or carry on without him.

> The Rev. Ian Paisley, in an angry table-thumping mood put his leader-ship of the DUP on the line at an executive meeting in Belfast that erupted in uproar. He apparently threatened to resign and at one stage a number of executive members stormed out in an unprecedented protest at his authority.[148]

Prominent members of the party opposed a proposal from the party officers for a joint election manifesto with the UUP. The *News Letter* quoted an insider as saying: 'It wasn't a leadership issue but a vote on party policy. But Mr Paisley jumped up, hammered the table and said "it is a matter of confidence in my leadership".'[149] The motion to maintain the pact was carried but not before pandemonium had broken out, with Paisley's colleagues accusing him of attempting to blackmail them into supporting him. Sammy Wilson said that while the meeting had been robust it had been democratic, adding that he hoped there would be no washing of dirty linen in public as this would play into the hands of the party's enemies. 'At the end of the day agreement was reached on policy and I assume all party members will loyally support it.'[150]

An example of the strength of feeling which the new public order legislation had aroused in the unionist community and the difficulties which this presented to political leaders was provided by an incident during one of the rallies which had been organised to protest against it. Under the headline 'Hot under the collar', the *News Letter* reported a fracas between Orange Order leader Rev. Martin Smyth and a Portadown man named Gordon Jackson. Smyth (who has commented that the public order legislation was 'one of the most devastating pieces of legislation . . . brought in, not to deal with republican parades but to give the Dublin folk some say over Orange parades)'.[151] was accused of assaulting the youth during a demonstration. The sixteen-year-old Jackson, who was a member of the Ulster Clubs, alleged that the South Belfast MP had struck him during an argument on 22 April. At a protest outside Stormont the youth criticised Smyth for his decision to comply with the seven-day ruling of the Public Order Order in the forthcoming Twelfth of July parades. Jackson chided Smyth that he would soon be inside Stormont negotiating terms of a settlement under the AIA, at which point Smyth told him to 'shut up'.[152] 'Mr Jackson persisted however, and Mr Smyth suddenly lashed out. He was restrained by his Official Unionist colleagues.'[153] Jackson said that he was merely exercising his democratic right to free speech and was considering taking legal action for assault. Whilst some may choose to say that only in Ireland could a cleric become involved in a street brawl, while others may interpret the incident as evidence that in Northern Ireland the Old Testament generally triumphs over the New, what was clear was the depth of division within the unionist community over the anti-Agreement campaign. *Ulster* magazine could not resist this opportunity to depict Smyth as a lukewarm Orangeman who was not prepared to match his words with his deeds and claimed that grass-roots loyalist opinion had swung away from the South Belfast MP:

> . . . many are now asking if they have been burning the wrong 'Lundy' all these years. An Orangeman of some 33 years standing described the Reverend as 'An unprincipled maverick of a bully-boy who attacked a Loyalist youth because the lad told the truth.' Being the leader of the Orange Order in name only is not sufficient and it is time that grass-roots Orangemen called for the removal of this coward, to make room for a leader with guts, and determination to win![154]

As for the actual campaign against the AIA, the end of April saw the preparation of a new initiative with the intention of bringing the protest to Britain. Code-named 'Campaign UK', it announced the launching of a national advertising drive sponsored by a number of unionist-controlled councils throughout Northern Ireland. Frank Millar declared that the campaign would involve a series of ten regional visits by unionist MPs to England and Wales. However, objectives such as highlighting 'the plight of the Ulster people' were extremely vague and unlikely to appeal to the radicals. In a characteristic display, Ian Paisley was making much more militant noises. Though he went along with Campaign UK, it is clear that his heart was elsewhere.

> Again let we warn the people of Ulster that the sooner they respond to my call to mobilise and prepare themselves for resistance by force, of the

agreement, the sooner they will destroy Thatcher's Judas Iscariot act of treachery. Sooner or later, whether people like it or not, it will have to come to a stand-up fight to the death.[155]

The effects of the new public order legislation continued to divide unionists during the summer marching season. The Orange Order itself appeared to be on the verge of a split over whether or not it should comply with the new regulations. It was announced in early July that angry loyalists were intending to stage a counterdemonstration to the main Orange parade to Drumcree in Portadown, scheduled for Sunday 5 July. The loyalists, some of whom were Orange Order members, were outraged by the decision of district officials to give the RUC the seven days' notice required under the Public Order Order. One protester commented:

> We believe the officials have gone against the decisions of their own men in Portadown. . . . The district meeting some time ago decided to give only the former five days notice to the parade, in protest at the Anglo-Irish agreement and also at police handling of parades in Portadown in recent years. . . . Then we heard that the Black institutions were going to give the full notice and it was then considered that the Orange Order should not be different. Many members of the Order feel betrayed by this.[156]

The Orange Order in Belfast, meanwhile, defended its decision to give police seven days' notice over its forthcoming Twelfth parade. On 8 July county grand master John McCrea said that, while Orangemen still had grave reservations about the Public Order Order, they were going to comply with the seven-day ruling because the system would eventually clog itself up. The premise here was that the requirement was so impractical it would not hurt the Orange Order to comply with it in the short term as it would not be feasible to continue such a practice in the longer run. It is difficult to say with any degree of certainty whether the Orange Order actually believed this hypothesis, though it is hard to understand how a two-day extension of notification would have placed an intolerable burden upon the RUC's administrative capabilities. However, it did enable the Order to climb down from a potential confrontation with the RUC during the marching season, a possibility which would have done nothing but damage to the unionist coalition and the anti-Agreement campaign. This desire of the Orange Order to minimise the danger of grass-roots indiscipline may provide the explanation for McCrea's rather optimistic hypothesis. McCrea's statement was treated with derision by DUP politician Jim Wells, who attacked the Belfast County Lodge's decision and described it as a disgraceful capitulation to Dublin rule in Northern Ireland.

> All denunciations of the Anglo-Irish Agreement made from Orange platforms next Monday will ring very hollow indeed when the Order's leadership have given a major boost to the agreement by complying with

one of its first demands . . . instead of carrying Orange banners at the front of the Belfast parade, Orange Order leaders should at least be honest with the people and carry white flags of surrender since that is exactly what they are doing by complying with Dublin rule in this province.[157]

This dispute created the bizarre situation where the Independent Orange Lodge were insisting, despite RUC reports to the contrary, that they were breaking the law. Independent Orangemen in the County Antrim village of Portglenone were determined to lodge their protest against the Public Order Order by holding their Twelfth parade without giving adequate notice to the police. County Antrim grand master and DUP politician James McClure rejected an RUC statement that adequate notice of the parade had been given, maintaining that only the normal five days' notice had been provided. 'We are determined to show our opposition to the new Public Order legislation and we had decided at Grand Lodge level to only give five days notice. That instruction, to my knowledge, was carried through.'[158] The Coleraine councillor rejected RUC reassurances and declared that he would regard himself as being in an illegal parade on 12 July. This unilateral action by the Independent Orange Lodge in Portglenone was in stark contrast to the policy of the Orange Order, which was to comply with the demands of the Public Order legislation until its internal contradictions proved its unworkability.

Electoral difficulties

Unionist factionalism increased in the run-up to the Westminster general election in June 1987, as the various protagonists hardened their opinions into alternative manifestos. One example of this came with the warning by Ulster Clubs chairman Alan Wright of the 'very real danger that the Unionist vote will drop' at the forthcoming election.[159] Wright was keen to attribute voter apathy to disillusionment with the unionist political leadership for their failure to establish a coherent and positive strategy for the anti-Agreement protest and it is clear that he had lost all confidence in the leadership of Paisley and Molyneaux.

> I feel totally let down, . . . I am just fed up. I have voted twice in the ballot box against the agreement, and twice with my feet at the City Hall in Belfast. The Unionists have had all the muscle a mandate could give them, but they have been ignored by the Government.[160]

The joint electoral pact remained intact in all but two constituencies, North Belfast where the outgoing MP Cecil Walker was facing a rival unionist challenge, and North Down. Walker commented that if returned he would not participate in a boycott of Westminster, and he urged his colleagues to do likewise. 'I don't intend to boycott Westminster. I am not an absentee MP and I don't intend to be.'[161] Walker was thus constructing a radically different political platform from his rival George Seawright, who played on his image as a loyalist firebrand and campaigned under the slogan 'The man who will not be silenced'.

A further blow was dealt to the unionist leadership on the eve of the general election, when the Rev. William Hamilton, the newly appointed president of the Methodist Church, dismissed them collectively with the comment: '. . . what a bunch. Some supporting anarchy, while others are content to play "trivial pursuits" with people's livelihoods and lives. If you have a vote tomorrow vote for compassion.'[162] If such criticism could be shrugged off by the unionist leaders as being unrepresentative of the community as a whole, the same attitude could not be taken to the results of the election, since their position at Westminster was weakened still further. In South Down, the outgoing UUP candidate Enoch Powell was defeated by the narrow margin of 700 votes by Eddie McGrady of the SDLP. The election results in general posed serious questions for the two main unionist parties in that they failed to reach the total number of votes cast for them in the by-elections of the previous year and in the general election of 1983. As Sidney Elliott commented in *Fortnight* magazine, the unionist strategy which set out to retain all fourteen previously held seats by putting forward an agreed candidate failed, due in part to Powell's defeat in South Down but also because they emerged from the election with a reduced vote.

> In the event, the loss of Enoch Powell's seat in South Down to the SDLP shifted the interpretation of the election, as in January 1986, to seats rather than votes. But the candidates party to the unionist pact altogether polled only 380,282 – 52 per cent of the total. This was 55,000 fewer than in 1983 and 38,000 fewer than in January 1986, when only 15 seats were fought.[163]

While the drop in the unionist share of the vote was seen by some (including Secretary of State Tom King) as evidence that their campaign against the AIA was losing support, the reality was rather more complicated. There is little evidence to suggest that unionists were becoming more amenable to the Agreement; many of them were simply frustrated at the way the anti-Agreement campaign was being conducted. This group of disaffected unionist voters fell into two broad categories, those frustrated and embarrassed at the ineffectual stunts and political own goals of their leaders, and a more radical group who took the opposing view that the campaign was too bland. This may help explain why the DUP share of the vote dropped from 14.6 per cent in 1986 to 11.7 per cent in 1987.[164] To conclude that the drop in the unionist share of the vote was the result of a growing acceptance of the AIA was merely wishful thinking on the part of the Agreement's supporters and architects. What was clear was that the anti-Agreement campaign was being mismanaged and that the two main parties were losing the support of the unionist community, whether this was from UUP supporters embarrassed at the violence which accompanied the civil disobedience campaign, or from DUP supporters aggrieved that the programme of street protest had decreased rather than accelerated.

In the two constituencies where the incumbent unionist MP was being challenged by another unionist, Cecil Walker of the UUP defeated George Seawright by over 8,000 votes in North Belfast, while in North Down, James Kilfedder survived an acrimonious battle. Prior to the poll, Kilfedder had claimed that a smear campaign was being waged against him by his opponents in North Down. The Popular Unionist leader maintained that he had been subjected to politically motivated harassment, both verbal and physical, on two occasions. He compared the tactics being used against him as being reminiscent of those employed during the rise of the Nazis in Germany. After his successful contest against Robert McCartney, Kilfedder marked his victory by accusing his rival of running a campaign of 'deception, lies, half-truths and smears.' [165] McCartney replied by commenting that: 'The man was showing all the signs, to put it kindly, of serious electoral strain.' [166]

The next aspect of the protest campaign to cause friction within the unionist pact came with the announcement on 5 October 1987 that the second anniversary of the signing of the AIA would not be marked by a rally at Belfast City Hall as had happened the previous year, but that the focal point of the protest would involve a lobby of parliament on Thursday 12 November. Possibly, the organisers' worry that another rally would be accompanied by the sort of violence which occurred twelve months earlier had been a determining factor in their decision not to hold a similar protest this time around. It is clear that there was little propaganda value to be had from such a demonstration, as it had all been done before to little avail. In addition, there was a risk that similar numbers may not come out a second time due to a combination of apathy from moderates and disillusionment from radicals. As the anniversary fell on a Sunday, the unionist leaders advocated holding a series of county demonstrations on Saturday 14 November. These would obviously be smaller gatherings than the previous year's Belfast rally; they would be more easily policed by stewards and less susceptible to infiltration by extremist elements from outside the area. This decision was heavily influenced by the leaders of the two main unionist parties and particularly by the Ulster Unionist Party, further illustrating the dominant influence of James Molyneaux over Ian Paisley. Molyneaux was delivering on his statement of a year earlier, that he would be reluctant to encourage mass street demonstrations in the future if they were likely to be accompanied by lawlessness and rioting. Whether Paisley was convinced by force of argument that a repeat of November 1986 would result in yet another propaganda own goal, or whether it was simply another example of the DUP leader's inability to take unilateral action which would wither on the vine without UUP support, is open to conjecture. What is clear is that the decision not to hold a mass rally in Belfast angered some sections within the DUP who were already frustrated at the low-key nature of the protest campaign. The former mayor of Castlereagh Cedric Wilson made it clear that some unionist politicians were going to go ahead with a rally at Belfast City Hall regardless of their leaders' wishes, as it was vitally important that the people of Northern Ireland should show the British government visually that they still said 'No'. [167]

The second year of the Agreement ended as it had begun, with resignations from disillusioned activists frustrated at the lack of coherent direction exhibited by those orchestrating the anti-Agreement campaign. The year had commenced in violent fashion with the mass demonstrations at Belfast City Hall marking the first anniversary of the Hillsborough deal and ended in a whimper, with an impotent display at Westminster.

It had been clear for some time that the Ulster Unionist Party were setting the political agenda of unionism and the DUP could do little else but follow suit. The lack of immediacy of the AIA was partly responsible for the UUP dominance over policy direction, as the wider unionist community were not as fearful of the Agreement's implications for their religio-cultural heritage as they had been in its first year. The realisation of many unionists that there was life after Hillsborough, when combined with the fact that Paisley's bellicose warnings of imminent Armageddon had failed to produce any shift in the British position, allowed Molyneaux to pursue his own policy, which was to wait for the internal tensions within the AIA to tear it apart. Molyneaux was convinced that the lack of significant improvements in both cross-border security and the administration of justice (the latter being in terms of the nationalist critique) would significantly dampen the ardour of the Agreement's supporters both in the minority community and in government circles. For Molyneaux it was this long-term attitudinal seachange which would lead to a policy shift by the British or perhaps even the Irish government and not the street protest, which was regarded by Ian Paisley as the only means of political leverage available. Molyneaux regarded the anti-Agreement campaign as the means of preserving the unionist coalition until the British government came to its senses and realised that it could not govern Northern Ireland without the consent of the unionist population. Paisley, on the other hand, believed that political unrest and threats of civil war would, as they had done in the past, successfully call the bluff of the British government.

The third year's protest against the Anglo-Irish Agreement was almost as notable for what did not happen as for the campaign of opposition which did exist. The widespread apathy of the unionist community (to the anti-

Agreement campaign rather than to the AIA, which was still intensely disliked) witnessed a decline in set-piece demonstrations. There was no intensification of unconstitutional action, much to the chagrin of many within the DUP, and there was only one street demonstration of any significance and even this was twinned with an Orange centenary celebration in an attempt to motivate the unionist community into supporting it and prevent further embarrassment. It seems clear from the evidence of the third year's protest that the political failures of the first two years of the anti-Agreement campaign had taken their toll. One potential avenue of progress, that of unconstitutional behaviour, ranging from exhorting their followers to drive on the wrong side of the road to the open advocacy of paramilitary activity, was closed off due to the disapproval of the UUP, while the other avenue of expressing popular support through mass demonstrations had become impossible to sustain.

The campaign of civil disobedience did labour on, though the political leaders seemed more interested in such token gestures of defiance than did their followers. An interesting episode in the campaign came towards the end of February 1988 when it was reported in the *Belfast Telegraph* that four Ulster Unionist MPs were going to prison in protest against the public order legislation, but were without their party leader James Molyneaux whose fine had mysteriously been paid for him through a Portadown firm of solicitors. Unionist Party headquarters issued a statement declaring that this had been done 'in defiance of his wishes'.[168] The fines were imposed for the MPs' participation in an illegal march through Belfast city centre the previous April. The four unfortunate MPs who did not have their fines paid were Rev. Martin Smyth, Harold McCusker, William Ross and Clifford Forsythe. Smyth commented on his leader's absence by saying that Molyneaux had 'most definitely' wanted to go to jail with his colleagues and he suggested that his fine might well have been paid by a government 'dirty tricks' department anxious to keep him out of prison thus minimising the propaganda value of the exercise.[169] John Taylor's recollection of this incident is rather less Machiavellian and he defended his own decision to resist the delights of Crumlin Road Jail by commenting:

> I noticed Mr Molyneaux didn't go to jail either incidentally. . . . It [the fine] was very conveniently paid at the last minute. Perhaps he thought along the same lines as myself! Mr Paisley of course, went [to jail], but then I think he thrives on going to prison every now and again you know.[170]

The latest in a dwindling number of organised set-piece demonstrations designed as part of the anti-Agreement campaign took place at Hillsborough in late October 1988. Speaking at the rally, the Belfast lord mayor Nigel Dodds commented: 'We reaffirm our determination never to allow this Ulster, which we love and for which so many have paid the supreme sacrifice, to be dragged under Dublin rule. This is where our fathers and forefathers stood. It is where we stand today.'[171] The *News Letter* reported that more than 20,000 Orangemen had demonstrated outside the gates of Tom King's official residence in Hillsborough on Saturday 29 October to say 'No' to the AIA. Significantly, however, the anti-Agreement rally was twinned with a celebration of the 300th anniversary of the departure of William of Orange from Holland to England in 1688 and his accession to the British throne. The most plausible explanation for this double-headed demonstration was the organisers' concern that it might be difficult to mobilise the unionist population simply to protest yet again at the AIA. Interestingly, neither Paisley nor Molyneaux was able to be present, as the Ulster Unionist leader was meeting the Friends of the Union group in London, while his DUP counterpart was in America. [172]

The significant aspect of this low-key approach was that the unionist political leadership could no longer mobilise the Protestant community. This accusation was denied by Ulster Unionist general secretary Jim Wilson. He declared that 'Our resistance to the diktat is as strong now as it ever was, although it may not be reflected in the streets.'[173] Maryfield (the centre of the secretariat) was picketed for an hour by a token loyalist presence, while at Stormont members of the Ulster Clubs laid a wreath at the Carson statue before handing a letter of protest to an NIO official. Three councils, North Down, Castlereagh and Ards, were represented at the gates of Maryfield. In typically extrovert fashion, Ian Paisley marked the third anniversary of the signing of the AIA with a torchlit protest march in Larne on the evening of 15 November. At the march the DUP leader claimed that Tom King was the 'blood-soaked ally of the IRA'. In his address, Paisley condemned the unionist politicians who were advocating talks with other political parties, accusing them of engaging in treachery against the Protestant people.

> Those, like Raymond Ferguson, eager to rush to Dublin can go. Those, like Ken Maginnis, eager to talk to the SDLP can go. But the unionist leadership will not be going back on their mandate – no negotiations until the agreement ceases to be implemented and Maryfield ceases to operate. The act of treachery has failed to produce peace, stability and reconciliation. Instead of peace – polarisation. Instead of stability – slaughter. Instead of reconciliation – rebellion. . . . We can not have it, we must not have it, we will not have it.[174]

Notwithstanding such stirring rhetoric, the November protest represented the final convulsions of a civil disobedience campaign which had been in its death throes for many months. Three years of unionist protest against the AIA had not only resulted in a cementing of relations between the British and Irish governments, but had also witnessed a further cultural separation and mutual alienation between Britain and the Ulster unionist community. The emphasis on street politics and civil disobedience was scaled down due to the leadership's inability to mobilise popular support within the unionist community. The final word on what they themselves would argue was an attempt to achieve political change through a demonstration of 'people power' should go to the current leader of the Ulster Unionist Party. David Trimble recollects that the anti-Agreement campaign was not able to sustain the initial level of support for the protest because this was not accompanied by successful results.

> We were able to mobilise opinion, which we did very effectively, but then of course, once you mobilise opinion that way, if there is no immediate results from that activity, people will then begin to lose heart, which they did to a certain extent.[175]

Notes

1   Rev. Ian Paisley, *News Letter*, 20 October 1986.
2   Sammy Wilson, interview with author, 20 November 1991.
3   John Alderdice, interview with author, 7 February 1996.
4   John Taylor, interview with author, 30 September 1991.
5   ibid.
6   Rev. Martin Smyth, interview with author, 22 November 1991.
7   Nigel Dodds, interview with author, 2 December 1991.
8   Michael McGimpsey, interview with author, 16 October 1991.
9   ibid.
10   ibid.
11   David Trimble, interview with author, 3 October 1991.
12   James Molyneaux, interview with author, 19 November 1991.
13   James Molyneaux, annual address to the Ulster Unionist Council, 30 March 1985.
14   James Molyneaux, interview with author, 19 November 1991.
15   Nigel Dodds, interview with author, 2 December 1991.
16   G. FitzGerald, *All in a Life* (Dublin, 1992), p. 497.
17   John Taylor, interview with author, 30 September 1991.
18   David Trimble, interview with author, 3 October 1991.
19   T. Wilson, *Ulster: Conflict and Consent* (Oxford, 1989), p. 194.
20   FitzGerald, *All in a Life*, p. 533.
21   James Molyneaux, interview with author, 19 November 1991.
22   Nigel Dodds, interview with author, 2 December 1991.
23   Rev. Martin Smyth, interview with author, 22 November 1991.
24   Michael McGimpsey, interview with author, 16 October 1991.
25   'Westminster sources said the unionist leaders warned of a possible loyalist backlash if she forged ahead with a reported agreement on a limited package with Eire.' *News Letter*, 2 September 1985, pp. 1–2.
26   ibid., 11 September 1985, pp. 1–2.
27   ibid.
28   ibid., p. 4.
29   ibid., 21 September 1985, p. 7.
30   Dorothy Dunlop, interview with author, 5 December 1991.

31   *Fortnight*, No. 233 (February 1986), p. 4.
32   ibid.
33   ibid.
34   ibid., p. 12.
35   *Fortnight*, No. 245 (November 1986), p. 3.
36   *News Letter*, 24 September 1985, p. 1.
37   ibid., 1 November 1985, p. 4.
38   ibid., 2 November 1985, p. 7.
39   ibid.
40   ibid., 14 November 1985, p. 17.
41   *Fortnight*, No. 230 (December 1985), p. 7.
42   *News Letter*, 15 November 1985, p. 12.
43   ibid., 16 November 1985, p. 3.
44   ibid., 18 November 1985, p. 5.
45   Garret FitzGerald, interview with author, 8 April 1992.
46   *News Letter*, 21 November 1985, p. 6.
47   ibid., 25 November 1985, p. 10.
48   James Molyneaux, interview with author, 19 November 1991.
49   Rev. Martin Smyth, interview with author, 22 November 1991.
50   *News Letter*, 6 January 1986, p. 6.
51   ibid.
52   ibid., 7 January 1986, p. 6.
53   ibid., 13 February 1986, p. 8.
54   ibid.
55   David Trimble, interview with author, 3 October 1991.
56   ibid.
57   Rev. Martin Smyth, interview with author, 22 November 1991.
58   Michael McGimpsey, interview with author, 16 October 1991.
59   Peter Robinson, interview with author, 8 November 1995.
60   *News Letter*, 1 March 1986, p. 3.
61   ibid.
62   ibid.
63   ibid., p. 7.
64   ibid., 3 March 1986, p. 6.
65   ibid., 4 March 1986, p. 5.
66   ibid., p. 3.
67   ibid.
68   ibid.
69   ibid.
70   ibid., p. 5.
71   ibid.
72   ibid., p. 12.
73   ibid., 13 March 1986, p. 8.
74   James Molyneaux, interview with author, 19 November 1991.
75   Sammy Wilson, interview with author, 20 November 1991.
76   ibid.
77   Nigel Dodds, interview with author, 2 December 1991.
78   ibid.
79   Peter Robinson, interview with author, 8 November 1995.
80   Rev. Martin Smyth, interview with author, 22 November 1991.
81   Peter Robinson, interview with author, 8 November 1995.

82 *News Letter*, 2 April 1986, p. 9.
83 ibid., 5 April 1986, p. 9.
84 ibid.
85 *Fortnight*, No. 236, (March–April 1986), p. 4.
86 *Ulster*, March 1986, p. 5.
87 Sammy Wilson, interview with author, 20 November 1991.
88 *News Letter*, 19 April 1986, p. 8.
89 ibid., 25 June 1986, p. 8.
90 ibid., 2 July 1986, p. 9.
91 ibid., p. 9.
92 *Fortnight*, No. 238, May 1986, p. 12.
93 *News Letter*, 21 April 1986, p. 2.
94 ibid., p. 9.
95 ibid., 26 May 1986, p. 1.
96 ibid., p. 2.
97 *Combat*, June 1986, p. 7.
98 *News Letter*, 28 October 1986, p. 2.
99 ibid., 29 October 1986, p. 1.
100 ibid., p. 3.
101 ibid.
102 ibid., 30 October 1986, p. 7.
103 ibid., 6 November 1986, p. 6.
104 ibid.
105 *Combat*, November 1986, p. 1.
106 *News Letter*, 11 November 1986, p. 1.
107 ibid., pp. 1–2.
108 ibid., p. 2.
109 ibid., p. 6.
110 ibid.
111 ibid., 13 November 1986, p. 8.
112 ibid.
113 ibid.
114 ibid., 14 November 1986, p. 10.
115 ibid., 18 December 1986, p. 8.
116 ibid., 17 November 1986, p. 12.
117 Sammy Wilson, interview with author, 20 November 1991.
118 *News Letter*, 15 December 1986, p. 4.
119 ibid., 18 December 1986, p. 3.
120 *Fortnight*, No. 232 (January–February 1986), p. 7.
121 *Fortnight*, No. 231 (December 1985–January 1986), p. 11.
122 *News Letter*, 2 January 1987, p. 3.
123 ibid., p. 10.
124 Peter Robinson, interview with author, 8 November 1995.
125 *News Letter*, 15 January 1987, p. 1.
126 ibid., 24 February 1987, p. 8.
127 ibid., 25 February 1987, p. 11.
128 ibid., 2 March 1987, p. 5.
129 Michael McGimpsey, interview with author, 16 October 1991.
130 *News Letter*, 20 March 1987, p. 8.
131 ibid., 25 March 1987, p. 1.
132 ibid., 10 April 1987, pp. 1–2.

133 ibid., 11 April 1987, p. 1.

134 ibid.

135 ibid., pp. 8–9.

136 ibid.

137 John Taylor, interview with author, 30 September 1991.

138 *News Letter*, 13 April 1987, p. 1.

139 ibid., p. 4.

140 John Taylor, interview with author, 30 September 1991.

141 Michael McGimpsey, interview with author, 16 October 1991.

142 David Trimble, interview with author, 3 October 1991.

143 ibid.

144 James Molyneaux, interview with author, 19 November 1991.

145 *News Letter*, 13 April 1987, p. 8.

146 ibid., p. 9.

147 ibid., 14 April 1987, p. 9.

148 ibid., 15 April 1987, p. 1.

149 ibid.

150 ibid., pp. 1–2.

151 Rev. Martin Smyth, interview with author, 22 November 1991.

152 *News Letter*, 23 April 1987, p. 15.

153 ibid.

154 *Ulster*, June 1987, p. 2.

155 *News Letter*, 29 April 1987, p. 14.

156 ibid., 3 July 1987, p. 10.

157 ibid., 9 July 1987, p. 10.

158 ibid., 10 July 1987, p. 10.

159 ibid., 6 June 1987, p. 7.

160 ibid.

161 ibid., 10 June 1987, p. 8.

162 ibid., 11 June 1987, p. 11.

163 *Fortnight*, No. 253 (July–August 1987), p. 11.

164 ibid.

165 *News Letter*, 13 June 1987, p. 8.

166 ibid.

167 ibid., 6 October 1987, pp. 1–2.

168 *Belfast Telegraph*, 24 February 1988, p. 1.

169 ibid.

170 John Taylor, interview with author, 30 September 1991.

171 *News Letter*, 31 October 1988, p. 16.

172 ibid.

173 ibid., 16 November 1988, pp. 14–15.

174 ibid.

175 David Trimble, interview with author, 3 October 1991.

CHAPTER 5

A Little Local Difficulty

It is clear that although there was widespread unionist support for the general objective of bringing down the AIA, there was from the beginning disagreement about the tactics which should be employed to achieve this common end. As there was no substantial edifice of the AIA which could be physically attacked, other than the Maryfield secretariat, unionists complemented their street politics campaign with a boycott of local government, education and health boards and other public bodies, as well as government ministers. As councillors were less concerned with the bigger picture and the general strategy of maintaining unionist unity, it was at the local level that cracks in the anti-Agreement campaign became most obvious. One of the first examples of dissent within the unionist campaign to boycott local government came when the lord mayor of Belfast, John Carson, attended a City Hall lunch despite the presence of Secretary of State Tom King. Carson's defence was that he attended in his capacity as a representative of Belfast and the office of lord mayor, and not as an Ulster Unionist politician.

> I have a responsibility to all the people of Belfast. In my role I have to be impartial. We must promote the city at all times and I felt I was doing my best for Belfast by attending this lunch.[1]

Carson was denounced by his unionist colleagues as a traitor and collaborator for deliberately ignoring the joint unionist strategy of boycotting government ministers. The UUP general secretary Frank Millar said Carson might well face expulsion from the party for his actions. 'I cannot say immediately that he will be [expelled] – that is not the way party discipline works – but his action has blatantly gone against executive policy as outlined earlier this week.'[2]

Ulster Unionist MP John Taylor recollects that he too had serious misgivings about the conduct of the anti-Agreement campaign at local government level. Taylor's view was that the policy of non-co-operation with government ministers or in local councils would not put the government under pressure and would only succeed in damaging their cause by dissipating what little support they had left in Britain.

> I was opposed to the initial stages of the campaign which involved boycotts. As you know, although I was an MEP at the time in Strasbourg, why even then I made the effort to appear at Westminster every week, and of course Enoch Powell was there every day. The rest of our colleagues of course took part in what was called boycott policy, both at Westminster and in our district councils. But I kept saying to them, 'look, I don't think it's going to make much of an eruption in 10 Downing Street if Mrs Thatcher's told that Moyle District Council isn't meeting.' You know you've got to get this thing in perspective, and it was a nonsensical campaign which of course, in time, unionists decided to abandon.[3]

In addition to the mass protest, non-co-operation with government ministers and the boycotting of Westminster and local councils, many unionist representatives resigned from the broader elements of local government. There was for instance a withdrawal of unionist councillors from the Belfast Education and Library Board in protest at the agreement, although not all were happy to do so. UUP member William Corry, the chairman of the board, claimed that he only joined the walk-out under duress from his colleagues, sparking demands that he should resign his council seat. Corry claimed outside the meeting that had he not joined the protest he would have been expelled from the party and that this was a counterproductive policy.

> It is not a satisfactory situation, when someone is told to do something rather than agreeing to do it. . . . I feel this policy is misguided. Unionists should be in fighting their case especially in education. The action is ineffective as well, because the board will go on as normal.[4]

This disillusionment at the UUP's decision to continue the pact with the DUP was felt very strongly at the local level, as after a difficult period in the early 1980s, Ulster Unionist councillors in Belfast felt that they had seen off the DUP challenge and had re-established their dominance in the city. Dorothy Dunlop, then a UUP representative in the Northern Ireland Assembly and Belfast city councillor, recollects that she was extremely disappointed that the Ulster Unionist leadership wanted to prolong what she regarded as an unsustainable and undesirable coalition.

> I was never on for the pact in the first place. After the elections of 1985 – the council elections – the DUP actually didn't do very well in comparison with 1981. They had had a big surge in 1981. In 1985 they didn't do so well, so we – particularly in Belfast – we were very much clearly the majority party by that time. And I was coming along the corridor of the [Belfast] City Hall, just at the end, at close of the declarations really, and I saw Jim Molyneaux and Ian Paisley standing together, making some kind

of a pronouncement that from now on we will go forward hand in hand more or less, and I took Jim Molyneaux aside and I said, 'what is this, what are you doing, tying yourself in with Ian Paisley like that?' 'Oh', he said, 'don't worry about it Dorothy, don't worry about it, it's just a loose arrangement, just a loose arrangement.' It wasn't, it was a lot more than just a loose arrangement. No I was very angry, because we had actually won a handsome majority over the DUP in that election.[5]

Fractures were beginning to appear in the anti-Agreement pact at local government level as early as January 1986. A dispute erupted at the end of January between Dorothy Dunlop, at the time chairperson of East Belfast Unionist Association, and the DUP, with Dunlop attacking the Democratic Unionists for their demonstration at St Anne's Cathedral against Cardinal Suenens on the eve of the Westminster by-elections. Dunlop blamed the low turnout in East Belfast for Peter Robinson on the activities of the Free Presbyterian zealots within the DUP and she went on to say that this had put the unionist pact in jeopardy.

> All unionists who genuinely believe in Christian love and breaking down religious divisions in our community will hope that our MP will dissociate himself from the actions of those public representatives of his party who were part of the Cathedral protest. If he cannot persuade them to see the errors into which they fall when they act so vehemently on such unfounded suspicions as seem to have sparked off their attack on Cardinal Suenens, then cooperation between the two unionist parties will indeed be in great peril.[6]

Dunlop was in turn criticised by DUP Assembly member for East Belfast Denny Vitty, who declared that her outburst was 'deplorable'.

> The unionist people at this time expect solidarity, determined leadership and a commitment to defeat the obnoxious Anglo-Irish Agreement. The electorate of East Belfast had a greater awareness of the issue than seemingly had Mrs Dunlop when 81 per cent of the voters registered their support for withdrawal of consent.[7]

By mid-February 1986 James Molyneaux felt obliged to meet the party's local government representatives in order to spell out the overall strategy and the way ahead. In fact he was forced to do this or risk a split in the unionist pact, not simply between the Ulster Unionists and the DUP, but also within the ranks of his own party. Many UUP councillors who had gone along with the boycott campaign out of loyalty and the wish to preserve unity, rather than any belief in the efficacy of the policy, were beginning to complain that the rules which governed their behaviour did not seem to apply to Unionist MPs or Assembly representatives. The UUP mayor of North Down, Hazel Bradford, did not hide her unease at the tactics being pursued by the party leadership.

> There is a degree of unhappiness that councillors are being asked to carry the banner while Assembly members remain in place and Westminster MPs carry out a role. . . . councillors have held the line pretty firmly but I believe they would like some reassurance that they are not simply cannon fodder and that their action won't be in vain.[8]

While Molyneaux's meeting with his local government officials alleviated some of the internal stress within the UUP, a further blow to the unionist pact was dealt shortly afterwards when a decision was taken by the Ulster Unionists not to resign their committee seats in the Assembly, despite the fact that the DUP had resigned theirs. Ian Paisley, Peter Robinson and Rev. William Beattie had all resigned in response to the government's refusal to allow civil servants to appear before the Assembly scrutiny committees. However, a UUP spokesman simply commented: 'We also condemn the NIO's blatant action but don't feel resignations from the committees is the right response.'[9] Peter Robinson reacted to this decision of the UUP chairmen and vice-chairmen of the six Assembly committees not to resign their posts by saying there was no division in the strategy of unionist Assembly representatives towards the anti-Agreement campaign. While admitting that there was a tactical disagreement, he commented that both parties were trying to achieve the same end. 'The Official Unionist Assemblymen's tactic is slightly different from our own but they also recognise Tom King's meddling and will not put up with it.'[10]

Allied to the fear outlined in the previous chapter, that unconstitutional behaviour such as the Day of Action would be morally repugnant to many Ulster Unionist voters as well as economically damaging, the UUP were also sensitive to the fact that the anti-Agreement campaign was becoming a chore for their own supporters. In Belfast, the loyalist adjournment policy, which was supposed to put pressure on the British government, was condemned by some for hitting unemployed and disabled people in the city. (On 19 November 1985 the eighteen unionist-controlled district Councils began an adjournment policy against the AIA and warned that they would not strike local government rates.) Twenty-five neighbourhood groups who provided a range of services for disabled, out-of-work constituents and pensioners were faced with closure as the adjournment policy meant that no money could be allocated by Belfast City Council from 1 April 1986, the start of the new financial year. Unease amongst Ulster Unionists at the policy is obvious from the following comment of Belfast councillor Alfie Redpath. Notwithstanding his caveat that short-term suffering should be accepted as the price for eventual liberation from the unwanted Agreement, his distaste for the adjournment policy is palpable.

> None of the members of my party are happy that we had to take this decision. We have no wish to damage the excellent work done by these

groups. However, we believe there is a more fundamental right at stake – the right to oppose the Anglo-Irish Agreement.[11]

Sammy Wilson's recollection of this dilemma, that in order to damage the AIA, unionist politicians were having to inflict wounds upon their own community, is characteristically strident and unambiguous.

> Well the fact of the matter was that the communities weren't hurt by it at all because there was a mechanism there whereby, if local government money was not being raised, a commissioner could come in. The government never actually did that . . . I can't think of any occasions when the main functions of local government stopped because of a shortage of money. Some groups may not have got grants, but . . . my view of a lot of the groups who didn't get grants was that they were never really necessary to the community anyway, and when they closed their doors, it was quite obvious they were wasting our money because nobody ever even noticed they had closed their doors.[12]

Problems with the adjournment policy

A major challenge to the unionist adjournment policy in local government came when the Alliance Party began legal proceedings against those who were preventing the councils from operating. This forced the issue, particularly within the UUP, as many councillors who were already sceptical of unionist tactics faced the possibility of being personally surcharged for being in contempt of court.

The allegation of disenchanted Ulster Unionist councillors that the local government boycott was hurting the very people that the unionists claimed to be championing was potentially more damaging to the Ulster Unionists than to the DUP. Aside from the sizeable chunk of middle-class Protestant support for the party, the UUP had a 'softer' vote than their DUP colleagues. While the latter often expressed the virtues of self-sacrifice and abstinence for spiritual rather than temporal gain, one of the central planks in the electoral platform of the former was based upon economic self-interest. Although it is difficult to generalise about voting behaviour, it would be fair to say that the UUP would be susceptible to a leakage of their vote if they were seen to be endangering the economic prospects of their supporters. As a result, the Ulster Unionists found the council boycott policy, and to a lesser extent the Westminster boycott, a much more difficult package to sell to their grass-roots than did their DUP counterparts. The following extract from a private letter sent to Jim Molyneaux by a leading figure on the Ulster Unionist group of Belfast City Council in April 1986 illustrates the unease with the council boycott strategy at local level.

> I think you will soon get another invitation to meet the Belfast City Councillors again. Many of us are increasingly disturbed at the damage

which we are being asked to inflict on our city in furtherance of the council boycott, and while it was vital that it should continue until we had downfaced the Alliance Party on the matter of the High Court action we are not now so convinced about its usefulness to the general campaign when it does not seem to be backed up by any action at Westminster.[13]

The councillor pointed out to Molyneaux that the boycott policy was increasingly becoming a political embarrassment because they were damaging the material welfare of their own people and delaying spending on capital projects in the city. The recommendation of this letter was either to end the pact with the DUP and return to the council chamber, or to continue with the council boycott on the proviso that Westminster MPs return to the Commons to lobby for their case.

> It would be better if we took a concerted decision, separate from the DUP if necessary, to go back before the cost to the rate-payers becomes too high. On the other hand, if we are to continue, as a back-up to our MP's, then we feel that it is vital that they should be at Westminster explaining what we are doing. On balance, I feel that if there is no positive result from Downing Street by May 1st, I must advise the [Belfast] City Hall group that the boycott is useless and they should go back to work.[14]

In response to what appeared to be the imminent disintegration of the council boycott strategy, the Ulster Unionist Party executive met on 24 April and issued the instruction that councillors were only to continue with the protest where there was no danger of court proceedings. This attempt at compromise by the leadership produced the ludicrous situation whereby UUP councillors who were in a minority situation simply abstained and allowed the councils to be run by nationalists while those in majority situations adjourned the council unless a court case was pending. At a Councillors' Association meeting held the next day, a debate took place to consider whether this instruction from the executive was acceptable. The following recollection of one of the councillors most critical of the boycott policy illustrates the extent of the division within the party over the local government strategy.

> I said to the Councillors' Association, 'You are the only people who can reverse this. You are the ones who are having your heads put on the line, but you are not making the decision. It's not a voluntary decision and it's no use looking to the executive to bail you out, they are not going to bail you out, the MPs are not going to bail you out. If you don't want to get into the situation, you have got to take the decision yourselves to avoid it.'[15]

The result of the meeting on 25 April was to continue with the boycott, although some of those on the losing side attacked the leadership for flouting normal procedures. Dorothy Dunlop recollects that the leadership attempted to get around a decision of the party executive in an effort to keep the adjournment policy and the pact with the DUP intact.

> Their decision was to continue with the protest. . . . But it was not a very democratic meeting. We had already had an instruction that we were only to continue with the protest where we were not in danger of court proceedings. . . . This was to come back to the executive on the following Tuesday after the Saturday that the councillors met, and the party leader and the party secretary – who was Frank Millar at that time – cancelled the adjourn[ment] meeting. They said we didn't need to hold this now, because the Councillors had had their own meeting and decided to go on with the protest. Now I don't believe that the party leader had that right, I don't think he had the right to overturn a decision of the executive, which was to hold another meeting before the date at which we were going to be in contempt of court.[16]

It is clear from the tension between dissident UUP councillors and the party leadership that the latter were committed to maintaining the joint unionist coalition with the DUP, even if that alienated a section within their own party. An effort was being made by both parties to preserve unity in the face of a common enemy – the AIA. However, when it came to discussing future strategies and how unionism should move forward with an alternative to the Agreement which would be acceptable to the British government, unity became a very rare commodity. Once unionists began to look beyond simple expressions of opposition and gave some attention to the development of their ultimate political goals, factionalism broke out within the unionist ranks.

Further criticism of the Ulster Unionist leadership from within the party provides evidence of the various cultural perspectives outlined in Chapter 2. The dispute arose when the Greater Belfast Young Unionist Association chastised the Glengall Street leadership over their decision to sever the remaining institutional links with the British Conservative Party. The association, which was then dominated by adherents to the gospel of political integration, condemned the insular attitudes being displayed by some of their colleagues and declared that the move was an insult to all those Tories who had supported their cause. 'These people are fighting our case in the face of the counter-productive boycott being carried out by many of the Ulster Unionist and DUP MPs.'[17]

While there appeared to be little common ground between integrationists and devolutionists over the future of unionism, a more immediate problem faced the joint pact at the beginning of May 1986 when five rebel Ulster Unionist councillors defied the leadership by voting to resume normal business at Belfast City Council. DUP members voted to continue the adjournment policy while one UUP councillor, Reg Empey, abstained. Crucially, the split in the unionist pact came hours before a High Court deadline which ordered councillors to resume business or face a £25,000 fine. The five rebels – Belfast lord mayor John Carson, William Corry, Margaret Crooks, Dorothy Dunlop and Alfie Redpath – were accused by their colleagues of betraying the party, the opposition campaign and the loyalist community. In moving the motion to resume business, Redpath stated: 'Our protests against the Anglo-Irish Agreement must not be a protest of rebellion because our people are not rebels. . . . methods must be found [to bring down the AIA] without wrecking and destroying this province.'[18]

The disinclination to rebel and the respect for law and order which are so deeply ingrained into the unionist psyche undoubtedly influenced the progress of the anti-Agreement campaign. The Rev. Martin Smyth recollects that the Protestant conscience played a major part in preventing the escalation of unconstitutional protest action as many unionists could not bring themselves to break the law, even when they considered it to be illegitimate.

> I think there has been a degree of inhibition in many people in Northern Ireland, because there are those who would want to go down certain paths, and because of their loyalty to Christ and their faith as such, they would not become willing murderers.[19]

Ian Paisley admitted that the protest campaign had suffered a setback after the events in Belfast City Council, but he maintained that the fight against the Anglo-Irish Agreement would continue, despite what he considered to be the treachery of the five UUP councillors. 'They have flown in the face of the overwhelming vote of the Unionist family, and decided to line up with the enemies of Northern Ireland.'[20] One of the rebel councillors Dorothy Dunlop, has pointed out that they voted for a resumption of council business because the boycott was a pointless exercise which put no pressure on the British government and would have dragged on indefinitely with detrimental consequences for Belfast and because the councillors were being placed in contempt of court by decisions taken by the leadership of the party rather than by themselves. In other words, one is only bound by collective responsibility when there is collective decision-making.

> There were big capital projects such as the Conference Concert Hall that were totally held up [by the boycott], and the government weren't going to do anything about that. I mean they were purely local government things but they were important to the city and we missed about two years as far as building the Conference Concert Hall is concerned. And I said to Jim Molyneaux, these are the things that are going to hurt Belfast, and he agreed with me up to a point, but he just shrugged his shoulders. The ordinary everyday running of the council was not a thing of any great significance, it could have gone on indefinitely if the Alliance Party hadn't gone to the courts.[21]

Dunlop pointed out that the decision of the Alliance Party to fight the boycott policy in the courts had put the unionist councillors in contempt of court, yet decisions over the local government strategy were being taken by the party executive. When asked if she felt any resentment at this fact and whether she believed that the Ulster Unionist Party was placing too high a burden on the councillors and demanding their complete loyalty, yet at the same time was relatively lax in enforcing the Westminster boycott, Dunlop replied:

> Oh absolutely, absolutely. I mean that was the whole thing about the contempt of court issue, because the decisions were taken, at least in the Ulster Unionist Party, by the overall body, the executive of the party, which meets every month in Glengall Street or every two months, representatives of the constituencies, but only a few of those people are actually councillors. So they were taking decisions for councillors that were going to put the councillors into contempt of court and hit their pockets etc. and get them disqualified and all the rest of it, and the Councillors' Association was extremely unhappy about it.[22]

Tempers within the UUP, raised by the difficulty of maintaining the boycott policy, were beginning to boil over by the summer of 1986, as the leadership found itself in the middle of both interparty and intraparty faction-fighting. On 20 June a further fracture appeared in the unionist pact at the local level with the eruption of a row between the Ulster Unionists and the DUP on Ballymena Borough Council. The DUP-controlled council was criticised by UUP councillor and Orange Order deputy grand chaplain, the Rev. Robert Coulter, who said that the pact was dead in all but name. 'As far as my Party is concerned the DUP has voted this pact out of existence.'[23] Coulter also accused the DUP of being reluctant to co-operate with his party.

> When we suggested that the position of Mayor and deputy-Mayor could be split between the two parties, all our approaches were spurned – what sort of unity is that? . . . The DUP was totally unbending so far as cooperation has been concerned. They could have been an example of unity to other councils and the electorate especially if they had at least given us one chairmanship of a council committee. . . . However, they have flatly refused to give us our place in the unionist partnership. They are happy enough to let the Official Unionists work in the United Unionist Action Committee, but when it comes to the representative positions, the DUP has blocked us.[24]

It would be inaccurate to suggest that these frictions were uniformly felt throughout the two parties, as undoubtedly personality clashes were in some instances disguised as policy differences. Nevertheless, much of the unity which did exist took the form of grudging forbearance rather than comradely co-operation, making the pact brittle from top to bottom. The violence and squabbling that surrounded the dissolution of the Northern Ireland Assembly on 23 June (from which more than twenty unionist politicians had to be forcibly evicted by the police) raised questions over the uneasy alliance, even within the hierarchies of the UUP and DUP where unity was easier to preserve than at the grass-roots level. Ian Paisley admitted that a difference in emphasis over protest tactics existed, but maintained that the two parties remained united in their opposition to the Agreement. The *News Letter* suggested that feelings were less ambivalent amongst Paisley's colleagues. 'It was clear, however, that many DUP Assemblymen were bitterly disappointed that only two Official Unionists joined them in their marathon protest sit-in at Stormont in the early hours of Tuesday morning.'[25]

James Molyneaux remained stoically silent over specific incidents such as this but it was well known that he took what was called 'the long view'. This was taken to mean that as long as the two parties agreed with each other in principle, they could vary in strategy and tactics to a certain degree. This brings us back to Molyneaux's broad perspective, namely that the existence of a united unionist front against the AIA was an end in itself. He saw the operation of the anti-Agreement campaign as a means of preserving unity and maintaining morale, rather than forcing the British government to abandon the policy. In his recollection of events, Molyneaux comments that he never regarded the campaign as a means of bringing down the Agreement, but saw it simply as an exercise in letting off steam, which had it not been released, may have been used for more destructive purposes. This strategy aimed to keep the protest alive until the British realised for themselves that the Agreement was not working.

> . . . we repeatedly said . . . that it never will be ceremonially burnt or torn up or anything like that, it will simply be a mumbo-jumbo. I could write the speech for the Secretary of State of the day, announcing that it was the end of it. He would say, 'Mr Speaker, time has moved on, this has proved to be a great basis for co-operation, however with the developments in Europe and in Eastern Europe, it makes sense that we should update our attitude to the Agreement itself.'[26]

This was less ambitious than the DUP view, which determined that civil disobedience would force the government to change course due to the breakdown of law and order in the region, while the withdrawal of consent to be governed as represented by the boycott policy would bring the government to its senses.

By the end of August a further split had occurred in the joint pact when it became clear that Ulster Unionist councillors in North Down had abandoned the council boycott policy. On the evening of 26 August the council voted by a margin of thirteen to six for a return to normal working, a decision which sparked an angry reaction from DUP members. The rebel councillors said that they were still opposed to the AIA, but that the boycott tactic had run its course.[27] This decision by North Down UUP councillors prompted a reaction from some party colleagues and from the DUP, who called for an escalation of the anti-Agreement campaign. The lord mayor of Belfast, DUP press officer Sammy Wilson, proposed mass resignations by councillors to show the NIO that opposition to the accord was undiminished. Ulster Unionist Councillors' Association chairperson Arnold Hatch said he was bitter about the North Down decision and declared that there would be a review of party tactics within the next few weeks. The decision by the North Down UUP to resume normal council business was attacked by Lisburn councillor Ronald Campbell who said that their behaviour was 'an act of gross betrayal and a stab in the back.'[28] The UDA, meanwhile, warned that it was impossible to maintain the facade of unionist unity if groups of councillors made their own policy independently of their party leaderships without being disciplined for doing so. In its editorial, *Ulster* criticised the North Down Ulster Unionists and concluded that such action would escalate if their behaviour went unpunished.

> Unity is strength. Everybody knows that much. To abandon the ship now while it is steaming forward is simply highlighting a yellow streak that must have always been just under the surface. These traitors must be isolated if Unionist unity is to be spared.[29]

By mid-September an attempt was under way to escalate the anti-Agreement campaign, with the DUP taking soundings over the willingness of members to resign their council seats. Discussions had already been held with the leaders of the various unionist party groups in council chambers throughout Northern Ireland, with the preliminary results suggesting that most if not all the 137 DUP councillors were prepared to resign. It soon became clear, however, that support for this tactic was not quite so evident within the Ulster Unionist Party. 'It is known that recently one leading party member admitted that they would be "lucky" if 20% of their councillors resigned in the joint-protest tactic.'[30]

Clearly the DUP were in favour of an escalation of the protest to a point where the administration of Northern Ireland was no longer possible. The Ulster Unionists were noticeably less enthusiastic about pursuing such a strategy. They were even less enamoured by the idea put forward by many in the DUP that constitutional politics was only the first phase of the anti-Agreement campaign. Whereas most Ulster Unionists would be unwilling to contemplate the breakdown of 'law and order' in Northern Ireland, many of their DUP colleagues saw this as a necessary and almost inevitable tactic, without which the British government would come under no pressure to change its policy and scrap the AIA. Thus, while UUP general secretary

Frank Millar urged the stepping up of the campaign through peaceful and lawful methods, the former DUP Assemblyman Ivan Foster suggested that loyalists might have to break the law to break the Agreement. 'We need to recognise that the Agreement will never be talked out of existence, or voted out of existence.'[31] Foster was speaking during a debate at Belfast City Hall which was then functioning as the unionists' 'alternative Assembly' set up after the Northern Ireland Assembly had been prorogued. The difficult relationship between the DUP and Ulster Unionists, which was already stretched to breaking-point, was not helped by the mischievous comments of maverick unionists such as John Taylor. The Strangford MP called on his fellow unionists to end the long-running council boycott and, in doing so, put himself in conflict with a UUP–DUP joint working party which was expected to recommend a mass resignation of council seats at meetings the following week. According to the *News Letter*, Paisley and Molyneaux were to announce proposals at these meetings which would intensify the campaign against the AIA and the paper accused Taylor of trying to disrupt the process and prevent an escalation of the protest campaign.

> Last night, however, Mr Taylor threw his own spoke in the mass resignation suggestion by describing it as the 'most hare-brained idea' he had yet seen. Speaking in Newtownards to his Constituency Association's executive, he warned that unionist opponents would either simply co-opt new members to replace unionist absentees, or trigger by-elections which could mean loyalists losing control of some town halls.[32]

Demonstrating once again that Ulster British mentality examined in Chapter 2, Taylor declared that resignation would not be in the interests of the unionist people as all it would achieve would be to hand local government power to nationalists and republicans on a plate. 'Resignation is a policy of political suicide. Unionists must never abdicate from their traditional role of service to the community. In despair we must not hand control over [to] the opposition.'[33] Sammy Wilson condemned Taylor's suggestion that the council boycott should be ended, commenting that he was doing the NIO's job for them. Wilson (who may have had his eye on Taylor's Westminster seat) suggested that the activities of the Strangford MP were even more damaging to the unionist cause than those who insisted on defying the council boycott strategy.

> As a politician of standing and experience Mr Taylor should know the effect of his suggestions when unionists call off their protest at council and Westminster levels, . . . this is just the kind of talk Tom King and the Northern Ireland Office wants to hear. It gives them heart and encourages them to continue to push unionists in the hope that cracks will appear and widen. . . . His careless talk only serves to make our job harder and it is good to see that very few are prepared to support him.[34]

During the course of all this squabbling, Paisley and Molyneaux held a meeting on 23 September and decided that the mass resignation of unionist councillors, which had been proposed earlier in the campaign, would not now be contemplated until after the first anniversary of the signing of the Agreement.[35] The most plausible explanation for this decision was that Molyneaux could not provide a guarantee to Ian Paisley that UUP councillors would support the resignation tactic. He was having enough difficulty in preventing the disintegration of the UUP's council boycott policy and may not have been convinced that sufficient numbers of his councillors would be willing to resign their seats. Paisley for his part did not want any further fractures to appear in the pact and most importantly did not want the DUP to embark upon any unilateral expeditions. In an attempt to offset the growing impression that the pact was breaking up, Molyneaux and Paisley agreed to tighten disciplinary procedures on both UUP and DUP councillors who refused to obey the party line. Letters were issued to the 350 unionist councillors in the North which told them to abide by official policy decisions or suffer the consequences. Paisley made it clear that anyone who refused to follow party directives risked being thrown out of their party.

> Any councillor, whether he be a member of the DUP or the Ulster Unionist Party, who fails to keep the party line, who dissents from the party line, or who votes in opposition to the party line, will be very seriously dealt with – that means possible expulsion.[36]

An attempt was made by the leadership to pacify the grass-roots by holding a 'talk-in' between the two party leaders and local government councillors. This was to centre on how the councillors saw the local government protest progressing in the approach to the first anniversary of the AIA. Essentially it was to act as a means by which dialogue could take place between the leadership and the local councillors. The 'talk-in' was held on the eve of Belfast City Council's monthly meeting and was not attended by the five Ulster Unionist rebel councillors who had voted in June for a resumption of normal business as they had lost the party whip and were prevented from attending.[37]

The threat issued from the unionist leadership to impose sanctions upon those councillors who insisted upon dissenting from party policy was realised when seven rebel Ulster Unionist councillors were expelled from the party. An eighth member, Belfast Education and Library Board chairperson William Corry, was suspended from the party '. . . until such time as he gives a written undertaking to adhere to Party policy'. Those expelled were five North Down members, Bruce Mulligan, Rev. McConnell Auld, Jack Preston, George Green and Samuel Hamilton and two members from Carrickfergus, Mollie Ardill, and Robert Patton. Ardill said she was 'absolutely shattered' by the news, though she claimed she had no choice but to attend the meeting and strike a district rate. 'It would have been totally illegal for me not to do. I was elected as a public representative and could not step outside the law.'[38] The seven rebels, who did not attend the disciplinary meeting, were expelled *in absentia* after the following formal statement by the party's disciplinary committee.

> In the absence of the seven councillors, and in the absence of any case in mitigation, or any assurance about their future conduct, the committee found the said councillors guilty and imposed a penalty of immediate expulsion from membership of the Ulster Unionist Party.[39]

One of the rebels, Robert Patton, said that he was quitting the party before they had a chance to expel him. The Carrickfergus councillor said he would be submitting a letter of resignation to Glengall Street and would remain in the council as an independent.[40] The North Down councillor Rev. McConnell Auld said that many Ulster Unionist councillors were conducting business covertly and he criticised the party's disciplinary committee for beginning a 'witch hunt' to root out those who believed in democratic politics rather than civil unrest. He maintained that all unionist councillors were opposed to the Anglo-Irish Agreement, but emphasised that debate in council chambers and at Westminster was the democratic way to get rid of it. Warming to his theme, Auld went on to say that the tactics of the unionist leadership seemed designed to

> . . . incite street violence leading up to the anniversary of the signing of the Anglo-Irish Agreement. . . . Continuous policy to adjourn council business is illegal under the Local Government Act. Also it is illegal to attempt to intimidate anyone into breaking the common law. Is the decision of the disciplinary committee such an illegal act?[41]

Auld also pointed out that as a member of the clergy he was unable to contradict the Christian ethic which demanded obedience to the government, the payment of taxes and freedom of conscience. 'The Ulster Unionist Party policy to bring local government to a standstill and the refusal to pay rates are directly contrary to the word of God.'[42] This was of course an interpretation of his role which differed starkly with that provided earlier by Ian Paisley. This demonstrates once again the important role religion plays in unionist politics, not in terms of theological wrangling but rather in the way in which spiritual beliefs influence political behaviour. Whereas Auld placed an emphasis upon obedience of central authority, Paisley took a more aggressive stance, maintaining that as foot-soldiers for Christ they had a duty to disobey temporal authority if this was found to be in conflict with the 'Word of God'. Needless to say, Paisley conferred upon himself the qualities and qualifications necessary to determine this issue.

The general pattern of interparty conflict during this period was characterised by DUP attacks on their Ulster Unionist colleagues for giving in and returning to normal council business. In October 1986, however, Castlereagh Council witnessed the figurative 'man bites dog' scenario when Belfast UUP councillors accused their DUP colleagues in Castlereagh of breaching the local government boycott.

> The fragile Official Unionist/DUP pact was exposed yesterday [22 October] when Belfast Official Unionist councillors confronted Castlereagh members for holding a special meeting. They protested that the meeting, to overturn the decisions taken by a one-day commissioner last week, was in breach of a directive issued by the two leaders, James Molyneaux and Ian Paisley, that no council business was to take place before November 15.[43]

The hardline maverick Denny Vitty, a former DUP Assembly member, said it had saddened him that some Ulster Unionists had 'neither the ability nor the brains' to appreciate what their Castlereagh colleagues were attempting to do. The UUP general secretary Frank Millar used the opportunity to hoist the DUP on their own petard, criticising the councillors for disloyalty to their unionist colleagues.

> We do have sufficient common sense to know when a directive is exactly that. . . . that directive instructed all local government councillors not to transact any business before November 15. It is wrong that there should be exceptions, and I can understand how the Belfast Members felt. . . . as far as we were concerned, no business means no business, and it is totally wrong that a certain section should go its own way.[44]

Despite Paisley's announcement that the Castlereagh meeting had been cleared by himself and James Molyneaux, it was later admitted by the UUP leader at a meeting of his party councillors that he had given no such clearance and had not even discussed the issue with Paisley before the council meeting. Jim Kirkpatrick, secretary of the Ulster Unionist group in Belfast City Council, commented after the meeting with Molyneaux that Peter Robinson, the mayor of Castlereagh, had persisted in going ahead with the contentious meeting before obtaining the clearance to do so and had thereby jeopardised the joint pact and the whole anti-Agreement campaign.

> We were very frustrated by the whole situation and feelings were running high . . . but the meeting has cleared the air and the only anger voiced at it related to the DUP's foolishness in risking the dismantling of the Unionist pact . . . we want to see the DUP working with us against the Agreement, especially in Belfast, and stopping the sort of one-upmanship that Mr Robinson and his colleagues obviously engaged in last week.[45]

Not everyone was quite so sanguine. There was clear unease within the ranks of Ulster Unionist councillors, who worried that their leader would shortly ask them to resign their council seats. Molyneaux had declared at Belfast City Hall that the abstentionist tactic had outlived its usefulness and, while it was widely viewed as a negative policy within the ranks of UUP councillors, many such as Omagh Council member William Thompson were worried that resignation would be worse, handing control of the councils over to nationalists. Under the headline 'We will not quit' the *News Letter* reported that councillors across Northern Ireland had refused to follow an instruction from the unionist leadership to resign their council seats.

> Worried councillors in both the Official Unionist Party and DUP were saying that now that they had considered fully the consequences of a total withdrawal from the Provinces's 26 district councils a halt had to be made to a move that would result in 'absolute disaster' for the loyalist community.[46]

Belfast high sheriff Herbert Ditty summed up the feelings of many of his colleagues with characteristic bluntness:

> The unionist electorate would never forgive us if we sold Ulster out in this way. In Belfast, the capital city of Northern Ireland, we would be handing over power to a crowd of republicans and if this happened loyalists would have no alternative but to bail out.[47]

It was soon obvious that a significant number of Belfast councillors were opposed to the resignation tactic, including former lord mayor Tommy Patton, Jim Kirkpatrick, Dixie Gilmore and Fred Proctor. Additionally, all four Independent Unionists were hostile, Frank Millar, Joe Coggle, Ted Ashby and Hugh Smyth. Once again unionists found that the only way they could register their opposition to the AIA was through actions which ultimately damaged their own political position and could be seen by everyone to be of no material benefit to the community they sought to represent. The Independent Unionist Frank Millar Snr summed this tactic up with the following observation.

> Any unionist who walked out of a council and allowed republicans to take over would be guilty of treachery. This is a mad-cap idea and absolutely nothing will be achieved by it. I for one will not be walking out and I am glad to know there are a number of other unionist councillors who think like me, even if it means being thrown out of the party.[48]

Once again it is clear that unionists were divided in their analysis. Sammy Wilson, speaking at an Ulster Resistance rally in Derry, took the opposite view, declaring that the only way forward was to make Northern Ireland totally ungovernable.

> Rather than talking, unionists must show themselves prepared to withdraw completely from political life in this Province. . . . The advice of both Mr

James Molyneaux and the Rev. Ian Paisley to withdraw from nominated boards and local government should now be heeded. There are many benefits from this course of action. Firstly, it would be an indication that we have no intention of coming to terms with this agreement. Secondly such action would leave local government totally unrepresentative and would without doubt force the closure of councils all over the Province.[49]

In late November a meeting was held at Glengall Street between the UUP councillors and the party leadership in an attempt by the latter to secure support for the resignation tactic. The meeting, held on Wednesday 26 November and attended by 126 out of the party's 190 councillors, ended with a clear majority voting to continue operating on the councils. It was decided by 82 votes to 44 to reject the recommendation of the party executive and remain in the councils.[50] Under the headline 'Molyneaux shrugs off "slap in face"' the *News Letter* reported Molyneaux's attempt to repair the damage to his dented authority as Ulster Unionist leader and his efforts to heal the rift in the pact which had opened over the council adjournment split. He said that he was determined to carry through the anti-Agreement policy whatever obstacles were thrown in his way.

> I don't pretend to like the kind of situation where a segment of the party refused to accept my guidance. But it is up to me to ensure that the campaign against the Anglo-Eire agreement is in no way weakened.[51]

Molyneaux rejected the allegation that the defeat was in any way a personal crisis for his leadership, saying: 'It was a defeat for sensible recommendations made by the councillors' own executive, with my support.'[52] Forty-eight hours after the Glengall Street decision, however, four leading Ulster Unionists came to the aid of their party leader by resigning from key council and education board positions. Dr William Brownlees, deputy leader of Ballymena Borough Council, tendered his resignation to Molyneaux, as did Arnold Hatch, chairperson of the Unionist Councillors' Association and a member of Craigavon Council. East Antrim MP Roy Beggs formally resigned as chairman of the North Eastern Education and Library Board, while UUP councillor Ron Jackson resigned from Castlereagh Borough Council. As for the DUP, the way was led by Peter Robinson who resigned as mayor of Castlereagh. A mass resignation of DUP councillors followed after a meeting of their party's executive on 31 November. Within the space of a week eight more Ulster Unionist councillors had submitted their resignations to James Molyneaux, bringing the total number of councillors 'on hold' to twenty. It was understood that eighteen more letters of resignation were imminent. These resignations like those which went before were 'letters of intent' which Molyneaux was empowered to use whenever he believed the time was right to do so. The term 'unionist sleeper' was never more appropriate. One of those councillors who had submitted a letter of intent, Alderman Ronnie Campbell of Lisburn Borough Council, told the Magheragall Ulster Unionist branch on 5 December that he was disappointed many of his fellow councillors had not been prepared to make the necessary sacrifice. 'I find it sad that a section of our party has been responsible for breaking up a united unionist opposition to the agreement.'[53]

Despite the existence of pockets of support within the UUP for the resignation policy, it was to prove to be an uphill struggle for the unionist leadership for two reasons. Firstly, it was a symbolic gesture which went against the grain of many UUP councillors who had entered local politics to achieve some practical objectives for their community. Secondly, by this point in the anti-Agreement campaign, grass-roots activists had grown disillusioned with their leadership due to the tactical compromises necessitated by the pact and the lack of success of the campaign generally. In other words, morale was low and momentum was non-existent. Leaders who in different circumstances might be able to rally their troops with the declaration that one more push would secure victory, were by this stage preaching to the unconverted. In November 1985 Ulster said 'No': by November 1986 however, Ulster had had enough. In David Trimble's recollection he implicitly accepts this judgement and suggests that the resignation strategy was hampered by the frustration felt by many individual councillors at the apparent impotence of the campaign to achieve any tangible results leaving them unwilling to embark upon another failed enterprise.

> It might have been better, in retrospect, to have jumped straight into that at the deep end and immediately called for whole-scale resignations at the same time as the Members of Parliament were resigning, rather than to do it by stages, because, some of the councillors were saying, by the time the leaders were asking for resignations, 'the campaign isn't going to succeed, so what's the point?'[54]

The anti-Agreement campaign appeared to be in chaos when on the evening of 5 January 1987 Ulster Unionist councillors staged a walk-out from Belfast City Council which effectively terminated the adjournment policy. Nine UUP councillors, including former lord mayor John Carson, walked out of the meeting before a DUP proposal that the council should continue to adjourn meetings in protest against the AIA had been voted upon. With the Ulster Unionists absent, SDLP and Alliance members voted by 22–14 against the DUP motion and, despite the latter's attempt to prevent the return to normal business with a combination of filibustering and interjections, 'normal service' was resumed. Fred Cobain, chairman of the Ulster Unionist group on the council, defended his colleagues' decision to walk out and claimed rather lamely that it was a tactical manoeuvre to thwart the NIO rather than a capitulation. Cobain asserted that it was party policy that councils in trouble with the courts should do limited business to avoid councillors being personally surcharged and to ensure that they did not, as he put it, become 'contempt of court fodder'.[55] However, if this was the position how do we explain the fact that the very same night as the Belfast adjournment policy collapsed, the UUP-controlled councils in Larne and Carrickfergus suspended business in defiance of threatened legal action, while Banbridge and Ballymena councils also adjourned their meetings? The action of Ulster Unionist councillors in Belfast confirmed the worst fears of many DUP members that their Glengall Street colleagues did not have the will to pursue the fight against the Agreement when the going got tough. Cobain denied DUP allegations that the UUP had taken their decision due to the fear of legal proceedings and with one eye on their bank balances.

> We have been in contempt of court since February. If we are to be fined we will be fined on our record. We are not running away. . . . Official Unionists believe the adjournment policy has run its course and that something new is needed . . . we hope that tactic is that the unionist community withdraws total consent.[56]

DUP councillor Nigel Dodds was rather less sympathetic, admitting that the decision of the Ulster Unionists in Belfast City Council had damaged the anti-Agreement protest and expressing his disbelief that they could alter their local government policy in such a brazen manner.

> I do regard the walkout as a major setback. I don't believe they could say one thing 12 months ago and do another now. . . . the decision has left us in a minority. It is a sad day whenever that has happened.[57]

Friction was intensified by the failure of Ulster Unionists who held positions on the Belfast Education and Library Board to resign on 5 January in contravention of Party orders to that effect. The following account illustrates how the local government campaign had degenerated to the point that it was beyond parody:

> . . . the four unionists present demanded payment for a board meeting last week. They had turned up intending to stage a boycott, only to find it was cancelled. The councillors Billy Blair, Tommy Patton, Joe Coggle and John Parkes walked out after losing a resolution that the meeting be adjourned by 16 votes to four. DUP Councillor Sammy Wilson – the Lord Mayor of Belfast – arrived 20 minutes later and told the meeting he had turned up to prevent the board suspending him for non-attendance before he could resign. . . . When the adjournment vote was lost its Official Unionist proposer, Mr Blair, left wishing members a Happy New Year.[58]

As a result of the collapse of the adjournment policy in Belfast and the lack of united action with regard to resignation from the Belfast Education and

Library Board, a crisis meeting was called to reconcile the differences of those involved in the protest campaign. The emergency meeting between the two sets of councillors was held on Monday 12 January at the instigation of James Molyneaux and party general secretary Frank Millar. Millar was understandably infuriated at the decision of his Ulster Unionist colleagues to resume business as this had made it extremely difficult for him to preserve the unionist coalition in any meaningful form. He commented that there was no question of the Official Unionist–DUP pact being terminated, but that local government had to be sorted out 'once and for all'.[59] Rather appropriately, Millar was frank in his assertion that the anti-Agreement campaign was going less than smoothly at local level and required a much greater degree of consistency if it was to have any realistic future.

> My view is that the present situation is a shambles . . . I am not specifically referring to Belfast but it does reflect the indiscipline which has undermined the bulk of the campaign and councillors bear considerable responsibility for this. . . . Councillors have to make their minds up, in conjunction with the leadership of the two parties, as to how they will heighten their campaign or the local government part of the campaign against the agreement will slide away.[60]

Millar denied reports that the forthcoming meeting of the ten Ulster Unionist MPs and chairmen of the party's constituency associations was anything other than a strategy meeting in preparation for a general election which was likely to occur within the year. The meeting of Ulster Unionist and DUP councillors on 12 January was a success to the extent that agreement was reached between the two sides over the future of the local government protest policy. The new strategy hammered out between the local government officers of the two parties at the UUP headquarters in Glengall Street was a compromise agreement which fell between adjournment of business and complete withdrawal from the councils.[61] The formula eventually arrived at allowed the UUP to attend just one district council meeting and then adjourn until the last meeting in 1987, thus creating a *de facto* rather than a *de jure* withdrawal from council business.

Regardless of such agreements, it was proving to be increasingly difficult to disguise the fault lines in the unionist pact. The tension between the two main unionist parties exposed by the lack of success which had characterised the anti-Agreement campaign was given a thorough airing in the media despite the yearning for unity within the hierarchies of both parties. Under the alliterative headline 'Former MP blasts the feuding factions', the *News Letter* reported criticism by former Newry and Armagh MP Jim Nicholson of his unionist colleagues for their public bickering and faction-fighting. He issued a blunt warning that this would prove detrimental to their own interests and the unionist case in general.

> If you persist there will be no unionist-held seats to argue over. . . . Council
> tactics will be of little consequence, for the union will have gone and both
> unionist parties will disappear for they will have failed those who elected
> them.[62]

Despite Nicholson's plea the interparty squabbling continued, while
rumours began to circulate that the DUP were ready to terminate the pact
and pursue a more radical policy against the Agreement. Under dramatic
headlines such as 'Defiant DUP threatens to go it alone', the local media
reported that DUP councillors were threatening to take unilateral action if
Ulster Unionists rejected the latest local government protest tactics. The
News Letter suggested that DUP members were becoming impatient with
their Ulster Unionist colleagues and quoted one as saying that UUP
councillors should either obey their executive and resign or capitulate
totally, instead of prevaricating over the matter.

> This confusion has gone on too long. The Official Unionist leader made it
> very plain that he wanted his councillors to resign. They have not come up
> with any decent alternative and now they should do the honourable thing
> and resign. . . . I think some Official Unionists do not realise that if they do
> not accept fresh proposals then they might as well throw in the towel and go
> back to the normal business. That is when we will part company, for I can
> think of no DUP councillor who is prepared to do that.[63]

Despite such ultimatums, the two main parties could not agree on a common
approach to the role local government should play in the anti-Agreement
protest. This division was illustrated in the aftermath of a meeting between
the two sides on the evening of 19 January, when disagreements emerged
between the DUP and Ulster Unionists over the next round of action
against the AIA. The DUP rejected the previously agreed formula which
allowed the UUP to attend just one district council meeting and then
adjourn until the last meeting in 1987. Castlewellan DUP member of
Carrickfergus District Council Ethel Smyth walked out of the meeting,
commenting that the proposal was a watering down of the adjournment
policy.[64] It appeared at this point that joint action in Northern Ireland's
council chambers by the main unionist parties was on the verge of collapse,
a fact admitted by Frank Millar after the breakdown of his negotiations to
establish an agreed strategy with the DUP over the local council protest.
Millar admitted that the situation was far from satisfactory.

> [The] whole thing is a mess. . . . We have now got to decide, is there going
> to be a local government protest or is there not. We do know that it cannot
> possibly carry on the way it is going now. We have got to cut through a lot
> of this bluff. . . . There has been a lot of one-upmanship in attempts to win
> or gain advantage for local personalities and that has afflicted local govern-
> ment protest from the beginning. There are faults and guilt on both sides.[65]

The widening gulf between the two main unionist parties on Belfast City Council was again illustrated when three Ulster Unionists, along with Independent Unionist Frank Millar Snr, approved the proposed rate for the coming year at a meeting of the General Purposes and Finance Committee, while the chairman and DUP leader on the council Nigel Dodds and his party colleague Ted Ashby voted against. Dodds commented that a pact existed in name only, with both parties operating as completely separate units with no common strategy and very little communication taking place between the two.

> What angered me was the fact that we are supposed to be in a pact and yet there was no consultation or compromise decision at all. . . . there must be a meeting of the two parties before the rate comes before the city council for approval at the February meeting. This cannot go on. There really is no agreement at all at the moment.[66]

Fractures were also beginning to appear within the DUP as not everyone in the party was content to abide by the boycott policy. The reason for this was not solely due to the lack of unanimity with the Ulster Unionists, but because of an increasing frustration with the existing campaign and a perception that the boycott strategy was a futile gesture which would only result in nationalists gaining control of local government. Kilkeel DUP councillor George Graham defended his decision to attend Newry and Mourne District Council meetings on the grounds that unionists could better oppose the AIA from within the councils than by simply refusing to attend, as it was quite apparent that this had so far failed to render local government unworkable. 'I have reviewed the whole situation and believe the boycott of nationalist-controlled councils has not been a great success. A lot of people in Kilkeel are saying we should be back there fighting our corner.'[67] Graham said that he had stuck rigidly by the boycott, but declared that absenteeism from local government was not enough and had to be replaced by more effective forms of protest. In an interesting role reversal, Bessbrook Ulster Unionist councillor Danny Kennedy accused his DUP colleague of acting in such a way as to perpetuate the Agreement, and stated that there was no way he would agree to resume normal business as long as the Agreement was in place. 'Conducting normal business on controlled councils is no different than operating normally on unionist-dominated councils and the sooner some unionists catch themselves on the sooner we will get rid of this iniquitous agreement.'[68]

By early February 1987 the council boycott strategy was in tatters as Ulster Unionists returned to conduct normal business in spite of venomous attacks from their DUP colleagues. The bitterness generated by the situation was highlighted by a fracas at the 3 February meeting of Lisburn Council after a DUP motion calling for the suspension of proceedings was defeated.

There were angry exchanges between the Official Unionist Mayor Walter Lilburn and the leader of the DUP grouping the Rev. William Beattie. When business started DUP members walked out and a group of Loyalists in the public gallery led by Banbridge DUP councillor Jim Wells, chanted abuse towards the chair and at those who tried to speak. At one stage an Eire tricolour was thrown towards the Mayor who threatened expulsion if there was further interruption. Eight of the twelve items on the agenda were rushed through and after twenty minutes the Mayor walked out followed by his Official Unionist colleagues.[69]

In Omagh the council adopted a rate, while in Ards business continued as usual for the third week in a row without the DUP, who walked out after their motion to adjourn was defeated by nine votes to five. Similarly, in Magherafelt and Fermanagh business was conducted by Ulster Unionist councillors to the anger of their DUP colleagues, who accused them of betraying the mandates on which they were elected.[70]

Evidence that there was a ground swell of opinion within the Ulster Unionist Party in favour of ending the boycott of local government was provided by the outcome of the election for new Ulster Unionist Councillors' Association officers. These elections, held in the second week in February, were a success for many previously regarded as liberals within their party, such as the association's new chairman Walter Lilburn, at that time mayor of Lisburn. The elections were seen as a green light by other UUP councillors to return to normal business in local government and consequently angered DUP members who had believed beforehand that a compromise settlement was still possible which would facilitate a united unionist protest in council chambers across Northern Ireland. However, as a result of the elections it seemed certain that in several councils Ulster Unionists were going to agree to strike a rate to avoid placing themselves outside the law, while DUP councillors were set to oppose them. Jim Wells, DUP Association secretary, commented on 9 February that to strike a rate would be to renege on previous promises given to the electorate. 'Our last full association meeting in Carrickfergus made that very plain. Members feel strongly that they cannot strike a rate, and then ask people not to pay them. . . . the DUP will continue to oppose this move in all council chambers.'[71]

In Belfast City Council a rate was struck on 16 February by a margin of twenty-one votes to fourteen due to the effective non-participation of the Ulster Unionist councillors who either were absent or abstained. This left the DUP in a minority on the council and thus powerless to prevent a rate being set, much to the annoyance of Sammy Wilson who launched a bitter attack on his UUP colleagues for their policy reversal.

> I think they have sold themselves short and people in the community short.
> . . . for the last 15 months we have been telling people it would be aiding

the Anglo-Irish agreement to pay their rates and now we strike a rate ourselves – it is totally contradictory.[72]

William McCrea accused those councillors who had returned to normal business of capitulation to the NIO and the Dublin government. He dismissed the argument put forward by many UUP members that their return to the councils was a tactical measure caused by the threat of court action, rather than a lack of moral fibre. The Mid-Ulster MP rejected assertions that these councillors were making a tactical withdrawal so they could fight another day, castigating them as self-interested individuals who were doing a disservice to Northern Ireland and betraying those who had given their lives in defence of the Protestant people.

> Local government in Ulster is being made to try out decisions of the intergovernmental conference at Maryfield and several so-called unionists in the east of the Province are deliberately complying with the wishes of Tom King and Peter Barry. It is a tragedy that a few self-seeking councillors can put our campaign of resistance into trouble. . . . Those who pedal a policy of capitulation to the Anglo-Irish accord insult the sacrifice made by our sons and daughters in defence of Ulster's position within the United Kingdom. I shall never permit my name to be associated with such betrayal.[73]

Sammy Wilson vented his anger on the Alliance Party, who had initiated the court action against those councillors boycotting council meetings, accusing them of being agents of the Northern Ireland Office. He declared that faced with the humiliating and embarrassing experience of dwindling electoral fortunes, the Alliance Party was attempting to intimidate councillors through threats of financial penalty, bankruptcy, disqualification and ultimately jail from carrying out the mandate given to them by their electorate.

> In effect, the barristers of the Alliance Party became the 'boot-boys' of the Northern Ireland Office. . . . It is true that some jelly-bean unionists like John Carson, Alfie Redpath and others did hoist the white flag in the face of court threats. Nevertheless, the assault on unionists by Alliance Party-initiated court action became little more than paradoxical failure since it succeeded in further strengthening, rather than weakening, unionist resolve. . . . The protests will go on more determinedly than ever, both inside and outside the law, until this detested dictatorial agreement is smashed. Dublin rule is no more acceptable 18 months after it was initiated than in the early months of its enforcement. And should it remain for yet another 18 months, unionists will still be forcefully registering their dissent by saying 'NO' in the councils of this province.[74]

March began as predictably as February had ended with regard to unionist interparty squabbling over the direction of the local government protest against the AIA. The *News Letter* reported a row which erupted in Belfast City Hall on Monday 2 March when three Ulster Unionists rebelled against an adjournment proposal. 'Taunts, threats and jeers rained down on former Lord Mayor John Carson, Dorothy Dunlop and William Corry, when they sided with the opposition to push out the Unionist-backed motion.'[75] The row concerned a motion from Alliance councillor Will Glendinning, which would have facilitated the automatic allocation of grants to community groups and other voluntary agencies, despite the adjournment of Belfast City Council. Independent Unionist Frank Millar proposed that the matter be deferred until a revised committee structure had been introduced. Millar's proposal, which would have forced an adjournment, was initially supported by twenty-three votes to twenty-two. However, refining the Wilson dictum that 'a week is a long time in politics', when the recorded vote was called several minutes later the motion was defeated by twenty-three votes to twenty-four. It was at this point that the three dissidents were rounded upon by those unionists who wanted the boycott policy to continue. A ten-minute shouting match then ensued between the rebels and their colleagues.

When peace was restored, Glendinning's motion was passed by eleven votes to seven. It ratified the allocation of grants including cash for staffing and maintenance in the leisure centres, repairs and salaries at Belfast Zoo and block grants totalling over £70,000 to community and welfare organisations. The decision of the three rebel councillors brought immediate condemnation and calls for their resignation from the DUP. The lord mayor of Belfast, Sammy Wilson, accused them of betraying both their party and the wider community who had given them the mandate they were now abusing, and he called on James Molyneaux to expel them from the UUP. 'Their party will have to make a move on this issue now. These people who have been masquerading as unionists, have been totally isolated. It is impossible for them to remain inside the party.'[76]

At the end of August 1987 it was clear that little progress was being made and that the council protest was still in chaos. On 26 August a fourth member of the DUP group on Lisburn council resigned from the party amid a storm of allegations directed at Lisburn DUP leader Rev. William Beattie. Councillor Robert Dunsmore, a member of the DUP for the previous six years, resigned from the Lisburn branch of the party after a public row with Beattie. Dunsmore accused Beattie of 'dictatorial arrogance' on the council and said he had engaged in an attempt 'to silence the right of free speech' of his party colleagues. Dunsmore's resignation was the fourth such move by exasperated DUP councillors who left the Lisburn branch of the party in acrimonious circumstances. Ivan Davis resigned two weeks earlier while Tommy Davis declared his intention to step down at the beginning of July. Denis McCarroll had left the party 'for personal reasons' earlier in the year. Dunsmore suggested that this haemorr-haging from the Lisburn DUP was Beattie's fault. 'Mr Beattie should review his own position on the council after the recent spate of resignations.'[77] Dunsmore claimed that Beattie had tried to stop his DUP colleagues giving their own opinion to the press and the former DUP councillor commented that as an elected representative he had a right to do so.

> I will not be gagged and I will not be moved. As an elected representative on the council I will speak my mind and speak to whom I will. . . . I will not bow down nor will I be black-mailed by empty rhetoric or sabre rattling.[78]

Dunsmore's resignation left four DUP members on Lisburn Council out of an original total of eight and there were rumours that another resignation was imminent. Dunsmore, who was to continue as an independent unionist on the council, said he deeply regretted his decision but was left with no alternative because of Beattie's behaviour. It is obvious from Beattie's response that this friction was a product of the joint pact between the two unionist parties.

> The DUP has taken a policy decision in Lisburn to enter into a pact with the Official Unionists and Mr Dunsmore must respect that decision. . . . We have thrashed out a local agreement which Mr Dunsmore does not support because of his anti Official Unionist stance. . . . I have never tried to gag him and his time would be better spent attacking his real enemies in the council such as nationalists and especially Sinn Féin.[79]

By the second half of 1987 it had become impossible to paper over the cracks of unionist division at local council level. At the beginning of October, it was announced that UUP and DUP councillors had met to relaunch the protest campaign against the AIA.

> Both associations agree that the council campaign is a shambles and needs to be drastically overhauled. They are now hoping solid proposals will be put on the table before the second anniversary of the signing of the London/Dublin deal next month. Since the beginning of the year, the council adjournment policy has fallen apart.[80]

By the beginning of 1988, the unionist boycott of local government had deteriorated to the point of virtual extinction, due to a combination of frustration at its lack of success, fractures in the unionist pact over its implementation and the fear of individual councillors that they would be held in contempt of court and personally surcharged if they continued their protest. The tensions created by the council adjournment policy demonstrated, once again, the genius of the AIA in policy-making terms, in that it could not be damaged by street protests or boycotts.

Looking back at the boycott

The inability of unionist politicians to attack the AIA without inflicting wounds upon themselves and their communities has been cited by leading figures in both main unionist parties as one of the most fundamental difficulties during the anti-Agreement campaign. 'Well the adjournment policy was fine as long as we weren't hurting ourselves with it.'[81] Nigel Dodds, meanwhile, agreed with the contention that the council boycott failed because, unlike previous British initiatives such as Sunningdale, there was nothing tangible to aim at other than the Maryfield secretariat.

> Well I think that undoubtedly, the way in which the Anglo-Irish Agreement has been set up and so on, there is nothing on the ground as it were, in Northern Ireland, that you can bring down or destabilise. I suppose yes that's right, unlike the Sunningdale Agreement as you say. I think that the local government [boycott] ran into trouble in the courts and so on, and obviously when that happened we had to change course.[82]

Implicit in Dodds's recollection of the council boycott strategy is a political realism, an understanding that such protests were of symbolic importance and were never capable of bringing real pressure to bear on the British government. Liberal unionists such as Michael McGimpsey reflected that the council boycott policy was counterproductive to unionist objectives, as such exhibitions of non-co-operation even within the confines of the meagre amount of responsibility devolved to Northern Ireland politicians was unlikely to entice Westminster to transfer more powers from London to Belfast.

> The trick was to oppose the Agreement without breaking the Union, and all those devices were ultimately damaging the Union and ultimately getting nobody anywhere. So they were protests and they went on far too long. I think they were necessary at the time as an outlet for steam and as opposed to the other outlets that we are so fond of over here, but they were never going to get anywhere.[83']

Once again this emphasises the multiplicity of strategic goals within the unionist community, as McGimpsey sought to oppose the Agreement without breaking the Union, while others such as Sammy Wilson were determined to 'smash the diktat' regardless of how this affected Northern Ireland's position within the Union. This is not to say of course that DUP strategists such as Wilson did not care whether their actions resulted in a weakening of the Union, or were unaware that this might occur; the crucial point was that for such radical unionists the Union was a political arrangement which was expendable if it compromised the religio-cultural heritage of what they believed to be the Ulster Protestant nation. The dispute over the boycott strategy was thus symptomatic of a cultural diversity within unionism, between those who viewed themselves as intrinsically British, sharing (despite the possession of a specific regional identity) a common heritage with the rest of Britain, and those who held more isolationist attitudes. For this group, Northern Ireland was 'a place apart', an identifiable nation in its own right with a cultural heritage that could stand on its own, outside the confines of the Union. This belief that the Union was expendable (though only as a last resort) enabled radicals such as Sammy Wilson to rationalise the boycott strategy and the other elements of the anti-Agreement campaign, without the reservations apparent in those with a more liberal perspective.

> The first thing that we had to do was to create an atmosphere in which people realised there was a crisis. Now that meant that things had to be abnormal, and whether they were abnormal with massive demonstrations out there, whether they were abnormal because the press was reporting that councils were being disrupted, or MPs weren't going to Westminster, or ministers weren't being invited to various functions or whatever, just creating that atmosphere of abnormality was important, and from that point of view the adjournment campaign worked, because it was all part of that scenario. Now some people say 'it didn't work, because eventually you had to go back to councils'. That is quite true, and if by working, you mean that the object was simply to stop councils from operating and stop people going to council meetings, then obviously that's not the case, but that was only a means to an end. You stopped councils working, because that's another way of saying that government in Northern Ireland is abnormal, and people are not co-operating with it. I mean, the adjournment campaign went on for a year and a half, two years, and during that time the press were continually focusing on council meetings and on the wrangles at council meetings, and that was the oxygen if you want, of the campaign. It kept it alive, and it always gave you a platform. Every time you went into a general council meeting, you were reminding people that 'Ulster Says No'. Every time we chased a minister, even if it was only five people standing outside a function . . . you were reminding people that 'Ulster Says No', and you were getting that into the press. So from that point of view I think that it was a success.[84]

David Trimble's recollection of the local council boycott was typically unambiguous and illustrates a less sanguine attitude than that exhibited by Sammy Wilson. When asked whether he thought the anti-Agreement campaign in general, and the council boycott in particular, had been a success, Trimble replied:

> No it wasn't particularly a success. It had some successes [mass demonstrations and by-elections], but the campaign as a whole wasn't a success. . . .
> The obvious consequence of the adjournment policy and that particular line . . . was actually a total withdrawal from local government, and this is what the party leadership tried to do. . . . It got to the point where the party leadership was asking all the councillors to sign letters of resignation and

hand them in to it, so they could be used when appropriate, and that's the point at which that form of protest broke down, because there was a revolt of the party councillors. . . . In some respects, the only way of fighting the Agreement would have been a whole-scale recourse to paramilitary activity, or to violence, and that was something that the leadership was very anxious to avoid.[85]

Rev. Martin Smyth provides yet another unionist perspective on the council boycott strategy by insisting that it could have succeeded in forcing the British government to at least modify the AIA if not remove it completely. Smyth was eager to allocate the blame for the failure of the adjournment policy to the councillors themselves, commenting that had it not been for the lack of discipline exhibited by some councillors the strategy would have been more successful.

> If the local councillors had done the same [as Westminster MPs] and all come out at that time, then we would have been in a different ball game. There were those who said, 'well, this government will ignore us', but the government could not have ignored us if two-thirds of councillors had absented them-selves. Even in the councils where they could have carried on, because there was a quorum of Alliance and SDLP and Sinn Féiners who could have carried on, in the end that was unsustainable. But for various reasons, take the classic one, [Peter] Robinson, who was part of the campaign planners, he kept Castlereagh Council in being, and as a result, there were unionist councillors all round the country who wouldn't come out if Castlereagh wouldn't come out. That was where it went wrong.[86]

What Smyth omits to mention in this recollection of the council boycott was that (as illustrated in Chapter 4) solidarity was no more apparent at Westminster, as Enoch Powell and John Taylor consistently attended the Commons in contravention of the strategy agreed by the unionist coalition. In addition, Smyth's suggestion that the DUP were responsible for the collapse of the local government adjournment policy stretches reality somewhat, as for the most part, it was rebel councillors within his own party, the UUP, who made the tactical decision to end their boycott and resume normal business rather than place themselves in contempt of court.

Another aspect which accounts for the breakdown of internal cohesion within the unionist community concerned the tensions within the two main parties during the progress of the anti-Agreement campaign. Many UUP councillors, such as Dorothy Dunlop and Hazel Bradford, were frustrated at the way strict party discipline was enforced at grass-roots level while their Westminster colleagues were not subjected to the same rules. Enoch Powell, John Taylor and Ken Maginnis, for example, broke the Commons boycott on a number of occasions yet were not threatened with expulsion by the party leadership. This angered the DUP, as they felt that their efforts to fight the AIA were being undermined.

At the same time many Ulster Unionist councillors became increasingly upset as the anti-Agreement campaign progressed, as they were given no input into the policy-making process and, as they saw it, were obliged to observe collective responsibility where there had not been collective decision-making. This became an unbearable situation for some UUP councillors when they were directed by the party executive to place themselves in contempt of court and make themselves personally liable to be surcharged.

The resentment expressed by UUP councillors, that they were being used as pawns by the leadership with little regard to either proper democratic consultation or adequate concern for the consequences of policy decisions, caused continual tension throughout the anti-Agreement campaign. This contributed to the political difficulties of the unionist coalition, as Molyneaux was under pressure from the DUP to escalate the scale of the anti-Agreement campaign and enforce the local government boycott, yet he could never be completely sure whether the grass-roots of his party would obey the decisions of the party executive. The ambivalent position of many Ulster Unionist councillors over the local government boycott and the general thrust of the initial phase of the anti-Agreement campaign provoked their DUP counterparts, who felt that the fight against the AIA was being held back by the UUP. These tensions were fed, of course, by the unionist experience of political failure between 1985 and 1988. This feeling of political impotence and realisation that their symbolic gestures and street demonstrations were having little impact on the policy-makers left many unionists within both main parties crying out for a more positive strategy.

This evolution from defiance to pragmatic negotiation will be examined in the following chapter. As for the anti-Agreement campaign itself, perhaps the last word should go, not to a politician, but to a poet. John Hewitt was an Ulster Protestant whose unionism was compatible with his Irish identity. The following extract from his poem 'Anglo-Irish Agreement' illustrates his frustration with the unionist political leadership at the time and lyrically encapsulates the unionist political mood in the mid-1980s.

> These days the air is thick with bitter cries
> as baffled thousands dream they are betrayed,
> stripped of the comfort of safe loyalties,
> their ancient friends considered enemies,
> alone among the nations and afraid.[87]

Notes

1   *News Letter,* 21 November 1985, p. 4.
2   ibid.
3   John Taylor, interview with author, 30 September 1991.
4   *News Letter,* 28 November 1985, p. 4.
5   Dorothy Dunlop, interview with author, 5 December 1991.
6   *News Letter,* 29 January 1986, p. 8.
7   ibid.
8   ibid., 14 February 1986, p. 3.
9   ibid., 18 February 1986, p. 8.
10 ibid., 19 February 1986, p. 8.
11 ibid., 14 April 1986, p. 1.
12 Sammy Wilson, interview with author, 20 November 1991.
13 Private correspondence supplied to author.
14 ibid.
15 Dorothy Dunlop, interview with author, 5 December 1991.
16 ibid.
17 *News Letter,* 29 April 1986, p. 9.
18 ibid., 7 May 1986, p. 2.
19 Rev. Martin Smyth, interview with author, 22 November 1991.
20 *News Letter,* 7 May 1986, p. 2.
21 Dorothy Dunlop, interview with author, 5 December 1991.
22 ibid.
23 *News Letter,* 21 June 1986, p. 7.
24 ibid.
25 ibid., 25 June 1986, p. 8.
26 James Molyneaux, interview with author, 19 November 1991.
27 *News Letter,* 27 August 1986, p. 1.
28 ibid., 28 August 1986, p. 2.
29 *Ulster,* September 1986, p. 3.
30 *News Letter,* 13 September 1986, p. 6.
31 ibid., 18 September 1986, p. 6.
32 ibid., 20 September 1986, p. 7.
33 ibid.
34 ibid., 29 September 1986, p. 4.
35 ibid., 24 September 1986, p. 1.
36 ibid., 25 September 1986, p. 14.
37 ibid., 30 September 1986, p. 8.
38 ibid., 18 October 1986, p. 6.
39 ibid.
40 ibid.
41 ibid., 21 October 1986, p. 7.
42 ibid.
43 ibid., 23 October 1986, p. 2.
44 ibid.
45 ibid., 28 October 1986, p. 6.
46 ibid., 25 November 1986, p. 1.
47 ibid., p. 2.
48 ibid.
49 ibid.

50 ibid., 27 November 1986, pp. 1–2.
51 ibid., 28 November 1986, p. 14.
52 ibid.
53 ibid., 6 December 1986, p. 3.
54 David Trimble, interview with author, 3 October 1991.
55 *News Letter,* 6 January 1987, pp. 1–3.
56 ibid.
57 ibid., pp. 1 and 3.
58 ibid., p. 8.
59 ibid.
60 ibid.
61 ibid., 13 January 1987, pp. 1–2.
62 ibid., 14 January 1987, p. 12.
63 ibid., 15 January 1987, p. 14.
64 ibid., 20 January 1987, pp. 1-2.
65 ibid., 21 January 1987, p. 4.
66 ibid., 24 January 1987, p. 8.
67 ibid., 31 January 1987, p. 6.
68 ibid.
69 ibid., 4 February 1987, p. 2.
70 ibid.
71 ibid., 10 February 1987, p. 8.
72 ibid., 17 February 1987, p. 3.
73 ibid., 20 February 1987, p. 17.
74 *Fortnight,* No. 249 (March 1987), p. 16.
75 *News Letter,* 3 March 1987, p. 1.
76 ibid.
77 ibid., 27 August 1987, p. 8.
78 ibid.
79 ibid.
80 ibid., 1 October 1987, p. 7.
81 Dorothy Dunlop, interview with author, 5 November 1991.
82 Nigel Dodds, interview with author, 2 December 1991.
83 Michael McGimpsey, interview with author, 16 October 1991.
84 Sammy Wilson, interview with author, 20 November 1991.
85 David Trimble, interview with author, 3 October 1991.
86 Rev. Martin Smyth, interview with author, 22 November 1991.
87 *Fortnight,* No. 245, (November 1986), p. 7.

PART III

CHAPTER 6

Coming in from the Cold:
From Belligerence to Negotiation

It was clear to many unionists by the beginning of 1987 that their protest campaign was going nowhere and that the only alternative left open to them was political negotiation with the British government and the SDLP on a devolved settlement. There were of course fundamental problems with this approach, not least the fact that a large element within the Ulster Unionist Party including its leader James Molyneaux favoured an integrationist solution. An added difficulty was caused by self-inflicted conditions imposed by the unionists before they would participate in talks with the British government. Their stipulation that the working of the Anglo-Irish Intergovernmental Conference and the Maryfield secretariat had to be suspended in advance was a difficult position to retreat from (even had they wanted to) without causing a further split within their ranks.

Perhaps the biggest problem for unionism at this stage was one of political culture. The main political organisations within the ideology were built upon protesting, defending stated positions and retrenching ground which had been lost or had been perceived to have been lost. The sense of being a besieged community has understandable historical foundations, but has produced, nevertheless, a defensive mentality which tends to inhibit progressive thought or action. The sense of being under attack from antagonistic forces of varying intensity, whether these be in Dublin, London, Belfast, Washington or, in more extreme cases, Rome, has produced a desire for solidarity. The electoral cohesion of unionism which has resulted, the maxim that 'united we stand, divided we fall', has tended to inhibit the establishment of an innovative or pragmatic ideology. While such a coalition was capable of harnessing a cross-class unionist alliance in support of that one great objective, the Union with Britain, it was less secure when it came to setting out a positive agenda for the future. The institutional division within unionism was another complicating factor. Despite the loose political alliances which existed, a power-struggle was going on in unionism – within the UUP itself, between it and the DUP and between the two main parties and loyalist paramilitaries – for control of the political agenda. Thus, policy positions were not adopted solely on the basis of rational calculation about the best course for unionism, but were also a means of internal positioning to outmanouevre competitors within the ideology. Clearly, this was not going to help unionism develop an effective political strategy which would further the central objective of strengthening Northern Ireland's position within the Union.

Loyalist paramilitary thinking

A good example of this counterproductive tendency was provided at the end of January 1987 with Ian Paisley's response to the first real sign of intelligent life within unionism for several years. Ironically, it emerged from the UDA, traditionally perceived by nationalists as being the most extreme group within unionism. Paisley rejected the UDA's blueprint for progress, entitled *Common Sense – An Agreed Process*, on the grounds that it proposed power-sharing devolved government, following agreement at an all-party constitutional conference. 'Power-sharing was rejected by the Northern Ireland people at the time of Sunningdale and we still reject the idea that any party should have seats in government as of right.'[1] The DUP leader declared that the sort of constitutional conference suggested by the UDA could only be entered into after the AIA had been scrapped and after the Maryfield secretariat had been closed down. Ulster Unionist leader James Molyneaux described the UDA proposals as 'irrelevant' as long as the AIA remained in operation.

> There isn't any problem in talking or considering any proposals from anybody if they were going to go anywhere but the reality is that this Government is not going to move in any direction or show any flexibility this side of a general election – if the Tories win the election there may not be movement then.[2]

The UDA plan was developed by its political wing, the Ulster Political Research Group (UPRG). It advocated the establishment of a cross-community government in a seventy-eight member legislative assembly elected by proportional representation.[3]

At face value, the proposal was extremely progressive and was welcomed as such by John Hume, the leader of the SDLP. Portrayed by the media as mindless psychopaths, the UDA produced a document which appeared to embrace the pantheon of modern liberal-democratic theory. In other circumstances, British civil liberties campaigners may have looked at *Common Sense* as a template for democratic reform, with its proposal for a written constitution and a bill of rights to protect minority interests. The conclusions of the constitutional conference would be put to the people in a referendum, with any subsequent agreement requiring not less than two-thirds support for implementation.[4] The UPRG maintained that *Common*

Sense would get over the Protestant siege mentality and the Catholic fear of being dominated by the majority population. *Common Sense* demonstrated its progressive intent when it declared that majority rule was no longer a viable option.

> Coalition is now the practice rather than the exception in modern pluralist societies. We have become so accustomed to equating democracy with majority rule that we tend to forget that majority is democratic only when there is alter[n]ation in office, or when there is broad consensus for it. Majority rule in deeply divided societies is likely to be profoundly undemocratic, and the only democratic system is one that allows participation in government by coalition of all groups, majority and minority, on a more or less permanent basis.[5]

Paisley's haste in rejecting *Common Sense* is interesting, especially as it proposed an internal settlement based upon legislative devolved government, a 'solution' which he had previously shown a fondness for. In reality, his reaction owed less to his concern that the UDA were about to 'sell out' the Protestant people and had more to do with a fear that his own place in the political hierarchy was being usurped. However, John McMichael was no Terence O'Neill, and shouting 'Lundy' at the UDA was to prove a futile exercise.

James Molyneaux was similarly wary of policy documents which did not originate from party HQ at Glengall Street. He was also alarmed that the UPRG proposals all but eliminated the link with Britain and simply presented an independent Northern Ireland in a glossy cover. The fact that Paisley's rejection of *Common Sense* owed more to his personal ambition than to the fear that the UDA had gone soft was borne out by the reaction of others within his party. Many expressed surprise at their leader's attitude and suggested that the UDA's power-sharing proposals deserved more careful consideration. Billy McDowell, a DUP councillor for Newtownabbey, said he could not understand why Ian Paisley and James Molyneaux had not even offered to talk to those who had drawn up the package.

> It is not perfect, but at least it shows that they [the UDA] are in touch with the grass roots. . . . There is only one way forward for the people of Ulster and that is together. The alternative to sitting down and talking is standing up and fighting . . . we can destroy the agreement if we go forward together with the plan. It should be given a chance.[6]

McDowell said that devolved government in Northern Ireland would have to be based on power-sharing and 'anyone who thinks otherwise is living in cloud cuckoo land'.[7] This was certainly not the view of Robert Lyle, vice-chairman of the Young Unionist Council, who commented at a party meeting in Belfast on 2 February that the *Common Sense* document 'should be rejected because of its inherent unstable and undemocratic nature'.[8]

Apparently Lyle did not agree that power-sharing was a feasible means of obtaining devolved power from Westminster, as such structures would be inherently weak due to the desire of well-meaning but ultimately muddle-headed people to allow the nationalist minority to participate in the administration of the state. He argued that government was primarily concerned with making decisions, and therefore the granting of a veto power to the minority representatives would make the operation of such government untenable.

> Power-sharing means including members of widely differing and incompatible political parties in the government. This will totally destabilise the work of that government. Different departments would end up reflecting the views of different parties. . . . In this way government would become 'shambolic' and devoid of any purpose or direction.[9]

Lyle's argument appeared to hinge on the fact that, while the demographic make-up of Northern Ireland might be a freak of the region's troubled past, it would be wise to make the best of it and allow the unionist majority to dominate any devolved administration as this is the only way it could effectively be run. However, to argue that good government was about decision-making rather than democracy was a dangerous position for a unionist to take in the 1980s, as the same principle could be used in defence of the AIA. Here, a decision was taken over the heads of the people to make it easier for the British government to run Northern Ireland in conjunction with the Irish Republic. Such sentiments could also be used to defend direct rule and unelected quangos as a more efficient means of governing Northern Ireland than a devolved administration based on power-sharing with all the difficulties which that would involve.

Opposition to the UDA's proposals was particularly apparent from supporters of integration and those campaigning for Labour Party representation in Northern Ireland, presumably worried that the plan might increase the momentum and enthusiasm for devolution within Northern Ireland. In a *Fortnight* article entitled 'The UDA Plan: Opening For Dialogue Or Sectarian Fix?' Mark Langhammer and David Young provided a predictably negative response to *Common Sense*. The first line of attack suggested that the UDA leadership was out of touch with its membership, and might not therefore be able to deliver their support for the promises which were made. The second criticism was on ideological rather than practical grounds, namely that if the *Common Sense* proposals were to become a reality, they would condemn Northern Ireland to a system of institutionalised sectarianism.

> The construction of an Executive along these lines [power-sharing devolved government] represents a form of permanent coalition which can only freeze politics in Northern Ireland into sectarian forms. . . . People can only

be represented in an isolated power-sharing government as 'Prods' or 'Taigs' – not as socialists, liberals, conservatives or communists. . . . A formal sectarian coalition of this sort would serve to suppress any tendencies in the society which wished to break with sectarian political activity. . . . The checks and balances which the UDA would seek to have written into the new constitution could only minimise the effects of feuding, not alter its inevitability.[10]

The advocates of equal citizenship seemed to be under the impression that sectarian conflict began with partition and the establishment of a provincial parliament at Stormont. As intercommunal strife existed in Ulster before the onset of 'institutionalised provincialism' – indeed before the Act of Union – it is difficult to believe the argument that this would cease once Northern Ireland was fully incorporated into and treated equally with the other regions of the United Kingdom.

Angered at the way in which the main unionist parties had ignored *Common Sense*, *Ulster* magazine attacked the chaos within unionist politics and laid the blame for this at the door of the political leadership. In an article entitled, 'Where to now?', the paramilitary journal launched a vitriolic attack on Paisley and argued that the development and articulation of a more positive agenda was necessary.

It is not enough to campaign for the Diktat to be done away with: . . . To be successful in our struggle against joint authority we must have a long-term aim – a political goal which will ensure that we do not have to suffer the indignity, humiliation and hardships of the last 12 months, indeed the last 17 years. The O.U.P. and D.U.P. have no such vision or long-term strategy. . . . Paisleyism is the politics of reaction, campaigning always against something but never actually for anything. In his 20 years in political life Ian Paisley has never created anything in terms of political gain as his is a position of always being on the defensive.[11]

Unionist politics was in crisis. Mainstream unionism had mobilised the community and prosecuted an extraparliamentary campaign against the AIA. The failure of that campaign to achieve its expected results was compounded by initiatives such as *Common Sense*. Molyneaux and Paisley were shackled together in a loveless alliance, married 'for the sake of the children' rather than out of respect for one another. The negative strategy of the joint unionist alliance, of boycotting local government and British officials, allowed the UDA to dominate the political arena. While Paisley and Molyneaux lifted their ball off the pitch and refused to play, the UPRG brought on another ball and kicked it towards the SDLP. How was mainstream unionism going to reassert its authority without seeming to capitulate on the principles inherent within the anti-Agreement campaign?

While it recognised the necessity of establishing a more positive political strategy, the UUP was hindered from achieving this for most of 1987 because it was preoccupied by its own internal divisions. Aside from the general breakdown in discipline, faction-fighting was endemic within the party between those who wanted devolution and those in favour of integration. The most prominent offender in this regard, whom the leadership considered was responsible for keeping the conflict going, was Robert McCartney. The former UUP Assemblyman, who had made his name by grabbing a microphone off Ian Paisley at a city-centre demonstration in Belfast to denounce the DUP, commented that he was ready to face a battle with those in the party hierarchy who wanted to discipline him. 'I will fight all the way. . . . At the moment it is like fighting a ghost. I don't know what the charge against me is, nor have I had any letter of warning from Glengall Street headquarters.'[12] It was decided at the party's executive meeting on 29 February, by thirty-four votes to seventeen, that action would have to be taken against him if civil war was to be avoided within the party.

By this stage the Belfast barrister was a loose cannon within the party whose acerbic criticisms of the leadership were in danger of damaging party morale. McCartney was anxious to ensure that the UUP adopted an integrationist policy position rather than the 'pygmy politics' he associated with devolution. One former colleague of McCartney's who was sympathetic to the integrationist case commented that his leadership of the Campaign for Equal Citizenship precluded their involvement in it, as he was too abrasive to work with.

> Oh Robert McCartney quarrelled with everybody . . . he treated everybody with such contempt. I couldn't believe that for anybody who wanted to be a politician, so to speak, that they could alienate their own, the people that they needed for support. . . . I certainly would have supported the CEC. I didn't get involved too much in it for the very reason that Bob McCartney was leading it, and I had had experience of him in the Assembly and I knew that anything he tried to lead he would ruin.[13]

McCartney called the effort to discipline him impetuous and emotional. With his typical air of being the only sane man in the room, he declared that the decision '. . . has shades of Alice in Wonderland to it. I'm half expecting the Mad Hatter and the March Hare to appear, along with Tweedledum and Tweedledee.'[14]

As the main unionist parties were politically divided, policy ideas began to emanate from more exotic sources to fill the intellectual vacuum which the anti-Agreement campaign had encouraged. The UDA's *Common Sense* is an obvious example of this, as was the document published on 2 March entitled *Strategy for Victory*. This unveiled a new initiative from the Ulster Clubs designed to get unionism onto its front foot once again. Their blueprint was to involve all fourteen unionist MPs and other loyalist groups in what was called a Northern Ireland Grand Committee to co-ordinate the protest campaign against the AIA. The Ulster Clubs denied that this was the first step towards a provisional government or UDI, though clearly it left such an option open to them as a last resort. The plan envisaged a system of subcommittees, each one of which would be chaired by an MP and set a specific task. Thus, one would organise the withholding of motor tax, another rates and so on. The Ulster Clubs' document called the Grand Committee an alternative to the NIO, the inference being that it might provide the basis for self-government in the future should their worst fears be realised. David Trimble rejected the UDI allegation, declaring that if that had been their intent, they would not have given primacy to elected representatives on the subcommittees. Clearly the intention here was to tie the hands of unionist politicians by setting the political agenda for them. By having political figures on the subcommittees, the initiative would lock unionist politicians into the success of the Ulster Clubs' policy. Subsequent failure of the initiative would further tarnish the image of constitutional politicians in their promise to deliver a peaceful means of destroying the AIA and thus increase the credibility and political clout of fringe groups such as the Ulster Clubs and the UDA. Conversely, should unionist politicians reject the initiative or refuse to participate in it, they would be open to the accusation that the anti-Agreement protest was going nowhere and that the constitutional politicians lacked the necessary commitment to smash the AIA. Reaction to the Ulster Clubs' document was mixed, Peter Robinson commenting that it was a substantial initiative which deserved a 'studied response rather than an off-the-cuff comment'.[15] His DUP colleague Jim Allister was more positive, commenting that the proposals gave a 'revitalised direction'[16] to the anti-Agreement campaign. He suggested that there were some within the unionist community who would be delighted if the initiative failed as they were more interested in stability than in stepping up the protest campaign. 'I trust these proposals will not be stymied by those happiest to do nothing rather than grasp the nettle of active opposition to Dublin rule.'[17] John McMichael's response on behalf of the UDA was to declare that he would talk to anyone, though the implication was that the initiative was no more radical than *Common Sense*.

> We would generally welcome the fact that both the Ulster Clubs and the recently-announced Unionist task force will now be in tune with our view that the resistance campaign will only be effective if the various loyalist factions are prepared to work in harmony with a mutually agreed strategy.[18]

March 1987 also witnessed some positive stirrings within the DUP, with a recognition that their current strategy was too insular and did not devote adequate attention to external opinion. Jim Wells announced that more attention had to be given to promoting the unionist cause outside Northern Ireland. Commenting after a number of meetings in England to publicise the anti-Agreement campaign, Wells appeared genuinely shocked at his discovery that mainstream British opinion equated unionism with some form of advanced dementia and proof that 'Mad Cow disease' had jumped the species barrier. This illustrates just how out of touch he was, as this attitude had been obvious to more detached observers for a number of years.

> At each one [anti-AIA meetings in England] the strong feeling has come across that there is absolutely no sympathy – still less understanding – of the unionist cause . . . I really do feel that the next phase of the campaign must involve widespread publicity in Great Britain. I get the impression that the British people feel that all we, as unionists, ever do is say 'no'. That is just not the case.[19]

Despite the ironic element of Wells's last remark he appears to miss the central point of his discovery. This was that further expressions by unionists of their 'just cause' would only serve to copper-fasten what they regarded as a stilted image of them in Britain. It is undoubtedly true that this stereotypical image sees Catholics and Protestants, nationalists and unionists, as indistinguishable from one another. Both are perceived in Britain as violently blinkered communities with a destructive obsession with the past. Many Protestant unionists who go to work in London are dismayed when they are referred to as 'Paddies', however endearing the context might be. A publicity campaign by unionists bemoaning the lack of democracy in Northern Ireland would be unlikely to win the 'battle of hearts and minds' in Britain, as the 'Irish' are generally seen as authors of their own misfortune. The absence of liberal-democratic structures of government, insofar as this is even recognised in Britain, is viewed as a result of the inadequacy of the political actors and their communities within Northern Ireland, rather than as the cause of such inadequacy.

Clearly, many unionists were not happy with negative campaigning, even if they were not sure precisely where they wanted to go. In a speech to the Ulster Unionist Constituency Association for Upper Bann in Lurgan on 4 April 1987, the UUP deputy leader Harold McCusker stated that saying 'no' was not enough. Unionists, he claimed, would have to come up with a clear strategy and an alternative to the AIA rather than simply calling for its removal.

> No one that I know or have spoken to believes that the destruction of the agreement is a sufficient end in itself. . . . In fact, no political realist believes that its simple destruction is achievable. There has to be a replacement, the Government must be convinced that an alternative not only exists but that it, unlike the present agreement, has a prospect of obtaining some of the objectives Mrs Thatcher claims to be her own.[20]

This statement is evidence that McCusker was facing up to the harsh realities of political life, unlike some of his colleagues who were still trying to huff and puff to blow the Anglo-Irish house down. McCusker, who was speaking at his reselection meeting as the Ulster Unionist candidate for Upper Bann in the forthcoming Westminster election, commented that some unpalatable realities had to be swallowed by the unionist community. He also made it clear that he was disappointed with the UUP response to the *Common Sense* document: 'Unionist politicians have been less than generous in their response to the document *Common Sense*, produced by the political wing of the UDA.'[21] He said that, at the very least, it should have been recognised as the most courageous political act taken by any group within the majority community in the past ten years, and should also have been acknowledged as an honest attempt to address some of the issues at the heart of the present conflict.[22]

As a result of the ineffective campaign to 'smash the diktat', together with criticism which ranged from the paramilitaries to Protestant church leaders such as the Rev. John Thompson who had described their tactics as being 'morally questionable', the DUP and UUP decided to establish a joint unionist Task Force. Its brief was to open dialogue with various groups in the wider unionist community, secure support for the anti-Agreement campaign and establish what consensus existed within the unionist community for political alternatives to the AIA. Michael McGimpsey's recollection was that the Task Force was a direct consequence of the violence which accompanied the first anniversary rally at Belfast City Hall. He believes that it was a product of the rapid disintegration in relations between the unionist community and the RUC which accompanied the police's role in rerouting Orange parades.

> The prime reason for that [the Task Force] was that at the second rally at the City Hall [15 November 1986], there was rioting as you remember, and violence, and the RUC riot squad was used, and Jim Molyneaux said he would never lend his name to another protest like that that would produce violence. Remember there was a campaign against the police and there was burning of police houses and all the rest of it, and Molyneaux said then that he was not going to have anything to do with any sort of policy that was going to result in violence. So they had to have a rethink then.[23]

It became clear in May 1987 that the Task Force ideas on a political way forward would not be included in the forthcoming joint election manifesto of the two main unionist parties. It was announced on 12 May by Ian Paisley that the Task Force document was not at a sufficiently advanced stage to be included in the manifesto. The DUP leader said that the publication of the report would have to come after the election and that there was no change in the two unionist parties' first priority, namely the setting aside of the AIA and the closing down of the Maryfield secretariat. Harold McCusker accepted that the election had precluded an early publication of the report, commenting stoically that 'It is better for our report to be given full and proper consideration rather than a rudimentary examination.'[24]

Frank Millar was also conciliatory in tone, declaring: 'The reality is that the election has intruded on the process and we would not wish to initiate substantial discussions on long-term policy issues in the run-up to polling day.'[25]

Amid the confusion surrounding just what the Task Force had recommended, the UDA sought to set their own political agenda in the hope that they could obtain support from unionists disaffected with the joint manifesto of the two main parties. John McMichael, chairman of the UPRG, attempted to exploit the weariness of the unionist community by commenting that it was time they stopped defending old positions and made a positive attempt to seize new opportunities. This was an implicit criticism of the existing unionist leadership and a suggestion that the UPRG could provide the new coherent direction which all unionists were longing to see.

> We are approaching one of the most interesting and important times in the history of Northern Ireland. Indeed, the next few months may well prove to be a watershed for unionism. We must decide whether we continue to crouch in the trenches of not-an-inch unionism forever defending, or whether we are prepared to break out and seize the initiative and advance on what we decide to be our objective.[26]

McMichael went on to elucidate *Common Sense* and put this forward as the UDA's manifesto.

> The unionist objective must be to achieve a situation where Northern Ireland is unquestionably established as part of the United Kingdom by the consent of the majority of people in both communities; and that Northern Ireland must have a government which has cross-community support and the necessary authority to deal with matters ranging from unemployment to hard-core terrorism.[27]

Ulster, meanwhile, rejected allegations by Robert McCartney that *Common Sense* was a sell-out. This provides an interesting example of the UDA's ability to tailor its message to fit a particular audience. Through McMichael and the UPRG it presented itself to the general public as the soul of moderation. Its house journal, consumed by a small number of urban working-class UDA supporters, conveyed a rather different impression. The implicit message here was that they had not gone soft and were simply engaging in astute political manoeuvring. *Ulster* made it quite clear that, despite the pleasant noises being made about *Common Sense* by John Hume, power-sharing was not on offer. This was an opinion which did not exactly coincide with the way McMichael was expressing the UDA position publicly at the time.

> It [the UDA] has been accused of a sell-out because it has the 'audacity' to advocate political consensus. The UDA's crime is to suggest that a form of 'qualified' majority rule should be considered for Northern Ireland. Of course the majority would rule, but minorities would have an input – albeit

a minority one. This qualified majority rule would also mean that the SDLP would have to agree that Northern Ireland is part of the U.K., until the vast majority of its people desired otherwise.[28]

This was clearly an attempt to assuage fears that the UDA had gone soft and were giving in to pressure from the British government to establish a power-sharing executive with the nationalists. To an extent, therefore, the UDA were attempting to 'have their cake and eat it'. At one level, *Common Sense* represented an effort to boost the political power of the UDA, by holding out mouth-watering possibilities for the British government and the SDLP. On another level, it sought to portray itself as the one progressive voice within an otherwise politically stagnant unionist community. Yet, as the above extract indicates, the implicit message being given to the Protestant working class through publications such as *Ulster* was that power-sharing was the continuation of majority rule by other means. Assessments of the UDA's commitment to the gospel of democracy must be tempered by the fact that they were actively engaged in murdering innocent Catholic civilians on an ongoing basis during the same period. There has been a tendency for commentators to get rather misty eyed about *Common Sense* and to hold it aloft as an example of loyalist paramilitary moderation. This would clearly be an overstatement of the case. Nevertheless, though nationalists were simply being offered minority influence within an internal settlement, the tone with which it was offered at least demonstrated an understanding of Catholic concerns. True, there was no movement towards a constitutional compromise, but the recognition of the need to build in mechanisms such as a bill of rights and supreme court to prevent majority domination of the executive was a positive signal for the future.

Reaction to the Task Force report

On the eve of its publication, scheduled for 2 July 1987, the CEC launched an attack on the Task Force report. The published report was to be an abridged version, with sections concerning the review of tactics of the anti-Agreement campaign being left out. While the report avoided setting out any specific model of government, it was known to be strongly pro-devolutionist and opposed to integration. This explains why the CEC president Robert McCartney and colleagues attacked it at a press conference in Belfast, claiming that unionist politicians were getting ready for a complete cave-in and an acceptance of a power-sharing initiative under the terms of the Anglo-Irish Agreement. CEC chairman Dr Lawrence Kennedy commented: 'This will be a clear indication to the Provisional IRA that unionists have abandoned the Union.'[29] The following day, Robert McCartney alleged that the Task Force had hatched a secret deal with the SDLP to keep Northern Ireland separate from the rest of the United Kingdom.

Even while they prattled publicly about unionism and the Anglo-Irish agreement, the so-called task force were secretly negotiating a deal with like-minded members of the SDLP which they hoped would maintain Northern Ireland's separateness from the rest of the United Kingdom. If this deal involved a role for Dublin, their attitude was, so be it.[30]

Not surprisingly, McCartney's allegations drew a response from his former colleagues, who accused him in turn of using dirty tricks in his attacks on the Task Force document. Frank Millar denied McCartney's contention that a contract had been established between the UUP and the SDLP, commenting: 'He is talking through his hat . . . there were never any discussions between us and the SDLP.'[31] McCartney brushed these denials aside: 'I stand over my remarks . . . my information is that contacts were made and my sources are at a high level in the SDLP.'[32] McCartney went on to allege that Austin Currie of the SDLP was involved in the liaison between the two parties, though Currie denied all knowledge of any such contact. 'I don't know what Mr McCartney is playing at. I have not met task force members for discussions nor have any feelers been put out to me about their report . . . you can take that as a categorical denial.'[33] McCartney also came under fire from the Alliance Party, its deputy leader Addie Morrow denouncing his reaction to the report as 'deeply disappointing'.[34] The Lisburn councillor Seamus Close accused McCartney of feeding his 'super ego trip' and described the CEC president as the 'best fairytale writer since Grimm'.[35]

The Task Force report (or rather the abridged version thought suitable for public consumption) was very well received in the local press. Rumours began to circulate that it could provide the basis for exploratory talks between unionist politicians and the government on the future administration of Northern Ireland.

The Task Force document, entitled *An End to Drift*, was released at a press conference on 2 July. Those involved in what amounted to a unionist version of the New Ireland Forum declared the main objective of unionism to be devolved government within the United Kingdom. They expressed their hope that 'talks about talks' would lead to formal and full-scale negotiations on an alternative to the AIA. The report contained the warning that, if the government rejected genuine attempts to get a new settlement, the unionist community would be forced to countenance independence. The Task Force trinity of Harold McCusker, Frank Millar and Peter Robinson asked the two party leaders to consider setting up a commission which would examine alternatives to the Union. They also requested that a convention be established to lead a new protest campaign and that a panel should oversee the initial stages of the talks to see if there was any basis for discussions 'without prejudice' with the government. No precise structures or models of government were outlined in the report, but it was clear that the authors favoured the creation of a devolved assembly with legislative powers, and specifically a plan along the lines of that enshrined in the Catherwood report, as a basis for negotiation. The authors rejected suggestions that their 'talks about talks' proposals represented a U-turn or climb-down over the demand that the AIA had to be removed. The report commented:

> In advance of any negotiation, we feel it must be made plain that failure to arrive at consensus would leave the unionist leadership no alternative but to seek an entirely new basis for Northern Ireland outside the present constitutional context.[36]

Most significantly for unionist politics, the report contained a thinly veiled attack on the two unionist leaders' performance since 1985.

> We have found absolutely no lessening in the unionist community's antipathy to the Anglo-Irish agreement. At the same time our investigations have unearthed deep disquiet about the current protest campaign and a simple disbelief that on its own it can, or will, persuade Mrs Thatcher to change course.[37]

Despite such conclusions some unionists have maintained that the report was not critical of the anti-Agreement campaign. John Taylor recollects, for example, that the title *An End to Drift* was a criticism of the AIA rather than a commentary on the campaign against it.

> Oh, an end to drift, yes, well, I don't consider that critical of the unionist leadership. I think it sums up the situation, we are in a period of drift. It's not a personal attack on Molyneaux or Paisley or anything like that, we are in a period of drift in Northern Ireland and continue to be.[38]

Notwithstanding such remarks, the report clearly provides a benchmark, indicating the increasing unrest and frustration within the unionist community at the drift of the campaign against the AIA. This negative feedback received by the authors is evident in the report's introductory declaration that '. . . protest can be no substitute for politics'.[39] In the conclusions section of the report, an obvious attempt was made to address the long-term problems facing the future of the unionist ideology, rather than simply reacting to them in a defensive manner. However, this new-found desire to come to terms with political reality and emerge from the bunker mentality of the past was unfortunately not shared by the leaders of the two parties. The report concluded with the realisation that Northern Ireland's constitutional status within the United Kingdom had been steadily and successfully undermined since the 1960s.

> This demand for action [stepping up the anti-Agreement protest] is tempered by a realistic appraisal of the limits of Unionism's negotiating strength and, on the other hand, by anxiety that a commitment to negotiate 'a reasonable alternative' should not be construed, in London or elsewhere,

as evidence of a willingness to come to terms with the Agreement itself. The temptation in such circumstances might be to do nothing. However we would consider this the ultimate abdication of responsibility. It seems to us that those who counsel against negotiation must make plain the alternative means by which they propose to determine the future of the people of Northern Ireland. . . . Negotiation need not be the precursor to 'sell-out' or 'betrayal'. . . . We must give hope to a community dangerously immune to disappointment and defeat.[40]

At a press conference on 8 July, Paisley and Molyneaux gave their official response to the Task Force report. Despite lavishing fulsome praise on the efforts of the three unionist politicians who had drafted the document, one gets the impression that they did so through gritted teeth. They announced that as a result of its findings a new round of talks would be initiated with the British government over future constitutional arrangements for Northern Ireland.

> As a result we put in hand (immediately Parliament opened), steps through the usual channels at Westminster, to get these probing talks going. These are not negotiations but talks to see if the Government is prepared to enter into negotiations to seek an alternative to and a replacement of the Anglo-Irish agreement. The ball is now firmly in the Government's court and we are led to believe that the response will be helpful.[41]

Along with this new user-friendly form of unionism, where politicians declared their willingness to consider various options and to negotiate with government, came the old-style belligerence which had done so much to blight unionist fortunes over the previous twenty years. Thus we get Rev. Martin Smyth warning that unionists would reintroduce their Commons' boycott if the government did not respond positively to the Task Force report. Smyth indicated that a positive move had to be made by the government, otherwise unionists would have no choice but to leave Westminster again and embark upon a new phase of civil disobedience. Despite the fact that such ultimatums issued in the past by the likes of Brian Faulkner and Ian Paisley had met with little success, Smyth illustrated once again the totally insular political world which many unionists appeared to inhabit. While it may have been important to Martin Smyth that he attended Westminster, it was of relatively minor interest to a British Prime Minister. Indeed, as British policy from 1920 has centred around removing the Northern Ireland issue from the agenda of British politics, the self-enforced exile of unionist politicians might have been looked upon as a blessed by-product of the AIA.

Despite the effusiveness of their public rhetoric, it was clear that Molyneaux and Paisley were underwhelmed by the findings of *An End to Drift*. David Trimble put it unambiguously when commenting retrospectively on the period:

> . . . well I mean it's fairly obvious that the Task Force report was shelved. It
> was going in a different direction, it was calling for almost a sort of copycat
> Forum [New Ireland Forum], a convention of unionists representing the
> entire unionist community, to consider 'where we go from here'.[42]

When it was suggested to him that this may have been a good idea from
the unionist point of view, as a prerequisite for a successful political strategy
is knowing what you want to achieve, Trimble replied:

> You see, the subtext of the Task Force report seemed to me to be indepen-
> dence. I think if you look closely at the Task Force – the bit that was
> published – the subtext is independence, that we head for a political
> confrontation with the British government, saying 'either you treat us as
> genuinely part of the United Kingdom or you get out'. That basically was
> the line that they were on, and the political leadership, particularly Jim
> Molyneaux, didn't want that to happen, and he shelved the Task Force
> report. He had an alternative strategy. . . . Jim's approach is a more cautious,
> a more gradualist one, and his strategy was the one of slowly engaging the
> government in talks, in the hope of gradually turning them around and
> away from the Agreement.[43]

It was put to Trimble that an alternative reason why the report was shelved
was because of the thinly veiled criticisms it made of the conduct of the
anti-Agreement campaign in general, and the performance of the two
unionist leaders in particular. The title of the report, *An End to Drift,* pre-
supposes that the protest had lost momentum and the people ultimately
responsible for this situation were Ian Paisley and James Molyneaux. It
was also suggested to Trimble that it was difficult to imagine that Frank
Millar (accused by the CEC and many on the more radical fringes of
unionism of being a closet 'power-sharer') could put his name to a document which espoused independence. Trimble's response was that, despite
Millar's presence, the report could be interpreted as being in favour of
independence as a last resort should Britain refuse to maintain the Union
in a form acceptable to the unionist community. 'Well, there you are. I
think Harold [McCusker] and Peter [Robinson] were the ones, in particular,
that that line came more naturally to, and Jim Molyneaux didn't want to
have that sort of political confrontation.'[44]

Trimble's belief that the Task Force report was shelved by the unionist
leadership seems accurate. However, his suggestion that this was due to
its advocacy of independence is more difficult to accept. Michael McGimpsey,
for example, while agreeing that the report was not vigorously promoted
by the unionist leadership, commented that this was because it came out
in support of power-sharing devolution at a time when the integrationist
faction were at their most powerful within the UUP hierarchy.

> They [McCusker, Millar and Robinson] produced a report which, rumour
> has it, was for some form of devolution with cross-community consent. I

don't know why it wasn't pushed forward, but there were a lot of tensions at that time about the Task Force report, and then of course, the integrationists in the [Ulster] Unionist Party were muddying the waters, saying that integration was the only answer. So the Task Force ended up really as a damp squib.[45]

It is clear from these different perspectives that the unionists could not even agree amongst themselves about the findings of the Task Force, still less reach a consensus on why the leadership appeared reluctant to implement its recommendations. Trimble attributes Molyneaux with having the wisdom of Solomon and the patience of Job for taking his 'long view', while McGimpsey views this as 'masterly inactivity' from a leadership overly concerned with appeasing its internal warring factions. James Molyneaux has denied the allegation that the full report was not published because of criticisms made of the unionist leadership, claiming that it was a practical necessity forced upon him by those who had compiled it. Molyneaux's recollection of events casts doubt upon Trimble's account, namely that Molyneaux shelved the report because its subtext advocated independence. Asked whether he thought that *An End to Drift* got the credit it deserved, Molyneaux replied:

Yes it did. The reason that it wasn't all published was that . . . we were presented with a draft outline of the report, which was about three times the size of the finished article, and we quite rightly concluded that, 'the main problem is that you can't quote what has been said to you in confidence by church leaders, by the CBI, by other political parties, because you told them on our insistence, when you invited them, that their contribution would be in strict confidence'. So you can't go quoting, which the draft did actually, the draft said that this that and the other group – naming them – said on behalf of such and such, suggested this. We said 'no, but you can't do that. You can give a summary of your conclusions, refer to it that all the people we talked to, or two-thirds of the bodies we talked to, or one-quarter of the people were in favour of A, B and C, but you cannot go around quoting them', and that was the reason why it had to be redrafted and condensed. I think that they may have seen that themselves, only they didn't insist on it while Paisley and I felt that we had a duty to insist on it. It was for that reason it was condensed.[46]

Although Molyneaux was keen to promote the idea that the unionist leadership were bound on ethical grounds from publishing *An End to Drift* in its entirety, he went on to outline the political problems posed by the document, and it is these which provide a greater clue to his reservations about the report: '. . . the Task Force built in things . . . which were going to be a complete departure from the Paisley–Molyneaux strategy'.[47] What he meant was that, through its declaration that no unionist leader should contemplate any structure of devolved government which would exist under the auspices of the AIA, the report tied the hands of the unionist leadership and created an inflexible brand of unionism that they were now trying to get away from. 'When they put in that clincher that "you Paisley, you Molyneaux, mustn't contemplate a devolved structure in which Dublin will have any role, consultative or other". I mean that put the kibosh on any progress.'[48] When it was put to him that some within the Ulster Unionist Party believed the Task Force report was dumped because its subtext espoused independence, Molyneaux disagreed, presenting yet another interpretation of the report to add to those who saw it alternatively as advocating a solution based upon power-sharing or isolationism.

> No, no, it wasn't that [independence]: They did talk to people in bodies that you can think of who were in favour of independence, and in the initial one [the original draft] they actually quoted the names of the people who had said that independence was the thing, 'and Mr so and so asserted that arrangements could be made with the British Treasury to provide a sub-vention to an independent Ulster'. I liked that one, as if any Chancellor would ever do that. But that was the bit that had to be obliterated. There is in the Task Force a mention of independence, but because of that ban that we placed on quotes from either individuals or institutions, having given them an undertaking in the first place that they wouldn't be quoted, we just simply wouldn't sanction it. But it didn't feature to any great extent, in actual fact the joke of it was that the conclusions when you put them together were in favour, not of independence or devolution, but of inte-gration, because they had to take an opinion poll, and they discovered that that, put together with their interviews, gave integration as the one thing on which there was the bones of agreement right across the board, on the basis that it was 'fair dos' for everybody. This place [Westminster] would legislate on the basis of its seven-hundred-year record of protecting minorities, therefore it was safer than certain other experiments.[49]

It would appear from this that Molyneaux was oblivious to the fact that, during Britain's 'seven-hundred-year record of protecting minorities', Ireland suffered Cromwellian genocide, the penal laws, the Great Famine overseen by a criminally negligent British government, countless attempts to suppress the native culture and oppression of the Presbyterian settler community in Ulster. From the unionist perspective, Westminster's attempts to introduce Home Rule and their eventual signing of the Anglo-Irish Treaty in 1921, not to mention the AIA in 1985, were hardly motivated primarily from a desire to protect the minority unionist community in the north-east of Ireland. However, whatever about his reading of history, it is clear from Molyneaux's recollection of *An End to Drift* that he viewed it as creating more problems than it was likely to solve. Perhaps the last word on this point should be left to Peter Robinson, one of the members of the Task Force. When Molyneaux's allegations – that the report was not published in full because of errors in its drafting – were put to him, the DUP deputy leader gave a characteristically blunt response.

> It is absolute nonsense. It is crazy stuff that! The position was that there were two parts to the Task Force report. One [the second part] was our findings, you got all of the findings. The first part was our analysis of the campaign against the Anglo-Irish Agreement. As you could probably conclude, there were some criticisms and very sharp criticisms [of the unionist leadership] contained within that which it was felt it would be inappropriate to publish.[50]

What was also apparent was the lack of consensus among leading unionists over what the conclusions of the Task Force were, with conflicting theories being advanced as to why its recommendations were not put into effect. Some unionists went as far as to suggest that the report was a successful exercise and that its findings were not submerged but were actively followed up, culminating in the Brooke–Mayhew Talks of 1991–92. The Rev. Martin Smyth suggested that it successfully opened up channels of debate and dialogue, not only within the unionist community, but eventually between unionist political leaders and the British government.

> I think that the Task Force report was quite a good report. It gave an opportunity for a cross-fertilisation of ideas, people were encouraged to bring their views in the knowledge that they would not be revealed. . . . The recommendations were largely followed through . . . and we finally got the governments to acknowledge that there was a possibility of a new agreement, and as a result we were prepared to go into that negotiating business [the Brooke Talks], and while we're being held responsible for nothing being done, if you look at the record you will discover that it was Jim Molyneaux who opened that door for negotiations to take place, and he has not been given much credit for that.[51]

This sympathetic attitude to the Task Force proposals was not shared by those on the radical wing of unionism, despite Peter Robinson's participation. The *News Letter* published a letter signed simply 'Leaderless Loyalist', which provided an example of the disappointment which some unionists felt at the findings of the Task Force, and in particular its offer of what amounted to an internal power-sharing arrangement.

> Having been misled into voting in the recent election for politicians, who had obviously decided to sell us out by agreeing to some form of the inclusion of the republican SDLP in a future devolved administration in Ulster, our so-called leaders have compounded their weakness by supporting the task force report in a meaningless and vague joint statement which deliberately omitted to mention the fact that power sharing is now on offer to John Hume and Seamus Mallon . . . the leadership prompted by the Millar–McCusker–Robinson trio have prepared the ground-work for a total

surrender to the SDLP. Everything we have fought for over the past years is
to be thrown out because the politicians in a position to do something
about it are not fit for the job.[52]

While this view was not necessarily representative of mainstream unionist
opinion, it was undoubtedly in tune with a strong undercurrent of discontent with the Task Force expressed by more radical elements within
the unionist community. Paisley, who had based his political career around
undercutting those unionist colleagues who displayed a willingness to
revise the old 'not an inch' rhetoric of unionism, was well aware of grass-
roots feeling within his party and was keen to ensure that he did not stick
his neck out so far that it could be chopped off by the mob. Paisley's fear
of the 'Lundy factor', that negotiation and compromise would be seen as
treachery rather than good politics, together with his desire to maintain a
pact with the UUP, helps to explain his apparently schizophrenic behaviour
during this period. While he welcomed the conclusions of the Task Force
report and thanked its authors for their diligence in producing a valuable
document for discussion, he took every available opportunity to denounce
its findings. In early May 1987, before the conclusions of the report were
public knowledge, Paisley denounced power-sharing and made it abun-
dantly clear to Messrs Millar, McCusker and Robinson that they had better
think again.

> In the midst of Ulster's turmoil certain people are now advocating as the
> only way forward seats in any future government of Northern Ireland as of
> right for republicans, whether SDLP or Sinn Féin. In other words, the old
> power-sharing of Brian Faulkner and the Sunningdale agreement in another
> guise. Let me make it crystal-clear – the DUP will have none of it.[53]

On the eve of talks between the unionist leaders and government civil
servants in August, Paisley's message to the authors of the Task Force
report had not changed. 'Talk of compromise by some unionists . . . is the
talk of surrender.'[54] Frank Millar illustrated his sensitivity to such accusations when he told the press conference on the morning of the report's
publication that *An End to Drift* was not an act of treachery against the
unionist people. 'There isn't a white flag flying over Glengall Street this
morning. I don't think the three of us are feeling particularly nervous,
having authored a document for betrayal or sell-out.'[55]

By the beginning of August, both Paisley and Molyneaux were coming
under criticism for their lack of enthusiasm in following up the Task Force
proposals. Concern began to be expressed that the 'talks about talks'
initiative, which the two leaders had announced, was not being followed
through. Questions were being asked by grass-roots unionists as to what
was happening about the main recommendations of the report. When was
the panel to be appointed that would try to establish a basis for formal

negotiations? Where was the unionist convention to lead a renewed anti-Agreement campaign? Where was the special commission or research body to consider and advise on alternative constitutional models? The silence on these matters was deafening.

It is clear that little serious thought had been given to 'talks about talks' with the other 'constitutional' parties in Northern Ireland by the two unionist leaders. Their preoccupation at this stage was with finding a means of re-establishing contact with British government ministers. The UUP leader commented that he did not see this as a quick exercise, his language giving the impression that he was less than enthusiastic about the entire idea. Here again Molyneaux displayed his 'long view', believing (erroneously as it turned out) that time was on the unionists' side. 'I envisage several more rounds of probing discussions with civil servants. Assuming there are no serious hiccups, these could extend over a period of months before we get to the stage of talks with Government Ministers.'[56]

As far as the Task Force was concerned, Molyneaux commented that its recommendations would, as he put it, '. . . be brought into play at the appropriate time and as they become relevant to the talks'.[57] Ian Paisley denied reports that *An End to Drift* had advocated power-sharing devolution and said that he was not intent on ignoring its findings. A report in the *Irish Times* said that both Paisley and Molyneaux were set to break with the Task Force agenda, or at least prevaricate for as long as possible, 'because of its pro-devolution stance and perceived challenge to their authority'.[58] Paisley replied to this by commenting:

> It is a tissue of lies to suggest that there is any rolling battle between myself, Mr Molyneaux and the task force. . . . The task force was set up by Mr Molyneaux and myself and was to report to us – that has been done. We were to decide if and how much of it should be published – that has been done also. So that part of the operation is now over. We will take into cognisance what the task force has said, just as we will take into cognisance what many other people and organisations have said – but there is no private battle going on between us.[59]

Paisley claimed that the Task Force report had not been the catalyst for the talks about talks process, and that *An End to Drift* would not set the framework for formal negotiations with the government should they ever get off the ground.

> Our mandate for these talks comes from the general election and our manifesto when we said we would be going to see if there has been a change of heart on the part of the Government . . . but our position has not changed, and the Government is aware that it has not changed. We want a replacement of the agreement – an alternative to it – and it must be suspended and Maryfield shut down. . . . There hasn't been and there won't

be any sell out. I am not a Chichester-Clark. I am not a Terence O'Neill or a Brian Faulkner – and neither is Jim Molyneaux. We know the unionist case and we are working for it.[60]

However, this perspective stands at odds with Sammy Wilson's recollection, which was that the findings of the Task Force were actively followed up, and formed the basis for most of the positive political activity from 1987 onwards. Speaking four years after the publication of the report, Wilson denied that its findings had been either deliberately or accidently submerged, claiming that they had culminated in the Brooke–Mayhew initiative of 1991–92. In his view, the Task Force report represented the second part of the anti-Agreement campaign. The initial stages, he maintained, were necessarily negative as 'you could have clouded the issue' by trying to be positive during the first two years of the protest.[61] The Task Force, therefore, was a secondary phase in the battle against the AIA, activated, according to Wilson, after it had been communicated to the unionist community that the AIA was inherently bad and would have to be removed.

> I think that eventually most of the recommendations that were in the Task Force report were actually put into being. It took a bit of time, but I think that there was some adjustment and at the end of the day, we did put proposals to the government. We did push the government to start talks, and although the initiative which eventually came from it was called the Brooke initiative, the truth of the matter was that it was a unionist initiative, because it was started when we presented the paper to the Secretary of State in January of 1988.[62]

Talks with the SDLP

It is clear that the unionist leadership reacted in a defensive manner to the Task Force report. However, other signs were more hopeful. One indication of embryonic progress in unionism's journey back to progressive political activity was provided by a series of secret meetings which took place in the autumn of 1987 between prominent members of the UUP, the SDLP and the Northern Ireland Office. While these were ostensibly conducted without the knowledge of the party leaders, this attempt at what Americans would term 'plausible deniability' was clearly designed to tease out possible scenarios for interparty talks at a low level and out of the glare of the media spotlight that would have accompanied the exercise had it involved party leaders. A senior source within the UUP confirmed that secret talks had been taking place but refused to discuss them. He would only say that one of the meetings with the SDLP took place on a nobleman's estate in Germany a few weeks earlier. 'The talks are an open secret in unionist ranks but nobody is prepared to talk about them.'[63] While few unionists were prepared to go on the record, others were not so reticent. Sean Farren, the SDLP's employment spokesman, admitted that informal talks had been going on with the UUP and the NIO.

> I would call them informal contacts rather than talks, because the term talks has a formal ring about it. Northern Ireland is a small community and these contacts are made in all kinds of circumstances. I have no doubt that issues are raised about the current political climate, but not on a formal basis. But the people are not talking with a mandate. The debate on the current political situation is healthy, but it is not formal.[64]

Seamus Mallon, meanwhile, denied any knowledge of the talks and said his information was that the party leader John Hume was similarly unaware that such contact was taking place. Robert McCartney weighed in to the escalating unionist crisis with his statement that a prominent SDLP member had confirmed to him personally that talks had taken place between unionists and nationalists.[65]

It soon became clear that a further meeting between the UUP and SDLP had taken place at the Cohannon Inn on the outskirts of Dungannon between April and June 1987. It was strongly rumoured that SDLP politician Paddy O'Hanlon was one of the two nationalists present, though he categorically denied any involvement. The devolutionist Charter Group were closely associated with the unionist involvement in these discussions. The group's leading spokesman David McNarry came under attack from Ian Paisley for suggesting that it was inconceivable that the DUP leader could have been unaware of the talks taking place behind his back. Paisley rejected McNarry's claim that he had turned a blind eye to the interparty discussions. In his typically strident manner, he went on to accuse McNarry of being more amenable to the SDLP than to his fellow unionists, the implication being that he was a compromiser and a traitor to the Protestant cause.

> The DUP is having no talks with the SDLP, either officially or unofficially, and his assertion that I know about such talks is an atrocious lie. I do, however, remember his visit to my home with Harry West in which their proposal was that the future government of Northern Ireland should consist of three Official Unionists and two SDLP members. All other unionists were to be excluded. Evidently Mr McNarry and Mr West prefer partnership with the SDLP than partnership with the Official Unionists and other members of the unionist family.[66]

Paisley also vetoed plans by the Church of Ireland primate, Archbishop Robin Eames, to hold interparty talks. The archbishop's proposal was that he would act as an intermediary to get the political leaders around the table for a series of informal private discussions. Eames claimed to have received support for the scheme from John Hume, James Molyneaux and

Alliance Party leader John Cushnahan. Paisley, who had delayed his response to the initiative, finally came out against it on 12 August, commenting that it would conflict with the talks that the two unionist leaders were having with the British government.

> I don't see any point in the party leaders talking at this stage until these talks with the Government that we are having come to a conclusion. It is early days yet. The wisest thing would be to let the exploratory talks go ahead with the Government.[67]

However, Eames's blueprint aimed at breaking the deadlock and getting Northern Ireland politicians engaged in dialogue was praised by the president of the Ulster Unionist Council Sir George Clark, who commented that Paisley's rejection of the interparty talks plan was a rebuff that the Church of Ireland cleric did not deserve.[68]

On 8 August, a positive meeting took place in London between the two unionist leaders, Sir Kenneth Bloomfield, head of the Northern Ireland civil service, and Sir Robert Andrew, permanent secretary at the NIO, for exploratory talks in advance of their proposed meeting with the government. Molyneaux declared that it could be some time before there were firm indications of the government's willingness to negotiate a replacement for the AIA. 'It is quite a complicated process and extreme caution is necessary. No one should be expecting too much too soon.'[69] It is obvious from Molyneaux's rhetoric that he was trying to play down the possibility of agreement with the government in case the momentum became too strong to stop and he was prematurely forced down the road of negotiation with the government. Despite his pedestrian approach to the pace of discussions, such contacts were an important step forward for unionist politics and an essential ingredient to talks with the British government.

By mid-August, some unionists were advancing the theory that informal interparty talks were on the increase because many unionists distrusted the UUP leader's ability to deliver on devolved government. This accusation was levelled by David McNarry of the Charter Group who said that the UUP was a devolutionist party which did not have a devolutionist leader. 'Over the last 15 months more and more unionists have been talking to nationalists on the quiet. All these talks have been on an informal basis because no-one has a mandate or approval to officially represent their parties.'[70] McNarry claimed that the reason for the increase in the amount of interparty traffic was the disillusionment with James Molyneaux and mistrust of where he was leading the party. The Charter Group spokesperson claimed that Molyneaux would never deliver devolution and this had caused some within the party to put out their own feelers to the nationalists in the hope that they could cobble together an agreement on devolution in spite of their party leader. Molyneaux was defended by leading members of the UUP including one of his close political friends,

Ballymena unionist councillor and prominent Orangeman, the Rev. Robert Coulter, from the North Antrim constituency. An angry Coulter attacked McNarry with the following statement:

> Mr McNarry's comments that Jim Molyneaux could not be trusted to negotiate devolution is a reflection of his own twisted thinking. Mr McNarry has proved that he is the one along with his co-conspirators who are in fact displaying the evidence of betraying Ulster more than anyone else. Those who have consulted with nationalists without the leader's blessing are the quislings of Unionism in Ulster's greatest crisis. They have no right to talk on behalf of Unionism and they have no place in unionist policy making. They should be exposed and drummed out of the party.[71]

Once again we see the tendency within the ideology to lash out at those who do not conform, branding anyone who dares seek dialogue with the nationalist community as a traitor to the cause. McNarry was a leading member of the Orange Order whose advocacy of an internal solution to the Northern Ireland conflict did not differ substantially from many of his more hardline colleagues.

Molyneaux responded to the growing attack on his leadership by warning that anyone indulging in interparty talks without his authority irrespective of their rank would be disciplined by the party executive. The UUP leader denied that he knew of any talks taking place with the NIO and that he was similarly unaware that unionists and SDLP members had met near Dungannon for bilateral discussions. Apparently the fifth meeting between unnamed members of the UUP and the NIO, scheduled to take place in Craigavad on the evening of 19 August, was swiftly abandoned due to the surrounding publicity. Molyneaux's declared ignorance of the Craigavad and Dungannon meetings was expressed in the following statement on 18 August:

> I was not told about talks in Craigavad or Dungannon and I have no knowledge of this activity. There is a difference to plotting to overthrowing the leader and actually bringing it about. . . . I am not going to jump overboard because that would destroy the Ulster Unionist Council which re-elected me. I am not worried by a leadership coup. There will be blood on the floor first.[72]

It is obvious from these comments that Molyneaux was extremely worried that the secret talks were primarily aimed at dislodging him from the leadership. His statement openly admitted that he had lost the support of a significant section of his party. His warning that, to overthrow him, his opponents would have to tear the party apart, illustrates both his tenacity and the precarious state of his leadership at the time.

As the summer of 1987 drew to a close, Molyneaux and Paisley resumed their talks with government officials at the NIO. The latest talks held at

Stormont Castle lasted for ninety minutes and a further meeting was arranged for early September. Clearly these meetings functioned on a number of levels. From the British perspective, the mechanism was all important. Such meetings acted as a lubricant to unionism's return to conventional political activity. The dulcet tones and listening ear of Sir Kenneth Bloomfield and other NIO officials offered hope to beleaguered unionist politicians that their case would be heard sympathetically by the British government. However, the subtext of these meetings was that the AIA was not a matter for negotiation. While the British were anxious to facilitate unionism's journey back to the mainstream, they were not planning concessions of any substance.

Due to his fear that the NIO were trying to trap them into talks from which it might be difficult to extricate themselves without making concessions over the AIA, Peter Robinson urged caution on the two unionist leaders in their impending discussions with the government. Speaking at the opening of a new Apprentice Boys' club in Portsmouth, the DUP deputy leader commented that the talks about talks process was simply an exercise to ascertain whether or not the AIA and the Maryfield secretariat could be suspended. He stressed that these contacts had no business negotiating future government structures for Northern Ireland.

> We are mandated never to accept the Anglo-Irish agreement nor support or accept any structure that exists within or runs alongside it. I intend to keep faith with the electorate . . . we would only find it profitable, therefore, to take part in negotiations that permitted us the means to negotiate an alternative to and replacement of the agreement.[73]

Unionist resignations

A further blow to unionist morale came with Frank Millar's shock announcement on 11 September that he was retiring from active politics. It was widely interpreted that Millar's departure to begin a career in journalism was the result of his political leader's back-pedalling on the Task Force proposals. Paisley denied that either himself or James Molyneaux had distanced themselves from the report.

> I have yet to read anywhere in the Task Force report where it advocates power-sharing as of right in any devolved government, and if Mr Millar's interpretation was for power-sharing as of right then his departure may perhaps not be wholly regretted.[74]

Party colleague Harold McCusker paid the following tribute to Millar, who had been the youngest ever general secretary of the Ulster Unionist Party: 'A very bright light in the unionist firmament has been snuffed out. . . . Unionist circles in general will be in darkness for quite some time.'[75] Clearly this can be read as a criticism of the unionist leadership as

McCusker's use of the phrase 'snuffed out' implies that Millar's political demise was not self-induced and that he may have stayed had the Task Force report been implemented more swiftly.

Millar's contribution to the unionist ideology and his specific cultural outlook which separated him from many of his political colleagues were astutely pointed out by an article in *Fortnight* entitled 'The Exit of the Young Turks'. Here Millar was rightly praised for being reluctant to merely 'bang the Lambeg drum' and for taking a less insular attitude to politics, recognising that the future of the unionist community was as much dependent upon convincing those outside the region of the validity of their case, as it was upon preaching to the converted within Northern Ireland.

> Much of Millar's work went unnoticed or unappreciated. He successfully convinced important sceptical Westminster journalists that the unionist cause still had merit. He was acutely aware of the weak position of unionism – without friends, its representatives simply were not thinking or speaking in terms that the rest of the world understood. But he was, at 32, too young to be party leader – not to mention too sharp, too impatient, too liberal and too intelligent.[76]

Millar's interpretation of unionist priorities, therefore, placed an emphasis upon winning friends in Britain over to the validity of the unionist case against the AIA, rather than simply living in splendid isolation within the confines of Northern Ireland. However, as Sammy Wilson's perspective on the anti-Agreement campaign illustrates, there was a difference of opinion between key figures in the two main unionist parties over fundamental strategy. When asked whether he thought that it was imperative for unionists to regain some degree of popularity for their case in Britain, Wilson replied:

> No I don't think it is. I think that if we waste our time trying to persuade people in England, who basically aren't interested in what happens here, . . . and if you put your time and your energy into trying to convince English people that they should do the right thing by you, I think that you will waste valuable resources.[77]

In September 1987, Wilson reiterated Peter Robinson's earlier appeal for the leadership to adopt a more democratic approach to discussions with the government. Robinson's suggestion that the leadership's mandate was simply to determine whether or not talks with the government were possible and did not extend to the actual conduct of negotiations was echoed by the DUP press officer. Wilson claimed that it was an ideal time for the party leadership to consult a wider section of the unionist electorate before the next round of talks in October. He suggested that the parties should canvass opinion in the unionist community to determine what type of political solution was acceptable to them, rather than to go into talks with the government and emerge with a deal which did not meet with the approval of their electors.

> Considering the willingness of Mr King to get involved in this latest round of talks and that another meeting has been pencilled in, I feel the leaders must indicate what progress they feel has taken place . . . I feel the time is right for the leaders to say to a wider group, 'well, what do you think we should do now? We would like to hear what you think'.[78]

This comment was indicative of some worry within the DUP that their leader was coming under the influence of James Molyneaux to an alarming extent and might be lulled into a compromise which would be unacceptable to the party, causing embarrassment to all concerned.

Not everyone within the unionist family was in a positive frame of mind in the autumn of 1987. Ulster Clubs chairman Alan Wright condemned a forthcoming meeting with Tom King, saying it was a disgrace that Molyneaux and Paisley could find time to sit down with their arch enemy and yet refuse to implement the unionist convention as proposed by the Task Force. Wright appealed to them to organise with people who really cared for Northern Ireland, instead of further capitulation to those who wished to destroy it.[79]

If Frank Millar's departure had rocked the Ulster Unionists, then Peter Robinson's announcement on 7 October that he was stepping down as deputy leader of the DUP had no less effect on his party. Clearly, his resignation was linked to the party's response to the Task Force report, both at a leadership level and among other colleagues who read it as advocating power-sharing with nationalists and a betrayal of the unionist people. Relations between Paisley and his deputy had been strained since the publication of the report in July and Robinson appeared to have taken a dim view of the leadership's virtual shelving of the report. Harold McCusker commented that Robinson's resignation had taken him by surprise. 'He didn't discuss it with me beforehand . . . I imagine it might well be to do with the Task Force.'[80] Despite the recent resignations of senior unionist colleagues, Paisley remained unrepentant, attacking what he called 'foolish, misguided' unionists who had joined with the SDLP and Alliance chorus that concessions must be made despite the continued existence of the AIA and the government's refusal to consider suspending the Maryfield secretariat. Paisley's message to such people was that 'We have no more concessions to make.'[81] This was certainly a criticism of Frank Millar's recent rhetoric and that of his own ex-deputy, that unionists had to be realists and would have to contemplate what had previously been anathema to them, if an internal devolved settlement was to be reached. Paisley remained adamant that any further concessions by the unionist community would be a departure from democracy and 'Nothing less than an obituary notice to a dead unionism.'[82]

Liberal unionists who wanted to see a more flexible approach taken by the unionist leadership were facing an uphill battle at the end of 1987. Evidence that such sentiments were not representative of unionist opinion was provided by delegates at the UUP annual conference in November, when a proposal by Ken Maginnis that the nationalist minority should be given a veto in any future devolved assembly was rejected. The conference denied Maginnis's assertion that the lack of such a veto power would impair the progress of devolution within Northern Ireland after the AIA was eventually removed. Instead, the conference backed a motion from the East Londonderry Association that the party would not accept a system of devolved government whose decisions were subject to a veto by a minority or decisions taken within the framework of the AIA.[83] Maginnis commented that the signing of the AIA changed the political environment within which the Ulster Unionists operated. The Fermanagh MP claimed that this new relationship between London and Dublin made it necessary for the party to re-evaluate both the anti-Agreement protest and their ultimate objectives if they were to act as an effective pressure group on the British government. 'It is not good enough just to re-state our orthodox position because that position for unionists changed on the day when London and Dublin agreed to share power in Northern Ireland.'[84] Maginnis went on to say that unionists had to be prepared to enter a dialogue with 35 per cent of the community which did not describe itself as unionist.

What Maginnis was recognising here was what the Task Force had also concluded, namely that the nationalist minority in Northern Ireland had, since 1972, held a veto over the unionist community. The practical reality of the situation was that no form of self-government would be devolved to Northern Ireland from Westminster unless it had the approval of the SDLP and the Southern government. Maginnis was clearly aware that an agreement between unionism and constitutional nationalism was essential if any political settlement was to have the slightest chance of success. Thus the traditional unionist strategy of trying to wring major political concessions from the British government over the heads of the SDLP or, worse still, in direct opposition to their wishes, was a futile exercise and needed to be revised. 'If we put obstacles in the way of such dialogue [with the SDLP] then we are placing a weapon in the hands of the two Governments who jointly rule us under the Agreement.'[85]

While such advice may not have been what the unionist faithful wished to hear, it was apparent to most that negotiation with the British government and the SDLP was the only way forward. To do this effectively, they would have to establish a political position which presented a practical alternative to the AIA, rather than engaging in the monosyllabic performance-art which had characterised the 'Ulster Says No' campaign.

New year resolutions

The realisation that conventional political behaviour was the only serious option left for the unionist coalition explains the set of proposals submitted to Secretary of State Tom King by the UUP and DUP in January 1988. However, the secrecy which surrounded this initiative and the unionist attitude to it would indicate that it was aimed more at securing some political leverage against the British government than forming the basis for an internal settlement.

Evidence of more realistic thinking within unionism was provided on 8 January 1988, when senior unionists from both parties met to form a policy think-tank which aimed to draft new political proposals to put to Tom King.[86] In response to this joint party initiative, the Charter Group announced the setting up of a new pressure group under the name of the Campaign for a Regional Parliament (CRP). This group was dedicated to achieving the abolition of direct rule, and thereby the AIA. The CRP, led by David McNarry and former unionist leader Harry West, was not received with open arms by all sections of the unionist press, and this was illustrated by a scathing attack the following month from *News Letter* columnist Alex Kane. He derided the latest initiative by the Charter Group and condemned others within the devolutionist camp, declaring that this was an idea which had passed its political 'sell-by' date.

> So, the devolution wheel has come full circle again. The Charter Group has metamorphisised into the 'Campaign for a Regional Parliament', the long awaited sequel to 'Indiana McNarry and the Raiders of the Lost Cause'. . . . Everyone may want it [devolution], but they want it for different and contradictory reasons. It may be ironic, but it is nonetheless true, that the very thing the parties, groups and governments have in common is the very thing they will not and cannot agree upon. They may as well search an oven for a snowflake as search for a form of devolution which is acceptable to them all.[87]

In their 'search of the oven', Ian Paisley and James Molyneaux met Tom King for three hours on 25 January to determine if any potential existed for political progress. At the meeting, the two leaders discussed their draft proposals on a way forward with the Secretary of State. These called for a suspension of the workings of the Agreement and a declaration by the British government that it would consider an alternative to the AIA as a precursor to negotiations. Both leaders refused to comment on the outcome of their talks with Tom King other than to issue a press statement simply declaring that a further meeting would be held in due course. Speaking in retrospect, James Molyneaux's recollection of the proposals was that:

> They were a development of the paper that went to Thatcher in August '85. They were taking account of the fact, of course, that we had seen the

document [the AIA], we had seen the flaws in it even from the point of view
of the Irish Republic, that it was far too narrow.[88]

These talks between the unionist leaders and Tom King concentrated on
the issue of administrative devolution. The unionists proposed a new
devolved assembly, with a network of committees answerable to it. It was
envisaged that these committees would administer matters covered by
most NIO departments with the exception of security, and that the Secretary
of State would deal directly with the committee chairmen. The chairmen
were to be appointed in accordance with party strength in the new assembly,
which one unionist source dismissed as a 'grandiose county council
without executive powers'.[89] This suggestion that the January proposals
were concerned merely with administrative devolution has subsequently
been denied by the DUP, Nigel Dodds recollecting that 'we wouldn't have
put forward any document that simply had administrative devolution'.[90]
Sammy Wilson was also keen to contest such allegations, recalling that the
DUP had always been and would remain committed to legislative devolution.

> . . . it was made quite clear in the proposals that we were looking for the
> widest possible devolution. We would never have put our signature to
> anything which was simply administrative devolution. We want to see
> administrative, legislative devolution. We wanted to see security powers
> devolved and we wanted the widest possible [devolution]. I know that there
> are boundaries, certain limits on any local government . . . there would be
> certain fiscal things and foreign things that we couldn't have possibly had,
> but we wanted to have as much power devolved here and not some kind of
> sham or shell.[91]

It soon became clear that NIO officials were not impressed by what they
had heard from unionist politicians in the talks. As shall become clear later
on, this lack of enthusiasm for the January proposals was not simply a
reaction to their modest content, but more fundamentally perhaps, a perception on the part of the NIO that the unionists were not really serious
about initiating interparty talks with the SDLP on the future government
of Northern Ireland.

Disillusioned with the lack of positive movement towards a regionally
based settlement, the Charter Group attempted to map out a stronger
devolutionist agenda within the UUP by launching a new pressure group.
Building on the foundations of the Campaign for a Regional Parliament,
the new group unveiled in March 1988 called itself the Campaign for a
Devolved Parliament (CDP). It advocated devolution on a partnership
basis with legislative authority and a written constitution, buttressed by a
bill of rights. The CDP document, entitled *A Better Deal Together*, contended
that the only way of ending political violence in the region was to create
the conditions whereby both communities learned to work alongside one

another, and became jointly responsible for maintaining law and order. The process would involve interparty dialogue, formal negotiations and a settlement put to the people for endorsement by a referendum. Like the UDA's *Common Sense* proposals, the message to nationalists was that they would be treated fairly under the law within an internal settlement. In other words, if they gave up being nationalists and accepted the legitimacy of Northern Ireland as part of the Union, they would be granted minority rights within the state. Everyone seems to be in favour of referenda these days, though there is less agreement about the area which should be balloted: Northern Ireland, the island of Ireland, the United Kingdom or the British Isles. Doubtless the supporters of such a plan as that put forward by the CDP would argue that nationalists were simply being asked to accept reality. That reality was that for the foreseeable future Northern Ireland would remain within the United Kingdom because a majority of its residents wanted it to. They could, under these circumstances, accept this reality while still aspiring to Irish unity. Nationalists might reply that such a scenario allowed unionists to have their cake and eat it, while they were only allowed to look at the pictures. While nationalists may not have fallen over themselves with enthusiasm about such proposals, they were at least a further sign that elements within the unionist community wanted to reach a negotiated settlement.

At the beginning of February, meanwhile, positive noises began to be made by Harold McCusker, when he called on his fellow unionists to devise a political formula which would satisfy the SDLP and the Irish government, as well as themselves. He added that while he could not see circumstances in which Sinn Féin would give up violence, thereby precluding unionists from having to talk to them, it was nevertheless possible that they could renounce the 'armed struggle' at some point in the future. He commented that in this eventuality he could not see how they or their descendants could be excluded from the talks process. As for the anti-Agreement campaign, McCusker claimed that the British government could '. . . live with the resistance which has not been as determined as I would have liked. It has not shaken the Agreement.'[92] The UUP deputy leader was tacitly admitting that the campaign against the AIA was not going to be successful in its present form, and would have to be accompanied by a more positive approach. In essence, therefore, he was admitting that the unionists were in the end going to have to negotiate their way out of the AIA, and the sooner they faced up to that fact the better.

Even though the unionist parties were flogging the dead horse of the anti-Agreement campaign at the beginning of 1988, positive noises were being made in unlikely quarters. Protestant paramilitaries argued that a more progressive strategy was required to replace the negative strategy of the main parties. *Combat*, the house journal of the UVF, castigated the abstentionist tactics of the unionist leadership, commenting in its February editorial that this was yet another petty exercise in futility which sidetracked the unionist community from the real issues. 'Someone should be pushing these issues day and daily instead of popping in and out of Crumlin Road Prison every other week for motoring offences!'[93] *Combat* proceeded to illustrate its populist secular outlook with an attack on the elitist nature of unionist political leadership. It is also clear from the following comment that its more positive political outlook was directly linked to a greater confidence about the external political environment – and particularly British government intentions – than is normally to be found within mainstream unionist parties.

> . . . Ulster's Protestant working class have been dead suckers for a good story. First it was the aristocracy and landed proprietors who appeared, as from another planet at election times . . . then came the merchants, the skin-the-goats who could be depended upon for a job as long as you were a Prod, vote for me, mind you, or the Pope will be here in the morning. With their military ranking they resembled a military Junta. . . . The military Junta has been replaced by a 'Vicars' Caucus'. There is not the slightest, not the remotest chance that Britain intends to hand us over to the Papal statelet down below. The examination of the most elementary criteria show it to be an impossibility without mass violence. Our politicians know this and if they do not know it, then they must be thick as well as bent.[94]

While the two main unionist parties were prepared in early 1988 to dip their toes into the ocean of political negotiation, they still exhibited signs of hydrophobia. In March, for example, Molyneaux made it clear that the unionists would not be participating in the review of the AIA scheduled for November.

> There will be no unionist input into the review, except in the sense that our views and objections are publicly known. We would be prepared to give public clarification of our position, if it was needed, but we have no intention of attending any conference on the review.[95]

Molyneaux again illustrated here his predisposition to select a neutral rather than a forward gear, his strategy for defeating the AIA being not to bellow at the government but to wait until they came around to his way of thinking. He rejected participation in the review on the basis that it was not of a sufficiently fundamental nature. 'What we are interested in is an alternative agreement – Government willingness to draft a new agreement. . . . The review would simply be looking at the mechanics of the deal and trying to find ways of improving it.'[96] In typical Molyneaux style, as the review option was an unattractive one, he refrained from advocating his own initiative, such as a New Ireland Forum style alternative review of the AIA by unionists. One of the main reasons he did not do this was because he knew that they would never reach agreement amongst themselves on a specific package to replace it. His only suggestion was that unionists should do nothing and wait for the tide of events to turn in their favour. 'The fact that the exchanges between London and Dublin have become more acrimonious since the agreement was signed shows that it is defective by any standard set by the two governments.'[97] Molyneaux expressed his irritation that he was being pressured into taking part in a review of the Agreement on the strict parameters set out within the existing treaty, a process which ignored the proposals which the unionists had given to Tom King in January. Commenting retrospectively, Molyneaux pointed out that the unionist proposals were ignored because the British government were scared of their radical content and the fact that this might disturb London's exclusive dialogue with the Dublin government. The British, from Molyneaux's perspective, did not want the unionists talking to Dublin for fear that the latter might find their proposals about a wider Anglo-Irish agreement attractive. This, according to Molyneaux, would have forced London to take some unpalatable decisions which might extend Dublin's influence over the 'mother country'. When asked why the unionists did not make more of an effort to publicise their proposals once it had become obvious that the British government and the NIO were not interested in following them up, Molyneaux replied:

> There was high comedy about that because there was no evidence that they did do very much about it. They certainly didn't ever show them to the Dublin government although we wouldn't have objected if they had done that, the reason being they were dead scared of them, the British government was. She [Margaret Thatcher] had laid down the law that there wasn't going to be one inch of a retreat from the Agreement in any shape or form, and she seemed to have [Tom] King pretty well scared, that he wasn't permitted to encourage us. I remember on one occasion I said to him [that] we were talking about widening the Agreement to give Dublin rather more say overall, in the United Kingdom's affairs, and he said, 'I don't know anything about their views'. 'Well', I said, 'why don't you ask them?' 'No I will do no such thing', he said. He just simply refused.[98]

If Molyneaux thought that his offer to widen the terms of the AIA to cover the rest of the UK, thus giving Dublin a consultative role in Britain's internal affairs, would have been an attractive policy option for the British government and would entice them out of the existing arrangements with the Republic, he could be justly accused of living in a fantasy world. There is a theoretical logic in his position, to the extent that the AIA was specific to Northern Ireland and did not remedy the grievances of Irish citizens living in Britain. However, to advocate an agreement which extended the influence of the Irish government into the rest of the UK was to miss the point entirely. The reason the AIA was signed was that Britain did not and never has thought of Northern Ireland as an indigenous part of the UK. In essence, they regard the region as a part of Ireland over which Britain legitimately rules for a variety of historical reasons, but primarily because the majority of the people living in Northern Ireland wish it to do so. Britain would not countenance the Irish government's interference in any aspect of 'mainland' politics, as this was of no legitimate concern to Dublin. For its part, of course, Dublin would not be interested in pursuing what Molyneaux described as 'A British–Irish Agreement which would relate co-extensively to the territory of both islands, both nations [*sic*].'[99] The underlying rationale of Molyneaux's scheme was essentially integrationist. It proposed an agreement which was non-specific to Northern Ireland and where Dublin would have precisely the same rights of consultation over the welfare of Irish people in Finchley as it would have in respect of those in Fermanagh. Molyneaux suggested that such arrangements would be much more practical than the present restrictive Agreement and would be a realisation of the political goals announced by Thatcher and Haughey in 1980.

> I mean that fits in with the [Tom] King document, the document we put to King, with my philosophy of a much wider British–Irish agreement co-extensive to the territories of both nations, with the Anglo-Irish Intergovernmental Council, with its secretariat based here in the Cabinet Office [Westminster], and if you want to have the other end of it in Dublin, that's all right with me. Looking at all those matters, the Irish in England, the prevention of terrorism and all its operations, security co-operation, everything can be done through that. We don't need this very restrictive Agreement [AIA] applying to only six counties out of the entire British Isles. I mean that's just plain daft. In fact that Anglo-Irish Agreement in '85 was a direct contradiction of the Charlie [Haughey]–Thatcher philosophy of 1980, because that wasn't the totality, that was a miniature of the relationship not the totality.[100]

It is hard to believe that Molyneaux proposed this scheme with any degree of seriousness. He was not a naive politician, and must surely have known that the British government, who have spent the best part of the century trying to keep Irish issues off the domestic political agenda, were not likely to grasp at this opportunity to have them placed firmly on it once again. In addition, while the British would not regard giving Dublin a consultative role in the affairs of Northern Ireland as a ceding of British sovereignty, they would most definitely regard any interference from an Irish government in 'mainland' politics as a breach of sovereignty. Though this may be anomalous in constitutional terms, it points up the fact that Northern Ireland is not seen by the British people as an indigenous part of the nation, but rather as a freak of historical circumstance which they have a responsibility to govern until some other arrangements are worked out.

If Molyneaux knew that this idea would never really be taken seriously by the British government, what then was his purpose in suggesting it? Clearly the January proposals were designed in such a way that they allowed the unionists to present broad ideas to the British government which they hoped would allow them to enter political discussions without conceding ground. The woolliness of the proposals allowed the unionists to maintain their coalition without the inevitable factionalism which would have emerged once they were asked to make some positive choices about where they wanted to go politically. In addition, the move allowed them to claim that they were not being totally negative, and that it was the British government who were the recalcitrant party. Molyneaux's policy of waiting for the inevitable collapse of the AIA due to the internal strains upon it was a typically passive approach from a politician who regarded political initiatives as inherently dangerous, raising expectations or fears which were often misplaced.

The respected commentator on Irish current affairs, Fionnuala O'Connor, subsequently reported that Molyneaux was not even promoting his own January proposals as the basis for political negotiations.

> Those still dealing out optimism might be interested to know that the OUP leader himself is keen to play down the significance of the document he handed over. 'What King has isn't a blueprint, you know,' he told an associate recently. 'I don't even agree with some of it. It's just an outline. Anyhow, it goes no farther than we did when we suggested administrative devolution back in 1979.'[101]

These comments would suggest that the January proposals were intended to create some political leverage for the unionists rather than act as a genuine stepping-stone to an eventual agreement on a devolved administration. The unionists it would seem, if Molyneaux's view was representative, were simply reiterating their previous position, which clearly cut no ice with London, Dublin or the SDLP. This reiteration was accompanied by a proposal for a widening of the terms of the Agreement which nobody except themselves was remotely interested in.

If the unionists were under no illusions that their latest proposals for devolution would not provide a basis for dialogue with the other protagonists – as described by Molyneaux, they pale into insignificance alongside the *Common Sense* document for instance – what then was their function? Clearly both Paisley and Molyneaux were more interested in achieving a suspension of the workings of the AIA and the Maryfield secretariat than they were in cobbling together a package for devolved government which the UUP leader did not particularly want anyway and the DUP leader realised he would have great difficulty in selling to his rank and file supporters. As they could not engage in any dialogue until the accord was suspended – a political reality if a self-inflicted wound – they clearly hoped that the January proposals contained just enough substance to entice London, if not Dublin or the SDLP, into pressurising for a suspension, in order to see if there was any mileage in the initiative. Sadly for the unionists their proposals lay dormant, ignored and unwanted. However, while their content was regarded by their political opponents as amounting to little more than 'yesterday's ideas today', they functioned as an important stepping-stone in the revitalisation of unionist politics, signalling the beginning of a more pragmatic approach.

It was no longer a question of whether the unionists would negotiate, it was simply a matter of when and on what basis. Building on the positive momentum of *Common Sense*, the UDA launched an appeal through the editorial columns of *Ulster* magazine for unionists to hold a democratic conference to which all constitutional parties would be invited to put proposals for the future government of Northern Ireland. The magazine warned that the longer the unionist leadership delayed taking a political initiative aimed at achieving devolved government, along the lines of the plan outlined by *Common Sense*, the more likely it was that support would increase for those groups which advocated independence.

> Force will only be productive as a flexible part of an overall political and propaganda campaign . . . the days of merely reacting to the symptoms of the problems are now over. From now on we must set the agenda – neither must we fall into the trap of giving the British establishment an excuse to get out. . . . The future campaign must be one to produce a settlement not to save the careers of failed politicians or to maintain outdated ideas . . . to this end it is essential that the carefully sculpted image of the UDA as being gangsters is laid to rest once and for all.[102]

Once again the emphasis here was on the development of a clear political strategy for a replacement of the AIA rather than a continuation of counterproductive political stunts with diminishing returns which had characterised unionist political activity since 1985. However, notwithstanding the positive rhetoric, the UDA were undergoing an internal reorganisation which led to their becoming the most active terror organisation in Northern Ireland.

The unionist leadership also came in for attack from Ulster Clubs chairman Alan Wright, who suggested that their apparent lethargy disguised a desire to compromise with the British government over the suspension of the AIA. Speaking at the movement's annual conference in Portadown, Wright maintained that the talks about talks with Tom King were supposed to be about establishing whether the government were prepared to be flexible in the operation of the AIA to the point of suspending it. As the government had repeatedly stated their commitment to the 'diktat', he wondered how much longer it would be '. . . wise for Mr Molyneaux and the Rev. Ian Paisley to continue with what can only be seen as a duplicitous exercise on the part of Tom King and the Northern Ireland Office'.[103] Wright's comments suggest that he feared some form of compromise was likely to result from these talks and he was eager to make it clear that such a 'sell-out' would not be tolerated by his organisation or by the mass of the Protestant community. 'We underline once again that no arrangement is acceptable which would bring a republican government here, or would give the Irish Republic any say in our affairs.'[104] Wright made clear that an Irish dimension was not acceptable, but suggested that dominion status would facilitate peace and democracy in Northern Ireland.

> We believe, with Harold McCusker, that another alternative must be sought. Our dominion status document is such an alternative, and would preserve our Ulster-British heritage, maintain our historic links with the Crown, and allow all the people of Northern Ireland to enjoy first-class citizenship and democratic control of our own affairs.[105]

What is interesting about Wright's criticism of the unionist leadership is that, despite implicit warnings that any compromise with the Republic would be unacceptable, his rhetoric is much more considered than was evident three years earlier. No longer do we hear blood-chilling warnings of Armageddon, of hoping for the best but preparing for the worst; the emphasis now was on the necessity for political discourse. It could of course be said that the Ulster Clubs' analysis was rather one dimensional, and that their proposals for dominion status were unrealistic. Nevertheless, it is interesting to note that the penchant for political movement as opposed to paramilitary action, so apparent within mainstream unionism over the previous six months, had permeated even the most exotic reaches of the Protestant community. While it would be inaccurate to cite such rhetoric as evidence that Alan Wright had hung up his red beret, his attempt to win the 'battle of the pamphlets' and influence policy within the unionist community was an indication that the initial reaction to the AIA, which saw civil disobedience as the only way of defeating the Agreement, was being subjected to its own revisionist analysis.

The rash of statements and speeches made by Ulster Unionists anxious to display their liberal credentials must have been disconcerting at the very least for their colleagues within the DUP. It was almost inevitable that a row would erupt between the two parties, as conciliatory noises about co-operation with Dublin emanated from Glengall Street. Predictably, Sammy Wilson was one of the first to voice his criticism over what he saw as an infringement of joint party policy by the Ulster Unionists on the issue of Dublin's involvement in the affairs of Northern Ireland. Wilson's comments came in the wake of a statement by Rev. Martin Smyth to the effect that the UUP would welcome the opening of an office in Northern

Ireland by the Southern government. Wilson declared that his party would not support their UUP colleagues if they were advocating a role for the Republic in the administration of Northern Ireland. Speaking on 24 May, on the eve of talks between the two unionist leaders and Tom King in London, Wilson urged Molyneaux to clarify his position, as the continuing speculation over his attitude to Dublin was

> . . . damaging, confusing and taking attention away from the real political objective which unionists have. The DUP has made it clear that we are not for talking to Dublin and that only after a devolved government has been obtained for Northern Ireland will there be any need to seek ways of building up a working relationship with the foreign country which shares the same island. Mr Molyneaux can do much to clear the air by making a clear unequivocal statement as to where he stands. The unionist community which has stood together over the last three years needs to know that there will be no divergence of tactics at this stage. . . . Mr Molyneaux needs to publicly clarify if he wishes to exchange papers with Dublin, or if he intends to talk with Charles Haughey outside the arrangements made with the DUP.[106]

Ivan Foster, meanwhile, denounced rumours that unionists were preparing to compromise and accept a greater role for the Southern government in the affairs of Northern Ireland. These had been sparked off by James Molyneaux's regurgitation of the old phrase 'the totality of relationships within these islands' and his observation that the Anglo-Irish dialogue of the early 1980s might provide the basis for political discussions. Foster indicated that this would damage the unionist pact irreparably.

> If, and I emphasise the if, today's press reports of unionist willingness to accept a greater role for Dublin as the price for the removal of the Anglo-Eire agreement are accurate then I do not think that the rank and file of the DUP will go along with such a proposal and a serious rupture of the unionist camp is inevitable. . . . It is hard to believe that the very phrase that sparked off the Carson trail protests, the totality of relationships within these islands, is now part of the vocabulary of some unionists. . . . No amount of enthusiasm on the part of some MPs can hide the fact that a complete climbdown by unionists is planned.[107]

This thinly veiled attack on James Molyneaux and other leading members of the UUP who had made conciliatory noises in Dublin's direction, together with the widespread disquiet within the DUP over such remarks, resulted in a statement by Ian Paisley that both he and Molyneaux were united in their approach to any future dealings with Dublin. 'There will be no negotiations with Eire in advance of agreement on an internal settlement within Northern Ireland.'[108]

Clearly the DUP were in no mood to compromise. However, by the middle of July 1988 there were signs that some members within the UUP were attempting to engage in positive dialogue with the Irish government.

An article appeared in the *Sunday Times* on 17 July which hinted that unionists were prepared to 'reopen' talks with the Irish government and would, under certain circumstances, talk to Sinn Féin. The Rev. Martin Smyth denied that there was any truth in the report, but added that any approach to his party from Taoiseach Charles Haughey would be received politely. Smyth maintained that unionists were still waiting for a reply from Secretary of State Tom King to the proposals they made in January, but admitted that there were some within his party who would talk to Sinn Féin if the IRA stopped its campaign of violence. The DUP press officer Sammy Wilson condemned the article as evidence that some unionists were

> . . . still intent on breaking the joint commitment to have nothing to do with Dublin until the Anglo-Irish agreement is put on ice. . . . The indication by Martin Smyth that unionists are prepared to reopen talks with Dublin confirms the DUP suspicion that some unionists were having clandestine meetings with representatives of the Dublin dictatorship in the past. . . . Such careless talk is music to the ears of the terrorists. . . . If Official Unionists want to talk to Sinn Féin they will be doing it by themselves. The DUP will have no part in such an exercise. We will never forgive nor forget the part which these people have played in bringing misery to our Province.[109]

This latest outbreak of internecine feuding within unionism forced James Molyneaux to issue a denial that either the UUP or DUP would meet Charles Haughey for talks on the future of Northern Ireland within the parameters of the AIA. He maintained that the position still remained that only when the workings of the Agreement had been suspended would such a conference even be considered.

> As far as Ian Paisley is concerned he has made it quite clear that there are certain conditions under which he will meet with Charles Haughey. . . . None of those conditions to my knowledge has been met, and in fact it is quite obvious none of these conditions have been met. Therefore the DUP will not be meeting with him at any stage until those conditions are met. . . . Jim Molyneaux has given a commitment that he will likewise only meet Charles Haughey under the conditions that first of all the working of the agreement is suspended, and secondly we will be meeting Charles Haughey as representatives of an administration here in Northern Ireland.[110]

This episode illustrates the manner in which unionist interparty differences acted as an obstacle to the development of positive momentum. Every attempt by Ulster Unionists to emerge from the trenches dug in 1985 was accompanied by shouts of betrayal from the DUP and a frantic scuttling back to their previous positions by the UUP.

Another example of this negative dynamic came with the announcement on 20 July 1988 that the two main unionist parties had rejected the proposal for a new top-level political commission drawn from throughout Britain and Ireland. Sammy Wilson commented that his party would have 'nothing to do' with plans which would see Westminster and Irish politicians forming an Anglo-Irish interparliamentary tier. James Molyneaux agreed with Wilson that this was part of the AIA and as a result unionists would play no part in it. Wilson summed up the general feeling that the initiative had been spawned by the AIA and would not therefore be supported by the unionist community or their representatives. 'We do not accept that the suggested parliamentary tier is outside the terms of the agreement and we do not believe it is in the interests of Northern Ireland.'[111] It was envisaged that about forty members drawn from throughout Britain and Ireland, including two unionists and one SDLP representative, would take part in this consultative body to air views about issues affecting the two countries. One of the commission's chief architects, Peter Temple-Morris, commented that this was a way of breaking the Anglo-Irish impasse and overcoming the inability of unionists to participate in political debate.

> We have to find a way ahead that will involve all parties. . . . we think that a permanent standing parliamentary body created now will be a way forward in which all can participate. We have nothing as such to do with the Anglo-Irish Agreement. We do appreciate very much the unionist position in regard to that. We want the unionists as part of the United Kingdom side of this new parliamentary body. . . . This presents an important and invaluable opportunity for unionists. The commission, once created, has nothing directly to do with the government. It is an invaluable opportunity for unionists to come in and to be part of the United Kingdom delegation to have a forum in which all these problems can be gone into.[112]

By the middle of September the DUP had recognised publicly that its strategy was not going to succeed without a more positive dimension which offered a political alternative to the British government. Consequently, it was decided at the party's annual conference to take a radical look at political ways forward for Northern Ireland. Party delegates unanimously approved an inquiry into constitutional alternatives after Peter Robinson told the conference that under the AIA the Union was under grave threat. It was confirmed that independence was one possibility to be examined by the party executive think-tank, though in reality this announcement had more to do with securing the continued compliance of grass-roots activists than with any serious analysis of alternative policy options. The old chestnut of independence was traditionally considered by the DUP to be a 'Sword of Damocles' which could be hung over the British government to prevent large-scale concessions being made on Northern Ireland's sovereignty. Robinson's comment on independence illustrates the point: 'The basis of the argument is that independence is not an alternative to the Union, but an alternative to any attempts to force unionists into a united Ireland.'[113]

Pragmatic unionism under strain

Despite this newly found appetite for constructive political thought, the unionists reiterated at the beginning of October 1988 that they would not be accepting Secretary of State Tom King's invitation to talks with the British government to negotiate a replacement of the AIA. In a radio interview, King commented that; 'If the unionists turn their backs on this, I think history will judge them very harshly.'[114] King insisted that the government was not going to bow to unionist pressure to have the Agreement suspended and the Maryfield secretariat closed, and declared that it was time for unionists to emerge from the trenches they had dug for themselves three years previously when the AIA was signed. Ian Paisley's response to the Secretary of State's challenge was unconvincing. He claimed lamely that the unionists were the ones in a position of strength and were not going to let the government off the hook at this stage.

> Mr King is deceiving the people. He is the one in the trench, and it is up to him to climb out of it. As for the review, unionists want no part of it. We are not interested in any tinkering with the agreement. We want it replaced by an acceptable alternative.[115]

A few days later, the DUP leader was active in another arena, illustrating once again his specific brand of unionism and the degree to which this jarred with the cultural perspective of some of his Ulster Unionist colleagues. His protest in the European Parliament at Strasbourg on 10 October over the impending visit of the Pope the following day illustrated the problems the DUP faced in adopting a more pragmatic strategy likely to attract sympathy from the policy-making community in Britain or the Irish Republic. Despite having his microphone switched off, the DUP leader's five-minute tirade against the forthcoming visit of the Pope was clearly audible. Chaotic scenes erupted minutes after the opening of the parliament when Fianna Fáil MEP Niall Andrews asked: 'Is there any way to ensure that Mr Paisley, considered by many to be an institutional terrorist, does not get the floor to get the publicity which would bring this house into disrepute?'[116] Several minutes later, Paisley launched a rebuke of three of his most disliked subjects: the Pope, Roman Catholicism and the Republic of Ireland. The DUP leader warned that he would be present the following day to challenge the Pope on his presence. 'I will be here tomorrow and I will make whatever protest I feel I should make. And if this house wants to condemn me and throw me out of this house I will be quite happy.'[117] Ensuring that at least his self-fulfilling prophecies were accurate, Paisley was indeed thrown out of the European Parliament after his protest against the Pope's presence. Appeals by the president of the parliament for Paisley to be quiet were drowned out as the DUP leader yelled at an amused-

looking pontiff: 'I renounce you as the antichrist.'[118] Paisley was man-
handled out of the chamber by fellow MEPs but remained unrepentant:

> My protest against Rome will never be over. I shall carry on until I'm dead. . . .
> The words I spoke in there were those of the very first Protestant Archbishop
> of Canterbury Thomas Cranmer. He was burned for his views and those
> Euro MPs would have burned me today if they had the chance.[119]

While Paisley defended his action by saying that the European Parliament was
dominated by Rome and by Roman Catholic interests, some of his unionist
colleagues were less than supportive. Paisley's fellow MEP John Taylor
castigated the DUP leader's behaviour, and in doing so provided a classic
illustration of the cultural gap which exists within the ideology. The Strangford
MP denounced the demonstration as a publicity stunt which not only reflected
badly on Paisley himself but also tarnished the rest of Northern Ireland.

> He has succeeded in turning the whole of the European Parliament against
> Northern Ireland. It is time the unionist community in Northern Ireland
> realised what a disgrace this man is on the international political scene, and
> what damage he is doing to the unionist cause.[120]

Paisley's remarks were even regarded as being beyond the bounds of
decency by members of the French National Front, one of whom was
among the first to try to hustle the DUP leader out of the chamber.

The row which erupted between Ian Paisley and John Taylor was
reminiscent of a similar dispute a year earlier surrounding the visit of the
President of the Irish Republic Dr Patrick Hillery to the European Parliament.
On both occasions the two unionists illustrated a totally different cultural
outlook and conflicting perceptions of what unionism was about. This
personalised dispute can be seen as a microcosm of the social and political
differences which divide the two parties. Thus while the UUP were able to
adapt their political strategy on the basis of rational pragmatism, the DUP
often found it difficult to accept that confrontation was not always an
effective form of political activity. John Taylor's recollection of the incident
emphasises the difference between the unyielding philosophy of the DUP
and the more tolerant attitudes prevalent within his own party.

> There again, you had the distinction between the two parties. I'm not a
> Roman Catholic, I'm a straightforward Presbyterian, but I don't believe in
> insulting people because of their religion, and Ian Paisley does. The
> presence of the Pope was to him like a red rag to a bull, he just went
> berserk, and he started a performance, which first of all was wrong in that I
> think it's wrong to attack people because of their religion. Even though I
> don't agree with the Roman Catholic Church, I'm not going to publicly
> attack the Pope everywhere he turns up. Secondly, it brought discredit on
> Northern Ireland, and therefore it was very damaging for the unionist
> people of Northern Ireland, because this was televised all across Europe,

and here they saw this man, presented as the unionist voice of Northern Ireland – because he did get the largest number of votes in Northern Ireland – as going out of his way to insult one of the main Christian churches in the world.[121]

This penchant for pragmatism exhibited by some Ulster Unionists and so detested by their colleagues within the DUP was once again illustrated in October by that *bête noire* of radical unionism, Ken Maginnis. The Fermanagh and South Tyrone MP called for a definite starting date for negotiations between the unionists and the SDLP, although this was of course dependent on the suspension of the AIA. Maginnis's suggestion appeared to have been ruled out by his party leader the following evening, when he commented, 'dialogue will not stop the gunmen'.[122] In a speech to the Greater Belfast Young Unionist Association, Molyneaux declared that interparty talks were just a smokescreen to distract attention away from the worsening security situation and the inability of the government to defeat the IRA. Anxious not to further exacerbate the rift within the party between conservative and liberal elements, Molyneaux stated after the Belfast meeting that his criticism was directed at the NIO and not in any way against his Fermanagh colleague. 'Ken has called for talks, but only if the agreement is suspended, which is firm party policy.'[123]

Honour among thieves

In October 1988, one of the few sources within unionism which had been seriously engaged in pragmatic thinking on possible ways forward, namely loyalist paramilitarism and particularly the UDA, was distracted by its own internal feuding. This was precipitated by the assassination of John McMichael by the IRA the previous year and his investigation of the deliberate misappropriation by some leading UDA officials of funds gathered through racketeering. The latest victim of this row to be murdered was the UDA leader in west Belfast, Jim Craig. The Ulster Freedom Fighters (UFF) admitted that Craig had been 'executed for treason' on 15 October, commenting that his activities had resulted in the deaths of innocent people, namely McMichael. The UDA announced that they would be boycotting Craig's funeral due to his alleged involvement in McMichael's assassination. Craig had built up contacts with the IRA during his imprisonment at the Maze in the early 1970s and had maintained these links after his release. He then formed a working relationship with the Provisionals in racketeering activities in Belfast. This allowed sectarian killings to continue while providing an avenue of communication between the UDA and IRA to ensure that such killings did not get in the way of business. This arrangement also ensured, of course, that his name never got to the top of an IRA death-list. Jim Craig used his republican contacts to set up for assassination a number of his colleagues within the UDA/UFF who were either encroaching on his territory or showing an unhealthy interest in how he financed his lavish lifestyle. In a chilling insight into the internal power struggles within the UDA and their exercise of *machtpolitik*, journalist Martin Dillon encapsulates Craig's brutalised character and his contempt for human life in his book *The Shankill Butchers*.

> A UDA member entered the club and told Craig he had a pistol which was 'jamming'. He handed the weapon to Craig who casually levelled it at shoulder height, his hand outstretched, and pulled the trigger. The gun fired and a bullet struck the head of a man playing pool, killing him instantly. Craig had the body removed from the premises and dumped in a nearby alleyway.[124]

John McMichael, who was trying to carve out a political niche for the UDA and develop positive proposals for 'responsibility-sharing' such as those contained within *Common Sense*, was worried at the public embarrassment which Craig's racketeering was causing the UDA. As a result, an internal inquiry was launched into how Craig funded his activities. McMichael was blown up by an IRA car bomb before the inquiry could be completed, though it is clear that republicans had acted on a tip-off from a highly placed source with an axe to grind within the UDA.[125]

The turmoil in the UDA created by McMichael's murder and the assassination of Jim Craig a year later resulted in a virtual evacuation of the political arena by the Ulster Political Research Group. This came as a welcome relief for the main unionist parties and particularly the DUP, who had come under intense pressure from the UDA over the previous two years to provide a positive lead to the Protestant working class. With the UDA absent from the political scene, the DUP felt reassured that the pressure to produce tangible results had been relieved.

UUP–DUP disagreement on the way forward

Having got the UDA off their backs the DUP continued to erect barriers to discussion with the British government. In October 1988, Sammy Wilson commented that the unionists would not talk to Tom King until they had received a response from the Secretary of State on their document submitted to him the previous January outlining unionist proposals for the way forward. Wilson rejected the suggestion that the unionists should make the proposals public, commenting that it would be wrong to reveal the unionist hand when the SDLP were still refusing to put forward their proposals. This, of course, led to widespread criticism that the unionist proposals must be superficial and not worth getting excited about. Wilson denied this, commenting that they were a sincere attempt to break the political impasse and establish some form of devolved structure in

Northern Ireland. 'They are reasonable and worthwhile and it is widely known that they do contain an outline for devolved government, a relationship between Northern Ireland and Dublin and a further one between London and Dublin.'[126] Commenting retrospectively, Wilson remains adamant that the unionists were correct not to publish the details of the January proposals, as this would have weakened their position in any subsequent negotiations with either the British government or the SDLP.

> No I don't think they should have published them, because initially they were only an outline anyhow, and we also felt that by declaring our hand we weakened our negotiating position, because once you set down what you've given on paper and make that public, that becomes the baseline from which all other negotiations start.[127]

However, the anomaly in Wilson's position was that, if the January proposals were only an outline of the general direction in which the unionist coalition wanted to proceed, publication of their contents would have committed them to very little in terms of specific reforms. A more believable explanation for the unionist decision not to publish this document, which ties in with the muted reaction to it from the NIO, was that a public debate on their proposals, however general, would exacerbate further division within the unionist pact. The January proposals were necessarily non-specific because, as David Trimble recollected when speaking about establishing a unionist consensus for moving forward, 'Sometimes I feel that you would have difficulty getting any two or three [unionists] to agree on anything.'[128]

Eventually in February 1990, the 1988 proposals flopped into the public arena when the *Irish Times* published their main contents. The plans for an internal assembly run by committees based on proportionality, with ill-defined North–South structures, attracted little attention from either the SDLP or the British government.

In an attempt to get the unionists off the hook of non-participation in the review of the AIA, which they had insisted in impaling themselves on, the sympathetic Friends of the Union group decided to put forward proposals of their own, which they hoped might prove acceptable to both the unionist community and the British government. At the end of October 1988 the Friends of the Union announced that they had presented Margaret Thatcher with a copy of a draft agreement intended to replace the Hillsborough deal and establish new more comprehensive relations between London and Dublin. One of its main proposals recommended that the two countries broaden the 1980–81 Anglo-Irish dialogue. James Molyneaux encouraged speculation that there was some mileage in the Friends of the Union initiative when he commented in late October that unionists could live with the 1980 set-up if the 1985 AIA was removed.[129]

It soon became clear that support for the Friends of the Union proposals was not universal within the unionist pact and James Molyneaux was typically accused of treachery and compromise by extreme elements within the DUP. It was alleged by Ivan Foster on 31 October that the UUP leader had betrayed his party's partnership with the DUP by supporting the idea of an Anglo-Irish intergovernmental council. Molyneaux's statement that unionists could live with the blueprint provided in the Thatcher–Haughey summit communiqué of 1980 and that these arrangements were preferable to those of November 1985 provoked an angry response from Foster, who recalled that in 1980 the DUP's position was one of total opposition to the council plan as laid out in the communiqué. 'The 1980 structures were but the skeleton on which the 1985 agreement was built. Anyone who fails to see that must, to coin a phrase, be out of his mind.'[130] Foster went on to say that the DUP had found so much fault with the Dublin communiqué they had mounted the Carson trail rallies and formed the Third Force in order to prevent the Thatcher–Haughey plans being implemented.

> Since the DUP is still of the opinion that there was much fault to be found in the communiqué, we can only conclude that James Molyneaux believes his unionist partners to be out of their minds . . . he knew the DUP was of this mind when the present partnership was formed. It says little for his integrity that he is prepared to enter a partnership with those he considers out of their minds.[131]

Foster was not alone in his criticism of Molyneaux's support for the idea of an Anglo-Irish intergovernmental council. In early November, Sammy Wilson denounced the UUP leader's stated position and warned that it could precipitate the break-up of the unionist alliance. 'If the OUP wishes to pursue an intergovernmental council it will do so by itself. If unionist unity is to mean anything, then there must be respect for the views and attitudes of each party.'[132] Wilson rebuked Molyneaux for speaking out before discussing the matter with Ian Paisley and for assuming that the two parties agreed on what he saw as a way forward.

Molyneaux's defence that both himself and Paisley had agreed to such an intergovernmental conference in their letter of August 1985 to Thatcher was denied by Wilson when he declared: 'Dr Paisley never put his signature to any document which would have accepted this arrangement.'[133]

This row between the two main unionist parties can be seen as a form of surrogate negotiation with the British government in advance of the review of the Agreement. Though the unionists did not talk directly to the NIO, the dispute over the Friends of the Union initiative functioned as a barometer of opinion within the two parties, and left the British government in little doubt that the review would have to result in significant reforms to the 1985 treaty, if it was to be acceptable to the unionist community.

While unionists were criticised by their political opponents for being intransigent over participation in the review, they in turn, together with the Alliance Party, attacked London and Dublin ministers on 2 November, after the review launch meeting of the AIA. Unionists described the Stormont Castle meeting as 'a deliberate slap in the face' by the government.[134] The joint communiqué issued after the intergovernmental talks said that the review was expected to be completed in the early part of 1989. The governments also agreed that the next Anglo-Irish Intergovernmental Conference would be held shortly, and that the business of the conference would go on during the review. It was this last point which proved unacceptable to even the most moderate politicians within the unionist community. Alliance Party representative Seamus Close condemned the fact that a suspension of the conference sessions was not going to occur during the review to facilitate a period where interparty talks might be possible in Northern Ireland. 'If the communiqué means another conference before the review is completed, then the decision dismays me. Such a move can only add to the present political paralysis affecting the Province's political parties.'[135]

How do we explain the uncompromising attitude of the British government to unionist sensitivities regarding meetings of the conference during the AIA's review? It is clear that during this period London was more interested in doing business with Dublin than with the Ulster unionists. The review process itself was little more than a formality, undertaken because of the procedural requirements of the original Agreement, rather than as a serious attempt to address core questions about its strategic purpose. From the London and Dublin perspective, there was very little else on offer as an alternative to the AIA and what was on the table (the unionist proposals of January 1988) were thought too minimalist to be worthy of serious consideration. Certainly as far as London was concerned, the latest morsels from the unionist camp were not of sufficient potential to merit suspending the Agreement and incurring the displeasure of the Irish government, the SDLP and the United States administration. Such a change in policy would also have ended the bipartisan approach to Northern Ireland at Westminster.

Ken Maginnis of the UUP accused the two governments of attempting to sabotage fresh hopes of political progress by holding another meeting of the Anglo-Irish Intergovernmental Conference while the review of the Agreement was taking place, thus ruling out the chance of interparty dialogue in the interim. However, Maginnis commented significantly that 'certain exploratory feelers' had been extended by the unionists to the SDLP, and that if a *de facto* suspension of the AIA had been created by means of a gap in the meetings of the conference during the review process, interparty dialogue may have taken place. The Fermanagh MP declared that the chances for progress had effectively been ended by the announcement in the joint communiqué that the two sides were to meet again in December.

> In the light of certain prospects of progress, we begin to wonder whether there has been a deliberate attempt by the two governments to sabotage progress that was possible, and I think both the Northern Ireland Office and Dublin know what I am talking about. . . . We have to ask whether all the encouraging signals being put out in relation to unionists and the SDLP are being knowingly undermined. . . . Each time unionists move to a position where progress can be made, another torpedo is launched. I know unionists will be asking if the SDLP had a hand in this torpedoing exercise.[136]

In an interview with the *News Letter* on the eve of the third anniversary of the AIA, Paisley and Molyneaux were asked about the possibility of unionists negotiating a replacement to the Agreement based on the Thatcher/Haughey summit communiqué of 1980 and the subsequent Anglo-Irish Intergovernmental Council of 1981. The DUP leader made it clear that his party would have nothing to do with reforms based on this foundation.

> We have had a meeting and a thorough discussion of the matter. It is quite clear what Jim was saying – that it was time the Government got away from the Anglo-Irish agreement and started to re-trace its steps. There was a difference between unionists back in 1981. My party held Carson trail rallies and other protests. But today both parties are united in a conviction that an intergovernmental council is no good to us. There may have been strains within the parties but our unity is unshakable. We have talked this over. There is nothing in an intergovernmental council for us.[137]

Molyneaux's rejoinder to his colleague's unequivocal attitude to the 1980–1981 position is interesting, as it appears to signal a shift in his earlier stance. 'I would rather not have had the 1980 [*sic* 1981] Anglo-Irish council at all, and I am not endorsing it now. If the two governments come to their senses, scrap the diktat and get back to the intergovernmental council, we can't stop them. But we would not be part of it.'[138] This backtracking by Molyneaux from his statement at the beginning of November that the 1981 Anglo-Irish Intergovernmental Council could replace the AIA provides evidence of his willingness to compromise with the DUP in order to maintain the unionist coalition. Molyneaux went on to warn that unionists might withdraw their January proposals for an alternative to the Agreement, adding that while this threat was his personal position, his colleagues on the UUP–DUP policy committee may well take account of his opinion. 'Given the absence of a serious Government response, there is a limit to the amount of time a plan can be allowed to lie on the table.'[139] This can be read as bravado on Molyneaux's part, an attempt to depict himself as more hardline and altogether more difficult to satisfy than the NIO and the British government appeared to think.

The difficulties associated with finding a positive agenda for superseding the AIA while maintaining the unionist pact added to the tension and internal fighting. Robert McCartney, still smarting from his expulsion from the UUP in 1987, was particularly vociferous in his attacks on the leadership of James Molyneaux. The former UUP Assemblyman denounced Molyneaux as 'Paisley's pup' on the eve of the 1988 Ulster Unionist Party conference in mid-November. McCartney claimed in a radio interview that trusting the UUP leader was not a profit-making business and that he had never known a politician who had 'produced such a catalogue of disasters as Jim Molyneaux and remained in office'.[140] Friction was also evident on the eve of the conference between liberal and conservative factions within the party. The defensive mind-set within the UUP at the time and the distance they still had to travel to establish a credible political position were illustrated by the following row. Opposition arose to a suggestion by Raymond Ferguson (leader of Fermanagh District Council) that the UUP should conduct low-level talks with the SDLP despite the continued existence of the AIA. On the day before the party conference, a delegate named Sammy Foster condemned Ferguson's motion. 'It is a view of Fermanagh unionism which has caused consternation within the ranks. . . . Indeed, it is a Lundy-type attack on the leadership and will bring joy to the Secretary of State.'[141]

Having taken some steps during 1988 to end their self-imposed isolation from the constitutional political process which began after the signing of the AIA in 1985, the leadership ran back behind the barricades at the party conference. Molyneaux described the AIA as stinking of betrayal and declared that it would continue to be opposed 'with all the strength that God can give us'. The Ulster Unionist leader spoke with disdain of the government's spurning of his earlier offer (the January proposals) to aid London and Dublin in efforts to end the ancient quarrel between the two countries and warned that further talking would be useless until the government came to their senses.

> Further proposals from us would be futile, and it may even be dangerous to leave on offer proposals already made, if there is to be no reciprocal response from the Government. The Whitehall mafia complain about unionist leadership. They say it is ageing and stubborn. . . . I can do nothing about the first adjective, and I will do nothing about the second.[142]

Molyneaux criticised those within his party who advocated that they should begin talking to the SDLP and the British government, not to mention Dublin. He suggested that it would be uncharitable to mention those who had 'lost their heads' and attacked himself and Ian Paisley, or those who had 'urged compromise to the point of betrayal'.[143] Molyneaux was adamant that his policy of long-term opposition was the correct one to adopt, rejecting the charge from liberal elements within the party that the current strategy was too negative. 'I am not ashamed of our strategy of battening down the hatches until those who have chosen the road of confrontation in the Anglo-Irish agreement come to their senses.'[144]

Those within the UUP who favoured a more active policy than Molyneaux's 'running on the spot' philosophy were to learn at the conference that progressive political thought was a creed which had few followers in the party. The advocates of talks with the SDLP were heavily defeated after a lively and heated debate. Raymond Ferguson came under fierce attack for suggesting that unionists had nothing to fear from dialogue with nationalists in Belfast and Dublin. Lagan Valley delegate Ronnie Crawford attacked this view as a naive bid to take the party into constitutional talks with the SDLP. 'How would talking to the SDLP bring the Provisionals to their knees?. . . . As long as the Anglo-Irish agreement is in force we will never be able to negotiate.'[145] William Baird, another Lagan Valley delegate, was subjected to slow hand-clapping and foot-stamping when he advocated talks with non-unionists. However, the South Down delegate Craig Sides appeared to reflect the consensus of opinion when he suggested that, while the party should develop a more positive strategy, this should not involve any political interference from the Irish Republic: '. . . less "no" and more "go", but "no go" to any input from Dublin'.[146]

Facing realities

At the end of the 1980s, the UUP knew that the existing campaign against the AIA had failed and that to have any impact on the political process they would have to enter talks with the British government and the SDLP. Their disinclination to engage in such activity was motivated partly by a fear that they would be denounced as traitors and 'Lundies' by the DUP. It was also the product of a concern that any reassessment of their tactics would look like weakness and be exploited by the NIO.

Embryonic movements towards interparty talks were hampered by the composition of the ideology itself. Unionism contains people whose cultural identities are so distinct that they are virtually separate political philosophies. This difference of opinion as to what unionism was about understandably overlapped, not just in their critique of the status quo, but also in the alternative political institutions which they sought for the future. One of the most obvious manifestations of this was the debate within the UUP between integrationists and devolutionists, with James Molyneaux occupying an ambiguous position between the two but being known to favour the former. The UUP leader therefore found himself in the position of having to advocate a political position which he did not fully believe in, and which he knew he could not deliver without causing a further split in his party. This problem of not being able to deliver a united community has been endemic within the unionist ideology since Stormont was prorogued in 1972. It is a problem which emanates from their history and from the fact that unionism is essentially a reactive rather than proactive ideology, the emphasis being on resistance to integration with the Republic and maintenance of existing constitutional links with Britain, rather than any search for new commonly accepted political arrangements.

In addition to having conflicting notions of where they wanted to go (with obvious implications for the development of a positive political platform) the unionist leadership was also hampered by practical realities. It had been realised by many unionists for some time that the negative tactics associated with the 1980s would have to be replaced by political negotiation with the British government and interparty talks with the SDLP. However, it was obvious that this would result in a weakening of the unionist position *vis à vis* the nationalists. The political reality which unionists have had difficulty facing is that the Anglo-Irish Agreement of 15 November 1985 will only be replaced by another Anglo-Irish agreement based upon legislative power-sharing with the nationalist community and some form of Dublin input into the new political structures. While nationalists often talk of the unionist veto, the sad fact from a unionist point of view is that devolution will only be granted to Northern Ireland in terms acceptable to both the SDLP and the Irish government and thus, almost by definition, unacceptable to unionists.

In 1988, therefore, the stuttering approach of the unionist leadership to political negotiations epitomised by the January proposals was not only the result of internal cultural diversity, but also emanated from a belief that such negotiation would inevitably damage the unionist position. After the AIA was signed it was obvious that any replacement would involve substantial compromise to the nationalists, and at least some input from the Dublin government. If the AIA was repugnant to unionists, then so too was the only conceivable alternative to it, namely power-sharing with the SDLP. Like the proverbial attendant arranging deck-chairs on the *Titanic*, unionist politics at the end of the 1980s demonstrated either an unwillingness to face up to or an ignorance of this political reality. Rather than strengthening the constitutional position of Northern Ireland within the United Kingdom, unionist political activity in the 1980s all but exhausted the dwindling supply of unionist friends on the British 'mainland'. The only way forward for unionism and Northern Ireland was through interparty talks. It took two more years and another Secretary of State to get these under way.

Notes

1   *News Letter*, 30 January 1987, pp. 1–2.
2   ibid.
3   *Common Sense* envisaged that the government would be composed of a ten-member executive. Using party strengths in the Northern Ireland Assembly as a model, the Ulster Unionists would have four places, the DUP three, the SDLP two and the Alliance Party would have one seat.
4   The UDA document also contained proposals for the creation of a supreme court. This institution was to be responsible for upholding constitutional law and safeguarding the individual in line with the bill of rights.
5   *News Letter*, 30 January 1987, p. 9.
6   ibid., 3 February 1987, p. 2.
7   ibid.
8   ibid., p. 5.
9   ibid.
10   *Fortnight*, No. 249 (March 1987), pp. 14–15.
11   *Ulster*, January 1987, pp. 12–13.
12   *News Letter*, 2 March 1987, p. 7.
13   Private conversation with author.
14   *News Letter*, 2 March 1987, p. 7.
15   ibid., 3 March 1987, p. 8.
16   ibid.
17   ibid.
18   ibid.
19   ibid., 4 March 1987, p. 9.
20   ibid., 6 April 1987, p. 7.
21   ibid.
22   ibid.
23   Michael McGimpsey, interview with author, 16 October 1991.
24   *News Letter*, 13 May 1987, p. 9.
25   ibid.
26   ibid., 25 May 1987, p. 16.
27   ibid.
28   *Ulster*, June 1987, p. 4.
29   *News Letter*, 2 July 1987, p. 8.
30   ibid., 3 July 1987, p. 9.
31   ibid., 4 July 1987, p. 7.
32   ibid.
33   ibid.
34   ibid.
35   ibid.
36   ibid., 3 July 1987, pp. 1–2.
37   ibid., p. 8.
38   John Taylor, interview with author, 30 September 1991.
39   *Fortnight*, No. 254 (September 1987), p. 6.
40   *News Letter*, 3 July 1987, p. 8.
41   ibid., 9 July 1987, p. 11.
42   David Trimble, interview with author, 3 October 1991.
43   ibid.
44   ibid.

45 Michael McGimpsey, interview with author, 16 October 1991.
46 James Molyneaux, interview with author, 19 November 1991.
47 ibid.
48 ibid.
49 ibid.
50 Peter Robinson, interview with author, 8 November 1995.
51 Rev. Martin Smyth, interview with author, 22 November 1991.
52 *News Letter*, 21 July 1987, p. 22.
53 *Fortnight*, No. 254 (September 1987), pp. 6–9.
54 ibid.
55 ibid.
56 *News Letter*, 1 August 1987, p. 6.
57 ibid.
58 ibid., 18 August 1987, p. 9.
59 ibid.
60 ibid.
61 Sammy Wilson, interview with author, 20 November 1991.
62 ibid.
63 *News Letter*, 11 August 1987. p. 2.
64 ibid., 12 August 1987, p. 1.
65 ibid., p. 2.
66 ibid., 13 August 1987, p. 2.
67 ibid.
68 ibid.
69 ibid., 8 August 1987, p. 4.
70 ibid., 14 August 1987, p. 1.
71 ibid., 15 August 1987, p. 7.
72 ibid., 18 August 1987, pp. 1–2.
73 ibid., 24 August 1987, p. 3.
74 ibid., 12 September 1987, p. 1.
75 ibid., p. 2.
76 *Fortnight*, No. 255. (October 1987), pp. 6–7.
77 Sammy Wilson, interview with author, 20 November 1991.
78 *News Letter*, 15 September 1987, p. 9.
79 ibid.
80 ibid., 8 October 1987, p. 11.
81 ibid., p. 3.
82 ibid., 10 October 1987, p. 3.
83 ibid., 9 November 1987, p. 23.
84 ibid.
85 ibid.
86 The new group was comprised of five members from each party, the Ulster Unionist team included Rev. Martin Smyth, Harold McCusker, party chairman Jack Allen, and its new general secretary Jim Wilson, whilst the DUP delegation contained senior party figures such as Peter Robinson, Sammy Wilson, Nigel Dodds and Rev. William McCrea. Robinson's appointment to the think-tank was accompanied by a resumption of his position as deputy leader of the DUP.
87 *News Letter*, 22 February 1988, pp. 14–15.
88 James Molyneaux, interview with author, 19 November 1991.
89 *News Letter*, 28 January 1988, p. 10.

90 Nigel Dodds, interview with author, 2 December 1991.
91 Sammy Wilson, interview with author, 20 November 1991.
92 *News Letter*, 3 February 1988, p. 15.
93 *Combat*, February 1988, p. 1.
94 ibid., p. 2.
95 *News Letter*, 11 March 1988, p. 12.
96 ibid.
97 ibid.
98 James Molyneaux, interview with author, 19 November 1991.
99 ibid.
100 ibid.
101 *Fortnight*, No. 262 (May 1988), p. 6.
102 *News Letter*, 27 April 1988, p. 19.
103 ibid., 4 May 1988, p. 8.
104 ibid.
105 ibid.
106 ibid., 26 May 1988, p. 2.
107 ibid.
108 ibid., 6 June 1988, p. 7.
109 ibid., 18 July 1988, pp. 1–2.
110 ibid., 19 July 1988, p. 8.
111 ibid., 21 July 1988, p. 8.
112 ibid.
113 ibid., 19 September 1988, p. 8.
114 ibid., 1 October 1988 p. 3.
115 ibid.
116 ibid., 11 October 1988, p. 5.
117 ibid.
118 ibid., 12 October 1988, p. 1.
119 ibid.
120 ibid., p. 4.
121 John Taylor, interview with author, 30 September 1991.
122 *News Letter*, 11 October 1988, p. 9.
123 ibid.
124 M. Dillon, *The Shankill Butchers: A Case Study of Mass Murder* (London, 1989), p. 322.
125 ibid., p. 324.
126 *News Letter*, 17 October 1988, p. 7.
127 Sammy Wilson, interview with author, 20 November 1991.
128 David Trimble, interview with author, 3 October 1991.
129 Under the proposed intergovernmental structure outlined by the Friends of the Union, there would be meetings at ministerial or official levels and a secretariat to service the council, but this would be sited in either London or Dublin and not in Belfast. The intergovernmental council would also give the armed forces and the police of the two countries the right to cross into each other's territory in pursuit of terrorist suspects. It was also proposed that an advisory committee be set up to deal with matters of mutual interest which could include members drawn from the UK and Southern parliaments. *News Letter*, 31 October 1988, p. 9.
130 ibid., 1 November 1988, p. 10.
131 ibid. The row between Molyneaux and Foster continued to fester when the former Assemblyman alleged that the UUP leader had made misleading and mischievous claims. He denied Molyneaux's assertion that the principles set out in the joint unionist

letter of 25 August 1985 to Margaret Thatcher were comparable with the principles set out in the 1980 communiqué.

> If nothing else, it clearly implies that Dr Paisley has done a complete U-turn since he campaigned strongly against the communiqué proposals. . . . The communiqué, in its reference to a consideration of the totality of relationships within these islands, conceded to Dublin the right to discuss Northern Ireland's constitutional position. . . . Mr Molyneaux's readiness to use the communiqué as a blue-print for a new deal has to my knowledge never been discussed with the DUP. Such a plan can only result in something ominously like the present Anglo-Irish agreement being built.

News Letter, 3 November 1988, p. 4.

132 ibid., 2 November 1988, p. 9.
133 ibid.
134 ibid., 3 November 1988, p. 1.
135 ibid., pp. 1–2.
136 ibid., 4 November 1988, p. 8.
137 ibid., 15 November 1988, p. 8.
138 ibid.
139 ibid., p. 9.
140 ibid., 18 November 1988, p. 4.
141 ibid., p. 6.
142 ibid., 21 November 1988, p. 8.
143 ibid.
144 ibid.
145 ibid., p. 9.
146 ibid.

CHAPTER 7

Ulster Unionism in the 1990s:
The Talking Begins

At the turn of the decade, unionism was at a low ebb. The campaign to destroy the Anglo-Irish Agreement had failed to produce the expected results, while its tentative efforts to offer a political alternative to the AIA based upon a minimalist return of devolved powers to a Stormont assembly had not deflected the British government from its partnership strategy with the Irish Republic. The apparent impotence of unionism to influence policy-making within Northern Ireland led to internal fracturing and the emergence of various groups such as the Campaign for Equal Citizenship and the Charter Group within the UUP and the Ulster Political Research Group within the UDA. These groups, together with non-aligned individuals disaffected with the respective leaderships, struggled for control of the intellectual direction of the ideology. These divisions, charted in some detail in previous chapters, further weakened unionism and left little energy for proactive engagement within the political arena.

At the end of the 1980s politics in Northern Ireland had ossified further, with the SDLP clinging to the AIA as a 'banker' position which was unlikely to be improved through talks with a moribund unionist leadership. This was highlighted at the beginning of 1990 by an uncompromising speech by the UUP's William Ross, a close lieutenant of James Molyneaux and not renowned as a hardliner within the party. Ross launched an attack on those 'pundits' who criticised unionists for contributing to the political vacuum and lack of progress within Northern Ireland.

> Undoubtedly some of those who talk about vacuums are deeply concerned about the state of affairs in Ulster but, given the conclusions at which they arrive, I sometimes think that the largest vacuum is between their ears. . . . Progress in their terms . . . means movement towards a united republican Ireland, therefore in terms of action, stalemate or lack of progress, means simply that they are frustrated by finding themselves confronted by the steady stubborn will of the Ulster Unionist Party.[1]

The message from Ross was the traditional defensive and negative one which had done so much to blight unionist political fortunes during the 1980s. In effect, this strategy said that: the system is against us; we cannot rely upon either our argument or our mandate as these will be ignored by government; we must stand still, because if we move, we will go backwards. Sadly for the unionists, while they chose to engage in the 'hokey-cokey' steps of Molyneauxism, where they put one foot into the political arena and then took it out again, the dance went on around them.

The appointment of Peter Brooke as Secretary of State for Northern Ireland on 24 July 1989 marked a new positive phase in the politics of Northern Ireland and the intellectual condition of unionism. In personality terms, the new Secretary of State was radically different to his predecessor. Tom King could be an acerbic politician who, like his leader Margaret Thatcher, appeared to place little value on consultation or consensus. A 'doer' rather than a 'thinker', King's axiom seemed to be not so much 'shoot first and ask questions afterwards', as 'why bother asking questions at all'. Neither community in Northern Ireland warmed much to him. While nationalists gave him a guarded respect for standing up to the unionists during their protest against the AIA (and on one occasion being physically attacked by some of them at Belfast City Hall), they suspected him for his unionist sympathies, which in fairness he made little effort to disguise. Unionists, of course, despised King for his role in implementing the AIA which led some to openly disparage him as 'Tomcat' King. For them, he was the front man for a government engaged in the process of edging them off what Peter Robinson referred to as the 'window-ledge of the Union'. Most opinion formers in Northern Ireland were similarly unmoved.

Clearly by the end of the 1980s he was not the man the British government needed if it was to present itself as a neutral arbiter in the conflict. It should be said that King's position was an invidious one, taking over in late 1985 at a time when tensions were at their highest in a number of years and the two communities had become polarised along the fault-line of the AIA. It is doubtful that Brooke would have performed much better during that period. In that sense, King was a man for his time in the same way Brooke represented the early 1990s.

Peter Brooke was a different fish entirely. A Tory of the old school, his public image was one of being pathologically polite, reluctant to offend anybody's sensibilities and eager to establish some common ground. While his verbal circumlocutions over political terms and conditions at times bordered on the garrulous, leading some to lampoon him as 'Babbling Brooke', he nevertheless won the respect and trust of both the political community and the general public within Northern Ireland. This was accomplished not simply though *bonhomie*, but by a shrewd sense that the only way to get political progress started was through 'constructive ambiguity', that is, answers would not immediately be demanded of the parties as nobody really understood what the question was. This approach was encapsulated in August 1990 when the political adviser of a leading nationalist advanced the following conundrum: 'Question: What do you get when you cross Peter Brooke with the Mafia? Answer: A question that you cannot understand but cannot refuse.'[2]

Brooke begins new strategy

The first signs of a new departure in government policy towards Northern Ireland came with an interview given by the Secretary of State to mark his first 100 days in office. Brooke hit an unusual note when he pointed out that the British government recognised that it could not defeat the IRA militarily and that it would respond in a manner that was both 'flexible and imaginative' if republicans renounced their campaign of violence. While unionists reacted angrily to this as a sop to the IRA and an encourage-ment to them to continue with the armed struggle, as 'one more heave' would precipitate concessions from a government who had lost the will to fight, they recognised at the same time that Brooke held out an opportunity for them to return from the political wilderness. This mood was reflected at the beginning of January 1990 when the UUP's European Parliament representative Jim Nicholson held a meeting with Brooke and commented afterwards that unionists should be receptive to any realistic attempt by the government to end the political impasse.[3]

Politics during this period were dominated by a number of smoke-signals sent out by Peter Brooke in various public speeches which were then interpreted by the protagonists in Northern Ireland. One of the most significant of these coded messages came in an address to a gathering of businessmen in Bangor, County Down on 9 January 1990. Brooke made an appeal here for interparty dialogue and commented that any co-operation reached between the parties in Northern Ireland that would improve the functioning of the AIA would be viewed 'seriously and sympathetically' by both the British and Irish governments. This was an attempt to assuage unionist fears that any dialogue engaged in by the 'constitutional' parties would have to be consistent with the operation and existing parameters of the AIA. From their perspective, there was little point in talking if this was conducted under the auspices of the 'straightjacket' introduced in November 1985. In an attempt to get unionists to the negotiating table, Brooke commented in his Bangor speech that:

> . . . the two governments have already stated formally that if in future it appeared that the objectives of the Agreement could be more effectively served by changes in the scope and nature of the Conference, the govern-ments would be willing in principle to consider making such changes. . . . I

> do believe the Agreement can be operated sensitively, in the interests of bringing about talks between political parties and giving them the best possible chance of success.[4]

If there is one thing that the Northern Ireland political community are good at, it is using their highly tuned antennae to pick up and decode messages such as this. Unionists certainly interpreted Brooke's remarks as a signal that the government had finally given up on the AIA and wanted to negotiate an alternative to it. Ken Maginnis, one of the more liberal figures within the UUP, lost no time in making this point when welcoming the content of the Bangor speech the following day.

> There is a relief in the unionist camp at Mr Brooke's apparent willingness to consider an alternative agreement. We would all like to do something positive for the Province and Mr Brooke has gone out of his way to indicate he understands the unionist position.[5]

Democratic Unionist Party leader Ian Paisley welcomed Brooke's remarks as a sign that the British government was penitent and would return to 'the proper democratic process, honour and the ballot-box'.[6] However, positive though he was, Paisley added that the main obstacle in the way of interparty talks had not been tackled by the Secretary of State's speech, namely the non-implementation of the AIA while negotiations were under way and the cessation of the working of the Intergovernmental Conference and the secretariat at Maryfield.

> Only when these conditions are fulfilled can any real movement be achieved. Unionists are all eager to set in train once more the democratic process, and the thing which delays that is not any reluctance on their part but the dragging of feet of Her Majesty's Government.[7]

This condition was one which came to bedevil the whole talks process as the British government tried to balance unionist demands with the opposition of the nationalist community and the Irish government to a formal suspension of the AIA. The SDLP were of the opinion that unionists were engaged in a ruse to achieve an open-ended suspension and then string out interparty negotiations to the point that a subsequent reintroduction of the AIA would prove to be a practical impossibility. In this analysis, as their full-frontal attack on it had failed, unionists were now embarked upon a campaign of stealth to damage the Agreement. It took some time of course for this dispute to play itself out. Back in January 1990, unionists were eager to at least articulate a mood of optimism and generate some positive headlines for a change. This may explain the comments made by John Taylor of the UUP in an RTE radio interview when he advocated that a new institution should be established, at which representatives from Northern Ireland and the Irish Republic could meet, as part of a political settlement. Delegates to this body would be drawn from a devolved assembly at Stormont and the Dublin parliament. 'Dublin is our immediate neighbour and there are certain things now in which we have a common interest in which we would not have had 20 years ago.'[8] In an effort to massage the problem concerning the entry of the UUP into interparty talks, Taylor went on to say that if the AIA was rendered 'non-operational' for a fixed period rather than suspended, then the way would be clear for talks to begin.

Further signs of progress were provided by a four-hour meeting between Peter Brooke and the leaders of the two main unionist parties on 22 May 1990. A formula was agreed here for an informal suspension of the Maryfield secretariat and a gap in meetings of the Anglo-Irish Inter-governmental Conference for the duration of interparty talks.

No sooner was this obstacle removed when another one appeared to impede political progress, on this occasion the time-scale for the involvement of the Irish Republic in the process. While sources in Dublin claimed that they would be engaged from an early stage in proceedings, unionists demanded that they should not be brought in until 'substantial progress' had been made in talks between the rival factions within Northern Ireland. In a speech to the DUP annual conference on 24 November 1990, Ian Paisley left little room for ambiguity.

> Dublin can have no place whatsoever at any talks about an internal settlement in Northern Ireland. That is a matter for the representatives of the Northern Ireland constitutional parties and of the United Kingdom Government and Parliament alone. And substantial progress and agreement must be made at such talks before there can be any further progress.[9]

The tortuous mechanics of the talks process continued in the lead-up to Christmas, when a further meeting between the leaders of the two main unionist parties and the Secretary of State on 13 December produced a formula to break the deadlock over the timing of the Irish Republic's entry into the process. It was agreed here that Peter Brooke would act as a referee, deciding when progress was at a sufficient stage to justify the involvement of the South.

The British government announced its intention to force the pace in the House of Commons on 14 March 1991, when Brooke declared a deadline for interparty talks to commence and gave the parties until Easter to decide if they were going to sign up to his plan. While unionists eventually accepted these terms, they were initially suspicious due to Dublin's enthusiasm for the process. The propensity of fear to produce defensive and negative reactions within unionism was amply demonstrated three days after Brooke's announcement when William Ross commented that, although he had not actually studied Brooke's proposals, he believed that London had conceded to the nationalist agenda and agreed to an early involvement of the Irish government.

> I have been a sceptic when it comes to the motives of the Dublin government and nationalists in general. Time after time it is Dublin which blocks talks. At the end of the day they are simply interested only in taking us into a united Ireland. They have not and will not budge from that. Clearly that is a road we cannot go down – there is nothing in it for unionists. We have been labelled as the wreckers but not once have we seen an acceptance by the nationalist community of the unionist position, and they [unionists] have little reason to trust the Conservative Party either.[10]

In addition to his primitive reading of Southern Irish political objectives, this statement by Ross emphasises once again the reactive dynamic within Ulster unionism which leads to such defensive and ultimately defeatist policy positions. The sad truth is that no unionist leader has ever lost the support of their community by being *too* hardline; they have only fallen from office when they have demonstrated a capacity to engage in progressive thought and action. Terence O'Neill, James Chichester-Clark, Brian Faulkner, William Craig and eventually James Molyneaux shared this similar fate. However, despite such siren voices, times had changed within unionist politics since the 1980s. Their experience of exclusion after the signing of the AIA had left an indelible mark upon their collective consciousness and few wanted to repeat the exercise. James Molyneaux typified this new mood with his declaration at the end of March 1991 that, twenty years after the end of the Stormont government and five years after the AIA, the time had come for unionists to become 'insiders rather than outsiders in the British political system'.[11]

By the end of March the four participants in the talks – the UUP, the DUP, the SDLP and the Alliance Party[12] – had accepted the terms and Peter Brooke outlined the structure of the talks in the House of Commons on 26 March. The negotiations were to have three strands. Strand One would deal with internal relationships within Northern Ireland, the object being to establish a consensus for devolved government. Strand Two was to signal the entry of the Irish government into the process when the talks would consider relations between North and South. Strand Three would deal with East–West relations between the Republic of Ireland and Great Britain. Crucially, in terms of maintaining unionist support, Strands Two and Three were to begin at an unspecified date when Peter Brooke decided that sufficient progress had been made between the parties on internal arrangements. To reassure all participants that their consent to any subsequent deal was necessary, the unwieldy diplomatic concoction 'nothing is agreed until everything is agreed' was devised. This caused one of the more moderate participants to comment sarcastically a few months later, when the process was on the verge of breaking down, 'well, we're halfway to a solution – nothing is agreed!' To satisfy unionist preconditions concerning the AIA, the Anglo-Irish Intergovernmental Conference and

Maryfield secretariat were suspended for a fixed period, providing a window of ten weeks for the politicians to reach an agreement before the AIA swung back into action in the autumn. Brooke's success in getting the four 'constitutional' parties into round-table talks was no small achievement, earning him a rare verbal bouquet from Ian Paisley, who praised the Secretary of State's 'honesty, uprightness and . . . great openness'.[13]

Predictably enough, the DUP leader was hurling brickbats shortly afterwards, as unionists first of all argued with the SDLP about where Strand Two should take place and then fell out with the British government over the proposed independent chair. While the SDLP wanted the talks to take place in Ireland, the unionists stipulated that, because of the Republic's territorial claim to Northern Ireland,[14] they must be held in London. Unionists also vetoed the suggestion that Lord Carrington should chair the Strand Two discussions. They had apparently read his autobiography and were less than impressed at his references to the 'bigotry and insobriety'[15] of Northern Ireland politicians. They were also suspicious that Carrington was too close to the Foreign Office, whose analysis had played a major part in the signing of the AIA, and felt that his role in the Rhodesian settlement was a 'sell-out' which was not going to befall them. It was an unedifying spectacle which did not augur well for the fate of the interparty talks. The uncertainty over the parameters of the talks was not solely the preserve of the general public as key personnel within the UUP appeared to be no better informed. When at last it appeared that it had been agreed that Sir Ninian Stephen[16] would chair Strand Two, a joint statement was issued by Ian Paisley and James Molyneaux on 15 June which said that a formal endorsement of Stephen would have to wait until intensive research had been conducted by them on his suitability. This was viewed with some consternation by officials in UUP headquarters at Glengall Street who commented: 'it would be putting it mildly to say we were surprised by the joint statement . . . as far as we were concerned, we understood the matter was settled'.[17]

The first plenary session of the talks eventually got under way at Stormont on 17 June 1991 when the SDLP and Alliance put forward their position papers. Even at this late stage a delay occurred which resulted in the meeting being delayed by two hours due to a last-minute hitch caused by the Alliance and SDLP refusing to sit down at the negotiating table until the DUP accepted Sir Ninian Stephen as chair of Strand Two. This led to the bizarre sight of Paisley and Robinson (who claimed that they were awaiting further information on the Australian) leaving Stormont and spending an hour at their party headquarters awaiting the much sought after clarification. This journey clearly satisfied them as, minutes after they arrived back, the much delayed Brooke Talks got going at 12.52 p.m. Fittingly, after eighteen minutes' discussion, the delegates broke for lunch!

Talks under strain

It was clear from an early stage that Peter Brooke's initiative was not going to produce a substantial degree of progress. A political time-bomb was ticking away underneath the talks in that the next meeting of the Anglo-Irish Intergovernmental Conference was scheduled for 16 July, leaving the participants a mere four weeks to establish agreement within a complex framework of negotiations. Clearly this time-frame was inadequate, though the difficulties presented were due largely to the time wasting which had occurred since March. Predictably, given the preconditions with which the unionists entered the process, the date of the impending resumption of the AIA came to dominate the minds and the agenda of the talks. One senior official within the DUP remarked that: 'we entered the talks only after the agreement's [sic] operations were suspended. If the two governments go back on that crucial decision while the talks are still going on, the implications could be drastic.'[18] To make up for lost time, the politicians decided to step up their work rate, holding a five-hour meeting on 18 June and agreeing to follow a more intensive timetable involving three days of talks each week. Despite these renewed efforts, sufficient trust did not exist between the parties to enable any significant movement to take place. Unionists felt that the two governments remained committed to the old structures of the AIA as they seemed unwilling to suspend the forthcoming ministerial conference, even given the prospect – however remote – of interparty agreement superseding the AIA which was the ostensible aim of the Brooke initiative. The SDLP, on the other hand, believed unionists were stalling in an attempt to achieve a further suspension of the AIA and ultimately make it extremely difficult for the two governments to reimpose it against the wishes of the unionist community, especially within a political context which articulated the principles of agreement and consent.

The curtain eventually came down on the Brooke Talks on 3 July 1991 as time had run out before the resumption of the AIA. In an agreed statement with the four party leaders, the Secretary of State attempted to put a brave face on events, declaring that the talks 'had been valuable and produced genuine dialogue'.[19]

The unionist position during the Brooke Talks was clear. While the Ulster and Democratic Unionists behaved formally as individual parties during the talks, they had a common negotiating position. This was based on the document developed by a UUP–DUP working party in December 1987 and presented to the British government in January 1988.[20] While much of the language was inclusive and spoke of involving the nationalist community in 'a very real way', the broad architecture of the plan indicated a depressing lack of political movement within unionism. Both the UUP and DUP argued that an assembly should be established with non-executive responsibilities and should be run through an elaborate committee system. Parties would be represented on those committees in accordance with the strength of their representation within the elected body. Nationalists interpreted this as an invitation to become proportionate minorities rather than disproportionate minorities. In addition, the unionist proposal for an assembly with an increased representation to that of the 1982 model was designed to ensure that political control of the committees would rest firmly in the hands of unionist political representatives. *Irish Times* London editor Frank Millar pointed this out when the plan was leaked in July 1991.

> In an explanatory note to his colleagues, the draftsman of the document says: 'the larger the committee, the larger the unionist majority and the risk (of loss of control) is consequently and proportionately reduced.' In deference to previous unionist opposition to executive power-sharing, the document says: 'As there is no executive, there is *ipso facto* no executive power-sharing. Yet the SDLP can rightly say that they are represented at the highest level.[21]

It is clear from the unionist position on Strand One of the Brooke Talks that they were still trying to devise a means of being 'top dog' in Northern Ireland rather than reach a compromise settlement.

This was not a power-sharing relationship in the sense that nationalists understood that term and consequently held little attraction for the SDLP. In return for the scrapping of the AIA, the SDLP were being asked to sign up to a package which was integrationist in tone. The limited powers of the assembly were designed on one level to create a strong Westminster–Belfast political axis in terms of legislative decision-making, and on another level to reduce the scale of the Irish dimension. Unionists were aware that a legislative rather than merely an administrative assembly would increase the stakes for the nationalist minority within Northern Ireland and would require a more proactive role by the government of the Irish Republic in acting as a guarantor for that community. In such an arrangement, this role would have to be defined in advance and institutionalised in a manner which would likely have built upon rather than detracted from Dublin's role in the AIA. However, merely implementing decisions taken at Westminster shifted the power balance from Belfast to London. The reforms suggested by unionists, such as ending Orders in Council and establishing a select committee, were designed to achieve a greater political and institutional harmonisation with the rest of the United Kingdom, do away with the 'special case' status of Northern Ireland and remedy the 'direct rule with a green tinge' policy evident since the signing of the AIA. To some extent the Agreement was a brooding presence throughout the duration of the Brooke Talks. The knowledge that it would be reactivated should significant interparty consensus not be forthcoming was a constant irritant to the unionist negotiators and did little to create the culture of compromise which was an essential ingredient for the success of the exercise. Against this, nationalists would doubtless point out that it was only the 'obnoxious' nature of the AIA which had got unionists to the negotiating table in the first place. The SDLP, on the other hand, saw the Agreement as a starting block to be built upon rather than an edifice which could be chipped away in discussions with those who had been trying to destroy it for the previous six years. In structural terms this allowed the SDLP to negotiate from a position of strength and produced an unpromising equation. Put simply, if they did not move they would get the return of the AIA; if the SDLP did, they would get an emasculated version of the AIA. This reality, together with their experience as they saw it of unionist gamesmanship during the course of the talks, did little to encourage a mood of compromise within the SDLP in 1991.

Despite the failure of his talks initiative, Peter Brooke embarked upon a damage limitation exercise by making it clear that the door had not completely closed and he wanted to 'explore the possibility of finding terms on which fresh discussions could be held'.[22] The immediate prospects did not look encouraging. Loyalist paramilitaries, who had called a ceasefire on 30 April for the duration of the talks, resumed their campaign of violence with much greater ferocity from 4 July.[23] The upsurge in violence together with the failure of the talks resulted in a hardening of the unionist position. At a Friends of the Union meeting in early November, James Molyneaux denounced the structure of the Brooke initiative and declared that his party would not participate in a similar exercise again. Instead, he advocated a minimalist approach with low-level political discussions leading to incremental progress.

> If only the Northern Ireland Office would permit us to get together without putting us under the glare of the TV cameras in mock summitry . . . we won't get involved in another high-wire act simply to satisfy the news industry. There is no reason why in the course of bilateral discussions we can't edge forward and make progress where it is possible.[24]

At the DUP annual party conference a month later, Ian Paisley also spoke of the Brooke Talks as a 'high-wire act' and claimed that any further political discussions should take a different format and be held at Westminster rather than being centred on Belfast. He remained adamant of course that, although the structure and location of future talks had to change, the unionist preconditions surrounding the AIA and the role of the Irish government must remain. 'The talks about the internal affairs of Northern Ireland are no business of the Dublin government. It intruded itself into the first talks – that cannot happen again.'[25]

Many unionists retain bitter memories of the Brooke Talks, blaming the SDLP and the Irish government for erecting obstacles during the process and being ambivalent in their commitment to the enterprise. One Ulster Unionist claimed that the procedural wrangling was caused when John Hume demanded at the beginning of Strand One that the parties must decide where they were going to meet the Irish government before the talks proceeded any further and that this 'precondition' to continue caused the whole process to degenerate to a point that serious negotiation was impossible. 'I think in retrospect, possibly unionists were outmanoeuvred. They appeared to be the ones who were breaking the talks, when in fact [it was] quite the opposite, they were the ones most anxious to get the talks rolling.'[26] It has to be said however that, despite these protestations of injured innocence, the unionists seemed all too eager to be drawn into petty squabbling over the modalities and did not demonstrate the requisite spirit of compromise necessary for progress to be made. Of course they were positive about Strand One and achieving agreement about internal structures of government for Northern Ireland, but they showed precious little commitment to go beyond this and bite the bullet concerning how North–South relationships could be developed to reflect the political and cultural identity of those within the North who were not unionists. Distrust between the unionists and nationalists hung over the talks like a 'spectre at the feast' and tended to undermine any chance of serious negotiations taking place in a positive atmosphere. The unionist attitude was that the SDLP had no incentive for making the talks work as they had the AIA to fall back on and were manoeuvring during the whole process to ensure that when they did eventually collapse the unionists would get the blame for it. One senior member of the Ulster Unionist Party presents anecdotal evidence to support his claim that the SDLP were working to a different agenda and were less than wholeheartedly behind the Brooke initiative.

> When the talks were all over . . . the unionists all went home when it was announced that day. And Jim Nicholson and Reg Empey went in [to the bar] for a beer, feeling very low, and the SDLP were having a party in the bar. They hadn't been in the bar the whole ten or twelve weeks they had been up at Stormont, Hume had kept them all closeted in their rooms. We never even met them, we never even met them in the corridors, I don't know whether they were smokin' or drinkin' or not, but they were never in the bar until the very last day and when Jim Nicholson and Reg Empey went in, they were whoopin' and cheerin' and drinkin' their heads off. So I think that tells you [that] they saw themselves [as] having succeeded.[27]

The SDLP have, unsurprisingly, contested this version of events, with one of their leading members who was involved in the talks claiming that this incident was simply a matter of letting off steam in a highly pressurised environment and that, while the outcome of the talks was not successful, this did not oblige the party to go around wearing sackcloth and beating their breasts in mortification.[28]

At the beginning of 1992 Brooke attempted to resuscitate his talks process by holding discussions with the leaders of the four main parties. After a meeting with the Secretary of State on 7 January, James Molyneaux announced that this had resolved what appeared to be artificial misunderstandings and that he hoped interparty discussions could begin at the earliest opportunity. While this latest attempt to re-establish political dialogue was beset by uncertainty surrounding the date of the forthcoming Westminster general election and a concern that this could potentially interrupt the process, the initiative was dealt a fatal blow on 17 January when the IRA massacre at Teebane Cross in County Tyrone coincided with Peter Brooke's performance on RTE television.[29] The response of the unionist community to the Secretary of State's unfortunate syncopation ranged from dismay to disgust and Ian Paisley lost little time in issuing another political death certificate. 'We don't believe that the Secretary of State can recover any ground in regard to this matter. . . . It has gone too deep. It has cut through to the very quick, to the very soul of Ulster and will remain there for a very long time.'[30] The UUP stopped short of calling for his resignation but said that he no longer had any personal credibility within Northern Ireland.

A rather different tone was struck by the political sketch-writer for the *Times* when discussing unionist demands for the resignation of the Secretary of State. The reaction in the English press, of which the following extract was the most eloquent, demonstrates the detached attitude of those in Britain to issues of primary concern within the unionist community.

> Mr Brooke serves as a standing example of how it is no good trying to be nice to Ulster Unionists. Every month or so, patient Mr Brooke stands up in the glare of the Commons TV cameras and is ritually insulted by Northern Ireland's MPs. Every month backbench colleagues wince as this courteous bumbling fellow turns the other cheek and tries, yet again, to be reasonable. Every month his gentlemanly decency meets with the same sour and graceless response. Every month he returns for yet more money for a yet larger subsidy for their constituents. Every month he secures it. Every month, dipping deeper into the wells of their bottomless ingratitude, they respond with the same angry complaint that it is not enough. Every month he arrives to report that he has still not quite persuaded the unionists to talk to anyone else on their island. Every month he departs undertaking to have one last try. Every month he fails.
>
> And, should a future PM ever decide to face the Unionists down, nice Mr Brooke will stand witness for the proposition that the other way has been tried already.[31]

While other commentators were more restrained in their analysis, this episode emphasises once again the inability of unionists to see themselves as others see them. In Britain generally, Brooke's misdemeanour was a relatively insignificant matter which did not exercise public opinion unduly.

From Brooke to Mayhew

At the beginning of February 1992, Albert Reynolds was elected leader of Fianna Fáil following the resignation of Charles Haughey and became Taoiseach after getting the approval of the Dáil. In the subsequent Cabinet reshuffle, David Andrews replaced Gerry Collins as Minister for Foreign Affairs. The month was not complete before the new administration had fallen out with the unionist leadership over the remit of future political talks on Northern Ireland. The unionist demand for a concession over the Republic's constitutional claim received a setback on 13 February when Andrews announced that Articles 2 and 3 could only be discussed 'within the sense of global talks'.[32] Two weeks later Ian Paisley left little room for misunderstanding when he rejected the new Taoiseach's claim that the 1920 Government of Ireland Act should be on the table for negotiation in addition to the Irish constitution.

> Mr Reynolds had better learn that the constitutional position of Northern Ireland is not on the table. . . . At no time in any future talks will the unionist leaders even contemplate discussing the Union with the Irish Republic. Mr Reynolds had better get the message loud and clear – it is none of his business.[33]

As all thoughts turned to the looming British general election, the UUP began to manoeuvre in the hope that a hung parliament could provide them with a pivotal role in the formation of the next government. On 22 March the *Sunday Times* suggested that the Conservatives might look to the Unionists rather than the Liberal Democrats for support.[34] Hoping no doubt that the government would adopt aspects of his agenda in the election campaign, Molyneaux made it clear prior to the election that he was looking for an integrationist framework to be established within which interparty talks would take place.

> The post-election Government will be forced to establish a clear understanding of the Union and then underpin it with constitutional arrangements which demonstrate that the citizens of Ulster are, like their colleagues in England, Scotland and Wales, citizens of the United Kingdom with identical rights and obligations. Only when the constitutional framework has been established, can useful discussions on the details within that framework take place. With that framework in place there should be no difficulty living in harmony with our neighbours south of the frontier.[35]

This represented a curious approach to negotiations, as Molyneaux wanted nationalists to concede to an essentially unionist framework *before* interparty talks even began and when they did commence, these talks would merely fine-tune internal relations and those 'with our neighbours south of the frontier'. Molyneaux was also displaying a rather optimistic outlook if he believed that the British government would countenance becoming further embroiled in Northern Ireland than it absolutely had to. The reason why the region has not been treated in the same manner as other areas within the United Kingdom is precisely because it is manifestly *not* the same as England, Scotland or Wales. In none of these three countries is there an alternative national allegiance and only Scotland exhibits any secessionist tendencies capable of obtaining substantial support.[36]

The Conservatives won the general election of 9 April 1992 with a reduced but workable majority and Peter Brooke was replaced as Secretary of State by Sir Patrick Mayhew, a former Attorney General considered by the nationalist community to be antipathetic to their position.[37] The unionist reaction to Mayhew's appointment was rather more favourable, James Molyneaux declaring that the new Secretary of State was renowned for his 'independence of mind and dispassionate decision-making'.[38] Mayhew made it clear immediately upon his arrival in Northern Ireland that, while he had no magic formula for achieving a political settlement, his main objective was to build upon the foundations laid by Peter Brooke and attempt to reach a political settlement through interparty dialogue between the four main constitutional parties.

Mayhew makes progress

Thankfully, much of the preliminary manoeuvring had been resolved during the Brooke initiative and the participants were able to move from procedural wrangling over where the talks should be held to more substantive issues with less acrimony and time-wasting. The format was to be the same as before, a three-stranded process which would address each of the key relationships. Unionist concerns over the AIA were met when the two governments agreed in the wake of the Anglo-Irish Inter-governmental Conference meeting of 27 April to a three-month suspension to facilitate interparty negotiations. The infamous 'nothing is agreed until everything is agreed' formula remained an integral part of the process. What became known as the Mayhew Talks began formally on 29 April with a two-hour plenary discussion among the parties.

It soon became obvious that the lack of trust between the parties which had bedevilled the Brooke Talks was also going to undermine the 1992 negotiations. On 14 May, John Hume accused the UUP of bad faith by leaking the SDLP's submission to Strand One which envisaged a European dimension to future internal structures of government within Northern Ireland.[39] Speaking from Strasbourg, Hume alleged that whoever released the document to the media was trying to wreck the talks. 'I'm extremely angry. It is very clear the party from which the leak came, because it was accompanied by a media attack on our document by that party.'[40] The UUP's reaction was predictable, John Taylor commenting disdainfully that 'as an Ulster Unionist, I totally and utterly reject the thinking behind the leaked document'.[41]

Despite the discordant mood-music which accompanied the talks, progress of a sort was being made. By early July, Strand Two was scheduled to begin after a preliminary agreement had apparently been reached over an internal assembly based on a representative committee system. Crucially however, the SDLP had not formally agreed to this structure, while unionists were saying that they had only agreed to move on to the next phase because the Secretary of State had confirmed that their preferred devolutionist option would form the outline of the Strand One settlement. Another sign of positive movement came with the beginning of Strand Three on 30 June, bringing the unionists – including the DUP – face to face with Irish ministers for the first time since the 1973 Sunningdale conference. David Trimble sought to defend his party's participation in these talks from the endemic fear of being labelled as a compromiser, a tag which has traditionally signalled fatality for unionist leaders. Speaking to a gathering of Orangemen in Glasgow, Trimble declared that his party was taking part in the talks as 'part of a process making Irish nationalism generally come to terms with reality – and partition'.[42]

At this point the various strands began to unravel. Despite unionist assertions, it was clear that agreement had not been reached over internal structures of government. It was also apparent that Strands Two and Three were proceeding without a guarantee from the Southern government that they would remove Articles 2 and 3 of their constitution.[43] After the talks eventually collapsed in November, unionists blamed the SDLP for going back on their word over the Strand One agreement. This was subsequently used to imply that the SDLP were chiefly responsible for wrecking the talks and were never wholly committed to them in the first instance because they had the AIA to fall back on.

However, as the leader of the Alliance Party John Alderdice recollects, the situation was a little more complex. In the effort to establish sufficient agreement over internal structures, a working subcommittee was set up where representatives from each of the four parties would devise the basis for a position on devolution which would enable the other two strands to commence.

> We thought, and I remember rather well because our representative was Steve McBride, and he came to me and said: 'Look, we've got this package. All of us have had to compromise a bit. I'm not totally keen about all this but it's the best that can be achieved at the moment. Will we run with it?' I

read through it and said . . . 'if it's the best we can do, then it's the best we can do and it's important we [progress]' and in any case we were going to be coming back to it because there were bits of it that were in square brackets . . . that weren't completely sorted out and I said, 'okay, we'll run with it'. The message came back the next morning that Paisley had agreed to run with it, Molyneaux agreed to run with it but that John Hume wasn't agreeable to run with it.

Now in fairness, it had not gone to the plenary. It had not been approved, it had simply been drafted by this small group. The understanding of it was that everybody had given a bit and got a bit and that was the best that could be done and it was going back for ratification. . . . So that was what happened and from then on – I mean things had already been difficult before that, that's why the committee was set up – but when that happened we really didn't seem to be going anywhere very fast.[44]

Alderdice is surely correct in saying that this disagreement signalled the beginning of the end of the Mayhew Talks. However, it still begs the question as to why the SDLP were reluctant to accept the compromise. When Jonathan Stephenson, later chairperson of the SDLP, was asked for his party's account of events, he emphasised that the SDLP did not renege on an agreement which had been reached, but merely failed to accept the opinion of the subcommittee. Stephenson added that the proof that his party was not against the details of the draft agreement was demonstrated by the fact that the SDLP endorsed similar proposals when they later emerged in another form.

The SDLP story on that was that the subcommittee which reached that so-called deal had to report back to the full plenary and did report back to the full plenary and then agreement wasn't reached. But it's not a question of Hume pulling the plug. But the one thing I would say about that is that *isn't it odd* that unionists have gone around making that particular statement about a document which they say was agreed, which essentially forms the basis of the British part of the Framework Documents[45] which they rejected?[46] I mean people say that the Framework Documents were a nationalist document, but the British Framework Document about the internal arrangements was based almost entirely on what the unionists say was the rejected bit, the bit that Hume pulled the plug on and which they had agreed. . . . They can't have it both ways, if that was their preferred option then, then it should be their preferred option now. It is something we can negotiate on. The internal proposals [of the Framework Document] were the panel which was incredibly cumbersome, which is why Hume and the full SDLP delegation didn't in the end go for it.[47]

In reference to this last comment, however, it has to be said that the SDLP's preferred option at the time of a European commission to administer internal devolution, composed of disparate elements from Northern and

Southern Ireland, Britain and the wider European Community, could hardly be described as a model of practicality. When Stephenson was asked if the SDLP opposed the unionist position on Strand One of the Mayhew Talks because the internal power-sharing dimension was not adequate or because of the relationship between this and the wider concept of the Irish dimension, he indicated that the party's position owed less to the actual details of the proposal than the surrounding framework within which the negotiations were being conducted. Once again this response demonstrated the lack of trust surrounding the talks and the way in which this damaged the ability of the participants to compromise with one another.

> The objection wasn't on the substance of the internal agreement. The objection was that we weren't going to agree that until we agreed everything else, because we had said 'nothing is agreed until everything is agreed'. Once you agree internal structures, the unionists would say 'right, that's it, we've got our internal structures'. Now we weren't going to have that. We were prepared to look at internal structures inside the context of the whole package.[48]

This lack of trust which bedevilled movement in the Mayhew Talks did not just characterise the relations between parties but was also to be found within them. Evidence was provided at the beginning of July 1992 that elements in the DUP could not come to terms with the compromises required in the interparty dialogue. When Strand Two of the talks got under way in London on 6 July, three DUP councillors resigned in a revolt over Ian Paisley's participation in talks with the Irish government. While it was perhaps a poetic irony that the man who had spent much of his long political career accusing other unionists of betrayal was now himself the subject – if only tacitly – of the same charge, it was a further example of the difficulties faced by any unionist who engaged in positive action and moved away from an existing position. The three Cookstown councillors, Alan Kane, Walter Millar and Kenneth Loughran, sent an open letter of resignation to Paisley and implicitly accused him of moving away from their principled stance on talks with the Irish government.

> It is with grave concern and personal regret that the situation has been arrived at where we write to you in the following terms. We consider that there is no place for unionists around a negotiating table with the Irish Republic's government. Not only does the Irish Republic claim jurisdiction over Northern Ireland, but more significantly in practical terms it freely harbours IRA murderers and terrorists and has consistently refused to operate any meaningful extradition arrangements. . . . Over the years we have been consistently told that the DUP would not sit down at the negotiating table unless a government was in place in Northern Ireland discussing matters of mutual interest.[49]

Paisley responded to the resignations by declaring the following day that they were a 'stunt' and that of the three dissidents only Alan Kane was a current party member 'and not a very active one at that'.[50] Of itself this incident was not a serious challenge to the DUP leader's position, though it was a warning to Paisley not to run too far ahead of hardline opinion within the party. While this was not an activity that he often appeared to engage in, it nevertheless illustrated the limitations of Paisley's position during the talks. It also demonstrated the reactive dynamic within unionism which sees any progressive movement as a potential threat which should be resisted, a predisposition which tends to act as a brake on ideological or political development.

While he survived this scare intact, Paisley was not caught out again. During the early part of September the Mayhew initiative approached the point of disintegration when the DUP walked out because a discussion of Articles 2 and 3 was not sufficiently high on the agenda of Strand Two of the talks. Ian Paisley issued a statement declaring that he had left two party members as non-negotiating observers who would alert him when the Irish Republic's territorial claim came up for debate and that this would signal his return to the process. 'We will not be negotiating at the talks until this issue comes up, and we have made this very clear.'[51] The latest crisis in what seemed to be a perpetually fraught exercise was heavy with irony as disagreements over the agenda between the Irish government and SDLP on the one side, and the unionists on the other, were put to a vote. There have not been many occasions in Stormont's history when a vote went against the unionists, while the DUP, who have traditionally placed a lot of emphasis on the sanctity of majoritarian democracy, then quarrelled with the legitimacy of the mechanism. Ian Paisley was clearly upset by the turn of events.

> We sought along with other parties to resolve this issue. Yet, when another paper was produced later suggesting an agenda that my delegation found unacceptable, there was no one interested in resolving the difference. This time, the Irish Republic sought to bulldoze the issue through by vote. . . .
> We re-state our consternation at the turn of events that has for the first time in the whole of the talks process introduced voting as a means of deciding issues. We had thought, wrongly, it would seem, that we were engaged in a process of resolving disputes. Never before during any Strand in this process has voting formed part of the procedure.[52]

The Ulster Unionist Party did not join the DUP in its boycott, though they were by this stage extremely uneasy about the direction of events and felt 'naked in the conference chamber' without their Democratic Unionist colleagues. Predictably enough, a few days after the DUP action James Molyneaux announced that his party would also vacate the talks table if Articles 2 and 3 were not addressed. This warning came against a background in which the British government had introduced a position paper on North–South co-operation which had enraged the UUP. The intention of this document was to initiate a debate on mechanisms which could be introduced to remedy the inadequate levels of communication and co-operation between Northern Ireland and the Irish Republic. The language used spoke of an 'agreed Ireland' and a specific North–South axis which was the antithesis of the UUP strategy at the time. Ulster Unionists were stressing the need for a British–Irish agreement to replace the AIA with an Irish dimension which would be non-specific to Northern Ireland. In this scenario, the North would be integrated into the rest of the United Kingdom and any consequent Irish dimension would apply equally to any region within the state. This explains why the UUP were so alarmed by the British government's discussion document as it appeared to be going in completely the opposite direction in response to a nationalist agenda. Their concern over the document, which was reportedly written by Sir Patrick Mayhew, also explains the UUP's threat to join the DUP in boycotting the talks table. When James Molyneaux wrote to the Secretary of State with an ultimatum that if the discussion paper was not withdrawn his party would walk out of the talks, the document was dropped by the British government.[53]

While it is clear that little substantive progress was made during the Mayhew Talks over the core issues of an internal system of devolved government in Northern Ireland and an Irish dimension which would reflect the nationalist identity, the mechanics of the process did demonstrate some positive signals within unionism. With all three strands of the process in operation, Mayhew did get further down the road of negotiation than his predecessor Peter Brooke, even if both journeys did lead eventually to a dead end. Both of the main unionist parties engaged in dialogue with the government of the Irish Republic while the UUP went to Dublin without the DUP on 21 September for discussions under the auspices of Strand Two of the process.

However, as one observer has astutely remarked, 'one should not assume that movement denotes progress'[54] and while there was a degree of movement by unionists over the modalities, there was little evidence of political compromise. Once again unionist disunity bedevilled the ability of the ideology to move away from old positions in a more progressive direction. While the Ulster Unionists took a brave step in going to Dublin as part of the Strand Two negotiations, the DUP's Rev. William McCrea attempted to undercut them by describing their decision as a 'betrayal of the loyalist people'.[55]

By October the Mayhew Talks were staggering towards inevitable collapse, as yet again unionist minds began to dwell upon the imminent resumption of the AIA on 16 November. While unionists submitted a new paper on 9 November which included a bill of rights to protect minorities and an 'Inter-Irish Relations Committee' which would establish a formal relationship between a devolved assembly in Northern Ireland and the Dublin parliament, these ideas came too late in the day to be given serious consideration and in reality showed little change from their previous position. The Mayhew Talks ended formally the following day when unionists withdrew due to the commencement by the Maryfield secretariat of preparations for the Anglo-Irish Intergovernmental Conference the following week. Sir Ninian Stephen, chairperson of Strand Two of the process, produced the most understated summary of events: 'the talks have not resulted in a comprehensive accommodation in relation to the deep-seated and long-standing problems they have been addressing'.[56] Perhaps a slightly more practical assessment was provided by Mark Brennock of the *Irish Times* when he noted that what was 'initially a search for a historic new agreement became a search for heads of agreement, for elements of agreement, for a "soft landing" to allow for an early resumption of talks and, finally, for an "agreed statement"'.[57]

Notes

1　*News Letter*, 6 January 1990, p. 8.
2　Quoted in B. O'Leary and J. McGarry, *The Politics of Antagonism: Understanding Northern Ireland* (London, 1993), pp. 312–13. See also Jonathan Bardon's *A History of Ulster* (Belfast, 1992), p. 811, where the same joke is attributed to Mary Holland writing in the *Observer* on 31 March 1991: 'A few weeks ago there was a joke doing the rounds in political circles in Belfast. Question: What do you get when you cross Peter Brooke with Don Corleone? Answer: An offer you don't understand but can't refuse.'
3　*News Letter*, 9 January 1990, p. 8.
4　ibid., 10 January 1990, p. 10.
5　ibid., 11 January 1990, p. 4.
6　ibid., 17 January 1990, p. 10.
7　ibid.
8　ibid., 29 January 1990, p. 4.
9　ibid., 26 November 1990, p. 1.
10　ibid., 18 March 1991, pp. 1 and 4.
11　ibid., 25 March 1991, p. 9.
12　While Sinn Féin had a greater democratic mandate at the time than Alliance, and despite the fact that the party's president Gerry Adams was the MP for West Belfast, the party were excluded due to their refusal to condemn the IRA campaign.
13　*News Letter*, 27 March 1991, p. 7.
14　Articles 2 and 3 of the Republic of Ireland's 1937 constitution define the 'national territory' as consisting of the thirty-two counties of Ireland, though acknowledge that, pending the reintegration of the national territory, laws would only apply to the jurisdiction of the twenty-six counties. These articles were given a further significance for unionists by the judgment of the Supreme Court in the McGimpsey case of 1990 that reintegration of the national territory was a 'constitutional imperative' for the Irish government.

15 P. Bew and G. Gillespie, *Northern Ireland: A Chronology of the Troubles 1968–1993* (Dublin, 1993), p. 246.

16 Sir Ninian Stephen was a respected Australian diplomat and former governor general of Australia.

17 *News Letter*, 17 June 1991, p. 1.

18 ibid., 19 June 1991, p. 7.

19 ibid., 4 July 1991, p. 6.

20 This document, entitled *Administrative and Legislative Devolution*, was leaked to the London editor of the *Irish Times* and former general secretary of the UUP, Frank Millar and published in the *Irish Times* on 3 July 1991, p. 2.

21 *Irish Times*, 3 July 1991, p. 1.

22 *News Letter*, 4 July 1991, p. 6.

23 The Provisional IRA did not call a formal ceasefire, or observe an informal cessation during the talks.

24 *News Letter*, 11 November 1991, p. 5.

25 ibid., 2 December 1991, p. 13.

26 Conversation between the author and a senior member of the UUP.

27 ibid.

28 Conversation between the author and a senior member of the SDLP.

29 Peter Brooke's credibility lay in ruins after he appeared on RTE's *Late Late Show*. While artistically his rendition of 'My Darling Clementine' may not have worried the 'Three Tenors', it was certainly politically ill-advised, given the fact that the IRA had killed seven Protestant workmen at Teebane in County Tyrone the same evening. While he staggered on until the 1992 general election, this incident effectively sounded the death-knell of his period as Secretary of State.

30 *News Letter*, 21 January 1992, p. 1.

31 Matthew Parris, *Times*, 21 January 1992, p. 18.

32 Bew and Gillespie, *Northern Ireland: A Chronology*, p. 257.

33 *News Letter*, 26 February 1992, p. 7.

34 Bew and Gillespie, *Northern Ireland: A Chronology*, p. 259.

35 *News Letter*, 27 February 1992, p. 13.

36 While there are close historical and cultural links between Scotland and Northern Ireland, the dynamics of their nationalist tendencies are not similar. The engine of the independence movement in Scotland is essentially driven by a sense of political disenfranchisement, rather than an allegiance to a competitor 'mother country'. Orthodox nationalists in Northern Ireland (whose number is difficult to determine and does not equate to the size of the Catholic population) do not just wish to secede from the state they are in, but want to join an entirely different state. Thus, while public support for Scottish nationalism is likely to dissipate in the event of devolution granting the region a substantial degree of regional autonomy from Westminster, this is unlikely to significantly alter the attitudes of nationalists in Northern Ireland.

37 As British Attorney General, Mayhew had enraged the Northern nationalist community and the Irish government in 1988 by deciding on the grounds of 'national security' not to prosecute a number of RUC officers despite evidence contained within the Stalker/Sampson Report of a cover-up over an alleged official 'shoot-to-kill' policy in Northern Ireland. Nationalist suspicions were reinforced by one of Mayhew's first appointments. On 14 April he named Michael Mates as Deputy Secretary of State with responsibility for security. Mates, a former officer in the British army, had previously intervened regularly in Irish affairs and was often wheeled out by the media as a unionist voice on the Conservative back-benches. One nationalist MP referred to him contemptuously as 'Colonel Blimp' upon his appointment.

38 *News Letter*, 13 April 1992, p. 5.

39 The SDLP paper called for a Northern Ireland executive commission as an overall body to govern the region. Under this plan, a six-member commission elected by single transferable vote would be composed of three members from Northern Ireland, and one each from Britain, the Irish Republic and the European community.

40 *News Letter*, 14 May 1992, p. 16.

41 ibid.

42 ibid., 6 July 1992, pp. 1 and 4.

43 It has rarely been acknowledged by unionists that the removal of Articles 2 and 3 is not immediately in the gift of any Irish government as the constitution can only be amended after a referendum is held and a majority within the state consent to such a change.

44 Dr John Alderdice, interview with author, 7 February 1996.

45 *Frameworks for the Future*, commonly referred to as the Frameworks Document. There were two parts to this British–Irish intergovernmental policy initiative. The first was a specifically British government document outlining its preferred form of internal political structures within Northern Ireland. The second document was drafted jointly by the two governments and was concerned with the relationships within Ireland and between the two governments. Stephenson was referring here to the first of the framework documents entitled *A Framework for Accountable Government in Northern Ireland*.

46 When Stephenson was reminded that the UUP did not reject the British part of the Frameworks Document he agreed, but added that as a package the initiative was rejected by the UUP as a basis for political progress. Jonathan Stephenson, interview with author, 21 November 1995.

47 ibid.

48 ibid.

49 *News Letter*, 7 July 1992, pp. 1 and 4.

50 ibid., 8 July 1992, p. 7.

51 *Belfast Telegraph*, 9 September 1992, in Bew and Gillespie, *Northern Ireland: A Chronology*, p. 272.

52 *News Letter*, 11 September 1992, p. 6.

53 Bew and Gillespie, *Northern Ireland: A Chronology*, p. 273.

54 P. Arthur, 'The Mayhew Talks 1992', *Irish Political Studies*, 8 (1993), p. 139.

55 ibid., p. 141.

56 Bew and Gillespie, *Northern Ireland: A Chronology*, p. 277.

57 Arthur, 'Mayhew Talks', p. 142.

CHAPTER 8

Unionism Before and After the Ceasefires

Nineteen-ninety-three was one of the darkest years in the history of the conflict in Northern Ireland. While the death toll in the North had not risen since the previous year,[1] the political climate left little room for optimism. The constitutional talks, which had stuttered along during the previous two years, had failed to secure a compromise settlement, while unionist and nationalist representatives appeared to be moving further apart rather than closer together.

The political debate was dominated for most of the year by what became known as the Hume–Adams talks, together with reaction to this dialogue by the British and Irish governments. The autumn, meanwhile, saw an acceleration of both political turbulence and violence to a point that led all but the most optimistic to despair.

Dialogic difficulties

The inconclusive ending of what had euphemistically become known as the 'constitutional talks' process led to an acceleration of the dialogue between John Hume, the leader of the SDLP, and Gerry Adams, president of Sinn Féin, which had been going on sporadically since January 1988. These contacts were crucial building-blocks to the IRA ceasefire of 31 August 1994 and the concerns of unionist politics reflected the development of the Hume–Adams debate and growing consensus within Irish nationalism. After the collapse of the Mayhew Talks, John Hume made it his personal priority to work towards obtaining a ceasefire from the paramilitaries to provide a new environment for political discussions to take place. The contact between the two leaders of Northern nationalism was made public after Gerry Adams was spotted visiting the home of the SDLP leader in Derry on 10 April 1993.[2] A joint statement was released by the two leaders on 24 April which, for both symbolic and practical reasons, heralded a new phase in the political development of Northern Ireland. In the early 1980s, especially in the aftermath of the IRA hunger-strikes of

1981, the SDLP and Sinn Féin were separated by an ideological chasm. The New Ireland Forum was established to bolster constitutional nationalism and exhibit an Irish nationalist consensus which excluded Sinn Féin and those who supported it, in order to contribute to its political demonisation and marginalisation. The joint statement issued on 24 April was in that sense an ideological *volte face* by the largest nationalist party in Northern Ireland. Adams was no longer a terrorist to be threatened with excommunication by the Catholic Church. He was now an equal, a partner in the 'peace process', a man who could be reasoned with and should be listened to. This was not a message wholly to the liking of the rest of the SDLP and was certainly not welcomed by unionists of any persuasion. While the joint statement of 24 April served an important symbolic purpose, its practical impact was to publicly align the political strategies of the SDLP and Sinn Féin and solidify Northern nationalism to a point that had not been seen since the civil rights movement in the 1960s. Both leaders agreed that 'an internal settlement is not a solution' and that 'the Irish people as a whole have a right to national self-determination'. Precisely how that was to be exercised was 'a matter for agreement between the people of Ireland'.[3]

Unionist reaction to the Hume–Adams dialogue was predictable. They saw this as a potential threat on a number of levels. On the one hand, it would provide the IRA with a renewed motivation and end the political marginalisation of Sinn Féin. On the other, it represented a public alignment of Northern nationalism into a relatively cohesive bloc which posed a much greater electoral threat to unionism than had hitherto been the case. The DUP's leading representative in Derry, Gregory Campbell, compared Hume's meeting with Adams on 10 April unfavourably with the recent meeting between Gordon Wilson and the IRA.[4]

> Gordon Wilson could have been overlooked for his meeting on the grounds of naivety but no such luxury can be afforded an experienced politician like Mr Hume. Instead of giving Sinn Féin and the IRA the legitimacy of treating them like people capable of a reasonable response Mr Hume should be encouraging his community to isolate them and hand them over to the police when acts of terrorism are known to them.[5]

Ian Paisley was reported as saying that, because of the ongoing meetings between Hume and Adams, he would boycott any future constitutional talks with the SDLP unless such contacts were ended. The DUP deputy leader Peter Robinson endorsed this sentiment and accused Hume of providing assistance to the IRA in their hour of need.

> I don't think any self-respecting unionist would be involved in any talks while the SDLP was engaged in the twin process of having discussions with Provisional IRA representatives. John Hume has given the Provisional IRA a considerable leg up at a time when their propaganda was much needed to

resolve the many problems they had within the organisation from the Warrington bombings. It seems almost as if John Hume has come to the aid of the IRA at a time when their spirits were low.[6]

It was not only unionists who expressed concern about the Hume–Adams dialogue. Robin Wilson, former editor of *Fortnight* magazine and one of the most important opinion-formers in Northern Ireland over the last ten years, commented that the joint statement of 24 April 'merely confirmed that Mr Hume is no more interested in talking to unionists about a serious political accommodation than they are to him'.[7] While much of the Northern media criticism of Hume was reasoned, elements of the Dublin press launched a vitriolic campaign against the SDLP leader. Foremost among the participants in this newly discovered blood sport was the *Sunday Independent*, which, on 3 October, devoted seven pages to an 'analysis' of Hume's peace strategy. One of the paper's most prominent contributors was Eamon Dunphy, former soccer player turned political commentator, who declared: 'He is clearly intent on sucking us into an immoral relationship with active terrorists.'[8] In light of future events, the words of Richard Kearney, one of the few writers in the 3 October issue of the *Sunday Independent* to defend Hume, turned out to be a far-sighted commentary not just on the political judgement of the SDLP leader but on that of Kearney's fellow contributors.

> Trying to persuade unconstitutional republicans to abjure violence and turn constitutional overnight is no mean task. We should be grateful to Hume for at least trying. If he succeeds, who will cry Judas? It is, I believe, far too easy for us sitting comfortably in our southern armchairs to scapegoat Hume.[9]

Clearly, the political atmosphere did not suggest that interparty talks could recommence with any realistic chance of a positive outcome. Nevertheless, disregarding the negative mood-music which reached most ears during April, Sir Patrick Mayhew made a speech at the Institute of Irish Studies in Liverpool on 23 April in an attempt to resuscitate the political process. In this address the Secretary of State recognised the British government's responsibility to provide 'a direction and focus to future talks'. He tried to talk up the 1992 discussions by saying that it was his view and that of the Prime Minister that 'much more success' had been achieved in 1992 than was publicly recognised.[10] Mayhew went on in his Liverpool address to say that while the government were preparing some practical guidelines they did not intend to impose a blueprint for talks but would act as a facilitator in the process, which he was sure contained the potential to deliver an acceptable political accommodation. The Secretary of State declared that 'the pieces are on the board, but the end game has not yet begun'.[11] In an attempt to coax the unionists along, Mayhew reiterated that the constitutional status of Northern Ireland would not change unless this became the express wish of the majority of people living there, while joint authority was rejected on a similar basis. With a rhetorical nod in the direction of James Molyneaux, the Secretary of State suggested that a Northern Ireland select committee might be established as a means of remedying the democratic deficit in the region.[12] Typically, the DUP reacted more negatively to Mayhew's Liverpool speech than did their Ulster Unionist colleagues. There were two underlying reasons for this opposition. Firstly, the DUP had never been overly keen on measures such as the introduction of select committees, seeing them merely as a token gesture to buy off their opposition and distract people from the greater betrayal which was being perpetrated by London and Dublin. Secondly, the DUP saw such speeches as an attempt to divide unionism and marginalise the DUP. Peter Robinson was clearly unimpressed by what he had heard and the DUP deputy leader duly castigated the Secretary of State for posing as '[Minister for Foreign Affairs] Dick Spring's lapdog' and said that Mayhew was 'dangling as bait' the prospect of a select committee on Northern Ireland to attract the UUP and leave the DUP on the sidelines.[13] It was interesting that David Trimble took a more positive message from the Liverpool speech, pointing out that the Secretary of State had ruled out the possibility of joint authority.[14]

As ever in Northern Ireland politics the timing was unfortunate. The chances of Mayhew's speech acting as a catalyst to political progress were undoubtedly damaged by the publicity surrounding the Hume–Adams dialogue. A few days earlier the Ulster Unionist Reg Empey attacked the leader of the SDLP and played down the possibility of holding constitutional talks. He called Hume 'hardline' and accused him of inflexibility and of 'holding the same piece of paper in his hands for almost 20 years'.

> It has not changed in any fundamental way, justifying the growing belief among the unionists that the slogans 'no surrender' and 'not an inch' more accurately reflect the static and intransigent SDLP approach than the flexible and open approach of Ulster Unionists. As we move towards a new form of dialogue between the constitutional parties, there is only one question being asked by our negotiators: 'is the SDLP really prepared to accept the realities of Northern Ireland and indulge in a compromise with their fellow citizens?' The pity is that more and more of our colleagues believe that the answer to that question is a resounding 'No'. I hope we are wrong.[15]

Empey went on to comment on the SDLP proposals during the Mayhew Talks, claiming that they would have changed the constitutional status of Northern Ireland from being an integral part of the United Kingdom 'to a protectorate statelet'. 'While the proposals of John Hume would not have been a total nationalist victory, they would have been a total unionist defeat.'[16] Again, this points out the difficulties surrounding conflict resolution in Northern Ireland given the often zero-sum nature of the dispute, since what one side views as a minor concession the other interprets as a total capitulation. John Hume's ill-advised response to criticism he received for his dialogue with Gerry Adams – that he did not give 'two balls of roasted snow' for the opinion of his critics – did little to make unionists more amenable to his analysis.

The Secretary of State's pleasure

While unionist opinion was hardening against John Hume due to his contact with Gerry Adams, the Secretary of State was also coming under increasing criticism. This discontent erupted after Mayhew gave an interview to the German magazine *Die Zeit*, in which he implied that Britain's commitment to the Union was less than solid. All the buttons in the unionist defensive mentality were pressed by this ministerial *faux pas* which was taken as proof positive that British government intentions were treacherous and that the unionist community would eventually be abandoned and left prey to the irredentist intentions of the Irish Republic. Mayhew was reported to have said in the interview that Britain could not have a selfish interest in retaining Northern Ireland within the Union given the economic costs of the region to the British exchequer:

> Many people believe that we would not want to release Northern Ireland from the United Kingdom. To be entirely honest, we would, with pleasure . . . no, not with pleasure. I take that back. But we would not stand in the way of Northern Ireland, if that would be the will of the majority. The Province costs us three billion pounds per year. Three billion pounds for one and a half million people. But, as long as the majority wants to remain in the United Kingdom, we will pay the three billion without complaining.[17]

To many unionist ears *complaining* was exactly what he was doing in this interview; they were not prepared to forgive the Secretary of State's slips, Freudian or otherwise, and his retraction was not accepted. The *News Letter* editorial of 26 April presumably spoke for many concerned unionists when it commented that the British government seemed intent on creating the conditions for the destruction of the Union.

> Sir Patrick Mayhew is doing little these days to dissipate the growing fears of many thinking unionists that he is deliberately pushing the Province towards a political chasm. A number of fissures have appeared in his previously stated commitment to the position of Northern Ireland as an integral part of the United Kingdom, and recently the cracks appear to be widening in an alarming way. Assuming that nothing has been lost – or added – in his interview with a German magazine, it can be fairly concluded that Sir Patrick is ultimately on the side of a united Ireland. And not because he

has any great love for Dublin, but because he believes the Province has become too much of a liability for the rest of the United Kingdom to bear![18]

While Peter Robinson described the article in *Die Zeit* as 'dynamite', a spokesperson for the Northern Ireland Office embarked on a damage limitation exercise, declaring that the position of the government was clearly outlined in the Secretary of State's speech in Liverpool. Perhaps with the 'Tower of Babel' in mind, the official offered the following lame explanation: 'Until we can check our records of the interview, we are unable to comment but it is worth remembering that the interview was conducted in English, translated into German and back into English.'[19] It soon became clear that unionists could recognise a snub in any language. Peter Robinson was characteristically forthright.

> No excuse will wash with the people of Northern Ireland. I, therefore, do not look for an apology or empty denial. These comments not only reveal Sir Patrick's gratuitously insulting manner but expose his Government's intentions and its desire to off-load Ulster to Dublin. Sir Patrick must be removed. There is no place for such attitudes in the position he holds. Mayhew must go.[20]

The Ulster Unionists were typically more restrained, James Molyneaux taking a more conciliatory approach than Robinson to the Mayhew interview. 'I think certainly Sir Patrick will have to clear it up himself with a very authoritative statement.' His party colleague John Taylor said that he was deeply concerned about Mayhew's remarks and that they had done 'enormous damage' to the confidence of the unionist community in Northern Ireland and the outcome of future talks.[21] Commenting after the district council elections of 21 May, the independent analyst Robin Wilson made the following pithy observation: 'Northern Ireland's zero-sum is of course a minefield. But it has been a peculiar achievement of the current secretary of state, as the results showed, so maladroitly to enhance republican defiance and loyalist paranoia *at the same time*.'[22] Mayhew did his best to limit the damage by subsequently claiming that his remarks had been 'shortened and misreported' but this did little to mollify critics such as Peter Robinson. 'The real Patrick Mayhew spoke and indicated how happy he would be to get rid of Northern Ireland. Then he realised what he has [sic] said and tried to erase it from the record.'[23]

Paranoic or not, Mayhew's remarks had burnt into the psyche of radical unionist opinion. At the end of April, Ian Paisley attacked the North Down Tory James O'Fee for his statement at a public meeting that the government had hardened its position in favour of the Union. The DUP leader illustrated the growing disillusionment over British intentions when he compared the relative positions of Northern Ireland and Scotland within the United Kingdom.

The Government produced a document entitled Scotland in the Union – Partnership for Good, and in it the Government states that no matter what the electorate of Scotland think the union that was established in 1707 will remain. In Northern Ireland their commitment lasts only until the minority opinion becomes the majority opinion. The bottom line is they want to get rid of us.[24]

It was clear that the DUP were in no mood for re-entering interparty talks, especially on the basis outlined by the Secretary of State. Paisley condemned Mayhew's Liverpool speech and his plan for reinvigorating the political process: 'We reject that document in its totality.' Perhaps in an effort to add another political scalp to his belt, the DUP leader declared that he no longer had any confidence in Mayhew and that he should be replaced by someone more capable of achieving a workable political settlement. Comparing the Liverpool speech with the *Die Zeit* interview, the DUP leader declared that the best thing the Secretary of State could do would be to pack his bags and allow John Major to consider someone in whom the majority of people in Northern Ireland could have some trust. 'It puts him outside the pale of being able to chair any meetings to deal with our present predicament. The true Paddy has stood up and it can be seen wearing green nationalist clothes.'[25]

Peter Robinson echoed his leader's statement and aimed a blow at the UUP who had demonstrated less hostility towards the plan for re-entering interparty talks. Referring to the Secretary of State's Liverpool speech, the East Belfast MP said that he was 'bewildered how any unionist can welcome this Mayhew document. This party won't accept a talks process based on a structure which will either lead to failure or betrayal.'[26]

The basis of the speech could only lead to greater involvement by the Irish Republic in Northern Ireland's affairs. Unionists should not be gulled into accepting talks on the basis of that document. Sir Patrick has indicated he would be glad to get rid of Northern Ireland.[27]

Such comments have to be read in the context of the forthcoming district council elections which took place on 19 May 1993.[28] Elections in Northern Ireland are traditionally a period when politicians become more hardline and attempt to outdo one another in a negative display of their political virility. It is a sad reflection on the wider unionist community that their politicians, who are naturally motivated by self-preservation, feel that the safest ground lies behind the trenches and the safest rhetoric lies in issuing the rhythmic mantra of 'No Surrender'. Two things were certain in the run-up to this poll: the relationship between the DUP and UUP would worsen as both competed to demonstrate their unionist credentials, and neither would accept Mayhew's invitation to renew interparty dialogue. Predictably, the DUP's election manifesto played to its traditional hardline gallery, attacking the Secretary of State and the UUP in equal measure. Mayhew's talks document, *Framework for a Just Settlement*, was rejected on the grounds that it was a 'framework for the betrayal of Ulster', drawn up with the connivance of the Irish government. It was condemned for accepting the 'illegal, immoral and criminal' territorial claim of the Republic over the North and for providing the basis for a greater Southern involvement in the internal affairs of Northern Ireland.

> The Official Unionist Party welcomed the Mayhew betrayal as 'a very balanced, practical speech.' The Dublin government also welcomed it. The Official Unionists are now prepared to proceed on the basis of a sell-out speech by Patrick Mayhew which outlines a way forward which is disastrous for Unionists and destructive of Ulster's constitutional position. In so doing they have forfeited any right to the confidence of true Unionists.[29]

In his personal message to party supporters in the election manifesto, Paisley made his customary messianic appeal to his believers. Ulster was in danger, time was short, enemies were abundant and only he could save the day. The following lurid excerpt illustrates the fine line the DUP leader trod between vitriol and incitement to violence. While he may have been preaching to the converted, he left objective observers in little doubt that the DUP would not be making a substantial contribution to political progress in the short term at least.

> The conspiracy to destroy Northern Ireland and especially its Protestant people gains added momentum every day. The hour is exceedingly grave for us all. The reaping of the whirlwind is upon us as a result of the sowing of the south wind of successive British Governments. The evil of appeasement has produced a monster of mayhem, Mayhew, murder and misery and the Government continues to feed the brute instead of slaughtering it. . . . [Dublin] and the SDLP seek to ride on the backs of IRA violence to victory. Hence the new Pan-Nationalist Front with the SDLP in cahoots with IRA Sinn Féin. . . . I say to the Loyalist and Unionist electorate 'Get Mad With Mayhew'. Give him the bloody nose he deserves. . . . The world awaits Ulster's answer.[30]

While the policy position adopted by the Ulster Unionists was typically less extreme, their attitude to interparty talks was inevitably coloured by an attempt to defend themselves from the accusations by the DUP that they had 'sold out' and could not therefore be trusted by the unionist community. Consequently, in their manifesto for the local government elections the UUP also made the point – albeit less directly – that Northern Ireland's position within the Union was in jeopardy, but insisted that they were the party which could best protect the unionist interest.

> It is more [important] now than at any time in our history to assert the fundamental concept of upholding and strengthening the Union of Great

Britain and Northern Ireland. The Anglo-Irish Agreement and the current neutral stance by Her Majesty's Government both stem from a policy designed to placate the enemies of the Union. The Ulster Unionist Party will maintain an unrelenting opposition to this policy line and the imposed interference in domestic affairs by the government of the Irish Republic.[31]

Clearly, in this atmosphere, political progress was unlikely. The UUP leader James Molyneaux rejected interparty talks because of John Hume's contacts with Gerry Adams. 'Imagine unionists sitting around the table for talks with John Hume having his own vote and a proxy for Gerry Adams. We are not going to dance to anybody's tune. We have the high ground and we are going to maintain it.'[32] The DUP press officer, Sammy Wilson, reinforced this uncompromising attitude when he rejected a plea by Minister for Foreign Affairs, Dick Spring, to resume talks after the local government elections. Wilson suggested that there was no reason to begin talks if the Irish government's illegal claim was not dealt with. 'It would be futile and dangerous to resume the talks, for Eire has made it clear there is nothing to talk about – and dangerous for more and more concessions would be sought from unionists without anyone else giving an inch.'[33]

At the beginning of June, Jeremy Hanley was replaced as Political Development Minister at the NIO by Michael Ancram, who immediately announced that he wanted to resuscitate the interparty talks. This was greeted unenthusiastically by one UUP official who intimated a minimalist approach to political dialogue. 'Barriers remain. Nothing has really changed. The Secretary of State may push ahead with plans to sound out each main party, but full-scale discussions are on the back burner.'[34]

Sir Patrick Mayhew, meanwhile, continued to give the impression that he opened his mouth merely to change feet. Having infuriated unionists with his *Die Zeit* interview months earlier, the Secretary of State did it again with remarks he made while waiting to go into the opera at Castleward, County Down on 26 June. When asked by a journalist about an incident at a west Belfast Orange parade where a loyalist who was 'policing' it injured himself when a grenade he was carrying in his pocket went off prematurely, the Secretary of State remarked: 'well, nobody is dead. At the end of this opera, everybody's dead.' Mayhew later apologised for 'any distress' his comment had caused.[35] The DUP clearly believed that the Irish government were not serious in their commitment to initiate constitutional change, while Mayhew's rhetorical fumbling illustrated that the British were all too serious in their desire to alter the constitutional status quo of Northern Ireland. Following comments made by the Secretary of State on the BBC's *On the Record* programme in mid-June concerning the ground rules for the commencement of political dialogue, Sammy Wilson claimed that Mayhew had 'put the nail in the coffin' of any new talks starting in the autumn. The DUP press officer added, 'Dublin has not given one inch on its territorial claim and for Paddy Mayhew to say otherwise shows how little the issue means to the Government. . . . Basically, the Government [wishes] unionists to sign up to a process which contains the destruction of the Union.'[36] Judging from comments made by Peter Robinson the same month, it would seem that even had interparty talks got under way they would not have resulted in a settlement. Anxious to contribute ideas to the security debate, the deputy leader of the DUP called for the RAF to 'wipe out' IRA headquarters in Belfast and Dublin with Baghdad-style air raids.[37]

The council of despair

While relations between the DUP and the British government were at a low ebb in the summer of 1993, temperatures also began to rise in Belfast City Council between the Democratic Unionists and their UUP colleagues. The row was caused when the Ulster Unionist group on the council abstained in a crucial vote which effectively gave Alex Atwood of the SDLP chairmanship of the Client Services Committee. Though a relatively small matter in itself, this issue illustrated the various attitudes within unionist politics towards the concept of power-sharing and the extent to which they were prepared to envisage a political accommodation of Northern nationalism. Nigel Dodds clarified the DUP position on the issue. 'We supported unionist candidates in other votes. When Client Services came up we put forward independent unionist Joe Coggle for the post. We will not support a pact with the SDLP.'[38] While the UUP insisted that there was no pact with the SDLP, the group's deputy leader in the council, Jim Rodgers, provided a more positive perspective than that evident within the DUP.

> If Belfast City Council and the city is to progress we need co-operation between constitutional parties. Even though the SDLP are not prepared to do that, we are going to honour our manifesto to the electorate which clearly put forward the idea of proportionality on committees and chairmanships.[39]

Rodgers's party colleague Chris McGimpsey insisted: 'It is amazing that during the Stormont talks, the DUP were prepared to accept SDLP chairpersons of departments covering Northern Ireland. Yet they are opposed to such procedures at council level where powers are relatively minuscule.'[40] The limits of the UUP's positivity in Belfast City Council were displayed when they – along with all the other parties on the council except the SDLP – rejected a request from Sinn Féin to have a meeting. Fred Cobain, leader of the Ulster Unionist group, commented that a letter from Sinn Féin's Alex Maskey asking for a meeting had been 'thrown into the fire'.[41] At times it seemed as though no issue could pass through Belfast City Council without raising unionist blood pressures.[42] A row erupted for

instance between the UUP and DUP over a civic reception for Irish moun-
taineer, Dawson Stelfox, at Belfast City Hall because the lord mayor of
Dublin, Gay Mitchell, was invited to attend. In another example of the
internal struggle within unionism between dogma and pragmatism, the
DUP's Sammy Wilson attacked Belfast lord mayor, Reg Empey, for inviting
his Southern counterpart.

> It is typical of Reg Empey that he should sneak the Lord Mayor of Dublin
> into Belfast only a few days after going down to Dublin himself. What kind
> of a groveller is it who goes out of his way to persuade Dublin politicians
> that some unionists wish to befriend them? The aggressive claim which
> Dublin makes against Northern Ireland would be dealt with far more
> quickly if Mr Empey took his stand against these people, instead of treating
> them like neighbours.[43]

This argument was perhaps fuelled by the visit of President Mary
Robinson to the North a few days earlier, which unionist politicians found
repugnant on a number of levels. The most immediate was her much-
publicised handshake with Gerry Adams in west Belfast, which was
condemned as providing official Irish state approval for Sinn Féin and
legitimising and encouraging the IRA campaign.[44] A more general unionist
gripe concerned the status of the visit, as Robinson managed to short-
circuit much of the politically sensitive protocol by attending functions in
a private rather than official capacity. This did little to reassure many
within the unionist community, who saw it as yet another example of Irish
mendacity and British complicity. David Trimble thus condemned President
Robinson's visit as being 'The physical embodiment of the aggressive
territorial claim in the Irish constitution', and the UUP MP for Upper Bann
went on to accuse Sir Patrick Mayhew of

> . . . turning a blind eye to her coat-trailing operations. . . . Important though
> the dalliance between the President of the Republic and notorious Sinn Féin
> leaders indoubtedly [sic] is, I consider that the question of the status of her
> visit is even more important. . . . She attends functions, such as that in West
> Belfast at which the prominent and powerful in the locality are invited. In
> Coalisland she 'officially opens' a publicly-funded heritage centre. These are
> activities appropriate for a State visit. Yet we know from Northern Ireland
> Office statements that she has not been invited nor has she consulted the
> rightful government of Northern Ireland. That is the crux of the matter. She
> is acting in Northern Ireland in an official manner as if she had an inherent
> right to do so – as if she was the president of all of Ireland.[45]

David Trimble's reaction to Mary Robinson's visit was typical of the
defensive mentality within unionism, as he viewed the point of principle
to be of paramount importance. Because unionists feel so insecure about

their constitutional position within the United Kingdom, they reacted to Robinson's visit in a way which few other British subjects within the United Kingdom could understand. While people in Britain saw a well-dressed and personable (almost regal) woman smiling broadly at everyone placed in front of her, including the leader of Sinn Féin, Trimble saw the matter as a cunning manoeuvre not by an individual but by an irredentist state. Once again, while this may have been an understandable reaction by Ulster unionists, it underscored the difficulties they faced in gaining acceptance from those in Britain whom they defined as their co-nationals. Quite simply, unionist concerns as reflected in the President Robinson visit were not shared by many of those who lived across the Irish Sea, because few there were unduly worried about the constitutional integrity of Northern Ireland or whether this was formally or informally abused.

Moving towards the abyss

The second half of 1993 was notable for an unofficial alliance between the UUP and the British government, an increase of paramilitary violence and yet another attempt by the London and Dublin administrations to reinvigorate the political process.

While few involved were prepared to admit it, the Ulster Unionists came to an 'understanding' with the government in July when John Major was facing a Commons defeat over ratification of the Maastricht Treaty. It seemed clear to observers that the UUP would not vote against the government if its survival was at stake, in return for the granting of a select committee for Northern Ireland, an end to Orders in Council and a commitment by London to the principle of consent before any constitutional change was contemplated in the North. However, as John Hume reminded the UUP after the Maastricht vote, 'if you can be bought on a Friday, you can be sold on a Saturday'. Some unionists declared publicly that the improved relationship between the UUP and the government was not simply the shabby exercise of *realpolitik*, but the product of a longer term realignment which heralded a more optimistic future for the Union. David Trimble, for example, claimed that Conservative MPs were becoming increasingly frustrated by the Irish government. 'The arrogance of Dick Spring, the lack of movement over articles 2 and 3, as well as their lack of security co-operation have all led to a re-think on the Conservative benches.'[46] If unionists such as Trimble thought that such stirrings would leave a significant imprint upon the government's policy towards Northern Ireland or lead London to imperil the Anglo-Irish relationship, then they were soon to be disabused. The Downing Street Declaration signed on 15 December 1993 was evidence that the central political axis lay between London and Dublin, not London and Belfast.

Loyalist paramilitaries were not interested in the machinations going on at Westminster or whether measures such as a select committee would be introduced. Their analysis saw these as essentially ephemeral and short term, when compared to the potential threat posed by what they (together with supposedly more 'respectable' figures such as Ian Paisley) characterised as the pan-nationalist front. These concerns were heightened on 25 September when John Hume and Gerry Adams issued a joint statement claiming that the two leaders had reached an interim agreement which would be forwarded to the Irish government.[47] The UDA called on unionist politicians to withdraw from all institutions of government in protest at the Hume–Adams dialogue. The paramilitary group issued the chilling statement that the time had come to 'bring the people to a state of readiness to act in defence' of their religious and political beliefs'.[48] John Taylor added fuel to the fire by warning that Northern Ireland's position within the United Kingdom had been put in jeopardy by the Hume–Adams agreement and could result in a loyalist backlash. The Ulster Unionist Strangford MP claimed that the sending of a report to Dublin authorities by Hume and Adams was evidence of the 'pan-nationalist front in operation', which was aimed at weakening the constitutional position of Northern Ireland.[49]

In an interesting historical parallel with their reaction to the Anglo-Irish Agreement in 1985, unionists wasted little time in rejecting the paramilitary advice to boycott all government institutions in the wake of the Hume–Adams agreement. UUP secretary Jim Wilson declared: 'I cannot think of a more inappropriate time for leaders of the unionist community to withdraw from elected office.' With breathtaking gall, considering his role in and reflections on the campaign against the AIA, DUP press officer Sammy Wilson observed that boycott tactics had failed during the anti-Agreement campaign. 'There is no point in asking people to take part in a tactic which is not going to succeed.'[50] From the unionist point of view some may say it is a pity Wilson did not take the same view in 1986.

While Ian Paisley subsequently referred to the 'blood-stained nationalist consensus', loyalists paramilitaries stepped up their campaign of violence and widened their definition (which always owed more to theory than practice anyway) of what constituted a legitimate target.[51] This had been evident from a number of incidents which had taken place over the summer and were blamed by loyalists on the Hume–Adams dialogue. On 19 July, bombs were placed under the cars of West Belfast SDLP MP Dr Joe Hendron and his party colleague, Brian Feeney. On 26 August, the Red Hand Commandos said they would bomb bars or hotels which held folk nights on the basis that Irish music was part of the 'pan-nationalist front'.[52] The homes of Joe Hendron and four SDLP councillors were the subject of bomb attacks by the UFF and excused by that organisation on the basis of the Hume–Adams contacts. While unionist politicians queued up to confirm the logic of loyalist paramilitarism and express their distaste for 'pan-nationalism', they distanced themselves further from re-engaging in interparty talks. In an *Irish Times* interview, Molyneaux declared that the UUP would not participate in three-stranded talks on the basis of the Mayhew model. The DUP, meanwhile, produced a new policy document entitled *Breaking the Logjam*, which demonstrated little new thinking and would clearly not appeal to the SDLP.

The Hume–Adams agreement was setting the political agenda in October 1993. However, paramilitary actions at the end of October dwarfed all other considerations. On Saturday 23 October, a bungled attempt to blow up the UDA leadership on the Shankill Road in west Belfast succeeded only in killing the bomber, Thomas Begley, and nine innocent people most of whom were women and children, bringing opprobrium down on the republican movement from every quarter. The decision of Gerry Adams to shoulder Begley's coffin further enraged unionist opinion and was not received well in Britain either. Typically, the *Sun* was the most vivid with the headline: 'Gerry Adams – the two most disgusting words in the English language'.[53]

The loyalist paramilitary response was predictable and immediate. The UFF declared that its members had been 'fully mobilised'.[54] Later the same day a Catholic delivery man was shot and fatally wounded in the Donegall Pass area of Belfast. This was purely a foretaste of the killing spree which was to follow. Over the following week, loyalist paramilitaries were to demonstrate their cruel logic, that they too could count to ten (and even beyond) and that they would draw blood in equal measure to the IRA with almost scientific precision. On Monday 25 October, the UVF shot a Catholic pensioner dead on the outskirts of Belfast. The following day, two Catholic workmen were shot dead and five others were injured by the UFF at a council refuse depot in Belfast. On Thursday 28 October, two Catholic brothers were shot dead by the UVF in their home in Waringstown, County Down.[55] On Saturday 30 October, one week after the Shankill bomb, the UFF completed their revenge when they attacked the Rising Sun bar in Greysteel, Country Derry, killing eight people and injuring many others.

> The door opened and in came two men wearing boiler suits and balaclavas and carrying an AK-47 rifle and a Browning 9mm automatic pistol. One of them called out, 'Trick or treat'. A woman, thinking it was a Hallowe'en prank, turned and said: 'That's not funny'. The man with the AK-47 shot her first, then walked through the lounge, firing as he went. The other gunman's pistol jammed after one shot, and he cursed as he tried to clear it. In all forty-five shots were fired in the attack. The man with the rifle emptied one clip of ammunition, reloaded and resumed firing. When they left, the walls and floors were splashed with blood from the nineteen people who had been injured.[56]

The political atmosphere offered little hope. Conscious that time might be running out for their strategy, Hume and Adams pushed the two governments more anxiously for a positive response while unionists moved in the opposite direction. The UUP and DUP groups on Belfast City Council decided to break off relations with the SDLP until the Hume–Adams agreement was abandoned and renounced by the party, while Ulster Unionist leader James Molyneaux stated that he would 'absolutely not' be rejoining any three-stranded talks process in the immediate future. A few weeks earlier, speaking to a meeting of the Upper Bann Young Unionists, David Trimble had urged Hume to distance himself from Gerry Adams in order to get back on side with the 'constitutional' parties as he could not envisage unionists talking to the SDLP if Hume continued to talk to Sinn Féin.

> The Hume strategy, even on his own terms, is mis-conceived and bound to fail. It is also bad for Ulster politics in the short term. It creates a distance between the SDLP and the constitutional political parties. Indeed, it has already created an obstacle for any discussions, whether bi-lateral or multi-lateral, between the SDLP and constitutional political parties.[57]

In October 1993, political progress looked out of the question and the only communication came out of the barrel of the gun. Northern Ireland looked into the sectarian abyss in a way that was perhaps unique in the history of the conflict since 1968. While there had been other periods during the preceding twenty-five years which had been equally violent, there was still a sense that this was maverick behaviour which could be resolved if only the politicians would get together and reach an agreement. October 1993 was different. All the political avenues had apparently been traversed to no avail. The revolving-door entrance to Stormont seemed somehow appropriate, as the politicos went round and round in circles before being ejected from the building. It appeared that politics (or what passed for it in Northern Ireland) had failed, the rival paramilitary groups had become leaner and fitter organisations, the two governments seemed to lack either the capability or the willingness to intervene positively and the prospect of civil war loomed as a realistic possibility. At the end of October 1993, Belfast closed down. Many of the city's bars shut early and Hallowe'en parties were cancelled. The following comment from a resident of west Belfast was typical of the fear felt by both Catholic and Protestant communities at the time. 'You go to the shops for a pint of milk, you go into town in a black taxi, you walk home from the pub at night and you're lucky if you come back alive.'[58]

Poisoned pen-pals

In response to both the Hume–Adams initiative and the spiralling rise in violence, in late October the Irish government produced what it called the

'Six Democratic Principles for Peace'; these were also known as the 'Six Spring Principles', after their main author, Minister for Foreign Affairs Dick Spring.[59] This was the Irish government's attempt to wrestle the initiative back from John Hume and put a Dublin spin on proposals for political development. Over the next two months, the Irish and British governments strove to find a form of words which could keep Sinn Féin interested in what they called 'the Irish peace initiative' without alienating unionists. The initial signs were good as Gerry Adams promised that Sinn Féin would be constructive and imaginative in helping to 'move the situation forward', while James Molyneaux expressed optimism at the Spring initiative and declared that the six principles were 'a great improvement' on the Hume–Adams agreement. From the unionist perspective, Spring had given a clear guarantee on the key issue of Irish national self-determination. While Hume–Adams also talked of unionist consent as central to self-determination, it remained ambiguous about exactly how this would be exercised. The Spring principles, however, stated explicitly that there could be no change in the constitutional status of the North without the freely given consent of the majority. Once again the DUP differed from the Ulster Unionist analysis, rejecting the Spring principles as simply a more subtle variant of Hume–Adams. The party's deputy leader, Peter Robinson, left little room for confusion with a forthright condemnation. 'They [the Spring principles] are the handiwork of the IRA and the SDLP – the product of the Hume/Adams talks. . . . The camouflage is still thin and the green nationalist ultimatum shows through.'[60] The DUP's Mid-Ulster representative, Rev. William McCrea, was similarly unimpressed, accusing the Dublin government of 'whistling their Republican tune over the graves of Ulster's innocent'.[61] Whether they liked them or not, the Spring proposals were used to sanitise the Hume–Adams agreement and transform it into a document which could be sold to the British government. The Spring proposals, after several heated negotiations between Albert Reynolds and John Major, became the foundation stone for the Downing Street Declaration of 15 December 1993.

The British government embarked upon a series of meetings with Molyneaux and Paisley to assure them that the consent of the unionist community remained a fundamental principle which would not be waived under any circumstances. During the course of separate meetings on 9 November, Major emphasised to both leaders that he would not do a deal with Dublin behind their backs and said that he was making progress in discussions with Dublin over Articles 2 and 3 of the Irish constitution. While both were told that there was no 'secret deal', the UUP leader was clearly more satisfied than his DUP counterpart by what he had heard. After the meeting James Molyneaux was upbeat, claiming that the talks had been 'more profitable than it would appear on the surface. A great deal of ground has been covered.'[62] Ian Paisley, on the other hand, continued to see his cup as being half empty rather than half full. The DUP leader vowed that his party would not talk to Dublin until Articles 2 and 3 were removed from the constitution and they would not talk to the SDLP 'while they are talking to IRA murderers'.[63]

For once, Northern Ireland was undoubtedly at the top of the British political agenda, witnessed by the fact that John Major made it the centrepiece of his speech to London's business community at the lord mayor's banquet on 15 November. In his Guildhall address, the British Prime Minister echoed the language of Albert Reynolds and even Gerry Adams, when he declared that all of those involved in the political process would have to 'show courage, court unpopularity, break down old barriers and take risks'. Major went on to say that Sinn Féin would be invited to the negotiating table if the IRA ended their campaign and indicated that the DUP would not be allowed to impose a veto on such a development.[64] The unionist response to Major's speech was mixed. Ian Paisley claimed it as evidence of British duplicity and a signal of their ultimate intention, which was to remove Northern Ireland from the Union against the wishes of the unionist community.

> I have warned the people of Ulster what is in store for them, and John Major's speech is the first instalment in the Anglo-Irish Agreement Mark II. . . . Let the British Prime Minister take note that there will be no concessions by the unionists of this province to the six points of Dick Spring – three of which bear the bloody thumb mark of the IRA/Hume document. The strength of feeling in this province is for the defeat of IRA-Sinn Féin, not a way made for them to the negotiating table.[65]

Opinion within the UUP was more varied. While the Strangford MP John Taylor appeared to take a similar line to Paisley, warning that the situation was 'exactly the same' as the prelude to the signing of the Anglo-Irish Agreement in 1985, Fermanagh MP Ken Maginnis adopted a more conciliatory tone. He advised his colleagues that a more constructive attitude may be more appropriate. 'We can't tuck ourselves away in a corner and pretend unpleasant decisions don't have to be made. That is the reality of politics in Northern Ireland.'[66] He might have added that this was precisely what they had engaged in with little success after the AIA was signed in 1985. Ian Paisley's humour improved dramatically after a further meeting with John Major on 24 November. The DUP leader had asked the Prime Minister about the accuracy of a leaked Department of Foreign Affairs draft paper, which intimated that the British would adopt the role of persuading unionists of the 'value of the goal of Irish unity' through agreement. Major had apparently told the DUP delegation that if this leaked document had been sent to him he would have 'kicked it over the house tops'. Paisley later enthused: 'I liked his language tonight. That's good Ulster stuff.'[67] Major reassured the DUP that his door was open to them and they were not to be sidelined in any forthcoming talks process. Paisley's mood would soon become as changeable as the Irish weather, as mid-December witnessed guttural storms in North Antrim and sunny dispositions in London and Dublin.

Revelations in the *Observer* at the end of November meanwhile that the British government had established a secret chain of communication with the IRA inflamed unionist opinion and added to the growing list of severe embarrassments suffered by the Secretary of State. Despite John Major's earlier assurances to unionist politicians that he would not talk to 'the men of violence', and his earlier statement in the House of Commons that it would 'turn my stomach' to talk to Sinn Féin, it emerged on 28 November that his government had being doing exactly that for several years. A number of intermediaries were used with the official approval of the Secretary of State to liaise with Martin McGuinness of Sinn Féin. A meeting was held between McGuinness and a British civil servant two days after the Warrington bomb in March 1993 which killed two children. Both sides exchanged key position papers and the British government expressed a desire to convene formal, secret negotiations with Sinn Féin in return for a two-week ceasefire by the following Easter.[68] The government's enthusiasm for this high-risk strategy began to wane as unionist support at Westminster became more important in the run-up to the Maastricht debate in the summer and as loyalist and republican paramilitary violence increased. Interestingly, John Hume claimed that he had been made aware of the contacts in May, yet it seems from the public positions at any rate that he did not share this information with Dublin. James Molyneaux did not seem to be as well connected as his SDLP counterpart. The initial reaction of the UUP leader was disbelief that government ministers had engaged in secret talks with the IRA.

> Shown *prima facie* evidence, Mr Molyneaux initially preferred to suspect a conspiracy between civil servants who had kept Ministers in the dark. Asked whether there could have been political complicity, he said: 'Not at a ministerial level.' But in confirming the IRA link, the *Observer's* British source said there had been no freelance or pirate operation – it had been carried out under political direction and authority. That could only have been done with Mr Major's blessing.[69]

If unionists were incandescent with rage, the Secretary of State was, to put it mildly, in a difficult position. On this occasion there were no language difficulties to blame or obscure German copy to be rumaged for, as Mayhew's previous rhetoric was flung back in his face to great effect. He had tried to be careful in the past to use the word 'negotiation' in his public statements concerning contacts with Sinn Féin. His semantic and legalistic use of this term (thus, as long as communications with Sinn Féin did not amount to negotiations, he could say they were not talking to them) led many to believe that he was being disingenuous at the very least. Few unionists were convinced that the British government was engaged in anything other than another treacherous act to damage the unionist position in Northern Ireland. An example of Mayhew's attempt to blur the dividing line between communication and negotiation was provided by an interview on BBC TV's *Breakfast Time* programme of 16 November. When asked by the interviewer if there had been any contact between Sinn Féin and anyone 'who could be regarded as emissaries or representatives of the Government', the Secretary of State's reply seemed clear. 'No, there hasn't. There has been *no negotiating* [my emphasis] with Sinn Féin; no official, as I see, is alleged to have been talking to Sinn Féin on behalf of the British Government. We have always made it perfectly clear that there is going to be no negotiating with anybody who perpetrates or justifies the use of violence. That's been our public policy . . . and we have stuck to it.'[70] When pinned down about his use of the word 'negotiation' and asked if there had been any official exploratory talks at any level, Mayhew stated a position which was clearly opposite to the reality.

> There has been no talking whatsoever . . . nothing of that kind at all. We have always said that there is to be no bargaining whatsoever with people who espouse, who perpetrate violence, and that's absolutely the case. Nobody on the part of the British Government has done that or anything like it.[71]

The best account of the government's response to the exposure of their contacts with Sinn Féin is provided by the Belfast journalists Eamonn Mallie and David McKittrick in their fascinating book *The Fight for Peace*. They quote the head of information services at the Northern Ireland Office, Andy Wood, recollecting that the Friday morning before the Sunday on which the *Observer* broke the story, the government machine sprang into action in an effort to limit the political damage.

> Wood rushed to the office. He recalled: 'Jonathan Stephens [one of Mayhew's aides] was the first guy I saw when I got into the office. He said: "We've been in contact with the Provos. You can read all about it in Quintin Thomas's file." At 7.40 a.m. I was given a file which read like the first draft of a Le Carré novel.'[72]

Mayhew responded to the revelations by saying that the contacts were not talks, but that an old channel of communication had acted merely as a conduit for a message sent by the IRA to the effect that they had given up but did not know how to disengage. A press statement was issued by the NIO on the eve of the *Observer*'s publication which set the official line: 'At the end of February this year a message was passed on to the Government from the IRA leadership. It was to the effect that the conflict was over but they needed our advice as to the means of bringing it to a close.'[73] Gerry Adams accused Mayhew of lying as no such message had been sent by the IRA and because the contacts amounted to much more than a conduit as 'outlines of policy were exchanged and discussed'. In the House of Commons on 30 November, the Secretary of State released a thirty-page document detailing the contacts between the government and Sinn Féin over the preceding ten months. He made a statement in parliament designed to clarify the situation but which succeeded only in implicating him further in a web of deceit. He stated:

> At the end of February this year a message was received from the IRA leadership. It said: 'The conflict is over but we need your advice on how to bring it to a close. We wish to have an unannounced ceasefire in order to hold dialogue leading to peace. We cannot announce such a move as it will lead to confusion for the volunteers because the press will misinterpret it as a surrender. We cannot meet the Secretary of State's public renunciation of violence, but it would be given privately as long as we were sure that we were not being tricked.' That message came from Martin McGuinness. I have placed in the library and the vote office all consequent messages which the Government has received and dispatched.[74]

It later became clear that no such message had been sent. Martin McGuinness claimed: 'the text he read is totally counterfeit. No such communication was ever sent.'[75] When Sinn Féin prepared to release their evidence of the contacts with the British government, the Secretary of State admitted on 1 December that, on reflection, there appeared to be more than twenty 'transcription and typing' errors in the documents he had placed on the public record. More recent evidence places further doubt on the British version of events. In an interview conducted in 1995 by Mallie and McKittrick, former Secretary of State Peter Brooke admitted that he had authorised the commencement of dialogue with Sinn Féin as early as 1990, thus contradicting Mayhew's timetable of events. Having taken advice from John Deverell, the head of intelligence in Northern Ireland, co-ordinator of the security services and in effect 'chief spook', that it might be beneficial to open an official channel of communication with the republican movement, Brooke decided that the risk was worth taking.

> It was bound to be a risk – it couldn't be but a risk because you were engaged, even indirectly, in conversation and the whole thing could blow up in your face. But equally if you were actually going to make any progress, that was a risk you were going to have to take. . . . we had a substantial debate about it. It was a debate which among other things discussed the identity, the process by which the linkage would occur. I mean – were we making statements which were not strictly true, in terms of

responding to the House of Commons? I certainly believed, in the context of the conduit which existed, that we could continue to say that we were not in direct contact. . . . It was not negotiation. I was not sanctioning a whole series of things – it was the opportunity to carry on conversation.[76]

Like Sinn Féin, the unionists also accused Mayhew of lying and the DUP demanded his resignation – again. The party's deputy leader Peter Robinson rejected Mayhew's version of events and took the opportunity to attack the UUP for being taken in by British treachery.

The Secretary of State cannot justify lying to the people of Northern Ireland, telling them on BBC television's breakfast time programme on the 16th of November that there had been no contacts between anyone who was a representative or an emissary of the British Government and Sinn Féin or the IRA.[77]

Robinson ridiculed the supposed 'understanding' between the UUP and the government and their claim to have an 'absolute veto' over what John Major would agree to: 'If Jim Molyneaux has an absolute veto, then he has something to answer because he failed to use it.'[78] When asked if he accepted the Ulster Unionist caveat that government contacts with the IRA had stopped because of the UUP deal with Major over the Maastricht Treaty, Robinson made it clear that he did not.

You seem to be believing the Secretary of State and I don't know why you would put your faith in a Secretary of State who has been proved to be a liar. IRA statements and our own evidence, suggest that the contacts are still going on. . . . the real fact of life as far as the Ulster Unionist Party is concerned, is why did Jim Molyneaux make a statement on Friday trying to pull the chestnuts out of the fire for the British government? He said in that statement that he advised the people of Northern Ireland, when information came out over the weekend, not to jump to conclusions . . . he is saying to people, 'I know the British government have betrayed you, but don't jump to any conclusions, don't get excited about it, stay asleep, but take more sedatives, take more chloroform, let it all happen.'[79]

Perhaps it was just as well that the revelations concerning British contacts with the IRA occurred on Sunday 28 November, as the DUP annual conference had been held the day before and the shock may have been too much for many delegates who appeared to have whipped themselves into quite a lather as it was.[80] It was the UUP rather than Mayhew who bore most of the criticism at the conference. Sammy Wilson responded to Ken Maginnis's ridicule of him as being 'the oldest swinger in town' at the UUP conference the previous month with a caustic rejoinder. 'I'll tell you one thing – I'd rather be a swinger than a traitor. For while I've been swinging, the political barrow-boys from Glengall Street have been selling, selling

Ulster out.'[81] In a speech characteristically dotted with religious imagery, violent metaphor and defiant rhetoric, the leader of the DUP used his conference address to attack the UUP and the British government for the course of political events.

> Ulster Protestants have been slandered throughout the world. They have been vilified by the tongues of the uncircumcised Philistines. They have been used by those who needed them most and then cast aside when their days of usefulness have ended. Their deepest wounds have been inflicted upon them in the house of their friends. Yet fearless and loyal they have kept on their way resolved to do and die for the cause of God and Ulster.
>
> In their dark hour of trial it was their own unionist leaders who like Brutus of old struck the fatal blow. Lundy is the Ulster synonym for Judas and the Lundy brats have been plentiful in Ulster's history. The names of these Iscariots have been buried in the ignominy of their own self-dug graves of shame but Ulster men and women true to their pledge have survived and today they ride again against their ancient foes. I must tell John Major and Patrick Mayhew and the British Government that Ulster men and women will never surrender to the IRA the murderers of their kith and kin.[82]

Declarations of peace

If the DUP were unhappy at their party conference, then their mood darkened still further after the British and Irish governments unveiled the Downing Street Declaration on 15 December 1993 (see Appendix II). The Joint Declaration for Peace, as it was officially known, was a diplomatic triumph for both governments and appeared to open the prospect of an end to the conflict. The latest attempt at a historic compromise formula for talks did not, of course, receive unanimous approval within Northern Ireland. The Joint Declaration seemed to hold more charm for those who could appreciate the draftsman's art and the guile of senior civil servants than for the protagonists to the conflict. Like previous initiatives, the declaration was a masterpiece of ambiguity, giving with one hand and taking away with the other. Perhaps the two most noteworthy sections are paragraphs 4 and 5. In paragraph 4 the British Prime Minister confirms the unionist guarantee that the constitutional status of Northern Ireland will not change until a majority express a wish for such a change. Conversely, nationalists are told that Britain is a neutral arbiter in the conflict and that their national aspirations are equally valid to those of the unionists, if for the moment being unachievable due to their minority status.

> The Prime Minister, on behalf of the British Government, reaffirms that they will uphold the democratic wish of a greater number of the people of Northern Ireland on the issue of whether they prefer to support the Union

or a sovereign united Ireland. On this basis, he reiterates, on behalf of the British Government, that they have no selfish strategic or economic interest in Northern Ireland. Their primary interest is to see peace, stability and reconciliation established by agreement among all the people who inhabit the island, and they will work together with the Irish Government to achieve such an agreement, which will embrace the totality of relationships. The role of the British Government will be to encourage, facilitate and enable the achievement of such agreement over a period through a process of dialogue and co-operation based on full respect for the rights and identities of both traditions in Ireland. They accept that such agreement may, as of right, take the form of agreed structures for the island as a whole, including a united Ireland achieved by peaceful means on the following basis. The British Government agree that it is for the people of the island of Ireland alone, by agreement between the two parts respectively, to exercise their right of self-determination on the basis of consent, freely and concurrently given, North and South, to bring about a united Ireland, if that is their wish. They reaffirm as a binding obligation that they will, for their part, introduce the necessary legislation to give effect to this, or equally to any measure of agreement on future relationships in Ireland which the people living in Ireland may themselves freely so determine without external impediment . . .[83]

There are several interesting features of this paragraph as hidden meanings and nuances abound, not just in the language but in its very punctuation. As a concession to James Molyneaux's rhetorical predilections, Major uses the term 'greater number' rather than 'majority' to describe the pro-Union community. More importantly, while the British government defend the unionist right to veto any constitutional change to Northern Ireland which removes it from the Union and places it in an all-Ireland context, they say nothing about what may occur to the region's governance between these two extreme points. In an attempt to move in the direction of Sinn Féin, the British government emphasise their impartiality between the rival claims of unionism and nationalism, give an explicit guarantee that they will facilitate the exercise of *Irish* self-determination, albeit exercised separately in both parts of Ireland, and even state that they would introduce legislation to remove Northern Ireland from the United Kingdom if this became the expressed wish of the greater number. The old phraseology introduced by Peter Brooke into the Northern Ireland political lexicon was also used to convince Sinn Féin that the government was neutral on the constitutional issue. However, as John McGarry and Brendan O'Leary have pointed out in a shrewd analysis of the Joint Declaration, the absence of a comma after the word 'selfish' in the phrase that Britain had 'no selfish strategic or economic interest in Northern Ireland' was symptomatic of the ambiguity which riddled the entire document. Thus, this could be read as meaning that, while Britain had no selfish *strategic* or *economic* interest, it still maintained a selfish *political* interest in remaining in Northern Ireland.[84]

Paragraph 5, meanwhile, outlined the Irish government's position on the exercise of self-determination, unionist consent to constitutional change and the conditions under which the republican goal of a unitary state could be achieved.

> The Taoiseach . . . accepts, on behalf of the Irish Government, that the democratic right of self-determination by the people of Ireland as a whole must be achieved and exercised with and subject to the agreement and consent of a majority of the people of Northern Ireland and must, consistent with justice and equity, respect the democratic dignity and the civil rights and religious liberties of both communities . . .[85]

Once again the text is replete with subliminal messages. While reference was made to the people of Ireland *as a whole* exercising self-determination, it was stated explicitly that unionist consent would have to be given and empirically measured before Irish unity could take place. By accepting the principle of consent and the statement in paragraph 4 that self-determination would occur concurrently North *and* South, the Irish government had subtly shifted the axis of orthodox Irish nationalism. Dublin was making it clear that Northern Ireland was not a part of 'the Irish nation' as of right, but must be opted into by the majority of the people living there. Meanwhile, 'by accepting the North's right to exercise self-determination independently of the South, the Government of the Republic of Ireland recognises the legitimacy of partition by treating Northern Ireland as a quasi-separate geo-political unit'.[86]

While John Major went to some lengths to point out that his government would not adopt the role Sinn Féin were looking for, of playing the role of 'persuaders' of the unionist community, he sent a clear message to the republican movement that their political future lay within the democratic process. Speaking at a packed news conference in the dining room of 10 Downing Street during the launch of the Joint Declaration, Major declared that the initiative offered the opportunity for Sinn Féin to become fully involved in the political process.

> I think the men of violence may have heard of this declaration at this meeting and I think we await to see whether they will respond or not. I think it is for them to tell us. . . . If the IRA will end and renounce violence for good the British Government is prepared to enter into preliminary dialogue with Sinn Féin within three months when cessation of violence has been clearly established. . . . If they lose this opportunity it may never come their way again. We believe there is such an opportunity and we hope they will take it.[87]

Downing Street detritus

Reaction to the Joint Declaration within Northern Ireland was mixed. The SDLP and Alliance gave it a broad welcome, while the Sinn Féin and unionist response was more ambivalent. The republican movement were unimpressed by the initiative but wanted to avoid giving too negative a reaction as this may have led to a propaganda defeat for Sinn Féin and assisted those who wished to see them being marginalised politically. Holding statements were issued by senior Sinn Féin officials pending a considered response from the party. In the interim, Mitchel McLaughlin, then Northern chairman of Sinn Féin and widely believed to be one of its most astute political strategists, sounded an ominous note of scepticism. 'Already, the general reaction among nationalists is one of disappointment. . . . We will be comparing this document with the Hume–Adams initiative, which has in our view the potential to move us out of conflict and towards peace.'[88] Anxious not to be cast in the role of negative party, particularly given their cultivation of the sensitive American audience, Sinn Féin spent the next eight months prevaricating over the declaration, seeking and eventually receiving 'clarification' from the British government over how it was compatible with the 'Irish peace initiative'. The republican leadership were faced with a difficult balancing act. They had to buy enough time to muddy the waters between the declaration and Hume–Adams while John Major applied public pressure for a positive response and their grass-roots supporters demanded its rejection.[89] The definitive response of Sinn Féin to the declaration did not come until July 1994 when it was discussed at a special conference in Letterkenny, County Donegal. While Sinn Féin would contest the view that they rejected it at this meeting, the repeated accusations that it reinforced the unionist veto and locked nationalists into the British state hardly amounted to an endorsement. The view of the Joint Declaration in the SDLP was rather different to that in Sinn Féin. Speaking in the House of Commons, John Hume immediately welcomed it as 'one of the most comprehensive declarations that has been made about British-Irish relations in the past 70 years. My appeal to all sections of our people is to read the entire statement in full and to have no knee-jerk reactions.'[90]

The response of the unionist political community to the Joint Declaration was equally ambivalent, for although the DUP were predictable enough in denouncing the initiative as a betrayal of Ulster, the UUP adopted a much less hostile position. Using his well-developed talent for street theatre, Ian Paisley stood outside Downing Street on the morning of 15 December and read out to waiting journalists a letter of protest he had just delivered to John Major. He angrily branded the Anglo-Irish deal as an act of treachery by the British government in conjunction with the IRA in an effort to destroy the Union. When the DUP leader was asked by reporters about what he was going to do about it, he replied enigmatically: 'actions speak louder than words'.[91] Subsequently, the DUP produced proselytising literature against the declaration with one pamphlet, luridly entitled *The Dagger of Treachery Strikes at the Heart of Ulster: An Exposure by Ian R.K. Paisley M.P. M.E.P. of the Major–Reynolds Joint Declaration*, showing on its cover a cartoon of a human heart with a map of 'Ulster' inside it and a dagger plunged into its centre drawing blood. The document included a copy of his letter to John Major.

Prime Minister

As you and your Secretary of State lied about your communications with the IRA men of blood, so you have deceived the Ulster people in your talks with Dublin. The declaration which you and Albert Reynolds sign and make public today, is not between you and him alone. It is a tripartite agreement – Reynolds, the IRA and you. You have sold Ulster to buy off the fiendish republican scum. . . . You will learn in a bitter school that all appeasement of these monsters is self-destructive. The hand which reaches for your blood-money will never be satisfied until it destroys you. In the name of those who have fallen in the battle to save our beloved Province, WE PROTEST![92]

Paisley added when speaking on BBC radio the same day that 'Ulster has been hung drawn and quartered by Mr Reynolds, Mr Major and his cohorts in the IRA.'[93] During the debate on the Joint Declaration at Westminster on 15 December, the DUP leader attacked Major for his suggestion that, after a three-month 'decontamination' period, Sinn Féin would be accepted as constitutional politicians and unionists would be expected to sit down and negotiate with those who had defended the campaign of violence against the unionist community. Paisley suggested to the Prime Minister that, while he may like sitting down with the 'Godfathers of violence' his party would not be doing so. Visibly angered by this attack, Major responded that:

. . . the purpose of this agreement and this document is to make sure that 25 years from now your successor does not sit there saying that to the Prime Minister of the day. . . . I wish to take action to make sure there's no more bloodshed of this sort, no more coffins carried away week after week because politicians will not have the courage to sit down, address the problems and find a way through. . . . I am prepared to do that – and, if you believe I should not, then you do not understand the responsibilities of the Prime Minister of the United Kingdom.[94]

The response of the Ulster Unionist Party to the declaration was more cautious than that of the DUP. There are several reasons which explain this. The first and most important was that, unlike the AIA, they were consulted about its contents beforehand and were satisfied that it did not compromise on the principle that unionist consent must be secured and measured before any change was made to the constitutional status of Northern Ireland. The UUP were also very concerned to present a positive and pragmatic image to the policy-makers and wider public in Britain. Their experience of political exclusion following the AIA of 1985 had convinced many senior figures in the UUP that the long-term future of the Union was dependent upon two parties desiring its continuation rather than unionists within Northern Ireland simply demanding that it be upheld. Conscious of the damage done to their relations with the rest of the United Kingdom after the AIA, the UUP leadership were trying to win friends and influence people and did not seem keen to conform to stereotype by joining in with the 'primal screams' being emitted from the mouths of DUP politicians. Another important factor in the UUP position on the Joint Declaration was the arithmetic at Westminster. John Major's dwindling parliamentary majority combined with fractures within the Conservative Party over European policy left his government reliant upon other allies within the House of Commons. The 'understanding' reached between the UUP and the government during the Maastricht debate was seen as a template for future action by the leadership of the UUP and as a means of exerting leverage and influence upon the political agenda of the government towards Northern Ireland. Thus, they were anxious not to reject the Joint Declaration out of hand but rather hold a 'watching brief', suspending their judgement in the knowledge that their dissent carried implications for the very survival of the government, who would thus assiduously try to avoid incurring unionist displeasure for reasons of self-preservation. The Ulster Unionist MP for North Belfast, Cecil Walker, gave the declaration a guarded welcome and declared that it did not present a threat to Northern Ireland's position within the United Kingdom. He urged all moderate unionists to welcome the Anglo-Irish initiative and said that he saw 'signs for optimism. . . . Having read the statement quickly, I think the province's position is protected and the Irish Government appears to be making meaningful gestures to unionists.'[95] John Taylor urged unionists not to give a 'knee-jerk' reaction to the declaration but to read it for themselves. 'The document isn't as bad as I had feared. . . . Read it very carefully and don't jump too quickly to conclusions.'[96] UUP leader James Molyneaux also gave a guarded welcome to the declaration, describing it as a tortuously complex document which was 'comparatively safe'.

> I think on balance when you have studied it very carefully, there will be some things with which we agree. But it does need to be decoded, because it has obviously been written by two sets of hands, written by two governments which hold opposite views on the future of Northern Ireland, so it's not surprising that it seems quite complex. . . . It depends entirely on what the constitutional parties make of it and I think it has cleared the way

for a speeding up and extension of the Ancram talks, which I think have been very very valuable already.[97]

This view, that it was merely a complicated document which was difficult to understand but relatively benign, was the antithesis of the DUP view. They found it all too easy to comprehend and saw its intent as uniformly malign despite its inclusive rhetoric. Parallels can be seen here with the anti-Agreement campaign, as the unionist parties' conflicting analyses of the meaning of the Joint Declaration led to a fundamental disagreement over political strategy. While the UUP saw it as a positive catalyst to dialogue and progress, the DUP viewed it as yet another act of British treachery and a further threat to the position of Northern Ireland within the United Kingdom. Predictably, these conflicting interpretations created friction between the two parties. Speaking on BBC radio on 15 December, Ian Paisley declared that he would be very angry if James Molyneaux supported the declaration, saying that if this were to happen, 'God help him. God Almighty have mercy upon him if he is going to go down the line . . . that will be the most cruel blow ever struck at the Ulster people.'[98] Peter Robinson launched a full-scale attack on the UUP attitude to the declaration, accusing them of complicity in the sell-out of Ulster.

> No intelligent unionist could read the Downing Street Declaration without acknowledging that it is the greatest threat yet to the Union. Any unionist party that suggests otherwise has prostituted itself to the Government and is unworthy of the trust of the people. This Declaration exists because of the complicity of Official Unionist MPs.[99]

The UUP position on the Joint Declaration also caused unrest within the party among grass-roots activists who were less concerned about the leadership's tactical manoeuvring at Westminster than they were with the tone and content of the document. Evidence of this discontent was provided when six UUP councillors on Castlereagh Borough Council issued a warning to the party leadership by siding with the DUP at the December monthly meeting of the council to condemn the declaration as a 'reward' for the IRA. Speaking after the meeting which was adjourned in protest, the UUP councillor John Bell commented: 'the unionist people are fed up. They are warning the leadership that, if the top is not going to come down to them, then the bottom will have to come up.'[100] It was reported in the *Belfast Telegraph* on 23 December that the UUP leadership were going to do exactly this by holding a series of meetings with party members to explain their attitude to the declaration in an effort to prevent an internal mutiny over the issue. One senior party source was quoted as admitting that the briefings were to assuage the 'widespread unease' at grass-roots level over the party's position. 'To say there is alarm among party members is putting it mildly – a lot of people are saying Jim and the rest of the

Parliamentary Party are completely out of touch with the grass-roots and are playing this all wrong. . . . People are very angry, they are not reassured about the constitutional position.'[101] Molyneaux's position on the Joint Declaration was the beginning of the end for his leadership of the UUP. Subsequently, with the British government's introduction of the next major Anglo-Irish initiative in February 1995, commonly known as the Frameworks Document, Molyneaux would be seen to have miscalculated the closeness of the unionist relationship with the British government and the degree of political leverage they could exert upon John Major.

In an attempt to wrestle back the political initiative, reduce the controversy concerning the party's reaction to the Joint Declaration and redefine the direction of interparty dialogue, the UUP unveiled their latest thinking in February 1994 in a document entitled *Blueprint for Stability*. The plan for an internal assembly with safeguards for minorities such as a bill of rights and an Irish dimension which would evolve through mutual consent after the abolition of Articles 2 and 3 was an unremarkable development which had been sitting with the British government since the previous December. At the launch of the initiative, Molyneaux clearly backtracked on the Joint Declaration and hardened his position on the resumption of interparty talks. The UUP leader claimed that, while the two governments clearly felt obliged to do something in December 1993, time had moved on. 'We're at the point now where her majesty's government, having tried their experiment (the declaration) will have concluded that the time has come to begin the restoration of democratic processes within Northern Ireland.'[102] Molyneaux declared that the old Brooke–Mayhew formula was no longer acceptable as it had proved to be a failure in the past and would inevitably be so again. 'We're not going to engage in three-stranded talks because that would be just as big a fiasco as it was last time.'[103] Ian Paisley derided this latest flurry of activity within the UUP as a crude exercise in damage limitation after having miscalculated over the Joint Declaration. 'The attempt by the Official Unionists to distance themselves from their previously stated positions is untenable. It will be seen for what it is – an attempt to cover up a series of political misjudgements based upon support for the Tory government at Westminster.'[104]

Unionist tensions increase

Unionist politics during the first half of 1994 were dominated by concern over what unionists referred to as the 'pan-nationalist front', that is, the apparent political consensus engineered by Hume–Adams, and the response of the British government to this consensus through its stewardship of the 'peace process' with the Irish government. Evidence of this concern came when the IRA announced a seventy-two-hour Easter ceasefire to run from

5 to 8 April. While no conditions were attached to this stoppage, the IRA statement made clear its hope that the British government would respond in a positive manner. Despite the fact that Taoiseach Albert Reynolds said he was 'disappointed', while SDLP leader John Hume declared: 'I didn't go through any peace process to get a ceasefire. I'm not interested in a ceasefire. I'm interested in a total cessation of violence',[105] some unionists saw this as an orchestrated attempt by 'pan-nationalism' to wrest concessions from the British government. As usual, the DUP leader Ian Paisley provided the most vivid copy. 'Mr Hume can't deliver a united Ireland, neither can Mr Reynolds, so they'll ride on the backs of the IRA through their killings and mayhem to get a united Ireland.'[106] This perspective was shared by the loyalist paramilitaries who claimed that the IRA's three-day ceasefire was an irrelevance and declared that their campaign would go on independently as its purpose over and above 'defence' was preventing 'Ulster's' slide into a united Ireland. Two senior UDA representatives told the media that they had learnt the lesson that the only way to gain political concessions was through violence and that they would consequently respond ferociously to any deal between the government and the IRA which threatened the Union. 'Our days of reacting to the IRA are over. As far as we are concerned our agenda is proactive. . . . We have our own agenda. . . . There must be a prize for the IRA to call a ceasefire. The reasons for it would have to be closely looked at.'[107]

As the June European elections approached, the leadership of the UUP began to react to internal opinion within the party by taking a much tougher line on the Joint Declaration. At the annual general meeting of the Ulster Unionist Council, the party demonstrated their unease by voting two prominent 'liberals' out of their posts as honorary secretaries, while party leader James Molyneaux tried to reposition the UUP.

> The UUP did not welcome or endorse the Joint Declaration. We simply acted in the interests of the greater number of the people of Northern Ireland in permitting the [British] government the necessary room in which to avoid being trapped by Sinn Féin. Our tactics should not be confused with our objectives.[108]

Molyneaux went on to tell the meeting that Articles 2 and 3 must be addressed by the Irish government before any real progress could be made, while he rejected a return to the 'circus format' of interparty talks along the lines of the Brooke–Mayhew model. Clearly, this was an attempt by the UUP leader to protect his party against an attack by the DUP and minimise the danger of losing support to their rival in the European election from disaffected voters worried that the Ulster Unionists had become too moderate and too close to the government. The DUP's manifesto for the European election concentrated on domestic politics, played on unionist fears, gave out dire warnings about the future and claimed that *they* were the only party capable of securing the unionist position.

> This election is of enormous significance and importance for Ulster's future. The world will be watching to see what Ulster thinks. Is her resolve as strong as ever? Is her determination undiminished? This election sees republicanism emboldened and more united than ever before. John Hume and Gerry Adams have come together in a joint political strategy. The SDLP leader and the   leader of IRA/Sinn Féin have joined forces with Dublin to pursue their common goal of a united Ireland. The Official Unionists have already declared that their main aim is to defeat the DUP. For the DUP the fight is with Sinn Féin and the SDLP and against the iniquitous Downing Street Declaration and its treacherous predecessor the Anglo-Irish Agreement. . . . This is the first opportunity that the Ulster people have in a Province wide election to deliver their verdict on the Downing Street Declaration and the process to bring Sinn Féin/IRA to the negotiating table and give Dublin an even greater say in Ulster's affairs.[109]

In their election manifesto, the Ulster Unionists tried to characterise themselves as the responsible and rational alternative to the DUP and their paranoid vistas of 'pan-nationalist' aggression, Dublin conspiracies and British treachery. To do this, of course, they had to attack Paisley's analysis concerning the health of the unionist position within the United Kingdom, present a more benign scenario than that of the DUP and convince the electorate that the UUP had a more positive strategy to strengthen their position within the Union. This electoral competition produced the following thinly veiled attack from James Molyneaux on the DUP.

> Against intense opposition, Ulster Unionists continue to defend the integrity of the United Kingdom. Unionists should beware of those whose negative attitude plays into the hands of the IRA and the Republic's Government by permitting them to exploit any suggestion of defeatism. If we allow others to mislead us into believing that we have been betrayed, we will lose the will to resist and be swept into an all-Ireland state.[110]

The bitterness between the two unionist parties reached a peak at the end of May when Paisley made a personal attack on Molyneaux, accusing him of being a traitor to the unionist community. At a press conference during the European election campaign, the DUP leader was asked how his relationship with Molyneaux had deteriorated, given their co-operation during the campaign against the Anglo-Irish Agreement. Paisley replied: 'well didn't Lord Jesus himself call Judas his friend?'[111] When a shocked reporter asked him to clarify whether he really meant this comparison to be taken seriously, Paisley refused to retract it. 'Yes he's a Judas Iscariot in the betrayal he's carrying on at the present time.'[112]

Such DUP scaremongering may have helped Paisley maintain his position at the top of the poll in the European election, though his first preference share of the vote actually dropped marginally from 29.93 per cent in 1989 to 29.15 per cent. Nevertheless, with over 160,000 votes, the DUP leader was able to claim that he had received a renewed mandate from the unionist community for his opposition to the Joint Declaration. The UUP candidate Jim Nicholson secured 23.8 per cent of the vote, a marginal increase on the 1989 result but not enough to claim a seat on the first count. Paisley's remark that 'the sweetest thing in this election was to hear Dr Paisley's surplus votes will now be distributed'[113] was a pointed reference to the fact that the UUP candidate had trailed in third – behind the SDLP's John Hume – and that Nicholson owed his election to the magnanimity of the DUP leader's supporters.

Unionist reaction to the IRA ceasefire

Throughout the summer of 1994, the two main unionist parties competed to promote their conflicting analyses of the political situation. While the DUP were concerned that the British government were dancing to an Irish tune, and that 'pan-nationalism' was threatening the Union, the UUP were taking a more cautious approach, on the understanding that no secret deals had been done behind their backs.

In a typically macabre way, the first signs that a ceasefire was imminent came when on 10 July the IRA killed the leading loyalist, Ray Smallwoods, one of the key political strategists in the emerging Ulster Democratic Party (UDP). Smallwoods, a former paramilitary jailed for the attempted murder of Bernadette McAliskey in January 1981, had more recently been acting as an intermediary in secret talks between unionist politicians and the Combined Loyalist Military Command (CLMC) in an effort to secure a temporary ceasefire. Ken Kerr, then a leading member of the UDP, warned loyalists to be careful because he believed that the IRA were having a 'final fling, a final show of strength and a final blood bath before Sinn Féin go to the talks table'.[114] This trend continued with the IRA killing of leading UFF members, Joe Bratty and Raymond Elder on 30 July, two of those held chiefly responsible by the IRA for the massacre at Sean Graham bookmaker's shop in Belfast in 1992 in which five Catholics died.[115]

The rumour-mill got into full swing in July when DUP deputy leader Peter Robinson alleged that the British government was holding secret talks with republican and loyalist paramilitaries to persuade them to take part in the peace process. He warned that the violence would be prolonged rather than curtailed if the government tried to do a deal with those who were not committed to democratic politics. Robinson cautioned John Major against bypassing the elected representatives as this would fuel the logic of the physical force argument. 'There is no point in having a democratic process, no point in people getting mandates if the Government won't listen to those who have the mandate and instead listen to those who have the biggest guns.'[116] Given their experience of exclusion since the Anglo-Irish Agreement and their distrust of British government intentions, unionist uncertainty grew as talk circulated about an impending IRA ceasefire. The question which began to dominate the thoughts of many was, *why* would republicans end their campaign undefeated, unless they had been offered substantial concessions by London? In an effort to allay such fears, John Major gave a pledge to James Molyneaux that the Anglo-Irish dialogue would not impose a political framework which would undermine the present constitutional status of Northern Ireland against the wishes of the unionist community. Speaking after an hour-long meeting with the Prime Minister, the UUP leader claimed that he had been given an assurance by Major that no secret deals had been done with Dublin or the IRA. Asked if he believed what he had heard, Molyneaux replied: 'Yes, because I've never known John Major to tell lies. I am convinced that he was speaking from the heart.'[117]

In a further sign of the strained relations between the UUP and the DUP, a confidential memo sent by the Ulster Unionists to the government was leaked at the end of July. This document claimed that Ian Paisley was unwittingly responsible for assisting the IRA in its campaign to weaken Northern Ireland's position within the United Kingdom by denouncing the Joint Declaration as a 'sell-out'. The UUP declared that the IRA strategy depended upon increased violence by loyalists and 'short-sighted scare-mongering' from politicians such as Paisley. This attack provoked a furious burst from the DUP leader who accused Molyneaux of having misjudged the threat posed by the Joint Declaration and having underestimated the fear within the unionist community.

> This is like blaming Churchill for Hitler's terrorism because he refused to enter any scheme of appeasement. By blaming me for IRA murders and mayhem they also blame more than 163,000 voters who helped me at the European Election to beat Jim Nicholson by some 30,000 votes. No wonder Molyneaux and Nicholson are licking their sores and spewing out their frustration.[118]

The belief that the IRA would not call an end to their campaign unless substantial concessions were made to their agenda by the British government sent pulses racing within the unionist community in the lead-up to the announcement of the IRA ceasefire on 31 August 1994. While the DUP suspected the worst, opinion within the UUP was more confused. On the eve of the ceasefire, possibly buoyed by the verbal assurances given to him by the Prime Minister, James Molyneaux urged his supporters and loyalist paramilitaries to exercise restraint and avoid 'hasty actions'. Michael McGimpsey on the other hand, a UUP representative on Belfast City Council, claimed that the unionist position was about to be undermined by a watering down of the 1920 Government of Ireland Act at a forth-coming Anglo-Irish summit meeting within a matter of weeks. McGimpsey claimed that a package had been put together by the government which included the prospect of fundamental constitutional change together with an open-ended visa for Gerry Adams to travel to the United States. He warned that any scheme to dilute the sovereignty of Northern Ireland would be 'the straw that breaks the camel's back'.[119] Unionist temperatures went up another few degrees after the release of a joint statement by John Hume and Gerry Adams which provided a broad hint that the conditions were in place for an IRA ceasefire. Even the normally taciturn James Molyneaux was upset by this statement, fearing that it signalled some concession to the nationalist agenda by a British government which had finally succumbed to pressure from Dublin and Washington. 'It is quite disgusting to see Mr Hume selling his soul to the devil and joining in a sordid attempt to blackmail the British, American and Irish governments into giving the Armalite supremacy over the ballot-box.'[120] Ian Paisley warned that Northern Ireland was entering another 'constitutional crisis' and demanded a meeting with John Major to find out precisely what was happening. Gerry Adams did not improve the DUP blood pressure when he indicated that he had informed the IRA that the current political conditions could 'create the potential to eradicate the underlying causes of conflict'. The party's press officer Sammy Wilson took this as further evidence that a secret deal had been arrived at between the IRA and the British government which would ultimately destroy Northern Ireland's position within the United Kingdom.

> What has been agreed privately one can only guess at, but it is our belief that a deal on prisoners, cross-border institutions, and Government efforts to promote a united Ireland have already been agreed. Why else would Gerry Adams be so upbeat?[121]

Wilson went on to say that, in the wake of the latest Hume–Adams statement, unionists should break off links with the SDLP at local council level and prepare for 'a state of political war'.[122] James Molyneaux tried to recover some ground by claiming that while there was indeed an anti-unionist plot afoot, UUP pressure on the government had succeeded in thwarting any significant constitutional amendments from being considered.

The immediate unionist response to the IRA ceasefire, effective from midnight on 31 August 1994, was mixed. This indicated once again the conflicting political analyses within the two main unionist parties. While James Molyneaux said 'everyone will be pleased' if the IRA intended their cessation to be permanent, Ian Paisley accused the IRA of 'dancing on the graves of Ulster's dead' and warned (not for the first time) that Northern Ireland could be close to civil war.[123] In the past this would have sent a chill through the body politic of Northern Ireland and the Catholic community in particular. Like the little boy who cried wolf, however, the impact of such declarations from the man whom former Northern Ireland Prime Minister Brian Faulkner referred to as the 'Demon Doctor' was reduced by the frequency with which he uttered them. This was especially the case in the autumn of 1994 as the wolf was issuing its own warnings in the guise of statements from the Combined Loyalist Military Command. Paisley raised the spectre of civil war on the grounds that he had asked for a meeting with the Prime Minister to establish whether or not the government had, as he suspected, cut a deal with the IRA in return for the ceasefire. As he had not been granted an immediate meeting with John Major, he suspected that the people of Northern Ireland would assume the worst and react accordingly.

Imagery is a crucial aspect of politics in Northern Ireland and often has a direct bearing on actual events. The political imagery in the aftermath of the IRA ceasefire was striking. On 6 September, two meetings took place, one in London the other in Dublin, which sent opposite messages around the world. Ian Paisley was granted his meeting with Major but it did not go the way he had planned. In what was generally considered to be a carefully choreographed ambush, the Prime Minister 'terminated' his meeting with the DUP delegation and practically threw Paisley out of Downing Street barely ten minutes after the politicians had sat down. The proceedings got heated after the DUP leader apparently told Major that he did not accept his word that the government had hatched no secret deal with the IRA in advance of their ceasefire. According to Paisley, the Prime Minister then told him: 'get out of this room, and never come back until you accept that I speak the truth'.[124] Demonstrating that this was not a flash of temper which was regretted after consideration, but was instead a carefully orchestrated tactical manoeuvre to outflank the DUP and promote the UUP position, the Northern Ireland Minister of State Michael Ancram reinforced Major's action immediately afterwards rather than engaging in damage limitation. Commenting on the disagreement later, Ancram said that he hoped Paisley would consider his position very carefully and return to Downing Street when 'he is prepared to accept what he is told'.[125] While Paisley lurched off licking his wounds he remained unrepentant, claiming that the DUP would 'unapologetically block the road to surrender'.[126]

The other central image of 6 September came from Dublin when the three leaders of Irish nationalism, John Hume, Gerry Adams and Albert Reynolds, posed for photographers on the steps of Government Buildings. Their triple handshake was the crowning moment of a day which Adams declared to be 'the beginning of a new era'. The imagery was vivid and could not have been more removed from the events at Downing Street. While Paisley was being sent out into the cold by one government, Adams was welcomed into the parlour by another, transformed from a 'terrorist' to a statesman almost overnight. While the DUP leader seemed excluded and rejected, the Sinn Féin president was centre stage, a key player in political events, a man connected up to the mains (though not in the manner some unionists might have preferred). The triple handshake was a deliberate symbol of the transition taking place in nationalist politics: Sinn Féin had entered the mainstream democratic arena. For a few hours on 6 September, Government Buildings was 'the White House lawn', where the world's media congregated to record the end of another conflict as they had photographed Rabin–Arafat and Mandela–De Klerk. Albert Reynolds described the scene:

> Outside on the steps, I shake hands with Gerry, I shake hands with John. Somebody shouts that we have to have it all together, and the two hands came and I put mine on top of them. This was the coming together of those who had driven the peace process. I can understand people who lost their loved ones and relatives feeling a bit sick when they saw me shaking hands with Gerry Adams on the steps. But if that handshake was to ensure that no more loved ones were going to be killed on either side, somebody had to do it. I felt honoured to have the opportunity of doing it.[127]

For many unionists this was an unholy trinity, an overhasty exhibition of the 'pan-nationalist front' and a further signal that their own position had been damaged. DUP secretary Nigel Dodds epitomised the distaste felt by those shocked by the speed of events.

> The rush by Reynolds to bring Gerry Adams into talks is nauseating to the unionists of Ulster. Reynolds cannot contain himself in his rush to embrace Sinn Féin while the IRA has made it clear that it does not renounce terrorism, that it will keep its weapons of war, and that it will refuse to declare the ceasefire to be permanent.[128]

Unionist reaction to the ceasefire was fashioned in part by the scale of nationalist euphoria in Belfast. At one level this was relief that the war was over, or at least appeared to be, that the 'nationalist nightmare' of discrimination and security-force harassment was drawing to a close. However, relief alone does not explain the festive mood in west Belfast, where people celebrated because they assumed they had won. Winning in this sense did not necessarily mean victory; the triumph came from a recognition that they had endured, survived, forced the British to sue for peace. One Catholic teenager on Belfast's Falls Road declared: 'I've waited all my life for this. It's like winning the World Cup.'[129] While few really expected an imminent announcement of withdrawal by the government, most people believed that some understanding, however long term or vaguely phrased, must have been reached between the IRA and the government. The only note of caution on that day of high-octane emotion was sounded by Bernadette McAliskey, veteran of the Northern Ireland political scene and, while no longer an active protagonist in the political arena, an honorary republican without portfolio. Borrowing as it turned out from Leonard Cohen, the former Mid-Ulster MP warned: 'the war is over and the good guys lost'. McAliskey's view was that no deal had been done with the British government, that Sinn Féin – like so many nationalists before them – had been sucked into the constitutional process by John Hume and Albert Reynolds and had little choice but to persevere with their current strategy. The IRA had been forced into a corner and there was no way out. Many people in the unionist community believed exactly the opposite and reacted accordingly. The following sketch by *Irish Times* journalist, Mark Brennock, provides a flavour of the immediate feeling on 31 August 1994.

> They did come out on the streets of Belfast. A 30-car horn-blaring convoy festooned with tricolours and nationalist posters was greeted with cheers and applause as it snaked through nationalist Belfast yesterday afternoon. They were out on the streets in at least one loyalist area too. This became clear as a barrage of stones and shouts of 'f—ing Fenian bastards' came over the high corrugated iron 'peace line' which separates a small north Belfast loyalist enclave from nationalist Ardoyne. Stones clattered on the cars as they desperately sought refuge in the side streets of the Catholic area.[130]

Unionist feeling on the Shankill Road in Belfast was one of apprehension and disappointment, fuelled by the belief that the IRA would not have called a ceasefire without some guarantee from the British that their demands would be met. *Irish Times* journalist, Suzanne Breen, conducted a vox pop in a local pub with spine-chilling results.

> 'The British have sold us down the river and the nationalists are celebrating,' said one customer called John. 'But just remember, it'll be very dangerous for Catholics in Northern Ireland after this. Loyalist paramilitaries have not called a ceasefire. It's still no surrender as far as they're concerned. Catholics talk about all the recent loyalist killings. They've seen nothing yet.'[131]

The loyalist paramilitary response to the IRA ceasefire began typically enough with a statement from the UFF on the eve of its announcement which held out little hope for a reciprocal gesture. It seems clear that their concern did not centre so much on the British government preoccupation of whether the republican cessation was 'permanent' or not, but rather, what price had been paid for it.

> It is not peace you are after, but surrender. Your aggression to the loyalist people by both word and deed and your phoney, so-called peace, process is

paramount in our thoughts at present. . . . Do you, the Irish, seriously believe we will sit back and allow ourselves to be coerced and persuaded into an all-Ireland? As we have stated before there is a price to be paid. You have not yet paid the price but you will.[132]

Attitudes within the UVF were more shrewd. While they were at one with the UDA in accepting that a loyalist ceasefire was not imminent, the UVF were more politically mature than their sister organisation, containing a greater proportion of former prisoners eager to map out a political strategy for loyalism which went beyond the barrel of the gun. This difference was epitomised when David Ervine of the Progressive Unionist Party (a political organisation which evolved out of the UVF) urged loyalist paramilitaries to react cautiously in the event of an IRA ceasefire and to wait to see what concessions, if any, the government had made to the IRA before taking action themselves.

> Those people who say they are prepared to fight and die for their country should also be prepared to wait and think. It is important for loyalists to take a calm approach to what is going on and properly analyse the situation. I would say to loyalist paramilitaries that if there is, indeed, a window of opportunity and a chance to end violence, don't let unionists and loyalists be the ones to close it.[133]

While they were by no means 'softer' than the UDA, a fact borne out by their massacre of six innocent drinkers watching the World Cup at the Heights Bar in Loughinisland, County Down, in June 1994 (one of whom, 84-year-old Barney Green, was shot in the back), it would be fair to say that the UVF had a more developed political consciousness than was apparent amongst other loyalist paramilitaries. The loyalist umbrella group, the Combined Loyalist Military Command, demanded that Paisley and Molyneaux meet John Major and answer the questions which all unionists were wondering about. 'Is our constitution being tampered with or is it not? What deals have been done? End the speculation.'[134] Although the UVF did not observe a tacit ceasefire in September, the loyalist para-militaries did scale down their activities, with a UVF spokesman telling the *Sunday Tribune* that 'I think genuinely there is an absolute desire within this community for peace. That is reflected within the Loyalist para-militaries.'[135] On 8 September a document was produced by the CLMC which marked a clear shift from the earlier rhetoric of the UFF. The CLMC listed a number of concerns which included ascertaining if the IRA ceasefire was permanent; ensuring that no deal had been done between republicans and the British government; and confirming that Northern Ireland's position within the Union was secure.[136] When the paramilitaries finally became convinced on these points, the CLMC announced the loyalist ceasefire on 13 October 1994. It contained two conditions. Firstly, the permanence of the cessation was to be entirely dependent upon the absence of republican violence, including that of the Irish National Liberation Army, which had not called a ceasefire by this point. Secondly, the CLMC made clear that their decision had been made on the assumption that the Union was safe. If this proved to be a mistaken calculation, then they would return to their campaign of violence. The most striking aspect of the ceasefire declaration (apart from its showbiz-like presentation) was the CLMC 'apology' for those who had died at their hands. 'In all sincerity we offer to the loved ones of all innocent victims over the past twenty-five years abject and true remorse. No words of ours will compensate for the intolerable suffering they have undergone during the conflict.'[137]

Unionism in the peace – the decline of Molyneaux

'Quiet calm deliberation disentangles every knot.' This axiom favoured by former British Prime Minister Harold MacMillan could equally describe the style and political career of James Molyneaux. It was once remarked of Ross Perot's vice-presidential running-mate in the 1992 American presidential election, a mercurial and seemingly permanently confused former military officer, that while he would be the least suitable man to run the country, he would make an ideal dinner companion. The reverse could perhaps be said of James Molyneaux, leader of the Ulster Unionist Party from 1979 to 1995. The adjective most frequently used of the man who took the 'long view' of politics, was 'taciturn', a player who built his political career not on the streets but in the committee room. In many ways the antithesis of Ian Paisley, Molyneaux did not possess the rhetorical or public relations gifts of his DUP counterpart. His leadership of the UUP could not be measured by the decibels of his speeches or his flourishing gestures, but centred instead around quiet diplomacy at Westminster. In many ways this exemplified the cultural differences within unionism explored earlier in this book. While Paisley saw 'Ulster' as his political base, Molyneaux operated on a wider canvas, spending the bulk of his working week at Westminster. He liked to think of himself as a shrewd judge of the political environment, a man on the inside track with friends in high places, capable of heading off threats to 'the greater number' in Northern Ireland and protecting the constitutional position of 'Ulster' within the Union; in contrast to his blustering colleague in the DUP, a man of sober judgement, respected and listened to by the decision-makers in government. This image was initially sharpened by Enoch Powell's growing influence within the UUP in the early 1980s, a man known to be one of Margaret Thatcher's political idols and assumed to know her thinking on Northern Ireland policy. This image of Molyneaux as a man 'in the know' took its first major dent in 1985 after the signing of the Anglo-Irish

Agreement. Powell's analysis that a deal between the British and Irish governments would not be signed unless Dublin removed the iniquitous Articles 2 and 3 of its constitution proved to be flawed. Molyneaux's backstage manoeuvring was seen to have been fruitless since he had not prevented (in unionist eyes at least) severe damage being done to the constitutional fabric of the Union. Whatever political dynamics explain the signing of the AIA, it was quite apparent in 1985 that James Molyneaux was not being listened to by his supposed friends at Westminster. This was undoubtedly his lowest point as leader of the UUP and caused him momentarily to consider resignation.

Over the next nine years, Molyneaux proved that any descriptions of his political style should add 'tenacious' to the obligatory 'taciturn' references. While his authority within the party never fully recovered from the failure of the anti-Agreement campaign, he managed to cling to power with limpet-like adhesion, to the chagrin of those within the party who thought him to have passed his political 'sell-by date'.

Molyneaux was pilloried by the DUP for first supporting, albeit tacitly, the Joint Declaration of December 1993 and then moving from this position to an attitude of hostility while at the same time shoring up the government's dwindling majority at Westminster. Notwithstanding his disappointment in 1985, Molyneaux recognised the tactical advantage to be had as a potential king-maker in the House of Commons. While Paisley decried him as a 'Judas Iscariot', Molyneaux gained a degree of political leverage over the government and achieved his much sought after parliamentary select committee on Northern Ireland affairs. This time he was convinced that he did 'have the ear' of the government and, due to the fortunate Westminster arithmetic, this was an ear which could be twisted on occasions. The penalty for getting it wrong a second time would be severe.

Molyneaux's political options were limited anyhow. He had experienced the futility of unconstitutional action and recognised, correctly, that unionism had to be on the 'inside track' in the policy process however difficult that might prove to be. One of his central difficulties in pursuing this strategy was that the tactical considerations of maintaining a relationship with the government often sat uneasily with grass-roots opinion, which felt increasingly threatened by the tide of events. When Molyneaux claimed after the IRA ceasefire that he believed government assurances that no deal had been done because he had never known John Major to tell lies, not everyone was quite so easily satisfied. Many unionists felt threatened after the ceasefires, not so much by immediate events but fears about the long-term implications for the unionist position within Northern Ireland. These fears were exacerbated of course by the DUP whose warnings of British treachery served a constituency which was altogether more sceptical. When Ian Paisley cranked up the volume at the end of

1994, Molyneaux was placed in the difficult position of trying to maintain a working relationship with the government while protecting the UUP from radical unionists such as Paisley who condemned any such co-operation as damaging to unionist interests. Speaking to the DUP annual conference in December 1994, Paisley announced that his party would be boycotting the forthcoming international investment conference, scheduled to be held at Belfast's Europa hotel on 13 December. American involvement in this British government initiative signalled President Clinton's faith in the ceasefires and his commitment to political progress and economic regeneration in Northern Ireland. Paisley took the opportunity to attack all of those involved for taking part in what amounted to little more than an attempt to buy off the unionist community and accused Molyneaux of treachery for his party's participation.

> Mr Major and those responsible with him are going to have to be brought to account for what they are doing. . . . Are we going to bow our necks and agree to a partnership with the IRA men of blood who have slain our loved ones, destroyed our country, burned our churches, tortured our people – and demand now that we should become slaves in a country fit only for nuns' men and monks' women to live in? . . . Are we like abject slaves to Salem, the new United States overlord sent to us by the Whitewater crook? Are we going to allow minor Majors or major minors to take us for a ride to the paedophile priests?[138]

While few unionists, or nationalists, would give anything other than a resounding 'no' in answer to such questions, the harsh attitude taken by the DUP to initiatives such as the Belfast investment conference of December 1994 reduced the political space within which the UUP operated and acted as a form of Chinese water torture on Molyneaux's leadership of the party.

The first public signals that Molyneaux had miscalculated the strength of his own position and his relationship with John Major's government came at the end of January 1995, when he issued a warning that the impending Anglo-Irish Frameworks Document for political progress was unacceptably close to joint authority and would not be endorsed by his party.[139] Speaking during a BBC interview, the UUP leader suggested that such proposals would be a recipe for 'instability and chaos' and could not therefore be defended by his party. 'It is joint authority in a very blatant fashion and an unacceptable fashion – which would be objected to by all right-thinking people and rejected also on the grounds of sheer unwork-ability.'[140] Molyneaux went on to warn the Prime Minister that he was straining the limits of their parliamentary understanding and if he insisted on acting against the best interests of Northern Ireland, 'then there could be no relationship'. This marked a serious blow to the Molyneaux strategy, coming as it did only a week after UUP votes saved the government from a humiliating House of Commons defeat on the European fisheries agreement. The media began to scent what for them was the perfume of decaying flesh.

> Mr Molyneaux's apparent disclosure of some of the document's contents and his reaction to them amount to a remarkable volte-face, and catapult him and his party into the midst of the first personal and political crisis in the North since the republican and loyalist ceasefires started.
>
>   The effect of his interview on the unionist body politic will be seriously to question the scope and value of his much-vaunted parliamentary 'understanding' with Mr Major and implicitly to query Mr Molyneaux's own political judgement.[141]

While this plan for North–South bodies proved to be ill-founded, a more accurate leak of the forthcoming Frameworks Document was provided by the *Times* in February. Once again, commentators suggested that the sort of cross-border structures envisaged could be disastrous for Molyneaux's leadership of the UUP.

> The publication of the Framework Document may well test the special relationship between the leader of the Ulster Unionist Party and John Major to breaking point. If it does it will also damage, perhaps fatally, James Molyneaux's leadership of the party. The *Times* leak of elements of the document has provided the Democratic Unionist Party with much material with which it can argue that its rejectionist stance on the Downing Street Declaration has been proved correct. Molyneaux is in danger of being perceived as having been credulously dependent on a supposed relationship of trust with a British prime minister for the second time in a decade.[142]

The Frameworks Document[143] was launched amidst much hullabaloo in Belfast on 22 February 1995. The unionist reaction was almost unanimously negative, with the *News Letter* summing up feelings the following day with its front-page headline: 'No Way!'[144] The DUP response was predictable enough, with the party claiming that Northern Ireland had been given an 'eviction notice' from the United Kingdom. Ian Paisley rehearsed what had become his leitmotif during periods of political instability. He refused to attend John Major's statement to the House of Commons on 22 February and told the Prime Minister *in absentia*: 'You have sold Northern Ireland out. You have sold out the Union.'[145] During the launch of the initiative, John Major appealed to people to take their time in considering it. 'Read it, study it, think about it, discuss it, talk about it . . . let it mature.'[146] This was presumably a triumph of hope over expectation as the verdicts came thick and fast from politicians and public alike. The document was deliberately made available in post offices across Northern Ireland in an attempt to facilitate such contemplation and remove the politicians' monopoly on shaping reaction. One elderly lady who picked up her copy at a Belfast post office clearly needed some convincing: 'I can tell you what this is without opening it . . . You British are just waving us goodbye.'[147] At a party press conference on 22 February, Ian Paisley exhibited similar sentiments, declaring that the Frameworks Document was simply the latest instalment of a 'malicious scheme by successive British Governments to push Northern Ireland out of the Union. . . . This is a finely-tuned one-way street, it only has one proposal and that is to go down the Dublin road.'[148]

Attitudes within the UUP were more wide-ranging. While they were equally disappointed at the terms of the document, a range of opinion was apparent. The emotional response was one of outright condemnation while simultaneously the intellectual reaction was given to a more cautious consideration of the initiative's importance to the subsequent debate, and its status as a 'framework' for progress in interparty talks. The UUP's East Londonderry MP, William Ross, typified the gut reaction of many in the party, saying it should be thrown in the bin: 'it is not a document for discussion but a manifesto leading to the creation of a united Ireland'.[149] David Trimble, though equally hostile to it, displayed a more subtle approach. 'It is a very complex document, very detailed . . . It requires study and we will study it, although my first reaction is to say that it is actually much worse than expected.'[150] Even Ken Maginnis, one of the more liberal minded within the leadership of the UUP, found little to enthuse over in the Frameworks Document. He warned implicitly that this had effectively undermined the Molyneaux strategy and played into the hands of those who had warned of British betrayal.

> What this document has done is made the whole issue so contentious that the ordinary man and woman in the street in Northern Ireland will be even more distrustful of what is happening than ever before. They will be saying to us: 'You mustn't be generous. You must hold on to everything very tightly. You must concede nothing.'[151]

In the event this was a shrewd analysis. The unionist community perceived the language and tone of the Frameworks Document to be nationalist rather than unionist, referring collectively to 'the people of Ireland' and advocating North–South structures with 'harmonising' functions over a broad range of designated areas. Regardless of John Major's claims that he cherished the Union, for many Protestants in Northern Ireland, the word 'harmonising' had never seemed so threatening. They were to be 'harmonised' into an all-Ireland state. One senior member of the UUP suggested that if the Frameworks Document turned out to be as bad as expected then Molyneaux's strategy would be destroyed along with his leadership.

> There are some who think he made a huge mistake by trusting John Major to the extent that he did, particularly after what Margaret Thatcher did in 1985. If the documents published today are viewed as a similar betrayal serious questions will be asked about the leader's judgement.[152]

From this point on, the question was not whether Molyneaux would resign but simply when he would choose to do so. In March it appeared that even this luxury would be denied to him, when a stalking-horse candidate, Lee Reynolds, announced that he would challenge Molyneaux for the leadership of the party. No one, including the challenger himself, believed that this Queen's University student would win as he had held no substantial office in the party hierarchy. The intention was to hold a vote of confidence on Molyneaux's leadership and demonstrate the scale of opposition which existed. Reynolds issued a press statement on 14 March mischievously entitled 'My Duty to the Greater Number', a rhetorical nod in the direction of the party leader who favoured the phrase.

> It is because I and many other ordinary Unionists feel that the Union is in danger not least because of the failure of the Leadership of the Party that I have allowed my name to be submitted for the Leadership election on 18th March 1995.
>   . . . The Leadership record since 1984 is one of successive defeats and an ongoing weakening of the Union. I have no personal animosity towards the present Leader but the facts are that he has on two major occasions, November 1985 on the occasion of the Anglo-Irish Agreement and in February 1995, totally miscalculated the Government's intentions and misled the pro-Union majority as to the security of the Union. His acquiescence in the Joint Declaration guaranteed the contents of the Framework Document. . . . The Party Leadership has regularly precipitated crises by its incompetence. It has then used each crisis as an excuse for stifling criticism and debate in the interests of Party unity. Each time Northern Ireland is pushed further to the Edge of the Union and each time those who might save it are excluded by those who cannot.[153]

While Molyneaux duly won the leadership contest on 18 March, Reynolds received a significant degree of support, ensuring that the victory was a pyrrhic one. Most observers were shocked when Reynolds received 88 votes out of 619 cast, 15 per cent of the poll, a much larger vote than had been expected and a humiliating signal of the disenchantment in the party with Molyneaux's leadership. Bloodied but unbowed, Molyneaux limped along as a lame-duck leader while others began positioning themselves for the forthcoming electoral contest.

The *coup de grâce* to Molyneaux's leadership of the UUP was provided when the death of Sir James Kilfedder, the Popular Unionist Party MP for North Down, forced a Westminster by-election in the constituency on 15 June 1995. Crucially for the eventual result, the UUP nomination of the relatively unknown Alan McFarland, rather than the close Molyneaux ally and higher profile Reg Empey, proved disastrous for UUP fortunes. McFarland's main competition came from UK Unionist Robert McCartney, former member of the UUP expelled from the party during the campaign against the Anglo-Irish Agreement in the mid-1980s. McCartney made his opposition to the Frameworks Document the centre-piece of his campaign which raised the whole question of James Molyneaux's political judgement and his miscalculation over the strength of the UUP's relationship with the British government. As a result of McCartney's policy agenda, the DUP, who had no chance of winning representation in one of the most affluent areas of Northern Ireland, decided not to contest the seat but to throw their weight in behind the McCartney campaign. McFarland was a cerebral though uninspiring candidate, while McCartney led a charismatic campaign, assisted by the fact that he was a well-known unionist figure and had contested the seat on a previous occasion. In the event, McCartney scored a comfortable victory, despite a turnout of only 38.75 per cent, the lowest ever recorded in a Westminster by-election in the region. Notwithstanding the low turnout, the defeat of the UUP in what should have been a natural constituency for the party was taken as a vote of no confidence in party leader James Molyneaux and proved to be the final nail in his political coffin.

The Siege of Drumcree

The summer marching season of 1995 proved to be the most combustible for several years with major flashpoints in Belfast and Portadown over the vexed issue of the re-routing of Orange parades away from nationalist areas. The context to this was the wider political uncertainty over post-ceasefire institutions. Nationalists wanted to test the sincerity of the state's commitment to 'parity of esteem' and equal treatment within the state, while unionists expressed their frustration and anger over what many regarded as British duplicity and a slide towards an Irish nationalist agenda. There were of course the usual immediate reasons for inflamed passions over Orange marches. The demonstrators wished to parade along their traditional routes while many nationalists who lived in these areas found this behaviour threatening and offensive. Despite the assertion from defenders of the Orange institution that such parades were held in a carnival-type atmosphere, this was not the nationalist experience in many parts of Northern Ireland. Sectarian tensions were heightened in 1995 because both nationalists and unionists were looking at events for subliminal messages about potential political trends on a wider level. Thus, increased re-routing would be taken by some to indicate a greater Dublin influence in Northern Ireland's internal affairs, while less may be regarded by others as evidence of British government insincerity over the peace process. At times the situation went beyond parody such as the occasion in Belfast on 12 July when a group of nationalists attempted to visit their nearest off-licence which just happened to be 500 yards inside a Protestant area.

The RUC said it was too dangerous. The nationalists insisted on using 'the Queen's highway', just as the Orange marchers had done earlier. A bizarre discussion ensued. The nationalists offered to walk in single file. The police said they could go through individually at 10-second intervals. Finally they were allowed to walk together, shadowed by an armoured RUC Land-Rover. They came to the top of Donegall Pass. Within seconds, scores of Protestants charged with bricks and bottles. A dozen RUC Land-Rovers screeched in to block the road. While the RUC pushed plastic bullets into their weapons and used riot shields against flying glass and stones, the Catholics hurried off to the off-licence. The bricks were still flying when they returned 10 minutes later, clutching white carrier bags and striding quickly back to their nationalist enclave.[154]

Since the signing of the Anglo-Irish Agreement in 1985, Portadown had been an area of tension during the July period because of the re-routing of Orange parades by the RUC away from Obin Street and the Garvaghy Road due to the opposition of Catholic residents. In March 1986, following the banning of an Apprentice Boys' parade in the town and subsequent rioting, Keith White became the first Protestant to be killed by a plastic bullet fired by the RUC.

In 1995, the battle to demonstrate the ethnic traditions of the 'loyalist' community reached a crescendo in the 'Siege of Drumcree'. On Sunday 9 July, the RUC blocked an Orange Order march from parading along the Garvaghy Road on the grounds that it was likely to lead to public disorder due to the opposition of local residents. Incensed by this threat to what they regarded as their fundamental right to parade regardless of community consent, the Orangemen refused to disperse and set up camp in Drumcree. Despite attempts at conciliation no compromise could be found which would satisfy the demonstrators. Predictably, the stand-off attracted unionist politicians anxious to display their loyalist credentials and gain valuable publicity as stout 'defenders of the Union'. On the evening of 11 July, Ian Paisley addressed thousands of protesters and claimed that the siege was a matter of life and death. In a typically fiery speech in a field on the Drumcree Road, Paisley told his followers with his usual touch of hyperbole that the protest must continue to the bitter end.

> Because of the seriousness of the issue all of us must be prepared to make the necessary sacrifice. . . . There can be no turning back on this issue – we will die if necessary rather than surrender. If we don't win this battle all is lost, it is a matter of life and death. It is a matter of Ulster or the Irish Republic, it is a matter of freedom or slavery.[155]

David Trimble, who shared the same platform as the DUP leader, appealed for a peaceful demonstration by the Orangemen and assured them of his confidence that they would eventually be allowed to parade down the Garvaghy Road. The event was given an added piquancy when representatives from the Ballynafeigh Orange Lodge appeared and were applauded as they walked to the Drumcree Church which had become the HQ of the protesters. Ballynafeigh Orangemen were engaged in their own battle with the RUC for the right to march down Belfast's Lower Ormeau Road in defiance of the wishes of the local Catholic community who lived there.[156] Supporters and bands from other areas arrived into Portadown in a show of solidarity with their embattled colleagues. The stage was set for a riot and it duly arrived on the evening of 10 July, when a group of demonstrators broke through the police lines and set off towards the Garvaghy Road. A running battle then ensued between the mob (many of whom wore Orange collarettes) and the RUC, who responded to the fusillade of bricks and bottles by firing plastic bullets at the rioters. The *News Letter* (a paper with a predominantly unionist readership) was in no doubt about the damage which the Drumcree riot had done to the Orange Order, condemning the violence in its editorial the following morning.

> Last night's appaling thuggery cannot be excused. The reputation of the Orange Order has been tarnished in the eyes of the watching world and the vast majority of law-abiding members who hoped that an acceptable and dignified compromise would result from their legitimate protest were instead caught up in scenes of civil disorder as vicious as any witnessed in this Province's turbulent history.[157]

However, some of those involved 'had a good war'. David Trimble was present at the stand-off as MP for the area and acted as an intermediary between the protesters and the police. While appealing for calm and a peaceful demonstration he was also keen to point out that the march had taken place without any compromise deal having been done with the residents of Garvaghy Road. This was despite claims by the RUC, local residents and the Northern Ireland Mediation Network that in return for a quiet Orange parade down the road without 'musical' accompaniment, a similar march on the following day – 12 July – would be re-routed. Trimble disclaimed any knowledge of this accommodation and entered Portadown town centre at the head of the parade to a tumultuous reception, hand in hand with Ian Paisley. The 'Siege of Drumcree' had been added to the Protestant folk memory which included the Battle of the Somme in 1916, the reaction to the Home Rule crisis, the Siege of Derry in 1689 and the tradition of banding together in solidarity against an apparently superior enemy.[158] The role played by Trimble had established his credentials as a true-blue 'Son of Ulster', a defender of his community, and would prove invaluable to him in another battle, the forthcoming election for the leadership of the Ulster Unionist Party.

Unionism under David Trimble

James Molyneaux announced his resignation as leader of the Ulster Unionist Party on 29 August 1995, effectively firing the starting pistol for the UUP leadership election.[159] This became very much a 'hare and tortoise' contest as the last candidate off the starting-blocks was first past the winning post. Initially, David Trimble announced that it was not his intention to stand for the leadership of the party, preferring possibly to be the junior partner in a 'dream ticket' with John Taylor. Only when he became convinced that he could win the contest did Trimble concede to popular demand and put his hat into the ring. 'I was not anxious to put myself forward. It would pose a heavy burden – not just on myself but on my family. But I found as the week went on that there was an expectation by many people that I should put myself forward.'[160] A *Sunday Tribune* poll carried out amongst a cross-section of the Northern Ireland electorate at the end of August indicated that Ken Maginnis was the front-runner with 39 per cent support, followed by David Trimble with 16 per cent, Rev. Martin Smyth and John Taylor with 14 per cent, and Willie Ross trailing in with 4 per cent.[161] Trimble was less likely to be swayed by these popularity contests than by the private soundings he was taking within the party itself. Perhaps the most crucial aspect of the leadership election, as Ken Maginnis was to find out to his cost, was that the electorate was not the Northern Ireland public but the UUP and in particular the nine hundred or so delegates of the party's ruling body, the Ulster Unionist Council. This body is traditionally composed of the 'active minority' and tends to be less liberal than the party as a whole.

The leadership election took place fittingly enough in Belfast's Ulster Hall on 8 September, in a night charged with drama and emotion. This was heightend by the form of proceedings as each of the five candidates was asked to give a speech after which a series of votes by the 806 delegates successively narrowed the field down from five to one. The writing was on the wall after the first ballot, as Trimble came top with 287 votes to Taylor's 226, with Rev. Martin Smyth trailing in last with a derisory 60 votes. Smyth's chances were dealt a fatal blow at Drumcree, with his star falling as quickly in Portadown as Trimble's had risen. Smyth's absence from the four-day confrontation, despite his leadership position as grand master of the Grand Lodge of Ireland, was seen by many radical unionists as desertion from his post in their hour of need. Smyth's defence, that no one had invited him to attend Drumcree and he was busy addressing other Orange gatherings, did little to convince his critics and fed a sustained campaign by the 'Spirit of Drumcree' group to remove him from his position within the Orange Order. After the second ballot, William Ross was eliminated and Ken Maginnis withdrew to save himself further damage. In the third and final vote, a straight fight between Trimble and Taylor, the Upper Bann MP won with a comfortable majority.[162]

> When it came to the final announcement, Mr Trimble looked set to explode with the tension. While Mr Taylor continued to laugh and joke with the party officers, Mr Trimble sat rubbing his hands together feverishly. Ken Maginnis, who withdrew after the second ballot, sat looking despondent with his head bowed.[163]

In his victory speech, David Trimble claimed that he liked to think of himself as a moderniser and announced his intention to hold meetings with 'all the constitutional parties' and with the Irish government, though any meeting with Dublin 'would not be for the purpose of formal talks but for the purpose of understanding each other's positions'.[164] While the new UUP leader rejected as 'too facile' any suggestion that his victory was a consequence of his role in the 'Siege of Drumcree', it undoubtedly played a significant part in his success. The UUC delegates clearly wanted a leader who would be the most able to navigate a course through the treacherous seas they found themselves in. Trimble, with his academic legal background on the one hand and hardline pedigree on the other (a member of the quasi-paramilitary Ulster Vanguard in the 1970s and Lisburn chairman of the Ulster Clubs in the 1980s), seemed to many to be the man for the job. Of all the candidates, Trimble had established a solid reputation at Westminster and was by far the best media performer, even if he did tend to glow bright pink when annoyed and look at times as though he was about to spontaneously combust in front of the camera lens.

Non-unionists regarded Trimble with trepidation, viewing him as the least moderate of the candidates, the most irascible, and a man who would do little to help the peace process or the long-term fortunes of his own party in coming to terms with Irish nationalism. David McKittrick, the doyen of Belfast's journalists, has observed that he was commonly regarded as the man with the shortest fuse in Irish politics and an unpredictable 'pair of hands'. One British government official scoffed at the *Times*'s portrayal of Trimble as a 'moderate'. 'I was having my breakfast when I read that . . . nearly puked up my frosties.'[165] In terms of ability, Trimble was undoubtedly the most able candidate to lead unionism into the twenty-first century. The big question remained, where did he want to go?

The initial signs suggested that Trimble intended to adopt a harder stance than his predecessor over the peace process and the conditions in which the UUP would engage in talks with Sinn Féin. During several interviews given on the day following his election victory, Trimble hinted that rather than treating weapons decommissioning as some sort of 'holy grail', he was more interested in establishing the IRA's commitment to 'exclusively peaceful methods' as set out in the Downing Street Declaration.

It is obvious that in the course of this (peace) process the existence of private armies should end. Obviously that must happen. We have got to have the proofs. What I am saying is that decommissioning, the handing up of some weapons, may not be enough.[166]

Over the course of the next twelve months up to the eve of the 'all-party' talks scheduled for 10 June 1996, Trimble did little to dent his image within unionism or nationalism as a hard-man with brains. Few people doubted his intelligence, but question marks remained over the sureness of his political touch.

In terms of leadership style, Trimble adopted a more collegiate approach than was apparent during Molyneaux's tenure, appointing John Taylor as deputy leader of the party. It became standard practice for Taylor to accompany Trimble to meetings with the British or Irish governments, in contrast to Molyneaux's penchant for cosy *mano a mano* chats and backstage whispers. Trimble indicated this intention to take a chaperone with him when he was asked before the leadership election what changes he intended to introduce. 'One small crucial change I would make: I would never go into Downing Street alone. One must be careful not to be seduced by personalities.'[167] This may have been a coded reference to the weight his predecessor placed on his relationship with members of the British establishment. '"He was always going on about being a friend of the Queen Mother and if only we could have heard what she had told him only last week then we would have no fears for the future of the Union," runs the most frequently told anecdote of the Molyneaux style.'[168] Commenting upon his new support role, John Taylor said that 'both David and myself, prior to the leadership election, felt this was one of the changes necessary in the party'.[169] This had the practical advantages of providing the new leader with support during difficult discussions (what cynics might refer to as a 'nasty-cop, nasty-cop' routine), keeping a powerful figure within the party who had just suffered an embarrassing defeat inside the tent spitting out rather than vice versa, and insulating Trimble from any accusations that he had misinterpreted any points of debate with his various interlocutors. Taylor used his new position to bark on his master's behalf, notably when he declared in February 1996 that Minister for Foreign Affairs Dick Spring was 'the most detested politician in Ireland' and claimed that he could see 'no difference between Dick Spring and Gerry Adams'.[170] Spring replied jokingly that Taylor's ratings in Kerry, the Minister's home county, were not that good either.

During the weeks after his election Trimble demonstrated his desire to present the UUP as a more professional and dynamic party than the rather somnambulant beast he had inherited from his predecessor. He met SDLP leader John Hume on 14 September, after which both men described their discussions in the time-honoured diplomatic euphemism as being 'very constructive'. He met his unionist colleague Ian Paisley on 18 September, who exhorted him – unsuccessfully as it turned out – to give his support to the DUP-sponsored unionist commission which advocated establishing a 'pan-unionist front' to rival the perceived consensus within Irish nationalism. Within days Trimble had also held discussions with Prime Minister John Major and Labour Party leader Tony Blair. Trimble even welcomed Dick Spring to the UUP's party headquarters at Glengall Street in Belfast.

Evidence of this new proactive style was provided at the end of September 1995 when the UUP announced the establishment of a 'North American bureau' with offices in Washington provided by US business-man, Tony Cully-Foster, a native of Derry city. The purpose of this trans-atlantic link was to capitalise on what the UUP claimed was the growing understanding of and sympathy for the unionist case in Northern Ireland. Aside from providing new fund-raising opportunities, the new office was primarily focused on lobbying the American political establishment and opinion-formers to get the unionist case across to key government personnel. A similar exercise was undertaken in May 1996 with the establishment of a 'Unionist Information Office' in London. The initials UIO were heralded by some of its architects as a humorous play on the Northern Ireland Office – NIO – the inference being that the UIO would remedy any disinfor-mation produced by the government. This assumption that British public opinion took a dim view of Ulster unionists and the Union in general because of government manipulation of the media is an optimistic one. A more cruel assertion might be that David Trimble and his colleagues mistook the British for a community 'who gave a damn'. The long-term effects of the UIO on British attitudes to the Union remain to be seen.

While the energy and dynamism of David Trimble's style of leadership are uncontested, his credentials as a moderniser of the party and its appeal are more debatable. He signalled shortly after his election victory that a key element in this unionist makeover would be an update of the relationship between the UUP and the Orange Order. Considering the circumstances of Trimble's success, it was ironic, to say the least, that he chose this as his first area of attention. Speaking to delegates attending the party's annual conference at Portrush in County Antrim in October, Trimble made clear that his intention did not amount to 'expelling the Orange delegates or cutting the link with the Orange institution'.[171] However, he indicated that he wanted to find another way to reflect the historical association between Orangeism and the UUP. It was clear from the debate on the issue at the conference that the need to reconstitute the relationship was not unani-mously viewed as a priority within the party. Drew Nelson, a UUP representative on Banbridge District Council and a member of the Orange Order, was greeted with heckles and booing when he advocated that action be taken on the issue.

> In a sense this party was a child of the Orange Order but the child has now grown up and it wants its independence whilst still recognising its roots. If we want to form a modern political party in which all supporters of the Union – Catholic, Protestant and others – can feel truly comfortable then we have to bite the bullet and break the link.[172]

Unfortunately, biting bullets is not an activity which comes naturally to the UUP and many view the enterprise with intense suspicion and distrust. During a BBC radio interview on 24 May in the lead-up to the Forum elections of 30 May 1996, David Trimble did not suggest that his initial plan for modernising the link between his party and the Orange Order was imminent.

> I think far too much significance is attached to this. The Orange Order has a historic connection with unionism, and there is a formal connection through delegates, but in practice what actually happens is that those posts are actually occupied by active members of the party, and the Order as such does not, and never has to my knowledge, tried to interfere with the internal operations of the party. So it's more a matter of appearance rather than of substance. . . . These matters will change, but to talk in terms of breaking what is a significant historic link is something that would run . . . counter to the wishes of people within the party. So while we're talking in terms of remodelling the relationship we're not talking of abruptly ending it.[173]

The first real test of Trimble's leadership came when the British government began to signal in October 1995 that they might be prepared to initiate all-party talks in advance of any decommissioning of weapons from republican or loyalist paramilitaries. This would have amounted to a revision of the Washington 3 guideline adhered to by the British for several months, namely, that the IRA would have to make a token gesture by handing in or destroying some of their military arsenal as a sign of good faith before Sinn Féin would be allowed to the talks table. The idea of a twin-track approach to arms decommissioning and political negotiations emerged after an Anglo-Irish Intergovernmental Conference meeting at Stormont between Secretary of State Sir Patrick Mayhew and Minister for Foreign Affairs, Dick Spring. Due to the intractability of the problem, the two governments agreed to establish an international commission to arbitrate on the matter and make recommendations for a resolution of the procedural difficulties. The UUP deputy leader, John Taylor, derided the twin-track idea as a 'silly nonsense'[174] but said nonetheless that his party would wait and see what developed from it before making a final judgement. No such reticence was apparent from the DUP. Ian Paisley took this as further proof of the British government's hidden agenda to surreptitiously concede to the demands of the IRA which had been secretly agreed when the IRA called their ceasefire in August 1994.

> The idea that the Secretary of State is prepared to explore the very thought of alternatives to actual decommissioning is evidence of yet another Government climb-down. The Government, under pressure from Dublin and the IRA, are actively engaged in giving ground to the IRA. No unionist worthy of the name will be deceived by the British Government's lies. They may be able to find a 'form of words' to suit the requirements of IRA/Sinn Féin but mere words will not convince any unionist that the IRA intends to even start a decommissioning process.[175]

British officials subsequently went to great pains to reassure unionists that no change had taken place in the government's position, that Washington 3 was still in place and that the twin-track approach did not signify any substantive change to the existing demands on decommissioning. The key aspect of Sir Patrick Mayhew's comments came in reference to the envisaged arms commission. While saying that only decommissioning would create the necessary political confidence and trust for all parties to get around the negotiating table together, the Secretary of State added: 'If an (international arms) commission can . . . come up with some means of generating that necessary confidence by some other means, then we would want to look at that very closely and look at that on its merits.'[176] As ever with Northern Ireland politics, the nuances contained in this remark were taken as highly significant and subsequent attempts by the NIO to 'put the toothpaste back in the tube' proved unsuccessful. Ian Paisley said the government was speaking out of both sides of its mouth, while David Trimble voiced concerns about the proposed international arms commission. 'What concerns me is the suggestion that this international body will somehow be a substitute for decommissioning by finding some other means of saying to people "We are satisfied there is a commitment to peaceful methods . . ." There is a shift there.'[177] What Trimble was anxious to ensure throughout the whole decommissioning debate was that it was left up to him, rather than to an international commission or anyone else, to declare when he was satisfied as to the IRA's commitment to 'exclusively peaceful methods'. In theory at least, this effectively left the timing of all-party negotiations in his gift, and allowed him to control the pace at which the political process moved.

Trimble's political strategy included 'spreading the word' in foreign fields, particularly in the United States. At the end of October 1995, a UUP delegation embarked on a series of meetings in America designed to lobby important politicians and opinion-formers. An illustration of the battle which faced unionists in getting their message across was provided when the *New York Times* published a hostile newspaper advertisement by the Irish-American Unity Council which compared David Trimble with

David Duke, believed to be a leading figure in the Ku Klux Klan. The advertisement focused its attention on the link between the UUP and the Orange Order and likened parades through Catholic areas to 'a Ku Klux Klan march through an African American neighbourhood, or a neo-Nazi march through a Jewish neighbourhood'.[178] While the delegation talked down the significance of this verbal ambush, it was an indication to them of the battle they faced in breaking down stereotypical attitudes to unionism. This struggle was made all the more difficult when senior figures in the party behaved in a manner which actually confirmed rather than dissipated such stereotypes. Commenting on the advertisement, David Trimble declared that such views would embarrass much of the Irish-American community and did 'not reflect the real desire for dialogue we see from the invitations to speak and to debate that we have received from Irish-American groups across the country'.[179] The UUP leader was soon to learn that being invited to speak was one thing, while convincing your audience was quite another skill entirely. When the delegation took their roadshow to Washington to meet politicians on Capitol Hill, it became clear that the unionist 'charm offensive' was failing to charm and actually offending their hosts. These events are run-of-the-mill networking activities for any normal democratic political organisation, who will use such opportunities for information gathering and building up personal relationships with officials and politicians. High-profile events such as the Washington meeting are normally carefully stage-managed affairs where diplomatic euphemisms will be employed to disguise any disagreements which arise. David Trimble introduced a new style to such events, of questionable propriety, by engaging in a public row with the very people who had invited him to speak and whom he was presumably trying to influence. The *Sunday Tribune*'s account of the meeting would suggest that the UUP had a lot to learn about the lobbying process, the first rule being to do some research about the people you are talking to before insulting them.

> US lawmakers who attended the mid-week session with Trimble and two of his MPs, Ken Maginnis and Rev Martin Smyth, were still fuming this weekend about what they believe was a 'display of intransigence' by the three-man Unionist delegation. . . . The dozen or so congressmen present – The *Sunday Tribune* could not find one who was satisfied by the meeting and who didn't use the word tense to describe it – were especially taken aback when the Fermanagh and South Tyrone MP Maginnis mounted a crushing verbal assault on James Walsh, a Republican Representative from New York. '. . . Didn't he know who Walsh is?' asked one congressional staffer. Of all of the congressmen present, Walsh was one of the more sympathetic to the Unionist cause; he is a member of the Friends of Ireland group of lawmakers on the Hill and not a supporter of the traditionally more nationalist Ad Hoc Committee on Irish Affairs.[180]

The American hosts were equally perplexed by unionist reactions to this diplomatic débâcle, and particularly David Trimble's lack of penitence for the turn of events and his indication that it was the congressmen who were responsible for the disagreement which had emerged. In an interview with the *Sunday Tribune*, the UUP leader remarked: 'I thought we had headbangers in the House of Commons.'[181] This event encapsulates perfectly the inherent flaws in David Trimble's leadership. While he seems to recognise the need for a modernisation of structures and mind-sets within unionism, he undoes much of this work by ill-tempered words and actions which are sometimes counterproductive to his stated objectives. A good example of Trimble's often gauche handling of his party's affairs – to outside eyes at least – was his response to a joint invitation by Sir Patrick Mayhew and Dick Spring to preparatory talks in December 1995. While the UUP were invited in the same manner as all of the other main parties in Northern Ireland to what was hoped would be the forerunner to full-scale interparty dialogue, in a rather petulant display, Trimble took exception to the joint invitation:

> I thought it was rather impudent of Dick Spring to invite me to talks about the future of Northern Ireland and how it should be governed. The correct person for me, as part of the United Kingdom, to direct my concerns to, is the United Kingdom government, who I will continue talking to.[182]

While many non-unionists may regard this as rather childish behaviour, it may partly be explained by political insecurity and the knowledge that the UUP were competing for the unionist vote with other parties who could claim to have presented a more accurate political analysis to their community, at a time of deep uncertainty about the direction of the peace process. Trimble has been open about the challenge to the UUP presented by Ian Paisley. 'I am very conscious of the fact that if he sees an opportunity to slip in and seize some areas of my support he will.'[183] Evidence of this came during the DUP's annual party conference at the end of November when a bitter attack was launched on the UUP by several leading party members, including Paisley himself. Much of the criticism centred around the Ulster Unionist attitude to the Downing Street Declaration of 15 December 1993, and the way in which this led directly to the Frameworks Document. The party's deputy leader Peter Robinson was scathing in his assessment of the UUP's performance.

> I consider Ulster to be facing the severest trial ever inflicted upon it and, by and large, unionism is ill-equipped to meet the challenge. Instead of responding to Ian's invitation to 'rally together' the Official Unionist Party linger and dither in the jaws of our sternest crisis. It is with genuine sadness that I say that Glengall Street has brought Ulster to the brink of disaster by

its craven endorsement of the Downing Street Declaration, by being the first, through Martin Smyth, to suggest talking with the IRA and by proposing all-Ireland executive structures through its Talks team. . . . Mr Chairman, the years have not dulled the resentment and hostility I feel towards the Anglo-Irish Agreement. That sense of outrage and hurt has not left me, nor will it ever fade. The message from this conference is simple, clear and, after a decade of the diktat, it is unchanged – 'the DUP still says NO'. . . . The matter that bewilders me most is how some unionists can with apparent sincerity stand shoulder to shoulder with us in our opposition to the Anglo-Irish Agreement yet give credit to the Downing Street Declaration which is a direct and consequent extension of it.[184]

Robinson went on in his speech to illustrate the defensive mentality within unionism, indicating that his political viewpoint was fashioned through fear. As the political environment was hostile, it was foolhardy of other unionists, notably the UUP, to continue giving the political process credibility by engaging in conciliatory gestures such as carrying on dialogue with the Irish Republic. Once again we see the way in which political behaviour is fashioned by conflicting analyses within the unionist community of their political surroundings. While the UUP were unhappy about the course of political events since the signing of the Downing Street Declaration, they understood the necessity to be inside the process rather than outside and believed that if unionists argued their case vigorously they would be listened to. DUP politicians such as Peter Robinson have a much darker vision, and their fear of the forces ranged against them acts as a barrier to innovative thinking or progressive action.

Today unionists are the punch-bag – the target – the prey. . . . You love your country. You are a patriot. You are not prepared to turn your back on your heritage. You do not despise your past. You are proud to be Protestant. You will not apologise for being a unionist and you will not surrender to murderers. . . . The DUP position is as consistent as it is right. We will not negotiate with the IRA – with its guns or without them. Sinn Féin's legitimacy as a political party would not be achieved simply by the hand-over of the IRA's illegal weapons. The IRA must disband and be no longer in existence. . . . Mr Chairman, this party has always recognised that unionists cannot have normal relationships with Dublin until Dublin removes its aggressive and illegal claim to our territory. That was the traditional unionist position. During the last Talks process and more recently under Mr Trimble's leadership, unionists with a Kamikaze-like intuition have involved themselves in negotiations about Northern Ireland with the Irish Republic. Quite amazingly they have sought to portray it as being the apex of unionist achievement.[185]

Ian Paisley's address to the conference was similar in tone to that of his deputy leader. The forces ranged against the unionist community were manifold and the only option open was not to attempt to seek a compromise or engage in innovative political action, but rather to return to older methods which had proved successful in the past. As unionists' enemies today are essentially the same as those faced by their Protestant forefathers, the best defence of the unionist interest was to look to the tactics which had thwarted ancient enemies. Paisley's speech failed to recognise that looks can be deceptive and one of the few variables to have remained unchanged was unionism itself.

> In the phraseology of the ceasefire habitat everything demanded by the murderers and their parrots backed by John Hume, Dublin, Clinton and the Vatican is reasonable. On the other hand, everything supporting the blatant denial of these demanded concessions is intransigent. . . . The spirit which inspired our forefathers to refuse to bow the knee to the enemies of liberty still burns in the breast of their sons and daughters. Its recent bursting into flame in Drumcree should be a warning to the Government and those who hound them on to neuter the Union that the last word will not be spoken by Whitehall Government but by the men and women of Ulster themselves. At the Somme it was rightly said that the men of Ulster were lions but the English officers directing the battle were asses. When the English asses are dismissed from the negotiations and Ulster men and women take charge, then and then alone will democratic progress be made. . . . I am invited by the Government to a twin-track negotiation structure where I talk to IRA/Sinn Féin, Dublin, and the SDLP while the IRA pressurises the outcome of such talks with the threat of the use of their arsenal of murder weapons. My answer to that proposal is no. 'No' unconditionally. 'No' emphatically and 'No Surrender' finally.[186]

While the UUP might laugh off attacks from Sammy Wilson who wondered aloud at the DUP party conference whether the Ulster Unionists were led by 'David and the Tremblers',[187] the vitriol hurled at his party clearly stung Trimble. The UUP leader tried to seize the moral high ground and condemned the DUP for shattering unionist unity.

> I am very sad at what has happened now. It seems that the commitment of some people in the DUP is only skin deep. The crude abuse that we saw is quite inconsistent with a desire for unity. I remember when I first met Dr Paisley, after becoming leader, I suggested to him that we should co-operate where we could and if the circumstances were such that we couldn't co-operate we should at least have a non-aggression pact. I have endeavoured to co-operate. . . . I'm sorry that the good mood created has now been dispelled by the immaturity of some members of the DUP.[188]

Even had he wanted to move in a progressive direction towards a compromise with the SDLP (which is unlikely), the catalogue of abuse detailed above has acted as a disincentive for Trimble to engage in such action. The fear of being undercut by the loudest voice – which for the last thirty years has been owned by Ian Paisley – has been an important dynamic within unionist politics. David Trimble has had first-hand experience of this damaging trait in unionist politics as he was a member of the Vanguard Party when its leader, Bill Craig, advocated the 'voluntary coalition scheme' in May 1975. For its day, this was a progressive proposal for internal power-sharing, albeit on a transitional and temporary basis, but it lost support within the unionist community when Ian Paisley condemned it as a compromise too far. While Trimble sided with Craig, Vanguard split, and both the party and Bill Craig's political career went into a terminal decline, many activists within the movement, including Trimble, eventually re-entering the UUP.

David Trimble has spent much of his time as leader of the UUP attempting to act as a brake on any efforts by the British government to concede ground to Sinn Féin and lobbying hard for the establishment in Northern Ireland of an elected body as an essential ingredient of any renewed round of interparty talks. He quickly made a linkage between accepting Sinn Féin's entry into the political process and the UUP's demand for the creation of an elected body.

There are several reasons which explain Trimble's attachment since his election to the concept of a locally elected assembly, and why this idea has also proved popular within the DUP. After the strict choreography associated with government initiatives such as the Brooke–Mayhew Talks of 1991–92, an elected body attracted unionists who wanted a greater degree of control over the political process. Rather than simply reacting to Anglo-Irish initiatives, unionists hoped that by moving the centre of the political universe to Belfast, they would be more able to control the pace and nature of political developments. Secondly, the institutionalisation of Strand One of the talks process is attractive to unionists because it compartmentalises (critics would say elevates) the internal element from the external dimension to the negotiations. In addition, it formally insulates Strand One against interference from the Irish government. Disagreement about the role of the Irish government in the political process – when and on what basis they would enter discussions – was a constant theme of the Brooke– Mayhew Talks.

In November 1995, Trimble took his ideas for an elected forum to the United States where, according to the UUP leader, President Clinton, Vice-President Al Gore and National Security Adviser Anthony Lake 'told me that they should be marked down on the list of those interested'.[189] Hardly a ringing endorsement but a start nonetheless. Trimble advocated an elected assembly in a *Sunday Tribune* interview on 5 November, promoting it as a mechanism to facilitate the entry of Sinn Féin into the democratic arena.

We are a long way from serious [peace] negotiations. Sinn Féin has a lot to do. There are a lot of difficulties – not least the human one of engaging and discussing with people who have not yet clearly and visibly changed. And that is one of the ways an assembly would be helpful because it will give them (Sinn Féin) an opportunity to show to people they have changed.[190]

The DUP were also adamant that the creation of an elected assembly was a necessary precondition before they would re-engage in another round of interparty negotiations. Apart, therefore, from its inherent desirability, by pushing it so consistently throughout 1995–96, the leaders of the two main unionist parties tied a certain amount of their own personal authority to the idea. While the final form of the Forum is significantly different in function to that originally conceived by Trimble and Paisley, in institutional terms at least they have succeeded in delivering to their supporters what they set out to achieve, a physical symbol of the integrity of the Northern Ireland state.

A further reason why the main unionist parties wanted elections before beginning interparty negotiations was as a means of insulating their own positions. David Trimble does not intend to be the first unionist leader of recent years to negotiate with Sinn Féin unless he is given a mandate to do so from UUP supporters. Similarly, Ian Paisley will not have forgotten the defections from his party during the dog days of the Mayhew Talks, occasioned by his entry into Strand Two discussions with Dublin in advance of the removal of Articles 2 and 3 of the Irish constitution. A process which is endorsed at the ballot-box, therefore, mandates Trimble and Paisley to act accordingly.

In an effort to overcome the difficulties surrounding the IRA's unwillingness to unilaterally decommission their weapons, and the adamant refusal by unionists to engage with Sinn Féin until such a verifiable process got under way, the former American senator and President Clinton's special economic adviser on Northern Ireland, George Mitchell, was asked to lead an international decommissioning body to advise on the matter.[191] The Mitchell Commission began its work in early December 1995 and having taken submissions from political parties (the DUP refused to co-operate on the grounds that by internationalising the matter Britain was compromising its sovereignty over Northern Ireland) and other interested groups and individuals, it published its report on 24 January 1996. In objective terms, the Mitchell Report was an admirable achievement, using Solomon-like judgement to address the obstacles in the way of political dialogue. The initial unionist reaction was unfavourable, due to the apparent removal of the Washington 3 principle (that some decommissioning must take place before talks commence). Ian Paisley condemned the report and claimed that from the beginning the commission had been a device to allow the British government to dilute the decommissioning issue.

> Any talks that took place on this basis would still be overshadowed by the spectre of the IRA gunmen. There would be no level playing field. Talks would be taking place with the IRA gun literally at the head of unionist negotiators. The IRA must be dismantled as an organisation so that it no longer threatens or intimidates anyone in Northern Ireland. . . . The setting up of this commission internationalised an issue which is at the very heart of the British government's sovereign jurisdiction and its recommendations were always going to be used as a stick with which to beat those who do not accept the legitimacy of IRA/Sinn Féin.[192]

The UUP reaction to the Mitchell Report was more restrained, though David Trimble did declare his concern that simply to recognise the IRA's unwillingness to decommission its weapons as a 'reality' was a problem which indicated that little had been changed by the commission. 'It's the same problem that we've had before, that we are not in a position to move towards all-party talks because of the refusal of one party to meet the requirements which were clearly spelt out in advance and which are not unreasonable. . . . I don't know that the report has changed anything.'[193] Trimble's mood improved considerably the same afternoon when John Major, who had received the Mitchell Report twenty-four hours earlier, stood up in the House of Commons and announced, not that the twin-track policy of all-party talks and parallel decommissioning would begin immediately, but that the best mechanism to facilitate these negotiations was through 'an elective process' in Northern Ireland. While David Trimble was happy that his longed-for elected body seemed to be on the brink of being achieved, nationalists in Northern Ireand were incensed. Notwithstanding the fact that the Mitchell Report set out six fundamental anti-violence principles which it saw as incumbent upon all the protagonists to accept and honour,[194] Sinn Féin president Gerry Adams had initially welcomed the findings of the commission. 'It provides a basis for moving forward so that all matters can be settled to the satisfaction of all sides as part of the process. It points to a possible avenue into all-party talks.'[195] However, after Major's statement at Westminster, nationalist opinion hardened, with John Hume launching a bitter attack on the Prime Minister in the House of Commons, while Gerry Adams condemned the British government for 'binning' the report. For the republican community in Northern Ireland, this was the *coup de grâce* for the peace process and a signal that the British government were not seriously interested in achieving a political settlement. John Major's response to the Mitchell Report was the final straw for the IRA ceasefire and led directly to the bombing of Canary Wharf in London on 9 February 1996 and the ending of the IRA's 'complete cessation of military operations'. Over the next four months, the British and Irish governments tried to keep the political process afloat by scheduling elections to a forum to be held on 30 May, leading directly to all-party negotiations on 10 June. The intention was to entice the IRA to renew their ceasefire by stipulating that this would be a condition of Sinn Féin's entry into the talks. The familiar diplomatic two-step then ensued as British and Irish officials tried to keep the various parties signed up to the process, an exercise destined ultimately to satisfy no one. The machinations surrounding the elections dragged out into a farce in an attempt to satisfy the competing demands of the various parties and ensure some representation in the Forum from the 'fringe' loyalist parties.

While the SDLP grudgingly agreed to go along with the elections on the basis that they were merely an irritating entry point to the all-party negotiations on 10 June, unionists also became less enamoured with the process. This was not just because of the hybrid electoral system which was used, which David Trimble alleged was destined to 'shred the unionist vote', but because the British government, under pressure from the Irish government and the SDLP, watered down the significance of the elected body to the point of decoupling it from the negotiating process. The original idea, as conceived by unionists, was that the assembly would be an integral part of the process which would inform, monitor and underpin the negotiations. In February 1996, the UUP published proposals for a ninety-member elected body and suggested that such a structure could lead to all-party negotiations over the internal governance and external relations of Northern Ireland. The document, entitled *The Democratic Imperative*, advocated the establishment of an assembly which would appoint committees, based on proportionality, to consider matters relating to all three strands of the negotiating process. Eventually, the body would prepare a report for the Secretary of State presenting its proposals for future political structures relating to Northern Ireland and these would be placed before the British parliament and the Northern Ireland electorate by means of a referendum before implementation.

The British government conceded the unionist demand for an elected body in return for the UUP's acceptance of the Mitchell Report, and in particular the dropping of the Washington 3 principle. The difference between Washington 3 and the eventual position of the British government, that decommissioning of weapons must be 'seriously addressed' as the first item on the agenda, is ambiguous, and, in the event of a renewed IRA cease-fire, would doubtless result in semantic wrestling over whether Sinn Féin were 'addressing' decommissioning or not. However, at the very least this was a symbolic climbdown by the government. When the scale of nationalist opposition to the idea of a Stormont assembly (however transitory) became clear, London tried to keep the SDLP on board by making a clear distinction between the all-party negotiations and the assembly. From this point the elected body was merely to be the reservoir from which the negotiating teams were drawn, and the power balance between the assembly and the negotiations duly became weighted in favour of the latter. Crucially, from the SDLP point of view, the assembly was free-standing; it did not have any power of veto over the negotiations nor would it be able to delay them. Initially, the SDLP were extremely concerned that the elected body would control the pace and have an input into the proceedings of all-party negotiations. Their worry was that unionists would prevaricate endlessly in the Forum about decommissioning and other concerns such as Articles 2 and 3, thus holding up the negotiations and extending the longevity of the internal arrangements.

These implications for the assembly's remit were not well received within certain sections of unionism. Speaking after the second reading of the election legislation in mid-April, Ian Paisley's ardour for the process had cooled noticeably. 'We see in this Bill a rigging of the election system. And we also see a great conspiracy to weaken the forum when it is elected. And I think that that is a tragedy.'[196]

The SDLP opposed the elections and the Forum on the practical grounds that elections created increased polarisation within the community which would make negotiation more difficult and that a 110-member body was hardly necessary to determine three-person negotiating teams. These were undoubtedly real concerns but SDLP opposition was more fundamental. Partly, this was a spillover from the general British handling of the peace process which many within the nationalist community regarded as being dominated by the government's reliance on unionist votes at Westminster. This perception – whether real or imagined – has damaged Britain's ability to present itself to Northern nationalists as a neutral arbiter. Many were angry with the British government and blamed them for wrecking the peace process, while at the same time recognising that the ultimate moral culpability rested with the IRA. As with any other political party, attitudes within the SDLP towards the elections and the assembly spanned a broad range of opinion. While few SDLP supporters were enthusiastic and recognised that at best the elections could be seen as a necessary evil, others believed they were a ruse by the British government to institutionalise the culture of an internal settlement. While Sinn Féin's attitude to the elections and assembly was both predictable and consistent (they would renew their mandate but boycott the assembly), the SDLP position evolved in accordance with the changing remit of the elected body.

The Forum elections

The elections of 30 May 1996 to supply delegates to the Forum from which negotiators would be drawn to enter into wide-ranging interparty talks produced few surprises. As expected, the weeks preceding the poll led to the creation of more heat than light. At least two things were certain to result from this exercise. Firstly, none of the traditional parties would move in a progressive direction towards their political opponents, and secondly, unionism would fracture along reactionary lines. In the normal run of affairs, unionists talk about unity between elections and tear at one another's throats during them. The Forum elections of 30 May did nothing to alter this trend, as unionists jockeyed with one another for the favour of the voters. An examination of the rival manifestos of the UUP and DUP demonstrates the point. While the UUP's *Building your future within the Union* provided a positive message about the future and the party's ability to deliver its vision, it couldn't resist taking a swipe at its main rival for the unionist vote. 'The UUP exists to serve the people by advancing and promoting the UNION. It has never been the party of extravagant talk and improvised stunts.'[197] Though the UUP manifesto is to be commended for saying that the party would be approaching the Forum and talks positively and that while vigorously defending the unionist case, they would also 'be listening to the views and concerns of others',[198] the party were not above scaremongering to mobilise their vote.

> The so-called hybrid electoral system to be used in the Forum election has been foisted upon us with the support of an unholy alliance between Dr Paisley and John Hume. It is cynically designed to SHRED the Unionist vote and weaken the pro-Union voice in the Forum. Up to 11 parties or groups will be seeking to obtain votes from pro-Union electors. This lunacy cannot continue without inflicting irreparable damage to the pro- Union cause. THE BEST WAY OF FRUSTRATING THIS PLOY IS TO GIVE THE UUP A MASSIVE AND RESOUNDING VOTE ON 30TH MAY.[199]

The DUP manifesto attempted to capitalise on the identity of the leader[200] and the fact that the party were seen by many unionists to have provided a more accurate analysis of the political situation since the signing of the Downing Street Declaration in December 1993. The DUP's election communication, entitled *The Unionist Team You Can Trust*, played on the fears of their supporters and warned that only the DUP were strong enough to protect them. The message was the oldest one in the unionist political lexicon: Protestants in Northern Ireland were under siege and only strong leaders who would give nothing away to their enemies could be trusted with Northern Ireland's political future.

> The central question in this election is simple. Who do you trust to negotiate your future and the future of Northern Ireland? The record shows that for unionists there can only be one answer. Over the years the DUP has proved it is the party which will fearlessly contend for the unionist cause and resist all attempts to undermine Ulster's constitutional position. The Forum and the negotiations are not places for faint-hearted or white-flag

unionists. What Ulster needs [are] men and women who will not be bribed, bought or intimidated into the surrender of any more ground to republicanism. The DUP's judgment of the bogus IRA ceasefire, the Downing Street Declaration sell-out and the treacherous Framework Document, has been totally vindicated. You can have no trust in those other unionists who got it completely wrong. . . . Never before has there been such a concentrated effort by republicans to destroy the very foundations of Northern Ireland. Never before has a strong DUP team led by Ian Paisley been more necessary. Ulster is at the crossroads.[201]

While the DUP literature for the elections was full of things they would not do – talk to Sinn Féin, engage in political compromise etc. – arguably the most positive statements were provided in the manifestos of the Ulster Democratic Party and the Progressive Unionist Party. While neither gave any indication that they would countenance a weakening of Northern Ireland's constitutional position within the United Kingdom, both placed the emphasis upon the political future of Northern Ireland rather than its past. Whether this sort of message was a vote-winner within working-class Protestant areas in Northern Ireland was another matter.

The rhetorical battle between the UUP and DUP went up several decibels as polling day approached and each accused the other of splitting unionism and letting the 'pan-nationalists' win by default. On a radio interview a week before the vote, David Trimble took a swipe at another leading unionist personality, Robert McCartney, for standing in the election under his party banner of UK Unionist.[202] When asked by a member of the public about McCartney's appeal for a pan-unionist pact in the Forum after the election to maximise their influence in the new structure, the UUP leader's response was lukewarm.

I think it's highly regrettable that we see new parties being formed, formed quite unnecessarily, and there is no need for this plethora of new parties being brought into existence simply to divide unionism further, and I think those that talk about unity would be better actually practising a little . . . we need to have a single unionist party, that's the long and the short of it. What we don't need to have is people coming and forming new parties and proceeding to divide unionism on the basis of their own personality. And I hope the voters will do what they can to unite unionism in the way they cast their preference.[203]

Three days before the elections the UUP deputy leader John Taylor told a press conference in Belfast that the DUP had played into the hands of nationalists by advocating a list system of proportional representation rather than the usual single transferable vote. As a visual aid, Taylor displayed a poster which showed a splintered Union Jack flag as a metaphor for the divided unionist vote. Taylor said that there were too many unionist parties standing and the fault lay with the DUP's promotion of the list. 'It is a means of dividing up the strength of the pro-Union vote throughout Northern Ireland. We regret very much that the DUP played into the hands of the SDLP and the Dublin Government, and supported this List system.'[204]

The DUP responded to this attack by accusing the UUP of being soft on the crucial issue of Northern Ireland's position within the United Kingdom. Ian Paisley claimed that it was the UUP rather than his party which were damaging the unity of the unionist community by agreeing that the Government of Ireland Act, which had in effect created Northern Ireland in 1920, could be on the table for discussion during interparty negotiations.[205]

> The split has come in unionism because Mr Trimble and Mr Taylor have split away from traditional philosophy. I never thought I'd live to see the day when the leader of the Unionist Party [sic] would make such a statement about the 1920 Act. You have to deal with two things in this election. You have to deal with the frontal attack on the Union, and you have to deal with the treachery inside the unionist camp. And it is an act of great treachery, for a unionist that claims to wear the mantle of Craigavon and Carson, to say that the Act that founded Northern Ireland is just a technical point, it could be repealed tomorrow and it wouldn't matter. It is a unionist leader, sitting at a negotiating table, who can do more damage to the Union when he takes up that attitude than the others can do. That is a major split and departure and it is my business to expose that. . . . I am critical of Glengall Street, because it is destroying the Union by their attitude. And I ask a question. If Mr Trimble, before he enters the talks, is prepared to have the repeal of the Government of Ireland Act and call it a technicality, what will he surrender when he's in the talks? I have seen his toing and froing to Dublin, so have the Ulster people. I happened to stop at a chip shop in Lurgan on Saturday, and the chip shop suddenly filled up with people who wanted to shake me by the hand, and one man said: 'Mr Paisley go home, you don't need to canvass, for every time Trimble opens his mouth he gets you thousands of votes.'[206]

This row presented in microcosm an example of the negative dynamics within unionist politics, caused on one level by the necessity of competing organisations to denigrate others in the search for electoral support, and motivated also by the alternative political cultures within the ideology which fashioned political behaviour. In this case, Trimble was the victim of seventy years of unionist rhetoric and, by suggesting flexibility over the Government of Ireland Act, he had opened himself to accusations of treachery. This was the latest in a long line of examples of the risk faced by any unionist leader in stepping forward and saying something new, as opponents within the ideology were sure to shout that betrayal was at hand. As Trimble was to find out, merely to be right in Irish politics does not mean that you will win the argument. Often, when myth and reality compete for belief, it is the former which triumphs over the latter. The dispute was also caused by the different political cultures within unionism along the lines of the ideological definitions explicated in previous chapters of this book. While the DUP exhibit an insular mentality and translate this into their political behaviour, refusing to participate in structures which do not meet with their approval, the UUP generally take a more pragmatic approach conscious of audiences beyond Northern Ireland. David Trimble demonstrated this when defending himself against Ian Paisley's attack.

> We are not putting the Union on the table. We will be there to defend the Union, unlike some other people who either won't be there or say they are going to run out [of] the room and leave the Union undefended. We will be there to ensure that the Act of Union, and it's the Act of Union that matters. . . . If the nationalists try to put the Act of Union on the table, we will take it off the table, and we'll be there to do that, so those people who want to see the Union defended, should realise that it's only the Ulster Unionist Party that's going to be actively doing that.[207]

Thus, while David Trimble stressed that the UUP would be engaged in the political process, the rationale he used to defend the party's position was a negative one. Scared of losing votes to those who presented the most frightening scenario to the unionist community, the UUP leader (whether he wanted to or not) was forced to do the same thing, by saying in effect, 'vote for the UUP because we will be better at saying "no" than the DUP'. This was a tactic of dubious propriety as no one in Northern Ireland can 'scare the horses' as effectively as the leader of the DUP. Trimble's attempt to raise fears about the security of the Union could therefore have succeeded merely in doing Ian Paisley's electioneering for him and scaring his own supporters into voting for the DUP. In the event, however, while the UUP vote was slightly down on previous elections it held up in relation to that of the DUP, gaining thirty seats in the Forum compared to the DUP's twenty-four seats. Despite Paisley's attempt to turn the event into a European election, the DUP did not top the poll but came third [in terms of percentage of the vote] behind the UUP and the SDLP.[208]

Undoubtedly the most dramatic result of the Forum election came within the nationalist rather than the unionist camp. Sinn Féin's vote rose to over 15 per cent while the SDLP vote was down slightly on previous contests. As ever with elections, attention focused on seats won rather than votes, and here the differential between the two main nationalist parties was reduced due to the idiosyncrasies of the electoral system, with Sinn Féin gaining seventeen seats to the SDLP's twenty-one.[209]

Perhaps the most interesting aspect of the election was the performance of the smaller parties, notably the fringe loyalists and the innovative Northern Ireland Women's Coalition. While neither the Progressive Unionist Party nor the Ulster Democratic Party won any seats from the constituency lists, both put up a creditable performance overall and comfortably came in the top-ten league table of parties, guaranteeing them two seats each from the top-up regional list to the Forum and any subsequent negotiations. The best result for the PUP came in North Belfast, where Billy Hutchinson narrowly lost out to the DUP for the last seat. Due to the vagaries of the electoral system, the PUP were the fifth largest party in North Belfast but did not win any of the five seats in the constituency.

A similar story was true of the Northern Ireland Women's Coalition, a cross-party group which came together to highlight the gender imbalance in Northern Ireland politics and provide the opportunity to promote women in the political process. While they realised the difficulty of winning a seat from the constituency list system, they polled sufficient votes across Northern Ireland to come ninth in the top-ten league table of parties. There are obvious problems with the Women's Coalition as it currently stands. Voting for women because they are women, rather than because of what they believe in or stand for, indicates a tokenistic and unsustainable mechanism for advancing women in the political process. In fairness this was not how they presented themselves. The message was not simply to vote for women, but rather to vote for women who were committed to a 'multi-cultural, multi-ethnic, multi-religious society with respect and equality for all'.[210] However, broad principles such as these may not be enough to ensure that the movement survives in its present form given the zero-sum nature of the current political environment. Despite these difficulties, the Women's Coalition have achieved their aim of getting the gender imbalance into the political debate, with most of the traditional parties feeling obliged to seriously discuss the issue and inform the electorate of what steps they are taking to promote women within the political process. From a standing start – not having so much as a fax machine six weeks before the election – they obtained a mandate from the Northern Ireland electorate and outpolled other parties with a much longer history and well-oiled machine such as the Workers Party. Clearly, in the more traditional single transferable vote form of proportional representation, a women's movement could expect to gain substantial transfers from both unionist and nationalist parties.

As far as unionism was concerned, the necessity, illustrated by the election, to defend traditional positions rather than engage in new thinking or more inclusive dialogue for fear of being undercut by competitors may explain David Trimble's reference, in an *Irish Times* article prior to the vote, to 'the little Hitlers in the Department of Foreign Affairs and their accomplices in Stormont Castle'.[211] While this may have been effective electoral politics, it was not leading the unionist community towards a political settlement with nationalists within Northern Ireland. Where David Trimble can lead the unionist community, rather than where he can follow them, will be his ultimate test as leader of the Ulster Unionist Party.

As for the future of the 'some party' talks, perhaps the most pertinent comment was provided by a noticeboard outside St Anne's Cathedral in Belfast, which read: 'You can play a part in the political talks. Drop in and say a prayer.'

Notes

1   In 1993 eighty-four people were killed in Northern Ireland as a consequence of political violence while in England three people died. In 1992 eighty-five people were killed as a direct result of the conflict.

2   Allegedly Eamonn McCann saw Adams on Hume's doorstep. The story appeared in the *Sunday Tribune* the following day. However, anyone with the slightest knowledge of republican politics knows that they can keep a secret when they want to. It would be fair to assume therefore that this rather cavalier approach to confidentiality indicated that the time had come to go public on the dialogue.

3   Public statement issued by John Hume and Gerry Adams after their meeting of 23 April 1993, in B. Rowan, *Behind the Lines* (Belfast, 1995), p. 47.

4   Gordon Wilson was the father of Marie Wilson, one of the victims of the Enniskillen bombing in 1987. He subsequently devoted his life to working for the end of political violence in Northern Ireland and was appointed to the Irish Senate in recognition of his commitment to peace. On 7 April 1993 Mr Wilson met with representatives of the IRA to ask them to end their campaign. While the IRA apologised to Mr Wilson for the death of his daughter, their subsequent statement suggested little movement. Mr Wilson admitted as much in a press conference on 8 April. 'It became very clear to me very early on that the response they had made was that there was no change in their position. Perhaps it was naive of me to suppose that because it was me they would change their position. . . . It seemed to me that their position was entrenched. It seemed to me that nothing that I had said had in any way moved them from their stated position.' In P. Bew and G. Gillespie, *Northern Ireland: A Chronology of the Troubles 1968–1993* (Dublin, 1993), p. 296.

5   *News Letter*, 12 April 1993, p. 7.

6   ibid., 13 April 1993, p. 11.

7   *Fortnight*, No. 317, May 1993, p. 5.

8   E. Mallie and D. McKittrick, *The Fight for Peace* (London, 1996) p. 216.

9   ibid. The high priest of this set was one-time Irish politician turned journalist Conor Cruise O'Brien. Not content with attacking John Hume, he spread his net in wider circles, alleging on one occasion that the respected independent journalist Mary Holland exhibited in her writing for the *Observer* 'a partisan attitude to the IRA'. While this resulted in the following humble apology several weeks later, (perhaps under threat of legal action), the episode was indicative of the venom which could be spat at those commentators who did not buy in sufficiently to the revisionist line of the *Sunday Independent* epitomised by O'Brien.

> In my letter of 17 July last . . . I stated that Mary Holland had a 'partisan attitude to the IRA.' I now accept that she did not have and does not have a 'partisan attitude to the IRA.' I therefore repudiate and withdraw the allegation contained in my published letter of 17 July 1994 and I express my sincere regret to Mary Holland for any hurt or upset caused to her as a result. *Sunday Tribune*, 11 September 1994, p. A17.

10   Rowan, *Behind the Lines*, p. 49.

11 *Belfast Telegraph*, 23 April 1993, p. 1.

12 Rowan, *Behind the Lines*, p. 50.

13 *Belfast Telegraph*, 23 April 1993, p. 1.

14 ibid.

15 *News Letter*, 21 April 1993, p. 6.

16 ibid.

17 ibid., 26 April 1993, p. 8.

18 ibid., p. 6.

19 ibid., p. 8.

20 ibid.

21 ibid., 27 April 1993, p. 8.

22 *Fortnight*, No. 318 (June 1993), p. 5.

23 *Belfast Telegraph*, 27 April 1993, p. 3.

24 *News Letter,* 29 April 1993, p. 1.

25 *Belfast Telegraph,* 28 April 1993, p. 6.

26 *News Letter,* 29 April 1993, p. 1.

27 *Belfast Telegraph,* 28 April 1993, p. 6.

28 The results of the elections were that the UUP returned with 197 seats and 29.0% of the first preference vote (in 1989 the UUP won 194 seats and 31.3%). The DUP won 103 seats and 17.2% of the vote (in 1989 the DUP won 110 seats and 17.7%). The SDLP won 127 seats and 21.9% (in 1989 the SDLP won 121 seats and 21.0%). Sinn Féin won 51 seats and 12.5% (in 1989 Sinn Féin won 43 seats and 11.2%). Alliance won 44 seats and 7.7% (in 1989 Alliance won 38 seats and 6.9%). In Bew and Gillespie *Northern Ireland: A Chronology,* pp. 299–300.

29 Ulster Democratic Unionist Party, 1993 local government election manifesto, *'93 Election Special* (Belfast, 1993), p. 1

30 ibid., p. 2.

31 UUP, 1993 local government election manifesto, *Accountable Democracy* (Belfast, 1993), p. 4.

32 *News Letter,* 6 May 1993, p. 2.

33 ibid., 17 May 1993, p. 7.

34 ibid., 7 June 1993, p. 6.

35 ibid., 29 June 1993, p. 1.

36 ibid., 14 June 1993, p. 5.

37 Robinson reportedly said: 'Prime Minister John Major has publicly indicated that the USA was completely justified in dropping 23 Cruise missiles on Baghdad because it is alleged they had attempted to carry out a bombing which would likely have resulted in the death of former President George Bush. On that same principle, the RAF should wipe out the IRA headquarters in Belfast and Dublin, who have not only attempted terrorist activities against the United Kingdom citizens, but who for years have been carrying them out.' *News Letter,* 29 June 1993, p. 7. The SDLP leader John Hume responded by saying: 'Dear God. Peter Robinson will make any statement to get publicity. I don't think his remarks will be taken seriously by anyone, including the vast majority of the unionist community.' ibid.

38 ibid., 17 June 1993, p. 4.

39 ibid.

40 ibid.

41 ibid., 18 June 1993, p. 9.

42 Belfast City Council is the largest seat of local government in Northern Ireland and traditionally one of the most divided along sectarian lines. The funniest characterisation of the council – if not necessarily the most representative one – is provided by the

Belfast-based journalist Francis Gorman. 'It's where Sam Peckinpah meets Brian Rix in a long running Hammer production, sponsored by the ratepayers. The *dramatis personae* are a motley, geriatric bunch of buffoons and banjo players. . . . Effectively, since the early '70s, Northern Ireland councils have only had real power over the B-Specials – bins, bogs and burials. Frequently during the first hour, the chamber degenerates into a bear pit. Then it gets worse. . . . Perched precariously on the press bench in the middle as the vitriol and venom flies, the screaming match is like an opera commissioned by Channel Four – cacophony No. 1 in No Particular Key.' 'Into the Bearpit', *Fortnight*, No. 318 (June 1993), pp. 17–18.

43 *News Letter*, 23 June 1993, p. 3.
44 It was not only unionists who took this view. Many politicians, cultural commentators and opinion formers in the Irish Republic took the view that Robinson's handshake with the Sinn Féin president was ill-advised. Such critics tended to be concentrated in that area of cultural geography known as 'Dublin 4'. It later emerged that the British government had advised against the visit but Taoiseach Albert Reynolds refused to ask the President to cancel it.
45 *News Letter*, 21 June 1993, p. 5.
46 Jonathan Moore, *Fortnight*, No. 320 (September 1993), p. 12.
47 Confusion surrounded the Hume–Adams agreement from the beginning, not just over issues such as the exercise of 'national self-determination' but with regard to its actual physical existence. The uncertainty was not helped by Hume's immediate departure for Boston where he was to attend a trade mission, while everyone in Ireland and Britain was left to 'twiddle their thumbs' until his return. The SDLP leader then admitted in Boston that no document actually existed which could be sent to Dublin but that he would give the Irish government a full briefing on his return. While the Hume–Adams agreement has not as yet been published, the heads of agreement reached between the two leaders are understood to contain the following assumptions. That the British government would declare publicly that it had no long-term interest in remaining in Ireland and would actively pursue unionist consent to that end. The right of the Irish people as a whole to national self-determination would be recognised by Britain and would be the price for the cessation of the IRA campaign. *Fortnight*, No. 322 (November 1993), pp. 32–3.
48 *Belfast Telegraph,* 27 September 1993, p. 1.
49 ibid., pp. 1 and 6.
50 ibid., 28 September 1993, p. 3.
51 On 21 September the *Belfast Telegraph* (p. 1) carried a statement from the UFF which said that it would continue to target 'pan-nationalists' while the Hume–Adams discussions took place.
52 *Fortnight*, No. 321, (October 1993), p. 32. This threat was withdrawn on 27 August.
53 While many people found Gerry Adams's action unpalatable, it was the product of Northern Ireland's harsh and unyielding *realpolitik*. Had the Sinn Féin president distanced himself from Begley, he would have committed one of the gravest sins within republicanism, weakened his personal position within the movement and damaged the chances of securing an IRA ceasefire. The analysis of Eamonn Mallie and David McKittrick of the incident is the most astute.

> He knew very well that this action would associate him with the worst excesses of the IRA, and would wipe out his years of work to put some distance between Sinn Féin and the IRA, but in republican terms he simply had no choice. . . . One of the most essential features of the republican attitude to the peace process, so important as to be really rule number one, was that if the republican movement

was to move away from violence it had to do so as a unified coherent entity. . . . Thomas Begley had been part of the republican movement and was carrying out IRA orders when he died: Adams disapproved of the attack itself, but could not disown the volunteer. He had carried the coffins of many IRA men during the troubles: his action in carrying Begley's created a stir in Britain but none in Belfast. In republican terms it would have been amazing for Adams to refrain from doing so, amounting to a dramatic renunciation of the IRA. It would have been nothing less than the end of him as a republican leader. Mallie and McKittrick, *The Fight for Peace*, pp. 201–2.

54 The following statement was issued by the UFF on 23 October 1993 in response to the Shankill bombing.

This afternoon the loyalist people of west Belfast were on the receiving end of a blatantly indiscriminate bomb attack supposedly aimed at the leadership of the UFF. The number of women and children killed is still unclear, but shows that this was a false claim. As and from 6pm all brigade area active service units of the UFF across Ulster will be mobilised. John Hume, Gerry Adams and the nationalist electorate will pay a heavy, heavy price for today's atrocity, which was signed, sealed and delivered by the cutting edge of the Pan Nationalist front. To the perpetrators of the atrocity we say: 'You will have no hiding place. Time is on our side.' And we would ask John Hume: 'Is this part of your peace?' *Belfast Telegraph*, 25 October 1993, p. 7.

55 *Fortnight*, No. 323 (December 1993), pp. 23–5.
56 Mallie and McKittrick, *The Fight for Peace*, p. 204.
57 *Belfast Telegraph*, 22 September 1993, p. 4.
58 *Guardian*, 1 November 1993, p. 2.
59 Dick Spring announced these in Dáil Éireann on 27 October. 'They were that: the people of Ireland, north and south, should freely determine their future; this could be expressed in new northern, north–south and east–west structures; there could be no change in the north's status without freely-given majority consent; such consent could be withheld; the consent principle could be inserted into the republic's constitution; and the republican movement could come to the table if violence were abandoned.' *Fortnight*, No. 323 (December 1993), p. 24.
60 *Belfast Telegraph*, 29 October 1993, p. 3.
61 ibid.
62 *Guardian*, 10 November 1993, p. 1.
63 ibid.
64 *Irish Times*, 17 November 1993, p. 4.
65 ibid.
66 ibid.
67 *Belfast Telegraph*, 25 November 1993, p. 6.
68 These contacts were so sensitive that Albert Reynolds, who was about to sign the Downing Street Declaration, was not told about them. The Irish government were annoyed by the revelations as, quite apart from the diplomatic subterfuge which had gone on behind their backs, it appeared that Britain had agreed to negotiate with Sinn Féin in return for a two-week ceasefire while in negotiations with Dublin, Britain had insisted that a permanent end to violence was essential before any contact could take place.
69 *Observer*, 28 November 1993, p. 1.
70 ibid., p. 3.
71 ibid. Mayhew could seemingly not get enough rope to hang himself with. On BBC Radio 4's *Today* programme on 16 November he declared: 'Nobody has been authorised to talk or negotiate on behalf of the British Government with Sinn Féin. We have always

made it clear that there will be no talking or negotiating with Sinn Féin or any other organisation that justifies violence.' On 22 November when questioned by the press, he again said that no official contact had taken place between the British government and Sinn Féin. When a reporter asked him how he would react if evidence came out which proved contrary to his statement, Mayhew said: 'I shall be very interested to see it.' ibid. Presumably he found the Sunday newspapers fascinating reading at the end of November.

72 Mallie and McKittrick, *The Fight for Peace*, p. 237.

73 *Irish Times*, 29 November 1993, p. 8.

74 ibid., 30 November 1993, p. 5. Mayhew's naming of McGuinness as being in the IRA leadership also begged the question as to why he did not have him arrested. As it's a proscribed organisation, it is a crime to be a member of the IRA. For the Secretary of State to identify him *in a leadership role* in such a matter of fact way seemed a trifle anomalous.

75 *Belfast Telegraph*, 30 November 1993, p. 15.

76 Mallie and McKittrick, *The Fight for Peace*, pp. 106–7.

77 *Irish Times*, 29 November 1993, p. 9.

78 ibid.

79 ibid.

80 The timing was curious, as the DUP was apparently the source of the leak (William McCrea claimed credit for obtaining the information) yet there were no direct references to it at the party conference when the story had already been released to the *Observer*. The explanation for this was that McCrea wanted to protect the source of the leak and wished to have the document authenticated before going public on the matter. He had the evidence in his pocket when the DUP delegation met John Major at Downing Street on 24 November but decided not to confront the Prime Minister for these reasons.

81 *Irish Times*, 29 November 1993, p. 11.

82 Rev. Ian Paisley, speech to DUP annual conference, 27 November 1993.

83 The Joint Declaration for Peace, para. 4, pp. 3–4.

84 J. McGarry and B. O'Leary, *Explaining Northern Ireland: Broken Images* (Oxford, 1995), p. 418.

85 The Joint Declaration for Peace, para. 5, p. 4.

86 F. Cochrane, 'Any Takers? The Isolation of Northern Ireland', *Political Studies*, 42(3) (1994), p. 395.

87 *Belfast Telegraph*, 15 December 1993, p. 3.

88 *News Letter*, 16 December 1993, p. 2.

89 While most observers knew that Sinn Féin and the IRA were not going to endorse the Joint Declaration, one authority on the organisation has pointed to the significance of the fact that they did not reject it out of hand given the extent of opposition which existed within the ranks. 'When the leadership sought the views of the brigades they found South Armagh totally against acceptance, Tyrone and Fermanagh ambivalent, Belfast divided. Overall, the IRA brigades came out about ninety to ten against the Declaration as it stood.' B. O'Brien, *The Long War* (Dublin, 1995), p. 303.

90 *News Letter*, 16 December 1993, p. 8.

91 *Belfast Telegraph*, 15 December 1993, p. 1.

92 *The Dagger of Treachery Strikes at the Heart of Ulster*, 1993, p. 3.

93 *News Letter*, 16 December 1993, p. 5.

94 ibid., p. 8.

95 *Belfast Telegraph*, 15 December 1993, pp. 1 and 6.

96 ibid., p. 6.

97 *News Letter*, 16 December 1993, p. 5.

98 ibid.
99 Peter Robinson, 'Gauntlet Thrown Down', Press Release, 21 December 1993, p. 1.
100 *News Letter,* 18 December 1993, p. 7.
101 *Belfast Telegraph,* 23 December 1993, p. 5.
102 *Irish Times,* 1 March 1994, p. 6.
103 ibid.
104 ibid.
105 ibid., 31 March 1994, p. 1.
106 ibid.
107 *Guardian,* 9 April 1994, p. 4.
108 *Irish Times,* 24 March 1994, p. 4.
109 Ulster Democratic Unionist Party, *European Election Manifesto* (Belfast, 1994), p. 1.
110 *Belfast Telegraph,* 17 May 1994, p. 6.
111 ibid., 31 May 1994, p. 4.
112 ibid.
113 ibid., 14 June 1994, p. 8.
114 ibid., 11 July 1994, p. 1. Interestingly, in view of the reaction which met Gerry Adams's
    carrying of Thomas Begley's coffin after the Shankill bombing in October 1993, DUP
    politicians Peter Robinson and Sammy Wilson were pictured carrying Smallwoods's
    coffin. While the two cases are not a direct parallel as Begley's victims were more recent
    and Smallwoods was convicted of less heinous crimes, to many nationalists it may
    have appeared that the two DUP politicians were demonstrating their solidarity with
    loyalist paramilitaries without the media batting an eyelid.
115 After the killing of Bratty and Elder in the flashpoint area of the Lower Ormeau Road
    in South Belfast, the SDLP councillor for the area, Alisdair McDonnell, advised his
    nationalist constituents to go on holiday if they could afford to.
116 *Belfast Telegraph,* 19 July 1994, p. 6.
117 ibid., p. 7.
118 ibid., 30 July 1994, p. 1.
119 *Irish News,* 29 August 1994, p. 3.
120 ibid., p. 1.
121 *Belfast Telegraph,* 30 August 1994, p. 6.
122 ibid., 29 August, 1994, p. 6.
123 *Irish Times,* 1 September 1994, p. 1.
124 ibid., 7 September 1994, p. 1.
125 ibid.
126 ibid.
127 Mallie and McKittrick, *The Fight for Peace,* p. 334.
128 *Irish Times,* 7 September 1994, p. 4.
129 *Observer,* 4 September 1994, p. 25.
130 *Irish Times,* 1 September 1994, p. 4.
131 ibid.
132 *Belfast Telegraph,* 30 August 1994, p. 6.
133 ibid., p. 1.
134 ibid., 31 August 1994, p. 3.
135 *Sunday Tribune,* 11 September 1994, p. 1.
136 Rowan, *Behind the Lines,* p. 116.
137 ibid., p. 127.
138 *Observer,* 4 December 1994, p. 7.
139 While the Frameworks Document was not finally published for another month, the
    version Molyneaux rejected was a plan for two intergovernmental bodies which would

be established as a default mechanism to supervise the smooth transition to democratic politics. One of these bodies would oversee a new assembly and executive while the other would concern itself with the operation of the services delivered by Northern Ireland's twenty-six district councils and health and education boards. These two Anglo-Irish bodies would be invested with the power to intervene and take over the functions of any of these subsequent structures if they failed to work effectively. *Sunday Tribune,* 27 January 1995, p. A4.

140 *Observer,* 27 January 1995.

141 *Sunday Tribune,* 27 January 1995, p. A4.

142 Henry Patterson, in *Sunday Tribune,* 12 February 1995.

143 More accurately referred to as *Frameworks for the Future,* it was actually two documents rather than one. The first was a document solely authored by the British government entitled: *A Framework for Accountable Government in Northern Ireland,* which dealt with possible ways of establishing devolution. The second, *A New Framework for Agreement,* was drawn up jointly by the British and Irish governments and concentrated on North–South relationships and British–Irish relationships.

144 *News Letter,* 23 February 1995, p. 1.

145 ibid.

146 *Times,* 23 February 1995, p. 1.

147 ibid.

148 *News Letter,* 23 February 1995, p. 7.

149 *Times,* 23 February 1995, p. 1.

150 *News Letter,* 23 February 1995, p. 6.

151 ibid.

152 *Belfast Telegraph,* 22 February 1995, p. 7.

153 Lee Reynolds, Press Release, 14 March 1995.

154 *Observer,* 16 July 1995, p. 7.

155 *News Letter,* 11 July 1995, p. 3.

156 The circumstances of the Lower Ormeau confrontation are specific as the Orange route took it past the Sean Graham bookmaker's shop where five people were shot dead by the UFF in February 1992. On 8 July the same year, when an Orange parade passed through the area, Orange marchers shouted 'Up the UFF' and held up five fingers in reference to the number who had died. While the Secretary of State Sir Patrick Mayhew commented that these actions 'would have disgraced a tribe of cannibals', it explains why Catholics in the Lower Ormeau area have taken a dim view of Orange processions past their district.

157 *News Letter,* 11 July 1995, p. 4.

158 A group was established within the Orange Order called the 'Spirit of Drumcree' and commemorative medals were struck in recognition of the roles played by David Trimble, and Jeffrey Donaldson of the UUP, and Ian Paisley of the DUP in the crisis. While these medals apparently initially spelt siege 'seige' – a word one might expect unionists to know how to spell – it perhaps signified how little they had to grasp on to for reassurance and how defensive many in the unionist community were feeling in 1995. Evidence of this was provided by the link made by some Orangemen between their desire to march and the wider political situation.

On 12 July the stand-off between Ballynafeigh Orangemen and the local nationalist residents was 'solved' when the police allowed the marchers to parade down Belfast's Lower Ormeau Road and blockaded all the side-streets, effectively trapping the residents in their houses. Robert Saulters, master of the Belfast Orange Lodge, made his position clear. 'We are being brain-washed by the peace process. We must be on our guard, study our history and fight for our institution as never before.' *Observer,* 16 July 1995, p. 7.

In Orange minds there was no confusion about what was at stake outside the town. The re-routing of an Orange parade in an isolated Co. Armagh laneside was inextricably linked to a much larger set of concerns: the future of the union, the threat of Irish unity they imagine is part of a ceasefire deal with the IRA, and their primeval fear of being swamped by Catholics. Ed Moloney, *Sunday Tribune*, 16 July 1995, p. 8.

159 As he was in his political life, so he was in his political death, taciturn. Molyneaux issued a two-sentence press release from Westminster on a bank holiday Monday morning, announcing his resignation and declaring that he would not be commenting further.

160 *Irish News*, 2 September 1995, p. 8.

161 *Sunday Tribune*, 3 September 1995, p. 7.

162 The result of the UUP leadership contest of 8 September 1995 was as follows.
First ballot: D. Trimble, 287; J. Taylor, 226; K. Maginnis, 117; W. Ross, 116; M. Smyth, 60. M. Smyth eliminated.
Second Ballot: D. Trimble, 353; J. Taylor, 255; K. Maginnis, 110; W. Ross, 91. W. Ross eliminated and K. Maginnis withdrew.
Third Ballot: D. Trimble, 466; J. Taylor, 333. D. Trimble elected.

163 *Irish News*, 9 September 1995, p. 1.

164 ibid.

165 *Independent*, 11 September 1995.

166 *Sunday Tribune*, 10 September 1995, p. 1.

167 *Irish News*, 2 September 1995, p. 8.

168 D. Sharrock, 'Preserving the Union?', *Fortnight*, No. 351 (June 1996), p. 15.

169 *Belfast Telegraph*, 18 September 1995, p. 6.

170 ibid., 5 February 1996, p. 5.

171 ibid., 21 October 1995.

172 ibid., 23 October 1995, p. 7.

173 BBC Radio Ulster, *Election Phone-In*, 24 May 1996.

174 *News Letter*, 18 October 1995, p. 1.

175 ibid. p. 4.

176 *Belfast Telegraph*, 18 October 1995, p. 1.

177 ibid., p. 5.

178 ibid., 31 October 1995, p. 5.

179 ibid.

180 *Sunday Tribune*, 5 November 1995.

181 ibid.

182 *Irish Times*, 6 December 1995, p. 5.

183 *Sunday Tribune*, 5 November 1995.

184 Peter Robinson, speech to DUP annual party conference, 25 November 1995.

185 ibid.

186 Rev. Ian Paisley, speech to DUP annual party conference, 25 November 1995.

187 Sammy Wilson told the best joke at a party conference for many years, a contention substantiated by the fact that it managed to force a smile out of Peter Robinson. Wilson knew his audience, and as the *Irish Times* journalist Gerry Moriarty reports, funny stories about the Pope are high on their list of approved subjects.

Sammy opened with a joke about the Pope. Pope John Paul has just flown in to the United States to meet President Clinton. A presidential aide greets him in a swanky limo. The Pope, complaining that it has been years since he has driven a car, begged for a turn behind the wheel. So the aide jumps into the back and Pope John Paul speeds off down the highway at 90 miles an hour. He's stopped by a motor-cycle cop, who seeing the Pope rushes back to radio his sergeant for advice. 'I've just stopped a big VIP, what'll I do?' the cop asked. 'Is the VIP a senator?' the sergeant asked. 'No, more important,' said the cop. 'Is it the vice-president?' 'No, more important,' said the cop. 'Don't tell me it's the president?' 'No, more important,' said the cop. 'Who can be more important than the president of the United States?' asked the anguished sergeant. 'I don't know,' said the cop, 'but the Pope's his driver.' *Irish Times,* 27 November 1995, p. 15.

188 *Irish News,* 28 November 1995, p. 1.

189 *Sunday Tribune,* 5 November 1995.

190 ibid.

191 The two other members of the commission were Mr Harri Holkeri, a former Prime Minister of Finland, and General John de Chastelain from Canada. The Mitchell Commission's remit was to provide an independent assessment of the decommissioning issue and to identify and advise the British and Irish governments on an acceptable method for decommissioning to be achieved. While the commission had no powers of enforcement, both governments had promised to seriously consider its recommendations.

192 *Belfast Telegraph,* 24 January 1996, p. 6.

193 ibid.

194 The six Mitchell principles required all participants to negotiations to affirm their total and absolute commitment:
- To democratic and exclusively peaceful means of resolving political issues.
- To the total disarmament of all paramilitary organisations.
- To agree that such disarmament must be verifiable to the satisfaction of an independent commission.
- To renounce for themselves and to oppose any effort by others to use force or threaten to use force to influence the course or the outcome of all-party negotiations.
- To agree to abide by the terms of any agreement reached in all-party negotiations and to resort to democratic and exclusively peaceful methods in trying to alter any aspect of that outcome with which they may disagree.
- To urge that 'punishment' killings and beatings stop and take effective steps to prevent such actions.

195 Mallie and McKittrick, *The Fight for Peace,* p. 361.

196 *Irish News,* 19 April 1996.

197 *Building your future within the Union,* UUP election communication (Belfast, May 1996).

198 ibid.

199 ibid.

200 Ian Paisley landed the first blow before the election even began by getting his party listed on the ballot paper as 'Democratic Unionist (DUP) Ian Paisley' rather than under its official title of the Ulster Democratic Unionist Party. This had two advantages. Firstly, by carrying Paisley's name alongside the name of the party, there was a greater chance of getting the sort of personal vote with which the DUP had topped the poll in the previous four European elections, compared to their more modest performances at Westminster general elections. Secondly, by dropping the word Ulster from their title, the DUP moved themselves up the ballot paper and avoided any potential confusion of voters caused by the plethora of parties with 'Ulster' in their title.

201 *The Unionist Team You Can Trust,* DUP election communication (Belfast, May 1996).

202 McCartney had obtained valuable publicity by signing up some high-profile running mates, notably the Southern Irish unionist Conor Cruise O'Brien and former Northern Ireland Housing Executive Chairman, John Gorman. The latter was paraded by McCartney to demonstrate that he was non-sectarian and did not discriminate against Catholics.

203 David Trimble on BBC Radio Ulster's *Election Phone-In*, 24 May 1996.

204 BBC Radio Ulster, *NewsBreak*, 27 May 1996.

205 The reason why the UUP were willing to be so accommodating on this issue was because the Government of Ireland Act is no longer crucial to the sovereign position of Northern Ireland within the United Kingdom and, save for a few clauses, has been superseded by legislation introduced in 1973 as part of the Sunningdale Agreement.

206 BBC Radio Ulster, *NewsBreak*, 27 May 1996.

207 ibid.

208 The DUP vote went up relative to that of the UUP partly as a result of the personality nature of the election and also because, with eleven pro-Union parties standing in the poll, votes were taken disproportionately from the UUP in comparison with the DUP.

   The DUP vote also held up in East Belfast where Peter Robinson and Sammy Wilson were both returned despite the surreal element introduced before the election when photographs were published in the Irish tabloid paper *Sunday World* of Sammy Wilson and a female friend cavorting naked in a field while on holiday. The effect of this embarrassment on what is traditionally a religiously conservative party was perhaps diminished by the fact that Wilson was standing in an urban rather than a rural constituency where the Free Presbyterian vote is less important than other radical aspects of their policy agenda.

209 The most dramatic result came in West Belfast where Sinn Féin polled almost twice as many votes as the SDLP and won four seats to the SDLP's one. The most ironic result in the election came in the Foyle constituency in Derry where Sinn Féin gained two seats and the SDLP three out of the five on offer. In an area then, which historically had been perhaps the greatest example of unionist gerrymandering during the years of the Stormont administration, unionists were left with no representation in the city. Sinn Féin's good performance was partly due to benefiting from general nationalist approval with the leadership of Gerry Adams and his relationship with SDLP leader John Hume; the existence of a *de facto* IRA ceasefire within Northern Ireland and consequently a degree of tactical voting from erstwhile SDLP voters in Foyle, South Down and Newry and Armagh in an attempt to demonstrate their anger with the British government and strengthen Gerry Adams's position within the republican movement to reinstate the IRA ceasefire.

210 *Vote For Change*, election communication from the Northern Ireland Women's coalition. Belfast, May 1996.

211 *Irish Times*, 29 May 1996, p. 12.

CHAPTER 9

Conclusion

I must be frank with you. I am sick to death of the daily chorus of division and diatribe from some of this party's headline hunters. They are all very keen to tell me what they think is needed. Well I know what this party needs –a lot less noise and a lot more loyalty. The Ulster Unionist Party is a broad church, but our interests are not served by a church so broad that it has several competing choirs and self-appointed preachers each with their own different gospels.[1]

David Trimble's plea to his party captures the essence of this book, namely, the difficulty unionism has had in agreeing on a common objective and devising a coherent strategy to achieve it. While this statement was made in 1999, it could just as easily have been made in 1985 or 1974.

This additional chapter to the book will take the story of unionist politics forward from 1997 until the UUP leadership challenge of March 2000. The analysis will concentrate on the trials and tribulations of unionist politics throughout this period, concentrating on the Good Friday Agreement (GFA) of 10 April 1998 and its faltering implementation. The chapter will end with some observations concerning the state of unionist politics today and the extent to which they have moved on since the first edition of the book was published.

Unionist politics before the Good Friday Agreement

The year preceding the Good Friday Agreement was a turbulent one, dominated by sporadic outbreaks of violence from loyalist and republican groups who were not on ceasefires, and glacial progress in the political negotiations at Stormont. The year 1997 was also a period of historic meetings and elections, which produced new governments in the United Kingdom and the Irish Republic, a renewed IRA 'cessation' and the first official meeting between Sinn Féin and the British government since the 1920s.

Unionist and nationalist politics were also dominated by elections in 1997. This determined much of the political discourse that took place, as most of the parties had one eye on each other in the negotiations, and the other on competitors within their own ideological bloc who might be competing for the affection of the voters. Within unionist politics, the familiar pattern of previous years was repeated, with the UUP casting their DUP rivals in the role of political vandals damaging the unionist cause, and themselves as the voice of reason, providing strategic leadership to the unionist community. The DUP for their part were keen to depict themselves as providing both principled and moral leadership, while castigating their UUP colleagues for being treacherous, untrustworthy and a danger to unionist political interests. It was predictable therefore that, while speaking to the annual general meeting of the Ulster Unionist Council (UUC) in March 1997, David Trimble tried to put clear water between the UUP and its main rival for the unionist vote.

> I disagree with the McCartneys and the Paisleys. . . . Their actions and attitudes have been counterproductive. They have let nationalists off the hook, they have driven London into the arms of Dublin. . . . The reasonable case we present is being obscured by aggressive, loudmouth unionists. This is not in the interests of the Union.[2]

Of course, the message that Trimble was sending to a frightened and defensive unionist electorate was that, regardless of their voluble rhetoric, the political competitors of the UUP were the ones jeopardising the unionist position. DUP deputy leader Peter Robinson condemned Trimble's remarks as 'vile, vicious and venomous'. In April meanwhile, Ian Paisley declared that 'David Trimble is going to sell out the Union.'[3] Clearly then, the political dynamics within unionism, generated by the imminent British General Election, did not augur well for the prospects of compromise within the multi-party talks taking place at Stormont.

In the event, the General Election that took place on 1 May 1997 resulted in a consolidation of the UUP position, winning ten seats and 32.7 per cent of the vote. The DUP meanwhile, with just two seats and 13.6 per cent of the vote, failed to gain support at the expense of its larger unionist partner. While this was good news for David Trimble's leadership of the UUP, few people noticed. It was Sinn Féin who stole the headlines, with 16.1 per cent of the vote and personal victories for Gerry Adams in West Belfast and Martin McGuinness in Mid-Ulster. McGuinness's election was a high-octane struggle between the Sinn Féin candidate (reviled by most unionists) and the sitting MP, Rev. William McCrea of the DUP. This contest was made all the more combustible by McCrea's appearance at a rally in support of loyalist paramilitary Billy Wright (aka King Rat) the previous year. Wright, leader of the Loyalist Volunteer Force, was believed by many to have been responsible for the murder of numerous Catholics within the constituency.

The General Election saw Tony Blair replace John Major as Prime Minister and Mo Mowlam succeed Sir Patrick Mayhew as Secretary of State. Hopes were high that these changes at the top would precipitate a restoration of the IRA ceasefire that had broken down in February 1996, according to republicans, because of Major's reliance on unionist votes at Westminster. However, on Blair's first visit to Northern Ireland on 16 May, unionist spirits were lifted by what he had to say while many republican hearts sank. In a speech given at the Royal Ulster Agricultural Show (also referred to as Blair's Balmoral speech), the Prime Minister set out to reassure nervous unionists that the new Labour government was not intent on promoting a nationalist agenda. 'My message is simple. I am committed to Northern Ireland. I am committed to the principle of consent. . . . My agenda is not a united Ireland. . . . The Union binds the four parts of the United Kingdom together. I believe in the United Kingdom. I value the Union.'[4] While Gerry Adams criticised Blair after his speech for recycling the 'old failed rhetoric of the past', Sinn Féin were happy to put it down to the fact that the *appératchiks* within the Northern Ireland Office had not yet been issued with their new orders! Blair's strategy was clear therefore from the first days he entered office: reassure nervous unionists, reduce their fear and insecurity that the peace process contained a preordained outcome, in the hope that this would produce a more positive attitude from unionists within political negotiations. This calming of unionist nerves would prove to be one of the most enduring *leit-motifs* of the peace process for the next several years.

The aim of the new government was to inject the peace process with fresh momentum by firstly, getting the IRA ceasefire restored and secondly, re-energising the negotiations at Stormont, ideally to include Sinn Féin following another IRA cessation. Few people were surprised when, on 20 July, the IRA announced an unequivocal restoration of the 1994 ceasefire. Events within unionist politics gathered pace after this point. On 21 July, Robert McCartney's United Kingdom Unionist Party and the DUP announced their withdrawal from the multi-party talks due to the imminent arrival of Sinn Féin into the negotiations. This surprised no one, the crucial question being whether the UUP would remain in the process when Sinn Féin formally joined the talks in September. In an ironic reflection of a familiar Sinn Féin tactic, the UUP embarked on a 'fact-finding' mission to canvass opinion from the grass-roots of the party. Despite some underwhelming support from his senior colleagues,[5] David Trimble refrained from committing himself either way, and used this consultation exercise as 'cloud cover' for the most pragmatic of prevarications. It would be reasonable to conclude that Trimble was waiting to gauge support within the party before committing himself either way on the issue. Given the nature of the party he was trying to lead, and the increasingly audible chundering from some of his senior colleagues, it is difficult to blame him.

On 29 August Mo Mowlam accepted the 'veracity' of the IRA ceasefire and Sinn Féin were formally invited to attend the negotiations, scheduled to resume on 15 September. One of the most enduring images of the peace process came two days later, when the UUP entered Castle Buildings at

Stormont in a phalanx with the loyalist parties the PUP and UDP, to finally begin negotiations with Sinn Féin. A slice of radical *chic* perhaps for the bespectacled leader, though an astute move by Trimble nonetheless. The message this sent out to the wider unionist community was that Trimble was not isolated and that his party had allies within the negotiations, despite the 'noises-off' being made by opponents such as Ian Paisley and Robert McCartney.

In form if not substance, this was an historic moment in unionist history and in the political history of Northern Ireland more generally. For the first time, all of the major parties (with the exception of the DUP) were in the same negotiating process, at the same venue, at the same time, and even in the same room together, in talks co-sponsored by the two sovereign governments with international third-party mediators led by George Mitchell.

In practice, however, many of the participants in the negotiations spent the rest of the year either not talking directly to one another, or else talking at one another without listening. While Sinn Féin accused the unionists of refusing to properly 'engage' with them or address the 'equality agenda', unionists responded that there was little point in doing so as Sinn Féin were 'on a different planet'.

If 1997 was an eventful year for unionism, then the following year was cataclysmic. The year 1998 was one that scaled euphoric heights upon the signing of the Good Friday Agreement on 10 April, and plunged to the depths of despair with the Omagh bombing that killed twenty-nine people on 15 August. This was a roller-coaster year of sticking points and turning points in the peace process, when the people of Northern Ireland waited to see if the 'war' really was over, and became directly involved themselves in making this a reality, by voting in a referendum on the Agreement in May. However, the year did not begin auspiciously. On 4 January 60 per cent of loyalist UFF/UDA prisoners in the Maze voted to 'withhold their support' from the peace process. Gary McMichael, leader of the Ulster Democratic Party (the closest political party to the UDA), made the Jesuitical distinction that this 'was a vote of no-confidence in the peace process', rather than a vote against the loyalist paramilitary ceasefire. Few people in Northern Ireland were encouraged by his pedantry. Billy Hutchinson meanwhile, a leading figure within the Progressive Unionist Party (the political party closest to the loyalist paramilitary Ulster Volunteer Force announced that 'we should withdraw from the process completely'. Amid this cacophony of despair, other unionist politicians were calling on Secretary of State Mo Mowlam to resign. Clearly then, at the beginning of 1998, there was still a long way to travel on the road to peace.

As loyalists voiced their disenchantment with the peace process, the Secretary of State took the unprecedented step of visiting loyalist paramilitary leaders in the Maze prison. It was the biggest gamble of Mo Mowlam's career which, luckily for her and everyone else supporting the peace process, paid off. However, as the political process staggered onwards, loyalists continued killing Catholics, causing concerns about the integrity of their 1994 ceasefire. When some of these murders were finally admitted by the UFF, their representatives in the Stormont talks, the Ulster Democratic Party, found themselves in breach of the Mitchell Principles and in danger of being expelled from the negotiations. On 26 January, amid calls by some of their unionist colleagues demanding their expulsion, the UDP jumped before they were pushed.

In February, as the political negotiations roadshow moved to Dublin, Sinn Féin were threatened with expulsion from the talks when the murder of an alleged UDA member was laid at the door of the IRA. However, unlike the UDP before them, Sinn Féin refused to go quietly. The negotiations were held up in utter confusion as Sinn Féin took legal action in an attempt to avert their exclusion, while the rest of the participants were not sure who was in and who was out. Sinn Féin President Gerry Adams, normally a smooth and unruffled media performer, demonstrated his frustration at the turn of events to the ever-present journalists. 'I am absolutely pissed off, with trying to make this thing work, and those who have no interest in making it work, seize upon two men being killed, to exploit it and to bring this process down.' Eventually, on 20 February, Sinn Féin were formally expelled from the talks until 9 March, with a warning from Mo Mowlam that one more breach of the Mitchell Principles would result in their permanent exclusion.

Violence accompanied the political negotiations like a dark shadow in 1998, with both republican and loyalist representatives in the talks trying to distance their organisations from it. This was classic behaviour from 'spoiler' groups opposed to the negotiations, who hoped to destabilise the peace process through violence. On 23 February a car bomb exploded in the centre of Portadown causing extensive damage to the town. The target was no accident, being a 'Protestant town' in the heart of David Trimble's constituency and the focus of the Drumcree protests since 1995.

In March 1998, the political spotlight moved across to Washington for the annual St Patrick's Day celebrations and the now traditional 'shot-in-the-arm' for the faltering peace process from President Bill Clinton. Like so many times before, his benign concern served to refocus minds and charge some faint-hearts with the energy to continue the negotiations with renewed vigour. In view of his domestic difficulties in 1998, it is ironic that President Clinton carried such moral authority with the conservative Christians who generally make up Northern Ireland's political class. Having drowned their shamrocks, the peace talks negotiators flew back to Northern Ireland with the following message from President Clinton ringing in their ears: 'This is the chance of a lifetime for peace in Ireland. You must get it done.' No one wanted to disappoint the President.

As the negotiators returned home, they were given a stark timetable for success by the talks chairman George Mitchell. They were told that the next session of the negotiations would begin on 6 April and would remain in session continuously until the negotiations were concluded. Mitchell set the deadline for completion for Thursday 9 April. The delegates were told to 'eat, sleep and negotiate'. It was a week of high tension and drama, fuelled by a hopeful public and a news-hungry media starved of real information, while the politicians closeted themselves into Castle Buildings at Stormont. Even the body language of the politicians was studied for evidence of progress. Was Gerry smiling or was it just a leer? Was David Trimble walking even faster? And what did it all mean? Mo Mowlam chivvied everyone along with her unusual mix of jolly-hockeysticks enthusiasm and mischievous brand of humour. The Secretary of State caused some consternation at a press conference on 1 April when she announced solemnly to the media 'Because of the extraordinary progress we made yesterday, the talks deadline has been moved forward to tomorrow . . . [pause] . . . APRIL FOOL.' As one observer remarked; 'Mo has the disarming air of a kindly schoolmistress charged with the task of keeping some unruly but basically loveable gangs from killing each other.'[6]

To force the issue and in the hope of bringing the negotiations to a positive *dénouement*, George Mitchell produced a draft document on 6 April, representing his best guess as to what all the parties involved might be able to agree to. This received a lukewarm reaction from Sinn Féin and a wholly negative reaction from all shades of unionism. Gerry Adams went into culinary mode when asked for his view of the Mitchell paper. 'I think the senator has dealt with all the issues. In that way of course it is like stew. We have all the ingredients but you have to cook it properly.'[7] To unionist taste-buds however, it seemed something of an Irish stew. Despite reassurances from Tony Blair, the UUP publicly rejected it as a 'Sinn Féin wish list'. UUP deputy-leader John Taylor was particularly disparaging, leaving his party leader in little doubt that he would not be supporting an agreement based on the Mitchell draft. 'Clearly this paper is unacceptable to unionists. I personally could not be identified with it. . . . It creates many difficulties and they have to be overcome. I wouldn't touch it with a 40-foot pole.'[8] The loyalist parties were also underwhelmed by Mitchell's best efforts, with UDP spokesperson David Adams declaring that 'as far as loyalism and unionism is concerned this document does not represent a realistic basis for a settlement.'[9]

As the clock ticked ominously towards 9 April with little sign of progress towards a settlement, reinforcements arrived at Stormont in the form of British Prime Minister Tony Blair and Irish Taoiseach Bertie Ahern. On his arrival, Blair provided some unconscious humour by appearing unable to follow his own advice. Nevertheless, he summed up the mood of the moment and indicated that there was now an irresistible momentum for a negotiated settlement. 'A day like today is not a time for sound-bites really, we can leave those at home, but I feel the hand of history upon our shoulder.' The drama took a further twist when Bertie Ahern's mother died and he had to leave the talks to attend her funeral. Despite his personal grief, he returned to Belfast the same evening as the deadline for agreement approached. Fearing that a deal was imminent, unionists opposed to the talks, led by Democratic Unionist Party (DUP) leader Ian Paisley, marched to Castle Buildings on 9 April to hold a press conference accusing the unionist participants in the negotiations of treachery. This was a well-trodden path by Paisley, but on this occasion he was ambushed by supporters of the loyalist parties, the PUP and UDP, who were inside the talks process. Heated exchanges followed between Paisley and the loyalists, emphasising the changes that had taken place in loyalist politics. Paisley looked an isolated and forlorn figure. The antipathy felt by the loyalist parties towards the DUP in general, and Paisley in particular, was summed up by David Ervine of the PUP who remarked 'Ian Paisley – he's been thrown out of more places than Alex Higgins.'[10] This incident may have been a sideshow, far removed from the serious negotiations being conducted inside Castle Buildings at Stormont. It was, nevertheless, a glimpse of the unionist emotions and fears that the UUP leadership would be forced to placate after the Agreement was reached.

Amidst such drama, the negotiators continued to talk. The deadline of 9 April came and went. The talking went on into the night and through the following day. Eventually, around mid-afternoon on Good Friday 10 April, rumours began to emerge that an agreement had been reached. Typically for a peace process that had lurched from euphoria to despair and back again throughout its long and winding history, there was a last-minute hitch. Jeffrey Donaldson, a leading member of David Trimble's party and a central figure in the UUP negotiating team, had apparently walked out of the talks in protest at the terms of the Agreement. While senior party figures tried to explain away his early exit, it soon became clear that Donaldson was not happy with the terms of the settlement, particularly over the issue of decommissioning. The see-sawing nature of the on-off Agreement was even reflected by the dramatic weather conditions on 10 April at Castle Buildings. 'Protracted bursts of sunshine gave way, without warning, to dark clouds, sudden downpours and then snow. All the seasons in one day and all the human emotions built in to the multi-party talks process – hope, fear, anxiety and expectation.'[11] When David Trimble began a press conference on the steps of Castle Buildings immediately after the Agreement had been reached, he was immediately pelted by a hail-shower. He could have been forgiven for thinking that it was a sign of stormy weather ahead for the Agreement and for his political leadership.

The final plenary session of the negotiations was delayed but eventually Trimble agreed to accept the deal. It was left to talks chairman George

Mitchell to draw the final curtain on proceedings. Typical of the man credited with having the patience of Job for chivvying Northern Ireland's politicians towards a settlement, his concluding remarks conveyed an appropriate sense of achievement and satisfaction at the successful outcome: 'I have that bitter-sweet feeling that comes in life, I'm dying to leave, but I hate to go.' British Prime Minister Tony Blair felt the hand of history on his shoulder again, explaining that the dynamic of the Agreement was rooted in a positive-sum rather than a zero-sum equation, in plainer language, a score draw rather than victory or defeat for either side.

> In these past few days, the irresistible force – the political will, has met the immovable object – the legacy of the past, and it has actually moved it. The idea that if one side wins something in Northern Ireland the other loses, is gone. The essence of what we have agreed is a choice. We are either all winners or all losers. It is mutually assured benefit, or mutually assured destruction.

The details of the Agreement were of little surprise to seasoned observers of politics in Northern Ireland. It was based on the return of devolved powers, to be exercised through a 108-member Assembly based on power-sharing. An executive would be formed from this assembly with seats being distributed on the d'Hondt principle, in other words, relative to the numerical strength of parties in the assembly. The Agreement also envisaged the establishment of a North/South Ministerial Council within Ireland that would develop cross-border links on matters of mutual interest. Finally, a British/Irish Council was to be set up to reflect 'the totality of relationships among the peoples of these islands'. The constitutional emphasis was placed on the consent of the people within Northern Ireland. To reflect this fact, the British Government would remove Article 75 of the Government of Ireland Act, while the Irish Government would seek to amend Articles 2 and 3 of its constitution, making it clear that Irish unity would only be pursued by peaceful means and with the consent of a majority of the people within both jurisdictions.

In addition to its central constitutional architecture, the Agreement promised reform on policing and an accelerated release scheme for paramilitaries judged to be on valid ceasefires. While this was not an amnesty, and prisoners were to be released on licence, it was too much for many unionists, and became the biggest debating point in the subsequent referendum campaign. Some nationalists believed that the unionist concentration on the early release of prisoners was a smoke screen to hide the fact that they were politically opposed to the terms of the Agreement and the principle of having to share power with the Catholic community.

The other key section in the Agreement concerned the decommissioning of illegal weapons. This was eventually to become the key sticking point in the Agreement's implementation, with First Minister designate David Trimble refusing to implement the deal before decommissioning had begun. Sinn Féin's argument, which found sympathy within the broad nationalist community, was that this was yet another precondition imposed by the unionists on their participation in government and reflected the unionist intention to try to re-negotiate the terms of the Agreement after the event. Arguments over Sinn Féin's responsibilities with regard to the decommissioning of IRA weapons were to bedevil the implementation of the Agreement in the months and years ahead.

Unionism after the Good Friday Agreement

Having accepted the terms of the Good Friday Agreement, its unionist supporters (namely the UUP, PUP and UDP) had to begin the difficult task of selling it to their parties and within the wider unionist population. It was clear before the Agreement was reached that this was going to be a difficult task. On the evening of 9 April, David Trimble was heckled by a small group of unionist protesters on his way into a meeting of his party executive to discuss details of the putative settlement. One of the demonstrators illustrated the type of insecurity and fear reminiscent of the post Anglo-Irish Agreement period (detailed earlier in this book) that had done so much to blight political thinking within the unionist community.'The talks are a disaster for unionists. Trimble is selling us out like de Klerk sold out the white South Africans.'[12] However, this was not the only demonstration taking place near the UUP headquarters in Glengall Street that evening. Another much larger gathering threatened to drown out the small gaggle of unionist discontents who had come out to protest against the UUP leader. This was a reminder that'normal' people actually live in Northern Ireland outside the confines and at times obsessive concerns of politics. This grouping on the other side of the street from the unionist protest were not waving placards at David Trimble, but had their eye on livelier prey, in the form of pop stars Ronan Keating of Boyzone and Bono from U2, who had arrived for the *Hot Press* music awards in the hotel opposite the UUP offices. Their message may not have been music to the ears of their unionist neighbours competing for pavement space, but it was just as fervently expressed:'We want to be in the same part of Ireland as Ronan'; 'We love Leonardo di Caprio as well'; 'Whatever Bono says we'll agree to'.[13] While such sentiments might not be universally applauded, these were the people that the Agreement's supporters would eventually have to mobilise and enthuse, if the settlement was going to develop.

It became clear at a very early stage, however, that the Agreement would turn a private split in the leadership of the UUP over the terms of a settlement into an increasingly public disagreement. Jeffrey Donaldson's disappearance on the afternoon the Agreement was signed was like a missing front tooth in the UUP delegation. While Donaldson was initially cautious about coming out against his party leader, refusing to talk to journalists before attending a meeting of his party executive on 11 April, some of his other senior colleagues were far from reticent. West Tyrone MP William Thompson nailed his colours to the mast emphatically.'It's a complete disaster. Trimble has conceded on almost every point he said he would stand on. It has weakened the Union and is completely unacceptable and I will be voting no in a referendum.'[14] East Londonderry MP Willie Ross also indicated before the same meeting of the UUP executive that he would be an important figure in the anti-Agreement campaign. 'The deal is certainly not accepted or acceptable to me and I don't believe it's a peace deal. It has all the attributes of what I would call a full-blown surrender to IRA demands.'[15]

The humour of anti-Agreement unionists was not helped by the fact that on 14 April, a mere four days after the settlement was reached, the Irish government released nine IRA prisoners from jail as part of the Agreement's early release scheme. This seemed to many unionists like indecent haste and few doubted that their release, days before a Sinn Féin *Ard Fheis* to debate the Agreement, was a political manoeuvre to placate the republican community. The DUP's Nigel Dodds suggested that this was a sign of what was to come as a result of the agreement reached on 10 April.'This is clearly a political move. It is a clear indication that the IRA will continue to be appeased and we are going to see more and more of convicted murderers and IRA terrorists being released under this agreement if it passes.'[16]

The first hurdles to be cleared before the Agreement could be implemented were the dual referenda in Northern Ireland and the Irish Republic. A six-week campaign on the Agreement followed, leading up to the referenda on 22 May. The unionist'No' campaign got under way immediately, strengthened by high-level defections from the UUP. At a rally in Belfast's Ulster Hall, several UUP Westminster MPs publicly aligned themselves with Ian Paisley and other opponents of the negotiated settlement. At a press conference to launch his party's opposition on 15 April, DUP leader Ian Paisley indicated (not for the first time) the graveness of the situation for the unionist community.'This is a struggle for the lifeblood of our country. We will not be bullied by a foreign country who want a say in our future.'[17] As much of this book illustrates, such'last-ditch'rhetoric had played well within unionist politics in the past. However, times had changed and the'Ulster Says No'mantra of the 1980s was beginning to sound rather dull to many unionist ears. One example of this change was illustrated by the editorial line of the *News Letter*, a morning newspaper with a predominantly unionist readership. While it had been very opposed to the Anglo-Irish Agreement in 1985, the editorial of the paper in April 1998 urged its readers to support the Good Friday Agreement and addressed in particular members of the Orange Order, who were an important constituency within the unionist electorate.

> Nothing will be gained by putting the boot into an agreement which, while imperfect in many ways, seeks in the area of human rights to underpin the right to freedom and expression of religion and calls on the Eire [sic] government to

take steps to demonstrate its respect for the Protestant tradition. These are statements which the Orange Order should be welcoming if it wants to contribute to an atmosphere in which its culture and tradition can be enjoyed by all, both in this generation and the next.[18]

However, under pressure from radical oppositionists within its ranks, the Orange Order at first dithered and finally came out against supporting the Agreement.

The referendum campaign was sharpened by continued sporadic violence from paramilitary groups not on ceasefire, as both the Loyalist Volunteer Force (LVF) and the Irish National Liberation Army (INLA) continued to draw blood in April 1998. The PUP accused the anti-Agreement unionists campaigning for a 'No' vote in the referendum of heightening fears within the unionist community and of being responsible for the increase in violence. Party spokesperson Billy Hutchinson did not pull his punches when he claimed that:

All of those people out there in the No campaign had better take responsibility. If they are going to frighten people with a united Ireland, then they will be responsible for creating more deaths. We have already seen a number in the past couple of weeks and those people who say we are on a road to a united Ireland had better realise that they are making people very, very nervous and this is making people pull triggers.[19]

The Agreement presented some problems for traditional political alignments, as the UUP and its supporters suddenly found themselves defending the same position as Sinn Féin, against other unionists who were opposed to the deal. This forced the unionist community to consider political coalitions that weeks earlier would have been anathema to them. The position of the UUP was especially ironic, as the *de facto* defection of senior party officers placed David Trimble in an uneasy alliance with the SDLP and (theoretically at least) Sinn Féin, as all of them were supporting a 'Yes' vote in the forthcoming referendum. At the same time, he was on the opposite side to other unionists and even senior colleagues within his own party who were campaigning for a 'No' vote in the referendum. One UUP supporter of the Agreement lamented the apparent malaise within his party. 'The No campaigners are making lots of noise and the Yes campaign has been dreadful. There has been no real organisation or enthusiasm from Glengall Street. The height of our campaign seems to be issuing press releases.'[20] The unionist electorate were understandably confused. One half of unionism was claiming to have strengthened the Union, but was going to be voting the same way in the referendum as Sinn Féin, who appeared to believe that the Agreement had weakened the Union. Those unionists who opposed the settlement seemed to be on the same side in the referendum as the Continuity IRA and appeared to have no clear political alternative to it.

The consequence of this political confusion was incoherence within the 'Yes' campaigns run by the political parties. Instead of presenting a united front to the Northern Ireland electorate, both the UUP and SDLP campaigned separately. This did little to convince the electorate that an historic compromise had been reached between unionism and nationalism. Their coherence was not helped of course, by the parties giving conflicting messages to an already suspicious public. As both David Trimble and Gerry Adams were looking over their shoulders at dissidents within their own parties, the former claimed that the Agreement strengthened the Union with Great Britain, while the latter announced that it was a transitional step to Irish unity. The 'No' campaign effectively exploited this confusion and gathered momentum. An independent 'Yes' campaign, drawn from elements of civil society within Northern Ireland and anxious to ensure that defeat was not snatched from the jaws of victory, made a major contribution to the eventual outcome. It engineered the most abiding visual memory of the period when, on 19 May, SDLP leader John Hume and UUP leader David Trimble appeared together on stage in Belfast at a U2 concert in support of the Agreement. Bono's careful choreography, when he held both politician's arms aloft in unity, was the defining moment of the campaign. In the end, those prepared to hope for a peaceful future triumphed over those determined to remain in the hopelessness of the past. Following the vote on 22 May, 71 per cent voted 'Yes' with 29 per cent voting 'No'. The turnout of over 80 per cent was the highest poll since 1921 and strengthened the mandate of the Agreement's supporters. In the Irish Republic meanwhile, though the turnout was lower, 95 per cent voted to endorse the Good Friday Agreement and amend the Irish constitution.

Ulster says 'Yes'

The next milestone on the road to peace was represented by the elections to the new Assembly on 25 June 1998. While the result of this election would clearly be crucial to the successful implementation of the Agreement, the campaign that preceded it was notable for the new tone that had entered the language of much of pro-Agreement unionism. This was epitomised by UUP leader David Trimble in a speech given to business and community leaders in Belfast on 22 June. The language expressed here is significantly different in tone to the traditional unionist tub-thumping in the run-up to an election. The reason for this was that pro-Agreement unionists found themselves in the unusual position of having achieved something, in the form of the 10 April settlement. Unlike the multitude of elections that had taken place since the prorogation of Stormont in 1972, the pro-Agreement unionists had actually achieved the return of devolved powers to a Stormont Assembly, brought the reviled Anglo-Irish Agreement to an end and secured much sought-after reforms to Articles 2 and 3 of the Irish constitution.[21] This altered the structure of intraunionist politics quite significantly. Unionist parties were not simply providing alternative critiques of British government policy to their constituencies. After the Agreement, the UUP were able to point to a tangible set of achievements and articulate a positive vision of the future as a result of such achievements. Anti-Agreement unionists, on the other hand, provided a much more pessimistic outlook to the unionist electorate, claiming that the Agreement had weakened the Union. This more insecure perspective was illustrated by a 'No' unionist who booed Tony Blair during a visit to Northern Ireland on 16 May.

> How am I going to tell my children in 10 years' time that they're British if I vote yes, when it's all just a way of leading us into a united Ireland? The British way of life in Northern Ireland will be gone, Irish will be taught in the schools, Ahern and Andrews will be able to come up here whenever they like. We know it's not going to happen straight away, but we're going to be blended into a united Ireland, and we'll still have the Continuity IRA firing at us. (*Irish News*, 17 May 1998, p. 5)

David Trimble's speech on 22 June, on the other hand, provided a much more positive and confident articulation of unionism. The language was inclusive, upbeat, visionary, progressive; traits that one would not normally have associated with unionist speeches immediately prior to an important election. He asked rhetorically on behalf of his party 'Can we promote what is good and honourable in our shared heritage? Can we show respect for what is particular to other traditions?'[22] Of course the UUP was still in the business of winning votes and securing the support of what one former leader liked to refer to as 'the greater number' of people within Northern Ireland. However, once the inclusive language is stripped away, the sub-text of this speech is that the UUP, by engaging with nationalists and republicans, by not running away from the negotiating table, and by doing all the things that their opponents criticised them for, had actually succeeded in strengthening the Union. Their pitch, therefore, despite the inclusive language, was still based in the traditional communal thinking of the past rather than in any post-conflict paradigm. The launch of the UUP's pro-Agreement campaign before the referendum was, after all, prefixed with the slogan 'Say Yes for the Union.' Nevertheless, Trimble painted himself and the organisation he led, as the party that had taken risks for peace, while the Agreement had empowered the people of Northern Ireland to decide their own political future. The criticism of anti-Agreement parties and the DUP in particular, was barely concealed.

> When the going was tough we didn't run away. Thanks to our determination, Northern Ireland's place within the United Kingdom has been secured and the 'consent principle' is universally accepted. . . . Others may fail to understand or lack the courage, but if we fail to take this opportunity our children will not be forgiving. To run away again, or to stay only to sabotage the hopes of society, would be utterly irresponsible. I promise you today: we will reach for the prize

on offer, and we have good men and women with us who will stay the course. On Thursday, [25 June] give us the tools, and we will do the job.[23]

It is difficult to imagine a unionist leader giving a speech of such a positive nature for most of the period covered within the rest of this book. However, the results of the election were less conclusive for supporters of the agreement than the referendum vote, as unionists opposed to the settlement made significant gains at the expense of the UUP. While the DUP gained a creditable twenty seats in the new Assembly, the loyalist Ulster Democratic Party failed to win a single seat, despite their high-profile role in the Stormont negotiations.

September saw another visit to Ireland from President Clinton. While he had come to put the Presidential seal of approval on the GFA, like many sequels his trip did not manage to reach the euphoric heights of the original in 1995. He was given a warm welcome by the Irish people, despite being besieged at home by the Lewinsky scandal. However, he was visiting a country still wracked by grief following the Omagh bombing. Despite his domestic problems, President Clinton was still prepared to tackle sticking points in the peace process. This visit produced the first face-to-face meeting between the First Minister designate David Trimble and Sinn Féin President Gerry Adams. Another landmine cleared on the difficult road to political progress. Speaking to an audience of politicians in Belfast, President Clinton gave a prescient summary of the tasks that lay ahead.

> You owe it to your country to nurture the best in your people, by showing them the best in yourselves. Difficult, sometimes wrenching decisions, lie ahead. But they must be made. And because you have agreed to share responsibility, whenever possible you must try to act in concert not conflict, to overcome obstacles, not create them, to rise above petty disputes, not fuel them.

When the President climbed back aboard Air Force One, the politicians set about doing exactly the opposite, as the tortured stand-off between unionists and Sinn Féin over the issue of weapons decommissioning continued. September also saw the first wave of prisoner releases by the British government under the terms of the Agreement. By the end of 1998, 200 prisoners had been released under the scheme. The scale of prisoner releases fed into the debate on decommissioning, with some unionists arguing that this should be stopped because of the republican and loyalist delay in handing over their weapons and explosives. Those unionists who had been opposed to the Agreement from the beginning put pressure on David Trimble effectively saying; 'I told you so!'

Shadow-boxing

Despite the difficulties in the peace process caused by the long-running sore of decommissioning, progress of a sort was taking place, at least as far as pro-Agreement unionists were concerned. Following the elections, September saw the creation of a shadow Assembly at Stormont with the UUP as the largest party. While the UUP remained reluctant to go into government with Sinn Féin in the absence of 'actual' decommissioning, they were at least able to provide their supporters with evidence of actual political progress while at the same time keeping the political agenda out of the hands of the DUP. At last, an inclusive assembly was in place at Stormont with all the political parties represented. It would be some months, however, before this 'shadow' institution was to result in a functioning executive with the devolution of powers from Westminster. Until that point (over one year later), the parties in the Assembly argued over rival interpretations of the Good Friday Agreement. What exactly were Sinn Féin's responsibilities within the terms of the Agreement *vis-à-vis* decommissioning? How many North-South cross-border bodies would there be? How many departments would comprise the Executive? And what would be the relationship between the ministerial departments and the cross-border bodies? The discussion of these questions plagued the political atmosphere into 1999, damaged the momentum in the peace process, and poisoned the relationships between the parties to the Good Friday Agreement. Instead of implementing the settlement as mandated to do following the referenda in May, the Assembly began less auspiciously. Notwithstanding David Trimble's opening assertion that 'I want this to be a pluralist parliament for a pluralist people'[24] the initial signs were not encouraging. The Sinn Féin President Gerry Adams, for example, asked if members could use the Irish 'ta' or 'nil' in the chamber rather than the Anglo-Saxon 'aye' or 'nay'. In a counter-bid for cultural recognition, the Ulster-Scots Language Society issued a thesaurus of terms for the Assembly. The DUP were henceforth to be known as 'the Claucht Pairtie of tha Fowk' while the Women's Coalition were given the dubious handle of 'the Weeminfowk's Cleek'![25] The absence of devolved responsibilities in the Assembly provided the opportunity for such tendentious debates to fill the vacuum. As the atmosphere within the institution steadily worsened (not least between First Minister designate David Trimble and Deputy First Minister designate Seamus Mallon, who were reported to be barely on speaking terms by the end of 1999), mistrust became the dominant feature of the political process. Every day that passed without progress towards establishing the Executive was another day in which David Trimble's authority over his party weakened and the anti-Agreement unionists began to pick away at the fears and insecurities of nervous unionists. These insecurities have been documented in much of this book and have often damaged the ability of unionists to move in a unified way towards their objective of securing the Union. While Trimble did everything but beg republicans to *begin* the process of weapons decommissioning, he had to try and manage an increasingly sceptical Assembly party, several of whom were openly anti-Agreement to begin with, and a

unionist electorate who were becoming disenchanted with the implementation of the Good Friday Agreement and (like the republican community)
convinced of the others' bad faith. Apart from the influence of the siren
voices of the DUP, unionists had watched prisoners being released from jail
and contemplated the prospect of RUC reform together with the imminent
arrival of Sinn Féin ministers in government, while the decommissioning of
paramilitary weapons failed to materialise. Nationalists called on Trimble to
show leadership of his party, and became increasingly convinced that his
hiding behind the skirts of the 'rejectionists' was a ploy to disguise the fact
that he was trying to re-negotiate the Agreement after the event and impose
preconditions on Sinn Féin's entry into government. While nationalists were
frustrated by the delay in the establishment of the Executive and cross-
border institutions, Trimble was certainly in an unenviable position by the
beginning of 1999, trying on the one hand to placate an increasingly frac-
tious Assembly party, while at the same time avoiding a meltdown in his
relationship with either Northern nationalism or the British government.

A breakthrough was eventually reached on 16 February, when Trimble
narrowly secured sufficient unionist support to allow the Assembly to accept
a proposal for new government structures, detailing the departmental
ministries, North-South structures, the Civic Forum and the British-Irish
Council. The vote was passed in the Assembly by a resounding 77 votes to
29. However, due to the necessity of attaining cross-community support
(which was ironically endangering the implementation of the Agreement),
the votes on the unionist side were vital. Crucially, the same number of
unionists (29) voted for the package as voted against it, thanks to a last-
minute defection to the 'Yes' camp by the UUP's Roy Beggs Jnr.[26] This vote
opened the way for Secretary of State Mo Mowlam to initiate the necessary
legislation at Westminster to allow the formation of the Executive and the
devolution of transferred responsibilities to Stormont.[27]

While the Assembly vote on 16 February eased the immediate pressure,
the ghost of decommissioning continued to haunt the political process and
allowed anti-Agreement unionists to accuse the UUP of conceding on their
principles. Following the vote, and a subsequent bilateral meeting between
the UUP and Sinn Féin, the leader of the DUP, Ian Paisley, accused David
Trimble of being 'eager to jump into bed' and of having an 'eiderdown relationship' with republicans.[28] While some of Paisley's rhetoric could easily be
shrugged off as bluster, this would be to underestimate the DUP leader's
ability to tap into unionist fears and insecurities. This book has demonstrated
that leaders of the UUP did this at their peril, as Paisley has managed to out-
last all of his contemporaries by articulating a negative primordial version of
unionism dressed up in the clothes of morality. When Paisley launched his
European Election campaign on 23 February (in Bessbrook Orange Hall) it
was clear that he was going to attempt to use the decommissioning issue to

convince the unionist electorate that he was the only unionist leader who could be trusted to deliver them from the imperilled position they found themselves in.

> The springing open of the prison gates and the release onto the streets of Ulster of multiple murderers, we are told, is a symbol of peace. The refusal of those same gunmen to surrender even one of their murder weapons, already stained with the blood of innocent victims, is painted as a picture of peace when in reality it is an encouragement to future slaughter. The actions of David Trimble in setting up the embryo of an all-Ireland parliament is declared to be a strong force for peace when, in reality, it is an act of vile and despicable treachery.[29]

This was hardly a new tune being sung by the DUP leader; however, in the absence of IRA decommissioning, it was music to the ears of many of those unionists disappointed at the way in which the Good Friday Agreement was being implemented. An opinion poll carried out for BBC television's *Hearts and Minds* programme at the beginning of March, for example, found that seven out of ten unionists would be opposed to a decision by David Trimble to enter government with Sinn Féin in the absence of actual weapons decommissioning. This survey also suggested, rather alarmingly, that a majority of the unionist electorate were now opposed to the Agreement. More encouragingly perhaps, when unionists were asked which leader was working most effectively to preserve the Union, David Trimble won 43 per cent support with Ian Paisley trailing significantly behind on 25 per cent.

Still time ticked by without movement taking place over the implementation of the Agreement. The UUP slogan of 'no guns, no government' was turning into exactly that. The proposed deadline for the Executive 'going live' (10 March) came and went without agreement. This was knocked back by Secretary of State Mo Mowlam until the 'natural deadline' of the week beginning on 29 March, the week of Good Friday. This was a case of *déjà vu* for the peace process, as Prime Minister Tony Blair and Taoiseach Bertie Ahern dutifully arrived to hold the hands and twist arms of the protagonists. While Blair had talked famously a year earlier about feeling the 'hand of history on our shoulders', one commentator remarked cheekily that this time around it was more a case of 'a finger of fudge'.[30] The fudge being attempted on this occasion was one that had underpinned the whole Agreement, namely, how to find a form of words over decommissioning that would keep the UUP on board and allow the political process to move forward into the implementation stage.

These discussions resulted in the Hillsborough Declaration on 1 April. The key points in the declaration related to what was now being called the choreography of 'jumping together' on the issues that divided the pro-Agreement unionists and Sinn Féin. The document suggested that while decommissioning was not a precondition of the Agreement, it was an 'obligation'. It also proposed that on a predetermined date, nominations would take place, under the d'Hondt procedure, of ministers for the Executive, after which a collective act of reconciliation would take place that 'will see some arms put beyond use on a voluntary basis'. The Hillsborough Declaration was initially welcomed by UUP leader David Trimble as having the 'potential' to resolve unionist concerns over decommissioning. Others within his party were less sanguine, however, with Jeffrey Donaldson declaring that its language was 'decidedly woolly'. The DUP suggested that the Declaration was simply a form of words that would achieve little in practise and did not provide any greater guarantee of decommissioning than did the Agreement itself. Sinn Féin, on the other hand, were incensed by the Hillsborough Declaration and believed that the British and Irish governments had caved in to unionist pressure and had effectively re-negotiated the terms of the Agreement. Sinn Féin's chief negotiator in the 1998 talks, Martin McGuinness, summed up the republican mood when he declared that'I don't believe the IRA are going to jump to any ultimatum issued by David Trimble or those elements within the British military establishment.'[31] Sinn Féin chairperson Mitchel McLaughlin stated that the Declaration was 'an attempt to rewrite important aspects of the Good Friday Agreement, especially the decommissioning section so that the establishment of the institutions are on unionist terms. This is an unacceptable departure from the commitments given on Good Friday 1998.'[32]

The consequence of the Hillsborough Declaration was that it alienated republicans who felt that it had moved the goalposts on decommissioning, while not impressing sceptical unionists that any substantive guarantees had been provided. It was back to the drawing board and more talks for the two governments. Eventually, following another marathon session of meetings, the British government set a deadline of 30 June for the full devolution of powers to Northern Ireland. The statement, prepared at a meeting between the two governments and major parties on 14 May, was notable for the fact that despite its positive tone, no specific commitments over weapons decommissioning were required before the formation of the Executive was to commence. The key passage in the 14 May document reads as follows:

> All parties agree to the full implementation of all aspects of the Good Friday Agreement including the objective of achieving total disarmament and complete withdrawal of all weapons from politics in Ireland. They accept the issue of arms must be finally and satisfactorily settled and will do what they can to achieve decommissioning of all paramilitary arms within the time-frame set down in the Agreement, in the context of the implementation of the overall settlement. The International Commission on Decommissioning will now begin a period of intensive discussions with all parties and report back on progress before 30 June. All parties anticipate, without prejudice to their clear positions on this issue, a devolution of powers by 30 June.[33]

Unionists were upset that this had fudged the decommissioning issue. While the UUP 'reserved their position', anti-agreement unionists were far from reserved, believing this (correctly) to be proof that decommissioning would not be required to take place before the Executive was established, and that (in unionist parlance) 'unreconstructed terrorists' would be allowed into government. Under pressure from his party, UUP leader David Trimble declined to ask his Assembly colleagues to endorse it until clearer guarantees were given in the case of the IRA defaulting on decommissioning. For the next several weeks leading up to the 30 June deadline, political discussions between the governments and the pro-Agreement parties took place to find a form of words that would satisfy all concerned. However, despite a concerted effort, the deadline set by the British government came and went without agreement. While Prime Minister Blair tried to talk up the situation, declaring that 'what we have witnessed over the past few days are historic seismic shifts in the political landscape in Northern Ireland[34], unionists were not convinced. David Trimble illustrated the unionist unease over the requirements placed on Sinn Féin over IRA decommissioning: 'Despite the spin, despite the smoke and mirrors, there has been no commitment made by the republican movement to decommission in terms that would be recognised by the unionist community.'[35]

Unionist stage fright and institutional meltdown

In the end, unionist fears over decommissioning led the UUP to refuse to form an Executive with Sinn Féin, throwing the Good Friday Agreement and the peace process into disarray. On the evening of 14 July, the UUP executive met at its party headquarters and decided (after a fifteen-minute discussion) not to participate in the d'Hondt procedure to appoint ministers to a new power-sharing Executive, intended by the British government to take place the following day. On the morning of 15 July, First Minister designate David Trimble announced his party's decision to boycott the meeting at which an Executive was to be established. At Stormont meanwhile, a political farce took place as the remaining parties in the Assembly went through the motions of forming an Executive without their UUP colleagues. While everyone looked at the rows of empty UUP seats, an absent David Trimble was given five minutes to nominate his first minister to the Executive. When the SDLP and Sinn Féin filled all ten ministerial portfolios (due to the other parties declining to nominate candidates) Assembly Speaker Lord Alderdice declared the whole procedure null and void due to the lack of cross-community participation. The crowning moment in this political non-event came when SDLP Deputy Leader Seamus Mallon resigned as Deputy First Minister, launching a scathing attack on the UUP in the process. Mallon accused the UUP of using the decommissioning issue to:

> . . . bleed this very process dry. They stand by their demand of prior decommissioning. A condition found nowhere in the agreement. A condition alien to its

principles. What they are doing is worse than failing to operate an inclusive executive. They are actually preventing its very creation. They are dishonouring the agreement. They are insulting its principles . . . It is therefore necessary that I resign as Deputy First Minister. I wish to inform the Assembly that accordingly I offer my resignation with immediate effect.[36]

As a result of the parties' failure to establish an Executive, the Good Friday Agreement entered a review phase, chaired yet again by the long-suffering Senator George Mitchell, the hope being that the pieces could be put back together again during the autumn. In keeping with the general pattern of the peace process, the review of the Agreement did not run smoothly. In September, the Patten Commission on policing presented its report, to the chagrin of many within the unionist community. The Patten Commission's recommendations for reform of the RUC (particularly the symbolic identity-based items such as the name change from the RUC to the Northern Ireland Police Service) was seen as yet another negative aspect of the Good Friday Agreement. The front-page headline in the pro-Agreement *News Letter* the day after the publication of the Patten Report was unambiguous. It read simply, 'Betrayed'.[37] UUP leader David Trimble was also scathing in his assessment of this aspect of the Good Friday Agreement. The report was, he declared, a 'gratuitous insult' to the RUC and 'the most shoddy piece of work I have ever seen'.[38] While the UUP executive formally rejected the Patten Report at a meeting on 13 September, anti-Agreement unionists declared that this was the inevitable outcome of the 1998 deal and further evidence that unionist supporters of the Agreement had brought such destruction upon their own heads.

The Mitchell Review lasted for ten weeks, until an acceptable sequence was agreed between the UUP and Sinn Féin that would see separate statements issued by both parties recommitting themselves to the Good Friday Agreement. On 18 November, following another exhaustive round of meetings with all the parties, Mitchell signalled that his review was complete and that the outcome was a positive one.

> I believe that a basis now exists for devolution to occur, for the institutions to be established, and for decommissioning to take place as soon as possible. Devolution should take effect, then the Executive should meet, and then the paramilitary groups should appoint their authorised representatives, all on the same day, in that order. I hereby recommend to the governments and the parties that they make the necessary arrangements to proceed, and call on them to do so without delay.[39]

Before the Mitchell Review had been completed, Mo Mowlam had been replaced as Secretary of State for Northern Ireland. Peter Mandelson was appointed to the job on 11 October 1999 and immediately signalled his commitment to the successful completion of the review process. 'There is no alternative to the Good Friday Agreement. There is no plan B. It is that or nothing.'[40] In return for the UUP agreeing to the triggering of the d'Hondt mechanism that would facilitate the forming of the Executive and the other institutions 'going live', the IRA would appoint a senior figure of its organisation as an 'interlocutor' with General John de Chastelain's decommissioning commission to establish a timetable for weapons to be 'put beyond use' by the original deadline in the Agreement of 22 May 2000. On 17 November, an IRA statement was released stating its commitment to a peaceful settlement and its intentions over decommissioning. This was a crucial part of the jigsaw that would be pieced together over the next two weeks and lead eventually to the implementation of the Agreement. The crucial section of the IRA statement declared that:

> In our view, the Good Friday agreement is a significant development, and we believe its full implementation will contribute to the achievement of lasting peace. . . . The IRA is willing to further enhance the peace process and consequently, following the establishment of the institutions agreed on Good Friday last year, the IRA leadership will appoint a representative to enter into discussions with Gen John de Chastelain and the Independent International Commission on Decommissioning.[41]

Everything now hinged on a meeting of the Ulster Unionist Council, scheduled for Saturday 27 November. A hothouse atmosphere pervaded the unionist community and the rest of Northern Ireland in the days leading up to this meeting, as Trimble made a concerted effort to sell what was a substantial compromise to his party and to the wider unionist community. In effect, Trimble was seeking to move from the old mantra of 'no guns – no government', which had underpinned his party's policy up to this point, to something akin to 'government, then guns'. Inevitably, of course, this exercise in political pragmatism entrenched the divisions within the UUP and was seized upon by anti-Agreement unionists. Trimble admitted that a shift in his position over weapons decommissioning had taken place, though argued that this was merely a tactical manoeuvre to achieve the same end, rather than a compromise over principle. Unsurprisingly, his opponents did not concur. On the day before the meeting of the UUC, Trimble made an appeal to the unionist community in an article in the *News Letter*. He argued that despite the proposed shift from 'no guns, no government', his policy offered the best hope for securing the Union and of building a peaceful future within Northern Ireland.

> The Mitchell review lasted 10 weeks. I now believe that the proposals agreed and on the table offer the best chance we will get to achieve both our objectives of decommissioning and devolution. Yes, it is not the same as prior decommissioning, but it provides the only mechanism deliverable to achieve guns and government. . . . It is time to put the Republican movement to the test. If this plan works, Ulster Unionists will have secured decommissioning and devolution. The prize is enormous. We have a chance on the eve of the Millennium to

build a society focused on the real issues that matter to our children. We must and I believe we will, do our utmost to create this better future.[42]

Trimble's opponents (including the majority of his parliamentary party) refused to accept that this policy change would result in the achievement of weapons decommissioning, arguing that the requirements of Sinn Féin and the IRA were much too vague and little more than aspirational. However, succour existed for pro-Agreement unionists in the logic provided by George Mitchell when he announced the outcome of his review on 18 November. Turning his attention to the decommissioning issue, Mitchell declared:

> There has been a lot of talk about guarantees. There is one guarantee. It is that if this process fails there will be no chance whatsoever for any decommissioning. If I may use a phrase I had not even heard of until I came to Northern Ireland: even the dogs in the street know there will be no decommissioning, no possibility of decommissioning, if Mr Trimble is rejected and if this process fails.[43]

Unfortunately for David Trimble, George Mitchell did not have a vote in the impending meeting of the UUC. A pivotal role was now held by UUP deputy leader John Taylor, who had hardened his position against the Mitchell Review in the weeks preceding the UUP vote. Taylor's political mood during the peace process seemed to be as changeable as the Irish weather, and few observers were surprised when unionism's 'maverick's maverick' eventually announced his support for the new sequencing policy being put to the UUC meeting. One of the delegates at the meeting in Belfast's Waterfront Hall on 27 November provided a metaphor which encapsulated not only Taylor's unpredictability, but also illustrated the rural background of many within the UUC itself. Taylor, they suggested, 'was like a Corncrake. You know there's one about – but you can never tell which field it's in!'

While Taylor's final position at the UUC meeting was important to the outcome of the meeting, a key concession was made to unionists who were reluctant to vote for the revised policy due to fear that the IRA would not deliver on its 'obligation' to decommission. In effect, a motion was put to the UUC that imposed a time limit on decommissioning and suspended the party's final position on the implementation of the Agreement until a further meeting, to take place some time in February. If this time limit was not met, then post-dated letters of resignation from the four unionists in the new executive, lodged with the party president Josias Cunningham, would be activated and the structures of the Good Friday Agreement would be collapsed. While Trimble and his senior colleagues believed that this was the price necessary to win the vote in the UUC, end the political stalemate over decommissioning, and begin the process of setting up the structures agreed in April 1998, the practical result of this motion was to undermine the Mitchell Review in the eyes of republicans. By unionists imposing their own time limit on the achievement of decommissioning, which was not part of the Good Friday Agreement or the Mitchell Review, the UUC had (certainly as far as the IRA was concerned) effectively introduced another precondition into the political process. In the event, Trimble narrowly won the vote at the UUC meeting by a margin of 58 per cent to 42 per cent.[44]

While the UUC vote opened the way for the triggering of d'Hondt, the establishment of the Executive and the devolution of transferred powers to Stormont for the first time in twenty-five years, the UUC's decision to with-hold final approval for these new structures until February destabilised the embryonic administration. Although unionists might point out that this was only because the IRA failed to meet their'obligation'to decommission, repub-licans saw this as a unionist precondition on the legitimate right of Sinn Féin to sit in government on the basis of their mandate, a sign of bad faith on the part of David Trimble and the UUP, and as an attempt at renegotiating both the Mitchell Review and the Good Friday Agreement itself.

Politics 'goes live'

Regardless of the difficulties that lay ahead, at midnight on Wednesday 1 December 1999, powers were transferred from Westminster to the Stormont Assembly. The following day an inclusive power-sharing Executive was established including not only Sinn Féin and the UUP, but also ministers from the DUP who were avowedly opposed to the new political system but who were unwilling to exclude themselves from power.[45] Finally, 601 days after the Good Friday Agreement was reached, a cabinet government was formed in under one hour. For the first time in a generation, locally elected politicians were able to exercise responsibility and do so as part of an inclu-sive agreed settlement.

It did not take long for the focus of politics to shift from constitutional issues to debates over the allocation of resources. Like Banquo's ghost, however, decommissioning hung over the new administration as did the impending meeting of the UUC in February 2000 to determine the eventual fate of the Executive and the future of the Agreement itself. On 11 February, on the eve of the UUC meeting, Secretary of State Peter Mandelson suspended the political institutions and returned the powers transferred in early December back to Westminster, before the UUC got the opportunity to cash in the post-dated resignations of the four UUP members of the Execu-tive. While Sinn Féin condemned this as another example of the British government caving in to unionist pressure, Mandelson claimed in his defence that had he not done so, the Good Friday Agreement would have suffered a harder crash-landing and greater damage in the longer term.

While David Trimble attempted to put a brave face on these developments, his policy at this point lay in tatters and his leadership of the UUP was called into question. While he narrowly survived a leadership challenge from UUP stalwart Rev. Martin Smyth on 25 March 2000, Trimble's leadership of the UUP was weakened by the reversals that took place in February as it was now inextricably linked to the policies he had been advocating since the Good Friday Agreement in 1998.

The deadlock over the reinstitution of the Executive was finally broken in May when an agreement was brokered over the sequencing of IRA decommissioning, together with a timetable for the return of the devolved powers revoked in February. The careful choreography saw a statement from the British and Irish governments on 5 May, an IRA statement declaring their intention to begin the process of 'putting arms beyond use' on 6 May, and a decision to return to government taken at a meeting of the Ulster Unionist Council on 27 May. The Assembly met again on 5 June to pick up where it had left off the previous February. Despite nationalist criticism of Peter Mandelson for collapsing the structures of the Agreement in February at the behest of the UUP, the practical benefits of this 'soft-crashing' were that the powers revoked were just as quickly returned, with the minimum of procedural fuss or delay.

The crucial part of the joint statement from the British and Irish governments issued on 5 May is the following:

> 3. The governments now believe that the remaining steps necessary to secure full implementation of the agreement can be achieved by June 2001, and commit themselves to that goal. They have drawn up, and are communicating to the parties, an account of these steps.
>
> 4. Subject to a positive response to this statement, the British government will bring forward the necessary order to enable the Assembly and Executive to be restored by May 22nd, 2000.
>
> 5. With confidence that there are clear proposals for implementing all other aspects of the agreement, the governments believe that paramilitary organisations must now, for their part, urgently state that they will put their arms completely and verifiably beyond use. Such statements would constitute a clear reduction in the threat. In response, the British government would, subject to its assessment of the level of threat at the time, on which it will continue to consult regularly with the Irish Government, take further substantial normalisation measures by June 2001.[46]

In an immediate response to this statement, the IRA released their most detailed account yet of its intentions on decommissioning, stating that it would co-operate with the de Chastelain Commission and put its weapons verifiably beyond use. In a statement issued on Saturday 6 May, the IRA detailed its commitment, the crucial paragraphs being the following:

> The leadership of the IRA is committed to a just and lasting peace. . . . The maintenance of our cessation is our contribution to the peace process and to the creation of a future in which the causes of conflict are resolved by peaceful

means. For our part, the IRA leadership is committed to resolving the issue of arms. . . . In that context the IRA leadership will initiate a process that will completely and verifiably put IRA arms beyond use. We will do it in such a way as to avoid risk to the public and misappropriation by others and ensure maximum public confidence.

We will resume contact with the Independent International Commission on Decommissioning and enter into further discussions with the commission on the basis of the IRA leadership's commitment to resolving the issue of arms.

We look to the two governments and especially the British government to fulfil their commitments under the Good Friday agreement and the joint statement. To facilitate the speedy and full implementation of the Good Friday agreement and the government's measures, our arms are silent and secure. There is no threat to the peace process from the IRA.

In this context, the IRA leadership has agreed to put in place within weeks a confidence-building measure to confirm that our weapons remain secure. The contents of a number of our arms dumps will be inspected by agreed third parties who will report that they have done so to the Independent International Commission on Decommissioning. The dumps will be re-inspected regularly to ensure that the weapons have remained silent.[47]

It was on the strength of this statement that David Trimble went to the UUC meeting at the end of May seeking the agreement of his party to re-enter government with Sinn Féin. At the meeting in Belfast's Waterfront Hall on Saturday 27 May, the UUP's ruling council backed their party leader, and agreed by 53 per cent to 47 per cent to reinstate the executive and return devolved powers to Northern Ireland.[48] Consistent with the nature of Trimble's leadership of his party during the peace process, he had got *just enough* support to continue at every stage. However, the split within the party and the wider unionist community was clear to be seen, and the reaction (both within the UUP and the wider population in Northern Ireland who supported the Good Friday Agreement) was one of relief rather than triumph. Everyone knew, not least those opposed to the settlement, that Trimble had to win every time, while those in the 'No' camp only had to win once to jeopardise the future of the Agreement.

At the press conference in the Waterfront Hall after the vote was announced, Trimble managed yet again to provoke negative headlines despite his hard-won victory. In a throw away answer to the questioning journalists, the UUP leader made disparaging remarks about Sinn Féin, illustrating that while the structures of the Good Friday Agreement had been restored, the human relationships still had some way to go. The message many nationalists took from this aside was that Trimble's mask had slipped and that despite his inclusive rhetoric, he remained the arrogant old-style unionist who had walked triumphantly with Ian Paisley in Portadown during the Drumcree protest in the mid 1990s. 'As far as democracy is concerned, these folk ain't house-trained yet. It may take some time before they do become house-trained and I think we do actually need to see the Assembly running so the checks and balances that are there eventually bring them to heel ... We are dealing with a party that has not got accustomed to democratic procedures.'[49]

Despite such remarks, it is the political structures rather than the personalities that are of long-term importance to the political future of Northern Ireland. The events of May and June represent a significant achievement for David Trimble's leadership of the UUP and for the leadership of his partners in government. Only time will tell whether the structures survive. Much will rest on the internal feuding within the unionist community and within the UUP in particular.

Assessing the Good Friday Agreement for unionism

Much has happened within unionist politics since the turbulent days in 1985 when political unionism united in opposition to the Anglo-Irish Agreement. The period covered in this book has been traumatic for many people within the unionist community who have felt either pessimistic or optimistic about the prospects for political change.

While many unionists remain opposed to the Good Friday Agreement, it is difficult to argue that they were in a stronger political position in the mid 1980s than they are today. It was once remarked by a senior unionist politician during the dark days of opposition to the Anglo-Irish Agreement, that it was essential for unionists to move from being outsiders to becoming insiders in the political process. Notwithstanding the problems associated with its implementation, the Good Friday Agreement has achieved that. For the first time since 1972 (and briefly in 1974) unionist politicians were transformed from being lobbyists of British government officials into being managers of resources, decision-makers and architects within the political process. Of course, opinion is divided within the unionist community over the Agreement. Its critics would claim that its architecture is fundamentally flawed and that the house will soon come crashing down on the heads of its occupants. An audit of the Good Friday Agreement from a unionist perspective, therefore, has to recognise that judgements of success and failure are predicated on wholly different, if not mutually exclusive, political objectives.

Looking at the situation from the point of view of a pro-Agreement unionist, it would be fair to say that significant gains were made for the unionist community in April 1998. These advances were of course trumpeted loudly by the UUP leadership during the referendum and election campaigns that took place during the summer of 1998. David Trimble and others within his party claimed that the Agreement had strengthened the Union, a point that was hotly contested by the DUP, who preferred to believe the republican analysis that it represented a transitional step towards Irish unity. Nevertheless, all shades of Irish nationalism, including (theoretically at least) the republican community who supported the Agreement, recognised that Northern Ireland would remain part of the United Kingdom until a majority of the people living there expressed a wish to change that status. The Irish Republic meanwhile, had voted in a referendum to reform Articles 2 and 3 of its constitution into a more aspirational form, another item on the lengthy unionist shopping list since the mid 1980s that was successfully ticked off in April 1998. Unionist supporters of the Agreement could also point to the fact that they had finally succeeded in getting rid of the Anglo-Irish Agreement, signed by the British and Irish governments in 1985. Memories in Northern Ireland are not renowned for being short. Unionists, therefore, will not forget that they believed the AIA to be a threat to their desire to remain British subjects, and that their political leaders conducted an extra-parliamentary civil disobedience campaign to bring it down. As this book amply illustrates, their campaign involved mass protests, strikes, boycotts, refusal to meet British government ministers, the imprisonment of several unionist politicians for refusing to obey the Public Order Act, torch-lit processions and an increase of loyalist violence against members of the RUC. Those involved in this campaign will also remember that it failed miserably to 'destroy the Diktat' and succeeded only in dividing unionism internally and decreasing their already tarnished image within Great Britain and across the rest of the world. Despite their huffing and puffing, unionist politicians spent the next several years 'outside the loop' of influence with the British government, who got on with the business of running Northern Ireland and solidifying their relationship with the Irish government within the structures of the AIA. Very long odds indeed would have been offered in 1985 for a unionist leader winning the Nobel Peace Prize, never mind establishing an inclusive devolved government at Stormont with Sinn Féin, based on a recognition of the 'consent' principle, not to mention the Irish Republic altering Articles 2 and 3 of its constitution into a more aspirational form. These are significant achievements and advancements for unionism and they have been secured by pro-Agreement unionism. They are no longer outside the loop of influence. They are no longer constantly saying 'No'. They are no longer without friends or influence in government or further afield within the United States administration. The Good Friday Agreement has provided a focus of achievement for unionism that has given it renewed intellectual coherence (though led to organisational chaos of Monty Python standards). Finally, with the 1998 Agreement, unionism (at least the majority of pro-Agreement unionists) had a plan, over and above the simple assertion that they wanted to retain the Union. In 1985, this seemed to many unionists to be a rapidly receding aspiration, while in 1998 it is actually built in to their support for a set of political structures with international support.

In contrast to the 'do-nothing' school of unionism that had dominated it for so long, and which the Anglo-Irish Agreement was in part a product of, the positive strategy conducted by unionist supporters of the Good Friday Agreement achieved the removal of the AIA, and allowed leaders such as Trimble to use the following positive, inclusive and visionary language during the elections to the new Stormont Assembly in 1998.

> Thanks to our determination, Northern Ireland's place within the United Kingdom has been secured and the 'consent principle' is universally accepted. . . . if we fail to take this opportunity our children will not be forgiving. To run away again, or to stay only to sabotage the hopes of society, would be utterly irresponsible. I promise you today, we will reach for the prize on offer.

These words, spoken in June 1998, warmed the cockles of many a unionist heart, though they perhaps sent a chill through those of an anti-Agreement persuasion. However, compared with the shambolic position of unionism several years earlier during their campaign against the Anglo-Irish Agreement, for a unionist leader to be able to use the language of empowerment, rather than the language of protest, was an achievement in itself.

Those unionists who have become disillusioned with the GFA since 1998 (or who opposed it from the beginning) may see little in it to enthuse over today. There is a strong sense within the unionist electorate that they have done all the giving, while nationalists have done all the taking. They will point to the fact that virtually the only aspect of the Agreement on which there has been little movement (and which saw the suspension of devolved government in February 2000) has been on the issue of the decommissioning of paramilitary weapons. Unionists have seen a power-sharing Executive established with two new Sinn Féin Ministers; the North-South bodies set up; action taken on the 'equality agenda'; the proposed reform (they might say disbandment) of the RUC following the Patten Report; and prisoner releases continuing throughout the period. Decommissioning on the other hand, has stood still from the unionist point of view. Strictly speaking of course, decommissioning is a *neutral* issue, in the sense that it refers equally to republican and loyalist disarmament, though many unionists have appropriated this psychologically to refer to IRA weapons. Their perception, therefore, is that the lack of progress on decommissioning is in some way detrimental for unionism and an illustration of bad faith specifically on the republican side.

While this chapter has demonstrated how the issue of decommissioning has bedevilled the implementation of the Agreement and caused a breakdown of trust among the parties, another deeper malaise suggests itself. This concerns the fact that many unionists have hitched their wagons to issues that are peripheral to their traditionally understood objective of 'preserving the Union'. Regardless of the vexed issue of weapons decommissioning, what is most likely to achieve their ultimate objective of securing the Union of Northern Ireland within the United Kingdom are those very things that many

unionists currently regard as obnoxious, namely: a power-sharing government with Sinn Féin tied into it, based on the recognition of Northern Ireland
as a legitimate political entity; a political and cultural recognition of nationalist aspirations through North-South cross-border bodies; and the creation of
a representative and accountable policing service. The fact that some unionists have seemed prepared to sacrifice their ostensible goal of strengthening
the Union on the altar of decommissioning, suggests to non-unionists that
they are not, ultimately, interested in preserving the Union *per se*, but rather in
preserving a particular version of the Union that closely reflects their traditional political identity.

While unionist concerns about the Agreement are sincerely held (their
worries would be easier to deal with if they were not) it might be worth
thinking about what their opposition to it is likely to achieve. If the structures
of the Good Friday Agreement are again suspended, as they were in February
2000, this will force pro-Agreement unionists onto the back foot and fuel the
agenda of their anti-Agreement colleagues, both within the UUP and outside
it. It will undermine and perhaps fatally wound David Trimble's leadership of
the UUP. In addition, any future suspension of the GFA will inevitably throw
the British and Irish governments closer together with the only conceivable
alternative to the Good Friday Agreement being some form of Anglo-Irish
administration based upon a creeping joint authority. These are hardly unionist objectives and hardly do much to strengthen the Union, but are entirely
conceivable if the GFA is damaged as a result of the internecine warfare
currently taking place within the unionist community.

The prospect in the event of a collapse of the Good Friday Agreement is for
unionism to find itself without power, without influence, without decommissioning, without the RUC (the Patten recommendations look likely to be
implemented regardless) without ideological unity, without effective political
leadership, and (given current demographic trends) without confidence about
its long-term political dominance. It is also very unlikely, if Northern Ireland
fails to grasp this opportunity to direct its own political affairs, that young
talent will be encouraged into politics, or be attracted by the challenges of
debating 'wheelie-bin' shortages or stray dog policies. The 'bright young
things' who are looking for responsibility and ways of making a positive
impact on their society are likely to look elsewhere. While this might be good
news for NGOs in Northern Ireland, it will be bad news for both unionist and
nationalist political parties. The prospects for unionism in the longer term
look even bleaker in a post-Apocalypse Good Friday Agreement scenario.
The two governments may finally conclude that the two main communities
in Northern Ireland are simply incapable of resolving their differences and
settle in for the long haul to share authority over the region.

While some unionists might find the idea of a return to direct rule more
appealing and more comfortable than the unknown challenges presented by

political change, even the most comfortable deckchair is of little use if it is on the *Titanic*. While some unionists have not quite summoned up the courage yet to abandon ship, the only logical choice for them at this point is to try the admittedly more slippery seats in the Good Friday Agreement life boat.

Notes

1   David Trimble speaking at the annual conference of the Ulster Unionist Party on 9 October 1999. *The Irish Times*, 11 October 1999, p. 7.
2   ibid., 24 March 1997, p. 5.
3   *Belfast Telegraph*, 15 April 1997, p. 11.
4   *The Irish Times*, 21 May 1997, p. 11.
5   Westminster MPs William Thompson and Willie Ross called for the UUP to withdraw from the 'squalid' talks process on 31 August.
6   *The Sunday Tribune*, 5 April 1998, p. 14.
7   *Irish News*, 8 April 1998, p. 4.
8   ibid.
9   ibid.
10 ibid., 9 April 1998, p. 5.
11 Frank Millar, *The Irish Times*, 10 April 1998, p. 6.
12 ibid., p. 5.
13 ibid., p. 6.
14 *Ireland on Sunday*, 12 April 1998, p. 4.
15 ibid.
16 *Irish News*, 15 April 1998, p. 1.
17 ibid., 16 April 1998, p. 4.
18 *News Letter*, 15 April 1998, p. 3.
19 *The Irish Times*, 7 May 1998, p. 8.
20 ibid.
21 Anti-Agreement unionists would of course contest the point and argue that these were not 'achievements' for either the unionist community or for Northern Ireland in general. However, within their own frame of reference, these were considered to be achievements by pro-Agreement unionists and heralded as so in the election campaign.
22 *The Irish Times*, 23 June 1998, p. 9.
23 ibid.
24 This was a conscious play on words by David Trimble for the politically literate, referring to an oft-quoted remark made by one of his predecessors, Sir James Craig, in 1934. The first Prime Minister of Northern Ireland claimed that what he wanted was 'a Protestant parliament and a Protestant state'.
25 *Irish News* 15 September 1998, p. 2.
26 The only UUP Assembly member to vote against this deal was Peter Weir. Weir had already lost the party whip in the Assembly on 18 January for voting against his party.
27 Under the deal agreed by the Assembly on 16 February 1999, the Executive would have twelve members, the First and Deputy First Ministers together with ten ministerial departments. The ten departments were: Agriculture and Rural Development; Environment; Regional Development; Social Development; Education; Higher and Further Education; Training and Employment; Enterprise, Trade and Investment; Culture, Arts and Leisure; Health, Social Services and Public Safety; and Finance and Personnel. The leadership of these departments was to be allocated under the d'Hondt system of representation, with departments being divided on the basis of party numbers in the Assembly. Thus, the UUP and SDLP were to get three ministries, while Sinn Féin and the DUP were to get two each.
      This agreement also paved the way for the establishment of six implementation

bodies: Inland Waterways; Food Safety; Trade and Business Development; Special EU Programmes; Language (Irish and Ulster Scots); and Aquaculture and Marine Matters.

Six specific North-South bodies had been agreed: Transport; Agriculture; Education; Health; Environment; and Tourism.

The creation of a 60-member Civic Forum was also agreed.

28   *The Irish Times,* 18 February 1999, p. 9.
29   *Irish News,* 24 February 1999, p. 5.
30   *The Irish Times,* 30 March 1999, p. 6.
31   *Irish News,* 8 April 1999, p. 2.
32   *The Irish Times,* 9 April 1999, p. 7.
33   ibid., 17 May 1999, p. 6.
34   ibid., 2 July 1999, p. 8.
35   ibid.
36   ibid., 16 July 1999, p. 7.
37   *News Letter,* 10 September 1999, p. 1.
38   ibid., p. 6.
39   *The Irish Times,* 19 November 1999, p. 6.
40   ibid., 13 October 1999, p. 9.
41   ibid., 18 November 1999, p. 1.
42   *News Letter,* 26 November 1999, p. 8.
43   *The Irish Times,* 19 November 1999, p. 6.
44   480 delegates (57.9 per cent) voted for, and 349 delegates (42.1 per cent) voted against the motion that 'The Ulster Unionist Council authorises the Leader and the Ulster Unionist Assembly party to proceed as outlined in the Leader's Report and instructs the President to reconvene the Council in February 2000 to take a final decision.' *The Sunday Tribune,* 28 November 1999, p. 11.
45   On November 29 1999, the d'Hondt formula was put into effect in the Assembly as the agreed mechanism for establishing the cross-party executive. This followed a procedural wrangle over whether or not Seamus Mallon had actually resigned as Deputy First Minister in July. In a breathtaking display of political chicanery, the pro-Agreement parties decided that although he had made a resignation speech and had offered his resignation, this had not been formally accepted by the Assembly and, therefore, the Deputy First Minister designate had not actually resigned, clearing the way for the nomination of ministers to proceed.

The most notable aspect of this procedure was the fact that the two Sinn Féin nominees, Martin McGuinness and Bairbre de Brún selected the education and health portfolios respectively, placing both at the centre of social policy in Northern Ireland. The ten ministers and their portfolios were:

Minister of Education, Martin McGuinness (SF). Minister for Regional Development, Peter Robinson (DUP). Minister of Agriculture and Rural Development, Brid Rodgers (SDLP). Minister of Enterprise Trade and Investment, Sir Reg Empey (UUP). Minister for Social Development, Nigel Dodds (DUP). Minister of Health and Social Services and Public Safety, Bairbre de Brún (SF). Minister of Environment, Sam Foster (UUP). Minister for Higher and Further Education, Training and Employment, Sean Farren (SDLP). Minister of Finance and Personnel, Mark Durkan (SDLP). Minister of Culture, Arts and Leisure, Michael McGimpsey (UUP). The executive was completed by Deputy First Minister Seamus Mallon (SDLP) and First Minister, David Trimble (UUP). The two DUP ministers announced that while they would fulfill their duties as ministers, they would not be sitting at the cabinet table due to the presence of Sinn Féin.

46   *The Irish Times,* 6 May 2000.
47   ibid., 8 May 2000.
48   The final winning margin was 459 votes in favour with 403 voting against. One vote was spoiled.
49   *The Irish Times,* 29 May 2000.

Text of the Downing Street Declaration
15 December 1993

The Joint Declaration made at Downing Street between British Prime Minister John Major and the Taoiseach of the Republic of Ireland, Albert Reynolds, on 15 December 1993

1. The Taoiseach, Mr Albert Reynolds TD, and the Prime Minister, the Rt Hon John Major MP, acknowledge that the most urgent and important issue facing the people of Ireland, North and South, and the British and Irish Governments together, is to remove the causes of conflict, to overcome the legacy of history and to heal the divisions which have resulted, recognising that the absence of a lasting and satisfactory settlement of relationships between the peoples of both islands has contributed to continuing tragedy and suffering. They believe that the development of an agreed framework for peace, which has been discussed between them since early last year, and which is based on a number of key principles articulated by the two Governments over the past 20 years, together with the adaptation of other widely accepted principles, provides the starting point of a peace process designed to culminate in a political settlement.

2. The Taoiseach and the Prime Minister are convinced of the inestimable value to both their peoples, and particularly for the next generation, of healing divisions in Ireland and of ending a conflict which has been so manifestly to the detriment of all. Both recognise that the ending of divisions can come about only through the agreement and co-operation of the people, North and South, representing both traditions in Ireland. They therefore make a solemn commitment to promote co-operation at all levels on the basis of the fundamental principles, undertakings, obligations under international agreements, to which they have jointly committed themselves, and the guarantees which each government has given and now reaffirms, including Northern Ireland's statutory constitutional guarantee. It is their aim to foster agreement and reconciliation, leading to a new political framework founded on consent and encompassing arrangements within Northern Ireland, for the whole island, and between these islands.

3. They also consider that the development of Europe will, of itself, require new approaches to serve interests common to both parts of the island of Ireland, and to Ireland and the United Kingdom as partners in the European Union.

4. The Prime Minister, on behalf of the British Government, reaffirms that they will uphold the democratic wish of a greater number of the people of Northern Ireland

on the issue of whether they prefer to support the Union or a sovereign united Ireland. On this basis, he reiterates, on behalf of the British Government, that they have no selfish strategic or economic interest in Northern Ireland. Their primary interest is to see peace, stability and reconciliation established by agreement among all the people who inhabit the island, and they will work together with the Irish Government to achieve such an agreement, which will embrace the totality of relationships. The role of the British Government will be to encourage, facilitate and enable the achievement of such agreement over a period through a process of dialogue and co-operation based on full respect for the rights and identities of both traditions in Ireland. They accept that such agreement may, as of right, take the form of agreed structures for the island as a whole, including a united Ireland achieved by peaceful means on the following basis. The British Government agree that it is for the people of the island of Ireland alone, by agreement between the two parts respectively, to exercise their right of self-determination on the basis of consent, freely and concurrently given, North and South, to bring about a united Ireland, if that is their wish. They reaffirm as a binding obligation that they will, for their part, introduce the necessary legislation to give effect to this, or equally to any measure of agreement on future relationships in Ireland which the people living in Ireland may themselves freely so determine without external impediment. They believe that the people of Britain would wish, in friendship to all sides, to enable the people of Ireland to reach agreement on how they may live together in harmony and in partnership, with respect for their diverse traditions, and with full recognition of the special links and the unique relationship which exist between the peoples of Britain and Ireland.

5. The Taoiseach, on behalf of the Irish Government, considers that the lessons of Irish history, and especially of Northern Ireland, show that stability and well-being will not be found under any political system which is refused allegiance or rejected on grounds of identity by a significant minority of those governed by it. For this reason, it would be wrong to attempt to impose a united Ireland, in the absence of the freely given consent of a majority of the people of Northern Ireland. He accepts, on behalf of the Irish Government, that the democratic right of self-determination by the people of Ireland as a whole must be achieved and exercised with and subject to the agreement and consent of a majority of the people of Northern Ireland and must, consistent with justice and equity, respect the democratic dignity and the civil rights and religious liberties of both communities, including:
- the right of free political thought;
- the right to freedom and expression of religion;
- the right to pursue democratically national and political aspirations;
- the right to seek constitutional change by peaceful and legitimate means;
- the right to live wherever one chooses without hindrance;
- the right to equal opportunity in all social and economic activity, regardless of class, creed, sex or colour.

These would be reflected in any future political and constitutional arrangements emerging from a new and more broadly based agreement.

6. The Taoiseach however recognises the genuine difficulties and barriers to building relationships of trust either within or beyond Northern Ireland, from which both traditions suffer. He will work to create a new era of trust, in which suspicion of the motives or actions of others is removed on the part of either community. He considers that the future of the island depends on the nature of the relationship between

the two main traditions that inhabit it. Every effort must be made to build a new sense of trust between those communities. In recognition of the fears of the unionist community and as a token of his willingness to make a personal contribution to the building up of that necessary trust, the Taoiseach will examine with his colleagues any elements in the democratic life and organisation of the Irish State that can be represented to the Irish Government in the course of political dialogue as a real and substantial threat to their way of life and ethos, or that can be represented as not being fully consistent with a modern democratic and pluralist society, and undertakes to examine any possible ways of removing such obstacles. Such an examination would of course have due regard to the desire to preserve those inherited values that are largely shared throughout the island or that belong to the cultural and historical roots of the people of this island in all their diversity. The Taoiseach hopes that over time a meeting of hearts and minds will develop, which will bring all the people of Ireland together, and will work towards that objective, but he pledges in the meantime that as a result of the efforts that will be made to build mutual confidence no Northern Unionist should ever have to fear in future that this ideal will be pursued either by threat or coercion.

7. Both Governments accept that Irish unity would be achieved only by those who favour this outcome persuading those who do not, peacefully and without coercion or violence, and that, if in the future a majority of the people of Northern Ireland are so persuaded, both Governments will support and give legislative effect to their wish. But, notwithstanding the solemn affirmation by both Governments in the Anglo-Irish Agreement that any change in the status of Northern Ireland would only come about with the consent of a majority of the people of Northern Ireland, the Taoiseach also recognises the continuing uncertainties and misgivings which dominate so much of Northern Unionist attitudes towards the rest of Ireland. He believes that we stand at a stage of our history when the genuine feelings of all traditions in the North must be recognised and acknowledged. He appeals to both traditions at this time to grasp the opportunity for a fresh start and a new beginning, which could hold such promise for all our lives and the generations to come. He asks the people of Northern Ireland to look on the people of the Republic as friends, who share their grief and shame over all the suffering of the last quarter of a century, and who want to develop the best possible relationship with them, a relationship in which trust and a new understanding can flourish and grow. The Taoiseach also acknowledges the presence in the Constitution of the Republic of elements which are deeply resented by Northern Unionists, but which at the same time reflect hopes and ideals which lie deep in the hearts of many Irish men and women North and South. But as we move towards a new era of understanding in which new relationships of trust may grow and bring peace to the island of Ireland, the Taoiseach believes that the time has come to consider together how best the hopes and identities of all can be expressed in more balanced ways, which no longer engender division and the lack of trust to which he has referred. He confirms that, in the event of an overall settlement, the Irish Government will, as part of a balanced constitutional accommodation, put forward and support proposals for change in the Irish Constitution which would fully reflect the principle of consent in Northern Ireland.

8. The Taoiseach recognises the need to engage in dialogue which would address with honesty and integrity the fears of all traditions. But that dialogue, both within the North and between the people and their representatives of both parts of Ireland,

must be entered into with an acknowledgement that the future security and welfare of the people of the island will depend on an open, frank and balanced approach to all the problems which for too long have caused division.

9. The British and Irish Governments will seek, along with the Northern Ireland constitutional parties through a process of political dialogue, to create institutions and structures which, while respecting the diversity of the people of Ireland, would enable them to work together in all areas of common interest. This will help over a period to build the trust necessary to end past divisions, leading to an agreed and peaceful future. Such structures would, of course, include institutional recognition of the special links that exist between the peoples of Britain and Ireland as part of the totality of relationships, while taking account of newly forged links with the rest of Europe.

10. The British and Irish Governments reiterate that the achievement of peace must involve a permanent end to the use of, or support for, paramilitary violence. They confirm that, in these circumstances, democratically mandated parties which establish a commitment to exclusively peaceful methods and which have shown that they abide by the democratic process, are free to participate fully in democratic politics and to join in dialogue in due course between the Governments and the political parties on the way ahead.

11. The Irish Government would make their own arrangements within their jurisdiction to enable democratic parties to consult together and share in dialogue about the political future. The Taoiseach's intention is that these arrangements could include the establishment, in consultation with other parties, of a Forum for Peace and Reconciliation to make recommendations on ways in which agreement and trust between both traditions in Ireland can be promoted and established.

12. The Taoiseach and the Prime Minister are determined to build on the fervent wish of both their peoples to see old fears and animosities replaced by a climate of peace. They believe the framework they have set out offers the people of Ireland, North and South, whatever their tradition, the basis to agree that from now on their differences can be negotiated and resolved exclusively by peaceful political means. They appeal to all concerned to grasp the opportunity for a new departure. That step would compromise no position or principle, nor prejudice the future for either community. On the contrary, it would be an incomparable gain for all. It would break decisively the cycle of violence and the intolerable suffering it entails for the people of these islands, particularly for both communities in Northern Ireland. It would allow the process of economic and social co-operation on the island to realise its full potential for prosperity and mutual understanding. It would transform the prospects for building on the progress already made in the Talks process, involving the two Governments and the constitutional parties in Northern Ireland. The Taoiseach and the Prime Minister believe that these arrangements offer an opportunity to lay the foundations for a more peaceful and harmonious future devoid of the violence and bitter divisions which have scarred the past generation. They commit themselves and their Governments to continue to work together, unremittingly, towards that objective.

Text of the Good Friday Agreement 10 April 1998

DECLARATION OF SUPPORT

1. We, the participants in the multi-party negotiations, believe that the agreement we have negotiated offers a truly historic opportunity for a new beginning.
2. The tragedies of the past have left a deep and profoundly regrettable legacy of suffering. We must never forget those who have died or been injured, and their families. But we can best honour them through a fresh start, in which we firmly dedicate ourselves to the achievement of reconciliation, tolerance, and mutual trust, and to the protection and vindication of the human rights of all.
3. We are committed to partnership, equality and mutual respect as the basis of relationships within Northern Ireland, between North and South, and between these islands.
4. We reaffirm our total and absolute commitment to exclusively democratic and peaceful means of resolving differences on political issues, and our opposition to any use or threat of force by others for any political purpose, whether in regard to this agreement or otherwise.
5. We acknowledge the substantial differences between our continuing, and equally legitimate, political aspirations. However, we will endeavour to strive in every practical way towards reconciliation and rapprochement within the framework of democratic and agreed arrangements. We pledge that we will, in good faith, work to ensure the success of each and every one of the arrangements to be established under this agreement. It is accepted that all of the institutional and constitutional arrangements – an Assembly in Northern Ireland, a North/South Ministerial Council, implementation bodies, a British-Irish Council and a British-Irish Intergovernmental Conference and any amendments to British Acts of Parliament and the Constitution of Ireland – are interlocking and interdependent and that in particular the functioning of the Assembly and the North/South Council are so closely inter-related that the success of each depends on that of the other.
6. Accordingly, in a spirit of concord, we strongly commend this agreement to the people, North and South, for their approval.

CONSTITUTIONAL ISSUES

1. The participants endorse the commitment made by the British and Irish Governments that, in a new British-Irish Agreement replacing the Anglo-Irish Agreement, they will:
   (i)   recognise the legitimacy of whatever choice is freely exercised by a majority of

the people of Northern Ireland with regard to its status, whether they prefer to continue to support the Union with Great Britain or a sovereign united Ireland;

(ii) recognise that it is for the people of the island of Ireland alone, by agreement between the two parts respectively and without external impediment, to exercise their right of self-determination on the basis of consent, freely and concurrently given, North and South, to bring about a united Ireland, if that is their wish, accepting that this right must be achieved and exercised with and subject to the agreement and consent of a majority of the people of Northern Ireland;

(iii) acknowledge that while a substantial section of the people in Northern Ireland share the legitimate wish of a majority of the people of the island of Ireland for a united Ireland, the present wish of a majority of the people of Northern Ireland, freely exercised and legitimate, is to maintain the Union and, accordingly, that Northern Ireland's status as part of the United Kingdom reflects and relies upon that wish; and that it would be wrong to make any change in the status of Northern Ireland save with the consent of a majority of its people;

(iv) affirm that if, in the future, the people of the island of Ireland exercise their right of self-determination on the basis set out in sections (i) and (ii) above to bring about a united Ireland, it will be a binding obligation on both Governments to introduce and support in their respective Parliaments legislation to give effect to that wish;

(v) affirm that whatever choice is freely exercised by a majority of the people of Northern Ireland, the power of the sovereign government with jurisdiction there shall be exercised with rigorous impartiality on behalf of all the people in the diversity of their identities and traditions and shall be founded on the principles of full respect for, and equality of, civil, political, social and cultural rights, of freedom from discrimination for all citizens and of parity of esteem and of just and equal treatment for the identity, ethos, and aspirations of both communities;

(vi) recognise the birthright of all the people of Northern Ireland to identify themselves and be accepted as Irish or British, or both, as they may so choose, and accordingly confirm that their right to hold both British and Irish citizenship is accepted by both Governments and would not be affected by any future change in the status of Northern Ireland.

2. The participants also note that the two Governments have accordingly undertaken in the context of this comprehensive political agreement, to propose and support changes in, respectively, the Constitution of Ireland and in British legislation relating to the constitutional status of Northern Ireland.

ANNEX A
DRAFT CLAUSES/SCHEDULES FOR INCORPORATION IN BRITISH LEGISLATION

1. (1) It is hereby declared that Northern Ireland in its entirety remains part of the United Kingdom and shall not cease to be so without the consent of a majority of the people of Northern Irealnd voting in a poll held for the purposes of this section in accordance with Schedule 1.

(2) But if the wish expressed by a majority in such a poll is that Northern Ireland should cease to be part of the United Kingdom and form part of a united Ireland, the Secretary of State shall lay before Parliament such proposals to give effect to that wish as may be agreed

between Her Majesty's Government in the United Kingdom and the Government of Ireland.

2. The Government of Ireland Act 1920 is repealed; and this Act shall have effect notwithstanding any other previous enactment.

SCHEDULE 1
POLLS FOR THE PURPOSE OF SECTION 1

1. The Secretary of State may by order direct the holding of a poll for the purposes of section 1 on a date specified in the order.

2. Subject to paragraph 3, the Secretary of State shall exercise the power under paragraph 1 if at any time it appears likely to him that a majority of those voting would express a wish that Northern Ireland should cease to be part of the United Kingdom and form part of a united Ireland.

3. The Secretary of State shall not make an order under paragraph 1 earlier than seven years after the holding of a previous poll under this Schedule.

4. (Remaining paragraphs along the lines of paragraphs 2 and 3 of existing Schedule 1 to 1973 Act.)

ANNEX B

IRISH GOVERNMENT DRAFT LEGISLATION TO AMEND THE CONSTITUTION

Add to Article 29 the following section:

7.

1. The State may consent to be bound by the British-Irish Agreement done at Belfast on the 10th day of April, 1998, hereinafter called the Agreement.

2. Any institution established by or under the Agreement may exercise the powers and functions thereby conferred on it in respect of all or any part of the island of Ireland notwithstanding any other provision of this Constitution conferring a like power or function on any person or any organ of State appointed under or created or established by or under this Constitution. Any power or function conferred on such an institution in relation to the settlement or resolution of disputes or controversies may be in addition to or in substitution for any like power or function conferred by this Constitution on any such person or organ of State as aforesaid.

3. If the Government declare that the State has become obliged, pursuant to the Agreement, to give effect to the amendment of this Constitution referred to therein, then, notwithstanding Article 46 hereof, this Constitution shall be amended as follows:

   i. the following Articles shall be substituted for Articles 2 and 3 of the Irish text:

   Airteagal 2

   Tá gach duine a shaolaítear in oileán na hÉireann, ar a n-áirítear a oileáin agus a fharraigí, i dteideal, agus tá de cheart oidhreachta aige nó aici, a bheith páirteach i náisiún na hÉireann. Tá an teideal sin freisin ag na daoine go léir atá cáilithe ar shlí eile de réir dlí chun bheith ina saoránaigh d'Éirinn. Ina theannta sin, is mór ag náisiún na hÉireann a choibhneas speisialta le daoine de bhunadh na hÉireann atá ina gcónaí ar an gcoigríoch agus arb ionann féiniúlacht agus oidhreacht chultúir dóibh agus do náisiún na hÉireann.

   Airteagal 3

   1. Is í toil dhiongbháilte náisiún na hÉireann, go sítheach cairdiúil, na daoine go léir a chomhroinneann críoch oileán na hÉireann i bpáirt lena chéile, in éagsúlacht uile a bhféiniúlachtaí agus a dtraidisiún, a aontú, á aithint gur trí mhodhanna síochánta amháin le toiliú thromlach na ndaoine, á chur in iúl go daonlathach, sa dá dhlínse san oileán, a dhéanfar Éire aontaithe a thabhairt i gcrích. Go dtí sin, bainfidh na dlíthe a achtófar ag an bParlaimint a bhunaítear leis an mBunreacht seo leis an limistéar feidhme céanna, agus beidh an raon feidhme céanna acu, lenar bhain na dlíthe, agus a bhí ag na dlíthe, a d'achtaigh an Pharlaimint a bhí ar marthain díreach roimh theacht i ngníomh don Bhunreacht seo.

    2. Féadfaidh údaráis fhreagracha faoi seach na ndlínsí sin institiúidí ag a mbeidh cumhachtaí agus feidhmeanna feidhmiúcháin a chomhroinntear idir na dlínsí sin a bhunú chun críoch sonraithe agus féadfaidh na hinstitiúidí sin cumhachtaí agus feidhmeanna a fheidhmiú i leith an oileáin ar fad nó i leith aon chuid de.

ii. the following Articles shall be substituted for Articles 2 and 3 of the English text:

Article 2

It is the entitlement and birthright of every person born in the island of Ireland, which includes its islands and seas, to be part of the Irish nation. That is also the entitlement of all persons otherwise qualified in accordance with law to be citizens of Ireland. Furthermore, the Irish nation cherishes its special affinity with people of Irish ancestry living abroad who share its cultural identity and heritage.

Article 3

    1. It is the firm will of the Irish nation, in harmony and friendship, to unite all the people who share the territory of the island of Ireland, in all the diversity of their identities and traditions, recognising that a united Ireland shall be brought about only by peaceful means with the consent of a majority of the people, democratically expressed, in both jurisdictions in the island. Until then, the laws enacted by the Parliament established by this Constitution shall have the like area and extent of application as the laws enacted by the Parliament that existed immediately before the coming into operation of this Constitution.

    2. Institutions with executive powers and functions that are shared between those jurisdictions may be established by their respective responsible authorities for stated purposes and may exercise powers and functions in respect of all or any part of the island."

iii. the following section shall be added to the Irish text of this Article:

    8. Tig leis an Stát dlínse a fheidhmiú taobh amuigh dá chríoch de réir bhunrialacha gnáth-admhaithe an dlí idirnáisiúnta.

and

iv. the following section shall be added to the English text of this Article:

    8. The State may exercise extraterritorial jurisdiction in accordance with the generally recognised principles of international law.

4. If a declaration under this section is made, this subsection and subsection 3, other than the amendment of this Constitution effected thereby, and subsection 5 of this section shall be omitted from every official text of this Constitution published thereafter, but notwithstanding such omission this section shall continue to have the force of law.

5. If such a declaration is not made within twelve months of this section being added to this Constitution or such longer period as may be provided for by law, this section shall cease to have effect and shall be omitted from every official text of this Constitution published thereafter.

STRAND ONE
DEMOCRATIC INSTITUTIONS IN NORTHERN IRELAND

1. This agreement provides for a democratically elected Assembly in Northern Ireland which is inclusive in its membership, capable of exercising executive and legislative authority, and subject to safeguards to protect the rights and interests of all sides of the community.

The Assembly

2. A 108-member Assembly will be elected by PR(STV) from existing Westminster constituencies.

3. The Assembly will exercise full legislative and executive authority in respect of those matters currently within the responsibility of the six Northern Ireland Government Departments, with the possibility of taking on responsibility for other matters as detailed elsewhere in this agreement.

4. The Assembly – operating where appropriate on a cross-community basis – will

be the prime source of authority in respect of all devolved responsibilities.

Safeguards

5. There will be safeguards to ensure that all sections of the community can partici-
    pate and work together successfully in the operation of these institutions and that
    all sections of the community are protected, including:
    (a) allocations of Committee Chairs, Ministers and Committee membership in
        proportion to party strengths;
    (b) the European Convention on Human Rights (ECHR) and any Bill of Rights
        for Northern Ireland supplementing it, which neither the Assembly nor public
        bodies can infringe, together with a Human Rights Commission;
    (c) arrangements to provide that key decisions and legislation are proofed to
        ensure that they do not infringe the ECHR and any Bill of Rights for Northern
        Ireland;
    (d) arrangements to ensure key decisions are taken on a cross-community basis;
        (i) **either** parallel consent, i.e. a majority of those members present and voting,
            including a majority of the unionist and nationalist designations
            present and voting;
        (ii) **or** a weighted majority (60%) of members present and voting, including
            at least 40% of each of the nationalist and unionist designations
            present and voting.
    Key decisions requiring cross-community support will be designated in advance,
    including election of the Chair of the Assembly, the First Minister and Deputy
    First Minister, standing orders and budget allocations. In other cases such deci-
    sions could be triggered by a petition of concern brought by a significant minority
    of Assembly members (30/108).
    (e) an Equality Commission to monitor a statutory obligation to promote equal-
        ity of opportunity in specified areas and parity of esteem between the two
        main communities, and to investigate individual complaints against public
        bodies.

Operation of the Assembly

6. At their first meeting, members of the Assembly will register a designation of
    identity – nationalist, unionist or other for the purposes of measuring cross-
    community support in Assembly votes under the relevant provisions above.
7. The Chair and Deputy Chair of the Assembly will be elected on a cross-community
    basis, as set out in paragraph 5(d) above.
8. There will be a Committee for each of the main executive functions of the North-
    ern Ireland Administration. The Chairs and Deputy Chairs of the Assembly
    Committees will be allocated proportionally, using the d'Hondt system. Member-
    ship of the Committees will be in broad proportion to party strengths in the
    Assembly to ensure that the opportunity of Committee places is available to all
    members.
9. The Committees will have a scrutiny, policy development and consultation role
    with respect to the Department with which each is associated, and will have a role
    in initiation of legislation. They will have the power to:
    • consider and advise on Departmental budgets and Annual Plans in the context
      of the overall budget allocation;
    • approve relevant secondary legislation and take the Committee stage of rele-
      vant primary legislation;
    • call for persons and papers;
    • initiate enquiries and make reports;

- consider and advise on matters brought to the Committee by its Minister.

10. Standing Committees other than Departmental Committees may be established as may be required from time to time.

11. The Assembly may appoint a special Committee to examine and report on whether a measure or proposal for legislation is in conformity with equality requirements, including the ECHR/Bill of Rights. The Committee shall have the power to call people and papers to assist in its consideration of the matter. The Assembly shall then consider the report of the Committee and can determine the matter in accordance with the cross-community consent procedure.

12. The above special procedure shall be followed when requested by the Executive Committee, or by the relevant Departmental Committee, voting on a cross-community basis.

13. When there is a petition of concern as in 5(d) above, the Assembly shall vote to determine whether the measure may proceed without reference to this special procedure. If this fails to achieve support on a cross-community basis, as in 5(d)(i) above, the special procedure shall be followed.

Executive Authority

14. Executive authority to be discharged on behalf of the Assembly by a First Minister and Deputy First Minister and up to ten Ministers with Departmental responsibilities.

15. The First Minister and Deputy First Minister shall be jointly elected into office by the Assembly voting on a cross-community basis, according to 5(d)(i) above.

16. Following the election of the First Minister and Deputy First Minister, the posts of Ministers will be allocated to parties on the basis of the d'Hondt system by reference to the number of seats each party has in the Assembly.

17. The Ministers will constitute an Executive Committee, which will be convened, and presided over, by the First Minister and Deputy First Minister.

18. The duties of the First Minister and Deputy First Minister will include, inter alia, dealing with and co-ordinating the work of the Executive Committee and the response of the Northern Ireland administration to external relationships.

19. The Executive Committee will provide a forum for the discussion of, and agreement on, issues which cut across the responsibilities of two or more Ministers, for prioritising executive and legislative proposals and for recommending a common position where necessary (e.g. in dealing with external relationships).

20. The Executive Committee will seek to agree each year, and review as necessary, a programme incorporating an agreed budget linked to policies and programmes, subject to approval by the Assembly, after scrutiny in Assembly Committees, on a cross-community basis.

21. A party may decline the opportunity to nominate a person to serve as a Minister or may subsequently change its nominee.

22. All the Northern Ireland Departments will be headed by a Minister. All Ministers will liaise regularly with their respective Committee.

23. As a condition of appointment, Ministers, including the First Minister and Deputy First Minister, will affirm the terms of a Pledge of Office (Annex A) undertaking to discharge effectively and in good faith all the responsibilities attaching to their office.

24. Ministers will have full executive authority in their respective areas of responsibility, within any broad programme agreed by the Executive Committee and endorsed by the Assembly as a whole.

25. An individual may be removed from office following a decision of the Assembly taken on a cross-community basis, if (s)he loses the confidence of the Assembly,

voting on a cross-community basis, for failure to meet his or her responsibilities including, inter alia, those set out in the Pledge of Office. Those who hold office should use only democratic, non-violent means, and those who do not should be excluded or removed from office under these provisions.

Legislation
26. The Assembly will have authority to pass primary legislation for Northern Ireland in devolved areas, subject to:
    (a) the ECHR and any Bill of Rights for Northern Ireland supplementing it which, if the courts found to be breached, would render the relevant legislation null and void;
    (b) decisions by simple majority of members voting, except when decision on a cross-community basis is required;
    (c) detailed scrutiny and approval in the relevant Departmental Committee;
    (d) mechanisms, based on arrangements proposed for the Scottish Parliament, to ensure suitable co-ordination, and avoid disputes, between the Assembly and the Westminster Parliament;
    (e) option of the Assembly seeking to include Northern Ireland provisions in United Kingdom-wide legislation in the Westminster Parliament, especially on devolved issues where parity is normally maintained (e.g. social security, company law).
27. The Assembly will have authority to legislate in reserved areas with the approval of the Secretary of State and subject to Parliamentary control.
28. Disputes over legislative competence will be decided by the Courts.
29. Legislation could be initiated by an individual, a Committee or a Minister.

Relations with other institutions
30. Arrangements to represent the Assembly as a whole, at Summit level and in dealings with other institutions, will be in accordance with paragraph 18, and will be such as to ensure cross-community involvement.
31. Terms will be agreed between appropriate Assembly representatives and the Government of the United Kingdom to ensure effective co-ordination and input by Ministers to national policy-making, including on EU issues.
32. Role of Secretary of State:
    (a) to remain responsible for NIO matters not devolved to the Assembly, subject to regular consultation with the Assembly and Ministers;
    (b) to approve and lay before the Westminster Parliament any Assembly legislation on reserved matters;
    (c) to represent Northern Ireland interests in the United Kingdom Cabinet;
    (d) to have the right to attend the Assembly at their invitation.
33. The Westminster Parliament (whose power to make legislation for Northern Ireland would remain unaffected) will:
    (a) legislate for non-devolved issues, other than where the Assembly legislates with the approval of the Secretary of State and subject to the control of Parliament;
    (b) legislate as necessary to ensure the United Kingdom's international obligations are met in respect of Northern Ireland;
    (c) scrutinise, including through the Northern Ireland Grand and Select Committees, the responsibilities of the Secretary of State.
34. A consultative Civic Forum will be established. It will comprise representatives of the business, trade union and voluntary sectors, and such other sectors as agreed by the First Minister and the Deputy First Minister. It will act as a consultative mechanism on social, economic and cultural issues. The First Minister and the

Deputy First Minister will by agreement provide administrative support for the Civic Forum and establish guidelines for the selection of representatives to the Civic Forum.

Transitional Arrangements

35. The Assembly will meet first for the purpose of organisation, without legislative or executive powers, to resolve its standing orders and working practices and make preparations for the effective functioning of the Assembly, the British-Irish Council and the North/South Ministerial Council and associated implementation bodies. In this transitional period, those members of the Assembly serving as shadow Ministers shall affirm their commitment to non-violence and exclusively peaceful and democratic means and their opposition to any use or threat of force by others for any political purpose; to work in good faith to bring the new arrangements into being; and to observe the spirit of the Pledge of Office applying to appointed Ministers.

Review

36. After a specified period there will be a review of these arrangements, including the details of electoral arrangements and of the Assembly's procedures, with a view to agreeing any adjustments necessary in the interests of efficiency and fairness.

ANNEX A
PLEDGE OF OFFICE

To pledge:
(a) to discharge in good faith all the duties of office;
(b) commitment to non-violence and exclusively peaceful and democratic means;
(c) to serve all the people of Northern Ireland equally, and to act in accordance with the general obligations on government to promote equality and prevent discrimination;
(d) to participate with colleagues in the preparation of a programme for government;
(e) to operate within the framework of that programme when agreed within the Executive Committee and endorsed by the Assembly;
(f) to support, and to act in accordance with, all decisions of the Executive Committee and Assembly;
(g) to comply with the Ministerial Code of Conduct.

CODE OF CONDUCT

Ministers must at all times:
- observe the highest standards of propriety and regularity involving impartiality, integrity and objectivity in relationship to the stewardship of public funds;
- be accountable to users of services, the community and, through the Assembly, for the activities within their responsibilities, their stewardship of public funds and the extent to which key performance targets and objectives have been met;
- ensure all reasonable requests for information from the Assembly, users of services and individual citizens are complied with; and that Departments and their staff conduct their dealings with the public in an open and responsible way;
- follow the seven principles of public life set out by the Committee on Standards in Public Life;
- comply with this code and with rules relating to the use of public funds;
- operate in a way conducive to promoting good community relations and equality of treatment;
- not use information gained in the course of their service for personal gain; nor seek to use the opportunity of public service to promote their private interests;
- ensure they comply with any rules on the acceptance of gifts and hospitality that might be offered;
- declare any personal or business interests which may conflict with their responsibilities. The Assembly will retain a Register of Interests. Individuals must ensure that any direct or indirect pecuniary interests which members of the public might reasonably think could influence their judgement are listed in the Register of Interests.

STRAND TWO
NORTH/SOUTH MINISTERIAL COUNCIL

1. Under a new British/Irish Agreement dealing with the totality of relationships, and related legislation at Westminster and in the Oireachtas, a North/South Ministerial Council to be established to bring together those with executive responsibilities in Northern Ireland and the Irish Government, to develop consultation, co-operation and action within the island of Ireland – including through implementation on an all-island and cross-border basis – on matters of mutual interest within the competence of the Administrations, North and South.

2. All Council decisions to be by agreement between the two sides. Northern Ireland to be represented by the First Minister, Deputy First Minister and any relevant Ministers, the Irish Government by the Taoiseach and relevant Ministers, all operating in accordance with the rules for democratic authority and accountability in force in the Northern Ireland Assembly and the Oireachtas respectively. Participation in the Council to be one of the essential responsibilities attaching to relevant posts in the two Administrations. If a holder of a relevant post will not participate normally in the Council, the Taoiseach in the case of the Irish Government and the First and Deputy First Minister in the case of the Northern Ireland Administration to be able to make alternative arrangements.

3. The Council to meet in different formats:
   (i) in plenary format twice a year, with Northern Ireland representation led by the First Minister and Deputy First Minister and the Irish Government led by the Taoiseach;
   (ii) in specific sectoral formats on a regular and frequent basis with each side represented by the appropriate Minister;
   (iii) in an appropriate format to consider institutional or cross-sectoral matters (including in relation to the EU) and to resolve disagreement.

4. Agendas for all meetings to be settled by prior agreement between the two sides, but it will be open to either to propose any matter for consideration or action.

5. The Council:
   (i) to exchange information, discuss and consult with a view to co-operating on matters of mutual interest within the competence of both Administrations, North and South;
   (ii) to use best endeavours to reach agreement on the adoption of common policies, in areas where there is a mutual cross-border and all-island benefit, and which are within the competence of both Administrations, North and South, making determined efforts to overcome any disagreements;
   (iii) to take decisions by agreement on policies for implementation separately in each jurisdiction, in relevant meaningful areas within the competence of both Administrations, North and South;
   (iv) to take decisions by agreement on policies and action at an all-island and cross-border level to be implemented by the bodies to be established as set out in paragraphs 8 and 9 below.

6. Each side to be in a position to take decisions in the Council within the defined authority of those attending, through the arrangements in place for co-ordination of executive functions within each jurisdiction. Each side to remain accountable to the Assembly and Oireachtas respectively, whose approval, through the arrangements in place on either side, would be required for decisions beyond the defined authority of those attending.

7. As soon as practically possible after elections to the Northern Ireland Assembly, inaugural meetings will take place of the Assembly, the British/Irish Council and

the North/South Ministerial Council in their transitional forms. All three institutions will meet regularly and frequently on this basis during the period between the elections to the Assembly, and the transfer of powers to the Assembly, in order to establish their modus operandi.

8. During the transitional period between the elections to the Northern Ireland Assembly and the transfer of power to it, representatives of the Northern Ireland transitional Administration and the Irish Government operating in the North/South Ministerial Council will undertake a work programme, in consultation with the British Government, covering at least 12 subject areas, with a view to identifying and agreeing by 31 October 1998 areas where co-operation and implementation for mutual benefit will take place. Such areas may include matters in the list set out in the Annex.

9. As part of the work programme, the Council will identify and agree at least 6 matters for co-operation and implementation in each of the following categories:
   (i) Matters where existing bodies will be the appropriate mechanisms for co-operation in each separate jurisdiction;
   (ii) Matters where the co-operation will take place through agreed implementation bodies on a cross-border or all-island level.

10. The two Governments will make necessary legislative and other enabling preparations to ensure, as an absolute commitment, that these bodies, which have been agreed as a result of the work programme, function at the time of the inception of the British-Irish Agreement and the transfer of powers, with legislative authority for these bodies transferred to the Assembly as soon as possible thereafter. Other arrangements for the agreed co-operation will also commence contemporaneously with the transfer of powers to the Assembly.

11. The implementation bodies will have a clear operational remit. They will implement on an all-island and cross-border basis policies agreed in the Council.

12. Any further development of these arrangements to be by agreement in the Council and with the specific endorsement of the Northern Ireland Assembly and Oireachtas, subject to the extent of the competences and responsibility of the two Administrations.

13. It is understood that the North/South Ministerial Council and the Northern Ireland Assembly are mutually interdependent, and that one cannot successfully function without the other.

14. Disagreements within the Council to be addressed in the format described at paragraph 3(iii) above or in the plenary format. By agreement between the two sides, experts could be appointed to consider a particular matter and report.

15. Funding to be provided by the two Administrations on the basis that the Council and the implementation bodies constitute a necessary public function.

16. The Council to be supported by a standing joint Secretariat, staffed by members of the Northern Ireland Civil Service and the Irish Civil Service.

17. The Council to consider the European Union dimension of relevant matters, including the implementation of EU policies and programmes and proposals under consideration in the EU framework. Arrangements to be made to ensure that the views of the Council are taken into account and represented appropriately at relevant EU meetings.

18. The Northern Ireland Assembly and the Oireachtas to consider developing a joint parliamentary forum, bringing together equal numbers from both institutions for discussion of matters of mutual interest and concern.

19. Consideration to be given to the establishment of an independent consultative forum appointed by the two Administrations, representative of civil society,

comprising the social partners and other members with expertise in social, cultural, economic and other issues.

ANNEX

Areas for North-South co-operation and implementation may include the following:
1. Agriculture – animal and plant health.
2. Education – teacher qualifications and exchanges.
3. Transport – strategic transport planning.
4. Environment – environmental protection, pollution, water quality, and waste management.
5. Waterways – inland waterways.
6. Social Security/Social Welfare – entitlements of cross-border workers and fraud control.
7. Tourism – promotion, marketing, research, and product development.
8. Relevant EU Programmes such as SPPR, INTERREG, Leader II and their successors.
9. Inland Fisheries.
10. Aquaculture and marine matters.
11. Health: accident and emergency services and other related cross-border issues.
12. Urban and rural development.
Others to be considered by the shadow North/ South Council.

STRAND THREE
BRITISH–IRISH COUNCIL

I. A British-Irish Council (BIC) will be established under a new British-Irish Agreement to promote the harmonious and mutually beneficial development of the totality of relationships among the peoples of these islands.

2. Membership of the BIC will comprise representatives of the British and Irish Governments, devolved institutions in Northern Ireland, Scotland and Wales, when established, and, if appropriate, elsewhere in the United Kingdom, together with representatives of the Isle of Man and the Channel Islands.

3. The BIC will meet in different formats: at summit level, twice per year; in specific sectoral formats on a regular basis, with each side represented by the appropriate Minister; in an appropriate format to consider cross-sectoral matters.

4. Representatives of members will operate in accordance with whatever procedures for democratic authority and accountability are in force in their respective elected institutions.

5. The BIC will exchange information, discuss, consult and use best endeavours to reach agreement on co-operation on matters of mutual interest within the competence of the relevant Administrations. Suitable issues for early discussion in the BIC could include transport links, agricultural issues, environmental issues, cultural issues, health issues, education issues and approaches to EU issues. Suitable arrangements to be made for practical co-operation on agreed policies.

6. It will be open to the BIC to agree common policies or common actions. Individual members may opt not to participate in such common policies and common action.

7. The BIC normally will operate by consensus. In relation to decisions on common policies or common actions, including their means of implementation, it will operate by agreement of all members participating in such policies or actions.

8. The members of the BIC, on a basis to be agreed between them, will provide such financial support as it may require.

9. A secretariat for the BIC will be provided by the British and Irish Governments in co-ordination with officials of each of the other members.

10. In addition to the structures provided for under this agreement, it will be open to

two or more members to develop bilateral or multilateral arrangements between them. Such arrangements could include, subject to the agreement of the members concerned, mechanisms to enable consultation, co-operation and joint decision-making on matters of mutual interest; and mechanisms to implement any joint decisions they may reach. These arrangements will not require the prior approval of the BIC as a whole and will operate independently of it.

11. The elected institutions of the members will be encouraged to develop interparliamentary links, perhaps building on the British-Irish Interparliamentary Body.

12. The full membership of the BIC will keep under review the workings of the Council, including a formal published review at an appropriate time after the Agreement comes into effect, and will contribute as appropriate to any review of the overall political agreement arising from the multi-party negotiations.

BRITISH-IRISH INTERGOVERNMENTAL CONFERENCE

1. There will be a new British-Irish Agreement dealing with the totality of relationships. It will establish a standing British-Irish Intergovernmental Conference, which will subsume both the Anglo-Irish Intergovernmental Council and the Intergovernmental Conference established under the 1985 Agreement.

2. The Conference will bring together the British and Irish Governments to promote bilateral co-operation at all levels on all matters of mutual interest within the competence of both Governments.

3. The Conference will meet as required at Summit level (Prime Minister and Taoiseach). Otherwise, Governments will be represented by appropriate Ministers. Advisers, including police and security advisers, will attend as appropriate.

4. All decisions will be by agreement between both Governments. The Governments will make determined efforts to resolve disagreements between them. There will be no derogation from the sovereignty of either Government.

5. In recognition of the Irish Government's special interest in Northern Ireland and of the extent to which issues of mutual concern arise in relation to Northern Ireland, there will be regular and frequent meetings of the Conference concerned with non-devolved Northern Ireland matters, on which the Irish Government may put forward views and proposals. These meetings, to be co-chaired by the Minister for Foreign Affairs and the Secretary of State for Northern Ireland, would also deal with all-island and cross-border co-operation on non-devolved issues.

6. Co-operation within the framework of the Conference will include facilitation of co-operation in security matters. The Conference also will address, in particular, the areas of rights, justice, prisons and policing in Northern Ireland (unless and until responsibility is devolved to a Northern Ireland administration) and will intensify co-operation between the two Governments on the all-island or cross-border aspects of these matters.

7. Relevant executive members of the Northern Ireland Administration will be involved in meetings of the Conference, and in the reviews referred to in paragraph 9 below to discuss non-devolved Northern Ireland matters.

8. The Conference will be supported by officials of the British and Irish Governments, including by a standing joint Secretariat of officials dealing with non-devolved Northern Ireland matters.

9. The Conference will keep under review the workings of the new British-Irish Agreement and the machinery and institutions established under it, including a formal published review three years after the Agreement comes into effect. Representatives of the Northern Ireland Administration will be invited to express views to the Conference in this context. The Conference will contribute as appropriate to

any review of the overall political agreement arising from the multi-party negotiations but will have no power to override the democratic arrangements set up by this Agreement.

RIGHTS, SAFEGUARDS AND EQUALITY OF OPPORTUNITY
Human Rights
1. The parties affirm their commitment to the mutual respect, the civil rights and the religious liberties of everyone in the community. Against the background of the recent history of communal conflict, the parties affirm in particular:
   - the right of free political thought;
   - the right to freedom and expression of religion;
   - the right to pursue democratically national and political aspirations;
   - the right to seek constitutional change by peaceful and legitimate means;
   - the right to freely choose one's place of residence;
   - the right to equal opportunity in all social and economic activity, regardless of class, creed, disability, gender or ethnicity;
   - the right to freedom from sectarian harassment; and
   - the right of women to full and equal political participation.

United Kingdom Legislation
2. The British Government will complete incorporation into Northern Ireland law of the European Convention on Human Rights (ECHR), with direct access to the courts, and remedies for breach of the Convention, including power for the courts to overrule Assembly legislation on grounds of inconsistency.
3. Subject to the outcome of public consultation underway, the British Government intends, as a particular priority, to create a statutory obligation on public authorities in Northern Ireland to carry out all their functions with due regard to the need to promote equality of opportunity in relation to religion and political opinion; gender; race; disability; age; marital status; dependants; and sexual orientation. Public bodies would be required to draw up statutory schemes showing how they would implement this obligation. Such schemes would cover arrangements for policy appraisal, including an assessment of impact on relevant categories, public consultation, public access to information and services, monitoring and timetables.
4. The new Northern Ireland Human Rights Commission (see paragraph 5 below) will be invited to consult and to advise on the scope for defining, in Westminster legislation, rights supplementary to those in the European Convention on Human Rights, to reflect the particular circumstances of Northern Ireland, drawing as appropriate on international instruments and experience. These additional rights to reflect the principles of mutual respect for the identity and ethos of both communities and parity of esteem, and – taken together with the ECHR – to constitute a Bill of Rights for Northern Ireland. Among the issues for consideration by the Commission will be:
   - the formulation of a general obligation on government and public bodies fully to respect, on the basis of equality of treatment, the identity and ethos of both communities in Northern Ireland; and
   - a clear formulation of the rights not to be discriminated against and to equality of opportunity in both the public and private sectors.

New Institutions in Northern Ireland
5. A new Northern Ireland Human Rights Commission, with membership from Northern Ireland reflecting the community balance, will be established by Westminster legislation, independent of Government, with an extended and enhanced

role beyond that currently exercised by the Standing Advisory Commission on Human Rights, to include keeping under review the adequacy and effectiveness of laws and practices, making recommendations to Government as necessary; providing information and promoting awareness of human rights; considering draft legislation referred to them by the new Assembly; and, in appropriate cases, bringing court proceedings or providing assistance to individuals doing so.

6. Subject to the outcome of public consultation currently underway, the British Government intends a new statutory Equality Commission to replace the Fair Employment Commission, the Equal Opportunities Commission (NI), the Commission for Racial Equality (NI) and the Disability Council. Such a unified Commission will advise on, validate and monitor the statutory obligation and will investigate complaints of default.

7. It would be open to a new Northern Ireland Assembly to consider bringing together its responsibilities for these matters into a dedicated Department of Equality.

8. These improvements will build on existing protections in Westminster legislation in respect of the judiciary, the system of justice and policing.

Comparable Steps by the Irish Government

9. The Irish Government will also take steps to further strengthen the protection of human rights in its jurisdiction. The Government will, taking account of the work of the All-Party Oireachtas Committee on the Constitution and the Report of the Constitution Review Group, bring forward measures to strengthen and underpin the constitutional protection of human rights. These proposals will draw on the European Convention on Human Rights and other international legal instruments in the field of human rights and the question of the incorporation of the ECHR will be further examined in this context. The measures brought forward would ensure at least an equivalent level of protection of human rights as will pertain in Northern Ireland. In addition, the Irish Government will:

- establish a Human Rights Commission with a mandate and remit equivalent to that within Northern Ireland;
- proceed with arrangements as quickly as possible to ratify the Council of Europe Framework Convention on National Minorities (already ratified by the UK);
- implement enhanced employment equality legislation;
- introduce equal status legislation; and
- continue to take further active steps to demonstrate its respect for the different traditions in the island of Ireland.

A Joint Committee

10. It is envisaged that there would be a joint committee of representatives of the two Human Rights Commissions, North and South, as a forum for consideration of human rights issues in the island of Ireland. The joint committee will consider, among other matters, the possibility of establishing a charter, open to signature by all democratic political parties, reflecting and endorsing agreed measures for the protection of the fundamental rights of everyone living in the island of Ireland.

Reconciliation and Victims of Violence

11. The participants believe that it is essential to acknowledge and address the suffering of the victims of violence as a necessary element of reconciliation. They look forward to the results of the work of the Northern Ireland Victims Commission.

12. It is recognised that victims have a right to remember as well as to contribute to a changed society. The achievement of a peaceful and just society would be the true

memorial to the victims of violence. The participants particularly recognise that young people from areas affected by the troubles face particular difficulties and will support the development of special community-based initiatives based on international best practice. The provision of services that are supportive and sensitive to the needs of victims will also be a critical element and that support will need to be channelled through both statutory and community-based voluntary organisations facilitating locally-based self-help and support networks. This will require the allocation of sufficient resources, including statutory funding as necessary, to meet the needs of victims and to provide for community-based support programmes.

13. The participants recognise and value the work being done by many organisations to develop reconciliation and mutual understanding and respect between and within communities and traditions, in Northern Ireland and between North and South, and they see such work as having a vital role in consolidating peace and political agreement. Accordingly, they pledge their continuing support to such organisations and will positively examine the case for enhanced financial assistance for the work of reconciliation. An essential aspect of the reconciliation process is the promotion of a culture of tolerance at every level of society, including initiatives to facilitate and encourage integrated education and mixed housing.

RIGHTS, SAFEGUARDS AND EQUALITY OF OPPORTUNITY
ECONOMIC, SOCIAL AND CULTURAL ISSUES

1. Pending the devolution of powers to a new Northern Ireland Assembly, the British Government will pursue broad policies for sustained economic growth and stability in Northern Ireland and for promoting social inclusion, including in particular community development and the advancement of women in public life.
2. Subject to the public consultation currently under way, the British Government will make rapid progress with:
   (i) a new regional development strategy for Northern Ireland, for consideration in due course by the Assembly, tackling the problems of a divided society and social cohesion in urban, rural and border areas, protecting and enhancing the environment, producing new approaches to transport issues, strengthening the physical infrastructure of the region, developing the advantages and resources of rural areas and rejuvenating major urban centres;
   (ii) a new economic development strategy for Northern Ireland, for consideration in due course by the Assembly, which would provide for short and medium term economic planning linked as appropriate to the regional development strategy; and
   (iii) measures on employment equality included in the recent White Paper ("Partnership for Equality") and covering the extension and strengthening of anti-discrimination legislation, a review of the national security aspects of the present fair employment legislation at the earliest possible time, a new more focused Targeting Social Need initiative and a range of measures aimed at combating unemployment and progressively eliminating the differential in unemployment rates between the two communities by targeting objective need.
3. All participants recognise the importance of respect, understanding and tolerance in relation to linguistic diversity, including in Northern Ireland, the Irish language, Ulster-Scots and the languages of the various ethnic communities, all of which are part of the cultural wealth of the island of Ireland.
4. In the context of active consideration currently being given to the UK signing the

Council of Europe Charter for Regional or Minority Languages, the British Government will in particular in relation to the Irish language, where appropriate and where people so desire it:

- take resolute action to promote the language;
- facilitate and encourage the use of the language in speech and writing in public and private life where there is appropriate demand;
- seek to remove, where possible, restrictions which would discourage or work against the maintenance or development of the language;
- make provision for liaising with the Irish language community, representing their views to public authorities and investigating complaints;
- place a statutory duty on the Department of Education to encourage and facilitate Irish medium education in line with current provision for integrated education;
- explore urgently with the relevant British authorities, and in co-operation with the Irish broadcasting authorities, the scope for achieving more wide-spread availability of Teilifís na Gaeilge in Northern Ireland;
- seek more effective ways to encourage and provide financial support for Irish language film and television production in Northern Ireland; and
- encourage the parties to secure agreement that this commitment will be sustained by a new Assembly in a way which takes account of the desires and sensitivities of the community.

5. All participants acknowledge the sensitivity of the use of symbols and emblems for public purposes, and the need in particular in creating the new institutions to ensure that such symbols and emblems are used in a manner which promotes mutual respect rather than division. Arrangements will be made to monitor this issue and consider what action might be required.

DECOMMISSIONING

1. Participants recall their agreement in the Procedural Motion adopted on 24 September 1997 "that the resolution of the decommissioning issue is an indispensable part of the process of negotiation", and also recall the provisions of paragraph 25 of Strand 1 above.

2. They note the progress made by the Independent International Commission on Decommissioning and the Governments in developing schemes which can represent a workable basis for achieving the decommissioning of illegally-held arms in the possession of paramilitary groups.

3. All participants accordingly reaffirm their commitment to the total disarmament of all paramilitary organisations. They also confirm their intention to continue to work constructively and in good faith with the Independent Commission, and to use any influence they may have, to achieve the decommissioning of all paramilitary arms within two years following endorsement in referendums North and South of the agreement and in the context of the implementation of the overall settlement.

4. The Independent Commission will monitor, review and verify progress on decommissioning of illegal arms, and will report to both Governments at regular intervals.

6. Both Governments will take all necessary steps to facilitate the decommissioning process to include bringing the relevant schemes into force by the end of June.

SECURITY

1. The participants note that the development of a peaceful environment on the basis of this agreement can and should mean a normalisation of security arrangements and practices.
2. The British Government will make progress towards the objective of as early a return as possible to normal security arrangements in Northern Ireland, consistent with the level of threat and with a published overall strategy, dealing with:
    (i) the reduction of the numbers and role of the Armed Forces deployed in Northern Ireland to levels compatible with a normal peaceful society;
    (ii) the removal of security installations;
    (iii) the removal of emergency powers in Northern Ireland; and
    (iv) other measures appropriate to and compatible with a normal peaceful society.
3. The Secretary of State will consult regularly on progress, and the response to any continuing paramilitary activity, with the Irish Government and the political parties, as appropriate.
4. The British Government will continue its consultation on firearms regulation and control on the basis of the document published on 2 April 1998.
5. The Irish Government will initiate a wide-ranging review of the Offences Against the State Acts 1939–85 with a view to both reform and dispensing with those elements no longer required as circumstances permit.

POLICING AND JUSTICE

1. The participants recognise that policing is a central issue in any society. They equally recognise that Northern Ireland's history of deep divisions has made it highly emotive, with great hurt suffered and sacrifices made by many individuals and their families, including those in the RUC and other public servants. They believe that the agreement provides the opportunity for a new beginning to policing in Northern Ireland with a police service capable of attracting and sustaining support from the community as a whole. They also believe that this agreement offers a unique opportunity to bring about a new political dispensation which will recognise the full and equal legitimacy and worth of the identities, senses of allegiance and ethos of all sections of the community in Northern Ireland. They consider that this opportunity should inform and underpin the development of a police service representative in terms of the make-up of the community as a whole and which, in a peaceful environment, should be routinely unarmed.
2. The participants believe it essential that policing structures and arrangements are such that the police service is professional, effective and efficient, fair and impartial, free from partisan political control; accountable, both under the law for its actions and to the community it serves; representative of the society it polices, and operates within a coherent and co-operative criminal justice system, which conforms with human rights norms. The participants also believe that those structures and arrangements must be capable of maintaining law and order including responding effectively to crime and to any terrorist threat and to public order problems. A police service which cannot do so will fail to win public confidence and acceptance. They believe that any such structures and arrangements should be capable of delivering a policing service, in constructive and inclusive partnerships with the community at all levels, and with the maximum delegation of authority and responsibility, consistent with the foregoing principles. These arrangements should be based on principles of protection of human rights and professional integrity and should be unambiguously accepted and actively supported by the entire community.

3. An independent Commission will be established to make recommendations for future policing arrangements in Northern Ireland including means of encouraging widespread community support for these arrangements within the agreed framework of principles reflected in the paragraphs above and in accordance with the terms of reference at Annex A. The Commission will be broadly representative with expert and international representation among its membership and will be asked to consult widely and to report no later than Summer 1999.

4. The participants believe that the aims of the criminal justice system are to:
   - deliver a fair and impartial system of justice to the community;
   - be responsive to the community's concerns, and encouraging community involvement where appropriate;
   - have the confidence of all parts of the community; and
   - deliver justice efficiently and effectively.

5. There will be a parallel wide-ranging review of criminal justice (other than policing and those aspects of the system relating to the emergency legislation) to be carried out by the British Government through a mechanism with an independent element, in consultation with the political parties and others. The review will commence as soon as possible, will include wide consultation, and a report will be made to the Secretary of State no later than Autumn 1999. Terms of Reference are attached at Annex B.

6. Implementation of the recommendations arising from both reviews will be discussed with the political parties and with the Irish Government.

7. The participants also note that the British Government remains ready in principle, with the broad support of the political parties, and after consultation, as appropriate, with the Irish Government, in the context of ongoing implementation of the relevant recommendations, to devolve responsibility for policing and justice issues.

ANNEX A
COMMISSION ON POLICING FOR NORTHERN IRELAND

Terms of Reference
Taking account of the principles on policing as set out in the agreement, the Commission will inquire into policing in Northern Ireland and, on the basis of its findings, bring forward proposals for future policing structures and arrangements, including means of encouraging widespread community support for those arrangements.

Its proposals on policing should be designed to ensure that policing arrangements, including composition, recruitment, training, culture, ethos and symbols, are such that in a new approach Northern Ireland has a police service that can enjoy widespread support from, and is seen as an integral part of, the community as a whole.

Its proposals should include recommendations covering any issues such as re-training, job placement and educational and professional development required in the transition to policing in a peaceful society.

Its proposals should also be designed to ensure that:
- the police service is structured, managed and resourced so that it can be effective in discharging its full range of functions (including proposals on any necessary arrangements for the transition to policing in a normal peaceful society);
- the police service is delivered in constructive and inclusive partnerships with the community at all levels with the maximum delegation of authority and responsibility;
- the legislative and constitutional framework requires the impartial discharge of policing functions and conforms with internationally accepted norms in relation to policing standards;
- the police operate within a clear framework of accountability to the law and the community they serve, so:

- they are constrained by, accountable to and act only within the law;
- their powers and procedures, like the law they enforce, are clearly established and publicly available;
- there are open, accessible and independent means of investigating and adjudicating upon complaints against the police;
- there are clearly established arrangements enabling local people, and their political representatives, to articulate their views and concerns about policing and to establish publicly policing priorities and influence policing policies, subject to safeguards to ensure police impartiality and freedom from partisan political control;
- there are arrangements for accountability and for the effective, efficient and economic use of resources in achieving policing objectives;
- there are means to ensure independent professional scrutiny and inspection of the police service to ensure that proper professional standards are maintained;
- the scope for structured co-operation with the Garda Síochána and other police forces is addressed; and
- the management of public order events which can impose exceptional demands on policing resources is also addressed.

The Commission should focus on policing issues, but if it identifies other aspects of the criminal justice system relevant to its work on policing, including the role of the police in prosecution, then it should draw the attention of the Government to those matters.

The Commission should consult widely, including with non-governmental expert organisations, and through such focus groups as they consider it appropriate to establish.

The Government proposes to establish the Commission as soon as possible, with the aim of it starting work as soon as possible and publishing its final report by Summer 1999.

ANNEX B
REVIEW OF THE CRIMINAL JUSTICE SYSTEM

Terms of Reference
Taking account of the aims of the criminal justice system as set out in the Agreement, the review will address the structure, management and resourcing of publicly funded elements of the criminal justice system and will bring forward proposals for future criminal justice arrangements (other than policing and those aspects of the system relating to emergency legislation, which the Government is considering separately) covering such issues as:

- the arrangements for making appointments to the judiciary and magistracy, and safeguards for protecting their independence;
- the arrangements for the organisation and supervision of the prosecution process, and for safeguarding its independence;
- measures to improve the responsiveness and accountability of, and any lay participation in the criminal justice system;
- mechanisms for addressing law reform;
- the scope for structured co-operation between the criminal justice agencies on both parts of the island; and
- the structure and organisation of criminal justice functions that might be devolved to an Assembly, including the possibility of establishing a Department of Justice, while safeguarding the essential independence of many of the key functions in this area.

The Government proposes to commence the review as soon as possible, consulting with the political parties and others, including non-governmental expert organisations. The review will be completed by Autumn 1999.

PRISONERS

1. Both Governments will put in place mechanisms to provide for an accelerated programme for the release of prisoners, including transferred prisoners, convicted of scheduled offences in Northern Ireland or, in the case of those sentenced outside Northern Ireland, similar offences (referred to hereafter as qualifying prisoners).

Any such arrangements will protect the rights of individual prisoners under national and international law.

2. Prisoners affiliated to organisations which have not established or are not maintaining a complete and unequivocal ceasefire will not benefit from the arrangements. The situation in this regard will be kept under review.

3. Both Governments will complete a review process within a fixed time frame and set prospective release dates for all qualifying prisoners. The review process would provide for the advance of the release dates of qualifying prisoners while allowing account to be taken of the seriousness of the offences for which the person was convicted and the need to protect the community. In addition, the intention would be that should the circumstances allow it, any qualifying prisoners who remained in custody two years after the commencement of the scheme would be released at that point.

4. The Governments will seek to enact the appropriate legislation to give effect to these arrangements by the end of June 1998.

5. The Governments continue to recognise the importance of measures to facilitate the reintegration of prisoners into the community by providing support both prior to and after release, including assistance directed towards availing of employment opportunities, re-training and/or re-skilling, and further education.

VALIDATION, IMPLEMENTATION AND REVIEW
VALIDATION AND IMPLEMENTATION

1. The two Governments will as soon as possible sign a new British-Irish Agreement replacing the 1985 Anglo-Irish Agreement, embodying understandings on constitutional issues and affirming their solemn commitment to support and, where appropriate, implement the agreement reached by the participants in the negotiations which shall be annexed to the British-Irish Agreement.

2. Each Government will organise a referendum on 22 May 1998. Subject to Parliamentary approval, a consultative referendum in Northern Ireland, organised under the terms of the Northern Ireland (Entry to Negotiations, etc.) Act 1996, will address the question: "Do you support the agreement reached in the multi-party talks on Northern Ireland and set out in Command Paper 3883?". The Irish Government will introduce and support in the Oireachtas a Bill to amend the Constitution as described in Annex B, as follows: (a) to amend Articles 2 and 3 and (b) to amend Article 29 to permit the Government to ratify the new British-Irish Agreement. On passage by the Oireachtas, the Bill will be put to referendum.

3. If majorities of those voting in each of the referendums support this agreement, the Governments will then introduce and support, in their respective Parliaments, such legislation as may be necessary to give effect to all aspects of this agreement, and will take whatever ancillary steps as may be required including the holding of elections on 25 June, subject to parliamentary approval, to the Assembly, which would meet initially in a "shadow" mode. The establishment of the North-South Ministerial Council, implementation bodies, the British-Irish Council and the British-Irish Intergovernmental Conference and the assumption by the Assembly of its legislative and executive powers will take place at the same time on the entry into force of the British-Irish Agreement.

4. In the interim, aspects of the implementation of the multi-party agreement will be reviewed at meetings of those parties relevant in the particular case (taking into account, once Assembly elections have been held, the results of those elections), under the chairmanship of the British Government or the two Governments, as may be appropriate; and representatives of the two Governments and all relevant

parties may meet under independent chairmanship to review implementation of the agreement as a whole.

Review procedures following implementation

5. Each institution may, at any time, review any problems that may arise in its operation and, where no other institution is affected, take remedial action in consultation as necessary with the relevant Government or Governments. It will be for each institution to determine its own procedures for review.
6. If there are difficulties in the operation of a particular institution, which have implications for another institution, they may review their operations separately and jointly and agree on remedial action to be taken under their respective authorities.
7. If difficulties arise which require remedial action across the range of institutions, or otherwise require amendment of the British-Irish Agreement or relevant legislation, the process of review will fall to the two Governments in consultation with the parties in the Assembly. Each Government will be responsible for action in its own jurisdiction.
8. Notwithstanding the above, each institution will publish an annual report on its operations. In addition, the two Governments and the parties in the Assembly will convene a conference 4 years after the agreement comes into effect, to review and report on its operation.

AGREEMENT BETWEEN THE GOVERNMENT OF THE UNITED KINGDOM OF GREAT BRITAIN AND NORTHERN IRELAND AND THE GOVERNMENT OF IRELAND

The British and Irish Governments:

Welcoming the strong commitment to the Agreement reached on 10th April 1998 by themselves and other participants in the multi-party talks and set out in Annex 1 to this Agreement (hereinafter "the Multi-Party Agreement");

Considering that the Multi-Party Agreement offers an opportunity for a new beginning in relationships within Northern Ireland, within the island of Ireland and between the peoples of these islands;

Wishing to develop still further the unique relationship between their peoples and the close co-operation between their countries as friendly neighbours and as partners in the European Union;

Reaffirming their total commitment to the principles of democracy and non-violence which have been fundamental to the multi-party talks;

Reaffirming their commitment to the principles of partnership, equality and mutual respect and to the protection of civil, political, social, economic and cultural rights in their respective jurisdictions;

Have agreed as follows:

ARTICLE 1

The two Governments:
   (i) recognise the legitimacy of whatever choice is freely exercised by a majority of the people of Northern Ireland with regard to its status, whether they prefer to continue to support the Union with Great Britain or a sovereign united Ireland;
   (ii) recognise that it is for the people of the island of Ireland alone, by agreement between the two parts respectively and without external impediment, to

exercise their right of self-determination on the basis of consent, freely and concurrently given, North and South, to bring about a united Ireland, if that is their wish, accepting that this right must be achieved and exercised with and subject to the agreement and consent of a majority of the people of Northern Ireland;

(iii) acknowledge that while a substantial section of the people in Northern Ireland share the legitimate wish of a majority of the people of the island of Ireland for a united Ireland, the present wish of a majority of the people of Northern Ireland, freely exercised and legitimate, is to maintain the Union and accordingly, that Northern Ireland's status as part of the United Kingdom reflects and relies upon that wish; and that it would be wrong to make any change in the status of Northern Ireland save with the consent of a majority of its people;

(iv) affirm that, if in the future, the people of the island of Ireland exercise their right of self-determination on the basis set out in sections (i) and (ii) above to bring about a united Ireland, it will be a binding obligation on both Governments to introduce and support in their respective Parliaments legislation to give effect to that wish;

(v) affirm that whatever choice is freely exercised by a majority of the people of Northern Ireland, the power of the sovereign government with jurisdiction there shall be exercised with rigorous impartiality on behalf of all the people in the diversity of their identities and traditions and shall be founded on the principles of full respect for, and equality of, civil, political, social and cultural rights, of freedom from discrimination for all citizens, and of parity of esteem and of just and equal treatment for the identity, ethos and aspirations of both communities;

(vi) recognise the birthright of all the people of Northern Ireland to identify themselves and be accepted as Irish or British, or both, as they may so choose, and accordingly confirm that their right to hold both British and Irish citizenship is accepted by both Governments and would not be affected by any future change in the status of Northern Ireland.

ARTICLE 2

The two Governments affirm their solemn commitment to support, and where appropriate implement, the provisions of the Multi-Party Agreement. In particular there shall be established in accordance with the provisions of the Multi-Party Agreement immediately on the entry into force of this Agreement, the following institutions:

(i) a North/South Ministerial Council;

(ii) the implementation bodies referred to in paragraph 9 (ii) of the section entitled "Strand Two" of the Multi-Party Agreement;

(iii) a British-Irish Council;

(iv) a British-Irish Intergovernmental Conference.

ARTICLE 3

(1) This Agreement shall replace the Agreement between the British and Irish Governments done at Hillsborough on 15th November 1985 which shall cease to have effect on entry into force of this Agreement.

(2) The Intergovernmental Conference established by Article 2 of the aforementioned Agreement done on 15th November 1985 shall cease to exist on entry into force of this Agreement.

ARTICLE 4

(1) It shall be a requirement for entry into force of this Agreement that:
  (a) British legislation shall have been enacted for the purpose of implementing the provisions of Annex A to the section entitled "Constitutional Issues" of the Multi-Party Agreement;
  (b) the amendments to the Constitution of Ireland set out in Annex B to the section entitled "Constitutional Issues" of the Multi-Party Agreement shall have been approved by Referendum;
  (c) such legislation shall have been enacted as may be required to establish the institutions referred to in Article 2 of this Agreement.
(2) Each Government shall notify the other in writing of the completion, so far as it is concerned, of the requirements for entry into force of this Agreement. This Agreement shall enter into force on the date of the receipt of the later of the two notifications.
(3) Immediately on entry into force of this Agreement, the Irish Government shall ensure that the amendments to the Constitution of Ireland set out in Annex B to the section entitled "Constitutional Issues" of the Multi-Party Agreement take effect.

In witness thereof the undersigned, being duly authorised thereto by the respective Governments, have signed this Agreement.

Done in two originals at Belfast on the 10th day of April 1998.

For the Government
of the United Kingdom of
Great Britain and
Northern Ireland

For the
Government
of Ireland

ANNEX I

The Agreement Reached
in the Multi-Party Talks

ANNEX 2

Declaration on the Provisions of
Paragraph (vi) of Article 1
In Relationship to Citizenship

The British and Irish Governments declare that it is their joint understanding that the term "the people of Northern Ireland" in paragraph (vi) of Article 1 of this Agreement means, for the purposes of giving effect to this provision, all persons born in Northern Ireland and having, at the time of their birth, at least one parent who is a British citizen, an Irish citizen or is otherwise entitled to reside in Northern Ireland without any restriction on their period of residence.

Select Bibliography

Books, articles and theses

Alderdice, J., 'Devolution Still Key to a Solution', *Fortnight*, No. 267 (November, 1988), p. 9

Allister, J., *Alienated but Unbowed* (East Antrim DUP, 1987)

Allister, J., *Anglo-Irish Betrayal – What Hope Now For Loyal Ulster* (Belfast, n.d.)

Armstrong, D. and Saunders, H., *A Road Too Wide* (Basingstoke, 1985)

Arthur, P., 'Anglo-Irish Relations Since 1968: A Fever Chart Interpretation', *Government and Opposition*, 16(2) (1983), pp. 157–74

Arthur, P., *Government and Politics of Northern Ireland*, 2nd edn. (London, 1984)

Arthur, P., 'Northern Ireland: The Unfinished Business of Anglo-Irish Relations', in P. J. Drudy (ed.), *Britain and Ireland Since 1922*, Irish Studies 5 (Cambridge, 1986)

Arthur, P., 'The Brooke Initiative', *Irish Political Studies*, 7 (1992), pp. 111–15

Arthur, P., 'The Mayhew Talks 1992', *Irish Political Studies*, 8 (1993), pp. 138–43

Arthur, P. and Jeffery, K., *Northern Ireland Since 1968* (Oxford, 1988)

Aughey, A., *Under Siege: Ulster Unionism and the Anglo-Irish Agreement* (Belfast, 1989)

Aughey, A., 'Unionism and Self-Determination', in P. Roche and B. Barton (eds.), *The Northern Ireland Question: Myth and Reality* (Aldershot, 1991)

Aughey, A., *Irish Kulturhampf* (Belfast, 1995)

Bardon, J., *Belfast: An Illustrated History* (Belfast, 1982)

Bardon, J., *A History of Ulster* (Belfast, 1992)

Barton, B., *Brookeborough: The Making of a Prime Minister* (Belfast, 1988)

Barton, B., *The Blitz: Belfast in the War Years* (Belfast, 1989)

Beckett, J. C., *The Making of Modern Ireland 1603–1923* (London and Boston, 1981)

Bell, D., 'Acts of Union: Youth Sub-culture and Ethnic Identity amongst Protestants in Northern Ireland', *British Journal of Sociology*, 38(2), pp. 158–83

Bell, G., *The Protestants of Ulster* (London, 1976)

Bew, P. and Patterson, H., *The British State and the Ulster Crisis: From Wilson to Thatcher* (London, 1985)

Bew, P., Gibbon, P. and Patterson, H., *The State in Northern Ireland* (Manchester, 1979)

Bew, P. and Gillespie, G., *Northern Ireland: A Chronology of the Troubles 1968–1993* (Dublin, 1993)

Bloomfield, K., *Stormont in Crisis* (Belfast, 1994)

Boyd, A., *Holy War in Belfast* (Kerry, 1969)

Boyd, A., *Brian Faulkner and the Crisis of Ulster Unionism* (Kerry, 1972)

Boyd, A., *Northern Ireland: Who is to Blame?* (Dublin and Cork, 1984)

Boyle, K. and Hadden, T., *Ireland: A Positive Proposal* (London, 1985)

Brooke, P., *Ulster Presbyterianism* (Dublin, 1987)

Brown, T., *The Whole Protestant Community: The Making of a Historical Myth* (Derry, Field Day Pamphlet No. 7, 1985)

Bruce, S.,'Ulster Loyalism and Religiosity', *Political Studies*, 35(4), pp. 643–8

Bruce, S.,'Prods and Taigs – The Sectarian Divide', *Fortnight*, No. 242. (July–September 1986), pp. 5–6

Bruce, S., *God Save Ulster! The Religion and Politics of Paisleyism* (Oxford, 1986)

Bruce, S., *The Edge of the Union: The Ulster Loyalist Political Vision* (Oxford, 1994)

Buckland, P., *Irish Unionism 1885–1923: A Documentary History* (Belfast, 1973)

Buckland, P., *The Factory of Grievances: Devolved Government in Northern Ireland 1921–39* (Dublin and New York, 1979)

Buckland, P., *James Craig* (London, 1980)

Cochrane, F.,'Progressive or Regressive? The Anglo-Irish Agreement as a Dynamic in the Northern Ireland Polity', *Irish Political Studies*, 8 (1993), pp. 1–20

Cochrane, F., 'Any Takers? The Isolation of Northern Ireland', *Political Studies*, 42 (3) (1994), pp. 378–95

Coughlan, A., *Fooled Again? The Anglo-Irish Agreement and After* (Cork and Dublin, 1986)

Coulter, C.,'The Character of Unionism', *Irish Political Studies*, 9.(1994) pp. 1–24

Cox, W. H.,'Who Wants A United Ireland?', *Government and Opposition*, 20(1) (Winter, 1985), pp. 29–47

Cox, W. H.,'Public Opinion and the Anglo-Irish Agreement', *Government and Opposition*, 22(3) (Summer, 1987), pp. 336–51

Craig, W., 'The Future of Northern Ireland', Speech at Ulster Vanguard's First Anniversary Rally, 1972

Crawford, R.G., *Loyal to King Billy: A Portrait of the Ulster Protestants* (London, 1987)

Dillon, M., *The Shankill Butchers: A Case Study of Mass Murder* (London, 1989)

Elliott, S. and Wilford, R., *The 1982 Northern Ireland Assembly Election*, Studies in Public Policy, No. 119 (Glasgow, 1983)

Farrell, M., *Northern Ireland: The Orange State* (London, 1976)

Farrell, M., *Arming the Protestants* (Dingle, 1983)

Faulkner, B., *Memoirs of a Statesman* (London, 1978)

Fisk, R., *Point of No Return: The Strike that Broke the British in Ulster* (London, 1975)

FitzGerald, G., *All in a Life* (Dublin and London, 1992)

Flackes, W. D. and Elliott, S., *Northern Ireland: A Political Directory 1968–88* (Belfast, 1989)

Foster, J. W. (ed.), *The Idea of the Union* (Vancouver, 1995)

Foster, R. F., *Modern Ireland 1600–1972* (London, 1988)

Gordon, D., *The O'Neill Years: Unionist Politics 1963–1969* (Belfast, 1989)

Guelke, A., *Northern Ireland: The International Perspective* (Dublin, 1988)

Hadden, T. and Boyle, K., *The Anglo-Irish Agreement: Commentary, Text and Official Review* (London and Dublin, 1989)

Harbinson, J. F., *The Ulster Unionist Party 1882–1973: Its Development and Organisation* (Belfast, 1973)

Harris, R., *Prejudice and Tolerance in Ulster* (Manchester, 1975)

Kennedy, L., *Two Ulsters: A Case for Repartition* (Belfast, 1986)

Kenny, A., *The Road to Hillsborough: The Shaping of the Anglo-Irish Agreement* (Oxford, 1986)

Loughlin, J., *Ulster Unionism and British National Identity Since 1885* (London and New York, 1995)

Lyons, F. S. L., *Culture and Anarchy in Ireland 1890–1939* (Oxford, 1982)

McCartney, R., *What Must Be Done: A Programme for Normalising Politics in Northern Ireland* (Belfast, 1986)

MacDonald, M., *Children of Wrath: Political Violence in Northern Ireland* (Cambridge, 1986)

McGarry, J. and O'Leary, B. (eds.), *The Future of Northern Ireland* (Oxford, 1990)

McGarry, J. and O'Leary, B., *Explaining Northern Ireland: Broken Images* (Oxford, 1995)

MacIver, M.A., 'Ian Paisley and the Reformed Tradition', *Political Studies*, 35(3) (September, 1987), pp. 359–78

McMichael, J., *Campaign against the Anglo-Irish Treaty* (Belfast, 1987)

Mallie, E. and McKittrick, D., *The Fight for Peace* (London, 1996)

Marrinan, P., *Paisley: Man of Wrath* (Tralee, 1973)

Miller, D., *Queen's Rebels: Ulster Loyalism in Historical Perspective* (Dublin and New York, 1978)

Moloney, E. and Pollak, A., *Paisley* (Dublin, 1986)

Moxon-Browne, E., *Nation, Class and Creed in Northern Ireland* (Aldershot, 1983)

Nelson, S.,'Protestant Ideology Considered', *British Sociology Yearbook*, No. 2 (London, 1975)

Nelson, S., *Ulster's Uncertain Defenders: Protestant Paramilitary and Community Groups and the Northern Ireland Conflict* (Belfast, 1984)

Northern Ireland Assembly Papers 237 (Belfast, 1986), Vols. I–III, *First Report from the Committee on the Government of Northern Ireland*

O'Brien, B., *The Long War* (Dublin, 1995)

O'Brien, C. C., *States of Ireland* (London, 1972)

O'Connor, F., *In Search of a State: Catholics in Northern Ireland* (Belfast, 1993)

O'Dowd, M. and Wichert, S. (eds.), *Chattel, Servant or Citizen: Women's Status in Church, State and Society* (Belfast, 1995)

O'Leary, B.,'The Anglo-Irish Agreement: Statecraft or Folly?', *West European Politics*, 10(1) (1987), pp. 5–32

O'Leary, B., 'The Anglo-Irish Agreement: Meanings, Explanations, Results and a Defence', in P. Teague (ed.), *Beyond the Rhetoric: Politics, the Economy and Social Policy in Northern Ireland* (London, 1987)

O'Leary, B. and Arthur, P., 'Northern Ireland as the Site of State – and Nation-Building Failures', in J. McGarry and B. O'Leary (eds.), *The Future of Northern Ireland* (Oxford, 1990)

O'Leary, B. and McGarry, J., *The Politics of Antagonism: Understanding Northern Ireland* (London, 1993)

O'Leary, C., Elliott, S. and Wilford, R., *The Northern Ireland Assembly 1982–1986: A Constitutional Experiment* (London, 1988)

Oliver, J. A., *Working at Stormont* (Dublin, 1978)

O'Malley, P., *The Uncivil Wars: Ireland Today* (Belfast, 1983)

O'Neill, T., *Ulster at the Crossroads* (London, 1969)

Pollak, A., *A Citizen's Inquiry: The Opsahl Report on Northern Ireland* (Dublin, 1993)

Probert, B., *Beyond Orange and Green: The Political Economy of the Northern Ireland Crisis* (London, 1978)

Purdy, A., *Molyneaux: The Long View* (Antrim, 1989)

Rees, M., *Northern Ireland: A Personal Perspective* (London, 1985)

Ridd, R. and Callaway, H. (eds.), *Caught up in the Conflict: Women's Responses to Political Strife* (London, 1986)

Roberts, D. A., 'The Orange Order in Ireland: A Religious Institution?', *British Journal of Sociology*, 22(3) (1971), pp. 269–82

Roberts, H.,'Sound Stupidity: The British Party System and the Northern Ireland Question', in J. McGarry and B. O'Leary (eds.), *The Future of Northern Ireland* (Oxford, 1990)

Robinson, Peter, *The North Answers Back* (Belfast, 1969)

Robinson, Philip, *The Plantation Of Ulster* (Dublin, 1984)

Roche, P. and Barton, B. (eds.), *The Northern Ireland Question: Myth and Reality* (Aldershot, 1991)

Rowan, B., *Behind the Lines* (Belfast, 1995)

Ruane, J. and Todd, J., 'Diversity, Division and the Middle Ground in Northern Ireland', *Irish Political Studies*, 7 (1992), pp. 73–98

Shannon, C. B., 'Women in Northern Ireland', in M. O'Dowd and S. Wichert (eds.), *Chattel, Servant or Citizen: Women's Status in Church, State and Society* (Belfast, 1995), pp. 238–53

Shea, P., *Voices and the Sound of Drums: An Irish Autobiography* (Belfast, 1981)

Smyth, C., 'The Ulster Democratic Unionist Party: A Case Study in Religious Convergence' (PhD thesis, QUB, 1983)

Smyth, C., 'The DUP as a Politico-Religious Organisation', *Irish Political Studies*, 1 (1986), pp. 33–43

Smyth, C., *Ian Paisley: Voice of Protestant Ulster* (Edinburgh, 1987)

Smyth, P. D. H., 'The Northern Ireland Assembly 1982–86: The Failure of an Experiment', *Parliamentary Affairs*, 40(4), pp. 482–500

Stewart, A. T. Q., 'The Transition in Presbyterian Radicalism in Northern Ireland 1792–1825' (MA thesis, QUB, 1956)

Stewart, A. T. Q., *The Ulster Crisis* (London, 1967)

Stewart, A. T. Q., *The Narrow Ground: Aspects of Ulster 1609–1969* (London, 1977)

Teague, P. (ed.), *Beyond the Rhetoric: Politics, the Economy and Social Policy in Northern Ireland* (London, 1987)

Thatcher, M., *The Downing Street Years* (London, 1993)

Todd, J., 'Two Traditions in Unionist Political Culture', *Irish Political Studies*, 2 (1987), pp. 1–26

Ulster Vanguard, *Ulster – A Nation* (Belfast, 1972)

Ulster Vanguard, *Ulster – Spelling It Out* (Belfast, 1972)

Ulster Vanguard, *Ulster – Community of the British Isles* (Belfast, 1973)

Utley, T. E., *Lessons Of Ulster* (London, 1975)

Walker, G., *The Politics of Frustration: Harry Midgley and the Failure of Labour in Northern Ireland* (Manchester, 1985)

Wallace, M., *Drums and Guns: Revolution in Ulster* (London and Dublin, 1970)

Wallace, M., *Northern Ireland: 50 Years of Self-Government* (New York, 1971)

Wallis, R., Bruce, S. and Taylor, D., *No Surrender! Paisleyism and the Politics of Ethnic Identity in Northern Ireland* (Belfast, 1986)

Wallis, R., Bruce, S. and Taylor, D., 'Ethnicity and Evangelicalism: Ian Paisley and Protestant Politics', *Comparative Studies in Society and History*, 29(2) (1987), pp. 293–313

Whyte, J., *Interpreting Northern Ireland* (Oxford, 1990)

Wilson, T., *Ulster: Conflict and Consent (Oxford, 1989)*

Wright, F., 'Protestant Ideology and Politics in Ulster', *European Journal of Sociology*, 14 (1972), pp. 213–80

Wright, F., 'Developments in Ulster Politics 1843–86' (PhD thesis, QUB, 1989)

Newspapers

Belfast News Letter
Belfast Telegraph
Daily Express
The Daily Telegraph
Guardian

The Independent
Irish Independent
Irish News
The Irish Times
Observer
Sunday Independent
Sunday Times
Sunday Tribune
The Times

Magazines and periodicals

Combat
Government and Opposition
Fortnight
Irish Political Studies
Magill
New Society
New Ulster Defender
Political Studies
Social Studies Review
The Equal Citizen
The New Nation
The Northern Ireland Assembly Papers
The Protestant Telegraph
The Revivalist
Ulster
Ulster Defiant
Workers' Weekly

Television and radio broadcasts

A Protestant Pilgrimage (Ulster Television, 1989)
For God and Ulster? Protestant Voices from the North (RTÉ Television, May 1996)
Prime Time (RTÉ Television, May 1996)
Spotlight (BBC [NI] Television)
Seven Days (BBC Radio Ulster, July 1992)
Talkback (BBC Radio Ulster)
The History-Makers (BBC Radio Ulster, 1989)
The View from the Castle (BBC [NI] Television, 1988)
This Week ('No Surrender', London Weekend Television, 1988)

Index

433